Footprint

East Coast Australia Handbook

Darroch Donald

Silence ruled this land. Out of the silence mystery comes, and magic, and the delicate awareness of unreasoning things.

Eleanor Dark, *Timeless Land* (1941)

1st edition

East Coast Australia Highlights

See colour maps at back of book

1 Sydney
Book a balcony seat at the *Doyle's Seafood Restaurant* in Watson's Bay and another balcony seat at the Opera House

2 Hunter Valley
Take a balloon flight at dawn over the vineyards

3 Iluka area
Lagoons, creeks, swamps and a World Heritage rainforest walk

4 Cape Byron
Watch dolphins surfing off the beach

5 Mount Warning
Be the first to see the Australian dawn from this summit in the Byron Bay hinterland

6 Gold Coast
Take on the tables at Conrad Jupiter's Casino

7 Surfers Paradise
Survive the Lethal Weapon thrill ride at Movie World

8 Moreton Island
Feed wild dolphins by hand at Tangalooma Resort

9 Eumundi Markets
Wander through these eclectic, colourful markets

10 Fraser Island
Get to grips with a 4WD, amidst the stunning scenery of the world's largest sand island

Bamaga

Gulf of
Carpentaria

Musgrave
Roadhouse

N

0 km   300
0 miles   300

NORTHERN
TERRITORY

QUEENSLAND

SOUTH
AUSTRALIA

NEW SOUTH WALES

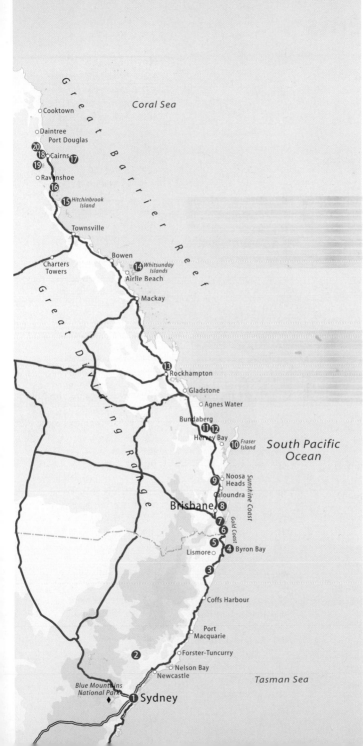

11 Bundaberg
Taste sweet molasses and sample Australia's finest rum – 'Bundy'

12 Mon Repos
Sit next to a huge turtle laying its eggs on the beach

13 Capricorn Caves
Listen to classical music and hear the incredible acoustics deep underground

14 Whitsunday Islands
Go island-hopping for around these beautiful islands

15 Hitchinbrook Island
An unspoilt wonderland of forested slopes, sheer cliffs and weird wildlife

16 Mission Beach
Get spooked by creatures of the night while night spotting in Lacey's Creek

17 Coral cay
Come face to face with an 'old wife' or a 'woobegong' off a coral cay

18 Barron Gorge
Take a cable-ride above the rainforest canopy

19 Atherton Tablelands
Get up for dawn to catch a glimpse of a duck-billed platypus

20 Kuranda
Act as a landing pad for some of the world's most beautiful butterflies in Butterfly World

Contents

5

Cairns to Cape York

Capricorn and Central coasts

Sunshine & Fraser coasts

Brisbane and around

Gold Coast

North Coast NSW

Around Sydney Sydney

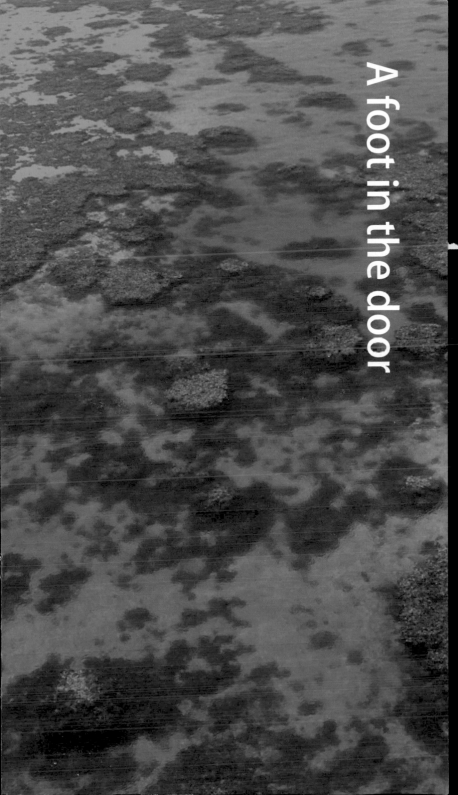

A foot in the door

Great Barrier Reef *(previous page)*
*Some 2,011 km long, the largest coral
reef in the world is an incredible natural
wonderland*
Sydney harbour *(right) Skiffs sailing
on the harbour that Clive James aptly
described as looking like "crushed
diamonds"*
Kangaroos 'grazing' *(below)*
Bucolic bliss just a short ride from Sydney

Watering holes *(above) Go down the pub
and blow the froth off a couple of cold ones*
Queensland Tree Fern *(right) A view from
the floor of the rainforest*
Sydney *(next page) Evening light plays on the abstract patterns
of the tiles that make up the 'sails' of Sydney's iconic Opera House*

Introducing East Coast Australia

It's easy to see why they call Australia the 'Lucky Country'. You only have to look at the East Coast with its countless beaches, headlands and islands. Here, on the edge of the world's largest and driest island, a remarkable biodiversity and range of habitats combine to form one of the most exceptional environments on earth. Where else on the planet would you find two completely different and accessible World Heritage parks – Daintree and the Great Barrier Reef – separated only by the tide? Yet these national treasures are just two mighty jewels in Australia's glittering crown. There are over 580 national parks and nature reserves in New South Wales alone, with some, like the Blue Mountains near Sydney, attracting more than one million visitors a year.

Of course all these natural assets create their own wealth of attraction and beauty, not to mention a vast array of amazing wildlife. But for many travellers 'doing the coast' the urban scene is of equal importance. Here too, you have the size and the diversity so typical of the country as a whole. The two state capitals, Sydney and Brisbane, are both equally absorbing but significantly different. Then there are the resorts with their pure tourist appeal: Byron Bay, well known for its artistic, 'alternative' community; the highrises and hyperbole of Surfers Paradise; and the picture postcard milieu of Noosa.

As such, the coastal journey between Sydney and Cairns is one of the most popular tourist routes in the world – and deservingly so. It is, in a way, a microcosm of all that the vast continent of Australia has to offer. Here, you can start your journey exploring the vibrant centre of humanity that is Sydney and be dwarfed by the shell-like structure of the Opera House and then end it exploring that other, even more diverse and colourful community, under the waves of the Great Barrier Reef. The East Coast is big and beautiful, weird and wonderful: a wholesale bombardment of the senses. You won't find a more varied and visually appealing stretch of coastline anywhere else – never in a month of Whitsundays.

Beauty and the beach

Bucket & space You will almost certainly lose count of the number of beautiful beaches and most will merge into one great swathe of sand in the memoryu, but that's not to say they won't be dramatically different. Sydney's Bondi Beach, or Surfers Paradise on the Gold Coast, are of course legendary and it does not take much imagination to picture the scene. But how about driving in a 4WD for mile upon mile along the golden fringes of Fraser Island? Befriending pelicans on a wharf, or watching dolphins surfing from Cape Byron? How about watching a sea turtle lay its eggs on a beach near Bundaberg? Or sea kayaking to a deserted island in the reef? This is what dream holidays are made of and the East Coast has it all by the bucket load.

A last resort Wherever there are beaches, there are resorts and the East Coast is no exception, far from it. However, like the beaches, cities and towns, they vary greatly. Perhaps given the far-reaching influence of Sydney, the coastal resorts of New South Wales, like Coffs Harbour and Byron Bay, can afford to be more sedate, or alternative, with little of the kitsch beyond an absurd plastic banana, or discount souvenir shop. However, once across the border into Queensland it is like the aftermath of some severe and chronic episode of resortomania. Suddenly the skyline erupts with holiday apartment blocks and roadside billboards all extolling the heady delights of Sea World, Wet World, Movie World and You Name It We've Got It World. Where else but the Gold Coast can you swim with dolphins, kiss Marilyn Monroe and wear a pink wig (after stirring your cocktail with it) without anyone batting an eyelid. Not likely, mate! No wonder then the pretty resort of Noosa, slightly further north, offers more natural and gracious surroundings without a highrise in sight.

Keeping it real Being larger, less aesthetically attractive and traditionally more concerned about providing essential services to the general population, Queensland's coastal towns usually prove less memorable than NSW's but this can make a refreshing change from the glitz. The sun-baked regional centres of Rockhampton, Mackay and Townsville, north of Brisbane, offer their own individual tourist attractions. In Townsville the weird and wonderful inhabitants of Billabong Wildlife Sanctuary will gladly share your lunch, then there are the incredible underground acoustics of the Capricorn Caves near Rockhampton. One exception to the rule is of course Cairns, Australia's most famous coastal town and one that has, after Sydney, developed into the country's most significant and popular tourist destination. Of course the reasons for that lie mainly offshore and below the surface on the Barrier Reef, but on terra firma, Daintree, Cape Tribulation and the Atherton Tablelands also provide a wonderful respite from the tourist hype.

Pastime paradise As if all of the beaches, activities, resorts and urban landscapes on the East Coast were not diverse and stimulating enough, there is another place that is yet more vital,more chaotic and colourful. To venture just a while into that incredible world below the waves on the Great Barrier Reef is simply awesome and for the goggle-eyed novice meeting goggle-eyed fish, it can be the greatest revelation of them all. With manta rays nibbling at your feet and shoals dancing before your eyes, you are sure to become hooked. Although the Barrier Reef is the obvious first choice for divers or novices there are numerous great dive locations along the entire length of the East Coast including the Solitary Islands, off Coffs Harbour, in New South Wales.

Movie World (right)
The most popular of
the Gold Coast's
theme parks
Lake Mackenzie
(below) The cool,
crystal-clear waters of
this lake can be found
at the heart of Fraser
Island – the world's
largest sand island

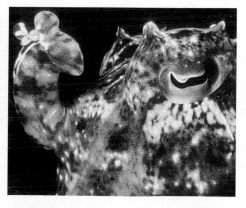

Hervey Bay (above) The bay's calm waters
provide an opportunity for pods of humpback
whales take a break, to socialize and play, before
continuing their journey to Antarctica
Cuttlefish (right) Pretty in pink

Koala (right) This koala takes a well-earned rest after all the hugging of visitors at a Queensland wildlife sanctuary
Lorikeets (below) Birds of a bright feather

Josephine Falls (middle) Near to Belligen, an artistic, 'alternative' village, this is great walking country
Kuranda Scenic Railway (above) This historic loco is a fine way to travel from Cairns to the village of Kuranda
Blue Mountains (right) Sheer beauty
Brisbane (next page) Vibrant and tropical, the city is well worth visiting

The wild west

With so much to see and do on the coastal route few venture inland despite the fact that not too far from the sound of the waves are many equally compelling attractions. In both states you can visit numerous national parks with dramatic scenery and an abundance of native wildlife: the Blue Mountains, Barrington Tops, Dorrigo and New England in New South Wales and Lamington, Springbrook and Eungella in Queensland to name but a few. In these parks, it is not unusual to find rainforest, rivers and waterfalls, considerable rainfall in winter, and even snow, which all combines to create a welcome break from the oppressive heat or sheer tourist numbers on the coast.

Walking in a wonder hinterland

For less active souls who prefer a glass of shiraz to a walk in the mountains, a detour inland can also prove worthwhile. The Hunter Valley, accessible from Newcastle and the New South Wales Central Coast, is one of Australia's prime wine regions. Home to close on a 100 vineyards and some of the finest labels in the country, it offers one of Australia's best opportunities to sample the fruits of her liquid labours.

Whose wine is it anyway?

Many of the coastal communities of northern New South Wales and the Sunshine Coast in southern Queensland originally grew around the alternative lifestyles of artists and artisans. Although this influence is still very much in evidence in many communities like Byron Bay and Eumundi near Noosa, the original principles are slowly being eroded by the tourist invasion. You'll find far more genuine communities thriving in the coastal hinterland. A diversion to Bellingen near Coffs Harbour or Nimbin in the Rainbow Region inland from Byron Bay will clearly demonstrate this fact and satisfy your inquisition. The wonderfully scenic drive along the Blackall Range inland from Noosa in Queensland is another trip worth taking.

A life less ordinary

Leaving the alternative lifestyle behind you can turn your attention to the more traditional Aussie existence of the legendary outback, without venturing too far inland. Some towns on the fringe such as Charters Towers, a mere two hours drive west of Townsville, offer a real insight into this most archetypal of Australian landscapes. Once a thriving gold mining town, Charters Towers remains proud of its heritage and still boasts some fascinating remnants, as well as offering just a taste of what life must be like 'out there' and 'outback'.

Gold rush

Australia's native wildlife should play a fundamental part of any visit to the country and no more so than along the coastlines of New South Wales and Queensland. The tracks and campsites of numerous national parks, or the captive wildlife sanctuaries along its entire length, provide an ideal opportunity to encounter a veritable 'Who's Who' of the animal and plant kingdoms – from the cute and cuddly to the downright bizarre. Even the names stir the imagination. Here you can marvel at the antics of the bandicoot, the bilby, the dibbler and the hopelessly appealing hairy-nosed wombat. And that's just the mammal department. How about the gastric brooding frog, the forty-spotted pardalote and the old wife? If you end up confused and unable to tell a duck-billed platypus from a bucketmouth, then take a break and enjoy that most Australian of pastimes – the Barbie.

Animal magnetism

Essentials

Essentials

Planning your trip

Where to go

With a combined landmass of over 2.5 million sq km, New South Wales and Queensland form an area 10 times the size of the UK. Although the interior does not possess the same diverse scenery as the UK and is certainly far less populated (14% of the population and 7% of the USA's) it is obvious that if you have no more than one or two weeks for a visit, you can dismiss the idea of trying to see too much of either state, and certainly of attempting to see very much of the outback – unless you intend to fly.

This is why the coastal route from Sydney to Cairns is so popular: a 2,685-km journey along a necklace by the sea, studded with numerous pearls. As such it can be approached in sections as well as in its entirety. The entire journey, stopping only to sleep, takes four days by car.

Where you choose to visit will primarily be determined by the time of year. Broadly speaking, the far north from October to April is extremely hot, humid and monsoonal. Cairns still gets visitors who want to see the Great Barrier Reef, but most visitors will want to enjoy the glorious summer weather in the southern regions and avoid the humidity up north. A visit during May to September not only opens up the north, but also allows an itinerary to range almost anywhere within the two states. See also Climate, page 19.

One- to two-week trip A trip of one or two weeks could only ever sample a specific area between Sydney and Cairns. The following tips suggest making the most out of Sydney, Brisbane, the Gold Coast and Cairns with your own transport. Other specific recommended destinations include the Myall Lakes National Park, Byron Bay, Fraser Island, Magnetic Island (off Townsville) and the Whitsunday Islands.

If you visit Sydney, see box 'A Long Weekend', page 65. Add to that a three-day trip to the Blue Mountains, a two-day trip to the Hunter Valley vineyards or, alternatively the Myall Lakes National Park. Brisbane will require at least two days and the Gold Coast at least three days with added exploration of Coolangatta, the Gold Coast hinterland national parks and (from Brisbane) Moreton or North Stradbroke Islands or Noosa also being recommended. Cairns and the Barrier Reef could occupy anyone for months, never mind a week or two. However the 'must see and do's' include a reef island trip with snorkelling or a dive (you can do an introductory dive even if you are not certified), Kuranda and the rainforest gondola, Daintree, Cape Tribulation and the perfect retreat from the coastal heat, the Atherton Tablelands.

Three- to four-week trip Ideally, this is the minimum amount of time a visitor from Europe or the USA should spend in the area. A three- to four-week trip could comfortably involve a few days in Sydney, then a trip north to Byron Bay, or the lesser visited Port Macquarie, or alternatively a visit to Brisbane and the Gold Coast then a rather hurried drive to Cairns. The one-way 2,685-km trip between Sydney and Cairns in four weeks by car is possible, but pushing it, so you may like to consider doing one of the above sections, then flying from Brisbane to Sydney or Brisbane to Cairns. Although there is not much in it, of the two coastal sections the Queensland trip (Brisbane to Cairns) is the best. Added to the city-based suggestions in the one-to-two week section above, you should consider the following locations:

Sydney to Brisbane Between Sydney (5 days) and Brisbane you can visit Port Stephens (2 days), Myall Lakes National Park (3 days), Hunter Valley (2 days), Port Macquarie (3 days), South West Rocks (2 days), Bellingen including the Dorrigo and New England National Parks (2-3 days), Coffs Harbour (2 days), Iluka and Woody Head (2 days) and Byron Bay (4 days). All are recommended.

Brisbane to Cairns Between Brisbane (3 days) and Cairns the Sunshine Coast and Noosa (3 days) are excellent locations for a short break along with an additional day trip along the hinterland Blackall Range. Fraser Island (3 days) is of course a major highlight, while Bundaberg (especially the turtle rookery) and the twin towns of 1770 and Agnes Waters are both great venues off the beaten track (2 days each). Around Rockhampton (1 day) try to take in Yeppoon and Great Keppel Island (2-3 days) and around Mackay the Eungella National Park (1-2 days). In and around Townsville don't miss Magnetic Island (3 days) and Charters Towers (1 day). Airlie Beach (2 days) and the Whitsunday Islands (2-3 days) are almost obligatory while just south of Cairns, Mission Beach (2 days) and Dunk Island (1-2 days) are also well worth visiting. With all that to consider, make sure you leave at least 5 days in and around Cairns and the Great Barrier Reef.

Over one month To make the trip by car or campervan between Sydney and Cairns, taking in the cities, the prime destinations mentioned above and other recommended side trips comfortably will require 12-15 weeks one way. You can then fly back to Sydney or, if you own a vehicle, endure the four-day drive. As well as the locations mentioned above other recommended short-stay destinations (with an emphasis on ecology and camping) include:

Sydney to Brisbane Barrington Tops National Park, Crowdy Bay National Park, Yuragyir National Park, and Byron Bay Hinterland national parks.

Brisbane to Cairns Cooloola Coast (Great Sandy National Park), Lady Musgrave Island (from Town of 1770), Heron Island (from Gladstone), Hinchinbrook Island (from Cardwell), Lizard Island (Great Barrier Reef from Cairns or Cooktown), Undara Lava Tubes (from Cairns), Cooktown, Chillagoe and, with 4WD, Cape York.

When to go

One of the joys of the East Coast is that at any time of year there is always some section where the weather is just right. The converse, of course, is that those particular about their destination need good timing. Broadly speaking, the peak season between Sydney and Brisbane is from mid-December through to the end of January. Conversely autumn, winter and spring (March to October) is considered the peak season north of Rockhampton (Tropic of Capricorn), when dry, warm weather is the norm. The 'stinger season' between October and May also presents its own dangers. See box, page 342. Generally, accommodation and tourist sites in both states stay open year-round, the main exceptions being in the far north in mid-summer (December to March).

Being a southern hemisphere continent, Australia's seasons are the opposite of those in the northern hemisphere

Watch out for school holidays and peak seasons, when some areas get completely booked out months in advance (particularly between Sydney and Brisbane). School holidays tend to take place during January, a week or two around Easter, a couple of weeks in June and July and another couple during September and October. If planning a long trip, say three months or more, try to make spring or autumn the core of your time.

Climate *Forecasts: T1900 926113, www.bom.gov.au* As a general rule of thumb, the further north you travel, and the further in time from July, the hotter it gets. And hot means very hot: days over 40°C (104°F) regularly occur in summer in the arid regions, and even cities as far south as Sydney average around 25°C. In the north of the country summer (November to April) is synonymous with 'the wet', a period characterised by high humidity, heat, tremendous monsoonal rainfall and occasional, powerful cyclones. Australia is the driest inhabited continent, and virtually nowhere further than 250 km inland gets more than an average of 600 mm (24 inches) of rain a year. About half the continent, in a band across the south and west, gets less than 300 mm and much of it is desert. Naturally, the East Coast and elevated areas along the Great Divide see much higher rainfall.

Essentials

Essentials

▶ **Tourist Commission offices**

Auckland *Level 13, 44-48 Emily Place, T09 915 2826.*

Bangkok *Unit 1614, 16th floor, River Wing East, Empire Tower, 195 South Sathorn Rd, Yannawa, Sathorn, T02 670 0640.*

Frankfurt *Neue Mainzer Str 22, D 60311, T069 274 00622.*

Hong Kong *Suite 1501 Central Plaza, 18 Harbour Rd, Wanchai, T2802 7700.*

London *Gemini House, 10-18 Putney Hill, T020 8780 2229.*

Los Angeles *2049 Century Park East, Suite 1920, T310 229 4870.*

Singapore *101 Thomson Rd, 26-05 United Sq, T255 4555.*

Sydney *Level 4 80 William St, Woolloomooloo, T02 9360 1111.*

Tokyo *C/o Australian Business Centre, New Otani Garden Court Building 28F, 4-1 Kioi-cho Chiyoda-ku, T03 5214 0720.*

The whole picture is complicated by ENSO (El Niño Southern Oscillation). This global climatic effect has a profound influence on the Australian climate. It starts out in the Eastern Pacific every two to eight years, with an abnormal increase in the temperature of the surface layers of the ocean bringing violent, destructive storms to the normally arid western coast of South America. As a counter to this the surface ocean off Eastern Australia is cooler than usual, lowering evaporation and cloud formation. Naturally low rainfall is decreased yet further and the net effects on much of the southern and eastern parts of the continent are drought, desiccation and sometimes horrific bush fires.

Festivals The main events that draw in the crowds are *Mardi Gras* in Sydney, February, and big sporting events such as the Rugby World Cup, which took place in Sydney in 2003. Obviously when large scale events such as these take place the area has a great party atmosphere which is well worth experiencing however you are strongly advised to book transport tickets and accommodation as far ahead as possible.

Tours and tour operators

There are a host of companies offering general or special interest tours. Most are district, state or multi-centre based. See individual town and city sections for details

There are several companies offering one- to 10-day trips along parts of the coast and many others venturing inland from the main centres. Most involve coach travel or some degree of 4WD manoeuvring and adventure activities. Make sure you ask around and chat to some of the operators before committing yourself. Ask about the average age and size of the tour group, the activity level, and details of the itinerary so you can be sure you will see and experience what you want to in a way that suits your ability and comfort level. One of the principal differences between the operators is in the sleeping arrangements they offer. One word of warning here, especially for backpackers: do not get cajoled into committing yourself to set itineraries along the coast unless you are sure this is what you want to do. Many find that once they reach the various tour destinations the very attractive choices of other accommodation and activities on offer are then out of their reach. Be aware, many of the chain backpackers put profits before your individual experience. Unless you are alone, independence is the key.

In Australia Major national players worth looking at include: *AAT King*, T02 9518 6095, www.aatkings.com.au, a high-profile national company offering a wide range of coach, 4WD and camping tours throughout Australia. *Goway*, T02 9262 4755, www.goway. com.au, offer national multi-day trips both luxury and budget including a 13-day Sydney to Cairns excursion. *Australia Pacific*, T1800675222 or T03 9277 8555, www.ap touring.com.au, offer a wide range of camping, independent, and escorted tours. *Scenic Tours*, www.scenictours.com.au, offer 8- to 28-day luxury tours of

Queensland. *Pegasus Coach Tours*, T02 9838 1733, www.pegasus coachtours.com.au, offer custom-designed tours throughout Australia.

The main backpacker-orientated coach company is *OZ Experience*, T02 8356 1766, www.ozexperience.com.au Of more specialist interest *Gondwana Discovery Tours*, T02 9567 7777, gondisc@ozemail.com.au, is NSW-based and offers a wide range of eco-orientated, escorted 4WD tours. *Swagman Outback Safaris*, T03 52222855, www.swagmantours.com.au, offer nine- to 32-day coach, truck and 4WD tours nationally with options in northern Queensland. *Surfaris*, T1800 634951, www.surfaris.com.au, offers surfing excursions with a week long Sydney-Byron Bay trip or a 4-day/3-night Byron-Noosa-Hervey Bay trip.

Travelbag, 3-5 High St, Alton, GU34 1TL, UK, T0870 9001350, www.travelbag.co.uk Reputable UK based firm offering a good range of general and tailor-made trips to Eastern Australia at reasonable prices. *Contiki Wells House*, 15 Elmfield Rd, Bromley, Kent, BR1 1LS, T020 8290 6777, www.contiki.com One of the world's largest travel companies catering primarily for the 18-35's market with numerous affordable Australian options. *Wildlife Worldwide Chameleon House*, 162 Selsdon Rd, T020 8667 9158, www.wildlifeworldwide.com One of the best wildlife oriented global operators offering tailor-made, mainly small group trips to Australia including Queensland's Lamington National Park and the Great Barrier Reef. *Australia Travel Centre*, 43-45 Middle Abbey St, Dublin, Ireland, T3531-8047188, Australia@abbeytravel.ie Good source of general advice for those travelling from Ireland.

In UK & Ireland

Abercrombie and Kent, 1520 Kensington Rd, Suite 212, Oak Brook, Illinois, 60523-2156, T800-323-7308, www.abercrombiekent.com Well-established US company offering a diverse range of luxury, locally guided global trips to Australia. *Absolute Australia*, 180 Varick St, New York, T212 627 8258, www.absoluteaustralia.com Diverse range of specialist trips to Eastern Australia with expert guides. *Earthwatch Research and Exploration*, PO Box 75, Maynard, MA 01754 USA, T978 461 0081, www.earthwatch.org Excellent eco-tourism trips to Eastern Australia in combination with conservation research on Australian wildlife. Offices in USA, UK and Australia.

In North America

Finding out more

Australian Tourist Commission, www.australia.com, and its state equivalents, see box, page 20, can be of great help, and there is also a wealth of all sorts of information to be found on the Federal and government websites (www.fed.gov.au). For general stats on all aspects of Australian life check out the website of the **Australian Bureau of Statistics**, www.abs.gov.au You can access the national database of telephone numbers and their accompanying addresses at www.whitepages.com.au **Yellow Pages®** also has its own site at www.yellowpages.com.au

Disabled travellers

Disabled travellers to Eastern Australia will find that although there are a good range of facilities meeting their needs, they can be spread quite thinly, especially outside the major cities. Although all public buildings have to meet certain government standards, the standards in the building can vary a lot. High-profile sights and attractions, and even parks generally have good access. The key to successful travel is planning, and there are several national and state organizations who can help with this, including **ACROD**, 33 Thesiger Court, Deakin, ACT 2600, T02 6282 4333, the industry association for disability services, and **NICAN**, PO Box 407, Curtin, ACT 2605, T02 6285 3713, who provide information on recreation, tourism, sport and the arts.

Also see www.australia.com and state sections

In Sydney the free leaflet 'CBD Access Map Sydney', available from the VICs or information booths, is a very useful map and guide for the disabled. For more detailed information contact the **Disability Council of NSW**, T02 9211 2866 (free call 1800 044 848) or **Disability Services Australia**, T02 9791 6599, www.dsa.org.au

Many organizations are equipped for handling TTY calls. For further information contact **Telstra Disability Services**, GPO Box 4997WW, Melbourne, VIC 3000, T1800 068424, 1800 808981 (TTYs), or T02 9396 1193. Publications include *Easy Access Australia: A Travel Guide to Australia* by Bruce Cameron (updated 2000, ISBN 095775101X).

As with many major airlines *Qantas*, T02 9957 7103 or 1800 652660 (both TTY), has considerable experience with disabled passengers. If you have to be accompanied by a support person on any internal flight, they offer the passenger and the nominated carer a 50% discount off. Contact **NICAN** for further details. Guide dogs may be brought into Australia, but are subject to quarantine, with occasional exceptions. Contact the **Australian Quarantine & Inspection Service**, T02 9832 4025. The interstate railways generally have facilities for the disabled but public transport is not always well designed for disabled travel without assistance. The major interstate bus operators are pleased to accommodate disabled travellers but prefer notice, though few coaches are equipped with lifts or lowered floors. The major hire car companies have adapted vehicles available. Disabled overseas parking permits may be used in Queensland. In New South Wales you will need to apply for a permit at a Roads and Traffic Authority office, T02 9218 6670, at least one month prior to arrival. Each state's permits are valid nationally. The website www.babs.com.au has a list of particularly well set up B&Bs. *WeCare Tours and Travel*, T02 9670 6668, wecaretours@fastmail.fm, are a New South Wales-based tour company specializing in tours for the disabled and elderly.

Gay and lesbian travellers

See also
www.gayaustralia
guide.com

The gay community in Australia is vibrant, vocal and visible in the larger cities. Sydney is the undoubted capital of gay and lesbian Australia, hosting every February the world's biggest Gay and Lesbian Mardi Gras. Outside the major cities, however, discrimination is not unknown and public displays of affection may not be enthusiastically received by the locals. **International Gay & Lesbian Travel Association (IGLTA)**, T02 9818 6669, is happy to help with advice. There are several national magazines keeping lesbians and gays in touch with what's going on, including *Lesbians on the Loose* and *DNA*. Checkout www.qbeds.com for lesbian- and gay-friendly accommodation.

Student travellers

There are various official youth/student ID cards available, including the widely recognized **International Student ID Card (ISIC)**, **Federation of International Youth Travel Organisations (FIYTO)** card, Euro 26 Card and Go-25 Card. Each also conveys benefits from simply getting discounts to emergency medical coverage and 24-hour hotlines. The cards are issued by student travel agencies and hostelling organizations. Backpackers will find a YHA or VIP membership card just as useful.

Travelling with children

Australia is an eminently wonderful and suitable place to take children. Far-fetched stories and rumours about poisonous snakes and insects, man-eating sharks and crocs, can put parents off but they shouldn't. If children are aware and sufficiently supervised, Australia will provide a memorable holiday experience for all the right reasons.

If you are concerned about the threat of the rumoured nasty native wildlife a trip to Sydney's Taronga Zoo, or indeed any of the numerous wildlife parks up and down the

National employment organizations

Agricultural work and station stays
Employment National, *T1300 720126,*
www.employmentnational.com.au,
provide good advice on where in the
country to find seasonal work and have
local agencies helping find specific
employment. **Visitoz,** *T07 4168 6106,*
www.visitoz.org, put you in touch with
outback stations looking for workers.
Willing Workers on Organic Farms,
T03 5155 0218, www.wwoof.com.au,
specialize in matching travellers with their

1,400 affiliated farms and stations. The
$45 membership gets you a guide book on
the scheme, friendly advice and insurance
against accidental injury.
Conservation holidays
Conservation Volunteers, *T1800 032501,*
www.conservationvolunteers.com.au,
organize volunteer conservation projects.
Overnight costs are $23 per day, including
accommodation, food and work-related
travel. In Sydney, the TNT magazine has
numerous employment agency listings.

Essentials

East Coast, will soon put your mind at rest. Wildlife in Australia, whether captive or not, offers one of the greatest natural history educational platforms for children on the planet. Encounters with amazing wildlife can become any foreign child's fondest.

As far as accommodation is concerned the vast majority of establishments, beyond the usual exclusive retreats for couples seeking a romantic weekend, welcome kids and offer reasonable financial concessions. Tourist based attractions and activities too, many of which are directed at the children's market, usually offer reduced rates for children and family concessions. When it comes to eating out, like most developed countries some eateries welcome children, while others – after being persecuted by the family from hell – may imagine having them spit-roasted, sans sauce. In general you are advised to stick to eateries that are obviously child-friendly or ask before making a booking.

In summary there are a multitude of excellent venues to take children or to keep them happily entertained. You will loose count of beaches of course, but we also highly recommend wildlife parks, the modern museums in Sydney and Brisbane and the theme parks on the Gold Coast.

Women travellers

In Australia the concept of chauvinism and the archetype Bruce and Sheila (the classic beer drinking male and do as you are told spouse) is fast becoming an old fashioned myth. Generally speaking women are given all due respect in all but the most backward of outback settlements.

For lone women travellers all the usual common sense recommendations apply. Australia is a big place and given so much space it seems logical you may find yourself alone and 'out there' some of the time. Indeed, the abduction and murder of male and female tourists, especially in the outback has occurred and will no doubt continue to. So try to avoid getting yourself in that situation and always let people know about your intentions. Hitch-hiking alone is not recommended for anybody, but especially women. Other than that; keep your wits about you and good company, especially at night.

Working in the country

The easiest work to get, though not to do, is generally fruit harvesting or packing. The pay isn't sensational, though hard workers can do alright, but it's sociable and can be fun. The main harvest periods are February to May in New South Wales and year-round in Queensland. If you do plan to rely on harvesting, bring a small tent, as accommodation can become problematic. Other outdoor work can also be found at farms and

A working holiday visa will be required for casual work, see page 24

stations. In the cities, work opportunities are usually tipped firmly in favour of women. The hospitality industry (hotels, pubs and bars) is the biggest employer of casual workers. Those with the right qualifications will find medical employment quite easy to come by. Jobs are advertised in local newspapers and on the internet, though the best places to start are the notice boards of backpacker hostels, or contacting them in advance. If working is going to form a major part of your travels, or you are thinking of emigrating to Australia, then consider a publication such as *Living and Working in Australia* by Laura Veltman (updated 2000, ISBN 1857036700).

Before you travel

Getting in

Visas   Visas are subject to change, so check first with your local Australian Embassy or High Commission. All travellers to Australia, except New Zealand citizens, must have a valid visa to enter Australia. These must be arranged prior to travel (allow two months) and cannot be organized at Australian airports.

Tourist visas do not allow the holder to work in Australia See also www.immi. gov.au/visitors

Tourist visas   These are free and are available from your local Australian Embassy or High Commission, or in some countries, in electronic format (an Electronic Travel Authority or ETA) from their websites, and from selected travel agents and airlines. Passport holders eligible to apply for an ETA include those from Austria, Belgium, Canada, Denmark, Finland, France, Germany, Greece, Hong Kong, the Irish Republic, Italy, Japan, Netherlands, Norway, Spain, Sweden, Switzerland, the UK and the USA. Tourist visas allow visits of up to three months within the year after the visa is issued. Six-month, multiple entry tourist visas are also available to visitors from certain countries.

See also page 23. Application forms can be downloaded from the embassy website or from www.immi.gov.au

Working holiday visa   A working holiday visa, which must also be arranged prior to departure, is available to people between 18 and 30 from certain countries that have reciprocal arrangements with Australia, including Canada, Denmark, Germany, the Irish Republic, Japan, Norway, Sweden and the UK. The working holiday visa allows multiple entry for one year from first arrival. It is granted on the condition that the holder works for no more than three months for a single employer. You must also demonstrate all the criteria necessary for a visitor visa ans must apply for it outside Australia – the current charge is A$150. For more information contact the Australian consulate in your native country or visit the Australian Immigration Department, www.immi.gov.au

Insurance   It's a very good idea to take out some form of travel insurance, wherever you're travelling from. This should cover you for theft or loss of possessions and money, the cost of medical and dental treatment, cancellation of flights, delays in travel arrangements, accidents, missed departures, lost baggage, lost passport and personal liability and legal expenses. Also check on inclusion of 'dangerous activities' such as climbing, diving, skiing, horse riding, even trekking, if you plan on doing any. Always read the small print carefully. Not all policies cover ambulance, helicopter rescue or emergency flights home. Find out if your policy pays medical expenses direct to the hospital or doctor, or if you have to pay and then claim the money back later. If the latter applies, make sure you keep all records.

If you have something stolen, get a copy of the police report – you will need this to substantiate your claim

Companies   There are a variety of policies to choose from, so it's best to shop around. Your travel agent can advise on the best deals available. Reputable student travel organizations often offer good value policies. Travellers from North America can try the *International Student Insurance Service (ISIS)*, which is available through **STA**, T800

Essentials

Australian Embassies and High Commissions

A full list can be found at
www.immi.gov.au

Canada *7th floor, Suite 710, 50 O'Connor St, Ottawa, Ontario, T613 2360841, www.ahc-ottaw.org*

France *(and visa processing for Luxembourg and Belgium), 4 rue Jean Rey, 75724 Paris, Cedex 15, www.austgov.fr*

Germany *(and visa processing for Switzerland, Denmark and Norway) Friedrichstrasse 200, 10117 Berlin, T030 8800880, www.australian-embassy.de*

Irish Republic *2nd floor, Fitzwilton House, Wilton Terrace, Dublin 2, T01 6761517, www.australianembassy.ie*

Italy *Corso Trieste 25, 00198 Rome, T06 852721, www.australian-embassy.it*

Japan *2-1-14 Mita, Minato-Ku, Tokyo, T03 5232 4111, www.australia.or.jp*

Netherlands *Carnegielaan 4, 2517 KH*

The Hague, T070 3108200, www.australian-embassy.nl

New Zealand *7th floor, Union House, 132-138 Quay St, Auckland, T09 3032429, www.australia.org.nz*

South Africa *292 Orient St, Pretoria, Arcadia 0001, T012 3423740, www.australia.co.za*

Spain *Pza Descubridor Diego de Ordás, 3, 28003 Madrid, T091 441 5025, www.embaustralia.es*

Sweden *Sergels Torg 12, 11th floor, 111 57 Stockholm, T08 613 2900, www.austemb.se*

United Kingdom *Australia House, The Strand, London, WC2B 4LA, T0207 3794334, www.australia.org.uk*

USA *1601 Massachusetts Ave, NW 20036, Washington D.C., T202 7973000, www.austemb.org*

7770112, www.sta-travel.com Other recommended travel insurance companies include **Access America**, T800 2848300, **Travel Insurance Services**, T800 9371387, and **Council Travel**, T888-COUNCIL, www.counciltravel.com Companies worth trying in Britain include **Direct Travel Insurance**, T0190 381 2345, www.direct-travel.co.uk, **Flexicover Group**, T0870 990 9292, www.flexicover.net.uk and **Columbus**, T020 7375 0011. Some companies will not cover those over 65. The best policies for older travellers are offered by **Age Concern**, T01883 346964.

Customs regulations & tax
See www.customs. gov.au for more details

The limits for duty-free goods brought into the country include: 1,125 ml of any alcoholic drink (beer, wine or spirits), and 250 cigarettes, or 250 grams of cigars or tobacco. There are various import restrictions, many there to help protect Australia's already heavily hit ecology. These primarily involve live plants and animals, plant and animal materials (including all items made from wood) and foodstuffs. If in doubt, confine wooden and plant goods to well-worked items and bring processed food only (even this may be confiscated, though Marmite is accepted!). Even muddy walking boots may attract attention. Declare any such items for inspection on arrival if you are unsure.

There are strict prohibitions when exiting Australia. Plant and animal life, including derivative articles and seeds, cannot be taken from the country. Australia's cultural heritage is also protected, and though a dot-painting or didjeridu are fine to take home, some art works and archaeological items are definitely not. See www.dcita.gov.au or call T02 6271 1610 for details.

Almost all goods in Australia are subject to a Goods and Services Tax (GST) of 10%. Visitors from outside Australia will find certain shops can deduct the GST if you have a valid departure ticket.

Vaccinations

No vaccinations are required or recommended for travel to Australia unless travelling from a yellow-fever-infected country in Africa or South America. Check with your local Australian Embassy for further advice. A tetanus booster is advisable, however, if you have one due.

Essentials

▶ **Snap happy**

Eastern Australia and especially Sydney presents endless photo opportunities and you will find a good camera is about as essential as a sun hat or a pair of Speedos. Given the harsh light in Australia, if you are at all serious about photography and getting good results, and have a digital or manual SLR (Single Lens Reflex) camera, then a polarising filter is essential. An orange 80A filter to warm up landscapes is also recommended. Film is expensive in Australia so you are advised to stock up before coming to Australia (especially in the USA) or at duty-free shops on arrival. For daytime shooting with transparency film, ASA50-200 Fuji or Kodakachrome 64 or 200 is recommended. For print photography, Kodak ASA100 is fine. For creative night shooting you will need a sturdy tripod but this may go beyond luggage capacity. If you are carrying an expensive camera and have travel insurance, make sure it is properly covered. This may involve an added premium and special listing.

What to take

Take more money and fewer clothes than you think you'll need

If you do forget some essential item you should be able to find it in Australia's major cities. Special respect must be paid to the Australian sun, especially if you will be spending long hours on the beach. A decent wide-brimmed hat and factor 30 sun-cream (cheap in Australian supermarkets) are essential. Light, long-sleeved tops and trousers cut down the necessity for quite as much sun-cream, help keep out the mosquitoes and keep you warmer in the early evening when the temperature can drop markedly. Even in the north it can get cold in winter so a few key warm clothes are also a good idea.

If you are 'roughing' it, a sleeping bag is useful in hostels and caravan parks as linen is not always supplied. In summer a sheet sleeping bag and pillow case usually suffice. Other useful items include: day bag, waterproof sandals, penknife (with bottle and can opener), padlock and length of light chain for security, a torch, a single-use underwater camera, water bottle (such as the *Platypus*), plastic lunchbox and a travel alarm clock.

If you're planning on doing some walking or trekking, come as prepared as you would do for wetter climes, including packing some decent boots. This said, most walking and camping equipment (other than boots) can be hired in the larger cities. It is quite easy to get lost on longer treks, so pack a compass and map (see Maps, page 43).

Money

The Australian dollar ($) is divided into 100 cents (c). Coins come in denominations of 5c, 10c, 20c, 50c, $1 and $2. Banknotes come in denominations of $5, $10, $20, $50 and $100. The currency is not legal tender in New Zealand, and NZ dollars are not legal tender in Australia. Exchange rates at the time of going to press were as follows: US$1 = A$1.48; £1 = A$2.51; €1 = A$1.76. All dollars quoted in this guide are Australian unless specified otherwise.

Banks, ATMs, credit & cash cards
Bank opening hours are Monday to Friday, from around 0930 to 1630

The four major banks, the *Challenge/Westpac*, *Commonwealth*, *National* and *ANZ*, are usually the best places to change money and travellers' cheques, though bureaux de change tend to have slightly longer opening hours and often open at weekends. You can withdraw cash from ATMs (cashpoints) with a cash card or credit card issued by most international banks, and they can also be used at banks, post offices and bureaux de change. Most hotels, shops, tourist operators and restaurants in Australia accept the major credit cards, though some places may charge for using them. When booking always check if an operator accepts them. EFTPOS (the equivalent of Switch in the UK) is a way of paying for goods and services with a cash card. Unfortunately EFTPOS only works with cards linked directly to an Australian bank account.

The safest way to carry money is in travellers' cheques, though travellers' dependence on them is fast becoming superseded by the prevalence of credit cards and ATMs. *American Express*, *Thomas Cook* and *Visa* are the cheques most commonly accepted. Remember to keep a record of the cheque numbers and the cheques you've cashed separate from the cheques themselves. Travellers' cheques are accepted for exchange in banks, large hotels, post offices and large gift shops. Some insist that at least a portion of the amount be in exchange for goods or services. Commission when cashing travellers' cheques is usually 1% or a flat rate. Avoid changing money or cheques in hotels as rates are often poor.

Travellers' cheques

If you need money urgently, the quickest way to have it sent is to have it wired to the nearest bank via *Western Union*, T1800 337377, www.travelex.com.au Charges apply but on a sliding scale. Money can also be wired by *Amex* or *Thomas Cook*, but may take a day or two, or transferred direct from bank to bank, but again can take several days. Within Australia money orders can be used to send money. See www.auspost.com.au

Money transfers

Accommodation, particularly outside the main centres, is good value, though prices can rise uncomfortably in peak seasons. Eating out can be indecently cheap. There are some restaurants in Sydney, comparable with the world's best, where $150 is enough to cover dinner for two. The bill at many excellent establishments can be half that. Transport varies considerably in price and can be a major factor in your travelling budget. Beer is about $4-6 a throw in pubs and bars, as is a neat spirit or glass of wine. Wine will generally be around 1½ times to double the price in restaurants that it would be from a bottleshop.

Cost of travelling
By European, North American and Japanese standards Australia is an inexpensive place to visit

The minimum budget required, if staying in hostels or campsites, cooking for yourself, not drinking much and travelling relatively slowly, is about $50 per person per day, but this isn't going to be a lot of fun. Going on the odd tour, travelling faster and eating out occasionally will raise this to a more realistic $70-100. Those staying in modest B&Bs, hotels and motels as couples, eating out most nights and taking a few tours will need to reckon on about $150-250 per person per day. Costs in the major cities will be 20-50% higher. Non-hostelling single travellers should budget on spending around 60-70% of what a couple would spend.

Almost all goods in Australia are subject to a Goods and Services Tax (GST) of 10%. Visitors from outside Australia will find certain shops can deduct the GST if you have a valid departure ticket. GST on Goods over $300 purchased (per store) within 30 days before you leave are refundable on presentation of receipts and purchases at the GST refund booth at Sydney International Airport (boarding pass and passport are also required). For more information T1300 363 263.

Many forms of transport and most tourist sites and tours will give discounts to all or some of the following: students, backpackers, the unemployed, the aged (all grouped as 'concessions' in this guide) and children. Proof will normally be required, a passport usually sufficient for children or the aged. See also page 22.

In general the cost of living in Australia is around half of that in the US and about 45% cheaper than the UK. Australia had three of the world's top 20 scoring cities in the Mercer Human Resource Consulting Group 2003 global quality of life survey. Sydney shares fifth place with Auckland, Copenhagen, Frankfurt and Bern, along with Melbourne (15th) and Perth (20th).

Cost of living

Essentials

▶ **Airline and agents in England and Ireland**

Council Travel 28a Poland St, London W1V 3DB, T020 7437 7767, www.destinations-group.com
Ebookers www.ebookers.com Comprehensive travel ticket booking website.
Expedia www.expedia.com Another web-only travel site, also with lots of background information.
STA Travel 86 Old Brompton Rd, London SW7 3LH, T020 7361 6161, www.statravel.co.uk Specialists in student

discount fares, IDs and other travel services. Also branches in most major cities and many college campuses.
Trailfinders 194 Kensington High St, London W8 6FT, T020 7938 3939, www.trailfinders.co.uk Particularly good on personalized itineraries and adventure travel.
Air New Zealand www.airnz.co.uk
British Airways www.britishairways.com
Emirates www.emirates.com
Qantas www.qantas.co.uk

Getting there

Air

As Australia is an island nation, and a considerable distance from anywhere except Indonesia and Papua New Guinea, the vast majority of visitors to Eastern Australia arrive in Sydney and come by air. There are international flights direct to Sydney, Brisbane and Cairns, and it is quite possible to have different points of arrival and departure that complement your intended itinerary. If there is not a direct flight to your primary choice there will usually be a same-day connection from Sydney, Melbourne or Perth. It is usually possible to book internal Australian flights when booking your international ticket, at lower prices than on arrival. Some do not even require a stated departure and arrival point. If you have any plans to fly within New South Wales or Queensland check this out with your travel agent prior to booking.

There are now enormous numbers of high street, phone and internet outlets for buying your plane ticket. This can make life confusing but the competition does mean that dogged work can be rewarded in a very good deal. Fares will depend on the season, with prices much higher during December and January unless booked well in advance. Mid-year tends to see the cheapest fares. *Qantas*, www.qantas.com.au, is Australia's main international airline and flies from a considerable number of international capitals and major cities. Most other major airlines have flights to Australia from their home countries or Europe.

The **internet** is great way of finding a bargain ticket, but can be frustrating unless you just want a straight return or single fare to a single destination. If you are considering a multi-destination journey it is worth checking out two or three agents in person.

One-way tickets are not necessarily a lot more expensive than half a return fare. If you are contemplating a lengthy trip and are undecided about further plans, or like the idea of being unconstrained, then a single fare could be for you. Australian immigration officials can get suspicious of visitors arriving on one-way tickets, however, especially on short-term visas. Anyone without long-term residency on a one-way ticket will need to show proof of substantial funds – enough for a stay and onward flight. Discuss this with your local Australian Embassy or High Commission before committing to a ticket.

Round-the-World (RTW) tickets can be a real bargain if you stick to the most popular routes, sometimes working out even cheaper than a return fare. RTWs start at around £750 (€1,184) or US$1,500, depending on the season. Sydney is easy to include on a RTW itinerary.

Airlines and agents in North America

Air Brokers International *323 Geary St,
Suite 4111, San Francisco, CA 94102, T800
8833273, www.airbrokers.com
Consolidator and specialist on RTW
and Circle Pacific tickets.*
Council Travel *205 E 42nd St, New York,
NY 10017, T800-COUNCIL,
www.counciltravel.com Student/budget
agency with branches in many other
US cities.*
Discount Airfares Worldwide On-Line
*www.etn.nl/discount.htm A hub of
consolidator and discount agent links.*
**International Travel Network/Airlines
of the Web** *www.itn.net/airlines
Online information and reservations.*
STA Travel *5900 Wiltshire Blvd, Suite 2110,*
*Los Angeles, CA 90036, T800 7770112,
www.sta-travel.com Discount/youth
travel company with branches in New
York, San Francisco, Boston, Miami,
Chicago, Seattle and Washington DC.*
Travel CUTS *187 College St, Toronto,
ON M5T 1P7, T800 6672887, www.travel
cuts.com Specialists in student discount
fares, IDs and other travel services.
Branches in other Canadian cities.*
Travelocity *www.travelocity.com
Online consolidator.*
Air New Zealand *www.airnz.co.uk*
United *www.ual.com*
Air Canada *www.aircanada.ca*
Singapore Airlines *www.singaporeair.com*

Essentials

When trying to find the best deal, make sure you check the route, journey duration, stopovers, departure and arrival times, restrictions and cancellation penalties. Many cheap flights are sold by small agencies, most honest and reliable, but there may be some risks involved with buying tickets at rock-bottom prices. Avoid paying too much money in advance and check with the airline directly to ensure you have a reservation.

From Europe

The main route, and the cheapest, is via Asia, though fares will also be quoted via North America or Africa. The Asia route usually takes from 20 to 30 hours including stops. There are no non-stop routes, so it's worth checking out what stopovers are on offer: this might be your only chance to see Kuala Lumpur. Stopovers of a few nights do not usually increase the cost of the ticket appreciably. The cheapest return flights, off-season, will be around £500 (€789), with stand-by prices rising to at least £800 (€1,263) around Christmas.

**From North &
South America**

There are direct *Qantas* flights from Los Angeles to Brisbane and Sydney, and from Vancouver and New York to Sydney. The cost of a standard return in the high season from Vancouver starts from around US$2,200, from New York from US$2,000 and from Los Angeles from US$1,700. Flights take around 10½ hours. There are also direct flights from Buenos Aires to Sydney.

**From New
Zealand**

There are direct *Qantas* and *Air New Zealand* flights from Auckland, Christchurch and Wellington to Cairns, Brisbane and Sydney. *Freedom Air*, www.freedom.co.nz, are another regional carrier servicing Sydney, Brisbane and the Gold Coast from various main centres in New Zealand. Expect to pay a minimum of NZ$400-500 for a return to the eastern seaboard. The journey takes about three hours.

**From South
Africa**

There are direct *Qantas* flights from Johannesburg to Sydney. *South African Airways*, www.saa.co.za, also fly direct, which takes around 14½ hours.

Departure tax

There are currently a various departure taxes levied by individual airports (ie, noise tax) and the government. One is a $10 contribution to funds for workers adversely affected by the collapse of the Ansett in 2001. All taxes are included in the cost of a ticket.

Road

Bus

If travelling by bus in Australia, always check the journey duration and time of arrival

McCaffertys/Greyhound, T13149/T132030 or (Sydney) T02 9212 3433, www.greyound. com. au or www.mccaffertys.com.au, have services throughout Australia and it is possible to get a direct, if long, ride from most of the mainland state capitals to Sydney, Brisbane or Cairns and most of the coastal towns in between. As well as scheduled routes and fares they offer two jump-on, jump-off passes. The Explorer Pass commits you to a set route, valid from 30 to 365 days, while the Kilometre Pass allows travel anywhere on the network over the course of a year. A 2,000-km pass is $281, concessions $253, with each extra 1,000 km costing around $100.

Touching down

Airport information

Sydney, Brisbane and Cairns are the main airports along this coast, and all have excellent services. All the main airlines fly to these airports with regular connections from international and national destinations. Facilities are good including banks and ATMs, tourist offices where help is on hand with accommodation booking and organizing tours and transport. They offer regular and efficient connections with the city centres either by coach or rail. See the respective sections for further details.

Tourist information

Generally speaking you are advised to stick with accredited VICs for the best, non-biased advice

Tourist offices, or Visitor Information Centres (VICs), can be found in all but the smallest Australian towns. Their locations, phone numbers, website or e-mail addresses, and opening hours are listed in the relevant sections of this guide. In most larger towns they have met certain criteria to be officially accredited. This usually means that they have some paid staff and will almost certainly mean they are open daily 0900-1700. Smaller offices may close at weekends, but given that many are run entirely by volunteers – something to bear in mind when someone struggles to find an obscure piece of information – the level of commitment to the visitor is impressive. All offices will provide information on accommodation, local sights, attractions, and tours. Many will also have information on eating out, local history and the environment, and sell local souvenirs, guides and maps. Most will provide a free town map. Their ethic is to provide information that does not favour one local establishment or operator over another so you may find it difficult to get a specific recommendation. Some also double as privately run booking agencies, however, and these may not give you comprehensive lists of accommodation or tours, but simply a list of those that pay a commission to the office. The booking service is free for visitors.

Local customs and laws

Tipping is not the norm in Australia, but a discretionary 5-10% tip for particularly good service will be appreciated. Smoking is illegal in restaurants, cafés and pubs where eating is a primary activity, and on public transport.

Safety

Australia certainly has its dangers, but with a little common sense and basic precautions they are relatively easy to minimize. The most basic but important are the effects of the **sun**. UV levels can soar in Australia, with safe exposure limits as low as three

Touching down

Business hours   *Generally 0830-1700 Mon-Fri. Many convenience stores and supermarkets are open daily. Late night shopping is generally either Thu or Fri.*

Electricity   *The current in Australia is 240/250v AC. Plugs have 2 or 3 blade pins.*

Emergencies   *For police, fire brigade or ambulance dial 000.*

Laundry   *Most larger towns have coin operated launderettes. Average cost, $5.*

Phone codes   *NSW 02, QLD 07.*

Time zones   *Australia covers three time zones: Queensland and New South Wales are in Eastern Standard GMT+10 hrs. NSW operate daylight saving: clocks go forward one hour from October and March.*

Essentials

minutes. A bad burn has ruined many a holiday, and unhealthy exposure can lead to much worse later. As well as sunburn, heat-stroke is also a danger, a common result of too much heat and too little fluid.

In **urban areas**, as in almost any city in the world, there is always the possibility of muggings, alcohol-induced harassment or worse. The usual simple precautions apply, like keeping a careful eye and hand on belongings, not venturing out alone at night and avoiding dark, lonely areas. There are two principal dangers on **country roads**. Fatigue is the cause of many Australian accidents, as are large native and stock animals. Hitch-hiking is not recommended. For more information on road safety see page 37, or contact one of the AAA associations, see page 41.

On the beach there is little to trouble the holidaymaker who sticks to the shore and swims between the patrolled flags, but swimmers must be aware of hidden dangers. The principal one is the **rip**, a strong, off-shore undertow that can sweep even waders off their feet, submerge them and drown them astonishingly quickly. Always look out for signs indicating common rip areas, and ask locals if at all unsure. See the **Surf Life Saving Australia** website, www.slsa.asn.au, for more information. Much publicized, but out of all proportion, is the danger from **sharks**. There are a handful of shark attacks in Australia each year, and usually one or two are fatal, but this must be balanced against the number of times someone goes for a swim or surf each year – hundreds of millions. Several other sea creatures are far more likely to do you harm, especially along the Queensland coast. Biggest of these are the **Estuarine crocodiles** ('salties') of the north. If given the opportunity they will ambush and eat any animal or person careless enough to stray near or into their river or estuary. Always check whether a waterhole or river is likely to be a crocodilian home, and if in doubt assume it is. Australian coastal waters are also home to a host of fish, jellyfish, octopus, urchins, coral and even molluscs that can inflict extremely painful, sometimes lethal stings and bites. See box, page 342.

In the water

Take precautions. Park rangers and the police are good sources of information. If you have the time learn about the various local poisonous marine creatures, their tell-tale wound-marks and symptoms, and the correct procedure for treatment. See page 342. Tell someone on-shore you are going for a swim. Avoid swimming alone, and keep swimming partners in sight. While snorkelling or diving, do not touch either creatures or coral. Even minor coral scratches can lead to infections, and it doesn't do the coral any good either. Wear a wetsuit or t-shirt and shorts even if the water is warm. This will lessen the effect of any sting and help protect against the sun. Wear water-proof sunscreen, and reapply frequently. If wading around in shallow water, particularly near reefs, wear a pair of old trainers or waterproof sandals. A large number of the little beasties that can do you serious harm do so when you tread on them. If you are bitten or stung, get out of the water, carefully remove and keep any spine or tissue, seek advice as to appropriate immediate treatment and apply it, and quickly seek medical help. When jumping off rocks into water, always first check that the depth is sufficient.

Essentials

▶ **How big is your footprint?**

- Follow the minimal impact bushwalking code for walking and camping. Details can be obtained from any park office.
- Choose a responsible operator. Ecotourism Association of Australia, T07 3229 5550, www.ecotourism.org.au, promotes ecologically sustainable and responsible tourism and runs an accreditation programme for tour operators.
- Try not to drive at dawn, dusk or at night, both to avoid killing native animals and for your own safety.
- Water is a precious resource in Australia – don't waste it or pollute it. In dry conditions camp away from waterholes so that animals are not afraid to approach the water.
- Make sure you are well prepared for the local conditions. Carrying sufficient water, food and fuel and appropriate clothing or equipment may save your life and avoid danger, expense and inconvenience for those who might otherwise have to rescue you.
- If you have to pass through gates in national parks or on private property the rule is 'leave them as you find them'.

On land   There are numerous creatures with very poisonous bites on land. Most will only bite, however, if trodden on, cornered or harassed. The most common poisonous **spider** is the tiny, shy redback, which has a shiny black body with distinct red markings. It regularly sets up shop under rocks or in garden sheds and garages. Outside toilets are also a favourite. Far more dangerous, though restricted to the Sydney area only, is the Sydney funnel-web, a larger and more aggressive customer entirely, often found in outdoor loos! There are dozens of venomous **snake** species in Australia. Few are actively aggressive and even those only during certain key times of year, such as mating season, but all are easily provoked and for many an untreated bite can be fatal.

See also Walking and trekking, page 50   The main dangers while **bushwalking** are dehydration from a lack of water, heat-stroke, and getting lost. Before setting out seek advice about how to access the start and finish of the track, the terrain you are planning to traverse, how long it will take given your party's minimum fitness level, the likely weather conditions, and prepare accordingly. Park rangers and the police are good sources of information. Learn about the various local poisonous snakes, their seasonal habits, tell-tale wound-marks and symptoms, and the correct procedure for treatment. Plan, if possible, to walk in the early morning or late afternoon when the famous golden glow often takes hold just before sunset. These are also the best times for viewing wildlife. Take a decent map of the area, a compass, and a first-aid kit. Take full precautions for the sun, but also be prepared for wet or cold weather. Take plenty of **water**, in hot weather at least one litre for every hour you plan to walk (a frozen plastic bottle will ensure cold water for hours). On long-distance walks take something to purify stream and standing water as giardia is present in some areas. Wear stout walking shoes and socks. Tell someone where you are going and when you plan to get back. Avoid striding through long grass and try to keep to tracks. If the path is obscured, make plenty of noise as you walk. If you do see a snake, give it a wide berth. If you need to squat to go to the toilet, or are collecting firewood, bash the undergrowth around your position. If you do get bitten by either a spider or snake stay calm and still, apply pressure to the bite area and wind a compression bandage around it (except for redback bites). Remain as still as possible and keep the limb immobile. Seek urgent medical attention. A description of the creature, and residual venom on the victim's skin, will help with swift identification and so treatment. Anti-venom is available for most spider and snake bites. Avoid walking alone, and keep walking partners in sight. Keep to paths and avoid cliff edges.

The three main professional emergency services are supported by several others, including the **State Emergency Service (SES)**, **Country Fire Service (CFS)**, **Surf Life Saving Australia (SLSA)**, **Sea-search and Rescue**, and **St John Ambulance**. The SES is prominent in co-ordinating search and rescue operations. The CFS provides invaluable support in fighting and controlling bush fires. These services, though professionally trained, are mostly provided by volunteers.

Emergency services
Dial 000 for the emergency services

Responsible tourism

All over the world the responsible traveller sticks to the creed of 'take nothing but photographs and leave nothing but footprints'. This applies to Australia too, where there are also some unique considerations. One of Australia's main attractions is the natural environment and its wildlife, and there are many opportunities for eco-tourism.

CALM promote a minimal impact bushwalking code aimed at protecting the environment, which is also a useful guide for minimizing your footprint in other natural environments. Fire is a critical issue in Australia's hot dry environments where only a spark is needed to create a fire that can get out of control and destroy an area the size of a small country in a day or two, perhaps threatening lives and property. The national parks around Sydney have been particularly badly hit in the last decade. For this reason, in some areas, there are total fire bans, either for a seasonal period or on days when a high risk of fire is predicted. In extreme circumstances a national park, scenic attraction or walking trail may be closed because the risk of fire is so high. Fire bans or restrictions usually apply in summer (November to March) in the south and during the late dry season in the north (July to November). Check fire restrictions before travel with the nearest parks, shire, police or tourist office as they may affect your preparations; on days of Total Fire Ban you will have to take food that doesn't need cooking.

Campers should always carry a fuel stove for cooking as many national parks or public reserves forbid campfires or the collection of wood or both. Fallen timber and hollow logs are an important habitat for wildlife. It is also good practice to keep your walking or camping gear clean between different environments, particularly in the southern forest areas affected by dieback, a fungus called *Phytophthora cinnamomi* that attacks the roots of plants so that they die of thirst. It is spread when soil or roots are moved, possibly via your boots, car or tent. Dieback areas are usually closed to the public but boot-cleaning stations are provided for high-risk walking tracks.

Travellers in Australia will also come across 'sacred sites', areas of religious importance to indigenous people, and naturally it is important to respect any restrictions that may apply to these areas. Permission is usually required to enter an Aboriginal community and you may be asked to comply with restrictions, such as a ban on alcohol. If you visit a community, or travel through Aboriginal land, respect the privacy of Aboriginal people and never take photographs without asking first.

If you want to know more about environmental issues or get involved in conservation, contact **Australian Conservation Foundation**, T02 9212 6600, www.acfonline.org.au or **The Wilderness Society**, T03 6234 9799, www.wilderness.org.au Other organizations include: **Queensland Parks and Wildlife Service**, T07 3227 8186, www.env.qld.gov.au (Brisbane); **National Trust of Australia**, T07 3229 1788, www.nationaltrustqld.org (Brisbane). The quarterly wilderness adventure magazine *Wild* is also a good source of information on current environmental issues and campaigns.

Essentials

▶ **Ten great hotels and resorts**

Rae's on Watego, *Byron Bay.*
Kingfisher Bay Resort, *Fraser Island.*
Palazzo Versace, *Gold Coast.*
Tangalooma Wild Dolphin Resort,
Moreton Island.
P&O Heron Island Resort, *Heron Island.*

Hayman Island Resort, *Whitsundays.*
Dunk Island Resort, *Dunk Island.*
Sanctuary Retreat, *Mission Beach.*
Sheraton Mirage, *Port Douglas.*
Lizard Island Resort, *Northern Great
Barrier Reef.*

Where to stay

*See inside cover for
price categories.
Accommodation is
identified by ■ on
maps in the guide*

East Coast Australia presents one of the most diverse and attractive range of accommodation options in the world, from cheap national park campsites alive with wildlife to exclusive and luxurious Great Barrier island retreats. The real beauty here, given the weather and the environment, is that travelling on a budget does not in any way detract from the enjoyment of the trip. On the contrary, this is a place where nights under canvas in national parks, or preparing your porridge on a campfire under the gaze of a possum is an absolute delight.

If we haven't provided the sleeping option that you desire, local VICs can supply full accommodation listings. Details of the centres are given throughout the book.

**Hotels, motels
& resorts**

At the top end of the scale, especially in Sydney, Brisbane, the Gold Coast, Moreton Bay Islands, Fraser Island, Whitsunday Islands, Cairns and the Great Barrier Reef Islands there are some impressive international-standard hotels and resorts, with luxurious surroundings and facilities, attentive service and often outstanding locations. Rooms will typically start in our L range. In the main cities are a few less expensive hotels in the A-B range. Most 'hotels', outside of the major towns, are pubs with upstairs or external accommodation. If upstairs, a room is likely to have access to shared bathroom facilities, while external rooms are usually standard en suite motel units. The quality of pub-hotel accommodation varies considerably, but is usually a budget option (C-D). Linen is almost always supplied.

Motels in Australia are usually depressingly anonymous, but dependably clean and safe, and usually offer the cheapest en suite rooms. Most have dining facilities and free, secure parking. Some fall into our D range, most will be a B-C. Linen is always supplied.

**B&Bs &
self-catering**

Bed and Breakfast (B&B) is in some ways quite different from the British model. Not expensive, but rarely a budget option, most fall into our B-C ranges. They offer very comfortable accommodation in usually upmarket, sometimes historic houses. Rooms are usually en suite or have access to a private bathroom. Bathrooms shared by more than two rooms are rare. Hosts are usually friendly and informative. Some B&Bs are actually a semi or fully self-contained cottage or cabin with breakfast provisions supplied. Larger ones may have full kitchens.

As well as private houses, self-contained, self-catering options are provided by caravan parks and hostels, and some resorts and motels with apartment-style units. Linen may not be supplied in self-catering accommodation. A couple of good websites are www.bedandbreakfastnsw.com (NSW) and www.bnb.au.com (QLD).

**National
parks, farms
& stations**

Some national parks and rural cattle and sheep stations have old settlers or workers' homes that have been converted into tourist accommodation, usually self-contained. They are often magical places to stay and include many old lighthouse keepers' cottages and shearers' quarters. Stations may also invite guests to see, or even get

Ten great hostels

Samurai Beach Bungalows, *Port
Stephens.*
Bellingen YHA Backpackers, *Bellingen.*
Arts Factory, *Byron Bay.*
Rainbow Retreat Backpackers, *Nimbin.*
Trekkers, *Southport, Gold Coast.*

Woolshed, *Hervey Bay.*
Platypus Bush Camp, *Eungella.*
Maggie's Beach House, *Magnetic Island.*
Global Palace, *Cairns.*
Cape Trib Beach House, *Cape
Tribulation.*

Essentials

involved in, the day's activities. Transport to them can be difficult if you don't have your own. Linen is often not supplied in this sort of accommodation.

There are a large network of good-value hostels (D-F). They are popular centres for backpackers and provide a great opportunity for meeting fellow travellers. Most will have at least one double room and possibly singles, sometimes with linen. Almost all hostels have kitchen and common room facilities. A few, particularly in cities, will offer freebies including breakfast and pick-ups. Standards vary considerably, and it's well worth asking other travellers about the hostels at your next ports of call. Most are effectively independent and but the best tend to be those that are owner-managed. The hostel associations **NOMADS** (T1800 819883, www.nomadsworld.com, no membership fee) and **YHA** (T02 9261 1111, www.yha.org.au) seem to ensure the best consistency of quality. International visitors can obtain a **Hostelling International Card** (HIC) from any YHA hostel or travel centre. For this you get a handbook to YHA hostels and around $3 off each night's YHA accommodation. YMCA and YWCA (T1800 249124, www.travel-ys.com) hostels are usually a clean and quiet choice in the major cities.

Hostels
*Many good choices
are listed as 'clean,
small and friendly'
hostels on
www.bpf.com.au*

Almost every town will have at least one caravan park with unpowered and powered sites, varying from $10-20 for campers, caravans and campervans, an ablution block and usually a camp kitchen or BBQs. Some will have permanently sited caravans (on-site vans) and cabins. On-site vans are usually the cheapest option (E-F) for families or small groups wanting to self-cater. Cabins are usually more expensive (C-D). Some will have televisions, en suite bathrooms, separate bedrooms with linen and well-equipped kitchens. Power is rated at the domestic level (240/250v AC) which is very convenient for budget travellers. Some useful organizations are: *Big 4*, T1800 632444, www.big4.com.au; *Family Parks of Australia*, T1800 682492, www.familyparks.com.au; *Top Tourist Parks*, T08 8363 1901, www.toptourist.contact.com.au

**Caravan &
tourist parks**
*Joining a park
association will
get you a discount
in all parks that are
association members*

Where Australian roads connect towns more than about 100 km apart there will usually be roadhouses on the way. They vary from simple fuel stops and small stores to mini-resorts with accommodation, small supermarkets, post offices, daytime cafés, evening restaurants and bars. They will often have single and double rooms in what look for all the world like converted shipping containers (they often are), known as ATCOs (after one of the principal manufacturers) or dongers. These usually fall into the B-C range.

Roadhouses

Some national parks allow camping, mostly in designated areas only, with a few allowing limited bushcamping. Facilities are usually minimal, with basic toilets, fireplaces and perhaps tank water; a few have BBQs and shower blocks. Enjoyable camping necessitates being well prepared. Payment is often by self-registration (around $3-10 per person), and BBQs often require 20c, 50c or $1 coins, so have small notes and change ready. In many parks you will need a gas stove. If there are fireplaces you must bring your own wood. Collecting wood within parks is prohibited, as logs and twigs are an important habitat for native animals. No fires may be lit, even stoves, during a Total

Camping
*Park notes with maps
are available for most
parks at local tourist or
parks offices, or at the
entrance point. Some
can be downloaded
from park authority
websites*

▶ ## Ten great national park and island campsites

Arakoon State Recreation Area, *Hat Head NP.*

Smoky Rest Area, *Hat Head NP.*

Woody Head Campsite, *Iluka NP.*

Platypus Bush Camp, *near Eungella NP.*

Green Mountains, *Lamington NP.*

Lady Musgrave Island *(Bundaberg).*

Masthead and North West Islands *(Gladstone).*

Heron Island *(Gladstone).*

Frankland Island *(Cairns).*

Hinchinbrook Island *(Cardwell).*

Fire Ban. Even if water is supposedly available it is not guaranteed so take a supply, as well as your own toilet paper. Bush camping in national parks is strongly regulated. The key rules are to be particularly careful with fire, camp at least 20 m from any waterhole or course, and to disturb the environment as little as possible. Nothing must be left behind, and nothing removed, even rocks. Toilet waste should be carefully buried, at least 100 m from any waterhole or course. Bear in mind camping in national parks is without doubt the best way to experience the natural environment in Australia and provides the best opportunity to see much of its unique and remarkable flora and fauna. Publications describing free roadside and bushcamping spots are widely available.

There are many spots outside parks where camping is also expressly allowed. A few are managed by forestry agencies and other local authorities, and there may be a small fee. On rare occasions there may be the basic toilets, water and fireplaces. Out of courtesy and regard for the environment, act as if you were in a national park. Some parking bays allow caravans or campervans to stop overnight. Even if not allowed, stop for a sleep if the choice is between that or driving while very tired.

Swags   Swags are large lined pieces of canvas that enclose a thin mattress and sleeping bag, for outdoor use, placed directly on the ground. They are very much a part of Australian folklore and are still widely used in the country. There's nothing quite like lying in bed and watching the sun rise in the morning as the cockatoos screech overhead. The main disadvantages to swags are their weight and the space they take up, and also that they are open to the elements and insects.

Campervans
See also Getting around, page 39

A popular choice for many visitors is to hire or buy a vehicle that can be slept in, combing the costs of accommodation and transport (although you will still need to book into caravan parks for power and ablutions). Ranging from the popular VW Kombi to enormous vans with integral bathrooms, they can be hired from as little as $30 per day to as much as $500. A van for two people at around $100 per day compares well with hiring a car and staying in hostels, and allows greater freedom. High-clearance, 4WD campervans are also available, and increase travel possibilities yet further. Kombis can usually be bought from about $2,500. An even cheaper, though less comfortable alternative is to buy a van or station wagon (estate car) that is big enough to lay out a sleeping mat and bag in.

The following are campervan specialists, though the major car hire companies also have campervans available, see page 41. *Apollo*, T1800 777779 or T07 3260 5466, www.apollocamper.com.au; *Backpacker*, T1800 670232 or T02 9667 0402, www.backpackercampervans.com; *Britz*, T1800 331454 or T03 9417 1888, www.britz.com; *Getabout*, T02 9380 5536, www.getaboutoz.com; *Maui*, T1300 363800 or T02 9597 6155, www.maui-rentals.com; *NQ*, T1800 079529 or T02 9380 7501, www.nqrentals.com; *Eastern State Specific Abbeys*, T1800 888401; *Wicked*, T1800 246869 or T0417 740307, www.wickedcampers.com.au

Ten great caravan and tourist parks

Shoal Bay Holiday Park, *Port Stephens.*
Sandbar Caravan Park, *Myall Lakes.*
Seal Rocks Camping Reserve, *Myall Lakes.*
Horseshoe Bay Beach Park, *SW Rocks.*
Emerald Beach Holiday Park, *Emerald Beach, Coffs Harbour.*

Broken Head Caravan Park, *Broken Head, Byron Bay.*
Noosa River Caravan Park, *Noosa.*
Beachcomber Caravan Village, *Mission Beach South.*
Happy Wanderer Village, *Hervey Bay.*
Cairns Coconut Caravan Resort, *Cairns.*

◀

Essentials

Getting around

Public transport in and around New South Wales and Queensland and its main centres, based on a variety of bus, ferry and train networks, is generally good and efficient, and often easier than driving. Most cities have metropolitan bus services, but some can be curiously regardless of tourist traffic and there is many an important outlying attraction poorly served by public transport, or even missed off the bus routes completely. Some cities are compact enough for this to be a minor irritation, others are so spread out that the visitor must invest in an expensive tourist bus service or taxis to get around. In such places staying at a hostel or B&B with free or low-cost bicycle hire can save a lot of money.

Road and street maps for all the major Australian regions, cities and towns can be found at www.arta.com.au

By far the best way of seeing the East Coast is under your own steam, or with a tour operator with an in-depth itinerary. See Tours and tour operators, page 20, and individual town and city sections for details. The further from the cities you go, the more patchy and irregular public transport becomes. Both New South Wales and Queensland have networks based on a combination of air, bus and train. Some of these services connect up at border towns but you are advised to check first. If short on time and long on funds, flying can save a lot of time and effort, both interstate and within New South Wales and Queensland. In some cases it is the only real option. Most other interstate options involve long-distance buses, and on a few routes, trains.

Air

Sydney, Brisbane and Cairns all possess an international airport, and almost every country town and outback station in Australia has at least an airstrip. Between them *Qantas*, *QantasLink* and *Virgin Blue* link most of the state capitals to each other and to many of the larger provisional towns and main tourist destinations. If one of them does operate a route they are likely to offer the cheapest fare, usually $100-700 one way. There are also several regional airways operating smaller planes on specialist routes. For up-to-date information on whether a destination is served by a scheduled or charter flight, contact your destination's tourist office.

Many provincial airports may not be staffed when you arrive. Check with the local tourist office regarding transport from the airport to the town

Road

State and interstate bus services offer the most cost-effective way of constructing an itinerary for a single traveller. The main operator throughout New South Wales and Queensland is *Travel Coach*, which now manages both *Greyhound Pioneer* and *McCafferty's*. Their network follows all the main interstate highways up and down the coast with offshoots including the Blue Mountains, New England (Hunter Valley), Armidale, Charters Towers, the Atherton Tablelands and so on. As well as scheduled routes and fares they offer two jump-on, jump-off passes. The Explorer Pass commits

Bus
A large selection of services can be found at www.buslines.com.au

Essentials

▶ **Main interstate and state airlines**

Qantas or QantasLink, T131313,
www.qantas.com.au
Virgin Blue, T136789, www.virginblue.
com.au, are the principal carriers.
Hazelton T131713, www.hazelton.com.au
that along with QantasLink offer regular
services between the main coast and
outback centres. In Queensland, again,

QantasLink T131313,
www.qantas.com.au in conjunction with
Macair T131313, www.macair.com.au are
the principal air carriers offering regular
services. Smaller regional charters and
airlines cover most Great Barrier Islands .
Specific local operators are mentioned in
the relevant text.

you to a set route, valid 30-365 days. Sydney-Cairns is around $300, eastern circuit $1,200. Slightly pricier is the Kilometre Pass, which allows travel anywhere on the network over the course of a year. A 2,000-km pass is $281, concessions $253, with each extra 1,000 km costing around $100.

The interstate
companies are
complemented by
state-wide bus/train
networks

If travelling by bus around Eastern Australia, always check the journey duration and time of arrival. Some routes can literally take days, each 24 hours long with just a couple of short meal stops. Many coaches are equipped with videos, but you may want a book to hand. It's also a good idea to take warm clothing, socks, a pillow, toothbrush and ear-plugs. There's a good chance you will arrive in the late evening or the early hours of the morning. If it is the case, book accommodation ahead and, if possible, transfer transportation. At least ensure you know how to get to your accommodation, and try to avoid walking around alone late at night. Also double-check times of connections: many travel arrangements have been disrupted by the discovery that a bus was on a different day than assumed. Many of the Transport sections in this guide do indicate departure times and days. These are, of course, subject to change and should not be relied upon as definitive.

Main interstate and state companies *McCafferty's*, T131499, www.mccaffertys. com.au, *Greyhound*, T132030, www.greyhound.com.au and *Premier Motor Service*, T131410, www.premierms.com.au, are the three principal long-distance, interstate coach service providers in New South Wales and Queensland, but there are many other smaller regional companies. Most are listed under the relevant destinations. *Countrylink*, T132232, www.countrylink.nsw.gov.au, also offer coach services to some centres in conjunction with rail schedules between New South Wales and Queensland.

Backpacker buses There are now several operators who make the assumption that the most important part of your trip is the journey. These companies combine the roles of travel operator and tour guide, taking from two to five times longer than scheduled services (a good indicator of just how much they get off the highway). They are worth considering, especially if you are travelling alone. In terms of style, price ($75-150 per day) and what is included they vary greatly, and it is important to clarify this prior to booking. Some offer transport and commentary only, others include accommodation and some meals, a few specialize in 4WD and bushcamping. The latter are not for everyone, but for many will provide an unforgettable experience. A few, including *Oz Experience* offer jump-on, jump-off packages, and are priced more on distance. The popular option of flying Sydney to Cairns and returning by *Oz bus* is $630. The main backpacker bus companies in NSW and Queensland are *Oz Experience*, T1300 300028 or T02 8356 1766, www.ozexperience.com, and *Travelabout*, T08 9244 1200, www.travelabout.au.com *Wonderbus*, T02 9555 9800, www.wonderbus.com.au, offer good tours of the Blue Mountains and a day trip to Port Stephens and the Hunter Valley vineyards. *The Adventure Company*, 1st floor, 13 Shields St, T40514777, www.adven

◀

Comparison of budget travel costs

The following table compares the costs of various ways of travelling. It is based on the approximate cost for two people travelling together, includes food (cooking rather than eating out), tours ($200 per week each without own transport, $100 otherwise), and where appropriate bus passes, fuel, NRMA or RACQ cover and insurance (not travel), depreciation and maintenance, and the purchase of camping equipment ($300). It assumes campers and those in campervans will bushcamp for free approximately half the time. For one person travelling alone the bus pass options are almost always the cheapest, unless you're planning a very long trip. The relative merits of each form of travel are, of course, not limited to cost alone. Prices are given in Australian dollars.

1   *Aus Experience* and stay in hostels
2   *McCaffertys/Greyhound* (by Explorer or km pass) and stay in hostels
3   Hire a campervan
4   Hire a car and stay in hostels
5   Hire a car and camp
6   Buy a car and stay in hostels
7   Buy a car or van and camp

	1	2	3	4	5	6	7
26 weeks 16,000 km	23,700	23,250	22,890	25,730	19,390	21,400	15,060
16 weeks 13,000 km	15,220	14,770	14,430	16,150	12,360	13,820	10,030
12 weeks 10,000 km	11,440	11,080	10,850	12,140	9,370	10,830	8,060
8 weeks 7,000 km	7,610	7,440	7,270	8,120	6,380	7,840	6,090
4 weeks 3,500 km	3,790	3,780	3,640	4,060	3,340	4,590	3,870
2 weeks 2,000 km	2,000	1,920	1,990	2,200	1,990	3,100	2,890

tures.com.au, and *Billy Tea Bush Safaris*, T40320055, www.billytea.com.au, are both Cairns-based adventure tour operators offering a good range of day and multi-day trips in Far North Queensland. *Wild-Life Tours*, T03 9534 8868, www.wildlifetours. com.au, offer some good eco-based options.

Car
There isn't a substitute in Australia for having your own transport

If you live in a small heavily populated country travelling by car in Australia will be an enlightening experience. Distances are huge and subsequent travelling times between the major cities, towns and sights can be huge, however, instead of getting bored and annoyed, sit back, put on some tunes and actually make driving part of the whole holiday experience. Conjestion, other than on a few routes in Sydney, isn't a problem.

As a general rule of thumb consider buying a car if you are travelling for more than three months. Consider a campervan if hiring or buying a car. Traffic congestion is rarely an issue on the East Coast route, only Sydney has anything like the traffic of most nations, so driving itineraries can be based on covering a planned distance each day. Up to, say, 100 km for each solid hour's driving. The key factor in planning is distance. It is pretty stress-free and as the distances can be huge, drivers can get bored and sleepy. There are a lot of single-vehicle accidents in Australia, many the result of driver fatigue.

Essentials

▶ **Distances and bus journey times along the East Coast**

New South Wales

Sydney to Katoomba	122 km	3 hours
Sydney to Newcastle	150 km	3 hours
Newcastle to Port Macquarie	253 km	4½ hours
Port Macquarie to Coffs Harbour	159 km	2½ hours
Coffs Harbour to Byron Bay	237 km	4 hours
Byron Bay to Surfers Paradise	100 km	1¼ hours

Queensland

Surfers Paradise to Brisbane	78 km	1½ hours
Brisbane to Noosa Heads	145 km	2½ hours
Noosa Heads to Hervey Bay	187 km	3½ hours
Hervey Bay to Bundaberg	125 km	2 hours
Bundaberg to Rockhampton	319 km	4 hours
Rockhampton to Mackay	348 km	4 hours
Mackay to Airlie Beach	160 km	2½ hours
Airlie Beach to Townsville	303 km	4¼ hours
Townsville to Cairns	361 km	5¾ hours

Also, especially if you stray from the coast and 'go outback', watch out for large animals. Kangaroos and emus can appear seemingly out of nowhere, particularly at dawn and dusk, and sheep and cattle frequently stray onto unfenced roads. Such collisions are not simply irritations: hitting a kangaroo, emu or sheep can write off the vehicle and cause injury. Drive only in full daylight if possible.

On country and outback roads you will also meet road trains. These trucks can be over 50 m long including up to four separate trailers strung along behind the main cab. Overtaking them takes great care – wait for a good long stretch before committing. If you're on a single-track bitumen road or an unsealed road pull right over when one comes the other way. Not only can dust cause zero visibility, but you will also minimise the possibility of stones pinging up and damaging your windows.

The other major factor when planning is the type of roads you may need to use. Almost all the main interstate highways between Sydney and Cairns are 'sealed', though there are a few exceptions. Many country roads are unsealed, usually meaning a stoney or sand surface. When recently graded (levelled and compacted) they can be almost as pleasant to drive on as sealed roads, but even then there are reduced levels of handling. After grading, unsealed roads deteriorate over time. Potholes form, they can become impassable when wet, and corrugations usually develop, especially on national park roads with heavy usage. These are regular ripples in the road surface, at right angles to the road directio that can go on for tens of kilometres. Small ones simply cause an irritating judder, large ones can reduce tolerable driving speeds to 10-20 kph. Generally, the bigger the wheel size, and the longer the wheel-base, the more comfortable journeys over corrugations will be. Many unsealed roads can be negotiated with a two wheel-drive (2WD), low-clearance vehicle, but the ride will be a lot more comfortable, and safer in a four wheel-drive (4WD) high-clearance one. Most 2WD hire-cars are uninsured if driven on unsealed roads. Some unsealed roads (especially in the outback) are designated as 4WD-only or tracks, though individual definitions of some differ according to the map or authority you consult. If in any doubt whatsoever, stick to the roads you are certain are safe for your vehicle, and you are sufficiently prepared for. With careful preparation, however, and the right vehicles (convoys are recommended), traversing the major outback tracks is an awesome experience. Always check with the hire company where you can and cannot take your 4WD vehicle (some

Car hire companies

Australia Avis, T136333, www.avis.com;
Budget, T1300 362848, www.budget.com.
au; Delta-Europcar, T1800 811541,
www.deltacars.com.au; Hertz, T133039,
www.hertz.com; Thrifty, T1300 367227,
www.rentacar.com.au
New Zealand Avis, T09 5262847,
www.avis.co.nz; Budget, T09 3752222,
www.budget.co.nz; Hertz, T09 3676350,
www.hertz.co.nz
North America Avis, T800 3311084,

www.avis.com; Budget, T800 5270700,
www.budgetrentacar.com;
Delta-Europcar, www.x.com.au; Hertz,
T800 6543001, www.hertz.com; Thrifty,
T800 3672277, www.thrifty.com
UK Avis, T0990 900500, www.avis.co.uk;
Budget, T0800 181181, www.budget.
co.uk; Delta-Europcar, T0870-607-5000
www.europcar.com; Hertz, T0990 996699,
www.hertz.co.uk; Thrifty, T0990 168238,
www.thrifty.co.uk

will not allow them off graded roads or on sand, like Fraser Island), and also what your liability will be in the case of an accident.

If you stray far from the coast, and certainly anywhere outback, prepare carefully before driving to remote areas. Even if there are regular roadhouses, carry essential spares and tools such as fan belts, hoses, gaffer tape, a tyre repair kit, extra car jack, extra spare wheel and tyre, spade, decent tool kit, oil and coolant, and a fuel can. Membership of the NRMA (NSW) or the RACQ (QLD) is recommended (see below), as is informing someone of your intended itinerary. Above all carry plenty of spare water, at least 10 litres per person, 20 if possible.

Rules and regulations To drive in Australia you must have a current driving licence. Foreign nationals also need an international drivers licence, available from your national motoring organization. In Australia you drive on the left. Speed limits vary between states, with maximum urban limits of 50-60 kph and maximum country limits of 100-120 kph. Speeding penalties include a fine, and police allow little leeway. Seatbelts are compulsory for drivers and passengers. Driving under the influence of alcohol is illegal over certain (very small) limits and penalties are severe.

Petrol costs Fuel costs are approximately half that in Britain, twice that in the US, fluctuating between 75c and $1 a litre in city centres and between 90c and $1.35 a litre outside the main cities. Anyone driving long distances in Australia will soon find that fuel expenses exceed those of food and rival those of accommodation. When budgeting allow at least $10 for every estimated 100 km (62 miles). On those long journeys follow the standard rules for minimizing costs: ensure correct tyre pressures, avoid using a/c if possible, pack luggage in the car rather than on the roof, check the oil regularly, stick to 90-100 kph (56-62 mph) and try to hunt out the cheapest fuel! A trip around the eastern or western circuits can easily involve driving 20,000+ km. Picking an economical vehicle and conserving fuel can save hundreds of dollars.

Motoring organizations Every state has a breakdown service affiliated to the **Australian Automobile Association (AAA)**, www.aaa.asn.au, which your home country organization may have a reciprocal link with. To join in Australia you need to join one of the state associations and note most have reciprocal services. In New South Wales it is the **NRMA**, T132132, www.nrma.com.au, and in Queensland the **RACQ**, T131905, www.racq.com.au Note also that you may only be covered for about 100 km (depending on scheme) of towing distance and that without cover towing services are very expensive. Given the sheer distances you are likely to cover by car, joining an automobile organization is highly recommended.

The general breakdown number for all associations is T131111

Essentials

Some companies will offer one-way hire on certain models and under certain conditions

Vehicle hire   Car rental costs vary considerably according to where you hire from (it's cheaper in the big cities, though small local companies can have good deals), what you hire and the mileage/insurance terms. You may be better off making arrangements in your own country for a fly/drive deal. Watch out for kilometre caps: some can be as low as 100 km per day. The minimum you can expect to pay in Australia is around $200 a week for a small car. Drivers need to be over 21. At peak times it can be impossible to get a car at short notice, and some companies may dispose of a booked car within as little as half an hour of you not showing up for an agreed pick-up time. If you've booked a car but are going to be late, ensure that you let them know before the pick-up time.

Buying a vehicle in Australia is a relatively simple process provided you have somewhere you can give as an address

Buying a vehicle   Cars and vans that should go the distance can be picked up for as little as $2,500, or $6,000 for a 4WD. Paying more increases peace of mind, but obviously increases possible losses when you sell it. If you're dealing with a second-hand car dealer you may be able to agree a 'buy-back' price, saving considerable hassle, and usually you will be offered some sort of warranty. Alternativley you can acquire a vehicle from fellow travellers, hostel notice boards and the classifieds. The principal advantage to buying privately is cost, and vehicles being sold by desperate travellers in a hurry to close a deal can be real bargains. State motoring organizations offer vehicle checks for around $100. Most cars in Australia are locally made or from Asia. An older vehicle may well need a little 'tlc' so the availability of spares should be a consideration. Availability is best for *Fords* and *Holdens*, but *Toyota* parts are also common.

Every car is registered within the state where it is first purchased, and the registration papers must be transferred at each sale. If a car is re-sold in a different state it has first to be re-registered in that state. You will need to formally complete the transfer of registration with the transport department, presenting them with the papers, a receipt (there is a stamp duty tax of about 5%), plus in some states a certificate of roadworthiness. The seller may provide the latter or you may have to get a suitable garage to check the vehicle. Registration must be renewed, in the state the vehicle was last sold, every six or 12 months. Do not, if you can possibly avoid it, let your vehicle registration run out in New South Wales. If you do, you will enter a bizarre and highly expensive bureaucratic world. The best option is to ensure the car you purchase has a registration covering the entire period of your stay and preferably longer to make a resale more viable. Third-party personal injury insurance is included in the registration. You are advised, however, to invest in third-party vehicle and property insurance, even in comprehensive cover if you cannot afford to lose the value of your vehicle.

Cycling   Long-term bicycle hire is rarely available, and touring cyclists should plan to bring their own bike or buy in Australia. Bicycle hire is available in most towns and cities and companies are listed in the book in the relevant sections. See also Sport and special interest travel, page 54. If you do plan on touring the coast by bicycle, the website, www.aussiecycling.com.au, is recommended.

Hitch-hiking   Hitch-hiking, while not strictly illegal in New South Wales and Queensland, is not advised by anyone. The tragic events near Barrow Creek in 2001 demonstrate that there will always be odd twisted souls who will assault or abduct people for their own evil ends. This is not to say that hitching is more dangerous in Australia than elsewhere else.

Train

Adult fares get considerably cheaper if booked in advance

Train travel up and down the east coast is a viable mode of transport and can be a delightful way to get from A to B, especially if you are short of time. Given the distances between the main centres Australia in many ways lends itself to rail travel and you may find routes with such evocative names as *Sunlander*, *Spirit of Capricorn* and

Savannahlander irresistible. That said a car or coach is a better option if you wish to explore or get off the beaten track as the east coast offers endless beaches and numerous national parks that are well away from any railway stations. If you do want to consider rail travel bare in mind the track gauges differ in NSW and Queensland so the crossing between the two takes in an intriguing transition by road. Also bear in mind that overnight travel by rail is possible but often expensive if you wish to find comfort in your own compartment and to do it in style. One thing well worth considering is a jaunt in to the outback from Rockhampton to Longreach, *Spirit of the Outback*, or Cairns to Forsayth *Savannahlander*.

In New South Wales **Countrylink**, T132232, www.countrylink.nsw.gov.au, offer rail and rail/coach services state-wide and to Brisbane. The line gauge differs from that of Queensland, so between the two states coach connections are provided from Brisbane for onward travel. The main *Countrylink Travel Centre* in Sydney is located at the Central Railway Station, Eddy Ave, T02 9955 4237. A useful website for general travel throughout New South Wales is www.webwombat.com.au/transport/nsw.htm

In Queensland **Queensland Rail**, T132232, www.qr.com.au, offer a range of rail services up and down the coast and into the outback. Roma St Transit Centre, Roma Street, Brisbane, T32363035, hosts offices for most major coach and rail service providers and is a fine source of general travel information. **Outback Queensland** is also well served by all of the above but stopovers and less frequent travel schedules are obviously the norm.

Maps

Several publishers produce country-wide and state maps. Regional maps are also available and the most useful for general travel. The best and cheapest of these are generally published by the motoring organizations; *NRMA* (NSW) or *RACQ* (QLD). *UBD Country Towns and Street Directory: New South Wales and Queensland* has good detail on towns (excluding Sydney or Brisbane which have their own UBD editions) and includes a road atlas for the whole state. Along the New South Wales coast look out for the excellent *Cartoscope Tourist Maps*, www.info2go.com.au They are free from most VICs and offer clear regional maps with town details on the back. *AUSLIG*, the national mapping agency, are publishing 54 x 54 km topographic maps, at 1:100,000 scale, of every such size area in Australia, recommended for any long-distance trekking or riding. Most areas are now in print, but if not black and white copies can be obtained. For a map index, place name search, details of distributors or mail order, contact T1800 800173 or T02 6201 4381, www.auslig.gov.au *AUSLIG* also publish a 1:250,000 series, covering the whole country, useful for those heading outback on 4WD trips. Specialist map shops include *Internet* (Australia) www.travelguidewarehouse.com In Sydney there are *The Travel Bookshop*, 175 Liverpool St (southern edge of Hyde Park), T02 9261 8200, or *Dymocks*, 350 George St, 261 George St and 34 Hunter St, T1800 688 319, www.dymocks.com.au In Brisbane *World Wide Maps and Guides*, 187 George St, T07 32214330, www.worldwidemaps.com.au

View and print off touring and street maps at www.arta.com.au

Keeping in touch

Communications

Internet access, and thus email, is widely available in hostels, hotels and cafés. Expect to pay about $2-5 for 30 minutes. State governments are keen for their citizens to have access to the internet and some have set up schemes to allow cheap or even free access. Based either in libraries or dedicated centres, they are usually also accessible to visitors.

Internet

Essentials

Post   Most post offices are open Monday to Friday 0900-1700, and Saturday 0900-1230. Sending a postcard, greeting card or 'small' letter (less than 130 x 240 mm, 5 mm thick and 250g) anywhere in Australia is 45c and should arrive within three days. Postage of larger letters starts at 98c. Airmail for postcards and greetings cards is $1 anywhere in the world, small letters (under 50g) up to $1.50. Parcels can be sent either by sea, economy air (a good trade-off option between speed and cost) or air. See individual town and city directories for details of local post offices.

Telephone   Most public payphones are operated by nationally-owned *Telstra*, www.telstra.com.au
Directory inquiries   Some take phonecards, available from newsagents and post offices, and credit cards. A
1223; International   payphone call within Australia requires 40c or 50c. If you are calling locally (within
Directory inquiries   approximately 50 km) this lasts indefinitely. STD calls, outside this area, will use up 40c in
1225; Service   the first 43 seconds if calling before 1900, and 78 seconds after. Subsequent time costs
difficulties 132203;   40c each time block. To check the likely cost of a call, T1800 113011. Well worth consid-
International service   ering if you are in Australia for any length of time is a pre-paid mobile phone. *Telstra*
difficulties 1221   and *Vodafone* give the best coverage and their phones are widely available from as little as $50. Calls are more expensive of course. By far the cheapest way of calling over-
seas is to use an international pre-paid phonecard (though they cannot be used from a
mobile phone, or some of the blue and orange public phones). Available from city post
offices and newsagents, every call made with them initially costs about $1 (a local call
plus connection) but subsequent per minute costs are a fraction of *Telstra* or mobile
phone charges.

There are no area phone codes. You will, however, need to use a state code if the
one for the state you are calling differs from the one for the state you are in: 02 for
ACT/NSW; 03 for VIC/TAS; 07 for QLD; 08 for NT/SA/WA (and Broken Hill). To call Eastern Australia from overseas, dial the international prefix followed by 61, then the state
phone code minus the first 0, then the 8-digit number. To call overseas from Australia
dial 0011 followed by the country code. Country codes include: Republic of Ireland 353;
New Zealand 64; South Africa 27; the USA and Canada 1; the UK 44.

Media

Newspapers   Each state has its own daily and Sunday newspaper and some of the larger states have
& magazines   two. Naturally these all have a parochial focus. In New South Wales the *Sydney Morning Herald* is considered the most influential and has a national readership. Perhaps given the relatively low national population figure (18 million) *The Australian* www.theaustralian.news.com.au, is the only national paper and has the biggest readership of them all (453,000). It is generally popular, politically 'middle of the road' and publishes a good glossy magazine with the weekend edition. Although some would vehemently disagree the *Sydney Morning Herald* is considered by many to be the unofficial national tabloid 'voice'. In Brisbane and southern Queensland the main newspaper is the *Courier Mail*.

Australians are avid consumers of magazines and even the smallest newsagent will carry a bewildering range on every subject from brides to surfing. The main current affairs magazine, the weekly *Bulletin*, includes a section of *Newsweek*.

Foreign newspapers and magazines are widely available in the main urban centres. It is also possible to buy special weekly editions of British papers such as the *Daily Mail* and *The Guardian*. There are Asian editions of *Time* and *The Economist*.

TV & Radio   There are five main television channels in New South Wales and Queensland; the pub-
SBS has the best   licly funded **ABC** and **SBS**, and the independent, commercial stations, *Channel 7*,
world news, shown   *Channel 9*, and *Channel 10*. **ABC** aims for Australian high quality content including
daily at 1830   many BBC programmes. **SBS** focuses on multi-national culture, current affairs, sport

Essentials

and film. In general they almost all lack depth especially if you were weaned on a staple of the world-class BBC.

ABC broadcasts several national radio channels: Radio National features news, current affairs, culture and music; Classic FM is self-explanatory; and Triple J is aimed at a young, 'alternative' audience. There are also many local commercial radio stations that feature a mix of news, talk-back and music.

Food and drink

The quintessential image of Australian cooking may be of throwing some meat on the barbie but Australia actually has a dynamic and vibrant cuisine all its own. Freed from the bland English 'meat and 3 veg' strait-jacket in the 1980s, by the skills and cuisines of Chinese, Thai, Vietnamese, Italian, Greek, Lebanese and other immigrants, Australia has developed a fusion cuisine that takes elements from their cultures and mixes them into something new and original. A menu from Sydney's *Rockpool* might feature Asian noodle salad with Australian abalone, flavoured with truffle oil, ginger and scallion; a blend of Asian and Italian flavours with fresh local seafood.

Restaurants and other places to eat are identified by a ● symbol on maps

Eating habits in Australia are essentially the same as most Western countries and are of course affected by the climate. The BBQ on the beach or in the back garden is of course an Aussie icon, but you will find that most eating out during daylight hours takes place outdoors. Going out for brunch on the weekend is hugely popular especially in the cities and often takes up the whole morning. Sadly fast food is also a major feature and the infamous *MacDonald*'s brand omnipresent. Organic foods is still something to be enjoyed and sought after by the minority, but like most countries the tide seems to be changing along with growing concern about genetically modified (GM) foods.

Cuisine

Asian ingredients are easily found in major cities because of the country's high Asian population and might include coriander, lemon grass, chilli and thai basil. Australia makes its own dairy products so cheese or cream may come from Tasmania's King Island, Western Australia's Margaret River or the Atherton Tablelands in Far North Queensland. Of course there is also plenty of seafood, including some creatures that will be unfamiliar to most travellers like the delicious crustaceans Moreton bugs, yabbies and crayfish. Mussels, oysters and abalone are all also harvested locally. Fish is a treat too; snapper, dhufish, coral trout and red emperor or the dense flavoursome flesh of freshwater fish such as barramundi and Murray cod. Australia's isolation and clean environment also ensures that all these ingredients taste as good as possible.

Freshness is the other striking quality of this cuisine, dubbed Modern Australian. This is achieved by using produce from the local area, and cooking it in a way that preserves the food's intrinsic flavour. The food shines for itself without being smothered in heavy or dominating sauces. Native animals are used, such as kangaroo, emu and crocodile, and native plants that Aboriginal people have been eating for thousands of years such as quandong, wattle seed or lemon myrtle leaf.

A word of warning however. This gourmet experience is mostly restricted to cities and large towns. There are pockets of foodie heaven in the country, but these are usually associated with wine regions and are the exception rather than the rule.

Eating out

Restaurants are common even in smaller towns. It is a general, but by no means concrete rule of thumb that the smaller the town the lower the quality, though not usually the price. Chinese and Thai restaurants are very common, with most other cuisines appearing only in the larger towns and cities. In Sydney, and Melbourne, which are the undisputed gourmet capitals of Australia, you will find the very best of Modern Australian as well as everything from Mexican to Mongolian, Jamaican to Japanese. Brisbane

Essentials

▶ **National treasures**

There are a few special foods that Australians produce and treasure. The meat pie is the favourite Australian fast food, about the size of your palm and filled with mince or steak and gravy. The quality can vary from soggy cardboard to something a French pastry chef wouldn't be ashamed of. If you are tempted your best bet is a fresh one from a bakery rather than a mass-produced one (sealed in a little plastic bag) that sits in a shop's warming oven all day. Fish and chips are also popular and these are often good in Australia because the fish is fresh and only light vegetable oils are used for frying.

Vegemite spread is a dark and sticky yeast extract that looks a bit like axle grease. It's the Aussie equivalent of British Marmite, though fans of one usually detest the other. Tim Tams are a thick chocolate

biscuit, very similar to the Brits' Penguin and reputedly the country's best selling snack. What Brits call crisps, Aussie's call chips ('hot chips' are fried chips), with Twisties a very Australian favourite.

Damper is bread made of flour, salt and water, best baked out bush in the ashes of a campfire. Nothing beats warm damper slathered with jam and butter. Another Aussie baking favourite is the lamington: a block of sponge that has been dipped in chocolate and rolled in coconut. The pavlova is a classic Australian desert, created for the visit of Russian ballerina, Anna Pavlova. The 'pav' is like a cake-sized meringue, served topped with whipped cream and fresh fruit. It is rarely consumed without an argument about whether it was actually invented in Australian or New Zealand.

also boasts some fine eateries. Corporate hotels and motels almost all have attached restaurants as do traditional pubs who also serve counter meals. Some may have a more imaginative menu or better quality fare than the local restaurants. Most restaurants are licensed for the consumption of alcohol. Some are BYO only, in which case you provide wine or beer and the restaurant provides glasses. Despite the corkage fee this still makes for a better deal than drinking alcohol in fully licensed premises, where any alcohol is provided by the proprietors. European-style cafés are only rarely found in the country, and as in many Western countries the distinction between cafés, bistros and restaurants is becoming extremely blurred.

If you can't do without your burgers or southern-fried chicken or fish and chips then fear not. Australians have taken to fast food as enthusiastically as anywhere else in the world. Alongside these are food courts, found in the shopping malls of cities and larger towns. These have several takeaway options, usually including various Asian cuisines, surrounding a central space equipped with tables and chairs. Also in the budget bracket are the delis and milk bars, also serving hot takeaways, together with sandwiches, cakes and snacks.

Eating in   If you cook for yourself you'll find just about everything in an Aussie supermarket that you would find in Europe or the USA, and at very reasonable prices. An excellent meal for two can easily be put together for under $20.

Drinks   Australian wine will need no introduction to most readers, as it is now imported in huge quantities into Europe and the USA. Many of the labels you might be familiar with, including *Penfolds* and the giant of the industry, *Jacob's Creek*, are produced in South Australia, but there are dozens of recognized wine regions right across the southern third of Australia, and several in the process of development. The industry has a creditable history in such a young country, with several wineries boasting a tradition of a century or more, but it is only in the last 25 years that Australia has become one of the major players on the international scene. Australians themselves drink more and

Aussie barbie

◀

"Throw another prawn on the barbie". *and beach foreshores. Unless free, a 20c,*
The image is very familiar to travellers well *50c or $1 coin will get you 15-30 minutes*
before they arrive, and for once this is no *of heat. You'll need to bring your own*
myth. Aussies love a BBQ, and many *utensils. At private BBQs, bringing your*
households will have a couple a week as a *own meat and alcohol is the norm, with*
matter of course. Public BBQs are common, *hosts usually providing salads, bread and*
often found in town and national parks, *a few extra snags (sausages).*

Essentials

more wine and less beer. The average rate of consumption is now 20 litres per person per year, compared to 8 litres in 1970. Beer has dropped from an annual 135 litres per person in 1980 to 95 litres now.

The price of wine is unexpectedly high given the relatively low cost of food and beer. Even those from Britain will find Australian wines hardly any cheaper at the very cellar door than back home in *Tesco's*. The joy of Australian wine, however, is in its variety and quality. There are no restrictions, as there are in parts of Europe, on what grape varieties are grown where, when they are harvested and how they are blended. The 'Mediterranean' climate of much of the south of the country is very favourable for grape-growing, and the soil is sufficient to produce a high-standard grape. Wineries range in size from vast concerns to one-person operations producing a few hundred bottles a year. Cellar doors range from modern marble and glass temples to venerable, century-old former barns of stone and wood. Some will open for a Saturday afternoon, others every day. In some you'll be lucky to get half a dry cracker to go with a taste, others boast some of the best restaurants in the country. A few are in small town high streets, others are set in hectares of exquisitely designed and maintained gardens. The truly wonderful thing is that this tremendous mix of styles is found within most of the various regions, making a day or two's tasting expedition a scenic and cultural as well as an epicurean delight. In New South Wales the Hunter Valley provides one of the best vineyard experiences in the world with over 100 wineries, world-class B&Bs and a range of tours from cycling to horse-drawn carriage.

The vast majority of beer drunk by Australians is lager, despite many being called 'ale' or 'bitter'. The big brands in New South Wales and Queensland are *Tooheys* (NSW) and *Castlemain XXXX* (QLD); both are very homogenous but equally refreshing on a hot day. If your palate is just a touch more refined, hunt out some of the imported beers on tap which are predominantly found in the pseudo Irish pubs found in almost all the main coastal towns. Beer tends to be around 4-5% alcohol, with the popular and surprisingly pleasant tasting 'mid' varieties about 3½%, and 'light' beers about 2-2½%. Drink driving laws are strict, and the best bet is to not drink alcohol at all if you are driving. As well as being available on draught in pubs, beer is also available from bottleshops (or 'bottle-o's') in cases (or 'slabs') of 24-36 cans ('tinnies' or 'tubes') or bottles ('stubbies') of 375 ml each. This is by far the cheapest way of buying beer (often under $1 per can or bottle).

Entertainment and nightlife

It is the pubs and bars that provide much of the country's entertainment. Many put on regular live music, DJs, karaoke, comedy and quiz nights, but it is perhaps gambling and the infamous 'pokies' (slot machines) that are the biggest draw, especially in rural areas. Even in the major cities many pubs look like a miniature Las Vegas and sound like a siren fest the minute you walk in the door. In some medium-sized towns pubs and

See also Sport and special interest travel, page 50

bars also operate a club or discotheque. These, like every developed country, vary from the rural Neolithic to the Sydney state-of-the-art. True nightclubs however are generally only found in the cities and then usually only open a few nights of the week. They charge an entry fee of around $5-15, but will usually be free on some mid-week nights or before a certain time. Australians are very much up on the play when it comes to trends in both fashion and music so don't go expecting to shake your flare-bottomed pants to ABBA or Village People (though that is often possible for sheer nostalgia value).

Though the broad epithet 'pub' is applied equally to British, Irish and Australian establishments, there is only a little overlap in terms of architecture: that of the brick Victorian edifice. There has been little other opportunity for convergence, and there are very few Aussie equivalents of the quaint old country pubs of England. Instead there is a country type all Australia's own, a solid brick and wood affair with wide first-floor verandahs extending across the front, and sometimes down the sides as well. These usually have separate public and lounge bars, a bottleshop (off-licence) off to the side, and increasingly a separate 'bar' full of pokies (slot machines or one-armed bandits). The public bar often doubles as a TAB betting shop.

Cinema is also still very popular in Australia and most larger towns have one, maybe even an outdoor screen. You'll pay around $13 for an adult ticket, but look out for early week or pre-1800 specials. Sydney, Brisbane and Cairns all have high-profile casinos on a prodigious scale. They are open 24 hours a day and, as well as offering gaming tables and ranks of pokies, have live music venues and good-value eating.

Shopping

Tourist shops exploit the cute and cuddly factor of Australian native mammals to the limit so most tourist merchandise seems to consist of soft toy kangaroos and koalas and brightly coloured clothing featuring the same creatures. Other typical items perpetuate the corny Australian stereotypes: hats strung with corks. Not only will you be slapped every five seconds and look foolish but no Australian has ever been spotted wearing one.

Clothing & shoes Corkless hats, however, are a popular and practical souvenir, particularly the distinctively Australian Akubras, made from felt in muddy colours. Along the same lines, stockman's clothing made by *RM Williams* is also popular and very good quality. Two of the company's best sellers are elastic-sided boots and moleskins (soft brushed-cotton trousers cut like jeans). The *Driza-bone* long oilskin raincoat is also an Aussie classic. Australian surfwear is sought after world-wide and is a good buy while in the country. Look for labels such as *Ripcurl, Quiksilver, Mambo* and *Billabong*.

Jewellery Australia is a good place to shop for jewellery with Sydney offering plenty of fine outlets. There are many talented craftspeople making exquisite metal and bead work and the country produces unique and precious gems such as opal, pearl and diamonds. The widest range will be available in the cities but, as in most countries, products are often cheapest at the source and a wonderful memento of a particular place.

Aboriginal art & crafts In the tourist shops Aboriginal art designs are as ubiquitous as cuddly toys and printed on everything from t-shirts to teatowels. Some of these designs can be beautiful but be *Some of the qualities to look for in paintings are fine application, skilful use of colour and a striking design* aware that many have no link to Aboriginal people and do not benefit them directly – check the label. *Desert Designs* is a successful label printing the stunning designs of the Great Sandy Desert artist Jimmy Pike on silk scarves and sarongs. It is possible to buy genuine Aboriginal art and craft but it is more commonly available in country areas close to Aboriginal communities or from Aboriginal-owned or -operated enterprises. This applies more to craft items such as didjeridus and scorched carvings than paintings and of course there are reputable vendors everywhere but if in doubt ask for more information. Buying art and crafts from reputable sources ensures that the money ends up in the artist's pocket and supports Aboriginal culture, skills and self-reliance.

Many people are keen to buy an Aboriginal dot painting, usually acrylic on canvas, but this can be a daunting shopping experience. Also there are different styles of Aboriginal art, often depending on the region the artist comes from. For example the x-ray paintings on bark only come from Arnhem Land. The best Aboriginal paintings sell for many thousands but there are also many thousands of average paintings sold for a few hundred dollars. A good painting will cost at least $800-1500. Simple works on canvas can be as little as $100 and make good souvenirs. Take your time and have a good look around. Visit public and private galleries where you can see work of the highest quality – you may not be able to afford it but you'll learn something of what makes a good piece of Aboriginal art. Sydney has a number of excellent commercial galleries selling Aboriginal arts and crafts, see page 120.

Holidays and festivals

Naturally Sydney and Brisbane are the focus for the most popular, high-profile festivals and events, but there are many others along the coastal route, some conventional and some highly unique. The following are merely a sample. For more detail on festivals and events see www.thisweekinaustralia.com or the relevant destination listings.

January *Sydney Festival and Fringe Festival* takes place through most of the month. It is a celebration of the arts including the best of Australian theatre, dance, music and visual arts and is held at many venues throughout the city. For many the highlight is the free open-air concerts in the Domain, including Opera in the Park and Symphony under the Stars, www.sydneyfestival.org.au The 26th sees the annual *Australia Day* celebrations with the focus being a flotilla of vessels flying the flag in the harbour, www.australiaday.com.au In Brisbane there are similar events including the notorious *Cockroach Races* and even a little 'frozen chicken bowling' (as you do!).

February Without doubt the most famous Sydney event is the legendary *Gay and Lesbian Mardi Gras Festival and Parade* held each February for a month. It is an opportunity for the gay community to celebrate, flaunt their being, entertain and shock: T9557 4332, www.mardigras.com.au

March/April *Royal Agricultural Easter Show* is held every Easter in Sydney and now uses the state of the art facilities at Olympic Park as a venue. April 25th sees the annual Anzac Day services in almost all main centres. The popular *Blues and Roots Festival* held every Easter weekend in Byron Bay attracts its fair share of international stars, 'wanna-bes' or 'has-beens', www.bluesfest.com.au

May For the fit the annual *Sydney Morning Herald Half Marathon* is a great attraction, especially when it involves crossing the Harbour Bridge, while far less sedate is the *Australian Fashion Week*, celebrations showcasing some of the country's top designers. 'Alternatively' you can roll up roll up for the annual *Nimbin Mardis Gras* near Byron Bay, which is a mad-cap celebration of the alternative lifestyle and a certain weed. May also sees *Queensland Racing Festival* in Brisbane.

June Mass popcorn crunching is on offer at the *Sydney Film Festival*, a two-week fest for film buffs featuring over 150 features from 40 countries, T9660 3844, www.sydney

filmfestival.org.au, while Queensland revels in its own equivalent, the *Brisbane International Film Festival* at the end of the month and the annual Queensland Day celebrations.

August   Increasingly popular and far less soporific than watching the big screen is the *Sun-Herald City to Surf*, a 14-km race from Bondi Beach to the Sydney City Centre, T1800 555 514. Far more rotund contenders can be seen at *Hervey Bay Whale Festival* in Queensland. The last week of August sees the start of the two-week *Riverfestival* in Brisbane which celebrates the 'city's lifeblood' with food, fire and festivities.

September   September sees the *Festival of The Winds* at Bondi Beach which is a colourful festival of kites and kite flying, while the avid sports fans fight over tickets and take several days drinking leave for the Rugby League and Rugby Union Grand Finals. Meanwhile Brisbane gets legless with the *National Festival of Beers* (Australia's biggest).

October   *2003 Rugby World Cup* kicks off in Sydney with games played at the Telstra Stadium and venues in Brisbane and Townsville. In Surfers Paradise the annual *Indy Car Races* are guaranteed to thrill the crowds.

December   Over Christmas, *Carols by Candlelight* is the main festive public celebration of song in the Sydney Domain, while the wild and wicked grab a beer glass and a patch of sand at the *Bondi Beach Christmas Party*, which usually ends up as a mass streak into the waves. Far more serious though no less chilly on the flotation devices is the *Sydney to Hobart sailing race*, which departs the inner harbour, winds allowing, every Boxing Day. *New Year* in Sydney and Brisbane kicks in with spectacular fireworks and celebrations that centre around The Rocks and the Harbour Bridge (Sydney) and South Bank (Brisbane).

Public holidays   New Years Day; Australia Day (26 January 2004); Good Friday (9 April 2004); Easter Saturday (10 April 2004); Easter Monday (12 April 2004); Anzac Day (26 April 2004); Queen's Birthday (14 June 2004); Bank Holiday (2 August 2004); Labour Day (4 October 2004 in NSW, 3 May 2004 in QLD); Christmas Day (25 December 2004); Boxing (Proclamation) Day (27 December 2004).

Sport and special interest travel

Politics and sport are Australia's two big passions, and the latter takes on a religious significance for many. Travelling around country Australia, you soon start to see just why they are so successful at, and passionate about sport. Even the smallest towns will have a footy pitch or cricket pitch and golf course, and they don't have to be much of a size to have tennis and netball courts, a swimming pool, and a horse-racing track. In most cases there is easy public access at reasonable rates, so if you feel you won't be able to go without a round or a set then bring the minimum of gear and expect to be able to get a game almost anywhere. If you're a real adrenaline junkie then Australia can offer quite a range of heart-stopping activities, most of them involving moving quickly over water, even faster over snow, slowly but precariously over or under rock, or with gut-wrenching inevitability through nothing but fresh air.

Spectator sports

Any sport Australia takes seriously it does well at, almost laughably well at. Their cricketers seem to score more runs than anyone else, their rugby players launch themselves for more tries, their swimmers outperform respectably fast fish, their netballers shoot more goals than anyone else, their top tennis players regularly beat even the Americans, and they have recently had world champions in everything from darts to squash. This awful challenge for their opponents converts to a glorious opportunity for visitors to Australia. If you choose to be a spectator at a sport the Aussies really get into, then you're in for a treat: world-class competition at relatively low prices. And you'll usually be in the company of thousands of exuberant locals yelling their lungs out. Should you manage to get tickets for one of the Grand Finals, or the Grand Prix, or an international match then all the better, but you'll need to have booked both tickets and accommodation well ahead.

Australian Rules Football

www.afl.com.au
Also called 'Aussie rules' or just plain 'footy'

This is the classic down-under game, to the casual observer a free-for-all that defies the gods in causing as few broken necks as it does. A derivative of the rough football that was being played in Britain and Ireland in the late 1700s, it shares some affinities with Gaelic Football, and indeed Ireland and Australia do meet to contest an 'international rules' cup.

As with rugby and soccer, it's a winter game, with most leagues playing between March and September. The game is contested on a huge oval pitch, up to 200 m long, between two teams of 18 players each. At each end of the pitch four high posts denote the goal-mouth, and it is through these that the teams attempt to get the oval-shaped ball. If the ball goes directly between the central two posts a goal is scored and 6 points awarded, if it goes between one of the central posts and an outer post, or is touched by the defending team on the way then a behind is scored and a single point awarded. Players may kick or hand pass the ball in any direction, but not throw it. To hand pass is to punch the ball from the palm of one hand with the clenched fist of the other. If the ball is kicked over 10 m and cleanly caught then the catcher can call a mark. He can't be tackled and has time to kick the ball toward goal or a team-mate unmolested. The game is split into four quarters, each lasting 25 minutes. Scoring is usually regular, and winning teams with an excess of 100 points are not unusual.

The national league, the AFL, www.afl.com.au, is followed most closely, in fact obsessively, though there are enthusiastic state and local amateur leagues right around the country. Most of the clubs are in and around Melbourne, where the game was invented, but the national league also has top-flight teams from Adelaide, Brisbane, Perth and Sydney. The most exciting place to see an AFL match is at one of the country's great stadiums such as the MCG in Melbourne, Subiaco Oval in Perth or the Gabba in Brisbane. After a series of round-robin and knock-out rounds the season culminates in the AFL Grand Final, always held at the MCG in September. A good way of getting into the spirit of the game is by watching Channel 9's mad-cap *Footy Show*, or simply chatting to a knowledgeable Victorian. In New South Wales the major team in the AFL is the Sydney Swans, while in Brisbane it is the Lions.

Rugby League & Union

www.rugby.com.au

If Victoria is the bastion of AFL, then the big game on the eastern seaboard is Rugby League, the game that broke away from Union in England in the 1890s. It became popular in Australia by 1910, but has remained confined in popularity to New South Wales and Queensland. The major differences between League and Union are the number of players (13 to 15), points scored (less for tries and penalties in League) and the League rule that the tackled player retains possession of the ball and kicks it back between his legs to another member of his team. The main league is the NRL, www.nrl.com.au, and like the AFL the season's Grand Final is in September. New South Wales and Queensland select teams to play 'state of origin' crunch matches every year and a full Australian side (the Kangaroos) is also regularly put together for international matches and tours. Needless to say, Australia is extremely good and can often claim to be the best in the world.

Rugby Union traditionally had much less of a grass roots following until the national side, the Wallabies, won the Rugby World Cup in 1991. In the decade since, they can claim to have always rated in the world's top five teams, and frequently vie with arch rivals, the New Zealand All Blacks, for status as world's best. Aside from the World Cup (which they won in 1999) and regular international tours, the Wallabies compete in an annual three-way competition (the 'Tri Nations') against South Africa and New Zealand. The winners of the Aussie vs Kiwi games gain possession of the much-prized Bledisloe Cup, which has been contested by the two countries since 1931. The other major seasonal series is the Australian Rugby Shield, the national competition between state capital and country teams held during June and August.

During October-November 2003 Australia hosts the four-yearly Rugby World Cup. Matches will be played at a variety of venues across the nation. The semi-finals are at Telstra Stadium (formerly Stadium Australia) in Sydney on Saturday 15 and Sunday 16, with the final Saturday 22. Tickets are not planned to go on sale until the latter half of 2003. For schedule and ticket information see www.worldcup.rugby.com.au

Cricket

For round-ups on Australian and international news, see www.cricket.org

Once the footy season ends around September a large number of Australian minds switch, almost like clockwork, to cricket, just another major international team sport at which Australians just happen to be, more or less, better than anyone else. If you're a fan of the sport then we hardly need tell you this, or that the Melbourne Cricket Club ('MCG') is the spiritual home of the sport in Australia. Their website, www.mcg.org.au, is a very good place to catch up on what's going on in Australian cricket.

If cricket is something of a mystery to you, then suffice to say that there are two main versions. The traditional game of 2 innings per team that takes four to five days and almost always seems to end in a draw, and the limited-overs game that is completed in a day. In both instances both teams get an opportunity to build up as many runs as possible, with the winner the team with the most runs. Some purists will point out that the one-day game lacks the glorious tactics of the full five-day campaign, but novice spectators will probably find the former faster flowing, easier to understand, more exciting and far less likely to end in a draw.

The national side is involved in an annual series against England (the Ashes) plus a few series against some of the major cricketing countries. There are two interstate competitions, both running from October to February, and involving full state sides. The ING Cup is the one-day competition, and the Pura Cup decides who has the best five-day team. The main state sides in New South Wales are the New South Wales Blues (the SCG, Sydney) and in Queensland, the Queensland Bulls (the Gabba, Brisbane).

Horse racing

One of the best and most well-maintained independent racing websites is www.racing australia.net

Australians are mad about the gee-gees. There are horse-racing or pacing (horse and trap) tracks all over the country, in all but the tiniest towns, and there are usually a dozen or so meetings every day, and dozens of races to satisfy the most dedicated of punters. Most of the country's betting is via the state TABs, a pooling system similar to the UK's Tote. There are some high street TABs, but most can be found in the public bars of the nation's pubs.

Netball & basketball

Australia's biggest participant sport is netball. A surprise to many, but not to their international opponents as the national side is currently the world's best. The big national competition is the Commonwealth Bank Trophy, which is competed for by city- and town-based teams between April and August. The official website for Australian netball is www.netball.asn.au As eagerly watched, though with far humbler expectations on the international scale, is basketball. The National Basketball League title, www.nbl.com, is competed for between October and March, and the Women's National Basketball League, home.vicnet.net.au/~wnbl, between November and March.

Swimming

It doesn't seem fair. Australia doesn't just have one or two international-standard swimmers, they have a small poolful. Sydney's own Ian Thorpe (the 'Thorpedo', size 17 feet) and others like Grant Hackett and Michael Klim are all giants on the international scene, often only having each other for serious competition. For this reason, the Australian National Championships are the best domestic competition in the world to go and see. They're held in March, see www.ausswim.telstra.com.au for details.

Unlike with their swimmers, Australia has for a long time had to depend on just one or two brilliant players to keep the male flag flying, and the women's game is surprisingly weak. The boys have got their timing down to a tee: just as Pat Rafter finds he may have to hang up his racquet, along comes Lleyton Hewitt, possibly the most exciting player on the international circuit since John McEnroe. Australia hosts one of the world's four Grand Slam competitions, the Australian Open, www.ausopen.org, in Melbourne in January.

Tennis
For round-ups on tennis news see www.tennis australia.com.au

Essentials

Participatory sports

Australia is one of the world's great adventure countries, and the East Coast can offer a tremendous range of activities. Many of the best experiences are offered by specialist tour and hire operators along the coast, and if you have some specific goals it is essential to check out your options carefully in advance as the time of year and availability of spaces can make a big difference to what is possible. *Wild Magazine* has a good website, www.wild.com.au, and publishes quite a few walking and adventure guides.

A certain amount of walking is necessary to see many of the country's great natural sights, but Australia can also boast a great range of short, day and overnight walks, mostly in the many national parks, and even a few multi-day treks that rank alongside the best in the world. In New South Wales the Blue Mountains and Warrumbungle national parks are particularly recommended while in Queensland the 32-km four-day/three-night Thorsborne Trail on Hinchinbrook Island between Townsville and Cairns is a classic. Book well ahead.

Walking & trekking
See also Taking care in the bush, page 32

Many of Australia's natural ecologies are particularly sensitive to human activity and you should take care to disturb as little as possible. All the state conservation authorities have a minimal impact bushwalking code, published on their websites and printed on the park notes for all the national parks. Most of the longer walks, and some even as short as two hours, have a walker registration system in place – essentially ensuring that if you get lost or injured someone will come looking. If there is no such system in place make sure someone (it can be the local park ranger or the police) knows where you are going and how long you plan to be.

Bushwalking clubs are a good source of local advice and often welcome visitors on their regular expeditions. For a comprehensive list of clubs see www.bushwalking.org.au The best series of books on walking in Australia has been penned by indefatigable walker Tyrone T Thomas, see www.members.ozemail.com.au/~tyronet

Skiing and trekking poles are becoming increasingly popular as walking aids, considerably easing the strain on knees and backs. The tough tungsten carbide points can, however, rip up vegetation, scratch rock surfaces and spread plant diseases such as the *Phytophthora* dieback fungus. A broad-bottomed wooden or rubber-tipped pole, planted firmly on the track rather than off its edges, is an ecologically sounder alternative.

Although much of Australia is flat as a tack there are a few fabulous climbing spots. Most of the recognized routes are in the eastern half of the country in the Great Dividing Range. To find out more get hold of *Climbing Australia: The Essential Guide* by Greg Pritchard, or see www.climbing.com.au, which picks out abseiling operators.

Climbing, abseiling & canyoning

Canyoning is a sport almost exclusively restricted to the Great Dividing Range of New South Wales, and involves a combination of climbing, abseiling, wading and swimming through the canyons and gorges of the Blue Mountains and Manning Valley.

Essentials

▶ **Parks aplenty**

Some of the world's earliest national parks and reserves were declared in Australia, with the Royal National Park, near Sydney, being gazetted in 1879. They generally constitute natural areas of ecological, cultural or simply aesthetic importance (often a combination of all three), and can claim to encompass almost all of Australia's most jaw-dropping and sublime natural attractions. In New South Wales alone there are over 580 national parks and reserves, ranging from a few hectares to the size of small countries, and the degree of public access allowed is as variable. Many have excellent basic camping facilities and the experience is highly recommended. National parks are generally managed by the state in which they are situated, with the N ational Parks and Wildlife Service (NPWS), www.npws.nsw.gov.au, in New South Wales and the Queensland Parks and Wildlife Service (QPWS), www.env.qld.gov.au, being the two main administrators. In some parks there is an entry fee ($6-10), in others entry is free to some or all. Where entry fees are charged it is usually possible to obtain a state-wide pass lasting one to two years. In New South Wales for example a Single Country Park Pass is $20-35 while an All Parks Pass costs $80/140. If you intend to visit many parks and are in the country for a while, this is often a sensible way to go, but bear in mind camping fees are generally extra. Passes can be purchased at park visitors centres and some major VICs. There is no national pass.

Horse riding Australia has a great number of both horse-riding schools and station stays offering recreational rides, and you can't travel far in the more populated regions without finding one. Rides can be from 30 minutes to several days' duration.

The great Australian image of the horse-riding cattleman was shaped by Banjo Paterson's electrifying poem *The Man from Snowy River*, and it is indeed in the high country between Mansfield, in Victoria, and Canberra that the most awesome Australian horse riding can be experienced. There are however many places along the East Coast that offer fine scenic trails or multi-day treks and these are listed in the relevant texts.

Cycling & mountain biking Bicycles are commonly available for hire in cities and major towns, but facilities are scarce otherwise. Huge as the country is, cycling around it is a popular pastime and some states, notably Victoria with their Rail Trails, are actively promoting the activity. If you plan to do most of your touring on a bike you will need to either bring your own or buy in Australia, as long-term hire facilities are virtually non-existent. One alternative is to join a cycle-based tour, such as those organized by organizations like *Boomerang Bicycle Tours*, ozbike@ozemail.com.au, over east. Sydney-based companies are also an excellent source of information. See page 126.

Wildlife & birdwatching The unique Australian wildlife experience is one that goes far beyond the cuddling of koalas, feeding friendly kangaroos and coming face-to-face with a potato cod on the Great Barrier Reef. Almost everywhere you go wildlife surrounds you and can be observed, from huge bats in Sydney's Botanical Gardens to Tiger Quolls bottoms up in the dish washing tub of New England National Park. The concept that almost all of it, beyond the humble roo, is out to clamp its jaws, fangs or stinging tentacles into you is greatly over exaggerated and certainly not helped by international Reality TV stars like the Crocodile Hunter. True, there are many venomous and potentially dangerous creatures out there, but nothing a bit of common sense and respect won't protect you from. In summary, provided you retain an open mind as well as open eyes you will return home with an armoury of interesting memories, stories and photographs that will confirm the fact that Australia is one of the best places to encounter wildlife on the planet.

Essentials

Tracking down wildlife on the East Coast

Many of the following creatures, though widespread, are not always easy to see. With patience sightings are virtually guaranteed in their natural environment at the following places (tours and entry fees sometimes apply):

Dolphins *Tin Can Bay and Tangalooma Dolphin Resort on Moreton Island (QLD)*

Dugong *Hinchinbrook Island National Park (QLD).*

Sea eagles *Almost anywhere along the East Coast, even around Sydney.*

Echidnas *Common in both rural and urban environments.*

Fairy or Little penguins *As far north as Coffs Harbour (NSW), occasionally even in Sydney Harbour. Broken Bay (Hawkesbury River entrance) is a known breeding site.*

Flying foxes *Botanical Gardens, Sydney; Grafton and Bellingen (NSW), Cape Tribulation (QLD).*

Kangaroos *Just about anywhere in open country especially early or late in the day.*

Koalas *Port Macquarie (NSW) and Magnetic Island (QLD).*

Platypus *Eungella National Park and Yungaburra, Atherton Tablelands (QLD).*

Saltwater crocodiles *Hinchinbrook, Daintree and Cape York (QLD).*

Turtles *Mon Repos, Bundaberg and Heron Island, Great Barrier Reef (QLD).*

Whales *Hervey Bay (QLD), occasionally in and around Sydney Harbour.*

Wombats *Common in both NSW and QLD, especially in river valleys.*

Fishing

One of Australia's favourite hobbies, fishing is in some areas the only recreational activity available to locals and is pursued with an almost religious obsession. As you head north, surfboards begin to disappear from vehicle roof racks, only to be replaced by the 'tinnies', short aluminium boats that allow the fishing family to go where they please.

Inland fishing, mostly for barramundi in the north and the feral trout in the south, requires a licence in some states, though beach and sea fishing do not. Whatever the case, tour operators and hire companies will usually organize that for you. Excellent offshore sportsfishing is widely available as a day tour, usually for around $150-200. There are several excellent websites on recreational fishing in Eastern Australia, with location reports and details of tour operators and retailers, including www.fishnet.com.au and www.sportsfishaustralia.com.au

History

Those interested in the human history of Eastern Australia will find it comes in two distinct flavours. The history of the indigenous Aboriginal peoples, though prodigious in terms of tenure, is sometimes conspicuous by its absence. The state museums and galleries usually have sections devoted to Aboriginal culture, with the Australian Museum in Sydney being especially good, but some independent Aboriginal cultural centres like The Dreamtime Centre in Rockhampton and better still, Tjapukai near Cairns are often the most interesting and enlightening of formal sources.

The preservation and display of the 'European' history in Australia is, as is to be expected, much more extensive. The major museums and art galleries in Sydney, Brisbane and Townsville are superb and well worth the time spent wandering their halls and galleries. Outside of the major towns and cities they can become very parochial and, to be honest, not hugely interesting to non-Australians. Another source of occasional frustration can be 'historic sites'. To Europeans used to plentiful ruins and glorious architecture it can be a disappointment to discover that a site is exactly that: nothing but re-vegetated ground and a memorial plaque! As in many countries a National Trust has been developed to buy and manage buildings of historic and cultural importance that do survive. Entry to National Trust properties is free to members of the National Trusts of several countries, including Canada, Japan, Netherlands, New Zealand, the UK and USA.

▶ Notes for novices

To be let loose proper with all the diving kit you must first pass the equivalent of an underwater driving test, or dive certification. This takes several days to achieve under the tutelage of a qualified instructor. Even once you are certified you must always dive with 'a buddy' – which is more of an oxygen insurance policy than a drinking or shopping companion – and stay within a certain depth, before further courses propel you ever onwards to an 'advanced' or 'dive master' status.

We strongly recommend that you gain an understanding of the sea, what dangers may lie ahead, what creatures to avoid, oxygen control and so on. This research is very often left up to you. If in Cairns, an effective and entertaining way in which to learn these safety issues is to visit Reef Teach, see page 370.

Surfing, windsurfing, kitesurfing & waterskiing

If an Aussie lives near the beach there's a fair bet they'll be a surfer; if they're inland and anywhere near water then waterskiing will probably be the go. This makes for a great many local clubs, tuition and equipment hire. Surfing is generally best in the southern half of the country with famous and often jealously guarded spots in places like Newcastle, Port Macquarie and, of course, Byron Bay in NSW, and Coolangatta, North Stradbroke Island, Maroochy and Noosa in Queensland. There are quite a few websites dedicated to surfing, one of Australia's national obsessions, including www.surfinfo.com.au, which links to a great many surfie retail and travel businesses, and www.realsurf.com which has condition reports from all the major spots around the country. Dedicated surfies will want to get hold of a copy of Mark Warren's *Atlas of Australian Surfing*.

Windsurfing and kitesurfing are also widespread, with Noosa (QLD) being a good place to learn the new art of kitesurfing. Information can be found at www.windsurf ing.org, with club, holiday and tuition details on the state pages.

Canoeing, kayaking & rafting

Australia may be the driest continent but there are actually quite a few opportunities for a river paddle. Tropical Queensland rivers can generate a bit of white water in winter, and the Snowy Mountains of New South Wales are the chief mainland destinations for those after a rough and exciting ride. Sea kayaking is obviously huge and there are numerous operators in almost every major coastal town along the coast. The Whitsunday Islands (QLD) or Great Barrier Reef Islands (Cairns) are especially recommended. The Australian Canoeing website, www.canoe.org.au, concentrates on competitive canoeing, but some of the state links, such as Tasmania, have good river descriptions and links to commercial operators. White-water rafting companies are mentioned in the text and predominate in Cairns, Mission Beach and Airlie Beach (QLD).

Diving

Given time constraints, most visitors to the East Coast, who are intent on diving, or learning to dive, stick to the Great Barrier Reef and this is obviously to be recommended. However there is good diving to be had south of the reef all the way to Tasmania. In NSW notable sites include the Solitary Islands off Coffs Harbour. The Islands form park of the 100,000-hectare Solitary Island Marine Park, which, due to the meeting of warm tropical waters to the north and cooler temperate waters in the Tasman Sea, creates one of the most biologically rich marine environments on the East Coast. Given the biodiversity of the Great Barrier that is saying something. For information about Coffs Harbour diving activities see page 195. Australia is of course famous for the Great Barrier Reef, and for decades backpackers have made a beeline their to earn their diving spurs. Websites www.diveoz.com.au and www.scubaaustralia.com.au both have some very useful general information as well as fairly comprehensive, though not qualitative, state-by-state directories including sites, dive centres and charter boats. Details of several multi-day diving trips can be found on www.divedirectory.net

Travellers basing their trip on diving on the East Coast should pick up a copy of *Diving Australia* by Coleman and Marsh to decide what sites will best suit them.

Gliding, hang gliding & microlighting

Gliding is particularly popular in inland towns, often bordering the wheatbelts, where there is a rich harvest of sunny days and strong thermals, most common out on the plains of inland New South Wales. For a comprehensive list of gliding clubs see www.gfa.org.au

Hang gliding, while still requiring thermals for extended flights, makes use of elevated areas for take-off and so is most popular in upland and coastal cliff areas. A few operators offer hang gliding and paragliding lessons, and some one-off flights. Most are based on the central Queensland coast and the northern New South Wales coast (particularly in Byron Bay). You'll find a listing at www.hgfa.asn.au, the website of the Hang Gliding Federation of Australia, T02 6947 2888.

Flying in microlights, effectively hang gliders with engines and wheels and also known as 'trikes', and ultralights, similar but more aeroplane-like, is a fast-growing activity in Australia where weather and space make it an ideal sport, or simply a way of getting around. A few operators around the country offer scenic flights in 2-seat versions, but if you're interested in getting more involved contact one of the local clubs listed at www.members.ozemail.com.au/~aerial

Parachuting & bungy jumping
A list of bungy operators can be found at www.bungee-experience.com

Some people don't just want to get up in the air in some kind of aircraft but also want to fling themselves out of it once they're up there. Many of the several dozen skydiving clubs in Australia offer short, usually one-day courses in parachuting (also known as 'skydiving'), including a jump or two, and some cut out much of the training by organizing tandem jumps where you're strapped, facing forward, to the chest of the instructor. If a quick thrill is all you're after then the latter is the better option as it usually involves 30 to 60 seconds of freefall, by far the most exhilarating part of the experience, and costs around $250-300. A list of skydiving clubs affiliated to the Australian Parachute Federation, T02 62816830, can be found at www.apf.asn.au, and there are numerous opportunities to make the big leap all along the East Coast and around Sydney. If you fancy jumping out into thin air without a parachute then bungy jumping, leaping off a platform with an elastic rope tied around your ankles, is just about the safest option going. The great Papua New Guinean invention (developed commercially in New Zealand) is available from a site just north of Cairns.

Golf

Almost every town in Eastern Australia has at least one golf course, even in the outback, though the feel of the greens may not be too familiar, and most welcome visitors. The very best courses are, unsurprisingly, close to Sydney and Brisbane, with high concentrations on the Sunshine and Gold Coasts. The list of the top 50 public access courses to be found on the excellent and very comprehensive website, www.ausgolf.com.au, features a lot in Queensland.

Health

Medical facilities in individual towns and cities are listed in the directories

See also www.health.gov.au

Australia has a national, government-funded health care scheme called *Medicare*. This, together with the supporting private network, is reckoned to be one of the best health care systems in the world, so you can rest easy with the thought that if you suffer an unexpected accident or illness you should be well looked after. Public hospitals are part of *Medicare*, a large number of pharmaceutical products are funded or subsidized by the scheme, and most doctors are registered so that their services can also be funded or subsidized by the scheme. Doctors who invoice *Medicare* directly, so charging the patient nothing on examination, are said to bulk bill. Those that don't bulk bill charge the patient who then has to reclaim the charge from *Medicare*. Large cities usually have clinics where you can walk in without an appointment. The Travellers Medical and Vaccination Centre ('TMVC' or 'The Travel Doctor') operates several clinics around the country.

Australia has reciprocal arrangements with a handful of countries which allow citizens of those countries to receive free 'immediately necessary medical treatment' under the *Medicare* scheme. The arrangements with New Zealand and the Republic of Ireland provide visitors to Australia with free care as a public patient in public hospitals and subsidized medicines under the Pharmaceutical Benefits Scheme. In addition to these benefits, visitors from Finland, Italy, Malta, the Netherlands, Sweden and the UK also enjoy subsidized out-of-hospital treatment (ie visiting a doctor). Most visitors under the arrangement are covered for their entire stay. Visitors from Malta and Italy, however, are covered for a maximum of six months. If you qualify under the reciprocal arrangement, contact your own national health scheme to check what documents you will require in Australia to claim *Medicare*. All visitors to Australia are, however, strongly advised to take out medical insurance for the duration of their visit. You do not need to pre-register with *Medicare* to be entitled to the benefits, but can register on your first visit to a doctor or hospital. Charges can be reclaimed either via the post or in person at a Medicare office, which can be found in all major towns and cities.

Before you go

Ideally, you should see your GP or travel clinic at least six weeks before your departure for general advice on travel risks, malaria and vaccinations. Make sure you have travel insurance, get a dental check (especially if you are going to be away for more than a month), know your own blood group and, if you suffer a long-term condition such as diabetes or epilepsy, make sure someone knows or that you have a Medic Alert bracelet/necklace with this information on it. Items to take with you should include: First aid kit; sunscreen; mosquito repellents; pain killers; ciproxin (antibiotic); immodium; MedicAlert (for those with a serious condition).

On the road

There are two main threats to health in Australia. One is global warming, and with that the spread of more tropical diseases such as Dengue Fever. The second are the ever present, poisonous snakes and spiders. Check loo seats, boots and the area around you if you're visiting the bush.

Diarrhoea & **Symptoms** Diarrhoea can refer either to loose stools or an increased frequency; both
intestinal of these can be a nuisance. It should be short lasting but persistence beyond two
upset weeks, with blood or pain, require specialist medical attention. **Cures** Ciproxin (Ciprofloaxcin) is a useful antibiotic for bacterial traveller's diarrhoea. It can be obtained by private prescription in the UK which is expensive, or bought over the counter in Australian pharmacies. You need to take one 500 mg tablet when the diarrhoea starts and if you do not feel better in 24 hours, the diarrhoea is likely to have a non-bacterial cause and may be viral (in which case there is little you can do apart from keep yourself rehydrated and wait for it to settle on its own). The key treatment with all diarrhoeas is rehydration. Try to keep hydrated by taking the right mixture of salt and water. This is available as Oral Rehydration Salts (ORS) in ready-made sachets or can be made up by adding a teaspoon of sugar and a half teaspoon of salt to a litre of clean water. Drink at least one large cup of this drink for each loose stool. You can also use flat carbonated drinks as an alternative. Immodium and Pepto- Bismol provide symptomatic relief. **Prevention** The standard advice is to be careful with water and ice for drinking. If you have any doubts then boil it or filter and treat it. There are many filter/treatment

Please give blood!

Practically any subtropical area in Australia that is damp underfoot is home to leeches and their rapacious thirst for blood is surpassed only by their particularly crafty and insidious method for finding it. By all accounts humans are ideal prey, as they stomp about making lots of noise and vibrations, especially while travelling in a row. When the leeches feel the vibrations they move towards the disturbance (often en masse and in quite the most repulsive and indescribable way) and then, like a wound up spring, jump on to your various bodily parts. Then, they actually work they way down to your skin, presumably sensing the heat, before settling down to dinner. The worst thing is you will know very little about this

particular dinner invitation, since, before latching on to your skin (and sucking away like the proverbial hover bag), they are kind enough to anaesthetise the area locally first, using a special saliva. But, despite their looks, and let's face it, their admirable hunting technique, leeches are in fact incredibly clean and will do you no harm. In fact, for centuries they have been used by witch doctors (both ancient and of the modern hospital variety), to keep wounds clean and the healing blood flowing around them. Of course, as hard as it may be, do not let the thought of imminent attack deter you from any inevitably enjoyable rainforest walks. Merely make sure your wear sturdy foot-wear and that your skin is well covered.

Essentials

devices now available on the market. Food can also transmit disease. Be wary of salads (what were they washed in, who handled them), re-heated foods or food that has been left out in the sun having been cooked earlier in the day. There is a simple adage that says wash it, peel it, boil it or forget it. Also be wary of unpasteurized dairy products, these can transmit a range of diseases from brucellosis (fevers and constipation), to listeria (meningitis) and tuberculosis of the gut (obstruction, constipation, fevers and weight loss).

Symptoms If you go diving make sure that you are fit do so. The British Scuba Association (BSAC), Telford's Quay, South Pier Road, Ellesmere Port, Cheshire CH65 4FL, UK, T01513-506200, F506215, www.bsac.com, can put you in touch with doctors who do medical examinations. Protect your feet from cuts, beach dog parasites (larva migrans) and sea urchins. The latter are almost impossible to remove but can be dissolved with lime or vinegar. Keep an eye out for secondary infection. **Cures** Antibiotics for secondary infections. Serious diving injuries may need time in a decompression chamber. Prevention Check that the dive company know what they are doing, have appropriate certification from BSAC or Professional Association of Diving Instructors (PADI), Unit 7, St Philips Central, Albert Road, St Philips, Bristol, BS2 0TD, T0117-3007234, www.padi.com, and that the equipment is well maintained.

Underwater health

Symptoms White Britons are notorious for becoming red in hot countries because they like to stay out longer than everyone else and do not use adequate sun protection. This can lead to sunburn, which is painful and followed by flaking of skin. Aloe vera gel is a good pain reliever for sunburn. Long-term sun damage leads to a loss of elasticity of skin and the development of pre-cancerous lesions. Many years later a mild or a very malignant form of cancer may develop. **Cures** The milder basal cell carcinoma, if detected early, can be treated by cutting it out or freezing it. The much nastier malignant melanoma may have already spread to bone and brain at the time that it is first noticed. **Prevention** Sun screen. SPF stands for Sun Protection Factor. It is measured by determining how long a given person takes to 'burn' with and without the sunscreen product on. So, if it takes 10 times longer to burn with the sunscreen

Sun protection

product applied, then that product has an SPF of 10. If it only takes twice as long then the SPF is 2. The higher the SPF the greater the protection. However, do not just use higher factors just to stay out in the sun longer. 'Flash frying' (desperate bursts of excessive exposure), as it is called, is known to increase the risks of skin cancer. Follow the Australians' with their Slip, Slap, Slop campaign. Slip on a shirt, Slap on a hat and Slop on the sun screen.

Dengue fever   **Symptoms** This disease can be contracted throughout Australia. In travellers this can cause a severe 'flu-like illness which includes symptoms of fever, lethargy, enlarged lymph glands and muscle pains. It starts suddenly, lasts for 2-3 days, seems to get better for 2-3 days and then kicks in again for another 2-3 days. It is usually all over in an unpleasant week. Children are prone to the much nastier haemorrhagic form of the disease, which causes them to bleed from internal organs, mucous membranes and often leads to their death. **Cures** The traveller's version of the disease is self limiting and forces rest and recuperation on the sufferer. **Prevention** The mosquitoes that carry the Dengue virus bite during the day unlike the malaria mosquitoes. Which sadly means that repellent application and covered limbs are a 24-hour issue. Check your accommodation for flower pots and shallow pools of water since these are where the dengue-carrying mosquitoes breed.

Hepatitis   **Symptoms** Hepatitis means inflammation of the liver. Viral causes of the disease can be acquired anywhere in Australia. The most obvious symptom is a yellowing of your skin or the whites of your eyes. However, prior to this all that you may notice is itching and tiredness. **Cures** Early on, depending on the type of hepatitis, a vaccine or immunoglobulin may reduce the duration of the illness. **Prevention** Pre-travel hepatitis A vaccine is the best bet. Hepatitis B (for which there is a vaccine) is spread through blood and unprotected sexual intercourse, both of these can be avoided. Unfortunately there is no vaccine for hepatitis C or the increasing alphabetical list of other Hepatitis viruses.

Tuberculosis   Australia has the fourth lowest level in the world for this disease and is well protected by health screens before people can settle there. The bus driver coughing as he takes your fare could expose you to the mycobacterium. **Symptoms** Cough, tiredness, fever and lethargy. **Cures** At least six months treatment with a combination of drugs is required. **Prevention** Have a BCG vaccination before you go and see a doctor early if you have a persistent cough, cough blood, fever or unexplained weight loss.

Snakes & other poisonous things   A bite itself does not mean that anything has been injected in to you. However, a commonsense approach is to clean the area of the bite (never have it sutured early on) and get someone to take you to a medical facility fast. It is better to be taken because the more energy you expand the faster poisons spread around the body. Do not try to catch the snake or spider. You will only get more bites and faster spread of poison for your troubles. For some snake bites a knowledgeable first aider can provide appropriate bandaging and if a poison is on-board specialist anti-venoms will be administered by an experienced doctor.

Sexual health   The range of visible and invisible diseases is awesome. Unprotected sex can spread HIV, Hepatitis B and C, Gonorrhea (green discharge), chlamydia (nothing to see but may cause painful urination and later female infertility), painful recurrent herpes, syphilis and warts, just to name a few. You can cut down the risk by using condoms, a femidom or avoiding sex altogether.

Sydney

Introducing Sydney

Sydney has come a long way since January 1788 and that seminal day in Australia's human history when Captain Arthur Phillip, commander of the 'First Fleet', weighed anchor in Port Jackson and – with perhaps just a modicum of arrogance – declared the entire continent a British penal colony. Now, after its bicentennial, where once stood a conglomerate of sorry-looking shacks and lock-ups full of desperate, hopeless convicts, stands a forest of glistening modern highrises. In their shadow, hordes of free-spirited, cosmopolitan city workers now seem to have every reason to be proud of their own unique identity and their beautiful city. A city that is lauded as the 'real' (if not administrative) capital of Australia, home to almost a quarter of its total population and undeniably the country's most celebrated. Ask any Sydneysider (except the homeless) what it is like to live there and they will instantly support an expression of one who has just bet their annual salary on a one-horse race. Not only is it stunning but there is of course the lifestyle (reputed to be one of the best in the world), the climate (hot but not too hot) and the almost perfect mix of natural and man-made aesthetics.

The success of the 2000 Olympics only added to the city's reputation. Record-breaking amounts of money were spent on inner-city rejuvenation, transportation and state of the art sports venues, all of which provided the infrastructure and the stage for what were dubbed the best games yet. Many cynics (the vast majority living outside Sydney) expected a huge slump after the Olympics – some kind of 'post traumatic hype disorder' – but it never occurred. It seems life just went back to normal.

But can a city really be this good? Sure, Sydney has its problems and in some ways is just like any other city its size. There are the drugs (the dark side of its party image and its glamour), the crime, the ever increasing number of homeless, the social, economic and cultural divides and the ceaseless urban sprawl. True, if you take away the Opera House, the harbour and the mighty bridge, things would be very different. Also, in the last decade, with alarming frequency and as a result of decades of poor land management and persistent drought, severe bush fires have ravaged the city fringes and surrounding national parks, taking both lives and property. Added to this fiery vulnerability, and even more recently, after the loss of many natives in the Bali bombing of October 2002, there is also the growing spectre of global terrorism. With the Australian government's controversial and somewhat extrovert support of US policy it must share in the growing paranoia of a new and insidious nemesis and accept that Sydney would be the obvious target.

But in essence, and certainly in looks, Sydney has become and remains undeniably world-class and has a great deal to offer both the resident and the visitor, including remarkable and instantly recognizable icons, fascinating museums and art galleries, top-class restaurants and beaches, world-renowned festivals and cultural events, 24-hour entertainment, state of the art sports venues and a whole host of exciting activities. Then there are its lesser known secrets: its colony of outrageously big bats, a talking dog, a ten-metre matchstick (a little ironic these days), and even the odd penguin sighting in the glistening waters off the Opera House.

But despite the many attractions, the modern glamour and the hype, it is worth remembering that Sydney is, in a way, still in shackles. To most it seems huge and dominant, yet in reality it has been and will forever be a tiny speck of humanity incarcerated on the edge of a vast continent ruled by nature. The aborigines learned that lesson, adapted accordingly and thrived for thousands of years. Still so young, so in love with its own voice and with the ancient culture so muted, it seems Sydney has yet to do so.

Sydney

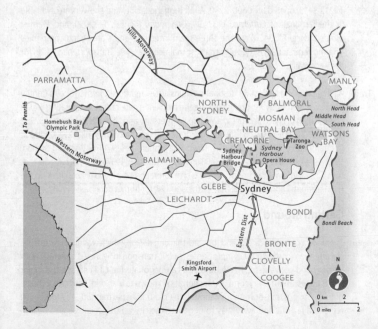

Sydney

Ins and outs

Getting there

Air

Phone code: 02
Colour map 1, grid C3
Population: 4,000,000

Sydney's Kingsford Smith Airport is 9 km south of the city centre. Given a major overhaul for the 2000 Olympic Games, its negotiation is pretty straightforward and the facilities are excellent. There is a Tourism New South Wales information desk in the main arrivals concourse where help is at hand to organize transport, accommodation bookings and flight arrival information, T9667 6065, www.sydneyairport.com Additionally, the Sydney Airport Help Desk is located in the centre of the terminal (Departures). Volunteer Airport Ambassadors (identified by gold jackets) are also on hand to answer any questions. Other airport facilities include ATMs, *Thomas Cook* and *Travelex Foreign Exchange*, car hire, post office and even medical centre (open 0400-2300 daily). Sydney's Domestic Terminal is a short distance west of the International Terminal. Due to terrorist attacks the locker service at Sydney Airport International Terminal is currently unavailable.

Public transport from the airport to the city centre (and between terminals) is readily available within a short walk of both terminal buildings. The green and yellow *Airport Express*, T131500, serves the city centre (daily 0500-2300) including the Central Railway Station, Circular Quay and Wynyard bus and principal rail stations (#300, $7, child $3.50, return $12, tickets from the driver). There are connecting services to Kings Cross, Bondi, Coogee (#350) and Darling Harbour, Glebe (#352). There is a ticket booth in the main bus area. A new rail link between the main city stations and the Domestic Terminal leaves every 10-15 mins, daily 0500-2400, from $10 one way (20 mins). Taxis are available outside the terminal (south). A trip to the city centre takes about 30 mins and costs around $25. Services from the airport to the city centre continue until the last flight arrivals. See Transport, page 128, for further details.

Bus

875 km from Melbourne, 292 km from Canberra, 984 km fromBrisbane, 2685 km from Cairns

The main coach station is located in the Central Railway Station, Shop 4-7, Eddy Av, T9212 3433, open daily 0600-2230. A left luggage facility and showers are available in the terminal. *McCaffertys*, T131499, *Greyhound Pioneer*, T132030, and *Premier Motor Service*, T133410, are the three main interstate and state coach companies offering regular daily schedules to most main centres. See Transport, page 128, for further details.

Train

All interstate and NSW state destination trains arrive and depart from Sydney's Central Railway Station, Eddy Av. *Countrylink* are the main interstate operators operating with a combination of coach and rail to all the main interstate and NSW destinations, T132232 (daily 0630-2200), www.countrylink.nsw.gov.au There is a Countrylink Travel Centre at Central Station, T9955 4237, while Town Hall Station, T9379 4076, Wynyard Station, T9224 4744, Circular Quay, T9224 3400 and Bondi Junction, T9379 3777, all have on-the-spot *CityRail* information booths. There is an information booth and ticket offices on the main platform concourse. See Transport, page 128, for further details.

Getting around

See Transport, page 126, for further details

Thanks to a history of careful and forward-thinking design, which was given extra-special attention for the 2000 Olympic Games, public transport in Sydney is generally both efficient and convenient. These days you can negotiate the city and see the major sights on just about every form of transportation known to mankind. You have a choice of ferry, car, bus, rail, or monorail, though the old traditional method – by foot – still remains a realistic and lively way to negotiate the city centre. Of course also bear in

◀

A long weekend

For sunrise get yourself in position at **Macquarie Point** *(harbourside) which offers the best views of the Opera House and the harbour bridge. Then head for the Opera House via the waterfront taking a short diversion into the heart of the* **Royal Botanical Gardens** *to see the aromatic bat colony. At the* **Opera House** *lose yourself in creative photography or simply awe amidst its shell-like structure and its views across to the bridge. From there, take your time negotiating* **Circular Quay** *perhaps stopping for a leisurely breakfast below the concourse. Then make your way to* **The Rocks**, *via* **Campbell's Cove** *where the Bounty is moored. Continue around to* **Dawes Point Park** *to marvel at the sheer size of the harbour bridge. Head back to The Rocks and down* **George Street**, *where, at the weekend, the bustling market is held. Book into a* **Bridge Climb** *for the following day. For lunch go to the Australian Hotel and get a pavement table.*

In the afternoon, catch a ferry from Circular Quay to **Taronga Zoo** *or for the soporific head for* **Balmoral Beach**. *In the evening return to* **Darling Harbour** *for dinner.*

Around the following put aside some time for your **Bridge Climb**. *Start early with a fascinating tour of* **Sydney fish market**, *and then, keeping your wallet firmly closed head via the* **Casino** *to the* **National Maritime Museum**. *Be sure to take the submarine tour then cross* **Pyrmont Bridge** *to the* **Sydney Aquarium**.

For lunch catch the ferry to **Watson's Bay** *to sample the seafood delights of Doyle's on the Beach, or join the fray at the al fresco Watson's Bay Hotel. Walk off your scran with a leisurely stroll to* **South Head**. *Hit* **Darlinghurst** *for dinner and perhaps* **Kings Cross** *for an eventful night on the town. Alternatively try* **Chinatown** *and for a less riotous nightout return to The Rocks or Darling Harbour.*

Sydney

mind that given the seemingly omnipresent, heavily embayed harbour you may find yourself on the water as much as land. The great hub of public transportation in the city centre is Circular Quay which sits like the doorstep to a huge termite hill at the base of the CBD (Central Business District). It is from there that most ferry (*Sydney Ferries*), suburban rail (*CityRail*) and bus (*Sydney Buses*) services operate. *State Transit* (*STA*) own and operate the principal suburban ferry and bus services. Other principal terminals are Wynyard on York St for northbound bus and rail services, Town Hall on George St, and the Central Railway Station. All have information booths supplying on the spot train and bus information. For information about all public transport in Sydney, T131500 (daily 0600-2200). Prior to arrival it is well worth having a muse at www.131500.com.au For the various attractive discount travel passes see box, page 127. Ferry and rail route maps are readily available from information centres and booths, see also the maps at the end of this guide. If you intend to be in the city even for a short time the free *Sydney Public Transport Directory*, available from the Sydney VIC, is very useful.

Tourist information

Beyond the visitor information booth at the airport international arrivals terminal, the first stop for any visitor should be the Sydney Visitor Centre, Cadman's Cottage, 106 George St, The Rocks, T9255 1788, T1800 067676 (free call from outside Sydney and within Australia), F9241 5010, www.sydneyvisitorcentre.com Open 0900-1800 daily. The centre provides a comprehensive service, including information, brochures, maps and reservations for hotels, tours, cruises, restaurants and other city-based activities. The centre can book stand-by accommodation (discounted rates), but this is a face-to-face service only. Alternatively visitors can contact some hotels and tour/activity operators via the free-to-use phones.

Sydney

▶ **Plastic fantastic**

Well, it has finally, and perhaps inevitably arrived – 'sightseeing by plastic' but it isn't nearly as deadly as Visa or MasterCard. **The SeeSydneyCard** is a new concept in sightseeing – a pre-paid tourist credit card that gives unlimited admissions to a wide variety of attractions, activities and tours, and offers reductions at some restaurants and shops. The card also includes optional public transport and comes with a free full colour guide book and maps. There are two types of card, adult and children's (5-15 years). Adult cards range from 1-day for $49 (with transport $62) to a week at $149 ($207) and children 1-day $29 (with transport $35.50) to a week at $89 ($118). For more information and purchasing contact the major VICs or call T9255 1788, www.see sydneycard.com It can prove worthwhile if you are short of time and plan to visit all the main attractions.

If you have a specific interest in museums and historical buildings you might also consider the **Ticket Through Time** (valid for 3 months) costing $23, children $10, family $40. Ask the VIC.

Another main VIC is at Darling Harbour, T19022 60568, www.darlingharbour.com Open daily 1000-1800. It offers much the same in services as the Rocks centre but has an emphasis on sights and activities within Darling Harbour itself. Neither centre issues public transport tickets.

Manly, Parramatta, Homebush Bay and Bondi also have local information centres. Small manned information booths are located: corner Pitt St and Alfred St, Circular Quay; opposite St Andrew's Cathedral near the Town Hall on George St; and on Martin Place, near Elizabeth St. Manly VIC, located on the forecourt, next to the ferry terminal, is an ideal first stop. It is well stocked with detailed leaflets covering everything from eating out to bicycle hire. Open daily 1000-1600, T9977 1088, www.manly.nsw.gov.au

There are several independent travel offices designed mainly to cater for backpackers including *Travellers Contact Point*, 7th floor, 428 George St, T9221 8744, www.travellers. com.au, open Mon-Fri 0900-1800, Sat 1000-1600, which also offers mail forwarding and employment advice; *Backpackers World*, Central Station, 482 Pitt St and Level 3 Imperial Arcade, 83 Castlereagh St, T1800 676763, www.backpackers world.com.au; *YHA Travel Centre*, Sydney Central YHA, T9281 9444 and 422 Kent St, T9261 1111, travel@yhansw.org.au; *Student Uni Travel*, Level 8, 92 Pitt St, T9232 8444, www.sut.com.au Most of these offices also have internet facilities. *Australian Travel Specialists* cater for the full range of traveller and have offices throughout the city, including one at Wharf 6, Circular Quay, T9555 2700.

The main daily newspaper in Sydney is the excellent *Sydney Morning Herald* which has comprehensive entertainment listings daily (specific in the pull-out *Metro* section on Friday) and regular city features. There are some excellent, free tourist brochures including *Sydney Official Guide*, *This Week in Sydney*, *Where Magazine*, the very interesting suburb-oriented *Sydney Monthly* and for the backpacker *TNT* (NSW Edition) or *Backpack Guide to Australia*. For entertainment look out for *The Revolver* and *3-D World*. All these and others are available from the principal VICs, city centre information booths, or from cafés, newsagents and bookshops. Some of the best Sydney websites are www.visitnsw.com.au, www.sydney.citysearch.com.au, www.discoversydney.com.au

Maps   Most of the free tourist brochures have useful maps but for more detail purchase a copy of the Sydway *Sydney Tourist Guide Map* ($6). Comprehensive city street (UBD) region and state maps are available in most major bookshops. *Travel Bookshop*, 175 Liverpool St (southern edge of Hyde Park), T9261 8200, is also a good source of Australian travel information, books and maps. Open Mon-Fri 0900-1800, Sat 1000-1700.

History

The European history of New South Wales and indeed the entire nation is not surprisingly inextricably linked to that of its great capital – Sydney. Long before the beautiful coves and inlets of Sydney harbour embraced the arrival of the 'First Fleet' and its shores played host to the 'new colony', a very much older colony had been established in the region, in the form of the **Eora Aboriginals**. Incredibly, for over 100 times as many years as it has since taken for the development of the mighty metropolis and the state we know today, the Eora thrived. Sadly, it took just 100 years of early European colonization to almost completely wipe them out. For this reason, and many others that would see drastic and holistic effects on the entire continent, from anthropology to ecology, there is no doubt that day in 1778 was the most seminal point in Australian history.

With the relative success of **Captain Cook's** voyage of discovery of the eastern coast of Australia in 1770, King George III of England decided the potential 'new lands' would make a good colony, and initially an ideal jail. Eight years later, on 13 May 1778, six vessels carrying about 300 crew and 800 convicts, under the command of **Captain Arthur Phillip**, set sail from Portsmouth. The voyage took 36 weeks; there was a loss of less than 50 lives – about average for the day. On 18 January 1788 the 'First Fleet' sailed into Botany Bay, south of Sydney harbour, the site of Cook's first landing. Much to Phillip's dismay it was far from the 'ideal' site Cook had reported it to be. There was no water and little shelter, but at least the 'natives' seemed amiable. After pondering their predicament and a brief and totally unexpected liaison with French explorer La Perouse, Phillip moved north and entered Port Jackson (Sydney harbour) named in 1770 by Cook. Finding it eminently more suitable Phillip named it **Sydney Cove** after British Secretary of State Viscount Sydney and Phillip himself was quickly sworn in as the first Governor of the newly proclaimed state of New South Wales.

Initial attempts at settlement proved disastrous, since the crew were ill-prepared, poorly supplied and unskilled in utilizing local resources. The Eora Aboriginals must have found the invaders perplexing, almost amusing, were it not for their superior attitude and the new diseases they brought with them that were by now reducing their number by the day. The hopeless new penal colony struggled on trying unsuccessfully to grow crops and teetering on the brink of starvation until 1790 when the discovery of more favourable soils further up the harbour at **Parramatta** turned despair to hope. For the next two decades Sydney and its surrounds developed and grew with the arrival of more convicts and the parole of others. With the departure of the weary governor, power-hungry soldiers (known as the New South Wales Corps) left in charge of the convicts, took advantage of the administrative vacuum and the sheer distance from the homeland, by granting each other rights to secure tracts of land and use convict labour for their development. In the absence of money, rum became the currency of choice, earning the new 'mafia' their nickname – the **'Rum Corps'**.

England's first attempt to restore official order in the form of Captain Bligh (from 'Mutiny of the Bounty' fame) failed and it took the Scotsman, **Lachlan Macquarie** to restore order to a colony he described as adhering to a system of 'infantile imbecility'. A great planner and fair man, Macquarie was instrumental in the transformation of the established colony from a insignificant port built on a base of local exploitation to a progressive society earning international recognition. By the mid-1800s new farms and settlements dotted the region and explorers Lawson, Blaxland and Wentworth had found a way through the seemingly impenetrable Blue Mountains, opening up the west of the state to agriculture and settlement.

In 1840 the transportation of convicts (many of whom had by now been relocated from Sydney to Port Macquarie) to New South Wales was finally abolished. The discovery of **gold** near Bathurst west of the Blue Mountains in the 1850s and mineral finds in Broken Hill dramatically increased the population of the state and almost doubled that of Sydney within a single decade to around 370,000 by 1890. It was not all progressive and positive however, with the inevitable **inequalities** in wealth creating a whole range of social problems from rampant disease and deprivation to widespread alcoholism and crime. The problems of racial disharmony and the continued annihilation of the Aboriginals and their culture also remained a major problem throughout the state and the developing nation as a whole.

With the creation of the **Commonwealth of Australia** in 1901 and a new capital – **Canberra** – in 1927, Sydney and New South Wales took a back seat in the affairs of the nation. The First and Second World Wars came and went and immigration increased rapidly. Sydney in particular was becoming a truly cosmopolitan city proud of its lifestyle. Through the 1950s and 1960s however, the infant nation still struggled to find its own identity and disenfranchise itself from its colonial past. In many ways the nation, New South Wales and Sydney in particular, all seemed utterly insecure, and perhaps inevitably became increasingly eager to take flight towards their own destiny. Yet, with the help of its two famous icons – **Sydney Harbour Bridge** completed in 1932 and the **Opera House** in 1973 – together with the passage of time and the inevitable consolidation of its population and its emerging character, gradually Sydney was well on course to becoming one of the best-loved and most dynamic cities in the world. With massive amounts of money being spent on the city in preparations to stage the **2000 Olympics** and their subsequent and undeniable success, the image of the city, the state and the nation was further enhanced.

Sights

Circular Quay and The Rocks

Log on to www.view sydney.com.au and see the sights of Circular Quay live on the web

Sydney is without doubt one of the most beautiful cities in the world and the main reasons for this are its **harbour**, the **Opera House** and the **Harbour Bridge**, situated in and around Circular Quay – which also serves as the city's principal hub of transportation. It draws visitors like bees to a honey pot. As well as all the numerous harbour cruises, activities like the Bridge Climb and the quay's trendy restaurants, a simple walk between the Opera House via **Opera Quays** to the historic and commercial Rocks area offers a truly memorable experience. Other 'quay' attractions that nestle in the shadows of the mighty highrises of the Central Business District (CBD) include the Art Deco **Museum of Contemporary Art**, **Customs House** and the **Justice and Police Museum**.

What is most remarkable about **The Rocks** – on the western fringe of Circular Quay – is not only its apparent success in combining a genuine historical ambience with tourism, but its transformation through time, from being a thoroughly despicable place rife with crime, prostitution, rum-fuelled street fights, to the orderly and healthy resurrection we see today. Despite being given a major facelift in recent decades it still retains much of its original architectural charm and now serves as one of Sydney's most popular tourist attractions. Old and new are married in an eclectic array of shops, galleries, arcades, cafés and some fine pubs and restaurants. It is a great place to spend a morning or afternoon strolling, shopping or dining – provided you can stand the constant sight of toy koalas and didjeridus.

Even for the fiercest sceptics of man-made invention and architecture, who believe nothing made of human brain or brawn can match anything in nature – like the natural Australian icons of Uluru (Ayers Rock) or the Great Barrier Reef for example – the magnificent Opera House cannot fail to impress. Almost 24 hours a day, every day since this bizarre edifice was opened, people have flocked to admire it, touch it, photograph it and even play on it, often without even a thought of its impressive interior or principal function. At times it seems its steps and concourse are places of near touristical worship, and if iconic architecture has a god then the Opera House is probably it. In many ways it is indeed just like some futuristic cathedral with naves both inside and out, yet with an interior functioning as a focus not for ecclesiastical congregations and tradition, but for the best of national and international performing arts. It was built in 1973 and is the result of the Danish architect Jorn Utzon's revolutionary design.

Sydney Opera House

The Opera House has five performance venues, ranging from the main 2,690-capacity Concert Hall to the small Playhouse Theatre, that combined host about 2,500 performances annually with everything from Bach to Billy Connolly. The Opera House is also the principal performance venue for Opera Australia, The Australian Ballet and Contemporary Dance Companies, the Sydney Symphony Orchestra and the Sydney Theatre Company. For the latest schedules contact the SOH Box Office situated in the main foyer. A performance will cost anywhere from $30 to $180 depending on its prestige and your seat. Bookings are essential and can be made on-line.

From the outside, the Opera House is best viewed not only intimately from close up, but also from afar. Some of the best spots are from Macquarie Point (end of the Domain on the western edge of Farm Cove) especially at dawn and from the *Park Hyatt Hotel* on the eastern edge of Circular Quay. Also of course any ferry trip westbound from Circular Quay will reveal the structure in many of its multifaceted forms. From directly above the symmetrical design is impressive too but unless you take an expensive scenic flight this view will elude you.

■ *Three tours and performance packages are available. Front of House Tour provides an insider's view of selected theatres and foyers; Backstage Pass takes you behind the scenes; and there is the historical Bennelong Walk. Tours are available on a regular basis 0830-1700 daily, 45 mins (some fit round performances or rehearsals). $15.40-25.20. Performance Package combines a range of performance, dining and tour options. Guided Tour Office, Lower Concourse, T9250 7209. An SOH store selling official souvenirs, cafés, bars and a restaurant is also located within the complex. Via Macquarie St, Circular Quay, T9250 7777, www.soh.nsw.gov.au Mon-Sat 0900-2030.*

Along the main walkway of Circular Quay between the Opera House and the Museum of Contemporary Art, look out for the 'Writers Walk' which is a series of plaques on the main concourse that quote famous Australian writers and celebrities. Australian celebrity and writer Clive James wrote in his book *Unreliable Memoirs* (1980), "In Sydney Harbour... the yachts will be racing on the crushed diamond water under a sky the texture of powdered sapphires. It would be churlish not to concede that the same abundance of natural blessings which gave us the energy to leave has the right to call us back."

Writers Walk

Sydney

Sydney centre

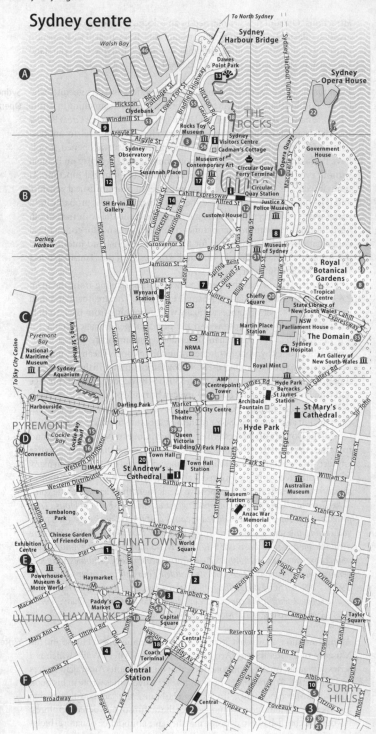

To North Sydney

Sydney
Harbour Bridge

Walsh Bay

Sydney
Opera House

Dawes
Point Park

THE
ROCKS

Hickson Rd
Pottinger St
Lower Fort St
Bradfield Highway
Hickson Rd
George St

Clydebank
Windmill St
Argyle Pl
Argyle St

Rocks Toy
Museum

Sydney
Visitors Centre
Cadman's Cottage

Government House

Hickson Rd
High St
Kent St

Sydney
Observatory

Susannah Place

Museum of
Contemporary Art

Circular Quay
Ferry Terminal

Circular Quay
Station

Macquarie St
Opera Quay

SH Ervin
Gallery

Cumberland St
Gloucester St
Harrington St

Cahill Expressway

Alfred St

Justice &
Police Museum

Customs House

Young St

Darling
Harbour

Grosvenor St

Bridge St

Loftus St

Museum
of Sydney

Royal
Botanical
Gardens

Jamison St

Spring St
Bent St
O'Connell St
Bligh St
Phillip St
Macquarie St

Margaret St

Wynyard
Station

Chiefly
Square

Tropical
Centre

Erskine St
Clarence St
York St
Kent St
Sussex St
Carrington St
George St
Pitt St

Hunter St

State Library of
New South Wales

King St

Martin Pl

NRMA

Martin Place
Station

NSW
Parliament House

Sydney
Hospital

The Domain

Pyremont
Bay

King St Wharf

National
Maritime
Museum

Sydney
Aquarium

Martin Pl

Royal Mint

Art Gallery of
New South Wales

Art Gallery Rd

AMP
(Centrepoint)
Tower

St James Rd

Hyde Park
Barracks
St James
Station

St Mary's
Cathedral

PYREMONT

Cockle
Bay

Convention

Harbourside

Cockle Bay
Wharf

Darling Park

Market
St

State
Theatre

City Centre

Queen
Victoria
Building

Park Plaza

Hyde Park

College St

Australian
Museum

William St

IMAX

Western Distributor

Town Hall
Station

St Andrew's
Cathedral

Druitt St
Town Hall

Bathurst St

Park St

Elizabeth St
Castlereagh St
Pitt St

Museum
Station

Anzac War
Memorial

Stanley St

Francis St

Tumbalong
Park

Chinese Garden
of Friendship

Exhibition
Centre

CHINATOWN

Liverpool St

World
Square

Darling Dr
Harbour St

Pier St

Dixon St

Goulburn St

Wentworth Av
Poplar St
Pelican St

Oxford St

Powerhouse
Museum &
Motor World

Haymarket

Paddy's
Market

Campbell St

Taylor
Square

ULTIMO   HAYMARKET

Macarthur St
Jarris St
Ultimo Rd

Capital
Square

Hay St

Reservoir St

Campbell St

Crown St
Denham St
Bourke St
Nichols St

Mary Ann St

Quay St

Rawson Pl

Central

Coach
Terminal

Eddy Av

Ann St

Mary St
Commonwealth St
Belmore St
Bellevue St

SURRY
HILLS

Central
Station

Thomas St
Lee St
Regent St

Broadway

Central

Kippax St

Foveaux St

Albion St
Fitzroy St

Detail map
A Kings Cross,
page 87

Related maps
Bondi, page 90
Glebe, page 83
Manly, page 94

Sydney

Sydney

Sleeping
1 All Seasons Darling Harbour *E1*
2 Bakpak *E2*
3 Capitol Square *E2*
4 Carlton Crest *F1*
5 Challis Lodge *C5*
6 Glasgow Arms *F1*
7 Grand *C2*
8 Inter-Continental *B3*
9 Lord Nelson *A1*
10 Medina on Crown *F3*
11 Millett's OZ *D2*
12 Observatory *B1*
13 Park Hyatt *A2*
14 Quay West *B2*
15 Royal Sovereign *F4*
16 Rucksack Rest *C5*
17 Russell *B2*
18 Sydney Central YHA *F2*
19 W Hotel *C4*
20 Wanderers Backpackers *D2*
21 Y on the Park (YWCA) *E3*

Eating
1 Aqua Luna *B3*
2 Australian Hotel *B2*
3 Bel Mondo *B2*
4 Bill's *E4*
5 Bill's 2 *F3*
6 Blackbird Café *D1*
7 Bodhi Vegetarian *E2*
8 Botanical Gardens Café *C3*
9 Brooklyn Hotel *B2*
10 Buon Ricordo *E5*
11 Café Centaur *F4*
12 Café Sydney *B2*
13 Casa Asturiana *E2*
14 Centrepoint *D2*
15 Chinta Ria – The Temple of Love *D1*
16 Coast *D1*
17 Dickson House Food Court *E2*
18 Emperor's Garden BBQ *E2*
19 Fishface *E4*

20 Forty One *C3*
21 Fuel *F3*
22 Guillaume at Bennelong *A3*
23 Harry's Café de Wheels *C4*
24 Hot Gossip *F5*
25 Hyde Park Café *E2*
26 Indian Home Diner *F4*
27 Kam Fook Seafood *E1*
28 Manta Ray *C4*
29 MCA Café *B2*
30 MG Garage *F3*
31 MOS Café *C3*
32 Oh, Calcutta *E4*
33 Orphee *F5*
34 Otto *C4*
35 Pavillion on the Park *C3*
36 Pitt St Mall *D2*
37 Prasit's Thai Takeaway *F3*
38 Quay *A2*
39 QVB Building *D2*
40 Restaurant VII *B2*
41 Rockpool *B2*
42 Shimbashi Soba on the Sea *C4*
43 Tetsuya's *E2*
44 Una's *E4*
45 Vivo *C2*
46 Wharf *A2*
47 Zenergy *D2*

Pubs & bars
48 Albury Hotel *F4*
49 Cargo *C1*
50 Durty Nelly's *F4*
51 Grand Pacific Blue Room *F4*
52 Hard Rock Café *D3*
53 Hero of Waterloo & Harbour View Hotel *A2*
54 Kitty O'Sheas *F5*
55 Mercantile *A2*
56 Orient *B2*
57 Oxford Hotel *E3*
58 Paddy McGuires *E2*
59 Scruffy Murphys *E2*
60 Scubar *F2*
61 Woolloomooloo Bay Hotel *C4*

Ⓛ LightRail Station
Ⓜ MonoRail Station

▶ **Urban jungle**

Amidst all the human activity on Sydney Harbour you may be astonished to learn that it is not entirely unusual to see a penguin dodging the wakes of boats in the inner harbour. Incredible as it may seem, little blue penguins live and breed in Sydney Harbour, and at the harbour mouth, in late winter and spring, migrating humpback whales are also regularly seen. Also, around The Rocks at dusk and after dark, keep your eye open for huge flying foxes (bats) that stray from the large colony resident in the Botanical Gardens.

Opera Quays At the eastern edge of the quay the new Opera Quays façade provides many tempting, if expensive, cafés and restaurants as well as an art gallery and a cinema, www.operaquays.com.au

Justice & Police Museum Housed in the former 1856 Water Police Court, the Justice and Police Museum features a magistrate's court and former police cells, as well as a gallery, and historical displays, showcasing the antics and fate of some of Sydney's most notorious criminals. The forensic evidence surrounding some of the most serious crimes and the rather incriminating 'mug-shots' of the perpetrators is interesting, but it is the impressive collection of weaponry that provides the most chilling reminder of their intent, attitude and determination. ■ *Sat/Sun 1000-1700, daily in Jan. $7, children $3, family $17. Corner of Albert and Phillip sts, Circular Quay. T9252 1144, www.hht.nsw.gov.au*

Customs House Nearby, facing the quay is the former 1840 Customs House which now houses several exhibition spaces, café/bars and, on the fifth floor, the poplar *Café Sydney*, a mainly seafood restaurant with superb views across the harbour. The Object Galleries (third floor) lend themselves to craft and design, while, on the fourth floor, the City Exhibition Space showcases historical and contemporary aspects of the city with a 1:500 model of the CBD as its main attraction.

Museum of Contemporary Art At the southwestern corner of Circular Quay it is hard to miss this rather grand museum. Opened in 1991, it maintains a collection of some of Australia's best contemporary works, together with works by renowned international artists like Warhol and Hockney. The museum also hosts regular national and international exhibitions. Overlooking the quay the in-house *MCA Café* is a popular spot for lunch or a caffeine fix. ■ *Daily 1000-1700. Free. Small charge for visiting exhibitions. 140 George St, The Rocks. T9241 5892, www.mca.com.au Tours available Mon-Fri 1100 and 1400, Sat/Sun 1200 and 1330.*

Cadman's Cottage A little further towards the Harbour Bridge is Cadman's Cottage which now sits looking somewhat out of place overlooking the futuristic Cruiseliner terminal. The cottage, built in 1816, is the oldest surviving residence in Sydney and was originally the former base for Governor Macquarie's boat crew, before playing host to the Sydney Water Police. The cottage is named after the coxswain of the boat crew, John Cadman, a former convict sent to Australia, apparently, for stealing a horse. Worse still, his evil and despicable wife Elizabeth was found guilty of stealing a hairbrush!

The cottage is now home for the far less heinous staff of the National Parks and Wildlife Service, Sydney Harbour National Park Information Centre, which is the main booking office and departure point for a number of harbour and island tours. A small historical exhibition is housed in the lower level.

■ *Mon-Fri 0930-1630, Sat/Sun 1000-1630. Free. 110 George St, The Rocks. T9247 5033, www.npws.nsw.gov.au*

Rocks Market

See page 125, for a Walking tours of the Rocks – the best way to appreciate the area

Rocks Market is just a short stroll from Cadman's Cottage, along George Street. This is perhaps the most popular market in Sydney, featuring a fine array of authentic arts, crafts, bric-a-brac and souvenirs. Be warned, however, it is a big market, and always very busy and so subsequently both cramped and exhausting. It is held every weekend from about 1000 to 1700.

Rocks Square

For live entertainment head for this square in the heart of the village where every day, from midday for a couple of hours, you'll hear jazz, classical or contemporary/traditional music. Also look out for two very camp and entertaining gentlemen on scooters, dressed as policeman, sporting skin-tight jodhpurs, leather boots and with blue flashing lights on their heads.

Rocks Toy Museum & Puppet Theatre

Children especially will love the Rocks Toy Museum housed in the former 1854 Coachhouse on Kendall Lane. It has over 3,000 toys spanning two centuries. Also on Kendall Lane is the even more child-friendly Puppet Theatre offering free shows at 1100, 1230 and 1400 weekends (daily during school hols).

Observatory Park & around

To escape the crowds, head up Argyle Street, and the steps to Cumberland Street, taking a quick peek at the historic row of cottages at **Susannah Place** at 58-64 Gloucester Street, below the popular **Australian Hotel** and pub (see page 106), before walking through the pedestrian walkway to Observatory Park.

The park offers some fine views of the bridge and is home to the **Sydney Observatory**, which is Australia's oldest. There is an interesting exhibition covering early Aboriginal and European astronomy as well as evening tours offering a chance to view the heavens. ■ *Daily 1000-1700. Free. Evening tour $10, children $5, family $25.*

Almost next door is the **SH Ervin Gallery**, at the National Trust Centre, that has a reputation for hosting some fine, small-scale exhibitions. ■ *Tue-Fri 1100-1700, Sat/Sun 1200-1700. Adults $6, child $4, T9258 0123.*

From Observatory Park it is a short walk further along Argyle Street to enjoy a drink and a bite to eat at the **Lord Nelson**, one of Sydney's oldest pubs, (corner of Kent and Argyle streets) before perhaps walking north down Lower Fort Street to **Dawes Point Park** with its dramatic bridge perspectives. At 43 Lower Fort Street, you may like to dip into **Clydebank**, a restored mansion with its period furnishings and collection of former Rocks memorabilia. ■ *Wed-Sat 1000-1800, $8. T9241 4776.*

Harbour Bridge

Harbour Bridge concedes the title of the world's longest single span bridge to New York's Bayonne Bridge, which beats it by a spanner's length

From near or far, above or below, day or night, it is impressive and imposing. Surely, along with its even more eccentric neighbour – the Opera House – the Sydney Harbour Bridge (or 'Coathanger' – as it is often called) is one of man's greatest urban constructions. Although even the first convicts entertained ideas about spanning the waters from Sydney Cove it was not until 1900 that an official tender was issued for designs. After considerable debate in 1924 under the guidance of one of Australia's greatest civil structural and transport engineers, John Bradfield (1867-1943) building began. It took 1,400 men nine years to complete using an astonishing six million rivets and at a cost of $A13.5 million. Sixteen men also died from work related accidents during its construction. Finally in March 1932, the bridge was officially opened creating an inevitable flood of development on the North Shore.

Today, it remains the second longest single span bridge in the world, with New York's Bayonne Bridge beating it by about a spanner's length. The deck supports eight lanes of traffic (accommodating around 150,000 vehicles a day), a railway line and a pedestrian walkway, which, along with the more recent 'out of sight, out of mind' subterranean Harbour Tunnel below, forms a crucial artery to the North Shore and beyond. The original toll across the bridge was 5c for a car and 2c for a horse and rider. Today, sadly, the horses are long gone and the toll for the modern-day car has risen to $2. Yet despite that and the incredible load of traffic the building costs were only paid off in 1988.

For over six decades the best views from the bridge were accessed by foot from its 59-m high deck, but now the **Bridge Climb** experience, that ascends the 134 m high, 502 m long span, has developed into an award-winning Sydney 'must-do'. See Tours and activities, page 122. Not as thrilling but far cheaper are the views on offer from the top of the **South-eastern Pylon Lookout**, which can be accessed from the eastern walkway and Cumberland Street, The Rocks. The pylon also houses the **Harbour Bridge Exhibition** (open daily).

From below, the best views of the bridge can be enjoyed from **Hickson Road** and **Deans Point** (south side) and **Milsons Point** (north side).

Harbour Islands Sydney harbour is scattered with a number of interesting islands, most of which hold some historical significance. **Fort Denison**, just east of the Opera House, is the smallest, the most obvious and by far the most notorious. Its proper name is Pinchgut Island, so called because it was originally used as an open-air jail and a place where former 'out'-mates were abandoned for a week and supplied with nothing except bread and water – for little more than stealing another inmate's biscuits. Furthermore, in 1796, the then governor of NSW left a sobering warning to the new penal colony by displaying the body of executed murderer Francis Morgan from a gibbet on the island's highest point. The island was later converted to a fort in the 1850s in fear of a Russian invasion during the Crimean War. ■ *Two tours are available: Brunch Tour, Sat 0900-1200, Sun 0915-1200. $47, children $43; and Heritage Tour, Mon-Fri 1130-1515 and 1500-1715, Sat 1130-1515 and 1500-1650, Sun 1130-1500 and 1440-1650. $22, children $18. There is a café on site.*

A little further east, off Darling Harbour, is **Clark Island** – a popular picnic retreat. East again, off Rose Bay, is **Shark Island**, so called because of its shape. It served as a former animal quarantine centre and public reserve, before becoming part of the Sydney Harbour National Park in 1975.

West of the bridge is the largest of the harbour's islands, **Goat Island**, which is the site of a former convict-built gunpowder station and barracks. This provides the venue for a range of entertaining **tours** including the Gruesome Tales Tour (*Sat 1800-2130, $24.20, adults only*) which recounts the island's grisly past and a standard Heritage Tour (*Mon, Fri, Sat and Sun, 1300-1515, $19.80, children $15.40, family $61.60*).

For all island access, tour information and bookings visit the Sydney Harbour National Park Information Centre, at 110 George Street, T9247 5033, www.npws.nsw.gov.au Open daily until 1630.

City Centre

Many visitors find the city centre – the modern corporate face of Sydney– a chaotic place. It is cooler owing to the modern highrises and disturbed by the collective din of corporate Australia. Yet despite that it is still worth taking the plunge and joining the purposeful floods of humanity through its gargantuan corridors to discover its hidden gems. Most notable are the scattered historic buildings that, though dwarfed by the mighty, have survived and stood up to the city's ceaseless modern development. Many of these can be found on **Macquarie Street**. Other places worth visiting are the **Sydney Centrepoint Tower**, which will give you a bird's-eye view on a fine day, and **Hyde Park** or the **Botanical Gardens**, for a rapid escape from the chaos of the city. Between these gardens is **The Domain** with its own high-profile attraction and colour in the form of the Art Gallery of New South Wales.

Museum of Sydney

Museum of Sydney (MOS) was opened in 1995 and is a clever and imaginative mix of old and new. Built on the original site of Governor Phillip's (the captain of the 'First Fleet') former 1788 residence and incorporating some of the original archaeological remains, it contains uncluttered and well-presented displays that explore the history and stories that surround the creation and development of the city, from the first indigenous settlers, through the European invasion and up to the modern day. Art is an important aspect of this museum and as well as dynamic and temporary exhibitions incorporating a city theme there are some permanent pieces, the most prominent being the 'Edge of the Trees', a sculptural installation that sits at the museum entrance. It is an intriguing concept and a clever mix of media and cultures that is a perfect reflection on the nature and substance of the city itself. ■ *Daily 0930-1700, $7, children $3, family $17.37. Phillip St. T92515988, www.hht. nsw.gov.au Shop and café on site.*

Macquarie Street

Macquarie Street, which forms the eastern fringe of the CBD, is Sydney's most historic street and the site of many original, important and impressive architectural establishment buildings. From north to south the first, set near the Opera House, in its own expansive grounds is **Government House**, a Gothic revival building completed in 1837. The interior contains many period furnishings and features giving an insight into the lifestyle of the former NSW governors and their families. ■ *Fri-Sun 1000-1500 (grounds daily 1000-1600). Guided tours only within the house, departing every half hour from 1030. Macquarie St. T9931 5222. Free.*

Further up Macquarie Street facing the Botanical Gardens is the **State Library of New South Wales**. Its architecture speaks for itself, but housed within its walls are some very significant historical documents, including eight out of the 10 known First Fleeter diaries. Also worth a look is one of the three intricate Melocco Brothers mosaic floor decorations that exist in the city. In this instance the foyer floor of the Mitchell Library entrance depicts the journey of Dutch explorer Abel Tasman in 1642-43. The library also hosts visiting exhibitions that are almost always worth visiting and offers an on-going programme of films, workshops and seminars. ■ *Mon-Fri 0900-2100, Sat/Sun 1100-1700 (Mitchell Library closed Sun), $16 for visiting exhibitions. Macquarie St, T9273 1414, www.slnsw.gov.au Shop and café on site.*

Next door, the original north wing of the 1816 Sydney Hospital (formerly known as the Rum Hospital) is now the **NSW Parliament House**. Free tours are offered when Parliament is not in session, and when it is you can visit the public gallery. Quite often the house becomes the focus for lively demonstrations that often terminate here after a procession through the city streets. The south wing of the hospital gave way to the **Royal Mint** in 1854 during the gold rush. No wonder it was called the Rum Hospital – with a plague of politicians on one side, locked-up gold on the other and a large crowd outside, screaming like banshees, it would turn anyone to the booze.

Hyde Park Barracks which lie on the northern fringe of Hyde Park were commissioned in 1816 by Governor Macquarie to house male convicts before being utilized later as an orphanage and an asylum. The renovated buildings now house a modern museum that displays the history of the Barracks, the grisly aspects of exiled convict life and the work of architect Francis Greenway. ■ *Daily 0930-1700. $7, children $3, family $17. Queens Sq, Macquarie St. Sydney Explorer Bus route, stop #4 T92238922, www.hht.nsw.gov.au Guided tours are available, with the unusual added option of staying overnight in convict hammocks. Café on-site.*

Central Business District (CBD) Rising from a manic buzz of retail therapy, the **Sydney Centrepoint Tower**, which has, since 1981, been an instantly recognizable landmark across the city. After the Opera House and Harbour Bridge the Sydney Tower is considered the city's third great icon, forming an incredible trio that could not be more diverse in architecture, aesthetics or engineering. The tower's 2,239-tonne golden turret is also known as 'Ned's Helmet', due to its resemblance to the famous Aussie bushranger (highwayman) Ned Kelly's protective headgear. Although aged in comparison to the futuristic Sky Tower, in Auckland, New Zealand (which on completion in 1995 pipped the Sydney Tower at 305 m by just a few metres), the view from Australia's highest building is no less impressive. As well as enjoying the stunning vistas from the tower's Observation Deck, you can also experience a virtual 'Great Australian Expedition' tour, or dine in one of two revolving restaurants (sadly, they only revolve sedately every 70 minutes, as opposed to seconds). Given the elevated price of entry to the Observation Deck alone, it goes without saying that you should keep an eye on the weather forecast and pick a clear day. ■ *Observation Deck open Sun-Fri 0900-2230, Sat 0900-2330. $19.80, children $13.20, family $55, virtual tour extra. 100 Market St, T9231 9300 (restaurant bookings T8223 3800), www.centrepoint.com.au*

Between the Sydney Tower and the Queen Victoria Building it is worth taking a peek at the impressive interior of the 1929 **State Theatre**. Much of its charm is instantly on view in the entrance foyer, but it is perhaps the 20,000-piece glass chandelier and Wurlitzer organ housed in the auditorium that steal the show. ■ *Self-guided tours are available Mon-Fri 11.30-1500. $12, concession $8. 49 Market St. T9373 6861.*

Just around the corner from the State Theatre, on George Street, boldly taking up an entire city block is the grand **Queen Victoria Building**. Built in 1898 to celebrate Queen Victoria's Golden Jubilee and to replace the original Sydney Markets, the QVB (as it is known) is most often touted as a prime shopping venue, containing three floors of boutique outlets, and selling everything from designer knickers to Aboriginal art. But shopping aside, the spectacular interior is well worth a look, with ornate architecture, stained glass windows, mosaics and two charming and intricate Automata Turret Clocks. At the northern end is the four-tonne Great Australian Clock that is the world's largest hanging animated turret clock. It is a stunning creation that took four years to build at a cost of $1.5 million. Once activated with a $4 donation (which goes to charity) the clock comes alive with moving picture scenes and figurines that would put any flock of colourful and operatic canaries to shame. At the southern end is the equally impressive Royal Clock, with its English historical theme. Among the many animated depictions is the execution of King Charles I, whose head goes up and down like a yoyo twelve times a day, poor soul. There are also a number of good galleries, historical displays, restaurants and cafés throughout the complex. ■ *Mon-Wed, Fri/Sat*

0900-1800, Thu 0900-2100, Sun 1100-1700 (some restaurants and cafés remain open after hours). 455 George St, T9267 4761, www.qvb.com.au Information desks on the ground floor and Level 2 Dome Area. Guided tours are available twice daily (T9264 9209). Explorer bus stop #14.

Across the street from the QVB is the **Town Hall**, built in 1888. It also has an impressive interior, the highlight of which is the 8000-pipe organ that is reputed to be the largest in the world. Self-guided tour brochure available in the foyer. Next door to the Town Hall is the newly renovated **St Andrew's Cathedral,** built between 1819 and 1868. There are regular choir performances and entry is free. ■ *Daily 0900-1700, free. Explorer bus stop #14. Corner of George and Druitt Sts, T9265 9007.*

Hyde Park itself is very impressive and a fine mix of aesthetics, from the historic grandeur of the 1932 **Archibald Fountain** and 1934 **Anzac War Memorial**, to the gracious sanctity of its spacious lawns and mighty corridor of trees. It provides a great place to escape the mania of the city and to people-watch. Here perhaps more than anywhere else in the city you will see a diverse mix of humanity, from camera-touting tourists to amorous lovers, from suits on a lunchbreak to the homeless on a no-break.

Hyde Park & around

At the northeastern edge of Hyde Park, on College Road, is the Catholic **Saint Mary's Cathedral**, which is well worth a look inside. It has an impressive and wonderfully peaceful interior, with the highlight being the Melocco Brothers mosaic floor in the crypt that depicts The Creation and took 16 years to complete. ■ *The crypt is open daily from 1000-1600. Free tours on Sun afternoons after mass at 1200. Free. College St.*

A little further south along College Street is the **Australian Museum** established in 1827. Considering the huge demands placed upon museums these days to keep the computer-age public satisfied by being at the cutting edge of technology, presentation and entertainment, the Australian Museum gets a credit, if not the gold star. The modern Indigenous Natural and Human History displays are well up with the play, but sadly, the Birds and Insect sections are a little tired and in need of attention. The numerous stuffed specimens still sport those traditional taxidermy facial expressions of the persecuted being electrocuted. Also housed in the museum is the magnificent Chapman Mineral Collection that has just about every 'ite' and 'zite' that syllables could possibly bond with. The colours and sheer diversity is mind blowing. Try to have your visit to the Indigenous Australian section coincide with the live didjeridu playing and very informative lectures given by aboriginal staff. Children and in fact anyone with a healthy sense of inquisitiveness will love the very impressive Search and Discover section. ■ *0930-1700, $8, children $3, family $19 (special exhibitions extra). 6 College St, T9320 6000, www.austmus.gov.au*

■ *Getting there: for the park and all the attractions mentioned here take Explorer Bus route, stop #7.*

The 30 ha Royal Botanical Gardens offers a wonderful sanctuary of peace and greenery only a short stroll east of the city centre and has done so for almost 200 years. In fact it was the location of the colonies first vegetable patch. It boasts a fine array of mainly native plants and trees, an intriguing pyramid-shaped Tropical House, rose and succulent gardens, rare and threatened species and decorative ponds. Along with the collection of plants, it is, without doubt, its large colony of wild **flying foxes** (bats) that is most absorbing. During the day they roost in their hundreds in the heart of the gardens, hanging on

Botanical Gardens

Sydney

Sydney

▶ **Bush fires**

Of considerable concern in recent years, not only locally but nationally, is the increasing recurrence of that age-old natural phenomenon – bush fire. In 1994, 1996, 1997, 2001 and most recently in 2002, fires ravaged the surrounding national parks and the fringes of the city, destroying numerous properties, taking

several lives and dulling Sydney's vivid colours with a cloak of grey, acrid smoke. However they start, they do provide a powerful reminder of modern man's impact on the Australian environment and his fragile place within it. They look set to continue until land management practices are drastically altered.

almost every available tree branch, like black and gold Christmas decorations, moving only now and again to groom, stretch a wing or argue with their neighbour. So close to a bustling city centre, replete with so many human urban icons, it really is an incredible sight. *Gardens Café and Restaurant*, see page 107, is located right in the heart of the gardens and is one of the best places to observe the bats – just follow the faint, musty smell of 'bat'. Bats are fastidiously clean animals but are not designed to smell like us, or alas, the roses.

There is a **visitors centre** and shop located on nearby Art Gallery Road in the southeastern corner of the park, where you can pick up a self-guided walks tour leaflet or join a free organized **tour** at 1300 daily. A specialist **Aboriginal tour**, explores the significance of the site to the Cadigal (the original Aboriginal inhabitants) and the first European settlers' desperate attempts to cultivate the site, is available on request for $16.50. Call T9231 8050.

Macquarie Point & Mrs Macquarie's Chair From the Botanical Gardens it is a short stroll to Macquarie Point and Mrs Macquarie's Chair, which offers one of the best vistas of the Opera House and Harbour Bridge in the city. It is a great place to be, especially at dawn or for the sunset – well before a constant procession of coach tours turn up, interspersed with newlyweds searching for those ideal snaps. As the name suggests, Mrs Macquarie's Chair is the spot where the first governor's wife came to reflect upon the new settlement, or perhaps yearn for her native Scotland. One can only imagine what her reaction would be now. ■ *0700-sunset. Free. Tropical Centre daily 1000-1600, $5. Explorer Bus route, stop #3. Mrs Macquarie's Rd via Art Gallery Rd. T9231 8111, www.rbgsyd.gov.au*

The Domain & Art Gallery of New South Wales The Domain is a pleasant green expanse of trees and open park sitting between the Art Gallery and Macquarie Place. It was declared a public domain in 1810 and is often used as a free concert venue especially over Christmas and during the Sydney Festival held every January.

At the southeastern edge of the Botanical Gardens and fronting The Domain is the Art Gallery of New South Wales – Australia's largest. Housed inside its grand façade are the permanent works of many of the country's most revered contemporary artists as well as a collection of more familiar international names like Monet and Picasso. In stark contrast the Yiribana Gallery is a major highlight, showcasing a fine collection of Aboriginal and Torres Strait Islander works that are well worth a muse. There are authentic half-hour dance and music performances in the gallery from Tuesday to Saturday at midday. The main gallery also features a dynamic programme of major visiting exhibitions. Be sure not to miss the quirky and monumental matchsticks installation by Brett Whitely that is located outside, behind the main building. Brett was one of the city's most celebrated artists and, until his recent death,

Snap happy

Sydney is without one of the most photogenic cities in the world, and anyone with a camera and an eye for capturing its gist will find opportunities at every turn, both during the day and at night. The following are just a few of the top spots, some with a recommendation as to the best time of day at which to get in position.

Circular Quay and the great icons of the Harbour Bridge and Opera House offer endless opportunities and perspectives. The best locations from which to capture the scale and angular complexities of the Harbour Bridge are from close up and below on Hickson's Road and around Dawes Point Park (southern end) and from the open parkland, waterfront and lookout point at Milsons Point (northern end). The Rocks also offer some great perspectives, especially from Lower Fort Street and Observatory Park. Observatory Park is an excellent place from which to shoot the brightly lit bridge at night.

The Opera House offers some superb opportunities, both from a distance and from close up. From a far, try Campbells Cove, Circular Quay (Park Hyatt Hotel), late in the day and from Mrs Macquaries Point at dawn. Other good spots to capture the bridge and Opera House together are from Macquaries Point, Cremorne Point, Bradley's Head next to the Zoo and McMahons Point on the North Shore. Hyde Park is excellent for city views, especially the Sydney Centrepoint Tower and the city centre, especially Phillip Street, Martin Place and Market St can also provide interesting human and highrise building perspectives.

To capture typical Sydney beach lifestyle Bondi Beach, Bronte and Manly Beach are all excellent at their busiest at weekends, or for a change, at dawn. The suburban streets of King in Newtown and Oxford in Paddington can also reveal typical city life. If you have an specific interest in architecture the Homebush Bay Olympic Park is great for the modern features, while Macquarie Street in the city is best for the more traditional Sydney is pretty flat so long distance shots are hard to come by, but North Head at dawn is well worth a visit.

Sydney

produced a broad range of works, in mixed media that are, like this piece, typically eccentric, unpretentious and often humorous. More of Whitely's work can be seen at the Brett Whitely Museum, Surry Hills, see page 88. The Greek-style edifice, originally built in 1885, is currently undergoing renovations to add a new Asian Gallery, conservation centre, coffee shop and restaurant.

■ *Daily 1000-1700. Free (small charge for some visiting exhibitions). Explorer Bus route stop #6. Art Gallery Rd, The Domain. T9225 1744, www.artgallery.nsw.gov.au*

Darling Harbour and Chinatown

Created with much aplomb to celebrate Sydney's Bicentennial in 1988, Darling Harbour has been revitalized to such an extent and so much success that even the waves seem to clap with appreciation. Here, day and night, ferries and jetcats bring hordes of visitors to marvel at its modern architecture and its high-profile aquatically themed attractions, or to revel in its casino and trendy waterside bars and restaurants. Framed against the backdrop of the CBD, it is intricately colourful, urban and angular.

In contrast, the Chinese Garden of Friendship towards the southwestern fringe provides a little serenity before giving way to the old and chaotic enclave of Chinatown, the epicentre of Sydney's Asian community – the city's most notable living monument to its cosmopolitan populace.

Sydney Aquarium

This modern, well-presented aquarium, with over 650 species, cannot fail to impress. On show, as well as tanks full of fish, are imaginative arrays of habitat arenas, where saltwater crocodiles, frogs, seals, penguins and of course the bizarre and enchanting platypuses all await your muse. Without doubt the highlight of the aquarium is the Great Barrier Reef Oceanarium. A huge, superbly crafted and stocked tank with vast walls of glass that give you an incredible insight into the world's largest living thing and the mind-bending array of other life that depends upon it. Of course, many visit the aquarium to come face-to-face with some of Australia's deadliest sea creatures. There is no doubt that such beauty and diversity has its dark side, as the notorious box-jellyfish, cone shell, or rockfish will reveal. ■ *0900-2000. $23, children $11, family $49. Aquarium Pier, Darling Harbour. T9262 2300, www.sydney aquarium.com.au Aquarium Pass with ferry from Circular Quay, $27.40, child $14.30. Getting there: Explorer bus stop #21.*

National Maritime Museum

If you have never been in a submarine before this is your chance

This museum, which was deliberately designed to look, from the outside, like the sails of a ship, offers a fine mix of old and new, in both diversity and scale. For many, its biggest attractions are the warship **HMAS Vampire** and submarine **HMAS Onslow**, that are the centrepiece of a fleet of old vessels that sit outside on the harbour. Both can be thoroughly explored with the help of volunteer guides. The interior of the museum contains a range of displays that explore Australia's close links with all things nautical, from the early navigators and the **First Fleet**, to the ocean liners (that brought many waves of immigrants), commerce, the navy, sport and leisure. Other attractions include a café, shop, sailing lessons and a range of short cruises on a variety of historical vessels. Try not to miss the beautifully restored 1874 square-rigger, **The James Craig** which is moored to the north of the museum at Wharf 7. After completion she will set sail again offering another historic cruise option. ■ *Daily 0930-1700. Tickets are priced according to the number of attractions and range from the basic gallery pass at $10 to the Super Pass at $20, children $6- $10, family $25-45. 2 Murray St, T9298 3777, www.anmm.gov.au Getting there: the Maritime Museum is easily reached by foot across the Pyrmont Bridge, or by MonoRail, LightRail or the Sydney Explorer bus, stop #19.*

Sky City Casino

Set back off the harbour and facing the city is the Sky City Casino. The general emphasis on brash modern architecture, nightlife and entertainment in this area is accentuated at the casino, where the melodic trickles of numerous water features fall like the tears of the luckless and the ruined. Even if you are not a gambler the complex is worth a visit, especially at night, when the water features that are incorporated in its curvaceous design spring to life in a water and light spectacular. The casino is open 24 hours and there are also two theatres, a nightclub, restaurants, cafés and bars, a hotel and a health club. ■ *Pirrama Rd. T9777 9000, www.starcity.com.au Getting there: best accessed by foot or by MonoRail, LightRail or the Sydney Explorer bus, stop #19.*

Sydney Fish Market

For anyone interested in sea creatures, the spectacle of the Sydney Fish Market is highly recommended. It is also a place where wildlife (albeit dead) and commercial trading combine in one fascinating arena. Every morning from 0530, over 2,700 crates of seafood, covering 100 species from fisherman's Co-ops and aquaculture farms in NSW, are sold to a lively bunch of 200 buyers using a computerized auction clock system. The best way to see the action and more importantly the incredible diversity of species is to join a tour group, which will give you access on to the auction floor. Normally the general public are confined to the viewing deck high above the floor, which, although giving an overview of the action, does not offer anywhere near the same aesthetic detail. Also within the market complex are cafés, some excellent seafood eateries and a superb array of open markets where seafood can be bought at competitive prices. The best time to arrive is about 0600. Things start to wind up about 1000. ■ *Bank St, Pyrmont, T9660 1611, www.sydneyfishmarket.com.au Tours operate Mon-Fri from 0700. Getting there: Sydney LightRail or bus routes #443 from Circular Quay and #501 from Town Hall (or walk from Darling Harbour).*

When it comes to collections the **Powerhouse Museum** is exactly that – a powerhouse of nearly 400,000 items collected over 120 years. Housed in the former Ultimo Power Station, there is an impressive range of memorabilia from aircraft to musical instruments, mainly with an emphasis on Australian innovation and achievement, and covering a wide range of general topics from science and technology, to transportation, social history, fashion and design. Of course only a fraction of the 400,000 pieces can be displayed at any one time, but there is undoubtedly something for everyone and it remains Australasia's largest museum and – according to itself – Sydney's most popular. Given its size and content you may need more than one trip, with half a day being barely enough to cover all the highly interactive displays. ■ *Wed-Sun 1000-1700, $10, children $5, family $20. 320 Harris St, T9552 3375, Pyrmont. Shop and café on site.*

Powerhouse Museum & Motor World

Only a short walk from the Powerhouse Museum is **Motor World**, where car buffs can drool over more than 150 rare and everyday vehicles, motorcycles and automotive memorabilia. ■ *Daily 1000-1700. $10, children $3, family $23. 500 Harris St, Ultimo, T9217 0111, www.phm.gov.au Getting there: MonoRail, LightRail or Sydney Explorer bus, stop#17.*

Facing Tumbalong Park in the southern section of Darling Harbour, and next door to the Chinese Garden, is **Australia's Northern Territory and Outback Centre**. It is little more than a glorified souvenir shop with a free 30-minute live show presenting outback imagery and featuring didjeridu playing in order to lure in the crowds. ■ *Daily 1000-1900. Performances Tue-Fri 1300, 1500, 1700, Sat/Sun 1300, 1400, 1500, 1700. T9283 7477, www.outbackcentre.com.au*

Other Darling Harbour attractions

Next door to the Darling Harbour VIC, on the Cockle Bay waterfront is the eight-storey **IMAX theatre**, which shows several one-hour films, with some in 3D. See Entertainment, page 116, for details.

Darling Harbour is spectacular at night when the **Waterscreens** show literally springs to life with a light and music spectacular, using multicoloured lasers that are projected on to two fine mist fountains in the middle of Cockle Bay. Shows alternate using classical, jazz and popular music and the animated images are excellent. From Wednesday to Sunday every half hour from 1930.

Further along George Street and occupying the southwestern corner of the CBD is the Haymarket district and Chinatown. The Chinese have been an integral part of Sydney culture since the Gold Rush of the mid-1800s, though today Chinatown is also the focus of many other Asian cultures, including Vietnamese, Thai, Korean and Japanese. The district offers a lively diversion, with its heart being the Dixon Street pedestrian precinct, between the two pagoda gates facing Goulburn Street and Hay Street. Here, and in the surrounding streets, you will find a wealth of Asian shops and restaurants, many of which stay open well into the wee hours. Some Westerners may however be

Dixon Street & around

Sydney

put off by the condemned sea creatures, kept in numerous aquariums that front most of the seafood restaurants.

Chinese Garden of Friendship

At the northwestern corner of Chinatown is the Chinese Garden of Friendship, which was gifted to NSW by her sister Chinese province, Guangdong, to celebrate the Australian Bicentenary in 1988. It contains all the usual beautiful craftsmanship, landscaping and aesthetics, including a teahouse that provides the ideal sanctuary from stresses of the city. ■ *Daily 0930-dusk. $4.50, children $2, families $10.*

Paddy's Market

In stark contrast to Chinatown is Paddy's Market on the corner of Hay and Thomas Streets, which is one of Sydney's largest, oldest and liveliest markets and also, it has to be said, one of the tackiest. ■ *Fri, Sat, Sun 0900-1630.*

City West

Separated by Sydney University and situated just to the west of Darling Harbour, the enclaves of Glebe and Newtown are renowned for their exotic and bizarre ranges of shops and their eclectic cosmopolitan cafés and restaurants. Nearby Leichhardt possesses a particular Mediterranean appeal and has been dubbed Sydney's 'Little Italy'. To the north the once seedy suburb of Balmain has seen a makeover in recent years with a desire to join the party. Further west are the contrasting attractions of the Homebush Olympic Park and the historic 'town within a city' – Parramatta.

Glebe & Newtown

To the southwest of Darling Harbour, beyond the small district of Ultimo, and separated by the campus of Sydney University (Australia's oldest), are Glebe and Newtown. **Glebe** prides itself in having an alternative New Age village atmosphere, where a cosmopolitan, mainly student crowd amble along its main drag Glebe Point Road to meet in the laid-back cafés, muse in old-style bookshops or bohemian fashion outlets, or seek the latest therapies in alternative health shops. The Saturday market provides an outlet for local craftspeople to sell their work as well as a mix of bric-a-brac, clothes and New Age essentials. It is held in the grounds of Glebe Public School on Glebe Point Road for a couple of hours in the morning, from 1100.

South beyond the university is King Street, the hub of **Newtown**'s almost bizarre and cosmopolitan range of shops, cafés and restaurants. Here you can purchase anything from a black leather cod-piece to an industrial-size brass buddah. A half-day muse, a Sunday brunch or an evening meal in Newtown's King Street is highly recommended. It is far less commercial or outwardly sleazy than Kings Cross. Don't miss *Gould's Secondhand Bookshop* at 32 King Street. Other interesting second-hand shops await your explorations at the southern end of King Street, beyond the railway station.

■ *Getting there: Glebe can be reached by bus from George St in the city, #431 or #434. Newtown can be reached by bus from Loftus St (Circular Quay) or George St in the city, #422, #423, #426-428. Newtown Railway Station is on the Inner West/Bankstown (to Liverpool) lines.*

Leichhardt

Although receiving less attention than the eccentricities of Glebe and Newtown, Leichhardt is a pleasant suburb, famous for its Italian connections and subsequently its eateries and cafés. There are numerous places to enjoy a fine expresso, gelato or the full lasagne with Norton Street being the main focus. See Eating, page 109. ■ *Getting there: bus from the QVB in the city, #440, #445.*

Straddling Johnstons Bay and connecting Darling Harbour and Pyrmont **Balmain**
with the peninsula suburb of Balmain is Sydney's second landmark bridge.
The **Anzac Bridge**, opened in 1995, is a modern, strangely attractive edifice
that, although unable to win a battle of aesthetics over the mighty Harbour
Bridge, still makes an admirable attempt. Just beyond its spoke, like suspensions, the former working-class suburb of Balmain is most often recognized
in name, rather than location, as one of Australia's best-known **rugby league**
teams. In recent years Balmain has, to use an analogy, undergone a quiet
metamorphosis from a nondescript moth to a vibrant butterfly. It's not that
the moth was ever dull, it is just that Balmain has come out of the shadows and

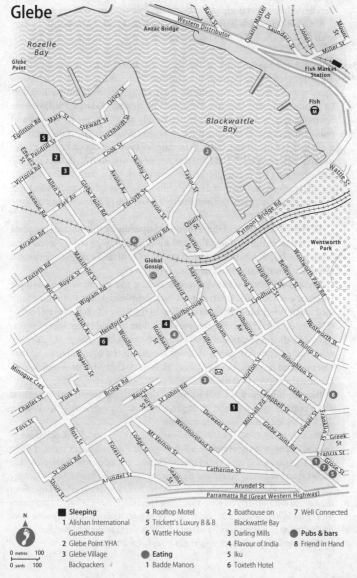

Glebe

Sydney

N

0 metres 100
0 yards 100

■ **Sleeping**
1 Alishan International
Guesthouse
2 Glebe Point YHA
3 Glebe Village
Backpackers

4 Rooftop Motel
5 Trickett's Luxury B & B
6 Wattle House

● **Eating**
1 Badde Manors

2 Boathouse on
Blackwattle Bay
3 Darling Mills
4 Flavour of India
5 Iku
6 Toxteth Hotel

7 Well Connected

● **Pubs & bars**
8 Friend in Hand

Related maps
Bondi, page 90
Kings Cross,
page 87
Manly, page 94
Sydney centre,
page 70

into the sun, in search of the tourist flowers. Now it seems Balmain loves nothing more than to flutter its new and colourful wings as a drag queen does her eyelashes. As a result Balmain and, in particular, its main drag of Darling Street now boast a small but eclectic range of gift shops, modern cafés, restaurants and pubs, which, either by road or preferably by ferry from Circular Quay, provide a pleasant half-day escape from the city centre. If you are there over lunch or in the evening try a drink or bite to eat in the Celtic and cosy *Sir William Wallace Hotel*, or the more traditional and historic 1857 *Dry Dock Hotel*. Its *Aviary Restaurant* is one of the suburb's best.

Balmain has hosted a popular Saturday market in the grounds of St Andrew's Church at the corner of Darling Street and Curtis Street for over two decades. The market begins at 0800 and finishes around 1600.

■ *Getting there: can be reached by bus from the QVB, #441-444, or by ferry from Circular Quay, Wharf 5.*

Homebush Bay Olympic Park

The best view of the entire complex is from the Observatory in the Novotel Hotel within the park

Although the vast swathes of Sydney's western suburbs remain all but an urban jungle for the vast majority of tourist, there are a few major and minor sights worth a mention. Topping the list is, of course, the multi-million dollar Homebush Bay Olympic Park with its mighty **Telstra Stadium**, the centrepiece of a vast array of architecturally stunning sports venues and public amenities. Telstra Stadium (formerly Stadium Australia) was the main focus of the games, being the venue for the opening and closing ceremonies, as well as track and field and soccer events. Although the Olympic flame has long been extinguished, it remains an important national venue for international and national rugby union, rugby league, Aussie rules football and soccer matches. ■ *Tours hourly 1100-1500 (45 mins). Adult $15.40, child $11.50.*

Next door is the state of the art **Sydney Superdome** that hosted basketball and gymnastics during the games and now offers a huge indoor arena for a range of public events from music concerts to Australia's largest agricultural show, the Royal Easter Show. ■ *Tours 1000-1600.*

Perhaps the most celebrated venue during the games was the **Sydney International Aquatic Centre** where the triumphant Aussie swimming team took on the world and left them standing in the wake of such stars as Thorpe ('Thorpedo') and Klim. The complex continues to hold international swimming and diving events and is now open to the public. The park has many other state-of-the-art sports facilities including the State Sports, Sydney International Tennis, Hockey, Baseball and Archery Centres and is surrounded by superb parkland.

Bicentennial Park is a 100-ha mix of dryland and conservation wetland and a popular spot for walking, jogging, birdwatching or simply feeding the ducks. Guided nature tours are available.

■ *Daily 0900-1700, T9714 7888, www.oca.nsw.gov.au For detailed information call or visit the Homebush Bay Olympic Park Visitors Centre, 1 Herb Elliot Av, near the Olympic Park Railway Station. Ask about the 'Superpass' that allows multiple facility access and a complimentary swim from $34.90. Getting there: 14 km west of the city centre, it is best reached by train (Western Line) from the city, or alternatively by RiverCat, from Circular Quay (Wharf 5) to Homebush Bay Wharf. From $20, child $10. Transportation around Olympic Park and to/from the station is on hand from $2.20 point to point, $11 per day. Olympic Explorer links with the ferry services from Circular Quay.*

Human 'Thorpedo'?

◀

Sydney's very own Ian Thorpe ('Thorpedo') is fast becoming the world's greatest ever swimmer. The 20-year-old has so far won two Olympic gold medals, two Olympic silver medals, 10 Commonwealth gold medals, eight World Championship titles and has broken 22 world records. He is still only 20 years old and has size 17 feet (which are clearly an asset), though few believe the rumour they are in fact webbed. His favourite animal? – the dolphin – of course.

Parramatta

Sydney

About 6 km further west from Homebush is Parramatta, often dubbed the city within the city. It is a culturally diverse centre and although its modern aesthetics are unremarkable, it does boast some of the nation's most historic sites. When the First Fleeters failed in their desperate attempts to grow crops in what is now Port Jackson in the city centre, they penetrated the upper reaches of the Parramatta River and established a farming settlement in 1788. Within three years the population had grown to over 100. The settlement was first known as Rose Hill before being renamed Parramatta – the name given to the area by the local Aboriginal tribe, the Burramatta.

Parramatta River, which quietly glides past the city, is without doubt its most attractive natural attraction and it features in a number of heritage walking trails. These and many other historical details are displayed at the Parramatta Heritage and Visitors Information Centre.

The oldest European site is **Elizabeth Farm**, a 1793 colonial homestead built for John and Elizabeth Macarthur, former pioneers in the Australian wool industry. The homestead contains a number of interesting displays and is surrounded by a recreated 1830s garden. ■ *Daily 1000-1700, $7, children $3, family $17. 70 Alice St, Rose Hill. T9635 9488.*

Also of interest is the 1799 **Old Government House** in Parramatta Park. It is Australia's oldest public building and houses a fine collection of colonial furniture. Ghost tours are also available every first and third Friday of the month from $22. ■ *Mon-Fri 1000-1600, Sat/Sun 1100-1600. $12. T9635 8149.*

Experiment Farm Cottage is the site of the colonial government's first land grant to former convict James Ruse in 1791. The cottage itself dates from 1834. ■ *Tue-Fri 1030-1600, Sat/Sun 1030-1600. $7. 9 Ruse St.*

■ *Getting there: train from the city centre (Western Line) or bus route #520 from Circular Quay. The best way to make a day of your visit is to take the 50 min Parramatta Rivercat journey from Wharf 5 Circular Quay. It winds its way up the Inner Harbour, offering great views back across the city, and ventures past the Homebush Bay Olympic Park. Parramatta Explorer Bus is a specialist service that explores the historical aspects of the city at weekends between 1000-1600. It stops at both the Rivercat Terminal and the main railway station every 30 mins, $10, child $5, T9630 3703.*

Featherdale & Australian Wildlife Park

There are two wildlife parks in the vicinity of Parramatta that offer your first, best hope to 'cuddle a koala'. It may sound crass but there is no experience beyond perhaps the smell of eucalypt or the sight of the Opera House that feels more Australian.

The best wildlife park in the city beyond Taronga Zoo is **Featherdale Wildlife Park** in Doonside. It has the largest private collection of native Australian wildlife in the country with over 2000 animals on show. Unlike its all dominant competitor, Taronga Zoo in the city, many of its inhabitants, such as the kookaburra and the enchanting tawney frogmouth (like a cross between a frog and an owl), roam free in the park, making themselves readily available for close inspection, photographs or a staring match. You can also hand-feed kangaroos, wallabies and emus and of course cuddle a koala. The on-site shop is also excellent. ■ *Daily 0900-1700. $15, children $7.50, family $38. 217 Kildare Rd. T9622 1644. Getting there: by car go via the M4 and turn off on to Reservoir Rd. After 4 km turn left on to Kildare Rd. Alternatively take the train from the city (Western Line) to Blacktown, then bus #725 from the station.*

Other face-to-face wildlife encounters can be had at the **Australian Wildlife Park** which is part of Wonderland Sydney, a vast amusement park with many highly staged aspects of Australiana from boomerang throwing to sheep mustering, as well as the usual vomit-enducing thrill rides and inevitably tacky souvenir shops. ■ *Daily 0900-1700. Wildlife Park only $16.50 (Wonderland $44), children $9.90 ($29.70), family $47.50. Wallgrove Rd, Eastern Creek. T9830 9100, www.wonderland.com.au Getting there: take the Wallgrove exit off the M4 westbound or Wonderlink, a transport and entry combo, T131500. Wonderland Express offers transits from major hotels, T9830 9187.*

Penrith	Sitting at the base of the Blue Mountains and beside the Nepean River, Penrith offers a number of exciting water-based activities that have been augmented with the creation of the **Penrith Whitewater Stadium** used as the canoe/ kayak slalom venue for the 2000 Olympics. Rafting sessions are now available to the public. Phone for details and directions, T4730 4333. **Sydney International Regatta Centre** has two purpose-built facilities used for the rowing and canoeing events of the 2000 Olympics. Much more user-friendly is the **Cables Waterski Park**, near the VIC, which offers cable-towed waterskiing, waterslides and pools.

City East

East of the city sit some of Sydney's most intriguing and well-known suburbs, famous for their nightlife, architecture, gay communities and of course, their sublime urban beaches. The most famous (and notorious) suburb is **Kings Cross**, which still lures visitors by the score, all intent on revelling in its seedy nightlife, or securing a bed in its rash of lively backpackers. Fringing 'The Cross' the suburbs of **Darlinghurst**, **Surry Hills** and, more recently, **Potts Point** and **Woolloomooloo** all offer more substance, hosting some of the city's best contemporary dining. West of Darlinghurst, beyond Oxford Street (the undeniable focus of Sydney's overt gay community) is the attractive suburb of **Paddington**, where Victorian architecture provides the backdrop to some major parks, sporting venues and city attractions including the Sydney Cricket Ground and Fox Studios. Further west are the beachside suburbs of **Bondi**, **Bronte** and **Coogee** with Bondi Beach being world famous for its enviably laid-back, quintessential Australian lifestyle.

Kings Cross & around *You need to have your wits about you – petty theft is common and intoxicated persons omnipresent*	Even before arriving in Sydney you have probably heard of Kings Cross, the famous, if not notorious hub, of Sydney nightlife and the long-established focus of sex, drugs and rock and roll. Situated near the navy's Woolloomooloo docks 'The Cross' as it is often called has been a favourite haunt of visiting sailors and Sydneysiders for years. Depending on your personality, age and life experience, you will either love or hate Kings Cross. The main drag through is **Darlinghurst Road** which is the focus of the action, while **Victoria Road** is home to a rash of backpacker hostels. At the intersection of both and the top of William Street, which

connects The Cross with the city, is the huge and iconic Coca Cola sign. You simply cannot miss it and it offers a great meeting point, though one wonders if a Capstan-Full Strength-Cigarettes advertisement with a flashing Government Health Warning would be more appropriate.

The best time to visit The Cross is, of course, in the wee hours when the bars, the clubs and ladies of the night are all in full swing. In daylight, and

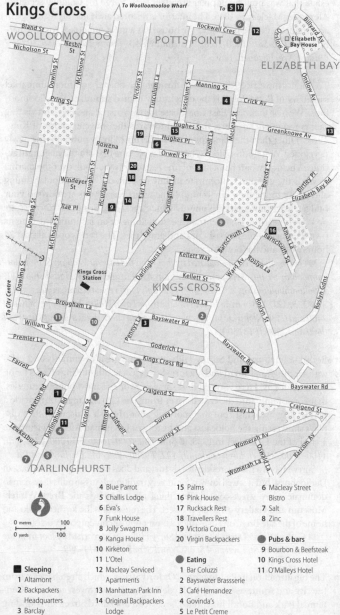

Kings Cross

Sydney

Sleeping	
1	Altamont
2	Backpackers Headquarters
3	Barclay

4	Blue Parrot
5	Challis Lodge
6	Eva's
7	Funk House
8	Jolly Swagman
9	Kanga House
10	Kirketon
11	L'Otel
12	Macleay Serviced Apartments
13	Manhattan Park Inn
14	Original Backpackers Lodge

15	Palms
16	Pink House
17	Rucksack Rest
18	Travellers Rest
19	Victoria Court
20	Virgin Backpackers

● **Eating**
1	Bar Coluzzi
2	Bayswater Brassserie
3	Café Hernandez
4	Govinda's
5	Le Petit Creme

6	Macleay Street Bistro
7	Salt
8	Zinc

● **Pubs & bars**
9	Bourbon & Beefsteak
10	Kings Cross Hotel
11	O'Malleys Hotel

Related maps
Bondi, page 90
Glebe, page 83
Manly, page 94
Sydney centre, page 70

particularly in the morning, it holds little appeal, with the words 'remains', and 'headaches' springing to mind. That said, Kings Cross is enormously popular with backpackers and Sydneysiders in general and it can provide a great (and often memorable) night out. It is also a great place to meet people, make contacts, find work and even buy a car.

Amidst its social mania there are a number of notable and more sedate sights in and around Kings Cross. **Elizabeth Bay House** is a revival-style estate that was built by popular architect John Verge for Colonial secretary Alexander Macleay in 1845. The interior is restored and faithfuly furnished in accordance with the times and the house has a great outlook across the harbour. ■ *Tue-Sun 1000-1630. $7, children $3, family $17. T9356 3022. 7 Onslow Ave, Elizabeth Bay.*

Woolloo-mooloo

Woolloomooloo is thought to be derived from the Aboriginal word 'wulla mulla' meaning male joey (young kangaroo)

To the northwest of Kings Cross, through the quieter and more upmarket sanctuary of Potts Point, is the delightfully named suburb of Woolloomooloo. 'Woo' is the main East Coast base for the Australian Navy and visiting sailors weigh anchor here, then head towards the souvenir shops of Kings Cross. Other than the warships and a scattering of lively pubs, it is the newly developed Woolloomooloo Wharf and a pie cart that are the major attractions. The new wharf has a rash of fine restaurants that look over the marina towards the city and concentrate mainly on seafood. It is a popular dining alternative to the busy city centre. If the wharf restaurants are beyond your budget, worry not, nearby is one of Sydney's best cheap eateries. *Harry's Café de Wheels* near the wharf entrance is something of an institution, selling its own $3 range of meat, mash, pea and gravy pies. The cart is open almost 24 hours a day and has been for years.

■ *Getting there: can be reached by foot from the city via William St or Woolloomooloo; by bus Sydney Explorer stop #9, Elizabeth Bay House stop #11, Woolloomooloo stop #13 (0840-1722 only) or regular bus services #311, 323-325, 327, 333 or train Illawarra Line from Town Hall or Martin Pl. Between 2400 and 0430 Nightride buses replace trains, but check times and stops between 0600 and 2200, T131500.*

Darlinghurst & Surrey Hills

Both Darlinghurst and Surrey Hills offer some great restaurants and cafés with Darlinghurst Road and Victoria Street just south of Kings Cross being the main focus. Here you will find some of Sydney's most popular eateries, that consistently lure the crowds over from The Cross at night or provide a perfect lazy breakfast spot the 'morning after'. **Jewish Museum** offers displays showcasing the holocaust and history of Judaism in Australia from the arrival of the First Fleet in 1788. ■ *Sun-Thu 1000-1600, Fri 1000-1400, Sun 1100-1700. $10, children $6, family $22. T9360 7999. 148 Darlinghurst Rd.*

Surry Hills is a mainly residential district and does not have quite the pzazz of Darlinghurst, but it is well known for its very traditional Aussie pubs that seem to dominate every street corner. One thing not to miss is the **Brett Whitely Museum and Gallery** on 2 Raper Street. The museum is the former studio and home of the late Brett, one of Sydney's most popular contemporary artists.

■ *Getting there: Darlinghurst and Surry Hills can be reached by foot from the city via William St, Liverpool St or Oxford St or by bus #311-399.*

Paddington

The big attraction in Paddington is **Oxford Street**, which stretches east from the city and southwest corner of Hyde Park to the northwest corner of Centennial Park and Bondi Junction. The city end of Oxford Street, surrounding Taylor Square, is one of the most happening areas of the city with a conglomerate of cheap eateries, cafés, restaurants, clubs and bars. It is also a major focus for the city's gay community. As the street heads west into Paddington proper it becomes lined with boutique clothes shops, art and book shops, cafés and a number of good pubs.

Many people combine a visit to Oxford Street with the colourful **Paddington Market**, held every Saturday from 1000. Behind Oxford Street heading north are the leafy suburbs, with their small, tightly packed Victorian terrace houses, interspersed with **art galleries** and old pubs, all of which that are the hallmark of Paddington. For a full listing of galleries pick up a free *Art Find* brochure from one of the galleries or the Sydney VIC. A stroll down Glenmore Road to the crossroads of Goodhope and Heeley Street will reveal some of the best of them.

South of Oxford Street is the old **Georgian Victoria Barracks** which has been a base for British and Australian Army battalions since 1848. It remains fully functional and visitors are welcome to see a flag-raising ceremony, a marching band performance and to join a guided tour on Thursdays at 1000. There is also a small museum open on Thursdays and Sundays. ■ *Bondi Explorer Bus stop #17.*

Just to the south of the Barracks in **Moore Park**, and in stark contrast, is the famous **Sydney Cricket Ground** (SCG) and next door the **Sydney Football Stadium** (SFS). The hallowed arena of the SCG is a place of near worship for many cricket enthusiasts which is considered by many as Australia's national sport. Though the Aussies have become so consistently good at so many in recent years it really is hard to tell. In winter, the SCG is taken over by the Sydney Swans Australian rules football team which has a local, though no less fanatical following. Sydney Football Stadium was for many years the focus of major national and international, rugby union, league and soccer matches but it now plays second fiddle to the mighty (and far less atmospheric) Telstra Stadium in Homebush. Tours of both stadiums are available to the public. Also within Moore Park, on Lang Road, are **Fox Studios**, which opened in 1999, costing over $300 million. They have been used in the filming of such recent blockbusters as *Mission Impossible II*, *Matrix II* and the *Star Wars* trilogy. Parts of the complex are open to the public, free of charge, and host a fairly unremarkable range of attractions including cinemas, shops, restaurants and markets. ■ *Bondi Explorer Bus stop #16.*

Just to the east of the Fox Studios Complex is **Centennial Park**, which at 220 ha is Sydney's largest. It provides a vast arena for walking, cycling, horse riding, roller blading and birdwatching. Parklands Sports Centre also provides tennis, roller-hockey and basketball. In late summer there is a nightly outdoor Moonlight Cinema programme, which often showcases old classics like *Monty Python* and *ET*. ■ *Getting there: the park can be accessed from the northwest corner (Oxford St) and Randwick to the south (Alison Rd). Bondi and Bay Explorer Bus stop #14.*

■ *Getting there: Paddington can be reached on foot from the southeast corner of Hyde Park in the city via Oxford St. Bus #378-382 or the Bondi and Bay Explorer from Circular Quay and Railway Sq.*

Watsons Bay

Watsons Bay sits on the leeward side of South Head that guards the mouth of Sydney Harbour. It provides an ideal city escape and is best reached by ferry from Circular Quay. As well as being the home to one of Sydney's oldest and most famous seafood restaurants – *Doyles* – it offers some quiet coves, attractive swimming beaches and peninsula walks. The best beaches are to be found at **Camp Cove**, about 10 minutes' walk north of the ferry terminal. A little further north is **Lady Bay Beach** which is very secluded and a popular naturist beach. The best walk in the area is the one- to two-hour jaunt to the 1858 Hornby Lighthouse and **South Head** itself, then south to the HMAS Watson Naval Chapel and the area known as **The Gap**. The clifftop aspect provides greats views out towards the ocean and north to North Head and Manly.

The area also boasts some interesting historical sites. Camp Cove was used by Governor Phillip, commander of the First Fleet, as an overnight stop before reaching Port Jackson in the Inner Harbour. **Vaucluse House**, on Wentworth Road, Vaucluse (south of Watson's Bay), was built in 1827 and is a fine example of an early colonial estate. It is furbished in period style and has a gift shop and tearooms. ■ *Tue-Sun 1000-1630. $7, children $3, family $17. T9388 7922.*

Many people spend a morning exploring Watsons Bay before enjoying a leisurely lunch at *Doyles*, which sits just above the beach and ferry terminal on Marine Parade. Next door to *Doyles* is the *Watsons Bay Hotel* which is a more casual affair offering equally good views of the city skyline and a superb outdoor BBQ area offering a range of fresh seafood. If you intend to dine at *Doyles*, bear in mind it is hugely popular, so pre-book. See page 112.

■ *Getting there: Watsons Bay is reached by ferry from Circular Quay Wharfs 2 and 4, or by bus #342 and 325 from Circular Quay.*

Bondi

There is a great stroll from Bondi to Bronte with good clifftop views. See Bronte below

Bondi Beach is by far the most famous of Sydney's many ocean beaches. It's hugely inviting stretch of sand is a prime venue for surfing, swimming and sunbathing – pastimes that are the very essence and epitome of Sydney lifestyle. Behind the beach, Bondi's bustling waterfront and village offers a tourist trap of cafés, restaurants, bars, surf and souvenir shops.

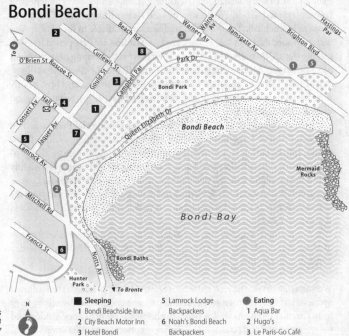

Bondi Beach

Related maps
Glebe, page 83
Kings Cross, page 87
Manly, page 94
Sydney centre,
page 70

N

0 metres 100
0 yards 100

■ Sleeping
1 Bondi Beachside Inn
2 City Beach Motor Inn
3 Hotel Bondi
4 Indy's Bondi Beach
   Backpackers

5 Lamrock Lodge
   Backpackers
6 Noah's Bondi Beach
   Backpackers
7 Ravesi's
8 Swiss Grand

● Eating
1 Aqua Bar
2 Hugo's
3 Le Paris-Go Café
4 Love in a Cup Café
5 Sean's Panorama

People-watching in Bondi is almost as entertaining as its beach activities. For years Bondi has been a popular suburb for alternative lifestylers and visiting backpackers keen to avoid the central city. It is also the place to see or be seen. Here, especially at the weekend, you will encounter everything from the British backpacker with milk-bottle-white legs sticking out of Union Jack boxer shorts, to troupes of laid-back local surf bums. However, having said that, if solitude and nature is your thing, then you can still find it on Bondi Beach. At dawn, when the sun creeps above the ocean, throwing only the occasional shadow of a local and his dog down the beach, it can be hard to imagine it becoming like a set from *Baywatch*.

If you intend swimming at Bondi bear in mind that like every Australian beach it is subject to dangerous rips, so always swim between the yellow and red flags clearly marked on the beach. Watchful lifeguards, also clad in yellow and red, are on hand for advice or, at worst, to pluck you from the surf if you get in to difficulty. Bondi Beach is the focus of wild celebrations on Christmas Day with one huge beach party, usually culminating in a mass dash naked into the sea.

■ *Getting there: reached by car from the city, via Oxford St, or bus on the Bondi and Bay Explorer or services #321, #322, #365, #366, #380. By rail first get to Bondi Junction (Illawara Line) then take the bus (numbers above).*

Bronte

To the south of Bondi Beach, and best reached by a coastal walkway, that connects Bondi to Coogee and offers one of the most popular walks in the city, is the small oceanside suburb of Bronte. This little enclave offers a smaller, quieter and equally attractive beach with a number of very popular cafés frequented especially at the weekend for brunch.

Clovelly & Coogee

Coogee is thought to be derived from the Aboriginal word meaning 'smelly seaweed'

A little further south still is Clovelly, which has another sheltered beach especially good for kids. Many people finish their walk at Coogee, which is in possession not only of a very silly name but a fine beach and a bustling waterfront, full of the usual cafés, restaurants and novelty shops. Although playing second fiddle to Bondi, it is also a popular haunt for backpackers or couples keen to stay near the beach. Contrary to the name, you will find the beach has no smelly seaweed. ■ *Getting there: bus #372-374 and #314-315.*

City North

North of the harbour bridge Sydney's 'other half' stretches all the way to the boundaries of the Ku-ring-gai National Park. The big attractions are the northern beaches, with **Manly**, near the Sydney harbour entrance, a self-contained beach resort providing an effortless day trip from the city centre. Fringing the harbour inland, some of the city's most sought-after real estate nestles in the pretty, well-heeled suburbs of **Mosman**, **Balmoral** and **Cremorne**. Amidst all this haughtiness the largest and best area of prime real estate is actually given over to the world famous **Taronga Zoo**, where monkeys and other animals live without a care in the world.

North Sydney

At night, the ferry trip across the harbour to the city from Cremorne Wharf is almost worth the trip in itself

On the northern side of the Harbour Bridge is a corporate 'sub-forest' of neon-clad highrises. There is little here for the tourist to justify a special visit, but there are some fine views of the city to be had in the area. **Blues Point Reserve**, on the shores of Lavender Bay, offers the best city views in McMahons Point. It can be reached via Blues Point Road which in itself boasts a number of fine cafés. If you are short for time the best vantage point is without doubt right below the bridge at **Milsons Point**. There is a lookout point which looks straight across to Circular Quay and the Opera House almost in the shadow of the bridge. Few folk realise they are standing right above the speeding traffic in the harbour tunnel below. Milsons Point is also home to the seldom used Luna Park, a former fun park complete with colourful ferris wheel that even in its haunting silence has become another icon of the inner harbour. Another attraction is the old Sydney Olympic Pool next door to Luna Park that offers spectacular city views.

Kirribilli is a serene little suburb that lies directly to the east of the bridge. Here you will find **Kirribilli House**, the PM's residence, a property that most Sydneysiders would argue possesses architecture and a garden with far more character and colour than Australia's most recent Prime Ministers, or indeed their phlegmatic Canberra colleagues. Along with **Admiralty House**, it sits overlooking the Opera House on Kirribilli Point. Both are closed to the public and are best seen from the water. Beyond Kirribilli are the congenial residential suburbs and secluded bays of **Neutral Bay** and **Cremorne**.

Mosman Mosman possesses a very pleasant village feel of which its well-to-do residents are rightly proud. Situated so close to the city centre yet almost like an island, it has developed into one of the most exclusive and expensive areas of real estate in the city. However, don't let this put you off. Mosman, much like its neighbour Balmoral, page 93, is a great escape by ferry from the city centre offering some fine eateries, designer clothes shops, walks and beaches, plus one of Sydney's 'must-see' attractions – Sydney's Taronga Zoo, see below. ■ *Getting there: best reached by ferry from Circular Quay (Wharf 4) to the Mosman Bay where a bus awaits to take you up the hill to the commercial centre. Alternatively take bus # 238, 250 or for Mosman and the zoo #247 from Wynyard Station in the CBD.*

Taronga Zoo This world famous, government-run establishment was first created in 1881 in the grounds of Moore Park, south of Centennial Park, Paddington, before being relocated to Bradley's Head, Mosman in 1916. It has an extensive collection of native Australian species, including the obligatory koala, platypus and marsupials, to add to a particularly impressive collection of colourful Australian birds. Of course, all the usual suspects are also in residence, including gorilla, tiger, elephant, bear, giraffe and the largest captive troupe of chimps in the world. Their antics alone will keep you spellbound for hours. One of the added attractions of Taronga is its position in relation to the city and its world-class views. There really can be no other zoo on the planet that is better placed aesthetically. You will almost certainly need a full day to explore the various exhibits on offer and there are plenty of events staged throughout the day to keep both adults and children entertained. The best of these is without doubt the Kodak Bird Show which is staged, twice daily, in an open-air arena overlooking the city. Even with no show it would be stunning, but once the various highly trained birds are put through their paces, it provides a truly memorable experience. Don't forget your camera and be prepared to duck! The keepers at Taronga are a dedicated and friendy crowd so don't be afraid to ask questions.

If you are especially interested in wildlife it pays to check out the dynamic programme of specialist public tours on offer. The new programme, 'Roar and Snore', is highly recommended. It involves a guided tour of the park after dark by a keeper, then a stay overnight in a three-man tent waking to a morning chorus of squawks and shrieks. As many of the animals are nocturnal you are able to see much more of them than you would by day. Additionally, from the zoo the view of the city at night is stunning.

■ *Daily 0900-1700. $23, children $12, family $57. Roar and snore costs from $120, child $88. A Zoo Pass combo ticket which includes ferry transfers and zoo entry costs $28.40, child $14.30. Bradley's Head Rd. T9969 2455, www.zoo.nsw.gov.au Getting there: best reached by ferry from Circular Quay (Wharf 2). Ferries go back and forth every half hour Mon-Fri from 0715-1845, Sat 0845-1845 and Sun 0845-1730. Taronga is built on a hill and the general recommendation is to take the bus from the zoo wharf up to the main entrance then work your way back down to the lower gate. Alternatively for a small additional charge on entry you can take a scenic gondola ride to the main gate.*

Balmoral

Balmoral Beach is one of the most popular and sheltered in the harbour. Other than the obvious attractions of this comfy, neighbouring, beachside suburb filled with fine eateries (see page 113) and great shopping, it offers quite a bizarre spectacle just after dawn. Here you will observe something that is quintessentially Sydney and Australian – the early morning, pre-work dip. From about 0630 it seems as if half the resident population turn out for their habitual morning constitutional or swim. It all looks incredibly delightful and healthy and offers the perfect place to finally decide to take up jogging or give up smoking.

Middle Head

On Middle Head, which juts out into the harbour beyond Mosman, you will find one of Sydneys best and most secluded naturist beaches – **Cobblers Beach**. Access is via a little-known track behind the softball pitch beyond the terminus of Military Road. In mid-summer a day spent here baring all and catching the rays can be hugely holistic and entertaining. The atmosphere is friendly and congenial and the crowd truly cosmopolitan. However, unless you are quite eccentrically gay and looking for a wild time, avoid the peninsula on the eastern edge of the beach. Venture up there in search of a memorable view and you may get a lot more than you bargained for. The beach is served several times a day by a refreshments boat that stocks soft drinks and ice cream.

Bradley's Head

The temporary site of the evil terrorist's house in 'Mission Impossible II'

Here you can enjoy the walk to the tip of Bradley's Head, below the zoo, with its wonderful views of the city. Park your car at the Ashton Park car park, about 1 km before the zoo wharf, and find the track to the west that skirts around near the water's edge. Alternatively just follow the path east from the zoo's lower entrance.

Manly

Manly is by far the most visited suburb on the North Shore, and for many visitors serves almost as a self-contained holiday resort, offering an oceanside sanctuary, away from the manic city centre. The heart of the community sits on the neck of the North Head peninsula which guards the entrance of Sydney Harbour. Manly Beach, which fringes the ocean or eastern edge of the suburb, is very much the main attraction. At its southern end, an attractive oceanside walkway connects Manly Beach with two smaller, quieter alternatives, Fairy Bower Beach and Shelly Beach.

As you might expect, Manly comes with all the touristical trappings, including an attractive tree-lined waterfront, fringed with cafés, restaurants, souvenir and surf shops that complement its wealth of accommodation options. Connecting Manly Beach with the ferry terminal and Manly Cove (on the western or harbour side) is the Corso, a fairly tacky pedestrian precinct lined with cheap eateries, bars and souvenir shops. Its only saving grace is the market which is held at its eastern end every weekend.

Sydney

Oceanworld is a long-established aquarium which although it could never compete with Sydney Aquarium in the Darling Harbour, it is still worth a muse, especially if you have childen. Its star attraction are of course its sharks, which play a leading role in its emphasis on 'dangerous' Australian creatures. Not all its charges are aquatic, with snakes, spiders and scorpions also on show. ■ *Daily 1000-1730. $16, children $8, family $25. West Esplanade. T9949 2644, www.oceanworldmanly.com   Regular tours are available and the sharks are fed on Mon, Wed and Fri at 1100.*

Manly Art Gallery and Museum showcases an interesting array of permanent historical items with the obvious emphasis on all things 'beach', while the gallery offers both permanent and temporary shows of contemporary art and photography. Given the price of entry it is worth a look. Manly Art Gallery and Museum also hosts the *Manly Arts Festival* held annually around September. ■ *Tue-Sun 1000-1700. $3.50, children $1.10. West Esplanade, T9949 1776.*

Manly offers a wealth of other activities including cycling, sea kayaking, roller-blading, diving and of course surfing. The VIC lists outlets and hire prices. Manly also hosts a major *Jazz Festival* in October and a *Food and Wine Festival* in June.

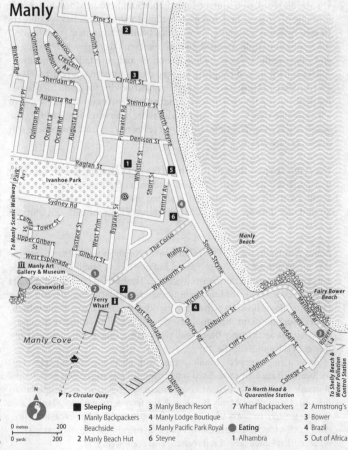

Manly

Related maps
Bondi, page 90
Glebe, page 83
Kings Cross, page 87
Sydney centre, page 70

0 metres 200
0 yards 200

To Circular Quay

Sleeping
1 Manly Backpackers Beachside
2 Manly Beach Hut
3 Manly Beach Resort
4 Manly Lodge Boutique
5 Manly Pacific Park Royal
6 Steyne
7 Wharf Backpackers

Eating
1 Alhambra

2 Armstrong's
3 Bower
4 Brazil
5 Out of Africa

The **10-km Manly Scenic Walkway** from Manly to Spit Bridge is an excellent scenic harbour walk. It starts from the end of West Esplanade and takes from three to four hours. You can catch a #144 or #143 bus back to Manly from the Spit, T131500. Before you attempt this walk try to get hold of the NSW Parks and Wildlife Service *Manly Scenic Walkway* leaflet from the Sydney or Manly VICs.

■ *Getting there: the best way is by ferry from Circular Quay (wharfs 2 and 3). The standard ferries cost $5, children $2.50 taking 30 mins while the JetCat takes 15 mins, $6.30. Both leave on a regular basis daily. Alternatively take bus #151 or #171 from Wynyard in the city, T131500.*

North Head & the Quarantine Station

The tip of North Head, to the south of Manly, is well worth a look if only to soak up the views across the harbour and out to sea. The cityscape is especially stunning at dawn. Just follow Scenic Drive to the very end. The Quarantine Station which takes up a large portion of the peninsula was used from 1832 to harbour ships known to be carrying diseases like smallpox, bubonic plague, cholera and Spanish influenza and to protect the new colony from the spread of such nasties. The station closed in 1984 and is now administered by the NSW Parks and Wildlife Service. ■ *T9247 5033. Tours daily except Thu, 1310. $11, children $7.70. More popular still is the daily 3-hr Ghost Tour at 1930 which includes supper, Wed $22.50, Fri-Sun $27.50. A 2-hr kids version is available at 1830, $13.20. Bookings recommended. Scenic Drive (bus #135 from Manly wharf).*

Northern Beaches

The coast north of Manly is inundated by numerous bays and fine beaches that stretch 10 km to Barrenjoey Head at Broken Bay and the entrance to the Hawkesbury River harbour. Perhaps the most popular of these are **Narrabeen**, **Avalon** and **Whale Beach** but there are many to choose from. Narabeen has the added attraction of a large lake that is used for sailing, canoeing and windsurfing, while Avalon and Whale Beach, further north, are smaller, quite picturesque and more sheltered.

A day trip to **Barrenjoey Head** is recommended. The most popular walk in the area is to the summit of Barrenjoey Head and the historic lighthouse, built in 1881. The views both north and south are spectacular. Access is from the Barrenjoey Boathouse car park and via the northern end of Station Beach (western side). The area is complemented by **Palm Beach**, a popular Sydneysider weekend getaway, with some fine restaurants, and of course, another great beach. Palm Beach has been made especially famous by the well-known Aussie soap opera *Home and Away* with much of the filming taking place on the beach. From here you can take day cruises up the **Hawkesbury River** (*$30, children $15*), or shorter excursions to **The Basin**, with its pretty beaches and camping areas in the Ku-ring-gai Chase National Park.

There are many water **activities** on offer in the area, focused mainly on **Pittwater**, a large bay on the sheltered western side of the peninsula. If you are particularly flush you can even fly into Pittwater from Sydney harbour by **floatplane**, T1300 656787, www.sydneybyseaplane.com

■ *Getting there: #L90 bus from Wynard in the city goes via all the main northern beach suburbs to Palm Beach. It leaves every 30 mins daily.*

Sydney

Hostelity

If you are backpacking around Australia beware of getting sucked into the hostel franchise chains and the numerous tour itineraries that set up onward travel and discounted accommodations at affiliated or associate hostels, especially heading north to Byron Bay, Fraser Island and beyond. This may suit some people, but it does limit your choice and your flexibility and, given the many accommodation options at these popular resorts, you may regret it later.

Essentials

Sleeping

See inside cover for price categories

Prices do rise in the high season and especially around Christmas and New Year in Sydney

Sydney has a wealth of accommodation of all types and to suit all budgets. Prices vary at all times so shop around. Most of the major luxury hotels are located around Circular Quay, Darling Harbour and the northern CBD (Central Business District), almost all priding themselves stunning views across the harbour or the city and with tariffs to match. Other more moderately priced hotels, motels and small boutique hotels are scattered around the southern city centre and inner suburbs. It is worth considering this option as many in the suburbs provide an attractive alternative to the busy city centre. Glebe is a particularly good option. Pub rooms are another alternative but standards vary and costs are generally quite high (from $80). Check out www.pubstay.com.au There are a few good B&Bs in the city. See www.bedandbreakfast.org.au for more options than we list in this guide.

There are a staggering number of backpacker hostels, with over 100 being scattered in and around the CBD, the inner suburbs and further afield in the popular beach resorts. The choice is vast and the standards again, vary. Most are centred around Kings Cross. If you intend to stay in hostels it is worth considering where you would like to be based before arriving and not necessarily jumping at the first deal you are offered. If you can afford the time, choose an area, pre-book in one hostel, then look around for what best suits you. Generally speaking, when it comes to hostels, there is the choice of the CBD for convenience, Kings Cross for the social life or the beachside resorts like Bondi and Manly for the iconic Sydney 'beach lifestyle'. The well-established, modern YHAs are recommended. Expect to pay $18-22 for a dorm bed, $45-55 for a double and $70 for an en suite. Most hostels will do weekly deals for about $120 or a few dollars off the cumulative daily rate. Almost all hostels have a laundry, kitchen and a common room with TV. Some have TVs in each room and almost all will arrange discounted tours on your behalf. Others can also assist in finding work. The vast majority of hostels offer internet access.

If you are intending to stay in Sydney for a few weeks then you should consider 'flatting' (flat share). The best place to look is in the Flats to Let section of the *Sydney Morning Herald* on Saturday or on hostel or café notice boards. Expect to pay no less than $120 per week, with the inner suburbs being even more expensive. As you might expect, there are a few motor camps or campsites in the city and a few hostels have camping facilities. The nearest and best motor parks are listed below. Numerous serviced apartments are also on offer in the CBD but you are advised to book early. *Medina*, T9360 1699, www.medinaapartments.com.au, are one example.

LL *Four Seasons*, 199 George St, T9238 000, www.fourseasons.com/sydney Well placed on the edge of Circular Quay and the CBD, this hotel has been refurbished and offers modern, well-appointed rooms, award-winning dining, specialist Australian herbal/spa therapies and has good facilities for families. **LL** *Park Hyatt*, 7 Hickson Rd, T9241 1234. Overlooking the Sydney Opera House and in the shadow of the Harbour Bridge, the *Park Hyatt* is a firm favourite, and given its waterside location this is hardly surprising. Offers all the expected sophistication and mod cons and has a fine restaurant on the ground floor, which is the ideal spot to watch the activity on the harbour and the sunset play on the Opera House. A full-scale replica of the *Bounty* is also moored right outside. **LL** *Quay Grand*, 61 Macquarie St, T9256 4000. On the eastern side of Circular Quay, this hotel is part of the ultra-modern Opera Quays complex. Provides stylish, fully self-contained apartments with spas and stunning views across Sydney Cove and the Harbour Bridge. Definitely a place to utilize room service.

Other popular 4- to 5- star options in The Rocks include the following. **LL-L** *Lord Nelson Pub and Hotel*, corner Kent St and Argyle St, The Rocks, T9251 4044, hotel@lordnelson.com.au Offers very pleasant, new and affordable, en suites above the pub. The added attraction here is the home-brewed beer, food and general ambience. The pub closes fairly early at night, so noise is generally not a factor. Recommended. **LL-L** *Old Sydney Holiday Inn*, 55 George St, T9252 0524, www.sydney.holiday-inn.com A reliable option ideally located in the heart of The Rocks with excellent views from most top rooms and especially from its memorable rooftop pool and spa. For something less commercial and very classy try, **LL** *Observatory Hotel*, 89 Kent St, T9256 2222. Nicely appointed rooms and surroundings, fine cuisine and a distinctly cosmic pool. Deservingly popular. **LL** *The Pier One Park Royal*, 11 Hickson Rd, Walsh Bay, T8298 9999, www.parkroyal.com.au This hotel is especially noted for its restaurant and direct views across the harbour and the bridge.

Slightly cheaper, yet still offering views of the harbour and also retaining a historic ambience, right in the heart of The Rocks, are **L-A** *Harbour Rocks*, 34-52 Harrington St, T9251 8944, www.harbourrocks.com.au, and **L** *Russell Hotel*, 143A George St, T9241 3543, www.therussell.com.au This hotel offers a good range of singles, en suites standard rooms and suites, and has an appealing rooftop garden. For a well-placed B&B try **LL** *Sydney Harbour B&B*, 140-142 Cumberland St, T9247 1130.

At the northern edge of the CBD, fringing Circular Quay, there are several more of the reliable chain hotels that still offer a peek across the harbour. **LL-L** *Hotel Inter-Continental*, 177 Macquarie St, T9230 0200. An impressive, well-facilitated hotel with 31 floors, 5 stars located in the former 1851 Treasury Building on Macquarie St and so within a stone's throw of the Botanical Gardens and the Opera House. As such it is often a first choice for visiting dignataries. Opulent surroundings with luxurious rooms and suites, an excellent café/bar and full health facilities all combine to make it one of Sydney's best. **LL-L** *Wynyard Vista Hotel*, 7 York St, T9290 1840. Another popular option in the CBD offering spacious self-contained rooms and suites with excellent city view, spa and Japanese rooftop garden. Well located with occasional attractive package deals. **LL** *Westin Hotel*, 1 Martin Place, T8223 1111. Right in the heart of the CBD, again at the top end and with all mod cons. It is near George Street for shopping, as well as being within walking distance of Circular Quay and Darling Harbour.

Exceptions in a sea of chain hotels are the following. **LL** *Carlton Crest Hotel*, 169 Thomas St, T/F9281 6888. Noted for its interesting architecture and popular pre-theatre restaurant, it also offers fine views back across the city centre, especially from its rooftop, outdoor pool. Nearby is the slightly cheaper, but perfectly adequate

Circular Quay & The Rocks
■ *On map, page 70*

There are some of the best, most luxurious hotels in the country in this area

City Centre
■ *On map, page 70*

Sydney

Sydney

LL-L *Country Comfort*, corner of George St and Quay St, T9212 2544. Other cheaper hotel options in the heart of Haymarket and Chinatown include **LL-A** *Aarons Hotel*, 37 Ultimo Rd, T9281 5555, that has basic en suite rooms, suites and deluxe rooms and a lively café with breakfast included. Right next door to the Capitol Theatre is the friendly boutique hotel **L** *Capitol Square*, corner of Campbell St and George St, T9211 8633, www.goldspear.com.au It has cosy en suite rooms, a good restaurant and can generally honour its claim as one of the best placed and most affordable 4-star hotels in the city centre. **L** *Stellar Suites*, Wentworth, 4 Wentworth Av, T1800 695 8284. Serviced apartments.

Pitched somewhere between a budget hotel and a hostel is **L-D** *Y on the Park (YWCA)*, 5-11 Wentworth Ave, T9264 2451, T1800 994 994, www.ywca-sydney.com.au It welcomes both male and female clients, has a good range of clean, modern, spacious and quiet rooms and boasts all the usual facilities. It is also well placed between the city centre and social hub of Oxford St.

Although most of the city centre backpacker hostels are to be found in Haymarket, one of the newest and the best is to be found right in the heart of the city. The all-new **B-D** *Wanderers Backpackers*, 477 Kent St, T9267 7718, www.wanderersonkent.com.au, is large, spacious and well facilitated, with fine doubles, twins and dorms. There are no kitchen facilities but with a cheap café and bar on the ground floor and a rash of eateries all around this is of little concern. It is very well run and also has to be the only backpackers with a stand-up solarium – great training for the outback or North Queensland! Recommended. Another newly refurbished budget establishment in the heart of the city is **A-E** *Millett's OZ*, Level 1, 161 Castlereagh St, T9283 6599, www.wakeup.com.au It has nicely appointed doubles/twins, some with en suite, and a range of dorms. It also has a newly established café, bar, travel desk and employment information.

Around Haymarket the hotels become cheaper and begin to be replaced by hostels

Some of these hostels are good and some are shocking, so shop around. **A-E** *Hotel Bakpak*, 2 hostels opposite each other at 412 Pitt St, T9211 4588, freecall T1800 013 186 (the newest) and 417 Pitt St, T9211 5115, freecall T1800 813522, www.bakpak group.com, are popular (mainly due to their position) and offer a good range of clean, modern rooms most with en suite, TV, fridge and telephone. The services which include tour bookings, and onward travel are also very good. Further south the edifice that is **C-D** *Sydney Central YHA*, corner of Pitt St and Rawson Pl, T9281 9111, sydcentral@yhansw.org.au, is even more popular and ideally placed next to Central Station and main interstate bus depot. The huge heritage building has over 500 beds split in to a vast range of dorms, doubles and twins, with some en suite. It also offers all mod cons including, pool, sauna, café, bar, internet, mini-mart, TV rooms, employment and travel desks. Its only downfall may be its size – for some it may be too impersonal.

A good 10-min walk further south of Central Station, down Chalmers St and across Prince Alfred Park, is **A-E** *Alfred Park Private Hotel*, 207 Cleveland St, T9319 4031, hotels@g-day.aust.com The former home of a whaling captain with 14 children it now serves as a cross between a budget hotel and a backpackers, offering the peace and quiet ill afforded the better known city establishments. It is well kept and very clean, offering tidy dorms, and spacious singles, doubles and twins. Pleasant courtyard, modern facilities and free guest parking.

Darling Harbour & Chinatown
■ *On map, page 70*

Darling Harbour itself is surrounded by large modern hotels, most of which offer fine views down into Cockle Bay and across to the CBD. On the western flank, there are several modern and well-facilitated options all just a stone's throw from all the action in Darling Harbour and a roll of the coin from the casino. **LL** *Grand Mercure Apartments*, 50

Murray St, T9563 6666. Overlooking Darling Harbour, these serviced apartments are very plush with all the facilites and comforts that you could want. **LL-L** *Novotel*, 100 Murray St, T9934 0000. Ubiquitous, reliable, large chain hotel. Something of a landmark, ideally located overlooking the harbour with easy access to all the major tourist attractions. Friendly service and well equipped for families. Good French restaurant. **LL-L** *Star City Hotel and Apartments*, above the Casino complex at 80 Pyrmont St, Pyrmont, T9777 9000. A fine choice amongst the many modern, luxury hotels fringing Darling Harbour with the added appeal of the casino, theatre, shopping, etc, all on site. Well-appointed standard rooms and suites with harbour views. Good mid-week or weekend specials.

Well placed, right next to the Chinese Gardens and Chinatown and at the southeastern corner of Darling Harbour, is the reasonably priced **L** *All Seasons Darling Harbour*, 17 Little Pier, T8217 4000. For tidy, more traditional pub/hotel stays within the city centre try **L-A** *Glasgow Arms Hotel*, 527 Harris St, Ultimo, T9211 2354. Good value, friendly, located just on the edge of Darling Harbour the hotel offers basic yet cosy rooms, entertaining bar (last order 2230) and an affordable pub restaurant with a courtyard downstairs.

Glebe This area is especially popular as an alternative backpackers' venue offering a village-type atmosphere with interesting cafés, shops and pubs all within easy walking distance. There are also one or two good mid-range options and an excellent B&B. **L-A** *Rooftop Motel*, 146-148 Glebe Point Rd, T9660 7777. A no-nonsense, quiet and clean motel, ideally located to all amenities. Single, doubles, twins and family rooms, pool and breakfast available. **LL-L** *Trickett's Luxury B&B*, 270 Glebe Point Rd, T9552 1141. A beautifully restored Victorian mansion, decorated with antiques and Persian rugs and offering spacious, nicely appointed en suites. Well worth the trip from the city centre. **L-D** *Alishan International Guesthouse*, 100 Glebe Point Rd, T9566 4048, www.alishan.com.au Pitched half way between a small hotel and a quality hostel, it is a spacious, renovated Victorian mansion with spotless doubles, twins and family en suites, all with TV and fridge. Shared accommodation is also available and overall the facilities are excellent. A great value budget option, especially for couples looking for a place away from the city centre.

City West
■ *On map, page 83*

B-D *Wattle House*, 44 Hereford St, T9552 4997, www.wattlehouse.com.au A lovingly restored Victorian house, smaller than the competition with a very cosy, homely feel and friendly owners. It has great double rooms and is especially popular for those looking for a quieter, more intimate place to stay. Book well in advance. Recommended. **B-E** *Glebe Village Backpackers*, 256 Glebe Point Rd, T9660 8133, freecall T1800 801 983, glebevillage@bakpak.com.au, is a large working backpackers' favourite. It offers a range of dorms and a few basic doubles and is friendly, laid-back and of course prides itself on finding work for guests. In-house café, pick-ups and regular day tours to beaches and other locations.

D-E *Glebe Point YHA*, 262 Glebe Point Rd, T9692 8418, glebe@yhansw.org.au A popular place with a nice atmosphere, offering fairly small twin and four-share dorms and modern facilities throughout. BBQs on the roof are a speciality. Regular shuttle into the city and transport departure points.

Newtown Newtown is yet to blossom with tourist accommodation, which is a shame given its atmosphere and aesthetics. One budget option offering a good range of en suites, standard rooms and dorms is **A-E** *Billabong Gardens*, 5-11 Egan St, T9550 3236, Free call T1800 806 419, www.billabonggardens.com.au There is also a fully equipped kitchen, lounge with TV, Internet and a heated pool.

Sydney

▶ **Great outdoors**

There are plenty of campsites and motor parks surrounding Sydney but within the inner city convenient parks are hard to find.

C-E Lane Cove River Caravan Park, Plassey Rd, North Ryde, T9888 9133, lccp@npws.nsw.gov.au 3 star, this is one of the best. Although nothing spectacular it offers powered and non-powered sites and a few basic yet comfortable cabins. It is 14 km north of the city centre, in a bush setting and within the bounds of the Lane Cove National Park. The site is owned and operated by the National Parks and Wildlife Service.

A-D Sydney Lakeside Narrabeen, Lake Park Rd, T9913 7845, www.sydneylakeside. com.au 4 star, it has a good range of quality villas, bungalows as well as powered and non-powered sites. It is located in Narrabeen, 26 km north of Sydney and near the beach.

A-D Grand Pines Tourist Park, 112 Alfred St, Ramsgate, T9529 7329, www.thegrand pines.com.au 3 star, it offers deluxe en suite and standard cabins and powered sites but no tents are allowed. In Ramsgate 17 km south of the city centre, near the airport and on public transport routes.

City East
■ On map, page 87

There are no shortage of hotels in Kings Cross and its surrounding suburbs, with everything from the deluxe 5-star to the basic and affordable

With over 35 backpacker hostels in and around Kings Cross the choice is vast and so there is fierce competition, therefore standards are generally good and well maintained and there are, inevitably, many similarities. All the hostels try to lure guests with some gimmick or other, be it a 'good time' reputation, their age, a café, free meal tickets, air conditioning in the rooms as opposed to a fan, 1 night in 7 free (mainly winter) and even beer, and so on. Most of the hostels are located along Victoria St, Orwell St or on the main drag (and in the heart of the action), Darlinghurst Rd.

Kings Cross LL-L *Millenium Hotel*, 12-14 Kings Cross Rd, T9356 1234, www.millsyd. com.au A recommended, large top-range hotel. Other similar options include **L** *Gazebo Hotel*, 2 Elizabeth Bat Rd, T9358 1999, **L** *Hampton Court*, 9 Bayswater Rd, T9357 2711, and the newly renovated, classy **L** *The Barclay*, 17 Bayswater Rd, T9358 6133, barclayhotel@bigpond.com Recommended.

B-E *Backpackers Headquarters*, 79 Bayswater Rd, T9331 6180, is immaculately kept and well run, the layout is a little odd but otherwise it is a fine choice in a quiet location, yet close to the action. **C-E** *Funk House*, 23 Darlinghurst Rd, T9358 6455, freecall T1800 247 600, goodtimes@funkhouse.com.au Set right on Darlinghurst Rd, this is definitely one for the younger party set. Zany artworks adorn the walls and doors. 3 to 4-bed dorms and double/twins all with fridge, TV and fan. Lots of freebies. Their almost legendary rooftop BBQ's are a great place to meet others. Good job-search assistance. **C-E** *Jolly Swagman*, 27 Orwell St, T9358 6400, freecall T1800 805 870, www.jollyswag man.com.au Another buzzing hostel set in the heart of the action. Professionally managed with all the usual facilities. TV, fridge and fan in most rooms. Excellent travel desk and job-search assistance. Social atmosphere. 24-hr check-in, fast internet and free beer on arrival.

C-E *The Original Backpackers Lodge*, 160-162 Victoria St, T9356 3232, www.original backpackers.com.au Possibly the best hostel in Kings Cross if not the city and certainly one of the best facilitated and managed. The historic house is large and homely, nicely appointed and comfortable, offering a great range of double, twin, single, triple and dorm rooms all with TV, fridge and fans (heated in winter). There is a great open courtyard in which to socialize or enjoy a BBQ. Cable TV. The staff are always on hand to help with onward travel, job seeking or things to see and do, while Blinkey the boxer dog

can ease any loneliness or the homesick dog owner. Recommended. Book ahead.
C-E *The Pink House*, 6-8 Barncleuth Sq, T/F9358 1689, freecall T1800 806 384,
thepinkh@qd.com.au, is a historic mansion offering a proper homely feel that is lacking
in many of the other Kings Cross hostels. Mainly because of that, it's deservedly popular, especially for those tired of the party scene. Lots of quiet corners and a shady courtyard in which to find peace of mind. Large dorms and some good doubles. Cable TV
and free internet.

C-E *The Palms* (Nomads), 23 Hughes St, T9357 1199, freecall T1800 737773, has a good
friendly atmosphere and a very social courtyard out front. All rooms have TV and fridge.
C-E *Travellers Rest*, 156 Victoria St, T9358 4606. Well-established hostel especially
popular with long-stayers. Dorm, single, twin and doubles some with TV, fridge, fan,
phone and kettle. Attractive weekly rates. **C-E** *The Virgin Backpackers*, 144 Victoria St,
T9357 4733, freecall T1800 667255, www.vbackpackers.com.au Quite modern and
chic, the 'V' offers good facilities, a nice balance between the lively and quiet. Tidy doubles and twins with TV and fridge and dorms. Well-travelled, helpful managers.
Internet café with good cheap meals.

Potts Point Heading north away from the mania of Kings Cross proper is **LL-L** *De
Vere Hotel*, 46 Macleay St, T9358 1211, www.devere.com.au Affordable long-estab-
lished boutique-style hotel with standard en suites and self-contained options.
In-house Chinese and Indian restaurants and off-street parking. Sufficiently close to
Kings Cross without being too affected with noise during the night. **L-A** *Macleay Serviced Apartments*, 28 Mcleay St, T9357 7755, macleay@nectar.com.au For an affordable apartments with great views across the harbour. **LL-A** *Victoria Court*, 122 Victoria
St, I9357 3200, T1800 630 505, www.VictoriaCourt.com.au, is a delightful and historic
boutique hotel in a quiet location. It comes complete with period antiques, well-
appointed en suites, fireplaces and 4-poster beds. The courtyard conservatory is excellent. Recommended. **A** *Manhattan Park Inn*, 8 Greenknowe Ave, T9358 1288,
www.parkplaza.com.au Art- Deco style highrise originally built in 1927. Standard,
affordable en suites some with good views across Elizabeth Bay. Restaurant. Often
offers good deals for families.

B *Challis Lodge*, 21-23 Challis Ave, T9358 5422, challislodge@wheretostay.com.au, is
another historic mansion, cheaper than *Victoria Court*, and therefore less salubrious,
yet with a good range of singles, twins and doubles, some with en suites. **C-E** *Eva's*, 6-8
Orwell St, T9358 2185, www.evasbackpackers. com.au This is another, clean,
well-managed hostel that offers a distinctly homely feel. Arty rooms with some en
suites. Rooftop space used for social BBQs and offering great views across the city. Similarly **C-D** *Kanga House*, 141 Victoria St, T9357 7879, offers a warm welcome and if you
are lucky you may be able to secure a room with a view of the Opera House, something
that would add a zero to your bed fee in the city. **C-E** *Rucksack Rest*, 9 McDonald St,
T/F9358 2348, is a long-established private hostel. It is basic and a little tired-looking
but good value, in a quiet location. Good double rooms. **C-D** *Blue Parrot*, 87 Mcleay St,
T9356 4888, freecall T1800 252299, is a new player on the hostel scene. As such, it has
all new fixtures and fittings which is an attraction in itself. Open fire. Quiet location.

Woolloomooloo **LL** *W Hotel*, 6 Cowper Wharf Rd, Woolloomooloo, T9331 9000. Stylish, warehouse-style, luxury hotel opened in 2000 and the showpiece of the Woolloomooloo Wharf. Has the added attraction of fine restaurants and a fine flotilla of luxury
launches right outside. Sumptuous, contemporary rooms often used by visiting pop
stars and well-heeled CEOs.

Sydney

■ *On map, page 87*   **Darlinghurst**   Separated only by a river of traffic Darlinghurst offers a fine alternative to Kings Cross and is still within a zebra crossing away. There are three very good, contemporary and immensely chic boutique hotels. **LL** *L'Otel*, 114 Darlinghurst Rd, T9360 6868, www.lotel.com.au, is very classy, yet, given its minimalist decor perhaps not everyone's cup of tea. No grandfather clocks, Persian rugs or tea cosies here. Even the carpet supports the hotel's name so there is no forgetting where you are. Quite unique, very hip and very much a place for the modern couple. Excellent personable service and a fine restaurant attached. **LL** *Hotel Altamont*, 207 Darlinghurst Rd, T9360 6000, www.altamont.com.au, is no less classy, yet supports a more traditional decor with beautiful spacious deluxe rooms with wooden floors and fittings. Recommended. **LL** *Kirketon*, T9332 2011, www.kirketon.com.au Modern, chic and minimalist decor with a bar and restaurant to match. In summary it is all very 'contemporary Sydney'. **A** *Royal Sovereign Hotel*, corner of Liverpool St and Darlinghurst Rd, T9331 3672, www.darlobar.com.au Stay here for something more traditional. The newly refurbished range of rooms above the popular *Darlo* bar are spotless and great value. Shared bathroom facilities.

Paddington and Surry Hills   These suburbs do not have a huge range of options. **LL-L** *Oxford Koala Hotel and Apartments*, corner of Oxford and Pelican sts, Surry Hills, T9269 0645, reservations@oxfordkoala.com.au A traditional, modern hotel and although fairly sterile it is highly convenient. **LL-L** *Hughenden Hotel*, 14 Queen St, Paddington, T9363 4863, www.hughendenhotel.com.au At the opposite end of Oxford St, this hotel is small, historic and suburban with plenty of character and located a stone's throw from the spacious sanctuary of Centennial Park. **LL** *Medina on Crown*, 359 Crown St, Surry Hills, T9360 6666, www.medinaapartments.com.au These apartments are expensive but, like the sister establishments throughout the city, very tidy. For quiet, friendly and low-key backpacker options try **C-E** *Oxford on Oxford*, 146 Oxford St, Woollahra, T9328 4450, freecall T1800 233343, www.oxfordonoxford.com.au, or the **C-E** *Kangaroo Bakpak*, 665 South Dowling St, Surry Hills, T9319 5915.

■ *On map, page 90*   **Bondi Beach**   It is perhaps no surprise to find that the older, well-established beachfront hotels in Bondi look a little garish, perhaps more befitting something on a pudding plate than a high street; however, their interiors will not disappoint, and they are, as boasted, only yards from the world famous beach.

LL *Swiss Grand*, corner of Campell Pde and Beach Rd, T9365 5666, freecall T1800 655 252, www.swissgrand.com.au The largest and most spectacular of the beachfront options. Luxury suites all with mod cons. Excellent views, a fine restaurant, gaming bar and an interesting foyer. The rooftop pool is stunning and a great escape from the hoards on the beach. Occasionally offers good-value 'Getaway' deals that are great for couples. **LL-L** *Ravesi's*, corner of Campell Pde and Hall St, T9365 4422, www.ravesis.com.au This hotel is slightly less obvious and more intimate than *Swiss Grand*. It has pleasant, good-value 3-star standard rooms, standard suites and luxury split-level suites, most with balcony's overlooking all the action. The newly refurbished balcony restaurant is one of the best in the area. **L-A** *Hotel Bondi*, 178 Campell Pde, T9130 3271, www.hotelbondi.com.au, is a little more traditional, with a popular public bar downstairs, a good café and a nightclub/performance space, *Zinc*, where you can 'shake your pants' to live bands and DJs or take part in pool competitions most nights. **L-A** *Bondi Beachside Inn*, 152 Campbell Pde, T9130 5311, www.bondiinn.com.au, is another beachfront option, pitched somewhere between a hotel and motel, offering tidy rooms and suites with kitchenettes and ocean views to match the more expensive hotels. Good for families or couples If you are looking for a quiet motel within walking distance of the beach. **A** *City Beach Motor Inn*, 99 Curlewis St, T9365 3100, is a good choice, having very neat, newly refurbished or new units, some with spa. Breakfast on request. Secure parking.

There are almost a dozen backpackers in Bondi, with some good, some not so good and all offering the usual gimmicks to lure your custom. Again it pays to look around and see what is on offer before booking long term. **C-D** *Indy's Bondi Beach Backpackers*, 35A Hall St, T9365 4900, www.indys.com.au This is one of the most popular. It is modern, friendly and has all the usual facilities, including doubles and twins with TV, fridge and fans and a very comfy cable TV room where you can catch that vital footy game from back home. It has a lively social atmosphere and its sheer range of free hires, from surfboards to roller blades, are an added attraction. Recommended. **C-E** *Lamrock Lodge Backpackers*, 19 Lamrock Ave, T9130 5063, www.lamrocklodge. com.au Also a good choice. It offers new, modern facilities and all rooms, dorm, single, twin and double, have cable TV, fridge, kitchenette and microwave. Good value. Recommended. **B-E** *Noah's Bondi Beach Backpackers*, 2 Campbell Pde, T9365 7100, www.noahs.com.au Perched on the hill, overlooking the beach as you descend into Bondi, this is a large place and popular owing to its position and price. As such it is not the quietest. Former hotel rooms converted to dorms, twins and doubles (some with ocean view). Rooftop BBQ area offers great views.

Coogee   Coogee is steadily growing in popularity as a viable and often cheaper alternative base to Bondi Beach. **LL** *Crowne Plaza Hotel*, 242 Arden St, T9315 7600, www.crowneplaza.com Offers nicely appointed rooms with great views across the ocean. **LL-A** *Coogee Bay Boutique Hotel*, 9 Vicar St, T9665 0000, www.coogeebay hotel.com.au Slightly cheaper than *Crowne Plaza* and offering very pleasant, newly refurbished, boutique-style rooms in addition to good traditional pub-style options. Both types are well appointed, en suite, have ocean views and are good value. The hotel itself is also a main social focus in Coogee both day and night. Recommended.

There are several backpacker hostels in Coogee. **C-E** *Surfside Backpackers*, 186 Arden St, T9315 7888, www.surfsidebackpackers.com.au This is the largest beachside option. It is very social with a solid reputation and all the usual facilities. Just as good, but smaller and with more character are the 2 houses (Wizard of Oz and Beachside) which, combined, form **B-E** *Coogee Beachside Backpackers*, 178/172 Coogee Bay Road, T9315 8511, www.sydneybeachside.com.au The rooms, especially the doubles, are excellent. Good facilities, friendly staff with good work contacts. 5 min walk to the beach. Ask about flat shares if you intend to stay long term. **B-D** *Beachouse Private Hotel*, 171 Arden St, T9665 1162. A quieter, personable option. Lone travellers, especially girls, are well looked after. Free breakfast.

Kirribilli   The quiet yet central suburb of Kirribilli across the water from The Opera House is an excellent place to base yourself, with a short, cheap and spectacular ferry trip to the CBD. There is little in the way of accommodation but that is part of its charm. **B-D** *Glenferrie Lodge*, 12A Carabella St, T9955 1685, www.glenferrielodge.com.au, is a vast, 68-room Victorian mansion that is under new management and looks set to explode on to the quality budget accommodation scene. The range of shared, single, twin or doubles are superb with some having their own balconies (from which, apparently, you might see John Howard – Australia's Prime Minister – jogging past from his Sydney residence nearby). Cheap dinners are on offer nightly. Very friendly. **C-E** *Kirribilli Court Private Hotel*, 45 Carabella St, T9955 4344, kirribillicourt.com.au Nearby, cheaper, functional.

City North

Sydney

■ *On map, page 94* **Manly** Being a well-established resort within the city Manly has no shortage of accommodation. The VIC on the forecourt beside the ferry wharf have detailed listings, maps and can help arrange bookings, T9977 1088, www.manly.nsw.gov.au

There are several hotels from the luxury to the pub traditional. **LL** *Manly Pacific Park Royal*, 55 North Steyne, T9977 7666, www.parkroyal.com.au Beachside, this is the most luxurious, offering all mod cons, ocean views, a rooftop pool and a good restaurant. **LL** *Radisson Kestrel*, 8-13 South Steyne, T9977 8866, www.radisson.com/manlyau At the southern end of the beach, this is also a pretty sumptuous choice. **L** *Manly Lodge Boutique Hotel*, 22 Victoria Pde, T9977 8655, www.manlylodge.com.au A more homely option and is both popular and good value. Recommended. **L-D** *Steyne Hotel*, corner of Ocean Beach and The Corso, T9977 4977, stay@steynehotel.com.au An older, cheaper and traditional pub-style hotel with standard, deluxe and backpacker rooms, including breakfast. **L-E** *Manly Beach Resort*, 6 Carlton St, T9977 4188, www.manlyview.com.au A 3-star motel option. All rooms are en suite and breakfast is included. Backpacker-style accommodation also available. Pool and spa. Of the hand-ful of B&Bs, **LL-L** *Periwinkle Guest House*, corner of East Esplanade and Ashburner St, T9977 4668, www.periwinkle.citysearch.com.au Centrally located, yet quiet and with character. There is a choice of shared bathrooms or en suites. Nearby **LL** *Corunna Manor*, 2 Osborne Rd, T04 0741 1510, corunna@tradepac.com.au Another good lux-ury option set in a century-old homestead with spa baths in each room. **L-D** *Manly Beach Hut*, 7 Pine St, T9977 8777, www.manlybeachhut.com.au, offers some quality, good-value twins and doubles for couples or the more mature independent traveller as well as shared accommodation, although also serving as a backpackers.

There are plenty of serviced apartment blocks in Manly. **LL** *Manly Paradise Motel and Apartments*, 54 North Steyne, T9977 5799, www.manlyparadise.com.au This is one of the best. 4-star. On the beachfront with ocean views, private balconies and rooftop pool. For slightly cheaper options try those on offer through the **LL-L** *Manly Waterside Holidays*, T9977 4459, www.manlyholidays.com.au

There are about a dozen or so pure backpacker establishments in Manly. **B-D** *Manly Backpackers Beachside*, 28 Raglan St, T9977 3411, manlybackpack@bigpond.com.au, Busy and well rated with some en suite doubles and small dorms. **C-E** *Wharf Back-packers*, 48 East Esplanade (right opposite the ferry terminal), T9977 2800. Arty and slightly cheaper, this is also popular.

Northern beaches **LL** *Jonah's*, 69 Bynya Rd, Palm Beach, T9974 5599, is a luxury boutique hotel and restauurant set high on the hill overlooking Ocean Beach. It offers 7 very cosy rooms with great views. The restaurant is French Mediterranean and recom-mended. Two backpackers stand out along the northern beaches. **B-E** *Collaroy YHA* (Sydney Beachhouse), 4 Collaroy St, Collaroy Beach, T9981 1177, www.sydney beachouse.com.au Superb. This is the *Hilton* of Sydney backpackers offering tidy dorms, twins, doubles and family rooms (some en suite) and great over all facilities, including a heated pool, spacious kitchen, dining areas, TV rooms, free equipment hire and organized day trips. Even free didjeridu lessons. It deserves its reputation as one of the best backpackers in the city. Recommended. Book ahead. Catch the L90 or L88 bus from Central, Wynyard or QVB. **C-E** *YHA Pittwater*, via Halls Wharf, Morning Bay, via Church Pt, T9999 2196, pittwater@rivernet.com.au, is a real getaway. Remote, located as it is in the Kuringai National Park and accessible only by ferry. It has dorms and a few doubles. Plenty of walking and water-based activities or simple peace and quiet. Phone for details, take all your supplies and book ahead. Palm Beach has plenty of excellent B&Bs especially suited to couples or families.

Eating

When it comes to quality and choice there is no doubt that Sydney is on a par with any *See inside cover for* major city in the world. It is a truly world-class eating destination, replete with over *price categories* 3,000 restaurants, brigades of world-class chefs and a rich array of fresh local produce (including the uniquely Australian kangaroo, snapper, barramundi, emu or crocodile). As well as excellent food there are also gallons of great national wines with which to wash it all down and in summary, you have to wonder where on earth to start.

As a general rule you will find the most lauded of the fine dining establishments that specialize in Modern Australian cuisine in and around Circular Quay, The Rocks, the CBD and Darling Harbour; however pockets of international speciality abound, from chow mein in Chinatown to pasta in Paddington. Sydney's thriving café culture is generally centred around the suburbs of Darlinghurst, Glebe, Newtown and the eastern beaches of Bondi and Bronte, which are the perfect locations for that vital coffee fix, or a congenial Sunday brunch. If there are any overall recommendations and if you are short for time, don't miss the seafood and views from *Doyle's on the Beach*, in Watson's Bay (cliché but for good reason); a cruise of the menus one evening along Newton's, King St (full of character); a night out overlooking Darling Harbour (very moderne); and a leisurely breakfast at Bondi or Bronte (which is so Sydney).

There are plenty of detailed 'Eating Out' guides to be found in the major bookshops, that will tickle your taste buds and point you in the right direction and, if you have access to the internet, the eating section of the site www.sydney.citysearch.com.au is also very helpful.

Given the stunning views and activity surrounding Circular Quay and the character and **Circular Quay** history surrounding the place, it is not surprising to find some of the best (and most **& The Rocks** expensive) restaurants and cafés in this part of the city. On the eastern side of the Quay ● *On map, page 70* you will find mid-range and expensive options with lots of atmosphere and memorable views under the concourse of the Opera House and within 'The Toaster' – a new *For the more* development whose appearance has earned it that rather derogatory label. The *expensive restaurants* cheapest eateries are to be found around the ferry terminals but unless you are desperate or want to put your cholesterol levels off the scale on the 'fatometer', these are best *book ahead* avoided. On the western side of the Quay and throughout The Rocks the choice is vast, from first-rate à la carte restaurants and historical pubs, to sidewalk cafés and stalls selling sweetcorn.

Expensive *Bel Mondo*, Level 3, Argyle Stores, 18 Argyle St, T9241 3700. Open for lunch Tue-Fri and daily for dinner. Set in a former elevated warehouse, providing a glimpse across the harbour, *Bel Mondo* offers Italian cuisine with plenty of imagination, a good wine list and (naturally) really good coffee. The service is also excellent without being too formal, adding to its consistently good reviews. *Guillaume at Bennelong Restaurant*, Opera House Concourse, T9250 7578. Open dinner Mon-Sat and lunch on Fri. Housed within one of the smaller 'shells', the Opera House complex, the newly renovated *Bennelong* offers unusual aesthetics and great food. Recent reports suggest this 'icon within the icon' under the meat cleaver of chef Guillaume Brahimi will more than live up to its former reputation and enviable setting. *Quay*, Upper Level, Overseas Passenger Terminal, Circular Quay West, T9251 5600. Open for lunch Mon-Fri and dinner daily. Closest to the water and offering unobstructed views of the bridge and the Opera House, the Euro-influenced *Quay* undoubtedly hurts the wallet, but guarantees a memorable experience and is considered by many locals as the head of the pack in the highly competitive arena of Circular Quay. Seafood is, not surprisingly, the speciality. Formal yet very relaxed, but don't go in sandals! *The Rockpool*, 107 George St, T9252 1888. Open for lunch Mon-Fri and dinner Mon-Sat. Located in the heart of The

Rocks, *The Rockpool* does lack the memorable views of other players around Circular Quay but remains a firm and reliable favourite. Offering highly imaginative cuisine with a distinct Euro/Asian edge, seafood dishes are particularly recommended and there is an excellent wine list.

Mid-range *Aqua Luna*, 2/18 Opera Quays, East Circular Quay, T9251 3177. Open Mon-Fri for lunch and daily for dinner. Housed within the nefarious 'Toaster' Aqua Luna is a slick-looking establishment, known for its fine and imaginative Italian and modern Australian cuisine. If you have never tried such daring dishes as risotto of organic rabbit than this is your chance. Given its location it is very popular prior to Opera House performances as much as for its mesmerizing views and its lively, distinctly trendy atmosphere. Book well ahead. *Café Sydney*, Level 5, 31 Alfred St, T9251 8683. Open daily for lunch, Mon-Sat for dinner. Set high above Circular Quay at the top of Customs House, *Café Sydney* is a firm favourite with city workers, offering superb views and al fresco dining. The food is traditional Modern Australian and nothing particularly remarkable, but, that said, it has an attractive laid-back atmosphere complemented with occasional live jazz. One criticism is the unavoidable traffic noise from the Cahill Expressway below. *Wharf Restaurant*, Pier 4, Hickson Rd, Walsh Bay, T9250 1761. Open for lunch and dinner Mon-Sat. Off the beaten track and a firm local favourite located at the end of the historic Walsh Bay pier beside the Sydney Theatre Company. Spacious, offering a great atmosphere and wonderful views of the busy harbour and the bridge. Ideal for a classy, pre-performance dinner. Modern Australian, nicely presented.

Cheap *Australian Hotel*, 100 Cumberland St, The Rocks, T9247 2229. Open daily for lunch and dinner. A fine venue for a true taste of Aussie food and beer, with a fine relaxed atmosphere. Generally good value, with al fresco dining and a menu, which includes pizza, croc, emu and roo steaks. Be sure to arrive early and secure a pavement table – they seem to have the almost magical ability of turning a lunch hour into an all-afternoon affair. *MCA Café*, 140 George St, T9241 4253. Open for lunch Mon-Fri and breakfast and lunch Sat/Sun. Located in the Museum of Contemporary Art the MCA is ideally located next to all the action on Circular Quay. It is a bit expensive but worth it, especially if you can secure a seat al fresco to watch the world go by. Seafood is particularly recommended.

City Centre
● *On map, page 70*

Again there is plenty of choice, especially when it comes to unremarkable convenience food and food courts. The sheer chaos and noise that surrounds you in the CBD is enough to put anyone off eating. However, if you are that way inclined, a retreat to the Botanical Gardens or Hyde Park is recommended, especially armed with a tasty takeaway.

Expensive *Forty One*, Level 41, Chifely Tower, Chifely Sq, T9221 2500. Open for lunch Mon-Fri and dinner Mon-Sat. Very popular, classy, spacious and congenial with the finest city views. With such a location one might expect the food to be insignificant, but it will not disappoint. Imaginative Modern Australian and an irresistible sweet selection. Book well in advance. *Restaurant VII*, 7 Bridge St, T9252 7777. One of the newest upmarket restaurants in Sydney, already earning a good reputation and offering imaginative Japanese cuisine with a French influence. Excellent service, classy decor and attention to detail only adds to its great cuisine, but you will pay for it! *Tetsuya's*, 729 Kent St, T9267 2900. Open for lunch Fri-Sat and dinner Tue-Sat. Without doubt one of Sydney's best restaurants. Chef Tetsuya Wakuda is world famous for his Japanese/Mediterranean creations. The restaurant has only recently been relocated to new and extremely swish premises. Book well in advance and, if you can afford it, try the 12-course degustation dinner.

Mid-range *Brooklyn Hotel*, corner of George and Grosvenor sts, T9247 6744. Open for lunch Mon-Fri. Renowned for its meat dishes (especially steak) with good, efficient service and plenty of inner-city pub atmosphere. Especially good mid-evening when 'city suits' loosen the ties and office gossip is replaced with laughter. *Pavilion on the Park*, 1 Art Gallery Rd, The Domain, T9232 1322. Open for lunch Sun-Fri 1200-1500. Sitting opposite the art gallery, the renovated 1960s, circular *Pavilion* provides the perfect escape from the city centre, offering al fresco dining with an eclectic Modern Australian menu. Perfect for a long lunch after a tour of the gallery and only a short stroll from the Botanical Gardens or Macquarie Point.

Cheap to seriously cheap *Botanical Gardens Café*, Mrs Macquarie's Rd, T9241 2419. Open daily 0830-1800. Offers sublime tranquillity amidst the Botanical Gardens and is set right in the heart of a fruit bat colony. In such a jungle-like setting it may not be everybody's cup of tea, but for environmentalists and botanists it's really hard to beat. The menu offers nothing remarkable but you will be so busy looking upwards it hardly matters. *Casa Asturiana*, 77 Liverpool St, T9264 1010. Open daily for lunch and dinner. Well known for its Mediterranean (Spanish) cuisine and its tapas in particular. Lots of genuine Spanish style decor, a good mix of clientele of all ages creates a lively atmosphere supported with regular live music. *Hyde Park Café*, corner of Elizabeth and Liverpool sts, T9264 8751. Open daily 0700-1630. Situated in a great spot for escaping the crowds, offering breakfast, light lunches, coffee and some excellent people-watching opportunities. Still within earshot of the inner-city traffic, it is a little noisy though. *MOS Café*, corner of Bridge and Phillip sts, T9241 3636. Open for lunch and dinner Mon-Fri from 0700 and Sat/Sun 0800-1800. A firm favourite, located below the Museum of Sydney, offering a congenial relaxed atmosphere and imaginative, good-value Modern Australian. It even offers porridge for breakfast – the finest sightseeing fuel available. *Paddy McGuire's*, corner of Kent and Erskine sts, T9212 2111. Open daily for lunch from 1100. New, spacious and characterful establishment offering good pub grub and fine European beers with the ever popular Irish edge. All very gimmicky, but dark and cosy and the ideal place to go before a trip to the cinema, theatre or a sporting event – provided you can drag yourself away. *Vivo*, 388 George St, T9221 1169. Open Mon-Fri 0700-2100. Set right in the heart of all the inner-city action offering a refreshingly wide choice of light meals at affordable prices and good coffee. Just beside the QVB, down Druitt St, is *Zenergy* (68), T9261 5679, which is great for healthy vegetarian wraps and sandwiches.

There are numerous underground **food courts** in the city centre offering a huge range of takeaway options for under $10, from pasta and burgers to wraps and chow mein. Good venues include the Pitt St Mall, Centrepoint and the QVB Building.

Darling Harbour and Chinatown both provide a great spot for lunch and dinner surrounded by plenty to see and do. Vegetarians should perhaps avoid the restaurants in Chinatown since they are not shy about displaying various poor sea creatures in squalid tanks prior to being boiled alive for your gastronomic pleasure.

Darling Harbour & Chinatown
● *On map, page 70*

Mid-range *Coast*, Roof Terrace, Cockle Bay Wharf, Darling Park, 201 Sussex St, T9267 6700. Open for lunch Mon-Fri and Sun and for dinner daily. A stalwart survivor in an arena where others have come and gone, offering a fine range of Modern Australian dishes, a formal, yet relaxed atmosphere and some of the best views across Darling Harbour. Great spot for lunch. Modern Australian with a Mediterranean edge.

Cheap *Bodhi Vegetarian Restaurant*, ground floor, Capitol Sq, George St, T9212 2828. Open daily 1000-1700. Considered one of the best places in town for

Sydney

Asian/vegan cuisine. Its Yum Cha is almost legendary. No-nonsense service and good atmosphere attracting a loyal and youthful following. *Chinta Ria-The Temple of Love*, Roof Terrace, Cockle Bay Wharf, 201 Sussex St, T9264 3211. Open daily for lunch and dinner. With a name like that who can resist? 'Welcome to the Pleasure Dome': while a rather plump and eminently satisfied Buddha looks upon a mixed crowd and a buzzing atmosphere, a mesmerizing open kitchen turns out quality Malaysian cuisine in generous quantity. Seafood is recommended and it is great for family groups. *Emperor's Garden BBQ*, 213 Thomas St, T9281 9899. Open daily 0900-0100. A reliable choice, usually bustling and particularly well known for its duck and suckling pig dishes. The decor is classically tacky, but with such a bombardment of the tastes and value for money, who cares? *Emperor's Garden Seafood*, 96 Hay St, Haymarket, T9211 2135. Open daily 0800-0100. One of the most reliable of the Chinatown restaurants. Always bustling, offering great service and again, great value for money. But with tanks of condemned sea creatures. *Kam Fook Seafood Restaurant*, Level 3, Market City, Hay St, Haymarket, T9211 8988. A huge establishment and the epitome of Chinatown, great for the claustrophobics and for seafood, but not for the faint hearted, the vegetarian or any fussy interior designers.

Seriously cheap *Blackbird Café*, Mid Level, Cockle Bay Wharf, T9283 7385. Open daily from 0800 til late. Deservingly popular, congenial, laid-back and good value, with a huge selection from pasta to steak served in generous quantity. Also good for that leisurely breakfast. *Dickson House Food Court*, corner of Little Hay and Dixon sts. Offers a wealth of the regulation cheap Asian takeaways, ubiquitous fast-food outlets and uninspiring counter meals, almost all for under $10.

City West
● *On map, page 83*

Glebe and Newtown Being so near the University, Glebe and Newtown take out the formalities and snobbery of the Sydney eating equation and replace it with value for money, huge choice and heaps of character. Glebe is home to many laid-back cafés and good pubs and in many ways the same applies to Newtown, except that Kings St has no end of attractive little restaurants offering everything from curry to charred emu. Both venues are also great for soaking up that lazy Sunday morning atmosphere.

Mid-range *Boathouse on Blackwattle Bay*, Ferry Rd, Glebe, T9518 9011. Open for lunch and dinner Tue-Sun. A quality upmarket (yet informal) seafood restaurant offering refreshingly different harbour views from those sought at Circular Quay and Darling Harbour. Here you can muse upon the lights of Anzac Bridge or the comings and goings of Sydney's fishing fleet while tucking into the freshest seafood. *Darling Mills*, 134 Glebe Point Rd, Glebe, T9660 5666. Open for lunch Fri and daily for dinner. Gracious, well-appointed sandstone restaurant with an imaginative Modern Australian menu, open fires, with plenty of comfort and charm. A fine and friendly escape from the city buzz and a little-known yet ideal venue for intimate romantics.

Cheap *Flavour of India*, 142A Glebe Point Rd, Glebe, T9692 0662. Open Sun-Thu 1800-2230, Fri-Sat 1730-2330. Quite simply Glebe's best Indian restaurant with a newly renovated, warm-coloured interior and imaginative decor providing lots of character. Great, efficient and friendly service and value for money. Tandoori dishes are particularly recommended. *Le Kilimanjaro*, 280 King St, Newton, T9557 4565. Open daily for lunch and dinner Mon-Sat. A fine opportunity to get away from ubiquitous Modern Australian dishes with exotic, good-value African cuisine extending well beyond the couscous. Very casual and relaxed. *Steki Taverna*, 2 O'Connell St, Newtown, T9516 2191. Open for dinner Wed-Sun. Popular citywide, this lively, small Greek restaurant is especially well known for its live entertainment, especially on Fri nights. Book ahead. *Thai Pothong*, 294 King St, Newtown, T9550 6277. Open for lunch

Sydney

Tue-Sun and daily for dinner. On a street with more Thai restaurants than chopsticks the *Thai Pothong* stands head and shoulders above the rest. Unremarkable spacious surroundings give it little intimacy but it is undeniably good for value, choice and service.

Cheap to seriously cheap *Iku*, 25A Glebe Point Rd, Glebe, T9692 8720. Open Mon-Fri 1130-2100, Sat/Sun 1130-2100. The first of what is now a chain of fine vegetarian and macrobiotic vegan cafés under the *Iku* banner, offering a delicious array of options that have put paid to the rabbit-food myth. *Tamana's*, 169 King St, Newton, T9519 2035. Open daily for lunch and dinner. Offers reliable no-nonsense Indian dishes that are great value for money. Eat in or takeaway. *Thanh Binh*, 111 King St, Newtown, T9557 1175. Open for lunch Thu-Sun, daily for dinner. Good-value Vietnamese offering delicious dishes from a vast array of noodles to more sophisticated venison in curry sauce. *Toxteth Hotel*, 345 Glebe Point Rd, Glebe T9660 2370. Open daily from 1100. A modern, spacious, traditional Australian pub serving mountainous plates of good pub grub at very reasonable prices. The omnipresent 'pokies' and pool tables spoil the atmosphere slightly but there are still areas where it is possible to escape the noise. *Badde Manors*, 37 Glebe Point Rd, Glebe, T9660 3797. Open daily 0730-late. Something of an institution in Glebe for many years, this favourite student hangout with its garage sale style decor. Can always be relied on for character and an appealing almost languid atmosphere, but don't expect American-style service. *Cinque*, 261 King St, Newtown, T9519 3077. Open daily 0730-late. One of the most popular of Newton's cafés located next to the Dendy Cinema and a small bookshop, which just adds to the attraction. Great all-day breakfasts and good coffee draw a relaxed, friendly and mixed crowd especially at the weekend. Local favourite. *Fishcafé*, 239 King St, Newtown, T9519 4295. Open daily 0730-2300. A charming little café decked out with strands of garlic and dried flowers and interesting bits and bobs. Definitely one of Newtown's best and most popular haunts. Like *Cinque* (above) especially popular for breakfast and for good coffee. Given its size it can however be a nightmare getting a seat. *Well Connected*, 35 Glebe Point Rd, Glebe, T9566 2655. Open 0700-2400 daily. One of the city's first internet cafés. Laid back with a whole floor upstairs full of well-used sofas dedicated to tired net surfers.

Leichhardt Renowned for Italian cuisine, some of the most popular venues for either coffee or something more substantial: *Bar Italia*, 169 Norton St, *Sorriso*, 70 Norton St, *Elio*, 159 Norton St, *Café Corso* at the Italian Forum and *Frattini*, 122 Marion St.

Kings Cross, Potts Point and Woolloomooloo Known as the 'Inner East' these three areas offer a truly eclectic range of choices, from the numerous fast-food outlets of Kings Cross, that cater for night owls and backpackers, to the chic and expensive options to be found along The Wharf at Woolloomooloo – a venue growing in reputation as one of the best for fine dining in the city. Paradoxically however, even there, the local trend for the cheap and cheerful is maintained by *Harry's Café de Wheels* with its famous 'pie and peas'.

City East
● *On map, page 87*

Mid-range *Manta Ray*, 7 The Wharf, Cowper Wharf Rd, Woolloomooloo, T9332 3822. Open for lunch Mon-Fri and dinner daily. Classy (and expensive) seafood restaurant. Some say one of the best in the city with a growing reputation. Located in a fine position overlooking a flotilla of extravagant launches backed by the city skyline and Sydney Centrepint Tower. *Otto*, 8 The Wharf, Cowper Wharf Rd, Woolloomooloo T9368 7488. Open Tue-Sun 1200-1500, 1800-2300. Very trendy, quality Italian with an imaginative menu and all the necessary trimmings including some very extrovert waiters.

Cheap *Bayswater Brasserie*, 32 Bayswater Rd, Kings Cross, T9357 2177. Open Mon-Thu 1700-2300, Fri 1200-2300, Sat 1700-2300. Always a reliable choice and immensely popular for its laid-back yet classy atmosphere, aesthetics and its imaginative Modern Australian cuisine. *Macleay Street Bistro*, 73 Macleay St, Potts Point, T9358 4891. Open daily from 7 till late. Well-established local favourite. Classy decor and good value, with a wide-ranging blackboard menu. *Shimbashi Soba on the Sea*, 6 The Wharf, Cowper Wharf Rd, Woolloomooloo, T9357 7763. Open daily 1100-2200. A fine Japanese restaurant that just adds to the sheer choice and quality to be found on the Wharf strip in 'Woolie'. Good mix of pure Japanese cuisine with more familiar meat and poultry dishes. Good value. *Zinc*, 77 Macleay St, T9358 6777. Not everybody's cup of tea, being very trendy, but there is no denying its ever increasing popularity, especially for breakfast. Good blackboard menu and friendly service.

Seriously cheap *Govinda's* 112 Darlinghurst Rd, Kings Cross, T9380 5155. Open daily from 1800. Restaurant and cinema combo offering great value 'all you can eat' vegetarian buffet along with the movie ticket. *Harry's Café de Wheels*, Cowper Wharf, Woolloomooloo. Open 0700-0200 Sun-Thu and 0700-0300 Fri/Sat. An oasis of informality, character and value for money, backed by the trendy, expensive options of The Wharf, Harry's is something of a Sydney institution, offering the famously yummy pies with pea toppings and gravy. One is surely never enough, as the photos of satisfied customers can testify. *Orange Thai*, corner of Hughes and Macleay sts, T9358 5666. Open daily 1100-2300. Cheap and cheerful (and clean) Thai eatery, right in the heart of Kings Cross, perfect for the pre-club munchies. *Café Hernandez*, 60 Kings Cross Rd, Kings Cross, T9331 2343. Great, eccentric 24-hr café serving Spanish fare, great coffee and with lots of character and an interesting clientele.

● *On maps, pages 70* **Darlinghurst, Paddington and Surry Hills** Darlinghurst and Paddington combine to dominate the city's café scene, with Oxford St, Victoria St and Darlinghurst Rd in particular enjoying almost legendary status. It isn't all baguettes and baristas however, there are some of the best restaurants in town to be found scattered amongst them. If you are looking for something off the beaten track, try the various options at the Five Ways crossroads at the end of Glenmore Rd in Paddington, where the leafy streets and almost iconic 'Paddo' architecture add to the overall appeal.

Expensive *Buon Ricordo*, 108 Boundary St, Paddington, T9360 6729. Open for lunch Fri-Sat and dinner Tue-Sat. Lively Italian that enjoys a citywide reputation offering pasta at its very best. Recommended. Bookings essential. *MG Garage*, 490 Crown St, Surry Hills, T9383 9383. Open for lunch Mon-Fri and dinner Mon-Sat. Highly unique convertible meets comfit option, with an ambience that only complements the class of the pricey cars that surround the tables. Delightful and imaginative (if expensive) Modern Australian cuisine, but it is certainly a memorable experience. Book ahead. *Salt*, 229 Darlinghurst Rd, Darlinghurst, T9332 2566. Open for lunch Mon-Fri and dinner daily. Very trendy, classy establishment with a clientele to match, offering some of the best Modern Australian in the city. But you will pay for it! Bookings essential.

Cheap *Bill's*, 433 Liverpool St, Darlinghurst, T9360 9631. Open for breakfast and lunch daily 0730-1500. One of the city's top breakfast cafés with legendary scrambled eggs. Small and at times overcrowded but that's all part of the experience. *Bill's 2*, the sequel, at 359 Crown St, Surry Hills, T9360 4762. Open for breakfast daily, lunch Mon-Sun 1200-1500, dinner Mon-Sat 1800-2200. Sister establishment to the above and an equal in popularity, choice and atmosphere. Can get too busy at times. *Billy Kwong*, 3/355 Crown St, Surry Hills, T9332 3300. Open daily for dinner from 1800. Pleasant decor, a relaxed atmosphere and great value make this a fine choice for Chinese, especially seafood and duck dishes. *Café Centaur*, 19 Oxford St, Paddington T9560 3200. Open daily 1000-2330. A pleasant quiet little café in a great bookshop that will delay your touristical wanderings for hours. Light fare, delectable sweets and good coffee. *Fishface*, 132 Darlinghurst Rd, Darlinghurst, T9332 4803. Open daily for dinner. Admirably secures the best base for fish and other seafood dishes in and around the inner east. Excellent fish and chips. *Fuel*, 476 Crown St, Surry Hills, T9383 9388. Open daily from 0800 for breakfast, lunch and dinner. Little sister to the unusual and popular *MG Garage Restaurant* (see above), offering more affordable but equally good bistro-style cuisine. Especially popular for weekend brunch. How does champagne sausage and oysters sound? *Go Bungai*, 8 Heeley St, Five Ways, Paddington, T9380 8838. Open for lunch Wed-Sun from 1200, dinner Tue-Sun 1800-200, Fri, Sat 1800-2300. Fine little Japanese restaurant with a loyal following, yet nicely set off the beaten track. A secluded courtyard adds to its appeal. *Oh, Calcutta*, 251 Victoria St, Darlinghurst, T9360 3650. Open for lunch Fri and dinner Mon-Sat. An award-winning Indian restaurant, by far the best in the Inner East and the closest you will get to the real thing in Sydney. Fresh tastes, cosy and great value. Book ahead. *Orphee*, 210 Oxford St, Paddington T9360 3238. Open Mon-Sat from 1000 and Sun 0800, closes around 1800. A well-established French-style restaurant considered one of the best in the city, offering a lovely homely atmosphere and imaginative menu. *Le Petit Creme*, 118 Darlinghurst Rd, Darlinghurst, T9361 4738. Open daily from 0800. Superb little French number with all the classics, from baguettes to cavernous bowls of café au lait. Great omelettes for breakfast or lunch. *Royal Hotel*, 237 Glenmore Rd, Paddington, T9331 5055. Open for lunch and dinner from 1200. One of the best choices at the increasingly popular Five Ways crossroads in Paddington. A grand old pub with gracious yet modern feel. Excellent Modern Australian cuisine is served upstairs in the main restaurant or on the prized verandah. Perfect for a lazy afternoon.

Seriously cheap *Bar Coluzzi*, 322 Victoria St, Darlinghurst, T9380 5420. Open daily 0500-1900. A well-established café that consistently gets the vote as one of Sydney's best. The character, the truly cosmopolitan clientele and the coffee are the biggest draw cards as opposed to the food. A place to go first thing to ease that nefarious 'Cross' hangover. *Indian Home Diner (Paddington)*, 86 Oxford St, T9331 4183. Open daily from 1100 till late. You really can't go wrong here with the usual great value (if mild), Indian combo dishes and, on this occasion, a small courtyard out back. Try a large butter chicken, and then try getting the stains off your t-shirt. *Prasit's Thai Takeaway*, 395 Crown St, T9332 1792. Open for lunch and dinner Tue-Sun. Great-value Thai restaurant and takeaway and the locally recommended cheap option in Surry Hills. Don't automatically expect to get a seat however. Plenty of vegetarian options. *Hot Gossip*, 438 Oxford St, Paddington T9332 4358. Open daily 0730-late. A well-established 'Paddo' café with retro '50s furnishings and an interesting clientele. Good food, healthy smoothies and a great cakes selection. *Mickey's Café*, 268 Oxford St, Paddington, T9361 5124. Open daily 0900-late. Local favourite with a huge range of value options from burgers to burritos. Especially good for lunch. *Una's*, 340 Victoria St, Darlinghurst, T9360 6885. Open daily 0730-late. Local favourite offering generous hangover-cure breakfasts and Euro-influenced lunches, including schnitzel and mouth-watering strudel.

Bondi, Bronte and Coogee A day spent at Sydney's world famous Bondi Beach is very much part of the city experience. It's a wonderfully laid-back suburb that hosts a truly cosmopolitan crowd, from pasty 'blue' Europeans in complete and utter awe of the sun, to bronzed surfies out to catch the day's best breaks. As well as Bondi, the suburbs of Bronte and Coogee are also top spots. A leisurely weekend breakfast at Bronte, followed by the clifftop walk to Bondi, is highly recommended.

● *On map, page 90*

Sydney

Sydney

Expensive *Doyle's on the Beach*, 11 Marine Parade, Watson's Bay, T9337 2007. Open daily for lunch and dinner. *Doyle's* is and has been for many years Sydney's most well-known restaurant. It has been in the same family for generations and has an unfaltering reputation for superb seafood, ideal location, atmosphere and harbour/city views that all combine to make it one of the best dining experiences in the city, if not Australia. If you can, book well ahead and ask for a balcony seat. Sun afternoons are especially popular. You can combine the trip with a walk around the heads, see page 90.

Mid-range *Hugo's*, 70 Campbell Parade, Bondi Beach, T9300 0900. Open daily for dinner, Sat/Sun for breakfast and lunch. A well-established favourite in Bondi, offering a combination of classy atmosphere, quality Modern Australian cuisine and fine views across the beach. *Sean's Panorama*, 270 Campbell Parade, Bondi Beach, T9365 4924. Open for lunch Sat/Sun and dinner Wed-Sat. Another Bondi classic, set at the southern end of the beach. Modern Australian with a European edge. Especially popular for breakfast. *Watson's Bay Hotel*, 1 Military Rd, Watson's Bay, T9337 4299. Open daily for lunch and dinner. Located right next door to the famous *Doyle's*, *Watson's* offers some stiff competition in the form of quality, value seafood al fresco, with lots of choice. You can even cook your own. Great for a whole afternoon especially at the weekend.

Cheap to seriously cheap *Aqua Bar*, 266 Campbell Parade, Bondi Beach, T9130 6070. Open daily 0630-1530. Healthy options, laid-back atmosphere. The view and excellent breakfasts make the *Aqua* a big favourite in Bondi. *Coogee Bay Hotel*, corner of Coogee Bay Rd and Arden St, T966 5000. Open daily from 1100. The most popular spot in Coogee day or night with multiple bars, huge open-air eating, value pub grub and life entertainment. *Le Paris-Go Café*, 38 Hall St, T9130 8343. Open daily 0700-1700. Very bohemian, laid-back and popular, with good healthy vegetarian options and generous all-day breakfasts. *Love in a Cup*, 106 Glenayr Ave, Bondi Beach, T9365 6418. Open Mon-Sat 0700-1700, Sun 0800-1700. A best-kept secret in Bondi, off the beaten track and very popular with the locals, especially for breakfast/brunch. Good value and good coffee. *Sejuiced*, 487 Bronte Rd, Bronte, T9389 9538. Open daily 0700-1830. Has competition on both sides, but is consistently the café of choice on the 'Bronte strip'. Favourite breakfast spot at weekends and a great start (or finish) to the cliff top walk between Bronte and Bondi.

City North   Given its location and its beaches Manly has for many years proved irresistible as an alternative accommodation base to the city. As such and as an equally popular venue for day trippers the 'resort' is blessed with numerous restaurants and cafés and a wide range of choice. As you might expect, much of that choice comes on the end of a cone, or between two sorry bits of white bread, but shop around and you will find more healthy and unusual alternatives.

● *On map, page 94*

There are no end of cheap takeaways along the concourse between the ferry wharf and Manly Beach

Manly Cheap *Alhambra*, 54 West Esplanade, Manly, T9976 2975. Open daily for lunch and dinner. A refreshing change from fast food and Modern Australian *Alhambra* offers Spanish/Mediterranean fare, with tapas, naturally, being a speciality. *Armstrong's*, Manly Wharf, T9976 3835. Open daily for lunch and dinner. Well positioned on the wharf overlooking the beach, good-value Modern Australian and locally recommended. *Awaba Café*, 100 yrds from Balmoral Beach, for great breakfasts of muesli and juices. *Bower Restaurant*, 7 Marine Pde, T9977 5451. Open daily for breakfast and lunch, Thu and some weekends for dinner. At the end of Marine Pde with memorable views back towards Manly Beach. Great spot for breakfast. *Out of Africa*, 43 East Esplanade, Manly, T9977 0055. Open for dinner Mon-Sun, lunch Thu-Sun. Good-value, authentic African cuisine with all the expected furnishings. It seems oddly out of place in Manly, but remains refreshingly different. *Mosman RSL*, 719 Military Rd, T9969

7255. Open daily for lunch or dinner. Offers 3 levels including a great value restaurant and al fresco bistro overlooking the main street and across the city. Choice of à la carte, pub food, or cook your own BBQ. Live entertainment at weekends. *Mosman Yacht Club*, opposite the Mosman Ferry Terminal, T9969 1244. A little-known option offering club prices in a classy setting overlooking the marina and plush properties. The lamb shanks are excellent. *Brazil*, 46 North Steyne, Manly, T9977 3825. Open daily from 0800 until late. Set right in the heart of the action overlooking Manly Beach. Standard Modern Australian and good coffee, but gets a bit busy in the evenings.

Balmoral Mid-range to expensive *Bathers Pavilion*, The Esplanade, Balmoral Beach, T9969 5050. Open daily from 0700. Ideally located in the historic pavilion overlooking Balmoral Beach. A superb spot for breakfast, for lunch, and dinner, with quality of food to match. Café or fine dining options. Great choice after a day spent on Balmoral beach. **Mid-range** *Watermark*, 2A The Esplanade, Balmoral Beach, T9968 3433. Open daily from 0800. Set in a beautiful location overlooking a beautiful beach, *Watermark* is well off the beaten track, but a wee gem, offering great Modern Australian with a seafood speciality. Also good for breakfast.

Bars

Sydney has some fine pubs in both the city centre and the suburbs to suit most tastes. Most are the traditional, street-corner Australian hotels, but there are lots of modern, trendy establishments, pseudo Irish pubs and truly historic alehouses on offer. Unlike Europe, generally speaking, you will find that most antipodeans do not buy 'rounds' which is standard practice, especially in the UK and Ireland. So beware, don't suddenly offer your group of new-found friends a tray full of pints expecting to get the kind offer returned. They will just think you're a exceptionally nice chap who's had too many with lots of spare cash to throw around. Many pubs, especially those along Oxford St and in Kings Cross, attract a cosmopolitan and happy mix of straight and gay clients which can at times make Woodstock look like a International Funeral Directors Conference. Although opening hours vary, most bars and pubs in Sydney with live entertainment stay open into the small hours especially at weekends, while the quieter establishments usually call last orders as early as 2230.

For the latest in club information and special events get hold of the free *3-D World* magazine, available in many backpackers, cafés or the clubs themselves, www.threedworld.com.au There is something called a Sydney Pub Trek, which is a very messy backpacker-based pub crawl on Thu nights. It includes plenty of price reductions and costs around $25, T9235 0999.

Circular Quay & The Rocks
● *On map, page 70*

The best single drinking venue in Sydney is undoubtedly The Rocks, where history, aesthetics, atmosphere and most importantly darn good beer combine to guarantee a great night out. *Orient*, 89 George St, T9251 1255. An old favourite set in the heart of Sydney's oldest precinct. Good range of beers and a good atmosphere but can get too busy at weekends and late at night. *Australian Hotel*, 100 Cumberland St, T9247 2229. Wedged on a street corner and one of The Rocks' most popular, it has a fine range of Aussie beers, good food and al fresco seating. A beer here is recommended. *Lord Nelson*, 19 Kent St, T9251 4044. The *Nelson* is Sydney's oldest pub and within its hallowed, nautically themed stone walls it brews its own ales and also offers some fine pub grub and accommodation. Get there early to secure a seat. The only drawbacks are the price of the beer is and its propensity to close just when the night is still young. A place for conversation. *Hero of Waterloo*, 18 Lower Fort St, T9252 455. Can be a bit of a squeeze but like the *Nelson* it is full of character and always entertaining. No-nonsense service and good beer. Pitched somewhere between a locals' haunt and a tourist venue. *Mercantile*, 25 George

St, T9247 3570. A pseudo Irish tavern, the 'Merc' is often busy, pretty wild and offers a fairly decent pint of Guinness, as well as great live traditional music until late. The place where everyone tends to end up on a Rocks pub crawl with some inebriated soul on stage with the band playing the tamborine and blowing bubbles.

City Centre
● *On map, page 70*

Scruffy Murphys, corner of Gouldburn and George sts, T9211 2002. A popular, well-established, yet rather tired Irish pub that always draws the crowds. It's a great place to meet people and the live bands and the beers are good, but there really is very little Irish about it. Open well into the wee hours. *Paddy McGuires*, corner of George and Hay sts, T9212 2111. A fine Irish-themed establishment that has just been refurbished and offers pleasant surrounds in which you can actually have a decent conversation or sample a fine range of beers. The pub food is good and there is also live entertainment on offer most nights. *Scubar*, corner of Rawson Pl and Rawson Lane, T9212 4244, www.scubar.com.au A popular backpacker-oriented pub that offers cheap beer, pizzas, pool, big TV screens and popular music until late.

Darling Harbour
● *On map, page 70*

Cockle Bay and Kings St Wharf in Darling Harbour have some very hip bars with outdoor seating areas that are great to watch the world go by during a sunny afternoon or balmy evening.

Cargo Bar, 52-60 The Promanade, T9262 1777. Laid-back and popular, especially good for that extended pub lunch. *Ettamogah Bar*, Harbourside Shopping Complex, Cockle Bay, T92813922. A distinctly gimmicky Aussie offering with lots of cartoon-style decor. Not everyone's pint of lager and a bit rowdy at times. *Cohibar*, Shop 359, Harbourside, Darling Harbour, T9281 4440. A fairly classy establishment popular with city suits and the trend-setters. Set on 2 levels with a terrace cocktail lounge, it is a great place to enjoy a cigar and/or the view across Cockle Bay.

City West
● *On map, page 83*

Glebe *Friend In Hand Pub*, 58 Cowper St, T9660 2326. Looks more like a venue for a international garage sale, but oozes character and also offers a bar café and Italian restaurant. Look out – the cockatoo does bite! *Toxteth Hotel*, 345 Glebe Point Rd, T9660 2370. A modern, traditional Australian affair. It is always pretty lively, has pool competitions and serves mountainous plates of good pub grub.

City East
● *On map, page 70*

Paddington *Albury Hotel*, 6 Oxford St, T9361 6555. Open until 0400. More an experience in debauchery than a bar and a firm favourite with the gay community, yet still welcoming a mixed and diverse crowd. While the drag queens frolick, the beer flows and the music pumps well into the wee hours. If you're single and confused, you won't be for long. *Durty Nelly's*, 9 Glenmore Rd, T9360 4467. The smallest, the best and most intimate Irish pub in the city, offering, nice aesthetics and a grand congenial jam session on Sun evenings (last orders 2330). *Grand Pacific Blue Room*, corner of Oxford and South Dowling sts, T9331 7108. Cool and trendy lounge bar popular with a mixed crowd. Frequent live entertainment and funky cocktails. *Lord Dudley*, 236 Jersey Rd, T9327 5399, www.lorddudley.com.au Last orders 2330. Located deep in the Paddington suburbs on the fringe with Woollahra the *Lord Dudley* is a grand historic rabbit warren looking much like a traditional olde English pub with aesthetics and beer to match. There is also some great, if expensive, pub grub on offer. Recommended. *Kitty O'Sheas*, 384 Oxford St, T9360 9668. A large mainstream Irish pub, very popular especially at weekends when live bands get the feet tapping and the beer spilling. If you need to escape the melee or have a white shirt on, try the bar upstairs. *Royal Hotel*, Glenmore Rd (crossroads with Goodhope and Heeley sts), T9331 2604. Offers a large atmospheric public bar downstairs and a fine restaurant on the second floor. Excellent both day and night with a good selection of beers.

Kings Cross *Bourbon and Beefsteak*, Darlinghurst Rd, T9358 1144. Large American-style pub and eatery conveniently open 24 hrs and as a result attracting all types in all stages of inebriation. *Hard Rock Café*, 121 Crown St, T9331 1116. Comes complete with the suspended automobiles, electric guitars and band memorabilia that have now been the trademark of the global outlets for 30 years. Roll in for their 'two-for-one drinks', Mon-Fri 1700-1900. *Kings Cross Hotel*, 248 William St, T9358 3377. A spacious, rowdy backpacker favourite with a weird interior and in the shadow of the huge Coca Cola sign. Remains open well into the wee small hours. *O' Malley's Hotel*, 228 William St, T9357 2211. Last orders around 0200. The local Irish offering with good live bands, but by no means the best Irish pub in the city. Live entertainment at weekends. *Woolloomooloo Bay Hotel*, 2 Bourke St, T9357 1177. Aussie-style establishment with karaoke nights and regular DJs. When you can no longer pronounce the name of the place it is definitely time to go home!

● *On map, page 87*

Bondi *Hotel Bondi*, 178 Campell Pde, T9130 3271. A lively bar popular with the surf set and backpackers, with live bands and a nightclub attached.

● *On map, page 90*

Coogee Coogee has lots of bars and places with playing live music. *Coogee Bay Hotel*, 9 Vicar St, Coogee, T9665 0000. This is the focus of Coogee nightlife. Beachside, it has a good atmosphere both night and day.

Newton *Marlborough Hotel*, 145 King St, T95191222, is popular with locals. Often hosts jazz and comedy. Open Mon-Sat until 0300, Sun until 2400.

This area is not particularly renowned for its nightlife. Especially for visitors, the pubs south of the bridge are more atmospheric options. **City North**

Clubs

Jacksons on George, 176 George St, T9247 2727. Mon-Fri 2000-0500, Sat 0600. From $15. Huge club spread over 4 floors with five bars, dining, dancing, live bands and pool, open 24 hrs. **Circular Quay**

Civic Hotel, 388 Pitt St (corner Gouldburn St), T8267 3181. Open nightly. Under $10. Although essentially a noted pub, cocktail bar and restaurant the *Civic* is a traditional weekend haunt for a cosmopolitan crowd who repeatedly come to enjoy old anthems and classics. *Gas*, 477 Pitt St, Haymarket, T9211 3088. Open 2200-0400. $15-25. *Gas* is one of the best venues for dance music in the city with excellent, clued-up DJs playing to the crowds a range of soul, funk, hip-hop, house and R&B, especially on Fri/Sat. *Globe*, corner of Park and Elizabeth sts, T9264 4844. Open daily 1100-2200, Fri/Sat 1100-0600. Fri $10, Sat $15. The place to go if you like funk and are funky. *Slip Inn*, 111 Sussex St, T9299 4777. Open daily. Free before 2200, $15 after. A trendy night spot with 3 rooms and a courtyard that fills with the young and beautiful. A mix of house and rave tunes. The night named 'Good Vibrations', on Sat, is especially popular. **City Centre**

Oxford Street is of course a major focus for nightlife and the main haunt for the gay and lesbian community. *Goodbar*, 11A Oxford St, T9360 6759. Open nightly, from $6. A well-established club and an old favourite amongst Sydneysiders, from the sexy young things to the sexually confused. Mixed music and good value in every respect. *Arq*, 16 Flinders St, T9380 8700. Mon-Thu free, Fri, Sat, Sun from $15. 2 large dance floors, plenty of space and a good balcony from which to watch a friendly crowd of both straight and gay.

Sydney

Darling Harbour   *Cave Nightclub*, Star City Complex, Pirrama Rd, T9566 4755. Very trendy establishment offering good dance and R&B combo. Coolest wares are obligatory. *Home*, 101 Cockle Bay Wharf, T9266 0600. Open 2200-0600. $15. One of the country's largest, state of the art nightclubs. Here, on 4 levels you will find lots of skintight pants and boob tubes getting on down to a vibe of mainly house and trance. Every Sat there is a *Kinkidisco*.

City East   **Kings Cross**   Although the main focus for travellers, particularly backpackers, 'The Cross' is not necessarily the best venue in town. A great night out (or certainly an experience) is on offer, but recent drug busts in some clubs have given the place a slight dodgy edge. There are quite a few popular clubs, most of which keep entry costs down to attract the backpacker crowd. *Icebox*, 2 Kellet St, T9331 0058. Open 2200-0500. $5-15. Offers more hardcore house and rave than most clubs in The Cross. *World*, 24 Bayswater Rd, T9357 7700. Fri-Sat $5 after 2200. Newly refurbished laid-back club set in grand surroundings and offering mainly UK house music. *Zen*, 22 Bayswater Rd, T9358 4676. Another new revamp, located next to *World*. As the name suggests, this time it is an Oriental theme that is the gimmick. Again it concentrates on progressive house music. Fri nights are especially good.

Bondi   *Bondi Pavilion*, Bondi Beach, T9130 3325, is a large venue that can throw a great party. Its position, overlooking one of the most famous beaches in the world, only adds to the laid-back atmosphere.

City North   **Manly**   *Aqualounge*, 42 North Seyne, T99772300, is considered the best venue in Manly and is located below sea level. Open Thu-Sat, every week.

Entertainment

From arias in the Opera House to giant chess in Hyde Park, there is always a wealth of things to entertain in Sydney, 24 hours a day, 365 days a year. For the latest information and reviews check the *Metro* section in Friday's *Sydney Morning Herald. The Beat* and *Sydney City Hub* are free weeklies that are readily available in restaurants, cafés, bars and bookshops in and around the city centre. Also try www.sydney.sidewalk.com.au The usual ticket agent is *Ticketek*, Sydney Entertainment Centre, Harbour St, Haymarket T9266 4800, www.ticketek.com.au They produce their own monthly events magazine *The Ticket. Ticketmaster*, T136100 also deal with theatre tickets. Discounted tickets can often be secured on the same day from *Halftix*, Darling Park, 201 Sussex St, T9286 3310. Bookings can also be made on www.halftix.com.au

Cinema   The biggest cinema attraction (literally) in Sydney is the huge 8-storey high **IMAX Theatre**, Darling Harbour, T9281 3300, www.imax.com.au Daily 1000-2200, $16.20, children $10.80, family $38. 3D movies from 1000. Explorer bus stop #22. In the city centre most of the major conventional cinema complexes are to be found along George St, between Town Hall and Chinatown. These include *Greater Union*, 525 George St, T9267 8666, *Hoyts* at 505, T9273 7431, and the *Village* at 545, T9264 6701. *Dendy*, 19 Martin Place, T9233 8166 and 2 East Circular Quay, T9247 3800. Elsewhere on Oxford St is the *Academy Twin* (3A), T9361 4453, *Chauvel*, corner of Oxford St and Oatley Rd, T9361 5398 and *Verona*, Level 2, 17 Oxford St, T9360 6296. *Chauvel*, in particular, showcases more retro, foreign or fringe films. *Hayden Orpheum Cinema*, 180 Military Rd, Cremorne, T9908 4344, on the North Shore, is a wonderful Art Deco cinema that offers an fine alternative to the modern city cinemas. A movie ticket will cost from $13, children $10. Half-price tickets are often offered on Tue nights. For listings see the *Sydney Morning Herald* or call *Movieline* T9218 2421. *Moonlight Cinema*, Centennial Park, T1900 933 899, movies@moonlight.com.au (23 Nov-23 Feb) and the *Open Air*

Cinema at the Royal Botanical Gardens near Mrs Macquarie's Chair (summer only) offer older classics under the stars. Take a picnic and plenty of cushions.

Rock The 3 main rock concert venues are the massive state of the art *Sydney SuperDome* in Homebush Bay Olympic Park, T8765 4321, www.superdome.com.au, the 12,000-seat *Sydney Entertainment Centre*, 35 Harbour St, City, T9320 4200 and the *Metro*, 624 George St, T9287 2000. Tickets for a major international band will cost anything 60-90. **Jazz** *Soup Plus*, 383 George St, T9299 7728, *The Basement*, 29 Reiby Pl, Circular Quay, T9251 2797, www.thebasement.com.au, and *Harbourside Brasserie*, Pier One, The Rocks, T9252 3000, are 3 major local jazz venues. For daily details of jazz gigs tune in to the *Jazz Gig Guide* at 0800 on *Jazz Jam*, 89.7FM Eastside Radio, Mon-Fri. The *Sydney Jazz Club* can be contacted on T9798 7294. **Australian** You will almost certainly hear the bizarre and extraordinary tones of the didjeridu somewhere during your explorations be it among the buskers on Circular Quay or in the many souvenir shops in the city. For actual live performances of the didjeridu and other traditional Aussie instruments try the Australia's Northern Territory and Outback Centre, 28 Darling Walk, Darling Harbour (Tue-Sun 1300, 1500 and 1700) or the *Reds Australian Restaurant*, 12 Argyle St, The Rocks, T9247 1011, daily with dinner 1745 and 1930. The *Didj Beat Didjeridoo Shop* in the Clocktower Square Mall, T9251 4289, just across the road is also a great venue to hear impromptu performances by the staff. **Blues** *Zambezi Blues Room*, 481 Kent St (behind Town Hall Square), T9266 0200, is a fine venue and free. **Folk** All the Irish pubs offer folk jam nights early in the week and live bands Wed-Sun. For some of the best try the *Mercantile Hotel*, 25 George St, The Rocks, the busiest *Scruffy Murphys*, corner Gouldburn St and George St, T9211 2002, *Kitty O'Sheas*, 384 Oxford St, T9360 9668 and *O'Malley's Hotel*, 228 William St Kings Cross, T9357 2211. Two excellent quieter options are *Paddy McGuires*, Corner of George and Hay, T9212 2111 and the best, *Durty Nelly's*, Glenmore Rd off Oxford St, which is a more intimate Irish pub offering low-key jam sessions on Sun afternoons.

National or international comedy acts are generally hosted by the smaller theatres, like *Lyric* and *The Belvior* (see below). *Club Luna* at the Basement, 29 Reiby St, T9251 2797, is excellent on Sun nights, from $13. A number of inner city hotels have comedy nights once a week including *Exchange Hotel*, corner of Beattie and Mullins sts, Balmain T98106099, Wed, from $5; and *Marlborough Hotel*, 145 King St, Newtown, T9519 1222, Tue, from $5. Both are recommended. Another long established venue is the *Unicorn Hotel*, 106 Oxford St, Paddington, T9360 3554, Mon, from $7. Other venues with more regular acts are *Comedy Store*, Bent St, Fox Studios, T9357 1419, Tue-Sat, from $10-27, *Laugh Garage*, 1st floor, *Macquarie Hotel*, corner of Gouldburn St and Wentworth Ave, T9560 1961, Thu-Sat, from $11-22, and *Comedy Cellar*, 1 Bay St, Ultimo, T9212 3237.

Gambling is big business in Australia with an estimated $10-12 billion being spent annually. Given the population of 19 million that figure is indeed staggering and makes Australians the most avid gamblers on earth. You will find that almost every traditional Australian hotel and pub in Sydney has the omnipresent rows of hyperactive pokies (slot machines). The main focus for trying your luck in Sydney is *Star City Casino*, 80 Pyrmont St, a coin's roll from Darling Harbour, T9777 9000, www.starcity.com.au It is a vast arena with 200 gaming tables, 1,500 pokies and lots of anxious faces. Open 24 hrs. Smart casual dress mandatory. Perhaps the best thing to do is just take a look inside, then throw a coin and make a wish in the splendid water features that front the Star City complex.

Music venues

Sydney

Comedy

Gambling

Performing arts   Naturally the focus for the performing arts in Sydney is the iconic **Sydney Opera House**. It offers 5 venues: **Concert Hall**, **Opera Theatre**, **Drama Theatre**, **Playhouse** and **Studio**, all presenting a diverse range of performances. The Concert Hall is the largest venue and home to the Sydney Symphony Orchestra. The Opera House is the home of Opera Australia, the Australian Ballet and the Sydney Dance Company. The Drama Theatre is a performing venue for the Sydney Theatre Company while the Playhouse is used for small-cast plays, more low-key performances, lectures and seminars. The Studio is used for contemporary music and performance. Prices and seats range from about $28-180. For details *Opera House box office*, T9250 7250, www.soh.nsw.gov.au

The beautiful and historic **State Theatre**, 49 Market St, City, T9373 6852 (info), T9266 4800 (bookings), www.statetheatre.com.au, offers a dynamic range of specialist and mainstream performances and cinema. Similarly the lovingly restored **Capitol**, 13 Campbell St, T9320 5000, offers a diverse range of performances, while **Theatre Royal**, MLC Centre, 108 King St, T136166, is noted for its musicals and plays. **Lyric Theatre** and **Showroom**, at the Star City complex, 80 Pyrmont St, T9777 9000, offer theatre, concerts, comedy, dance and musicals. Around $40-80 for a major performance. **Wharf Theatre**, Pier 4 Hickson Rd, The Rocks, is a main house for the Sydney Theatre Company and the Bangarra Aboriginal Dance Company, T9251 5333. *Wharf Restaurant* next door, see page 106, is superb for pre-performance dining. Behind the Scenes Tours are available, T9250 1777, $5. **Belvoir Theatre**, 25 Belvoir St, Surry Hills, T9699 3444, is another less well-known venue offering a good range of performances. **City Recital Hall**, Angel Pl, City, T9231 9000, www.cityrecitalhall.com.au, offers a program of regular classical music performances from around $35. The newly refurbished **Sydney Conservatorium of Music**, near the Botanical Gardens off Macquarie St, T9351 1222, info@greenway.usyd.edu.au, also hosts occasional live performances. **Sydney Entertainment Centre**, 35 Harbour St, City, T9320 4200, is one of the city's largest and most modern performance venues, hosting a wide range of acts, shows, fairs and sporting events. Bangarra are an exciting contemporary Aboriginal dance group and are based at Wharf 4, Walsh Bay, The Rocks, T9251 5333, www.bangarra.ozemail.com.au   They often perform in the Opera House.

Festivals

As Australia's largest, most vistited and undeniably attractive metropolis, Sydney offers a variety of festivals and events to rival any major city in the world. Without doubt the most famous and high-profile of the annual festivals is the gay and lesbian *Mardis Gras* which has, since its foundation in 1978, grown to become the most spectacular event of its kind on the planet. But it is not all pink boob tubes and leather codpieces. With its enviable climate, its stunning harbour and beaches, state of the art sports facilities and iconic cultural venues, it seems Sydney can offer something for everyone from surf fests to sonnets. In essence the remarkably diverse list of events fit into three main categories: sports, cultural and the arts, with the added spice of its own invariably colourful take on international or national traditional celebrations like the fireworks display at New Year, or the annual *Australia Day* celebrations, both of which are centred around the perfect backdrop of the harbour and Circular Quay.

The following is a summary of the major festivals held annually, or those major events specific to 2003/4. For comprehensive listings check out *This Month in Sydney* booklet free from the VIC, the weekend *Sydney Morning Herald* and www.sydneycity.nsw.gov.au

January   Every *New Year* kicks in with spectacular fireworks and celebrations that centre around The Rocks and the Harbour Bridge. Other good vantage points include

Milsons Point, The Opera House and Cremorne Point. *Sydney Festival* and *Fringe Festival* takes place through most of the month. It is a celebration of the arts including the best of Australian theatre, dance, music and visual arts and is held at many venues throughout the city. For many the highlight are the free open-air concerts in The Domain, including *Opera in the Park* and *Symphony under the Stars*, www.sydney festival.org.au The 26th sees the annual *Australia Day* celebrations with the focus being a flotilla of vessels flying the flag on the harbour, www.australiaday.com.au

February Without doubt the most famous Sydney event is the legendary *Gay and Lesbian Mardi Gras Festival and Parade* carrying on for the whole month. It is an opportunity for the gay community to celebrate, flaunt their being, entertain and shock. The highlight is a good shake of the pants and codpieces (or very lack of them) during the spectacular parade from Liverpool St to Anzac Parade (held at the end of the festival), T9557 4332, www.mardigras.com.au

March *Royal Agricultural Easter Show* is held every Easter and now uses the state of the art facilities at Olympic Park as a venue.

April The 25th sees the annual *Anzac Day – dawn service* at the Martin Place Cenotaph and a parade down George St.

May For the fit the annual *Sydney Morning Herald Half Marathon* is a great attraction, especially when it involves crossing the Harbour Bridge. Far less sedate are the *Australian Fashion Week* celebrations, showcasing some of the country's top designers. There is also another fashion week in Nov to preview the best of the winter collections.

June This month sees the crunching of popcorn at *Sydney Film Festival*, a 2-week fest for film buffs featuring over 150 features from 40 countries, T9660 3844, www.sydneyfilmfestival.org.au

August Increasingly popular and far less soporific than watching the big screen is the *Sun-Herald City to Surf*, a 14-km race from Bondi Beach to the City Centre, T1800 555514.

September September sees the *Festival of The Winds* at Bondi Beach which is a colourful festival of kites and kite flying, while the avid sports fans fight over tickets and take several days' drinking leave for the *Rugby League* and *Rugby Union Grand Finals*.

October The annual weekend *Manly Jazz Festival* is a gathering of Australia's best along with some fine foreign imports. Stages located in several public arenas including the beachfront and the Corso, as well as hotels, restaurants and bars, T99771088. The *2003 Rugby World Cup* kicks off in Sydney with games played at the Telstra Stadium and venues around the country.

November Activity is the highlight once again with the annual *Sydney to the Gong (Wollongong-80 km) cycle race*. For details contact Bicycle NSW, T9283 5200, www.ozemail.com.au/~bikensw

December Over Christmas, *Carols by Candlelight* is the main festive public celebration of song in The Domain, while the wild and wicked grab a beer glass and a patch of sand at the *Bondi Beach Christmas Party*, which usually ends up as a mass streak into the waves. Far more serious though no less chilly on the flotation devices is the *Sydney to Hobart sailing race*, which departs the inner harbour, winds allowing, every Boxing Day.

Sydney

Shopping

Whether it's top international fashion labels or jewellery, open-air markets or seafood, Sydney can offer a superb, world-class shopping experience to suit all tastes and budgets. The most popular shopping venues are naturally to be found in the city centre, but many of the suburban high streets also support a wide range of interesting outlets and colourful weekend markets. In the city, most of the large department stores, arcades, malls and specialist boutiques are to be found along George St and in the area around Pitt Street Mall, Castlereagh St and King St.

Not to be missed is the magnificent Queen Victoria Building (QVB), which is a vast and historic edifice in which the levels of retail therapy are almost legendary, see page 76. Nearby, connecting George St (412) with Pitt St is the smaller, yet no less attractive and historic Strand Arcade, T9232 4199, www.strandarcade.com.au, which was originally built in 1892.

The suburbs of Newtown (Kings St) and Glebe (Glebe Point Rd) have some fascinating shops selling everything from codpieces to second-hand surfboards. Double Bay, Mosman and Paddington (Oxford St) are renowned for their stylish boutique clothes shops and The Rocks is definitely the place to go for a didjeridu or cuddly koala.

Aboriginal art, contemporary fine art & photography There have been some very disturbing stories in recent years surrounding the authenticity and methods with which some, even reputable dealers commission their art from Aboriginal artists. This has reputedly included the unbelievably sad practice of paying artists a few tins of beer in return for artworks that are then sold on for thousands of dollars, none of which the artist will ever see. If you intend to buy original Aboriginal art ask plenty of questions that relate to the particular works' authenticity and look out for the **National Indigenous Arts Advocacy Association** Label of Authenticity. **Traveller Consumer Helpline** also has details, T1300 552001.

For the best in authentic and original Aboriginal art try: *The Aboriginal and Tribal Art Centre*, 1st floor, 117 George St, The Rocks, T9247 9625 (open daily 1000-1700); *The Coo-ee Emporium and Aboriginal Art Gallery*, 98 Oxford St, Paddington, T9332 1544 (open Mon-Sat 1000-1800, Sun 1100-1700); *Hogarth Galleries* nearby, at 7 Walker Lane, T9360 6839; and *The Gavala Aboriginal Art Centre*, Shop 377, Harbourside, Darling Harbour, T9212 7232. Further afield the *Boomalli Aboriginal Artists Co-operative*, 191 Parramatta Rd, Annandale, T9560 2541, is also recommended.

There are many art galleries showcasing some of the best Australian contemporary artists with most being in The Rocks or Paddington. Try to get hold of the free *Art Find* brochure from one of the galleries or the Sydney VIC. Ken Done is one of the most famous Sydney-based artists. He has a colourful, almost childlike style which you will either love or hate. His main outlet is at 123 George St, The Rocks, T92472740, www.gallery@done.com.au

For some excellent panoramic Australian photographs check out the *Ken Duncan Gallery*, George St, The Rocks (opposite the VIC) or the ubiquitous *Peter Lik Gallery* in the QVB, George St, www.peterlik.com.au

Australiana From the iconic Akubra hats (minus the corks) and *RM Williams* boots to the *Driza-bone* oilskin coats, you'll find all the main brands and outlets in Sydney. Generally speaking these world famous brands and products are all beautifully made and well worth the money. A pair of 'RMs' for example will, provided you look after them, last a lifetime. *RM Williams* outlets can be found at 389 George St and Shop 1-2 Chifely Plaza, corner of Hunter and Phillip sts, www.rmwilliams.com.au Akubra hats, *Driza-bones* and – should you have a horse in tow – a fine range of saddlery, can be found at the *Goodwood Saddlery*, 237-239 Broadway, T9660 6788, open Mon-Fri 0900-1730, Thu until 2000, Sat 0900-1700, Sun 1000-1600, or *Strand Hatters* in the Strand Arcade, 412

George St, T9231 6884. For unusual Australian crafts try the *Craft Australia Boutique* in David Jones department store, Market St, 4th floor, T9266 6276. *Object*, 3rd floor of the Customs House, 31 Alfred St, near Circular Quay, T9247 9126, www.object.com.au, also showcases the best in authentic Australian crafts. For a good range of souvenir products the many outlets in The Rocks (and Rocks Market) are a good source along with *Australia's Northern Territory and Outback Centre*, 28 Darling Walk, Darling Harbour, T9283 7477, www.outbackcentre.com.au You can purchase didjeridoos and the ubiquitous boomerangs all over the city but perhaps the best outlet is *Didj Beat Didgeridoo Shop* in the Clocktower Square Mall, The Rocks, T9251 4289. It has over 2000 'didjies' on show and the staff are delighted to pass on their impressive playing skills. A free 1-hr workshop is offered with your purchase ($55-1500) and they also stock a good selection of original Aboriginal art. Open 1000-1830 daily, www.didjibeat.com.au

Dymocks is the major player having outlets throughout the city. The largest (and apparantly the largest bookshop in Australasia) is at 428 George St with other outlets at 350 George St, 261 George St, and 34 Hunter St, T1800 688 319, www.dymocks. com.au Open Mon-Wed/Fri 0900-1800, Thu 0900-2100, Sat/Sun 0900-1700. *Travel Bookshop*, 175 Liverpool St (southern edge of Hyde Park), T9261 8200, F9261 8481. Open Mon-Fri 0900-1800, Sat 1000-1700. For travel guides and maps and a good source of information too. For smaller more traditional bookshops or second-hand try the 2 *Gleebooks* shops (new books at 49 Glebe Point Rd, T9660 2333, and childrens and secondhand at 191, open 7 days) and *Sappho Books*, 165 Glebe Point Rd, T9552 4498. Open 7 days 1000-2200. Paddington's Oxford St is also home to 2 good independent stores, *Ariel* (42), T9332 4581, and *Berkelouw's Books* (19), T9360 3200. The latter also sells a great range of second-hand books and has the added attraction of a café. Both are open until late. The largest and most bizarre secondhand bookshop in the city is the 'lost world'of *Goulds Book Arcade*, 32 King St, Newtown. **Bookshops**

You will find all the major international labels in Sydney with most having outlets in the major central city shopping streets, arcades and deparment stores (see below). Oxford St in **Paddington** and also the suburbs of **Double Bay**, and to a lesser extend **Chatswood**, are renowned for their boutique clothes stores and Australian designer labels. Names and labels to look for include Helen Kaminski, Collette Dinnigan, Morrissey, Bare, Isogawa and Bettina Liano. For designer bargains try the Market City above Paddy's Markets in Haymarket. Finally, if you are looking for something completely different – perhaps a pair of pink dayglo hot pants or fluffy ear muffs – then head for King Street in Newtown. **Clothes**

On Market St there are 3 great Sydney institutions, the characterful department stores of *Grace Bros*, T9238 9111, www.gracebros.com.au, *David Jones*, T9266 5544, www.davidjones.com.au and *Gowings*, T9287 6394, www.gowings.com.au **Department stores**

For a taste of Australian foods take a look at the food hall in the elegant *David Jones* department store, Market St, T9266 5544. Even if you don't like seafood a trip to the **Sydney Fish Market**, Pyrmont, is fascinating with stalls setting up their displays of Australia's best from about 0800, see page 80. For late night food shopping *Coles Express Supermarket*, corner of George and King sts, City and at the Wynard Station and Kings Cross are open 0600-2400 daily. **Food & wine**
Wine isn't any cheaper here than in the supermarket back in England

If you are a novice or even a seasoned wine buff, before purchasing any Australian labels you might benefit from a trip to *Australian Wine Centre*, 1 Alfred St, Circular Quay, T9247 2755, www.wine.ptylimited.com.au The staff are very knowledgeable and are backed by a great collection of over 1,000 wines. They also offer a world-wide delivery service. Open daily.

Sydney

Jewellery   Given the fact Australia produces over 90% of the world's opals it is not surprising to find a wealth of specialists dealing in their almost surreal beauty and worth. Some of the best include: *Flame Opals*, 119 George St, T9247 3446, wwwflameopals.com.au, open Mon-Fri 0900-1845, Sat 1000-1700, Sun 1130-1700; *Opal Minded*, 36-64 George St, T9247 9885, open daily 1000-1800; *Australian Opal Cutters*, Suite 10, 4th floor, 250 Pitt St, T9261 2442; and *Gems from the Heart*, Shop 33 in the QVB, George St, T9261 2002. To ensure authenticity and good workmanship only purchase opals from retailers who are members of **Australian Opal and Gem Industry Association Ltd** (AOGIA) or **Jewellers Association of Australia**. Pearls from the great Australian 'pinctada maxima' oyster, that range from gold to snow white, are also big business in Sydney and for some of the best and biggest look no further than *Bunda*, Shop 42, ground floor, QVB, George St, T9261 2210.

Markets   There are plenty of weekend markets held in the inner city that offer an eclectic and colourful range of new and second-hand clothes, arts, crafts and foods. The most popular is **The Rocks Market** held every Sat/Sun at the top end of George St, The Rocks. This is supplemented on Sun with an uncluttered open-air market on the Opera House concourse, which concentrates mainly on arts, crafts and souvenirs. The biggest, in the city centre, is the lively and fairly tacky **Paddy's Market** in Haymarket which is open Thu-Sun.

Good inner-suburbs markets include **Paddington Market** held every Sat in the grounds of the church at 395 Oxford St; **Balmain Market** at St Andrew's Church, corner Darling St and Curtis St, again on Sat; **Glebe Market**, in the grounds of Glebe Public Schools, Glebe Point Rd, every Sun; and the beachside **Bondi Markets** on Campbell Pde, also held every Sun. Last, but by no means least, is the fascinating Sydney Fish Market, see page 80.

Outdoor   Kent St is the place to start looking for camping and outdoor equipment. *Paddy Pallin* (507), T9264 2685, www.paddypallin.com.au, *Mountain Equipment* (491), T9264 5888, www.mountainequipment.com.au, and *Patagonia* (497), T9264 2500, are all within a guy-rope of each other. *Adventure Sports Australia* are based at 722 George St, T9281 6977. For *Rent-A-Tent* outlets call T998 74924 in Hornsby Heights or T9653 1631 in Galston.

Tours and activities

See page 130 for travel agents who organize trips further afield   With all there is to see in Sydney, visitors rarely have time to partake in specialist activities beyond the beach and most let their feet take over while sightseeing. However, the city does offer a number of attractive possibilities, with most, given the almost omnipresent harbour, involving either propeller, sails or paddles.

Bridge Climb   The most high-profile activity in the city is the award winning Bridge Climb, which involves the ascent of the 134-m Harbour Bridge span. For the vast majority of its 70-year life the huge 52, 800-tonne network of metal girders was the domain of engineers, maintenance crews and painters, but in recent years some bright spark came up with the idea of guiding public groups to its heady, windswept crown. The 3- to 4-hr climb can be done day or night and in most weather conditions besides electrical storms. Before setting out you are suitably garbed and given a thorough safety briefing. Many say that as well as the stunning views from the top it is the excitement of getting there that is most memorable. Although it is fairly easy going and is regularly done by the elderly the sight and noise of the traffic below adds a special edge. You must wear the overalls and harnesses provided and you cannot take your own camera on the trip – photographs of your group will be taken at the top. The reason for this is of course safety. *Bridge Climb* headquarters is located at 5 Cumberland St, The Rocks. Open 0700-1900, climbs during the week cost from from $130, children $100, weekends $160, children $125. Night climbs during the week cost from $160, children $125, at weekends $180, children $150. T8274 7777, www.bridgeclimb.com

There are a wealth of good-value harbour cruises on offer with most being based at **Cruises**
Circular Quay. Trips vary from a sedate cruise on a replica of the *Bounty* to paddle steamers and fast catamarans. There are 3 principal companies offering a wide range of cruises on mainly modern craft *Captain Cook* and *Sydney ferries*, based at Circular Quay, and *Matilda*, based at Aquarium Wharf, Darling Harbour. Other companies offering cruises on older or specialist vessels include the charismatic replica of *The Bounty*, *The Sydney Showboat Paddlesteamer*, *The Vagabond*, *Ocean Spirit*, *The Majestic*, *The Americas Cup Spirit* and the 1874 *James Craig*. Here are a few options in a sea of many.

Captain Cook, with a fleet of 12 large, modern catamarans, offer a wide range of excellent cruises throughout the day and evening, very often including lunch or dinner and quality musical or operatic entertainment, or entry to major attractions. Cruises range from $20, children $15 for a basic 1¼-hr harbour highlights cruise to $99/55 for a 2½-hr à la carte dinner cruise. All cruises depart from Wharf 6. T9206 1112, cruise@captaincook.com.au

The most nostalgic and sedate way of cruising the harbour is on board the beautiful *The Bounty*, a fully functional, scale replica of the famous 18th-century tall ship, used in the film of the same name, starring Australia's most famous actor Mel Gibson. There are a number of daily and special weekend cruise options including lunch, dinner, buffet lunch, pre-dinner and Sunday brunch. The weekday 2-hr Lunch Sail departs at 1230 (from $65) and the Dinner Sail at 1900 (from $99). On Saturday the 2½-hr Buffet Lunch Sail departs at 1230 (from $95), the 1½-hr Pre-Dinner Sail (from $53) at 1600 and the 2½-hr Dinner Sail (from $99) at 1900. On Sun times are the same as Sat except for the 1½-hr Brunch Sail (from $53) that departs at a very congenial 1000. 29 George St, The Rocks, T9247 1789, www.thebounty.com.au

Majestic is a beautiful 34-m modern launch (the kind you always dreamed of owning) and they offer a 2-hr 'Cruise 'n' Café' option, from $20, children $15; a 1¾-hr Seafood Buffet, from $58, children $43.50; and a 2-hr Seafood Platter, from $99. Tickets can be bought at the Sydney Harbour Cruise Centre, King St Wharf, Darling Harbour. Cruises depart from Campbell's Cove near *The Bounty*. T9552 2722, www.blue linecruises.com.au

Majestic also own and operate the *Sydney Showboat Paddlesteamer* fleet which are replicas of the original vessels that use to ply the harbour in the 1800s. A range of cruises are on offer from the basic 1½-hr Harboursights, from $19, children $11.40 (departs 1510, 1530, 1715) to the 2-hr à la carte Twilight Dinner Cruise, from $85, children $51 (departs 1930). The steamers depart from King St Wharf, Darling Harbour and pick up at the Eastern Pontoon in Circular Quay. T9552 2722, www.bluelinecruises.com.au

Also bear in mind there are some excellent cruise options up the **Hawkesbury River** from Palm Beach, north of Sydney, T9997 4815. As an example *Sydney Ferries* offer a 1-hr Morning Cruise from $15, children $7.50, family $37.50 (daily 1000 and 1115); a 2½-hr Afternoon Cruise, from $22, children $11, family $54 (daily 1300 and 1330) and a 1½-hr Evening Harbour Lights Cruise, $19, children $9.50, family $47.50 (Mon-Sat 2000). All cruises leave from Wharf 4.

Although diving is best left to the Barrier Reef if you intend heading north to **Diving**
Queensland, NSW and Sydney do offer some surprisingly good diving. The southern beaches, La Perouse and the Botany Bay National Park are the best spots. There are many dive shops in the city and several companies offering tuition and trips. These include the popular *Pro Dive*, 478 George St, T9264 6177, www.prodive.com.au, with

Sydney

4-hr boat trips from $109 ($169 with gear hire) and *Dive Centre* bases at both Manly (10 Belgrave St, T9977 4355) and Bondi (192 Bondi Rd, T9369 3855), www.divesydney.com Both companies offer Open Water Certificates from around $270. The website www.scubaaustralia.com.au is also useful.

Fishing   Despite all the harbour activity, both the fishing and the water quality in Sydney Harbour is said to be pretty good, with species like flathead, whiting and trevally being regularly caught, especially downstream from the Harbour Bridge. Offshore, the fishing obviously improves dramatically and Sydney is home to its own fishing fleet that regularly catch such exotics as marlin and tuna. There are a number of fishing charters available including *Charter One*, T04 0133 2355, www.charterone.com, based in Manly. Trips range from a 4-hr jaunt from $65 to full-day $125, including tackle hire. *Quayside Charters*, T9555 2600, are based at Circular Quay. Others include *Fishfinder*, T4446 4466, *Bounty Hunter*, 378 Pitt St, T9661 9430, and *Gemini*, T04 1822 8729.

Roller skating   Roller skating is very popular, especially along the beachfronts of Manly and Bondi, in Centennial Park and around Farm Cove in the Botanical Gardens. Hire costs about $12 per hour with $6 extra for every hour after that or around $20 for all-day hire. Skates can be hired from *Action Inline* or *Manly Blades*, North Steyne, Manly. In Bondi try *Bondi Boards and Blades*, 148 Curlewis St, and for Centennial Park *Total Skate*, 36 Oxford St.

Jet boating   Inevitably perhaps Circular Quay and Darling Harbour are home to a couple of jet boating companies that zip up and down the inner harbour taking in the world-class scenery. At Circular Quay *Oz Jetboating* rule the roost and are based at east Circular Quay, T9660 6111, www.ozjetboating.com They offer ½-hr trips departing daily from 1000, from $30, children $20, family $90. At the western shore of Cockle Bay in Darling Harbour, *Harbourjet* offer similar trips and prices, T9929 7373, www.harbourjet.com.au

Sailing   *Sydney Mainsail*, T9979 3681, www.sydneymainsail.com.au, offer 3-hr trips on Tue *Aesthetically Sydney* with highly experienced skippers, from $75. *Australian Spirit Sailing Company*, T9878 *Harbour offers some* 0300, www.austspiritsailingco.com.au, also offer similar trips. National Maritime *of the best sailing* Museum is also a good place to enquire, being the base for *Sydney by Sail*, which runs *in the world* introductory lessons from $55 (1½ hrs), plus B&B and dinner trips, T9280 1110. The office is based below the lighthouse. Other possibilities include the *Australian Sailing School and Club*, The Spit, Mosman, T9960 3077 and the *Balmoral Windsurfing and Sailing School*, 2 The Esplanade, Balmoral Beach, T9960 5344. Pittwater to the north of Sydney is also a hugely popular spot for sailing and offers numerous opportunities. Get hold of a copy of the *Northern Beaches Visitors Guide* from the VIC for listings.

Scenic flights   Although the sights of Sydney blow you away with your feet firmly planted on the ground, seeing it from above can be exhilarating and provide an entirely different aspect, especially of icons like the Opera House. There are a number of fixed-wing and helicopter scenic flight companies including *Sydney Heli-Aust*, T9317 3402, www.heliaust.com.au, that offer 30-min (from $150) to 35-min (from $199) helicopter flights around the inner harbour and a 5-hr luncheon trip to the Hunter Valley (from $599). They are based at the airport but offer pick-ups from the city. Interesting alternatives are the scenic flights offered by *Sydney Seaplanes* T1300 656787, www.sydneyby seaplane.com.au, based in Rose Bay. They offer a 15-min flight around the harbour from $120, children $60 while a 90-min trip taking in the harbour, beaches and Blue Mountains costs from $620, children $310.

Sea kayaking   Sea kayaking is a great way to cruise the harbour and explore the backwaters and bays of the inner suburbs. The Middle Harbour that branches off between Middle Head and

Clontarf snakes over 10 km into the lesser-known North Shore suburbs and is especially good. It is not entirely unusual to see the odd sea eagle or fairy penguin. Kayaks
can be hired from *Sydney Kayak Centre*, Spit Rd, Spit Bridge, T9969 4590; *Sydney Harbour Kayaks*, 3/235 The Spit Rd, Mosman, T9960 4389, info@4shk.com (also offer
guided trips); and *Q.Craft*, Shop 3/200 Pittwater Rd, Manly T9976 6333,
www.qcraft.com.au Typical prices are from $15 per hour or full-day from $70.

Surfing

The best spots in Sydney are of course Bondi and Manly but most of Sydney's beaches
offer great possibilities. For up-to-date surf conditions, check the website
www.wavecam.com.au
   Companies include: *Manly Surf School*, North Steyne Surf Club, Manly Beach, T9977
6977, www.manlysurfschool.com.au, offer good-value daily classes 1100-1300, from
$45 one lesson to 10-day lessons from $220; *Dripping Wet Surf Company*, Shop
2/93-95 North Steyne, Manly, T9977 3549, offer boards, body boards, flippers and
wetsuits for hire, board hire costs from $15 per hr; and *Aloha Surf*, 44 Pittwater Rd,
Manly, T9977 3777, who offer similar rates. In Bondi try the *Bondi Surf Company*, 2/ 72
Campbell Pde, T9365 0870.

Sky diving

You can also try your courage at sky diving in and around Sydney. Companies include
Simply Skydive, CM12, Mezzanine, Centrepoint, City, T9231 5865, www.simplyskydive.
com.au *Atomic Dog*, T1300 655622, *NSW Tandem Skydive*, 20 Allandale Rd, T1800
000759 and the *Sydney Skydiving Centre* based out at Bankstown Airport, T9791 9155.
Jumps start from about $275.

Swimming

South of the Heads the beaches at Bondi, Bronte, Clovelly and Coogee are hugely popular while to the north, Manly, Collaroy, Narrabeen, Avalon, Ocean Beach and Palm
Beach are also good spots. Lifeguards patrol most beaches in summer and you are
strongly advised to swim between the yellow and red flags. Most of the city beaches
also have safe, open-air, salt-water swimming pools to provide added safety, especially
for children. Indoor heated pools are not a rarity in Sydney either and three in particular
offer great facilities: *Sydney Aquatic Centre*, Homebush Bay Olympic Park, open
Mon-Fri 0500-2145, Sat/Sun 0600-1945, T9752 3666; *Cook Phillip Park Aquatic and
Fitness Centre*, 6 College St, next to Hyde Park, T9326 0444, $5, children $3.80 (impressive for its construction underground); *Sydney Olympic Pool*, below the Harbour Bridge,
Alfred St, Milsons Point, North Shore, T9955 2309, $4, children $2 (offers the best view
from any public swimming pool in Australia). *McCallum Pool* is a smaller outdoor public
pool on Cremorne Point (off Milsons Rd). Great views across the harbour.

Walking

The best way to see **The Rocks** properly is to join the official Rocks Walking Tour, which
is an entertaining and informative insight into both past and present. Bookings can be
made at the Sydney VIC, 106 George St or at the *Walks Office*, Shop K4, Kendall Lane.
The tours take 1½ hrs, departing at 1030,1230 and 1430 weekdays and 1130 and 1400
weekends. $17.50, children $10.50, family $45.55, T9247 6678, booking recommended.
   Within the city centre the walk along the Farm Cove foreshore from the **Opera
House to Macquarie Point** (1 hr) is excellent and best done at dawn or dusk. **Opera
House, past The Rocks to Dawes Point** (2-5 hrs) or back is always memorable. To the
east of the city, the scenic oceanside walks from **Watson's Bay to the Gap** and South
Head (2 hrs) and from **Bondi to Bronte** (1½ hrs) are both recommended. **Centennial
Park** offers a vast area of parkland tracks and small lakes. On the North Shore the walk
to **Bradley's Head** (1 hr) from Taronga Zoo offers lovely city views as well as historical
aspects and you have the option of carrying on to the views and fortifications of **Middle Head**. The walk to soak up the views from the **Barrenjoey Head lighthouse** can
provide just one highlight of a full-day trip to Palm Beach.

Transport

Local

Bus drivers do not automatically stop at bus stops – you must signal

Bus *STA* (Sydney Buses) are the principal operators with the standard buses being blue and white, the **Airport Express** green and yellow, the **Sydney Explorer** red and the **Bondi Explorer** blue. Standard bus fares start at $1.50-4.70 depending on distance and susequent zone. If you intend to travel regularly by bus a Travel Ten ticket is recommended ($11-39) while further savings can be also be made with the TravelPass and Sydney Pass system. See box, page 127. The Explorer buses cost $30 for the full return trip ($50 2-day). There is an on-board commentary and you can hop on and off at will. Both leave at regular intervals from Circular Quay. For all of the above bus fares, children travel half-price and there are also family concessions. Most Explorer buses operate between 0840 and 1722 only. The local green **Olympic Explorer** offers trips around the Homebush Bay site and links with ferry services from Circular Quay ($20 with ferry, $10 without), while the weekend blue and yellow **Parramatta Explorer** leaves every 20 mins from the RiverCat ferry terminal in Parramatta, $10 (ex RiverCat). Children travel half-price and there are also family concessions on most fares. For information about suburban buses in Sydney, T131500, www.131500.com.au

Car Travelling by car around Sydney is a nightmare with numerous tolls, expensive parking and omnipresent parking wardens to add to your woes. There really is no need to see the sights by car, but if you do, take lots of coinage for parking machines. For car rental companies, see page 128.

Cycling Travel by bike within the city centre can be hairy to say the least. Size matters! That said, it is a great way to see more of the city than you would on two legs and you are able to explore at will. The suburbs are a little less manic. Several companies offer bike hire from about $30 per day or $170 per week. Companies include *Bicycles in the City*, 722 George St, T9281 6977 (offer not only hire but maps and touring information); *Inner City Cycles*, 151 Glebe Point Rd, Glebe, T9660 6605; *Woolly's Wheels*, 82 Oxford St, T9331 2671; and the *Manly Cycle Centre*, 36 Pittwater Rd, Manly, T9977 1189. For general advice contact *Bicycle NSW*, Level 2, 209 Castlereagh St, T9283 5200, www.ozemail.com.au/~bikensw For *Sydney Cycle Ways* maps and additional information contact the *RTA*, T9218 6816.

See also page 123 for Harbour cruise details

Ferry A trip on one of Sydney's ageing, almost iconic green and gold harbour ferries is a wonderful experience and an ideal way to see the city, as well as reach many of the major attractions and suburbs. A short return voyage from the busy Circular Quay terminal to the zoo, Mosman or Cremorne on the North Shore, during both day and night, is highly recommended. The principal operator is *Sydney Ferries*, who operate the iconic 'green and golds' and also the fast *JetCats* to Manly and *RiverCat* to Homebush Bay/Parramatta. Several independent companies also operate out of Circular Quay, offering a wide range of cruises as well as suburban transportation and water taxis.

Like the buses, ferry fares are priced according to zone and start at a single trip for $4.20. A DayTripper Pass (one day) costs $13.40. If you intend to travel regularly by ferry a FerryTen ticket (from $26.50) is recommended, while further savings can be also be made with the TravelPass and Sydney Pass system (see box, page 127). Various travel/entry combo tickets are offered to the major harbourside sights including Taronga Zoo. Children travel half-price and there are also family concessions on most fares. For ferry information T131500, www. sydneytransport.com.au The main **Sydney Ferries Information Centre** can be found opposite Wharf 4, Circular Quay.

LightRail The new LightRail network is Sydney's newest transport system linking Central Station with Lilyfield, via a number of stops within the southwest CBD and Darling

◀

Sydney Suburban Travel Passes

There are numerous, popular travel pass systems in operation through the STA. The new and very attractive DayTripper Pass gives all-day access to Sydney's trains, bus and ferries within the suburban area from $13.40, child $6.70. Tickets can be purchased at any rail, bus or ferry sales or information outlet or on the buses themselves. TravelPass allows unlimited, weekly, quarterly or yearly combined travel throughout designated zones or sections. A 7-day pass for example, covering the inner (orange) zone, costs $34, child $17.50. For

the tourist staying only a few days, however, the best bet is the The Sydney Pass which offers unlimited travel on ferry and standard buses as well as the Sydney and Bondi Explorer routes and the four STA Harbour Cruises. They are sold as a 3-day ($90, child $45), 5-day ($120, child $60) or 7-day ($140, child $70) package. Return Airport Express transfers are also included and family concessions apply. Note that discount, ten-trip 'TravelTen' (bus) and 'FerryTen' passes are also available and recommended, from $11.

Harbour, as well as the Casino, Fish Market and Glebe. It is a 24-hr service with trains every 10-15 mins 0600-2400 and every 30 mins 2400-0600. There are 2 fare zones starting at a single journey at $2.60. A Day Pass with unlimited stops costs $8. Children travel at half price. For information, T9285 5600, www.metromonorail.com.au

MonoRail Opened in July 1988 as a gift to Sydney in celebration of Australia's Bicentennial, the MonoRail runs in a loop around Darling Harbour and southwestern CBD and provides as much of a novelty journey as a convenient way of getting from A to B. Even if you never use it you will doubtless see it as it slips gently past above your head like a legless metal centipede. The carriages run every 3-5 mins, Mon-Thu 0700-2200, Fri/Sat 0700-2400 and Sun 0800-2200. The standard fare (1 loop) is $4 while a Day Pass costs $8. Children under 5 years travel free and discounts are available to some major attractions.

Taxi/water taxi Sydney's once rather dubious taxi service was given a major revamp for the 2000 Olympics and it is now much improved. Ranks are located near every railway station, at Circular Quay and numerous spots in the CBD, otherwise hail one as required. From 2200-0600 higher tariffs apply. The minimum (hailed) flagfall is $2.20 with about a $110 charge per km thereafter. On short journeys tipping is not expected. There are several companies including: *Combined* T8332 8888, *ABC* T132522, *Premier* T131017, *Legion* T131451 and *RSL* T132211. Water taxis operate all over the harbour with most being based on the western edge of Circular Quay. The main operators are *Taxis* Afloat T9955 3222, *Harbour Shuttle* T9810 5010 and *Water Taxis Combined* T9555 8888.

Train Sydney's excellent 24-hr double-deckered train services are a convenient way to reach the city centre and outlying areas, or to link in with bus and ferry services. Much of the CBD line is underground. Fares are generally quite cheap and start at $1. Savings of up to 40% can be made with 'Off-Peak Tickets' which operate after 0900 on weekdays. Further savings can be made with the TravelPass and Sydney Pass system (see box, page 127). Children travel half-price and there are also family concessions on most fares. There are numerous 'coloured' routes with the green or purple City Circle (Central, Town Hall, Wynyard, Circular Quay, St James and the Museum) and blue Eastern Suburbs Line (Central, Town Hall, Martin Place, Kings Cross, Edgecliff, Bondi Junction) being the most convenient for visitors. For information about suburban trains in Sydney, T131500, www.131500.com.au, and at major train stations.

Sydney

Long distance
Information and flight arrivals/departures, T9667 6065, www.sydney airport.com.au

Air From **Europe** the main route, and the cheapest, is via Asia, though fares will also be quoted via North America or Africa. The Asia route usually takes 20-30 hrs including stops. There are no non-stop routes, so it's worth checking out what stopovers are on offer: this might be your only chance to see Kuala Lumpur. Stopovers of a few nights do not usually increase the cost of the ticket appreciably. The cheapest return flights to Sydney, off-season, will be around £500 (789 Euros), with stand-by prices rising to at least £800 (€1,263) around Christmas. Other airlines flying from Europe include *Air New Zealand*, www.airnz.co.uk *British Airways*, www.britishairways.com *Emirates*, www.emirates.com and *Singapore Airlines*, www.singaporeair.com

From **New Zealand** there are direct *Qantas* flights from Auckland, Christchurch and Wellington to Sydney. *Air New Zealand*, www.airnewzealand.co.nz, and *Freedom Air*, www.freedom.co.nz, are the other two main carriers, both offering routes that *Qantas* do not. Expect to pay a minimum of NZ$500 for a return to Sydney.

From **North and South America** there are direct *Qantas* flights from Los Angeles, Vancouver and New York to Sydney. The cost of a standard return in the high season starts around US$2,200 from Vancouver, US$2,000 from New York, and US$1,700 from Los Angeles. There are also direct flights from Buenos Aires. Other airlines flying from North America include *Air New Zealand*, www.airnz.co.uk; *United*, www.ual.com; *Air Canada*, www.aircanada.ca and *Singapore Airlines*, www.singaporeair.com

Round-the-World (RTW) tickets can be a real bargain if you stick to the most popular routes, sometimes working out even cheaper than a return fare. RTWs start at around £750 (€1,200) or US$1,500, depending on the season.

Bus Sydney Coach Terminal is in the Central Railway Station, Shop 4-7, Eddy Av, T9212 3433, open daily 0600-2230. Interstate services from Sydney include: **Adelaide** McCafferty's, 1-2 daily, 23 hrs, $116-121. **Brisbane**, *McCafferty's*, 5 daily, 20 hrs, $85. **Broken Hill**, *McCafferty's*, 1 daily, 16 hrs, $121. **Byron Bay**, *McCafferty's*, 4 daily, 18 hrs, $85. **Cairns**, *McCafferty's*, 5 daily, 46 hrs, $260. **Canberra**, *McCafferty's*, 10 daily, 5 hrs, $32. **Katoomba**, *McCafferty's*, 2 daily, 2 hrs 20 mins, $29. **Melbourne**, *McCafferty's*, 5 daily, 14 hrs 20 mins, $59. **Perth**, *McCafferty's*, 4 daily, 59 hrs, $360. *Greyhound* offer additional services in conjunction with *McCafferty's*. **Premier Motor Services** also offer similar services.

Car hire All the usual suspects have offices at the airport (Arrivals south) including *Avis*, T9667 0667, *Hertz* T9669 2444, *Thrifty* T9317 4161, *Budget* T132848, *National* T9207 9409 and *Red Spot* T9317 2233. In the city try Avis, Budget and Ascot centred on or around William St, Darlinghurst. Cheaper, more localized companies include *Dollar*, Sir John Young Crescent, T9223 1444 and *Bayswater Rentals*, 180 William St, Kings Cross, one of the cheapest standard hotels T9360 3622. Rates start from about $55 per day.

Campervan hire and dealers For hire: *Maui*, freecall T1300 363800/T38379 8891; www.maui-rentals.com.au, *Britz*, freecall T1800 331454, www.britz.com.au Car and campervan dealers (second-hand) include: *Travellers Auto Barn*, 177 William St, Kings Cross, T1800 674374, www.travellers-autobarn.com.au, *Kings Cross Car Market*, Ward St Car Park, Kings Cross, T1800 808188, www.carmarket.com.au (good buy and sell venue).

Train First class and economy fares vary so you are advised to shop around and compare prices with the various coach operators. Ask about their **Backtracker Pass** which offers unlimited journeys on entire rail and coach network, including Brisbane, 14 days $165- 6 months $330. **East Coast Discovery Pass** gives you 6 months, economy class travel, one way, either north or south with unlimited stopovers, Melbourne $93.50, Cairns $247.50. The railway station also houses the main interstate city coach terminal

(*McCaffertys* and *Greyhound*). For information T131500, www.sydneytransport.net.au

Interstate and NSW destination rail services from Sydney include: **Adelaide**, Great Southern (Indian Pacific), Mon/Thu, 23 hrs, $176. **Brisbane**, *Countrylink* (XPT), 2 daily, 14 hrs, $110. **Broken Hill**, *Great Southern* (Indian Pacific), Mon-Fri, 15 hrs, $117. **Byron Bay**, *Countrylink* (XPT), 3 daily, 12 hrs, $98. **Cairns**, *Countrylink/ Queensland Rail*, 2 daily, 50 hrs, $292. **Canberra**, *Countrylink*, 3 daily, 4 hrs, $47. **Katoomba**, *City Rail*, Regular daily, 2 hrs, $15. **Melbourne**, *Countrylink* (XPT), 2 daily, 10½ hrs, $110. **Perth**, *Great Southern* (Indian Pacific), Mon/Thu, 57 hrs, $459.

Directory

Airline offices *CBD unless otherwise stated*

Aerolineas Argentinas, 580 George St, T1800 222215; *Air Canada*, Level 12/92 Pitt St, T9232 5222; *Air China*, Level 11/115 Pitt St, T9232 7277; *Air Fiji*, Level 5,17 Bridge St, T8272 7889; *Air France*, 64 York St, T9244 2100; *Air New Zealand*, Level 4,10 Barrack St, T132476; *Air Pacific*, Level 10, 403 George St, T9244 2626; *American Airlines*, Mezzanine Level, 141 Walker St, North Sydney, T1300 650747; *British Airways*, Level 19, AAP Centre, 259 George St, T1300 767177; *Continental Airlines*, 64 York St, T9244 2242; *Eastern Australia Airlines*, Qantas Airways Domestic Terminal, Mascot, T9691 2333; *Garuda Indonesia*, 55 Hunter St, T9334 9900; *Hazelton Airlines*, Building 305, Eleventh St, Mascot, T131713; *Impulse Airlines*, Eleventh St, Sydney Kingsford Smith Airport, Mascot, T9317 5400; *Japan Airlines*, Level 14, 201 Sussex St, T9272 1111; KLM Royal Dutch Airlines, 5 Elizabeth St, T1800 505747; *Lufthansa*, 143 Macquarie St, T9367 3800; *Skimax-Qantas*, Level 3/263 Clarence St, T9267 1655; *Singapore Airlines*, 17-19 Bridge St, T9350 0100; Sydney Harbour Seaplanes Pty Ltd, Lyne Park Rose Bay, T 9388 1978; *Thai Airways*, 75 Pitt St, T9251 1922; *United Airlines*, Level 6, 10 Barrack St, T9317 8933; *Virgin Atlantic Airways*, Level 8/403, George St, T9244 2747.

Banks & ATMs

All major bank branches with ATMs are readily available on all principal shopping and eating streets in Sydney, especially along George St.

Communications

Post offices There are post shops dotted around the city marked with the prominent red and white circular logo. The main General Post Office is at 159 Pitt St (Martin Place), T131318. Open Mon-Fri 0815-1730, Sat 1000-1400. Poste Restante is based at the George Street branch, 310 George St (across the road from the Wynyard Station entrance). Log your name in to the computer to see if any mail awaits. The city centre Poste Restante code is NSW 2001. Open Mon-Fri 0830-1700.

Internet Internet is widely available throughout the city centre with the southern end of George and Pitt sts (between Liverpool and Hay) and the western end of Oxford St (between Crown and College) having numerous outlets. *Global Gossip* have outlets at 34 Wentworth Ave and 770 George St in the CBD and 317 Glebe Point Rd, Glebe. Most backpackers offer their own internet facilities and outlets in the outer suburbs are listed in the relevant text. Expect to pay $3-8 per hr. Be careful to confirm your start and finish time with the person on duty. Overcharging or convenient 'rounding up' seems to be common. Most internet outlets, newsagents and grocery stores advertise a copious number of allegedly 'spectacularly cheap, international phone cards, claiming to have rates to far-flung countries for as little as 9c per minute. Be careful – most are based on weird off-peak times and are dependent on the location from which you call.

Dentists

After Hours Dental Emergency, 144/313 Harris St, Pyrmont, T9660 3322.

Embassies

Belgium, 12A Trelawney St, Woollahra, NSW, T02 9327 8377. **Canada**, Level 5, 111 Harrington St, Sydney, T02 9364 3000. **France**, 31 Market St, Sydney, T02 9261 5779.

Germany, 13 Trelawney St, Woollahra, NSW, T02 9328 7733. **Netherlands**, 500 Oxford St, Bondi Jnc, Sydney, T02 9387 6644. **New Zealand**, Level 10, 55 Hunter St, Sydney, T02 9223 0222. **Sweden**, Level 5, 350 Kent St, Sydney, T02 9262 6433. **Switzerland**, 500 Oxford St, Bondi Jnc, Sydney, T02 8383 4000. **UK**, Level 16, The Gateway, 1 Macquarie Pl, Sydney, T02 9247 7521. **USA**, 19-29 Martin Pl, Sydney, T02 9373 9200.

Emergencies For emergencies, police, fire brigade or ambulance, dial 000. General enquiries T9690 4960. City of Sydney Police Station, 192 Day St, T9265 6499.

Foreign Foreign exchange is readily available on the arrivals concourse of Sydney Airport. In the **exchange** city there are many outlets especially around Circular Quay and along George St including *Thomas Cook*, QVB Walk, Shop 64, T9264 1133, *Visa Customer Centre*, 91 George St, The Rocks, T1800 180900 (open 1000-1800) and *American Express*, 124 and 50 Pitt St, T9239 9226/T1300 139060.

Laundry *City Laundromat*, Millennium Tower, corner Sussex St and Bathurst St, T9264 6661.

Libraries **State Library of NSW** (see page 75), **Sydney City Library**, 456 Kent St, T9265 9470. Open Mon-Fri 0800-1900, Sat 0900-1200.

Lost property *CityRail*, T8202 2000 and *Sydney Ferries*, T9207 3101. Also visit www.131500.com.au/lost_property.asp

Medical **Hospitals** **St Vincent's Hospital**, Victoria St, Darlinghurst, T9339 1111. **Royal North** **services** **Shore Hospital**, Pacific Highway, St Leonard's, T9926 7111. **Prince of Wales Hospital**, High St, Randwick, T9382 2222. **Sydney Children's Hospital**, T9382 1111. **Pharmacies** *Crest Hotel Pharmacy*, 60A Darlinghurst Rd, Kings Cross, T9358 1822 (open late), *City Pharmacy and Chase Medical Centre*, 136 Macquarie St, T9247 2390.

Travel agents The major travel agents have numerous branches throughout the city including *American Express Travel*, Level 5, 89 York St, T9279 1233, *Flight Centre*, 14/580 George St, T9267 2999, *STA Travel*, 855 George St, T9212 1255. Others include *Australian Travel Specialists*, Quay 6, Circular Quay, T9252 0401, *Backpackers Travel Centre*, 87 Glebe Point Rd, Glebe, T9552 4544. *YHA* have their own travel offices at the *Central Hostel*, Rawson Pl, T9281 9444 and 422 Kent St, T9261 1111. There are numerous companies offering a wide range of trips to the Blue Mountains. VIC has details.

Around Sydney

Introducing Around Sydney

One of the wonderful things about Australia's largest city is that you are never too far away from water or the green tranquillities of city parks, nature reserves or national parks. To the west, less than two hours away, some 70 km delivers you to the fringes of some of the state's largest and most celebrated national parks, that sit collectively within the **Greater Blue Mountains** region. Named after the visual effects of sunlight on eucalyptus oil released by the cloak of gum trees that liberally swathe the valleys and plateaus, the 'Blueys' now attract over one million visitors a year, that flock to delight in the stunning vistas, walk its

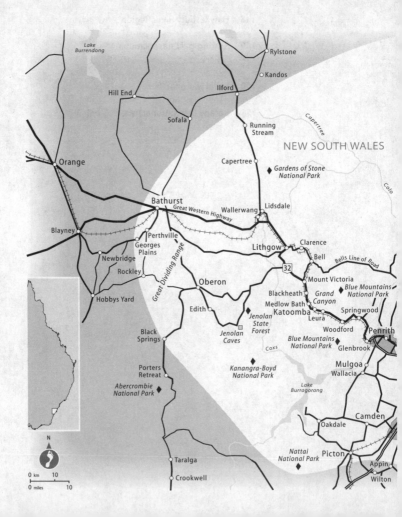

numerous tracks or simply relax in its many quaint and characterful accommodations. For many domestic visitors, an added bonus here, amidst the higher elevations, is also the rare and welcome hint of seasons.

Bounding the city to the northwest is the **Hawkesbury River region**, an area that is often missed by visitors, yet an area possessing its very own aesthetic charm. It provides a quieter escape than the Blue Mountains and its own little gems like the Settlers Arms in the historic settlement of St Albans. There, an afternoon drink can easily turn in to a memorable overnight stay.

Closer to home, the **Ku-ring-gai Chase National Park** to the north of Sydney and the **Royal National Park** to the south, sit either end of the voluminous suburbs like two great green bookends. Then between the two, like some highlighted historical manuscript, is the tiny **Botany Bay National Park** the site of Captain Cook's first landing in April 1770.

Around Sydney

Wollemi National Park
Hunter Valley
Wollombi
69
Yengo National Park
Kulnura
Colo Heights
St Albans
Wyong
Hawkesbury
Dharug National Park
Wisemans Ferry
Brisbane Water National Park
Gosford
Richmond
Marrammarra National Park
Woy Woy
Bouddi National Park
Windsor
Cattai National Park
Ku-ring-gai Chase National Park
Hornsby
Parramatta
Ryde
Sydney Harbour National Park
Bankstown
Sydney
Liverpool
Bondi
Kingsford Smith International
Campbelltown
Princes Highway
Botany Bay
Heathcote
Bate Bay
Heathcote National Park
Royal National Park
Helensburgh

Blue Mountains

Around Sydney

Colour map 1, grid B2   *The Blue Mountains form part of the Great Dividing Range, containing no less than five national parks covering a total area of 10,000 sq km. Although just as impressive, they are not really mountains but a network of eroded **river valleys**, **gorges**, and **bluffs** that have formed over millions of years. The result is a huge wonderland of natural features, from precipitous **cliffs** to dramatic **waterfalls** and **canyons**, not to mention the most dramatic limestone **caves** on the continent. Although once the happy home of the **Daruk Aboriginals**, the Blue Mountains were initially seen by the first Europeans as a highly inconvenient barrier to whatever could be plundered on the other side. Incredibly, for almost a quarter of a century they remained that way, before finally being traversed in 1813 by explorers Blaxland, Wentworth and Lawson.*

*To this day the impenetrable geography still limits transportation, with essentially the same two convict-built roads and railway line completed over a century ago reaching west through a string of settlements from Glenbrook to Lithgow. The strange thing is, by merely passing through you are almost blissfully unaware of the dramatic precipices, canyons and viewpoints that exist at the end of almost every other street or cul-de-sac. For decades the 'Blueys' have been a favourite weekend or retirement destination for modern-day Sydney escapees, who welcome the distinctly cooler temperatures and the colourful seasons that the extra elevation creates. But superb aesthetics and climate aside, the Blue Mountains also present some excellent **walking** opportunities, as well as other, more fearsome activities like **abseiling**, **canyoning** and **rock climbing**. Given the region's popularity there are also a glut of good restaurants and a wide range of accommodations from showpiece backpackers to romantic hideaways.*

Ins and outs

Getting there   Although public transport to and around the Blue Mountains is generally good you are advised to take your own vehicle or hire one, allowing you to make the most of the numerous viewpoints and sights within the region. From Sydney take the M4 ($2 toll), eventually crossing the Neapean River, before it forms the Great Western Highway at Glenbrook (65km), the first town on the borders of the region. The rather peculiarly named Bells Line of Road provides another access point across the mountains from Windsor on the east to Mount Victoria on the Great Western Highway (77 km).

The train is the best option for those without transport. They leave Sydney's Central Station (*Countrylink* and/or *CityLink* Platforms) on the hour daily well into the evening, stopping at all major towns through the Blue Mountains to Mount Victoria and beyond, T132232/T131500. It takes 2 hrs to Katoomba and costs $15 return.

CityRail, T131500, in conjunction with *Fantastic Aussie Tours*, T1300300915, offer a number of rail/coach tour options with *Blue MountainsLink* operating Mon-Fri and *Blue Mountains ExplorerLink* operating daily. Price includes return transport and tour on arrival in Katoomba. *Greyhound*, T132030, offer standard daily coach transportation on the westbound run to Dubbo. Numerous coach companies also offer day sightseeing tours from Sydney. Backpackers should ask any of the main hostels which are currently offering the best deals and which are currently recommended. Some may allow overnight stops. For others the main accredited VIC in Sydney can assist with the extensive choice and bookings. Most of the buses leave from Circular Quay. *Aerocity Shuttles*, T4782 1866, offer direct links from Sydney Airport.

The route through the Blue Mountains by car from Sydney is easily negotiable. From Glenbrook, you begin the ascent of the main plateau, following the same route as the railway line. You pass through Blaxland, Springwood, Faulconbridge and Woodford, before arriving at Wentworth Falls. It is in Wentworth that you essentially reach the top of the main plateau at an average height of just above 1000 m. From Wentworth Falls, the road then continues west through the northern edges of Leura and Katoomba, then north, through the heart of Blackheath and Mount Victoria. From Mount Victoria you then begin the descent to Lithgow (154 km). Katoomba is the largest of the towns and is generally accepted as providing the best amenities.

Getting around
*See Transport,
in each town section,
for further details*

The main accredited VICs are in Glenbrook (just off the Great Western Highway, T1300 653408, open Mon-Fri 0900-1700, Sat/Sun 0830-1630), Katoomba (Echo Point, T1300 653408, open daily 0900-1700) and Lithgow (1 Cooerwull Rd, off the Great Western Highway, at the western end of town, T6353 1859, www.tourism.lithgow.com, open daily 0900-1700) and Oberon, near Jenolan Caves (137-139 Oberon St, T6336 0666, open Mon-Fri 0830-1630, Sat/Sun 1000-1600. You can stock up with the free visitor's guide and maps. All regional centres offer a free accommodation booking service.

**Tourist
information**
*See www.blue
mountainstourism.
org.au for further
VIC information*

For detailed information on all the national parks detailed below, books covering the numerous walks within the parks, as well as topographical maps, etc, contact or visit the main NPWS office at the Heritage Centre, near Govetts Leap, Blackheath, T4787 8877, or the NPWS office in Richmond, Bowman's Cottage, 370 Windsor St, T45885247. There is also a NPWS Conservation Hut, at the end of Fletcher Road, Glenbrook, T4757 3827, open daily 0900-1700.

The national parks

The Blue Mountains region contains a conglomerate of five national parks that, combined, cover an area of 10,000 sq km, with half of that being considered 'wilderness area'.

The largest, at an expansive 4,876 sq km (and the second largest in the state after Kosciuszko National Park) is **Wollemi National Park** which sits to the north of the Bells Line of Road. It incorporates the state's most extensive officially recognized wilderness area and is by nature very rugged and therefore very inaccessible. It is in essence like some modern-day Jurassic Park which was highlighted in no uncertain terms in 1994 with the chance discovery of the Wollemi pine a species that once flourished over 60 million years ago. The exact location of the small stand of trees is understandably kept a closely guarded secret. As well as its complex geology, topography, Aboriginal art sites and botanical features, it is also home to a rich variety of birds. For once, this is a place where nature is getting a little of its own back, quite literally, by quietly repossessing the two former industrial towns of **Newnes** and **Glen Davis**. Of all the parks in the region it is the one for the well-prepared modern-day explorer. ■ *Basic NPWS campsites at Wheeny Creek, Colo Meroo, Dun's Swamp and Newnes. Main access is from Putty Rd 100 km northwest of Sydney or via Rylstone.*

The most famous and accessible park is the 2470 sq km **Blue Mountains National Park** that straddles the Great Western Highway and a string of mountain villages and towns, from Glenbrook in the east to Lithgow in the west. Only recently expanded in the 1980s, it contains natural features that range from deep canyons and forested valleys to pinnacles and waterfalls, as well as a rich abundance of flora and fauna. Although now receiving over one million visitors a year, much of the park remains extremely inaccessible, with over 500 sqkm considered official wilderness area. Sadly, the Blue Mountains,

Around Sydney

like so many national parks in NSW, have suffered in recent years not so much from the impact of tourism, but from the temporary impact of widespread bush fires. ■ *Basic NPWS campsites at Euroka Clearing near Glenbrook, Ingar near Wentworth Falls and Perry's Lookdown near Blackheath. You can also camp anywhere within 500 m of roads and facilities. Access is from many points east and west off the Great Western Highway, or from the Bells Line of Road 70 km west of Sydney.*

Next up is the beautiful 680 sq km **Kanangra-Boyd National Park** which sits to the southwest of Katoomba. Fringed by the Blue Mountains National Park on all but one side it contains a similar geology and topography to the Blue Mountains but is particularly famous for outstanding natural features, the Jenolan limestone caves and the Kanangra Walls (a series of outstanding bluffs). Both are well worth visiting, with the latter considered one of the great walks in the region. ■ *There is a basic NPWS campsite at Boyd River. Access is via Mount Victoria and the Jenolan Caves 180 km west of Sydney.*

To the southeast of Kanangra-Boyd and the Blue Mountains National Park is the 860 sq km, **Nattai National Park** gazetted in 1991. It touches the region's largest body of water, Lake Burragorang, and contains the region's largest populations of eastern grey kangaroos as well as many rare plants and animals like the Camden gum and the superbly named long-nosed potoroo. ■ *Basic NPWS camping near the lake. Access is 110 km south of Sydney between the Warragamba Dam and Wombeyan Caves Rd.*

The smallest national park in the group is the 12,000 ha **Gardens of Stone National Park**, north of Lithgow. Adjoining Wollemi, it's most noted for its prominent and shapely limestone outcrops and sandstone escarpments. Bird life is prolific. ■ *No campsites. Access is 30 km north of Lithgow via Mudgee Rd.*

Glenbrook to Wentworth Falls

Proud of its European roots and its railway heritage, the pretty village of **Glenbrook**, just beyond the Nepean River, acts as the unofficial gateway to the Blue Mountains. Fringing the village, south of the highway, is the southern section of the Blue Mountains National Park and access to numerous attractions. **Red Hands Cave** is a fine example of Aboriginal rock art. The distinctive hand stencils made on the cave wall are thought to be over 1,600 years old and were made by blowing ochre from the mouth. You can reach the caves either by road or by foot (8 km return) from the Glenbrook Creek causeway, just beyond the park entrance. There are also shorter walks to the **Jellybean Pool** and the **Euroka Clearing** with a basic NPWS campsite and the ideal spot to see grey kangaroos, especially early or late in the day. To reach the park gate ($5 day-use, walkers free), take Ross Road behind the VIC on to Burfitt Parade and then follow Bruce Road. The lookouts at **The Bluff** at the end of Brook Road (slightly further east off Burfitt, then Grey) are also worth a look and provide a taste of better things to come. North of the highway in Glenbrook you can also follow signs to the **Lennox Bridge**, the oldest in Australia, built by convicts in 1833. Built the way it was (within a year) it certainly looks as if it will remain so well into the new millennium. Nearby in Knapsack Park the **Marge's and Elizabeth Lookouts** provide great views back towards the western suburbs and Sydney.

Beyond Blaxland and Springwood is the small settlement of Faulconbridge, home to the **Norman Lindsay Gallery and Museum**. Lindsay (1879-1969) is just one of many noted artists that have found the Blue Mountains conducive to their creativity. He was particularly well known for his depictions of female nudes, which at the time caused more than a little controversy. In contrast, his children's book *The Magic Pudding* (1918) is an Australian classic. His studio (if not his models) remains very much the way he left it. ■ *Daily 1000-1600, $8, child $4, T4751 1067. 14 Norman Lindsay Crescent.*

For most, it is the stunning lookouts across **Wentworth Falls** and the **Jamieson Valley** that offer the first memorable introduction to the dramatic, precipitous and spacious scenery of the Blue Mountains. But having said that, don't count on it. Sometimes, when the clouds seem intent on meeting you personally, the experience can be little more than an unremarkable view of the car park. However, if the weather is good, the car park heralds the start of some superb walking tracks that take in viewpoints around the falls and some mighty precipitous sections down to their base. The best is the four-hour **Wentworth Pass Walk** that crosses the top of the falls, and then descends precariously down to the valley floor. If that were not enough, the track skirts the cliff base, through rainforest, before climbing back up via the dramatic Valley of the Waters gorge to the Conservation Hut. There you can reward yourself with a good coffee before completing the adventure with an easy walk back to the car park. Another alternative is the five-hour **National Pass Walk** that quite remarkably follows a cutting half way up the cliff that was miraculously carved out in the 1890s. Both are hard and certainly not for the agoraphobic, involving steep sections around cliff edges and laddered sections, but if you are able, either one is highly recommended. Give yourself plenty of time and make sure you get maps from the Conservation Hut before setting out. Some improvements are being made to both tracks and the base section of the Wentworth Pass can also be a little vague at times, so go prepared. If you are short of time, or are looking for something less demanding, try the **Den Fenella Track**, which will take you to some good lookouts, then you can return or preferably keep going (west) to the Conservation Hut along the Overcliff Track. Better still is the magical **Undercliff Track** to Princes Rock Lookout.

Around Sydney

Sleeping & eating

Wentworth has plenty of good **B&Bs** that offer a quieter alternative to those in Leura and Katoomba. VIC in Glenbrook or Katoomba or see www.bluemountainstourism.org.au for options. Book ahead. The café in the **Conservation Hut** (see Tourist information) offers light snacks and good coffee (as well as info, maps, etc). Open daily 0900-1700.

Transport

Blue Mountains Bus Company, T4782 4213, runs between Katoomba and Woodford.

Leura

Although the pretty village of Leura plays second fiddle to Katoomba, the two, essentially merge. With its distinct air of elegance, the residents of Leura are proud of their village and in particular their gardens that all change colourfully with the seasons.

Colour map 1, grid B2
Population: 4,000
107 km west of Sydney, 3 km east of Katoomba

The **Mall** forms the main thoroughfare with plenty of interesting shops, cafés and restaurants. **Candy Store** in the Strand Arcade will send anyone with a sweet tooth into a veritable frenzy, while **Megalong Books** on the Mall is the place to go for Blue Mountains books and maps. If you have kids in tow, or have a muted interest in toys and railways, then the **Leuralla and NSW Toy and Railway Museum** is well worth a muse, hosting lots of the old favourites including 'Noddy', 'Action Man' and 'Barbie', as well as train sets and memorabilia galore. ■ *Daily 1000-1700. $6, child $2. T4784 1169. Olympian Parade.*

A short stroll west of the museum is the **Gordon Falls Lookout**, which is worth a wee look. There are several other walks and lookouts around the cliff fringes in Leura with the best being the short 500 m walk to the aptly named **Sublime Lookout**. Reached alongside the equally sublime golf course on Watkins Road, this viewpoint offers arguably the best view of the Jamieson Valley and Mount Solitary. Follow signs from Gladstone Road, west of The Mall.

Everglades Gardens provide the best horticultural showpiece and has done since the early 1930s. ■ *Daily 1000-1700, $6, child $2, T4784 1938. 37 Everglades Ave.*

Sleeping & eating
On map, page 138

Leura has many excellent historic B&Bs and self-contained cottages. **LL** *Manderley*, 157 Megalong St, T47843252, www.bluemts.com.au/manderley, and the more affordable **L-A** *Peartree Cottage*, Holmes St, T94899195, www.bluemts.com.au/cottages, are 2 fine self-contained options, while **LL-L** *Peppers Fairmont Resort*, 1 Sublime Point Rd, T4782 5222, www.peppers.com.au, has a fine reputation and offers luxuriously appointed rooms and suites, as well as all the usual amenities including a restaurant, bar, pool, spa and massage. It is also very handy to the golf course. Of the many fine restaurants and cafés the *Silk's Brasserie*, 128 The Mall, T47842534, offers fine modern Australian cuisine. Open daily for lunch and dinner. Book ahead.

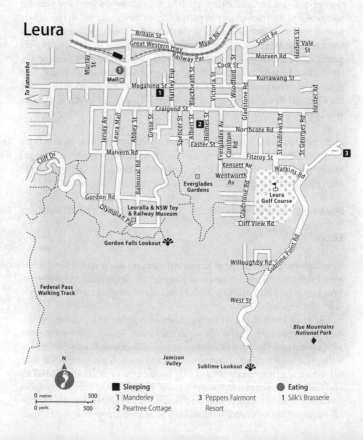

■ **Sleeping**
1 Manderley
2 Peartree Cottage

3 Peppers Fairmont Resort

● **Eating**
1 Silk's Brasserie

Katoomba and around

Considered the capital of the Blue Mountains, the historic town of Katoomba offers an interesting mix of old and new and a truly cosmopolitan ambience that attests to its development over the decades from a small mining village and well-to-do tourist destination, to a bustling commercial conglomerate. As well as the wealth of amenities and activities based in the town many come here simply to see the archetypal, two-dimensional postcard image of the Blue Mountains transformed into the real thing from the famous **Three Sisters** lookout at Echo Point.

Colour map 1, grid B2
Population: 18,000
122 km west of Sydney, 43 km southeast of Lithgow

Getting there The train station is the main transport hub of the area with the main coach companies offering services to and from Sydney and other main centres. **Getting around** Once you get to Katoomba there are a number of operators offering general local transportation or specialist sightseeing trips further afield. Main St itself runs parallel with the Great Western Highway and forms a junction with Katoomba's main drag Katoomba St. Katoomba St then runs due south to Lilianfels Ave, and Echo Point Rd, terminating at Echo Point, the VIC and the Three Sisters Lookout. **Tourist information** In addition to the VIC, see page 135, there is a Backpackers Travel Centre, 283 Main St, T4782 5342.

Ins & outs
See Transport, pages 134 and 143, for further details

A steady stream of tourist traffic floods consistently and relentlessly down Katoomba's main drag towards **Echo Point** where cascades of sightseers celebrate the Blue Mountains' most famous vista – the **Three Sisters**. Like the golden ramparts of some grandiose tectonic castle they offer the perfect glowing foreground to the expansive backdrop of the forested **Jamieson Valley** and the distant sandstone bluffs of **Mount Solitary**. It is little wonder the place is so popular, since here you can see, in effect, the true essence of the Blue Mountains, their grandeur and their colour in a scene that seems ever changing with the weather and the light. Built precariously 170 m above the valley floor the lookout also seems to defy gravity. The only low point is the crowds that come and go, so go at dawn and sunset, or in the evening the stacks are spotlit (though strangely, after the spectacle in sunlight, this can be disappointing).

Sights

From the lookout it is possible to walk around to the stacks and descend the taxing **Giant Stairway Walk** (30 minutes) to the valley floor. From there you join the **Federal Pass Track**, back through the forest below the cliffs to the **Katoomba Cascades** and **Orphan Rock**. As the name suggests it is a single pillar that became separated from the nearby cliff over many centuries of erosion. From Orphan Rock it is a short walk to a choice of exits: the hard option, on foot, up the 1,000-step Furbers Steps, or for the less adventurous, the **Scenic Railway**. Give yourself three hours for the complete circuit.

Other than the Federal Pass challenge (above), Katoomba presents many other excellent walking options, including the **Narrow Neck Plateau** (variable times) and **The Ruined Castle** (12 km, seven hours). The latter starts from the base of the Scenic Railway and can be made as part of an extended overnight trip to the summit of Mount Solitary. Recommended, but go prepared. **Grand Canyon** walk (5 km, four hours) from Neates Glen, Evans Lookout Rd, Blackheath, is also a cracker.

West of Echo Point, the junction of Cliff Drive and Violet Street will deliver you to the highly commercial **Scenic World**, with its trilogy of unusual scenic transportations and insidious attempts to make you revisit your breakfast. **Scenic Railway** option takes you on an exhilarating descent to the valley floor on what is reputed to be the world's steepest 'inclined funicular railway' –

Around Sydney

another way of describing a hairy 415 m tandem skydive in a tram. At the bottom you can then take a boardwalk through the forest to see an old coal mine with an audio-visual display and bronze sculpture. In contrast, the **Scenic Skyway** option at least keeps the angles and nerves within the realms of worldly physics and biochemistry, as well as providing a bird's-eye view of the

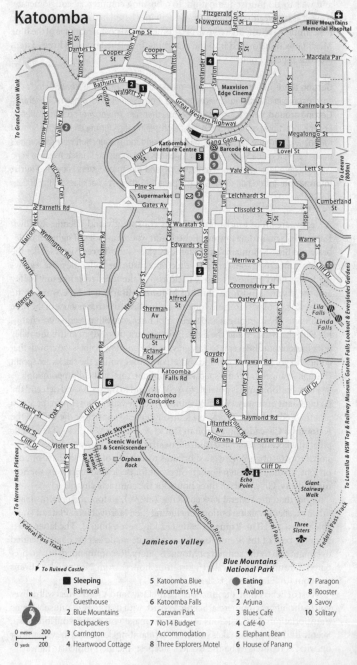

Katoomba

Around Sydney

■ Sleeping	5 Katoomba Blue	● Eating	7 Paragon
1 Balmoral	Mountains YHA	1 Avalon	8 Rooster
Guesthouse	6 Katoomba Falls	2 Arjuna	9 Savoy
2 Blue Mountains	Caravan Park	3 Blues Café	10 Solitary
Backpackers	7 No14 Budget	4 Café 40	
3 Carrington	Accommodation	5 Elephant Bean	
4 Heartwood Cottage	8 Three Explorers Motel	6 House of Panang	

valley floor and the surrounding cliffs. The last in the trio, and the latest addition, is the modern **Scenicscender**, which is like a combination of the two. If you survive that there is a cinema showing a Blue Mountains documentary and a revolving restaurant. ■ *Daily 0900-1700, Railway and Scenicsender $12 (one way $6), Skyway $10. T47822699, www.scenicworld.com.au*

Maxvision Edge Cinema, with its six-storey, 18 m high, 24 m wide screen, is worth seeing, offering an action packed and distinctly precipitous film of the Blue Mountains. Of more environmental and historical interest is the segment about the Polemic Pine, an entirely unknown and distinctly senescent species that was discovered in the deepest wilderness areas of the Wollemi National Park, apparently causing an almost audible stir within the world's botanical community. ■ *Daily, shows at 1030/1200/1330/1425 and 1730. $13.50. T4782 8900. 225 Great Western Highway.*

There is plenty of choice in and around Katoomba, from historic hotels to showpiece backpackers. Prices rise at weekends and at any time of year, but especially winter, you are advised to book ahead.

LL-L *Carrington Hotel*, 15-47 Katoomba St, T4782 1111, www.thecarrington.com.au, is an old classic hotel, built originally in 1882 and lavishly refurbished in 1998. It offers an elegant, historic and congenial atmosphere, with everything from open fires and stained glass windows, to a classy billiards room. The rooms are beautifully appointed and there is a fine à la carte restaurant, bar, nightclub and spa. Recommended. For a motel option try the locally recommended and unconventional **L-B** *Three Explorers Motel*, 197 Lurline St, T4782 1733, www.3explorers.com.au They also offer a nice fully self-contained 2-bedroom cottage. There are a fine choice of historic B&Bs, lodges and self-contained cottages in and around town including the long-established **LL-L** *Balmoral Guesthouse*, 196 Bathurst Rd, T4782 2264, www.bluemts.com.au/balmoral, that has been welcoming guests since 1876. It is large and has plenty of old world charm, period decor, en suites with spa, log fires, bar and is close to all amenities. More modern is the **L** *Heartwood Cottage*, 56 Station St, T4782 3942, a charming, quiet and cosy, self-contained, 2-bedroom cottage with a log fire. Excellent complimentary breakfast.

Pitched both at mid-range and backpackers is **A-E** *Katoomba Blue Mountains YHA*, 207 Katoomba St, T4782 1416, bluemountains@yhansw.org.au Recently and beautifully renovated within an Art Deco building it is something of a showpiece hostel for the YHA and fast developing a reputation as one of its best. It's modern, spacious, well facilitated, friendly and most certainly recommended. Trips are gladly arranged and there is bike hire and internet. Other budget options include the long-established and sociable **C-E** *Blue Mountains Backpackers*, 190 Bathurst St, T1800 624226. The owners also run the Katoomba Adventure Centre, so there is plenty of good advice surrounding local activities, especially walks. **C-E** *No14 Budget Accommodation*, 14 Lovel St, T4782 7104, www.bluemts.com.au/no14, is another alternative providing a peaceful, relaxed atmosphere in a old former guesthouse with double/twin, single and family rooms. **A-E** *Katoomba Falls Caravan Park*, Katoomba Falls Rd, T4782 1835, is well located and offers standard cabins, powered and non-powered sites and a camp kitchen.

Being so close to Sydney and attracting so many rampant gourmands, Katoomba and the Blue Mountains generally pride themselves in offering some classy restaurants and fine cuisine. For the more expensive restaurants you are advised to book ahead.

Expensive *Solitary*, 90 Cliff Dr, T4782 1164, is a very classy award winner with a fine reputation offering imaginative modern Australian cuisine and fine views across the

Sleeping
■ *On map, page 140*

See inside front cover for price categories

Eating
● *On map, page 140*

See inside front cover for price categories

Around Sydney

Jamieson Valley. Open lunch Sat/Sun and public/school holidays and dinner Tue-Sat. *The Avalon*, 18 Katooma St, T4782 5532, is a more relaxed but classy restaurant located upstairs in the town's old Art Deco theatre. It is especially noted for its generous servings and its valley views.

Mid-range   *The Savoy*, 26 Katoomba St, T4782 5050, is locally recommended for good value and especially for its conventional and kangaroo steak dishes. Open daily 1100-2200. *Arjuna*, 16 Valley Rd, T4782 4662, is the best Indian restaurant in the region and the views are almost as hot as the curry. Open Thu-Mon from 1800. Book ahead. Also offering fine views is *The Rooster Restaurant*, *Jamieson Guest House*, 48 Merriwa St, T4782 1206. It is an old favourite that serves good-value French-influenced cuisine. Open daily for dinner and for lunch Sat/Sun. The accommodation is also very good.

Cheap   *House of Panang*, 183 Katoomba St, T4782 6222, is a good value, no nonsense Malaysian restaurant. For a great breakfast in a relaxed atmosphere try *Café 40*, 40 Katoomba St, T4782 4063. Open daily 0700-2200. *Elephant Bean*, 159 Katoomba St, T4782 4620, is another fine café and recommended for lunch. Open Wed-Mon 0800-1500. For vegetarian food look no further than *Blues Café*, 57 Katoomba St, T4782 2347. Open daily 0900-1700. Finally if you have a sweet tooth you just cannot afford to miss out on a Katoomba institution – the Art Deco *Paragon*, 65 Katoomba St, T4782 2928. Open daily 0800-1700. The main supermarket is on Parke St opposite the post office.

Shopping   Camping equipment/adventure activity supplies and hire *Katoomba Adventure Centre*, 1 Katoomba St, T1800 624226, and *Paddy Pallin*, 166 Katoomba St, T4782 4466.

Tours & activities
The VIC has full listings

Walking, rock climbing, canyoning, mountain biking and abseiling are the 5 major activities in the Blue Mountains and several Katoomba-based operators offer supervised package deals. Other options include horse riding, 4WD adventures and numerous day tours to several major attractions like the Jenolan Caves or the stunning Kanangra-Boyd National Park.

Local operators include the very clued-up and eco-friendly folks at the *Katoomba Adventure Centre*, 1 Katoomba St, T1800 624226, www.kacadventures.com.au, offering great advice on independent walking as well as numerous adventure options, including abseiling from $99, canyoning (rappelling) from $99, rock climbing from $109 and adventure walks (Recommended), from $64. Others companies include *High 'N' Wild*, 3/5 Katoomba St T4782 6224, www.high-n-wild.com.au, who offer good mountain biking trips in particular. *Australian School of Mountaineering*, 182 Katoomba St, T4782 2014, www.ausmtn.com.au, offer hard-core professional rock climbing and bush craft trips (amongst others) and the reputable *Blue Mountains Adventure Company*, 84a Bathurst Rd, T4782 1271, www.bmac.com.au, is another worth looking at. For japes on 4 legs try *Blue Mountain Horse Riding Adventures*, T47878688, www.megalong.cc, located in the Megalong Valley west of Katoomba, offering hour/half/full and multi-day rides from $22. Their Pub Ride holds infinite appeal. *Getabout 4WD Adventures*, T9831 8385, www.getabout.com.au, offer professional 4WD tours with a tag-along option allowing you to take your own vehicle. For eco tours ask about Ranger Guided Walks and activity adventures with the NPWS at the Heritage Centre at Govetts Leap, Blackheath. Tim Tranter's *Tread Lightly Eco-tours*, T4788 1229, www.treadlightly.com.au, are good, with plenty of Aboriginal insight.

There are a number of operators offering general local transportation or specialist sightseeing trips further afield. *Blue Mountains Explorer Double-Decker Bus*,

T4782 4807, www.explorerbus.com.au, offers a local service with 27 stops around Katoomba and Leura, hourly between 0930 and 1730. An unlimited jump-on/off day pass costs $25, child $12.50. Alternatively, the *Blue Mountains Bus Co* T47824213 offer a standard Hail 'n' Ride service around Katoomba, Leura and Wentworth Falls Mon-Fri from 0745-2025, Sat 0800-1530, Sun 0915-1530, from $2. *Mountainlink,* 285 Main St, T1800801577, operate a 29-stop trolley bus tour around the main sights of Katoomba and Leura, with an all day unlimited stop travel pass, daily from 1015-1615, for $12. *Fantastic Aussie Tours* (located just outside the train station), 283 Main St, T4782 1866, www.fantastic-aussie-tours.com.au, offer a wide range of tour-based options from coach and 4WD adventure tours, to gourmet trails, visiting sights as far away as the Jenolan Caves.

Bike hire Available from *Cycletech*, 182 Katoomba St, T47822800, 19-50 per day. **Bus** *Greyhound*, T132030, offer standard daily coach transportation on the westbound run from Sydney to Dubbo, stopping behind the train station near *Gearin Hotel*, Great Western Highway. *CityRail*, T131500, in conjunction with *Fantastic Aussie Tours*, T1300300915, also offer a number of rail/coach tour options with *Blue MountainsLink* operating Mon-Fri and *Blue Mountains ExplorerLink* operating daily. Prices include return transport and a tour on arrival in Katoomba. **Car hire** Available from *Thrifty*, 80 Megalong St, Leura, T4782 4288. **Train** Katoomba train station, T4782 1902, acts as the main transport hub within the town and is conveniently located off Main St, at the northern end of Katoomba St. *Countrylink*, T132232, offer daily services to/from Sydney hourly. **Taxi** *Katoomba Radio Cabs*, T4782 1311 operate a 24 hr taxi service between Mount Victoria and Wentworth Falls.

Transport
See also Tours & activities above for getting around the area

Banks Most major bank branches with ATMs are located along Katoomba St. **Communications** Internet: available at *Barcode 6ix Café*, 6 Katoomba St, T4782 6896. Open daily 0900-2100. Good coffee. *Katoomba Adventure Centre*, 1 Katoomba St, T1800 624226. **Post office: Katoomba Post Office**, behind Katoomba St, on Pioneer Pl. Open Mon-Fri 0900-1700. **Medical services** Hospital Blue Mountains Memorial, Great Western Highway, 1 km east of the town centre, T4784 6500. **Useful numbers** NRMA: T4782 2280. **Police**: 217 Katoomba St, T4782 8199.

Directory

Medlow Bath, Blackheath and Megalong Valley

From Katoomba the Great Western Highway heads north through the pretty villages of Medlow Bath, Blackheath and Mount Victoria. Although not as commercial as their bustling neighbour, all provide excellent accommodation and restaurants, and are fringed both north and south by equally stunning views and excellent walks. To the west is the easily accessible **Megalong Valley** which is particularly well known for its horse trekking, while to the east, in contrast, is the **Grose Valley**, largely inaccessible aesthetic stunner and the great barrier to many an early Sydney explorer. The **Evans** and **Govetts Leap** Lookouts, east of Blackheath, provide the best easily accessible viewpoints, but there are also some lesser known spots well worth a visit.

Colour map 1, grid B2

In Medlow Bath nature's architecture gives way momentarily to the human form, with the historic **Hydro Majestic Hotel**. Built in 1903 it was, at the time, the longest building in Australia and, given its clifftop position, could also boast some of the most beautiful views. Though a hotel in its own right, its original, primary function was as a sanatorium, offering all manner of health therapies, from mud baths to spas, not to mention the strict abstinence from alcohol. At the time the rarefied air in the Blue Mountains was hailed as a

Medlow Bath

Around Sydney

▶ **Who was Govett and did he survive?**

Govetts Leap is named after pioneer surveyor William Govett, who was not, as the name of the lookout suggests, Australia's first hang glider, but a man renowned for possessing a desire to throw rocks off any high place he encountered.

Mr Govett, in the absence of modern-day technologies, was a man using basic physics to gauge the height of any particular precipice. By counting the seconds it took for the rock to fall to the bottom he could (so he said) calculate the height to the exact metre. Apparently, on more than one occasion, he was spot on! Govetts Leap is a heady 160 m.

remedy for all city ills and people flocked to the Hydro to 'take the cure'. Today although the mud baths (and thankfully the prohibition) have gone, the hotel still provides fine accommodation and a great spot for afternoon tea.

Blackheath Blackheath is a sleepy little village with a lovely atmosphere enhanced in autumn when the trees take on golden hues like some European autumnal flag. There are two lookouts well worth visiting.

The first, **Evans Lookout**, is accessed east along Evans Lookout Road and provides the first of many viewpoints across the huge and dramatic expanse of the Grose Valley. One of the best walks in the region, The Grand Canyon Trail, departs from Neates Glen, off Evans Lookout Road (5 km, five hours). From there you descend down through the rainforest and follow Greaves Creek through moss-covered rock tunnels and overhangs, before climbing back up to Evans Lookout. It is recommended.

The other lookout, **Govetts Leap**, is a stunner and has the added attraction of the Bridal Veil Falls, the highest (though not necessarily the most dramatic) in the Blue Mountains. It is certainly a memorable view and one Charles Darwin once described in 1836 as 'stupendous' (which these days equates to something far stronger!). Just before the lookout car park is the NPWS Heritage Centre, which is worth a visit providing up-to-date walks information, maps, guide and gifts. Fairfax Heritage Track, built to accommodate wheelchairs, links the centre with the lookout. From Govetts Leap you can walk either north to reach Pulpit Rock or south to Evans Lookout via the falls.

Although Govetts and Evans are both stunning, three other superb lookouts await your viewing pleasure and can be accessed from Blackheath. These are often missed, but no less spectacular. The first, **Pulpit Rock**, can be reached by foot from Govetts (2.5 km, 1½ hours) or better still by 2WD via Hat Hill Road. The lookout, which sits on the summit of a rock pinnacle, is accessed from the car park by a short 500 m walk.

From the same car park then continue north (unsealed road) to Anvil Rock, being sure not to miss the other short track to the bizarre geology of the wind-eroded cave. **Perry Lookdown** is 1 km before Anvil Rock and a path from there descends into the valley to connect with some demanding walking trails.

Also well worth a visit is **Hanging Rock**, a Blue Mountains icon. It can be reached along a rough, unsealed track (Ridgewell Road), on the right, just beyond Blackheath heading north. Although best suited to 4WD it is just possible to take a 2WD vehicle slowly in dry conditions. But if in doubt – don't. You can always resort to a local 4WD tour since most venture there. At the terminus of the track you reach the impressive **Baltzer Lookout**. But just to the right and out of immediate view, Hanging Rock will, on first sight, take your breath away. It is indeed aptly named and the heights are simply mind bending. Watch your footing and DO NOT attempt to climb to the point as tempting as it may be. It is a favourite abseiling spot, but only for the well equipped and utterly insane. Like all the other lookouts on the southern fringe of the Grose Valley, sunrise is by far the best time to visit.

This valley, accessed on Megalong Valley Road, west of Blackheath town centre, provides a pleasant scenic drive and is one of the most accessible and most developed of the wilderness Blue Mountains valleys. **Megalong Australian Heritage Centre** is described as an 'Outback Ranch in the Mountains' and although the word 'mountains' does not (like the rest of the Blueys) exactly fit with convention, the homestead actually does, offering a whole range of activities from horse trekking and 4WD adventures, to livestock shows. Accommodation is also available and there is a bistro restaurant. ■ *Daily 0730-1800. Horse trekking from $22, T4787 8688, www.megalong.cc.au*

Megalong Valley

LL *Hydro Majestic Hotel*, Great Western Highway, Medlow Bath, T4788 1002, www.hydromajestic.com.au Worth staying in purely for the historical aspect, the architecture and especially the views. Recently completely renovated inside, it offers luxury rooms and suites (some with spa and valley views) plus all the amenities you might expect. **LL-L** *Possums Hideaway*, 185 Evans Lookout Rd, Blackheath, T4787 7767, www.possumshideaway.com Ideal for a romantic night is this series of studio-style poled cabins in a quiet bush setting, with log fires and double spas. **LL-L** *Jemby-Rinjah Eco Lodge*, 336 Evans Lookout Rd, Blackheath, T4/877622, www.jembyrinjahlodge.com.au Offers either 1- or 2-bedroom, self-contained, modern cabins (one with a Japanese hot tub), log fires, all in a beautiful bush setting close to the lookout and walks. Dinner, bed and breakfast packages are also available. **L-B** *Glenella Guesthouse*, 56 Govetts Leap Rd, Blackheath, T4787 8352, is a well-known, surprisingly affordable, historic guesthouse, with a reputable restaurant attached, plus all the comforts including sauna, open fires and cable TV. **LL-C** *Imperial Hotel*, 1 Station St, Mount Victoria, T47871878, www.bluemts.com.au/hotelimperial, is reputedly the oldest tourist hotel in Australia. Beautifully restored, it is a fine place to soak up the history. Wide range of well-appointed rooms from the traditional to the 4-poster with double spa. Breakfast included, good restaurant, bar and live entertainment at the weekends. **A-E** *Blackheath Caravan Park*, Prince Edward St, Blackheath, T47878101. In a quiet suburban bush setting and within walking distance of the village. On-site vans, powered and non-powered sites, BBQ and kiosk, but no camp kitchen.

Sleeping

These villages provide excellent overnight options away from the bustle of the Blue Mountains capital

Other than the *Glenella Guesthouse* and the *Imperial* (see above) there are several notable eateries in Blackheath. The very classy French-style *Cleopatra*, 118 Cleopatra St, T4787 8456, is actually a guesthouse, but has won so many awards for its cuisine; it is often dubbed the 'restaurant with accommodation'. It is expensive but worth it. Open Tue-Sun for dinner, lunch on Sun. A more affordable but equally well-known Blackheath institution is *Vulcans*, 33 Govetts Leap Rd, T4787 6899. Superb coffee and great meals, but its only drawback is the limited opening times, Fri-Sun for lunch and dinner.

Eating

Medlow Bath, Blackheath and Mount Victoria are all on the main local bus/train routes to/from Katoomba. See Katoomba, page 142, for operator listings. The train station is in the centre of Mount Victoria off the Great Western Highway and on Station St, off the Great Western Highway.

Transport

Around Sydney

Lithgow

Colour map 1, grid B2
Population: 11,500
161 km from Sydney

Lithgow marks the western boundary of the Blue Mountains and was founded in 1827 by explorer Hamilton Hume. An industrial town and Australia's first producer of steel, its main tourist attraction is the nearby, remarkable **Zig Zag Railway**, as well as a scattering of historical buildings. The town also acts as the gateway to the **Jenolan Caves**, see below, and **Kanangra-Boyd National Park** to the south, see page 136, and the wilderness **Wollemi National Park** to the north, see page 135.

Sights There are three fairly low-key museums in the town. Firstly there is the **State Mine and Heritage Park and Railway** that outlines the town's proud links with coal mining and the railway. ■ *Sat/Sun 1000-1600, State Mine Gully Rd (off Atkinson St)*. Then there is **Lithgow Small Arms Museum**, that recalls the history of a local small arms factory. ■ *Sat/Sun 1000-1600, $4, child $2*. Finally there is **Eskbank House Museum**, a Georgian homestead built in 1842, complete with period furnishings and Lithgow pottery. ■ *Thu-Mon 1000-1600, $2. Corner of Inch and Bennett sts.*

Of far more natural historical appeal are the ruins of **Newnes** and **Glen Davis** that lie to the north of Lithgow, between the scenic Gardens of Stone National Park and the western fringe of the Wollemi National Park. Both were once thriving villages supporting a population of thousands that worked in the two large oil-shale refineries during the early 1900s. Now lying derelict and being gradually repossessed by the surrounding bush, both possess some fascinating old buildings, which combined create an eerie atmosphere, interrupted only by the calls of birds and the occasional clatter of pigeons' wings. South of Newnes an added attraction is the old 400 m rail tunnel that was once part of a busy line that connected the shale plants with Clarence Station. Now left dark and forbidding, the tunnel is now the silent home of **glow worms** (gnat larvae), which light up its dank walls like a miniature galaxy of stars. All along the unsealed roads to both Newnes and Glen Davis keep your eye open for the prolific bird life, from huge wedge-tailed eagles and raucous flocks of sulphur-crested cockatoos to tiny, iridescent fairy wrens. ■ *Getting there: you need your own transport as there is no public transport and it isn't within walking distance.*

In Clarence, 10 km east of Lithgow, you will find the **Zig Zag Railway**. It is a masterpiece of engineering originally built between 1866 and 1869. Operated commercially up until 1910 as a supply route to Sydney, it now serves as a tourist attraction with lovingly restored steam trains making the nostalgic 8 km (one hour and 20 minutes) journey from Clarence to Bottom Points (near CityRail's Zig Zag Station). ■ *Steam trains leave Clarence on Wed/Sat/Sun at 1100/1300 and 1500. On other weekdays motorized trains take over – same times. $14, child $11. T6353 1795, www.zigzagrailway.com.au Request drop-off if you are arriving by CityRail from Sydney/Katoomba at the Zig Zag Station.*

Transport Lithgow is on the main local and westbound bus/train routes to/from Katoomba and Sydney. The train station is on Main St, *Countrylink*, T132032, and *CityRail*, T131500, both offer regular daily services east and west. See Katoomba, page 142, for tours listings.

Bells Line of Road

Bells Line of Road is named after Archibald Bell, who in 1823, at the age of 19 and with the help of the local Aboriginals, discovered the 'second' route through the Blue Mountains to Lithgow from Sydney. Starting just west of Richmond in the east, then climbing the plateau to fringe the northern rim of the Grose Valley, it provides a quieter, more sedate, scenic trip across the Great Divide and is particularly well renowned for its gardens – best viewed in spring and autumn – and also for its spectacular views.

Just beyond the village of Bilpin, west of Richmond, the huge basalt outcrop of **Mount Tomah** (1,000 m) begins to dominate the scene and supports the 28 ha cool-climate annexe of the Sydney **Botanical Gardens**. Opened in 1987 the garden's rich volcanic soils nurture over 10,000 species, including a huge quantity of tree ferns and rhododendrons. Although the gardens are well worth visiting in their own right, it is the views, the short walks and the restaurant that make them extra special. ■ *Daily 1000-1600, $6, T45672154, www.rbgsyd.nsw.gov.au* Just beyond Mount Tomah is the **Walls Lookout**, with its expansive views across the Grose Valley. It requires a one-hour return walk from the Pierces Pass Track car park but the effort it is well worth it.

Back on the Bells Line of Road and just a few kilometres further west is the junction to the pretty village of **Mount Wilson**, 8 km further on, which is famous for its English-style open gardens. These include Linfield Park. ■ *Daily. $3. Mount Irvine Rd and Nooroo*. Also of interest is the **Cathedral of Ferns**, which are located on the left, at the northern end of the village. **Wynnes and Du Faurs Lookouts** can also be reached from Mount Wilson and are signposted, east and west of the village centre.

Back on the Bells Line of Road you can then head south at Bell (8 km) to join the Great Western Highway at Mount Victoria, or continue west to Clarence (16 km) and Lithgow (29 km).

Jenolan Caves

Jenolan Caves on the northern fringe of the Kanangra-Boyd National Park, south of Lithgow, comprise nine major, and 300 in total, limestone caves considered to be amongst the most spectacular in the southern hemisphere. After over 160 years of exploration and development (since their discovery in 1838 by pastoralist James Whalan), the main caves are now well geared up for your viewing pleasure with a network of paths and electric lighting to guide the way and to highlight the bizarre subterranean features that have taken aeons to form. The strangely shaped stalactites (form downwards) and stalagmites (form upwards) never fail to run riot with the imagination and the guided tours (see below for details) ensure you can learn about their formation and the cave's unique natural history.

Colour map 1, grid B2
Population: 7,000
190 km west of Sydney, 60 km south of Lithgow

If you are short for time the **Lucas Cave** and **Temple of Baal Cave** are generally recommended containing the widest variety of formations. **Chifely Cave** is the most historic and along with **Imperial Cave** it has partial wheelchair access. **River Cave** is said to be one of the most demanding. On your arrival at the caves you immediately encounter the **Grand Arch**, a 60 m wide, 24 m high cavern that was once used for camping and even live entertainment to the flicker of firelight. Nearby the historic and congenial **Caves House** has been welcoming visitors since 1898.

■ *The main caves can only be visited by guided tour, either selectively, or in a combination package, daily 1000-2000, prices range from 1 hr $15, child $10, 2 hr $27.50, to a 3-cave combo from $38.50, child $26.50, T6359 3311, www.jenolancaves.org.au As well as guided cave tours, some other caves have been set aside for adventure caving and, above ground, a network of pleasant bush trails satisfy the claustrophobics.*

Around Sydney

Sleeping & eating There is plenty of accommodation in and around Jenolan, from the historic *Caves House* and quiet self-contained cottages, to basic campsites. The grand and multi-facilitated **LL-F** *Jenolan Caves Resort*, T6359 3322, www.jenolancaves.com.au, includes the gracious *Caves House* that offers a range of traditional rooms and suites, as well as modern lodge units, self-contained cottages and a basic campsite. The resort is very well facilitated with an à la carte restaurant, bistro, bar and a host of organized activities. Another good, affordable alternative is **L-A** *Jenolan Cabins*, Porcupine Hill, 42 Edith Rd, T6335 6239, www.bluemts.com.au/JenolanCabins Each self-contained cabin accommodates 6 with 1 queen size and bunks, a log fire and TV. The owners also operate local tours, www.bluemts.com.au/Jenolan4WD

Transport There is no public transport but numerous tour operators in Katoomba and Sydney can oblige with day-tour packages. A basic day tour to the caves will cost about $70 exclusive of cave tour, $80 with one cave inspection and $150 with one cave inspection and a spot of adventure caving. The VICs in Katoomba or Sydney have full details.

Hawkesbury River Region

Colour map 1, grid B3
184 km return

The Hawkesbury River Region and the small villages of Wisemans Ferry, and St Albans in particular, provides a very pleasant day trip and quiet escape from the city. Hawkesbury River is one of New South Wales' longest and most historic waterways. It terminates in a large, scenic harbour at the northern fringe of the Ku-ring-gai Chase National Park. The harbour itself, which is a playground for boaties, is of considerable geographical importance dividing two regions. The southern shore, essentially the Ku-ring-gai Chase National Park, is the boundary or fringe of Greater Sydney and the northern shore is the start of the Central Coast.

From the historic village of **Wisemans Ferry**, it is possible to cross the river on the oldest ferry crossing in Australia. Remarkably the three-minute crossing is still free and open 24 hours. Once across, head north through the beautiful **Mogo River Valley** into the southern fringes of the Darugh and Yengo national parks to **St Albans** (21 km). From St Albans or Wellums Lake you can then take the road on the other side of the river back to Wisemans Ferry and Sydney.

The accredited VICs in Clarendon, Bicentenary Park, T4588 5895, or Brooklyn 2/5 Bridge St, T9985 7947, www.hawkesburyriver.org.au, have detailed information on this area. Local information is available in the *Coffee House* on Old Northern Road, T9651 4411. Open daily 0900-1700.

Sleeping & eating **L-A** *Settlers Arms*, 1 Wharf St, St Albans, T4568 2111. This is a superb 1830s pub, with a tiny stone-floored bar and outdoor seating area. It is an ideal spot for lunch and a lazy afternoon. If you feel like a walk, head a few kilometres further north until the road takes a bend. From there you can walk on a secluded, rough track up to a natural rock lookout across the valley (ask at the pub for directions). On your return, and perhaps after another pint at the *Settlers*, you might want to stay in one of their charming en suite rooms for the night or have a meal by candlelight in the cosy restaurant. Apparently, many of the old colonial pillars of society did so many years ago, in the company of young ladies looking far too young to be their wives. **A** *Wellums Lake Guesthouse*, Lot 1, Wellums Lake, Settlers Rd (3 km south), T4568 2027. Also offers comfortable accommodation and has a great café.

Day cruises up the Hawkesbury River ($30, children $15), or shorter excursions to The Basin (pretty beaches and camping areas in the Ku-ring-gai Chase National Park) are also available from the Palm Beach public wharf, T9997 4815. For more information visit www.sydneynorthernbeaches.com.au

Tours & activities

There is no public transport to Wisemans Ferry or St Albans. By road, from the Sydney CBD, take the Pacific Highway (Highway 1) northeast to Hornsby. Just beyond Hornsby take a left on to Galston Rd to join the Northern Rd (Highway 36). Gradually you will leave the shackles of urbanity behind and begin to reach scenic countryside through Glenorie and Maroota prior to sighting the magnificent Hawkesbury River at Wisemans Ferry (97 km, 45 mins from the CBD).

Transport

Ku-ring-gai Chase National Park

Though a few wealthy Sydney entrepreneurs might see Ku-ring-gai Chase as little more than 14,883 ha of wasted prime real estate, thankfully the rugged sandstone country that fringes the mighty Hawkesbury River, with its stunning views and rich array of native wild animals and plants, is safe from further suburban encroachment and has been since some bright spark, with infinite foresight, decreed it such in 1894. The park is named after the Guringai (Ku-ring-gai) Aboriginals who occupied the region for over 20,000 years before the arrival of nasty European entrepreneurs.

Colour map 1, grid B3 26 km north of Sydney

The park is a great place to see NSW much celebrated state flower – the warratah – in bloom (mid-spring to early summer)

Without doubt the highlight of the park is the **West Head Lookout** that sits high above the peninsula overlooking Pittswater and **Broken Bay** – the mouth of the **Hawkesbury River**. To the north is the beginning of the central coast and Brisbane Water National Park, while to the west is the tip of the Northern Beaches and the historic Barrenjoey Lighthouse.

The park also offers some lovely bush walks, secluded beaches and regionally significant Aboriginal rock art. **West Head** is criss-crossed with walking tracks that start from West Head Road. Aboriginal rock art can be seen along the **Basin Track**. This track leads to **The Basin** which can be reached either by ferry from Palm Beach or by foot taking 2½ hours (7-km long). Here is the Basin Beach campsite (see below) and the arrival/departure point of the Palm Beach ferry, and the 3.5 km **Red Hand Track** (Aboriginal Heritage Track). **Bobbin Head**, at the western end of the park, is a popular base for water-based activities and hosts the VIC plus several more interesting walks around the Cowan Creek foreshore. The VIC on Chase Road (between Mount Colah and Bobbin Head), T9457 9853, open daily 0900-1700, has all the details. See also NPWS Bobbin Head Information Centre, Bobbin Inn, Bobbin Head Road (western side of the park), T9472 8949, daily 1000-1600.

A great place to stay is the **C-E** *Pittwater YHA*, T9999 2196 (see Northern Beaches section, Sydney). The only camping area within the national park is The Basin open all year round to both campers and day picnic visitors. **E The Basin,** T02-99741011, reached by ferry or water taxi from the wharf at Palm Beach or by foot from West Head Rd. Access $9, child $4.50.

Sleeping & eating

Bus/ferry A better alternative to the train is catching bus #L90 to Palm Beach (eastern side) then catch the ferry to Basin Beach. Services leave Palm Beach Wharf for The Basin, every hour on the hour. There is also a daily service leaving from Palm Beach at 1100, arriving at Bobbin Head at 1245. The return service leaves Bobbin Head at 1345 and returns to Palm Beach at 1530. Ferry cruises also run to Bobbin Head (see page 95.

Transport

Around Sydney

Car Access is via Bobbin Head Rd, via the Pacific Highway (from the south) or from Ku-ring-gai Chase Rd via F3 Freeway (from the north). Access to the eastern side (West Head Rd and West Head Lookout) is from Mona Vale Rd, Northern Beaches. Vehicle entry costs $10 per day. **Train** *CityRail*, T131500 (Northern Line) from Central Station to Berowa, Mount Ku-ring-gai and Mount Colah, then walk to Bobbin Head (3-6 km).

Royal National Park

Colour map 1, grid C3
32 km south of Sydney

The 15,080 ha Royal National Park was the first national park in Australia, gazetted in 1879. Before the Europeans arrived the park looked very different from the scene that confronts you today. Back then, before European farming practices and the loss of native wildlife caused drastic changes to the vegetation, the park looked something akin to English parkland with short grasslands interspersed with huge eucalyptus. Today the vegetation has altered, with smaller gums competing with much more ground cover. This ironically has created what today is the park's greatest threat – fire. More than once in the last decade the Royal has been almost completely (but temporarily) destroyed by bush fires that feed on the copious fuel that once never existed. So today, as well as providing over 100 km of walking tracks, many taking in terrific ocean views, and hosting some beautiful beaches and other activities ranging from swimming to scuba diving, it is in a way, above all, a monument to modern man's ultimate folly and his systematic and often unconscious destruction of the fragile Australian environment.

The main hub of human activity centres around historic **Audley** at the park's northern entrance, where you will find the NPWS Royal National Park Visitors Centre, Farnell Avenue, T9542 0648. Open daily 0830-1630. They can provide park maps, detailed information on walks and all other activities. Ranger-guided walks are often available.

Wattamolla, **Garie** and **Burning Palms** are said to be three of the states most beautiful beaches, which is a hard call! Given the considerable competition, whether they actually live up to that reputation is debatable, but there is no doubting that they are areas of great beauty. The choice of walks ranges from the 500 m (wheelchair accessible) **Bungoona Track** to the 26 km **Coast Track** (Bundeena to Otford) that is a regional favourite. It guarantees some glorious coastal views and from June to September the odd whale sighting.

Sleeping
F The main NPWS campsite is at Bonnie Vale (on Bundeena Drive at the northeastern corner of the park near Bundeena) from $7.50, child $4. There are other more basic campsites at North Era Beach along the coast track and at the Uloola Falls on the Uloola Track.

Tours &
activities
You can hire rowboats and canoes at the Audley Boatshed, near the visitors' centre for a leisurely paddle up Kangaroo Creek. Mountain bikes are also available for hire but trail routes are limited and there is good surfing at the patrolled Garie Beach. Several freshwater pools also provide sheltered swimming with the Deer Pool, near Marley Beach, being the most popular.

Transport
Car From Sydney take the Princes Highway south and follow signs for Audley (left, at Loftus on Farnell Ave and McKell Ave). 40 mins drive. Vehicle entry costs $10 per day.
Train Take *CityRail*, T131500 (Illawara line) from Central Station to Loftus (4 km from

Audley), Engadine, Heathcote, Waterfall or Otford. You can also alight at Cronulla and take the short crossing by ferry to Bundeena at the park's northeastern corner, T9523 2990, from $3.

Botany Bay National Park

Botany Bay holds a very special place in Australian (European) history as the site of Captain Cook's first landing in April 1770. The landing site is near what is now **Kurnell** on the southern shores of Botany Bay, which, along with **La Perouse** on the northern shore, comes under the auspices of the 458 ha Botany Bay National Park. As well as possessing highly significant historical sites for both the European and Aboriginal cultures it presents plenty of walking opportunities and ocean views. Joseph Banks, the naturalist on board *The Endeavour*, named the bay on arrival in 1770.

Colour map 1, grid C3
15-30 km south of Sydney

Within the small **northern sector** of the park, around **La Perouse** on the northern headland, you can take a tour of **Bare Island Fort** which was erected amidst wartime paranoia and the perceived threat of foreign invasion. ■ *Guided tours on Sat/Sun, $7.70, child $5.50, T9247 5033.* Also located on the headland is the **La Perouse Museum and Visitors Centre** that stands on the actual site of the first landing of the First Fleet in 1788. The museum explores the great historical event and the fate of French explorer Captain La Perouse, as well as local Aboriginal and European heritage. ■ *Wed-Sun 1000-1600, $5.50, child $3.30, T9311 3379. Cable Station, Anzac Pde.*

The **southern sector** is larger and hosts the NPWS Discovery Centre (see below) and the best walks including the short, 1 km **Monument Track**, that passes several historical markers surrounding Cook's landing and the more demanding **Coast Walk** to Bailey lighthouse.

In the southern sector of the park the NPWS Botany Bay National Park Discovery Centre, Cape Solander Drive, T9668 9111, is a good source of park and walks information and hosts an interesting display surrounding Cook's landing as well as the usual natural history aspects. Open Monday to Friday 1100-1500, and Saturday to Sunday 1000-1630.

Bus Access to the northern sector is via Anzac Pde. *Sydney Buses*, T131500, offer regular daily bus services from Railway Sq (#393) or Circular Quay (#394) in Sydney's CBD. **Car** To get to the southern sector by car, follow the Princes Highway south, take a left on to The Boulevarde, and then follow Captain Cook Dr. Vehicle entry to the park costs $6. **Train** From Sydney's Central Station, take *CityRail* T131500, to Cronulla (Illawara line), then *Kurnell Bus*, T9523 4047, #987 to the park gates.

Transport

Around Sydney

Botany Bay National Park

Introducing North Coast NSW

The north coast of New South Wales stretches almost 900 km from Sydney to Tweed Heads and forms a near utopia for both mind and body, with its seemingly endless string of **coastal towns** and **national parks**, replete with beautiful beaches, bays, headlands and river mouths. There are so many, so similar, that, after a while, they all seem to merge to form a single fond memory, with images of sun-drenched golden sand and crystal clear waters all brought alive to the sound of rolling surf, which becomes like a constant companion. With all this inherent beauty a journey without any planning and afforded little time can often result in an exercise in frustration, as you inevitably clock far more hours on the beach than kilometres on the milometer. But before the great coastal journey begins, just beyond the urban embrace of Greater Sydney, it would perhaps be rude not to tickle your taste buds amidst the vines of the **Hunter Valley**. Hosting over one hundred vineyards and some of Australia's finest labels it offers one of the best opportunities in the country to experience the industry and its quintessential atmosphere.

Back on the coastal trail the industrial landscapes of **Newcastle** quickly give way to the sublime coastal landscapes that will become almost omnipresent. From the attractive settlements fringing **Port Stephens**, through the aquatic playgrounds and surf beaches of the **Myall Lakes National Park**, you are offered a mere taste before **Port Macquarie** provides a brief return to humanity. From there **South West Rocks** is a delightful stop-over before **Coffs Harbour**, **Angourie**, and **Bundjalung National Park** come and go simply adding to the fun and the fast developing tan. For many the most popular destination on the NSW coast is the laid-back tourist Mecca of **Byron Bay** which is often the last port of call before crossing the border in to Queensland. But if you can try to break up the journey with the odd trip inland, especially to the arty village of **Bellingen** with its colony of smelly fruit bats or beyond that the **Dorrigo and New England national parks** that host plenty more bizarre wildlife. In land from Byron Bay the **Rainbow Region** also offers yet more wonderful scenery and a scattering of 'alternative' settlements.

As far as activities are concerned it will be no surprise to encounter the obvious like surfing, swimming, fishing, diving, sailing and sea kayaking in abundance, but there will also be the odd surprise, from spotting wild koalas and kitesurfing, to standing in the shadow of a huge model banana.

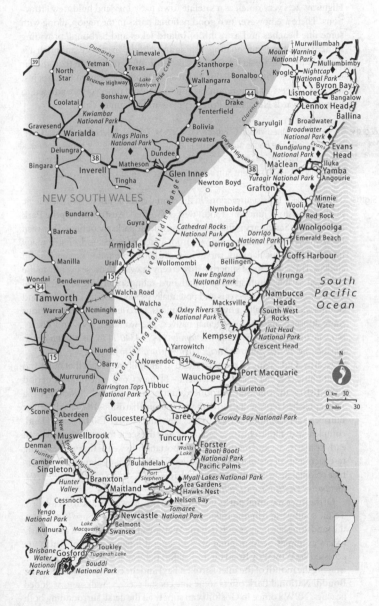

Sydney to Newcastle

Distance:163 km

The coastal region from Sydney (Broken Bay) to Newcastle is referred to as the **Central Coast** and is essentially by-passed by the Sydney-Newcastle Freeway (Highway 1). The region's largest settlement, **Gosford**, on the Pacific Highway, acts very much as a satellite town to Sydney and holds few attractions. There are however two good national parks in the region, along with some fine **beaches** and a wealth of **inland lakes** and harbours, providing some excellent walking, boating, fishing and surfing. In essence, although it is a hugely popular weekend getaway, the area offers little more than the far more accessible Pittwater, Palm Beach and the other Northern Beaches just north of Sydney. Therefore, unless you have lots of time, you are advised to press on towards Newcastle, Port Stephens, or the Hunter Valley.

Ins & outs
See Transport, page 157, for further details

There are accredited VICs in Gosford: 200 Mann St, Terrigal, Rotary Park, Terrigal Drive, Woy Woy, 8-22 The Boulevard, and The Entrance, Marine Parade. For general information and bookings, T4385 4430/T1300 659285, www.cctourism.com.au Most are open daily 0900-1700 except Sun when they close at 1400.

Sights

The two major tourist attractions in the central coast lie just west of the Pacific Highway Gosford Junction, 13 km west of Gosford. **Australian Reptile Park and Wildlife Sanctuary** is the first of many wildlife parks encountered between Sydney and Cairns. Recovering well from a recent fire that sadly killed many inmates, this particular park carves its niche by concentrating on reptiles and spiders. There are lots of superb native creepy crawlies to muse over from the common harmless huntsman or goliath bird-eating spiders and blue-tongued lizards, to the more dangerous and potentially deadly saltwater crocodiles and death adders. Naturally, any phobic leanings are countered with numerous more approachable and congenial natives, like wombats, roos and koalas. ■ *Daily 0900-1700. $17, child $8, family $44. T4340 1146, www.reptilepark. com.au Signposted from the Pacific Highway turn-off to Gosford.*

Nearby, **Old Sydney Town** tries hard to faithfully represent that quiet and quaint little colonial seaside settlement – Sydney Cove – the utopian period 1788-1810 – the one that introduced luxury convict travel. Basically it is a rather polished representation of the realities and hardships that faced the first European settlers upon arrival in the 'new lands'. Over 150 ha of parkland, complete with replica historic buildings, sets the scene for various displays of early crafts, trades and methods of transportation, as well as the more exciting re-enactments of pistol duels, floggings and other such pleasant forms of former colonial justice. ■ *Wed-Sun 1000-1600, $24, child $13.50, T4340 1104. Signposted off the Pacific Highway Gosford turn-off.*

Of the three **national parks** in the region, two are within 20 km of Gosford. To the southwest, fringing the northern arm of the Hawkesbury River Inlet, the sandstone landscapes of **Brisbane Water National Park** host a few fairly recent examples of Aboriginal art and a good lookout, both of which are accessed via Woy Woy Road off the Pacific Highway at Kariong. Further east, fringing the mouth of the inlet (Broken Bay) and the coast, the more popular **Bouddi National Park** offers some fine coastal scenery, walks and secluded beaches. NPWS office in Gosford can supply all the detail surrounding both parks and there is a small information centre at Maitland Bay in the Bouddi National Park. ■ *Vehicle entry is $6 at Putty Beach, T4368 2277.*

The coast north of Bouddi has yet more great **surf beaches** with **McMasters**, **Avoca** and **Terrigal** all being excellent.

North Coast NSW

The Central Coast also has a wealth of saltwater lakes and harbours with **Brisbane Waters**, south of Gosford, and **Tuggerah Lake**, north of Terrigal, being the largest. North of that the Central Coast Region gives way to **Lake Macquarie** which stretches all the way to Newcastle. Lake Macquarie is even larger than Brisbane and Tuggerah and four times the size of Sydney Harbour. Obviously with so much seemingly omnipresent and relatively calm water in the region, **sailing** sits at the top of the activities list with a wide range of other water sports also being well represented. VICs have full details. The waterways also attract lots of avian visitors with groups of friendly **pelicans** being a common sight. Their admirable displays of bucket-mouthed gluttony can be seen en masse at Memorial Park, The Entrance, daily at 1530.

Sleeping

The Central Coast is a popular weekend getaway from Sydney so there are plenty of modern motels, resorts and mid-range B&Bs, especially along the coast. Pre-booking is advised. **B-E** *Terrigal YHA*, 12 Campbell Cr, Terrigal, T4385 3330. Small and friendly, beachside location, dorm, double/twin, single and family room options (some cabin with en suite), internet, free use of surf/body boards. Motor parks include the well-placed and well-facilitated **LL-D** *Blue Lagoon Beach Resort*, Bateau Bay Rd, Blue Lagoon, 9 km north of Terrigal, T4332 1447, www.bluelagoonbeachresort.com.au For more solitude you might consider the **NPWS campsites** in the Bouddi National Park. Car-based camping is available at **F Putty Beach** (no campervans), with toilets, BBQs and no water, while backpack camping is available at **F** *Little and Tallow Beaches*.

Eating

When it comes to eating and fine dining try the long established, multi-award winning *Cowrie Restaurant*, 109 Scenic Highway, Terrigal, T02 43843016. Open daily for lunch and dinner. Sitting at the highest point in the town it offers sweeping ocean views and some of the best seafood in the region. For a relaxed lunch and coffee in Gosford itself *Caroline Bay Brasserie Café*, Gosford Regional Gallery and Edogawa Japanese Garden, 36 Webb St, T02 43248099, is perfect. Open daily for breakfast, lunch and dinner.

Transport

Air *Central Coast Airbus*, T1300 367 470, provides a daily shuttle services to Sydney Airport. For floatplane services between Sydney and the Central Coast, T1300 656 787, www.sydneybyseaplane.com **Bus** Long-distance coach company *Greyhound*, T132030, stop in Gosford outside the train station and provide daily services north and south. *Busways*, T4392 6666, and *Red Bus*, T4325 1781, are the 2 main local bus companies offering an extensive daily service. Many stop at the train station in Gosford, located behind the VIC on Mann St. **Ferry** A small local ferry crosses Broken Bay between Palm Beach and Wagstaff or Ettalong, Mon-Fri, T9918 2747, www.palmbeach ferry.com.au **Train** *Cityrail*, T131500, offer regular services to Sydney and Newcastle, while *Countrylink*, T132232, provide state-wide services.

Newcastle

As one of the most industrialized cities in Australia – with a main drag and a city centre mall as inspiring as a bowl of week-old porridge – it may come as a surprise that there are one or two things worth doing: a walk down **Tyrrell Street***, one of the leafiest streets on the planet; admiring the intricate and attractive façades of some of the historic buildings in the* **CBD***; visiting some of the best* **surf beaches** *in the State; and from the attractive headlands at* **Nobby's Lighthouse***, you can even embrace the city's lingering industrial function, by watching the huge freighters awaiting docking offshore. That said, Newcastle is mostly used as a convenient base from which to explore the* **Hunter Valley Vineyards** *and if you are*

Colour map 1, grid B4
Population: 270,000
150 km north
of Sydney, 348 km
south of Brisbane

North Coast NSW

thinking of using it merely as a stopover on the way north, you would be far better to head for Port Stephens and Nelson Bay, 50 km further north, where more pleasant aesthetics and an increasing wealth of activities beckon.

Ins & outs
See Transport, page 161, for further details

Getting there Newcastle has its own airport and there are regular coach and train connections with the main surrounding cities and tourist centres, with frequent daily services from Sydney and Port Stephens. **Getting around** A good network of bus and ferry services exists though you can explore the main centre on foot. **Tourist information** Newcastle VIC is in Wheeler Place, opposite the Civic Rail Station, 363 Hunter St, T4974 2999, www.newcastletourism.com Open Mon-Fri 0900-1700, Sat/Sun 1000-1530. Ask for the free *Newcastle Visitors Guide* which contains locality and street maps. NPWS do not have an office in Newcastle.

History

From its humble beginnings as a penal colony, almost a century ago, the industrial potential of the Hunter River and its deepwater harbour were quickly realized. Proving ideal for shipping vast amounts of coal from the productive Hunter Valley fields, the city rapidly developed to become one of the largest coal ports in the world. Additional industries proliferated, with major steel production predominating before its rapid decline within the last decade. This decline highlighted the city's almost inevitable susceptibility to the vagaries of the national economy. Less inevitable perhaps, but no less highlighted, was a major earthquake that struck the region in 1989. Labelled as Australia's worst in modern times, it resulted in the loss of 12 lives and caused considerable structural damage.

Sights

The city's fine viewpoints are a good place to start

The **Obelisk** on Ordnance Street, above the city centre, offers good views across the city, the harbour and the coast. Reach it via Tyrrell Street to put pay to the city's reputation for pure industrial aesthetics. Those aesthetics are however

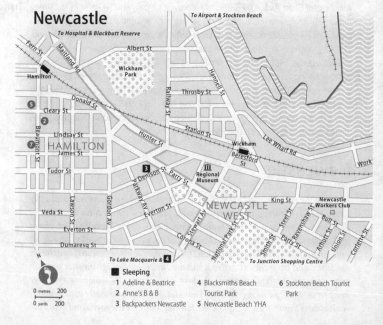

Newcastle

To Airport & Stockton Beach

To Hospital & Blackbutt Reserve

Fern St · Maitland Rd · Albert St · Wickham Park · Hamilton · Donald St · Cleary St · Lindsay St · HAMILTON · James St · Beaumont St · Tudor St · Railway St · Throsby St · Hannell St · Station St · Hunter St · Lee Wharf Rd · Wickham · Beresford St · Work · Denison St · Parry St · Regional Museum · Parkway Av · Lawson St · Gordon Av · Veda St · Everton St · Everton St · King St · Newcastle Workers Club · Stewart Av · NEWCASTLE WEST · National Park St · Smith St · Parry St · Ravenshaw St · Arthur St · Bull St · Union St · Corlette St · Dumaresq St · Corona St

To Lake Macquarie & [4]

To Junction Shopping Centre

N

0 metres 200
0 yards 200

■ **Sleeping**
1 Adeline & Beatrice
2 Anne's B & B
3 Backpackers Newcastle
4 Blacksmiths Beach Tourist Park
5 Newcastle Beach YHA
6 Stockton Beach Tourist Park

North Coast NSW

immediately obvious with a glance out to sea where fleets of huge vessels wait offshore to enter the harbour. Fine coastal vistas are afforded from **Fort Scratchley** on Nobby's Road, at the mouth of the harbour, which also houses the local **Maritime and Military Museum**. ■ *Tue-Fri 1000-1600, Sat/Sun 1200-1600. Free.* Finally, the all-prominent **Queens Wharf Tower**, Wharf Road, is also worth climbing though beware of encountering that eminently weird, obsessive creature known as a 'ship spotter'.

Newcastle can boast some very fine and gracious historical buildings, including the 1892 **Christ Church Cathedral**, the 1890 **Courthouse** and several classics on and around Hunter and Watt streets, including the post office (1903), the railway station (1878) and Customs House (1877). One rather unique remnant still functioning is the **Bogey Hole** on the shore off King Edward Park – a bathing pool built by convicts in 1820 for the then commandant of the penal colony, Major James Morriset. There are a number of good galleries and museums in the city with the **Regional Museum** and the **Newcastle Regional Art Gallery** both being worthy of investigation. ■ *Both closed Mon. Free.*

The VIC can supply a self-guided heritage walk leaflet, but by far the best way to experience the city's historical sights is on board the **Newcastle Tram** which departs from the railway station. ■ *On the hour daily 1000-1500, 45 mins. From $10, child $6.50. T4963 7954.*

The beaches on the eastern fringe of the city are superb and well known for their excellent surfing, swimming (patrolled in summer) and fishing. The main beach, **Newcastle Beach**, is located at the end of Church Street. To the north of the beach a rocky platform has been utilised to create the man-made **Ocean Baths** before the sand returns to form **Nobby's Beach** and the peninsula known as **Nobby's Head**. **Bar** and **Merewether beaches**, located south of the city centre, also provide their fair share of world-class surf breaks. **Lake Macquarie** fringes the southern city suburbs and forms a huge saltwater harbour providing another favourite spot for water-based activities.

North Coast NSW

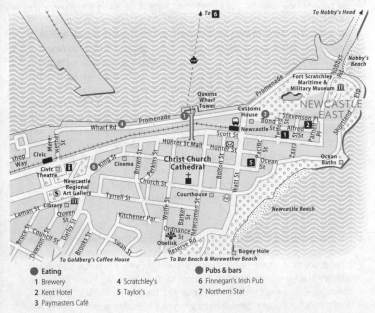

● Eating		● Pubs & bars
1 Brewery	4 Scratchley's	6 Finnegan's Irish Pub
2 Kent Hotel	5 Taylor's	7 Northern Star
3 Paymasters Café		

Remarkably, it is over four times the size of Sydney Harbour. Visit the VIC office or their website, www.lakemac.com.au, for detailed information on the locality. If you get fed up with all this sand between your toes you can find a green sanctuary and observe native wildlife at the 180-acre **Blackbutt Reserve**, 10 km west of the city centre. It has some good bush walks and wildlife exhibits with the inevitable koala talks on weekends at 1130 and 1430 (feeding daily 1400-1500). ■ *Daily 0700-1700. Free. T4952 1449. Off Carnley Ave, New Lambton. Getting there: bus #232/#363.*

Essentials

Sleeping
■ *On map, page 158*
See inside cover for price categories

There is plenty of accommodation for demand - seldom do you need need to book well in advance

LL *Rafferty's Resort*, 1 Wild Duck Dr (via Rafferty's Rd, Cams Wharf), Lake Macquarie, 27 km south of the city centre, T4972 5555, www.raffertysresort.com.au The most modern, luxury resort in the area offering self-contained cottages, suites, pools, spa, restaurants, café and sporting facilities. In very pleasant lakeside surroundings. Around the city centre **LL** *Holiday Inn* (former *Esplanade Hotel*), Shortland Esplanade, T4929 5576, www.holiday-inn.com/esplanade, is an old favourite with all the usual comforts, overlooking Newcastle Beach. **LL-L** *Novocastarian Motel*, 21 Parnell Pl, T4926 3688, www.novo.au.com Nearby, but slightly cheaper, this motel is another city icon in the ideal position and with a good restaurant. **LL-L** *Adeline & Beatrice*, Telford St, Newcastle East, T4929 4575 A much-loved historic option in a terrace house. This is a popular self-contained option, suitable for families and close to the historic precincts and city beaches. **LL-L** *Anne's B&B*, Ismebury, 3 Stevenson Pl, T4929 5376. A similar choice to *Adeline & Beatrice*. Of the handful of hostels in the city, **B-E** *Newcastle Beach YHA*, 30 Pacific St, T4925 3544, is something of a showpiece for the organization, being housed in a gracious heritage building, complete with chandeliers, ballroom, large open fireplaces and leather armchairs. Given its charm it is deservingly popular and offers numerous spacious dorms and doubles and the odd family and single room. Added to that the facilities are pretty faultless and spacious to say the least. Also on offer is internet, free use of surf/boogie boards. They seem to have the finger very much on the pulse of local activities, events and entertainment. An added attraction are the weekly all-you-can-eat BBQs and $4 pizza nights. **C-E** *Backpackers Newcastle*, 42-44 Denison St, Hamilton, T4969 3436, www.newcastlebackpackers.com.au Three kilometres west, the less grandiose and more intimate, suburban *Backpackers Newcastle* offers a fine alternative, with a nice laid-back, friendly atmosphere close to Hamilton's lively 'eat streets' (see below). It offers large dorms and double/twins and spacious adequate facilities. There is even a bath! Internet, free surf lessons (with $10 board hire). Of the numerous motor parks in the area, the well-facilitated **B-E** *Stockton Beach Tourist Park*, Pitt St, Stockton, T4928 1393, is recommended. Bear in mind however it is a 21-km car ride from the city centre, or alternatively, a short passenger ferry ride from the city centre ($1.80 per trip, or $33 weekly, combination bus/ferry pass). This is part of the charm but may not suit everyone. **E-F** *Blacksmiths Beach Tourist Park*, Gommera St, Blacksmiths, 29 km south on Highway111, is one of many outlying alternatives. It is in a beachside position near the inlet to Lake Macquarie affording guests the best of both aquatic worlds. No cabins or camp kitchen but plenty of powered and non-powered sites and BBQ facilities.

Eating
● *On map, page 158*
See inside cover for price categories

The main venues for fine dining in Newcastle are Queens Wharf and The Promenade beside the river. Three kilometres to the west in the suburb of Hamilton, Beaumont St – often dubbed the 'city's best eat street' – provides the widest selection of lively and affordable café, pub and international options. Darby St, off Hunter St, and Pacific St in Newcastle East are also worth looking at. On The Promenade (200 Wharf Rd), *Scratchley's* has become something of a regional institution over the last decade combining excellent cuisine – comprising mainly seafood and steak – with great views across the river, T4929 1111, www.scratchleys.com.au Open daily for lunch, Mon-Sat for dinner. Book ahead. Just a little further west the Queens Wharf buildings offer some other good alternatives including the more affordable *Brewery Restaurant*, 150 Wharf Rd, T4929 5792. It is also one of the city's best nightspots and during the day provides a great al fresco balcony from which to watch the ferries and the huge ships ply the river. Open for breakfast Sat/Sun 0800-1100, lunch and dinner Mon-Sat. Three good café options (from east to west) are: the historic and characterful *Paymasters Café*, 18 Bond St, Newcastle East, T4925 2600; *Scott Street Café*, 19 Scott St, T4927 0107, offering fine modern Australian fare; and the locally popular *Goldberg's Coffee House*, 137 Darby St, T4929 3122, with its shady courtyard and old English pub feel, open daily 0700-2400. Of the many options along Beaumont St, *Taylor's Restaurant*, (54), T4962 1553, comes recommended. Many of the traditional and often historic pubs in the city provide quality, quantity and good value, including the *Kent Hotel*, (59), T4961 3303, which also hosts jazz on weekend afternoons. *Coles supermarket*, The Junction Shopping Centre, corner of Glebe and Union sts, is open 24 hrs and the Market Square Shopping Centre, Hunter St Mall, has a food court.

Bars & clubs When it comes to pubs there are plenty from the traditional to the modern, providing lots of atmosphere and live entertainment. For something traditional try *Northern Star* or *Kent* on Beaumont St. For something new try *Finnegan's Irish Pub*, corner of Darby and King sts. For dancing, the hip *Brewery Hotel and Bar* on The Promenade (Queens Wharf), or the more down to earth *Newcastle Workers Club*, corner of King and Union sts, are locally recommended. Both stay open well into the wee hours, most nights.

Entertainment *Civic Theatre*, opposite the VIC, 387 Hunter St, T4929 1977, is an excellent regional theatre hosting some of the best travelling shows and plays in the country. For up-to-date listings visit www.civictheatrenewcastle.com.au or consult *Newcastle Herald* on Thu. The city-centre **cinemas** are located at 183 King St, T4926 2233 (*Union*); 31 Wolfe St, T4929 5019 (*Showcase*); and 299 Hunter St (*Kensington*). Tue night is cheap night.

Festival *Surfest*, held annually in **Mar**, is an internationally recognized competition and celebration of the art of staying upright on a Surfoplane, see below.

Tours & activities Other than the obvious attraction of the city's beaches and its convenience as a base from which to secure a tour of the Hunter Valley Vineyards, Newcastle has reluctantly given over the region's activity capital status to Nelson Bay. Many of the activities on offer there (and listed in that section) can be organized from Newcastle. Particularly exciting are the various 4WD, ATV and horse-trekking trips along the dune landscapes of Stockton Beach that stretches over 30 km to Anna Bay, just south of Port Stephens. Several rusting shipwrecks add to its appeal. The VIC can supply full listings of local activities including the many Hunter Valley tour operators. *Shadows*, T49907002, offer an interesting and entertaining day trip (0930-1630). It is aimed at younger folk and on board an old double-decker bus, from $35. For surf information and equipment hire contact *Pacific Dreams*, 7 Darby St, T4926 3355, or for something new Surfoplane, a sort of cross between a lie-lo and a surf board, 39 Darby St, T4929 1244, www.surfoplane.com

Transport **Local** *Newcastle Bus and Ferry*, T131500, provide local bus and ferry services. Fares start at $2.50 and allow an hours unlimited travel with an all-day pass costing $7.40. Bus/Ferry and Train/Bus/Ferry passes are also available from $33 per week. *Ferry Services*, T131500, link central Newcastle (Queens Wharf) with Stockton 0515-2400 Mon-Sat, 0830-2200 Sun, $1.80, child 90c one-way, tickets on board. **Bike hire** is currently unavailable in Newcastle. **Taxi**, T4979 3000.

Long distance Air Newcastle Airport, T4965 1925, is 24 km north of the city centre. *Qantas*, T131313/T4929 5821, newcastle@Qantas.com.au *Coastal Air Services*, T1800 262782, www.coastalairservices.com.au, also operate a fleet of amphibious aircraft from Sydney. *Thrifty*, T4942 2266, *Hunter Valley Connections*, T4934 6163, and *All Travel*, T4955 6777, all provide shuttles to the airport from $36 one-way. **Bus** Long-distance coaches stop next door to the train station. *Greyhound*, T132030, and *McCafferty's*, T131499, offer daily Sydney and north/southbound services. *Countrylink Travel Centre* acts as booking agents. *Port Stephens Coaches*, T4982 2940, www.psbuses.nelsonbay.com, also provide daily services to Sydney and Port Stephens. If you intend to pass through the Great Lakes Region and Myall National Park, *Great Lakes Coaches* (Kings Bros), T4983 1560, offer daily regional bus services between Taree and Sydney, via Tuncurry Forster, Bluey's Beach, Hawks Nest and Newcastle. **Train** The main train station is located at the far end of Hunter St (where it merges with Hunter St). *Cityrail*, T131500, offer regular daily services to Sydney. *Countrylink*, T4962 9438, have a travel centre at the station (open daily 0900-1700) and luggage storage. Note state-wide service connections are from Broadmeadow, 5 mins west. *Countrylink*, general info T132232.

Directory Banks Most of the major bank branches with ATMs can be found along the Hunter St Mall. **Car hire** *Thrifty*, 113 Parry St, T49611141, and *ARA*, 86 Belford St, T4962 2488, from $40 per day. **Communications** Internet: VIC Hunter St. Also, free with a purchase at the *Regional Museum Café*, 787 Hunter St (see above) or at the **Regional Library**, Laman St, T4974 5300. Open Mon-Fri 0930-1700, Tue 0930-200, Sat 0930-1700. Book ahead. **Post office**: 96 Hunter St. Open Mon-Fri 0830-1700. **Medical services** John Hunter, New Lambton, T4923 6000. **Useful numbers** Police: corner of Church and Watt sts, T4929 0999. **NRMA**: T4938 1191.

Hunter Valley

Colour map 1, grid B3

The best time to visit is in autumn for the colours of the leaves

*For most people, the Hunter River Valley is synonymous with world-class vineyards and fine wine – a little piece of Australia that conjures up images of **mist-covered valleys** and **rolling hills**, networked by patchworks of grape-laden **vines**. Ironically however, if not paradoxically, the true heritage of the Hunter lies not above ground, but below it, with the dark and foreboding mineshafts that once accessed the region's 'other' great resource – **coal**. These days vineyards dominate with over 100 in the region, producing mainly shiraz, semillons and chardonnays. They range from large-scale producers and internationally recognized labels to low-key boutiques. Despite the number, the emphasis in the Hunter Valley is definitely on quality rather than quantity and, although not necessarily producing the best wines in Australia, it is without doubt one of the best venues in the country to learn something of the process or sample that classic vineyard ambience and enjoy the congenial conviviality of fine wine, fine food and fine accommodation.*

History

As early as 1801 the 'black gold' was extracted with rapacious alacrity from the region's rich subterranean seams, earning the country considerable wealth and the region a string of familiar and traditional British working-class place names like Newcastle, Swansea and Stockton. Even the Hunter River was originally called **Coal River** before being renamed, along with the valley, in 1797 in honour of John Hunter the then Governor of NSW. However, over the years there has been an steady transformation of both working practices and aesthetics from unsightly coal pits to colourful vineyards. With the mix of a fine climate and successful marketing it seems that wine and tourism will continue, for the forseeable future, as the Hunter Valley's raison d'etre.

The first tentative endeavours into grape growing came about in the 1830s through the careful nuturings of **James Busby**, a Scots civil engineer sent over in 1824 to supervise mining operations throughout the region. Ever since that first cutting took root it seems the climate and the soils were destined to take care of the rest and, having greatly accelerated during the vineyard boom of the 1970s, the region has never really looked back.

Ins and outs

The nearest airport is at Newcastle, see page 162. Shuttles ferry people to and from the airport to the Valley. There are plenty of coaches and tours from Sydney, Newcastle and Port Stephens, see page 166. Train services arriving at Maitland and Scone.

Getting there
See Transport, page 166, for further details

Given the fact that copious wine tasting and responsible driving do not mix organized tours are by far the best way to tour the vineyards (see box). Another fine alternative is to visit the various vineyards by bike.

Getting around

Hunter Valley (Wine Country Tourism) VIC, Allendale Rd (2 km north of the town centre), T4990 4477, www.winecountry.com.au, open Mon Fri 0900-1700, Sat 0930-1700, Sun 0930-1530, is the principal centre, well set up to provide detailed vineyard information as well as accommodation and tour bookings. Local VICs in the region include Maitland, corner of High St and New England Highway, T1300 652 320, www.visitmaitland.com.au (daily 0900-1700); Singleton, 33 George St, T6571 5888 (Mon-Fri 0900-1700, Sat/Sun 0930-1630); and Muswellbrook, 87 Hill St, T6541 4050, www.muswellbrook.org.au (daily 0900-1700) in the Upper Hunter.

Tourist information

The Hunter Valley is most often described as two distinct regions, the Lower Hunter Valley and the Upper Hunter Valley with the vast majority of vineyards (over 80) in the Lower region. Both are bisected by the Hunter River and the New England Highway. The Lower Hunter Valley encompasses a region which extends from Newcastle on the coast, through Maitland, to Singleton, with Cessnock to the south considered the 'capital' of the Lower Hunter's vineyards centred in a few kilometres square to the northwest. Further west, the extensive wilderness of the Wollemi National Park dramatically halts almost all forms of human incursion, let alone grape vines. The Upper Hunter Valley vineyards extend from Singleton to Scone with most centred around Denman and Musswellbrook. All comprehensively signposted around Cessnock, however, you are strongly advised to pick up the free detailed maps from the VIC.

Orientation

Sights

For many, their first introduction to the great wine growing region are the decidedly drab and disappointing aesthetics of **Cessnock**, with its uninspiring main street reflecting a heritage borne mainly of coal, not wine. However, disappointment very quickly turns to satisfaction as you head west and north to the vineyard communities of **Pokolbin**, **Broke** and **Rothbury** where you find almost every preconceived image of rolling hills and valleys blanketed in endless lines of vines.

With over 80 vineyards in the Lower Hunter choosing which to visit can be tough. Obviously the many tour options on offer can pre-empt the problem

Lower Hunter Valley

North Coast NSW

but if you have no preconceived plan, live for beer not wine, or have no particular vintage favourites, then you are advised to mix some of the large, long-established wineries and labels with the smaller boutique affairs. Although many of the 'big guns' are well worth a visit, you will find a more relaxed and personalized service at the smaller establishments. Also be aware that almost every vineyard has received some award or another and this is not necessarily a sign that they are any better than the next. The following wineries are recommended and often considered the 'must-sees' but it is by no means is it a comprehensive list. Of the large long-established vineyards (over a century) **Tyrells**, **Draytons** and **Tullochs** (all in Pokolbin) are recommended, providing fine wine and insight into the actual wine-making process. Tyrells also has especially nice aesthetics. **Lindemans** and **McGuigans** (again in Pokolbin) and **Wyndhams** (Branxton), are three of the largest and most well known labels in the region, offering fine vintages and a broad range of facilities. McGuigans and Wyndhams also offer guided tours. Of the smaller boutique wineries **Oakvale**, **Tamburlaine** and **Pepper Tree** – with its class restaurant and former convent guesthouse an added attraction – are also recommended. Then, for a fine view as well as vintage, head for the **Audrey Wilkinson Vineyard**, DeBeyers Road, Pokolbin.

If you tire of the wineries there are many fine **art galleries** and even a few places to entertain the **kids** like the McGuigans Vineyard adventure playground and miniature steam train (see McGuigans above). See the VIC for further details.

Upper Hunter Valley Beyond Singleton, the aesthetic delights and sheer stupifications of the Lower Hunter Valley's glut of vineyards gives way somewhat to the more traditional rural landscapes of the Upper Hunter Valley, dotted with unsightly coalmines and electricity pylons. Thankfully, once you roll fearfully into **Denman** or **Musswellbrook**, the historic and congenial atmosphere returns and vineyards once again dominate the landscape. Though not nearly as saturated or well facilitated as the Lower Hunter, 'Brother Upper' still provides some fine vineyards and venues for accommodation and fine dining.

There are about a dozen wineries in the Upper Hunter with **Arrowfield** (between Denman and Jerry's Plains) and **Rosemount** (near Denman) being the oldest and most highly regarded. Both are fine labels and offer daily tastings. Other notable vineyards include **Reynolds** and **Cruickshanks** (both in Wybong). The VICs in Cessnock or Musswellbrook can provide information, maps and full accommodation listings.

Essentials

Sleeping & eating
In the midweek accommodation tariffs tend to decrease

There are literally dozens of B&Bs, guest houses, self-contained cottages and restaurants set amongst the vineyards, mainly around Pokolbin and Rothbury, which combined, have become very much a part of the Hunter Valley experience. The vast majority of restaurants and cafes are centred in and around the Lower Hunter Valley and this is by far the best place to go. The following establishments are considered just a few of the 'Hunter classics' or are listed for being unusual or convenient. Given the emphasis on taste and the great expectations surrounding the cuisine on offer in and around such classy vineyards you can expect to pay more for a meal here (most often with a main between $20-$30), but the quality almost always makes up for it. Book well in advance. Bear in mind that if you want to avoid driving between your accommodation and restaurant *Vineyard Shuttle Service*, T4998 7779, can oblige.

Lower Hunter Valley LL *Peppers Convent*, Halls Rd, Pokolbin, T4998 7764, www.peppers.com.au As the name suggests, this is a renovated convent with 17 rooms all beautifully appointed and with a tariff to match. It has all the usual extras, including pool, spa and the obligatory open fires. *Robert's Restaurant*, Halls Rd, Pokolbin, T4998 7330, www.robertsatpeppertree.com.au Open daily for lunch and dinner, bookings essential. This rustic restaurant is considered by many to be the best in the region. **LL** *Peppers Guesthouse*, Ekerts Rd, T4998 7596, www.peppers.com.au Delightful, facilitated and expensive. *Chez Pok*, Ekerts Rd, T4998 7596. This is a popular, top-class restaurant, offering local fare with a French, Asian and Italian edge. Open daily for breakfast, lunch and dinner. Again, bookings essential. **LL** *Casuarina Restaurant and Country Inn*, Hermitage Rd, T4998 7888, www.casuarina-group.com.au Completes the trio of world-class establishments combining fine accommodation with fine dining. It offers 9 exquisite, beautifully appointed, themed suites from the 'French Bordello' to the 'British Empire'. The restaurant offers superb cuisine with a Mediterranean/Asian focus. Open daily for dinner, bookings essential. **LL** *Hunter Valley Gardens Lodge and Harrigan's Irish Pub and Accommodation*, corner of Broke and McDonald's rds, T4998 7600, www.hgv. com.au Slightly more down to earth (but only slightly), this option offers excellent suites and guestrooms, with all facilities, including, of course, a fine pint of Guinness. *Seasons Restaurant* (open daily) has a choice of à la carte or the 'cook your own' Australian fare BBQ and wood-fired pizzas in the pub. Nearby, *The Cellar Restaurant*, Broke Rd, T4998 7584, is also highly regarded. Open daily for lunch, Mon-Sat for dinner. **B** *Wollombi Horse Riding and Barnstay*, Singleton Rd, T4998 3221. If you love horses as well as wine and want to combine trekking with comfort and value, this place can oblige.

Of the lowly, much maligned motels in the region **LL-L** *Hunter Country Lodge*, 220 Cessnock-Branxton Rd, North Rothbury, T4938 1744, www.huntercountrylodge.com.au, is a quirky motel/restaurant combo with log-cabin-style rooms. The unusual and colourfully decorated *Shakey Tables Restaurant* adds to the charm (open daily). In and around Cessnock some of the old traditional hotel/pubs can offer attractive rates, perfectly comfortable accommodation and value dining, including the **A-B** *Bellbird Hotel*, 388 Wollombi Rd, T4990 1094, www.bellbird.com Although it may seem rude to stay in a motor park, if you have no choice financially or otherwise, you will find **L-E** *Valley Vineyard Tourist Park*, Mount View Rd, 2 km west of Cessnock town centre, T4990 2573, the best facilitated with a fine range of cabins, powered and non-powered sites, pool and camp kitchen.

Upper Hunter Valley *Rosemount Restaurant* is highly regarded. Open Tue-Sun for lunch and morning teas, T6547 2310.

Festivals

Harvest time is February-March

The highlight of the busy events calendar is the wonderfully hedonistic and convivial *Lovedale Long Lunch*, held over a weekend every **May** where several top wineries and chefs combine with music and art to bombard the senses. Other alluring events include the musical extravaganzas of the *Jazz in the Vines Festival* and *Opera in the Vines*, both held in **Oct**.

Shopping

If you get sick of wine you can greatly increase the potential for stomach cramps at *Hunter Valley Chocolate Company*, Shop 5, Hunter Valley Gardens Village, Pokolbin, T4998 7221, open daily 0930-1730, or *Hunter Valley Cheese Factory*, McGuigans Wine Hall, McDonald's Rd, Pokolbin, T4998 7744, open daily 0900-1700.

Tours & activities

The vast majority of smaller operators will pick you up from your hotel. Many can supply lunch or dining options

They say by far the best way to truly experience the area's delights, is to save your cents and splash out on 3 days of relaxation, vineyard tours, fine dining and one of its dozens of cosy B&Bs. However, for the vast majority a day tour taking in about five wineries with numerous tastings and the purchase of one or two bottles of their favourite vintage to take home for special occasions, will sadly have to suffice.

As you can imagine there is a healthy crop of tour operators awaiting your custom, with a whole host of options and modes of transport, from the conventional coaches and mini-vans to horse-drawn carriages and bikes. Besides offering entertainment and insight they also prevent you from ending up behind bars with a drunk driving conviction. Many of the major conventional coach companies like *Hunter Valley Tours*, T4991 1659, and *Rover Coaches*, T4990 1699, offer exhaustive day tours from Sydney and Newcastle with a typical price (including lunch) from about $120.

Smaller more personalized mini-van tours from Sydney are offered by *Oz Trails*, T9387 8390, who also visit the Hawkesbury River and Lake Macquarie regions, from $100, and *Hunter Valley Wine Tours*, T9498 8888. Local mini-van companies include *Vineyard Shuttle Service*, T4998 7779/T4991 3655, offering both flexibility and good value, from $27. *Hunter Valley Limousines*, T4961 0816, can offer the upmarket, smooth approach. *Pokolbin Vintage Tours*, T4358 3298, is the period costume and senescent bus option, while *Shadow's*, T4990 7002, the great value, old commuter method, on board a double-decker bus (from Newcastle), from $35. No less unusual are *Pokolbin Horse Coaches*, T4998 7305, or *Paxton-Brown Carriages*, T4998 7362, for the congenial equestrian edge; or *Grapemobile*, T0500 804 039, for traditional peddle power, from $30. There is even a *'Golf 'n' Grape' Tour option*, T4991 1074, though if you can imagine playing a round like Tiger Woods after three bottles of vino, with his hands tied behind his back, then your somewhere close to the eventual score, if not the inevitable handicap!

There are also companies offering the more conventional activity based opportunities. It seems no vineyard region comes complete without colourful hot air balloons gently drifting above the vines and the Hunter is no exception. There are 3 companies all offering competitive prices and sunrise flights usually with about 1 hr in the air and a cooked breakfast and champagne inclusive of the price. *Balloon Aloft*, T4938 1955, based in Rothbury, have been adding colour to the skies for over 20 years, from around $225 ($250 at weekends). If you find such graceful airborne meanderings rather mundane, then you can always up the ante considerably with a tandem skydive. *Hunter Valley Tandem Skydiving*, T4990 1000, www.tandemskydive.com, can oblige from around $275 (budget accommodation also available). Other regional activities on offer include abseiling, ATV safaris, horse trekking, wildlife tours and even rally driving.

Transport

Air The nearest major airport is in Newcastle (see page 162). Newcastle-based *Hunter Valley Shuttles*, T4936 2488, or *All Travel Connections*, T4955 6777, offer shuttle services from the airport to Hunter Valley accommodations. *Coastal Air Services*, T1800 262 782, www.coastalairservices.com.au, also operate a fleet of amphibious aircraft from Sydney (or coast) to the Hunter Valley. **Bike hire** You can secure independent hire with *Grapemobile*, corner of McDonalds Rd and Palmers Lane, Pokolbin, T0500 804 039, from $30 per day. **Bus** Long-distance coach companies *Greyhound*, T132030, *McCafferty's*, T131499, and *Keans*, T4990 5000, stop at all major towns along the New England Highway, with daily services from Sydney. *Rover Coaches*, 231 Vincent St, Cessnock, T4990 1699, offer services between Newcastle and Cessnock. **Train** The nearest train station is Maitland which links with Newcastle and Sydney's *Cityrail* T131500. *Countrylink*, T132232, offer state-wide services to Queensland via Scone. **Taxi** *Vineyard Shuttle Service*, T4998 7779/4991 3655, based in Cessnock, offer local transfers or call a conventional taxi, T4990 1111.

Nelson Bay (Port Stephens)

*Port Stephens is a name loosely used to describe both the large natural harbour (Port Stephens) and the string of foreshore communities that fringe its southern arm and, in particular, the beautiful **Tomaree Peninsula**. The recognized capital among these communities is **Nelson Bay**, which proudly flies the tourism banner for a region and is fast developing into a prime New South Wales coastal holiday destination. As a result of its growth and undeniable beauty it is now rightfully luring many domestic holidaymakers and transient travellers away from the industrialized urbanities of Newcastle, providing the ideal first base or stopover from Sydney. Other than the tremendous aesthetics and views afforded by the **Tomaree National Park** and from **Tomaree Heads** across the harbour to **Tea Gardens** and **Hawks Nest**, there are an ever-increasing number of activities on offer from dolphin watching to camel rides. There is even the odd wild koala sanctuary and naturist beach though thankfully, despite the incredible tourist growth and rapacious activity-niche-filling in the area, trips to either are not yet organized.*

Colour map 1, grid B4/5
Population: 30,000
57 km north of Newcastle, 300 km south of Port Macquarie

Getting there The nearest airport is at Newcastle, 30 km away, with regular connections to main centres. Long-distance coaches serve Nelson Bay or you can travel to Newcastle and get a local bus connection. **Getting around** Port Stephens is small enough to navigate on foot. Local regional buses connect the town with surrounding attractions. **Tourist information** Port Stephens VIC is located next to the Marina on Victoria Parade, T1800 808 900/49811579, www.portstephens.org.au Open daily 0900-1700. Ask for free *Port Stephens Guide*. NPWS, 12B Teramby Rd (Marina Complex), T4984 8200, hunter@npws.nsw.gov.au, provide national parks and camping information.

Ins & outs
See Transport, age 171, for further details

North Coast NSW

Sights

Even if you do nothing else around the Nelson Bay area except laze about on its pretty beaches do climb to the summit of **Tomaree Head**, at the far west end of Shoal Bay, which is particularly spectacular at sunrise or sunset. The views that reward the 30-minute, strenuous ascent is truly memorable.

The best beaches in the area are to be found fringing the national park, east and south of Nelson Bay. To the east, **Shoal Bay** is closest to all amenities while farther east still, within the national park boundary, **Zenith Beach**, **Wreck Beach** and **Box Beach** all provide, great surfing, solitude and scenery. Two kilometres south of Shoal Bay the glorious beach that fringes **Fingal Bay** connects Point Stephens with the mainland. You can access the headland and its fine walking tracks at low tide. South of Fingal Bay, though not connected to it by road, **One Mile Beach** is another regional gem while **Samurai Beach**, just north of that, is the local naturist beach. West of One Mile Beach **Boat Harbour** gives way to **Anna Bay** which forms the northern terminus of **Stockton Beach**. This endless swathe of sand extends over 30 km all the way down to Newcastle and is well worth a visit simply to see the lengthy perspectives and its endless sweep of dunes. If you have 4WD you can 'let rip' but a permit must be obtained from the Council (or the VIC). See also Tours and activities.

There is a healthy suburban population of **koalas** in the region with the best place to see them being the fringes of Tomaree National Park or wooded areas of the Tilligerry Peninsula (via Lemon Tree Passage Road, off

Nelson Bay Road, 30 km south of Nelson Bay). If you are unsuccessful you can always satisfy the desire to see them at the low-key **Oakvale Farm and Fauna World**, opposite the Lemon Tree Passage and Nelson Bay Road Junction. It is mainly suited to children with numerous patable farm animals but some koalas are on show, along with the usual free roaming native Australian species. ■ *Daily 1000-1700, $11,child $6.50, T4982 6222*. While you are in the area you may also be tempted to visit **Tanilba House**, one of the oldest homesteads in Australia, built by convicts in 1831. ■ *Wed/Sat/Sun 1030-1630, from $5.50, child $2, T4982 4866. Caswell Corner, Tanilba*. Still on the historic theme, but closer to Nelson Bay, is the **Nelson Head Inner Lighthouse** set just above Little Bay, 1.5 km east of the town centre. On offer are guided tours, great views and a small café. ■ *Daily 1000-1600, T4984 9758*. Little Bay is also a great place to encounter pelicans as they wait patiently for fishermens' handouts late on in the day.

Finally, if you have kids in tow, you can secure endless hours of entertainment for the little devils at **Tomteland Fun Park**, 173 Nelson Bay Road, Williamtown, T4965 1500, or **Taboggan Hill Park**, Salamander Way, Nelson Bay, T4984 1022. Both open daily.

Essentials

Sleeping
■ *On map, page 168*
See inside front cover for price categories

Book ahead at peak holiday periods

There is plenty of choice in and around Nelson Bay, from resorts and modern self-contained apartment blocks to tidy B&Bs and koala infested hostels. Hotel options include the classy and indulgent **LL** *Peppers Anchorage*, Corlette Point Rd, T4984 2555, www.peppers.com.au, which offers luxurious rooms and suites (some with spa), a heated pool, sauna, massage, open fires, gym and the *Merretts Restaurant* (mainly good seafood). **L-A** *Shoal Bay Country Club Hotel*, Shoal Bay Rd, T4981 1555, www.shoalbaycountryclub.com.au Friendly, overlooking the bay and near to all amenities. It has apartments, suites, family and standard rooms (all en suite) with B&B or half board, pool, à la carte, casual dining and a lively bar.

Nelson Bay (Port Stephens)

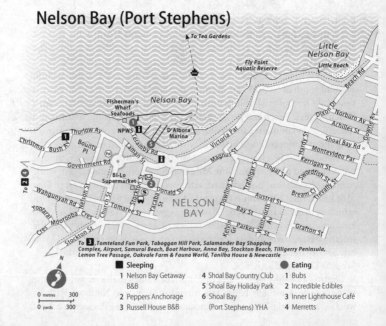

■ Sleeping		● Eating
1 Nelson Bay Getaway B&B	4 Shoal Bay Country Club	1 Bubs
2 Peppers Anchorage	5 Shoal Bay Holiday Park	2 Incredible Edibles
3 Russell House B&B	6 Shoal Bay (Port Stephens) YHA	3 Inner Lighthouse Café
		4 Merretts

There are plenty of self-contained options including the colourful and nicely appointed (but expensive) **LL-L** *Casablanca*, corner of Gowrie Ave and Intrepid Close, T4984 9100, www.portstephens.org.au/casablanca It is in a fine location between Nelson Bay and Shoal Bay and close to Little Beach. There are several good B&Bs in the region including: **LL-L** *Nelson Bay Getaway B&B*, 31 Thurlow Ave, T4984 4949, www.nelson baygetaway.com.au Offers both B&B and self-contained, spas, is the closest to the town centre and friendly; and **LL** *Russell House B&B*, 114 Salamander St, T4984 4246. Popular B&B which combines old-world charm with luxury, offering beautifully appointed suites (one with a 4-poster bed), in-house massage and a great traditional cooked breakfast.

Of the hostels in the region the eco-friendly **A-E** *Samurai Beach Bungalows*, corner of Frost Rd and Robert Connell Cl, Anna Bay, T4982 1921, samurai@nelsonbay.com, is recommended. Although on the bus route, it is some distance from Nelson Bay (5 km) but its position amidst bush at the edge of the Tomaree National Park gives it a great relaxed atmosphere to add to its undeniable character. Accommodation options range from dorm to en suite double bungalows (with TV and mini kitchen). The general facilities are also excellent and there is also the odd resident koala and supervised (harmless) snake encounter. Free sand, surf and boogie board hire, bike hire (free with 3-night stay) and pick ups. Recommended. The other alternative, with far less character, is the beachside, motel-style **C-E** *Shoal Bay (Port Stephens) YHA*, 59 Shoal Bay Rd, Shoal Bay, T4981 0982. En suite dorms, doubles and family rooms close to all amenities. For a good motor park, look no further than the excellent **LL-E** *Shoal Bay Holiday Park*, Shoal Bay Rd, T4981 1427, shoalbay@beachsideholidays.com.au Beachside, modern and friendly, close to all amenities and offering the full range of accommodation options, including camping. Great camp kitchen.

Other useful contacts include *Nelson Bay Real Estate*, T4984 1621, www.nelson bayrealestate.com.au, and *K.D Winning*, T4981 199, for holiday lets and apartments and *Port Stephens B&B Association*, www.BandB.nelsonbay.com, for local B&Bs.

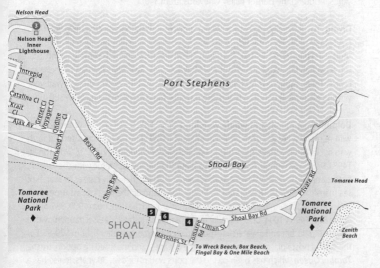

5 Pure Pizza & Robs on
the Boardwalk

North Coast NSW

Eating

● On map, page 168
See inside front cover
for price categories

For something different consider the dinner cruise options with *Moonshadow* (see Tours and activities below). On dry land most of Nelson Bay's eateries are to be found in the D'Albora Marina Complex on Victoria Parade. There you will find an award-winning, fine dining option at *Robs on the Boardwalk*, T4984 4444. Open daily 1000-late. It's fully licensed and comes recommended, especially for seafood. *Merretts Restaurant* in the *Peppers Anchorage* (see above) also has a good reputation for à la carte and seafood. Cheaper options include *Pure Pizza*, upstairs in the Marina Complex, T4984 2800, that offering dine in and free deliveries (open daily 1100-late). Then there is *Bubs*, T4984 3917, open daily from 1100-1800, located a short stroll further west, for good fish and chips. *Fisherman's Wharf Seafoods*, T4984 3330, opposite, provides fresh seafood straight off the boats should you prefer to cook your own. For good coffee and sandwiches head for *Incredible Edibles*, Shop 6 Nelson Sq, Donald St, T4981 4511. For great harbour views *Inner Lighthouse Café*, Nelson Head, above Little Beach, T4984 9758. Open daily 1000-1600.

Shopping

There is a small *Bi-Lo supermarket*, corner of Stockton and Donald sts. The larger chain supermarkets are to be found within the Salamander Bay Shopping Complex, 3 km west.

Tours & activities

For something different try the trip to the beautiful, uninhabited Broughton Island, off the Myall Coast

There is an ever-increasing range of mainly water-based activities on offer in and around Nelson Bay and Port Stephens, with the town marina being the base for most operators. The VIC opposite has a comprehensive list of daily tours and excursions and can assist with bookings. Tour schedules are reduced across the board in winter.

Pitched (quite literally) somewhere between water- and land-based trips is the amphibious *Duck Dive*, T4981 5472, www.duckdive.nelsonbay.com, that makes Coffs Harbour's 'Big Banana' seem positively archaic. It is a novel way to see the sights as well as proving a range of additional activities including diving, snorkelling, boom netting and boogie boarding. Departs 0900/1200/1500 in summer, 1030/1400 in winter from the Little Beach Boat Ramp, from $40, child $30. *Hades*, T4967 5969, and *Baydreamer*, T49820700 (good value), offer more conventional road tours to local and regional sights including the Hunter Valley vineyards (from $40).

Diving   To get really close to a whole array of interesting sea creatures *Pro Dive*, D'Albora Marina, Teramby Rd, T4981 4331, prodive@hunterlink.net.au, offer dive and snorkelling trips from $40-160. The depth of Port Stephens creates some interesting local sub aqua habitats highlighted in the Fly Point Aquatic Reserve, 1 km east of the town centre. There, numerous nudibranchs, wobbygongs and the odd seahorse await your viewing pleasure. Broughton Island also provides some excellent diving from $80-130.

Dolphin (year round) and **whale watching** (July-Oct)   These are top of the agenda with numerous vessels from large catamarans to old chug-along ferries setting forth with decks laden with camera-toting hopefuls. *Moonshadow*, Shop 3/35 Stockton St, T4984 9388, www.moonshadow.com.au, are the biggest operator with the largest, fastest and most comfortable vessels (Supercats). They offer daily cruises in search of sea mammals (from $18-39), trips to Broughton Island off the Myall Coast (from $59) and also twilight dinner and entertainment trips around the Port, from 1900, $55. *Spirit of the Bay*, T4984 1004, offer a similar range of trips on a smaller vessel (launch) with a boom net, spa, bar and a waterslide (potentially messy combination!), from $20-55. For the sake of nostalgia, or simply to secure the cheapest and most sedate option, try the *Tamboi Queen* which has been plying the ports waters for over 30 years. It also has a boom net and a bar. Cruises start from $14, family $38. *Imagine*, T4984 9000, www.imagineportstephens.com.au, offer comfortable and less crowded cruises on board a sail catamaran, from $20-50. Broughton Island, from $50. Recommended.

Sea kayaking The most intimate encounters with local pods of dolphin are of course most likely on a sea-kayaking trip. *Blue Water Sea Kayaking*, T4981 5177, www.sea kayaking.com.au, can oblige with guided day or sunset trips, and for the more experienced, excursions further afield around Broughton Island and up the Myall River. Tours start from $35 (1½ hrs) and they offer pick-ups. Recommended. Local trips are also offered by *Sea Kayak Adventure Tours*, T4982 7158, from $35.

Other watersports There are many other charter options for fishing as well as independent yacht, houseboat and jet ski hire companies. The VIC has details. **Surfing** lessons and surf gear hire are available with *Eon*, T4984 9796, from $33 (hire from $33, 2 hrs). If it is a fast 'bottom breaking' jet boat ride with full 360-degree spins you seek then contact *X-Jet*, T4997 2555, from $40, child $20.

4WD and ATV tours Stockton Beach, south of Nelson Bay, with its incredible dune habitat and wrecks, provide a major playground for 4WD and ATV (4 or 8WD motorbikes) tours with the odd set of horseshoes also making an impression. There are numerous, very similar, options with: *Dawson's Scenic 4WD Tours*, T4982 0980; *Port Stephens 4WD Adventure Tours*, T04 2784 6475; *Horizon Safaris*, T4982 6266; and *Port Stephens 4WD Tours*, T49827277, all providing fun and excitement with 1-hr/1½-hr/2-hr/half- and full-day trips from $14-50. Lunch and sand boarding are often included. *Port Stephens Dune Adventures*, T0500 550066, www.bushmobile. com.au, offer the 'Arnie Swatzanegger of vehicles', with a 6X6, yellow, go anywhere monstrosity with the 1½-hr, standard Dune Adventure (all weather) 1100/1230 with sand boarding and a spot of horseshoe tossing costing $20, child $15, while their extended 2½-hr trip taking in 'Tin City' (a hidden ramshackle settlement, threatened by the encroaching sand) costs from $30, child $20. *Sand Safaris*, T4965 0215, www.sandsafaris.com.au, offer an award-winning 2½-hr, 3-hr, 20/30-km trip on ATVs, with sand boarding included, from $99, child $54. This option provides an element of exhilaration and independence lacking on the other tours. Recommended. *Tag-Along Tours*, T4984 6112, offer guided trips taking your own vehicle along the beach. Alternatively, depending on your experience, a far less predictable mount awaits with *Beach and Bush Riding Adventures*, 2630 Nelson Bay Rd, T4965 1387. They are the horse trekking operator located closest to the dunes, offering trips of 1-3 hrs, from $30. Other operators include *Sahara Trails*, T4981 9077 (from $25, accommodation also available), and *Rambling Sands* (very flexible with trips), Janet Parade, off Nelson Bay Rd, Salt Ash, T4982 6391.

Transport

Air The nearest airport at Newcastle, 30 km south, T49651925. *Qantas*, T131313, offer daily flights from Sydney. *Coastal Air Services*, T1800 262 782, www.coastalairservices. com.au, also operate a fleet of amphibious aircraft from Sydney. **Bike hire** At 63 Shoal Bay Rd, Shoal Bay, T4981 4121. **Bus** *Baydreamer*, T4982 0700, offer shuttles, while *Port Stephen's Coaches*, T4982 2940, www.psbuses. nelsonbay.com, offer regular bus services between the airport and Port Stephens, local bus services and a daily Sydney service. Long-distance coaches stop on Stockton St in Nelson Bay. Another alternative is to use the Newcastle bound services (see Newcastle section), then catch the regular daily service from Newcastle to Port Stephens, with *Port Stephen's Coaches*. If you intend to pass through the Great Lakes Region and Myall National Park, *Great Lakes Coaches* (Kings Bros), T4983 1560, offer regional bus services between Taree and Sydney via Tuncurry-Forster, Bluey's Beach, Hawks Nest and Newcastle. **Ferry** Services, T4981 3798, then link Nelson Bay with Tea Gardens, daily 1000/1200/1430/1630, $17, child $9 return. **Taxi** T131008. **Train** Train services to Newcastle with onward bus connections.

Directory

Banks Most of the major branches with ATMs are to be found along Stockton or Magnus sts, Nelson Bay. **Car hire** *Nelson Bay Rent-A-Car*, 28 Stockton St, Nelson Bay,

North Coast NSW

T4984 2244, or *Avis*, Newcastle Airport, T4965 1612. **Communciations** Internet: *Tomaree Library*, Salamander Shopping Centre, T4982 0670. Open Mon/Wed/Fri 1000-1800, Tue/Thu 1000-2000, Sat 0930-1400. **Post office**: corner of Stockton and Magnus sts. Open Mon-Fri 0900-1700. **Police** Government Rd, Nelson Bay, T4981 1244.

Barrington Tops National Park

Colour map 1, grid A4
80 km northwest of Newcastle, 150 km southwest of Port Macquarie

The 40,453-ha Barrington Tops National Park encompasses a 25-km long plateau extending between a series of extinct volcanic peaks in the Mount Royal Ranges, north of the Hunter Valley. Rising to a height of 1,577 m at **Polblue Mountain**, the plateau forms one of the highest points on the Great Dividing Range and as such, contains a diverse range of habitats from rainforest to alpine meadows with many waterfalls and glorious views. The high elevation also results in unpredictable **weather** year-round and an annual rainfall of over 2 m, with sub-zero temperatures and snow in winter. Given its geographic position and make-up the park hosts a diverse range of species including lyrebirds, bandicoots and spotted tailed quolls. At the very least you are almost certain to encounter kangaroos as well as small squadrons of elegant and very vocal black cockatoos. The aesthetics and wildlife alone make a day-trip well worth while, though given the many excellent B&Bs, campsites, walks and activities available you may well be tempted to extend your stay.

Ins & outs
Entry to the park costs $7.50 per day

NPWS office, Church St, Gloucester, T6538 5300, Gloucester@npws.nsw.gov.au, is the nearest to the park. Open Mon-Fri 0830-1700. There is also an office in Nelson Bay, Port Stephens (see above). Visit www.barrington.com.au The main regional VIC handling Barrington Tops information is the Great Lakes VIC in Forster (see below). There are local VICs in Dungog, 191 Dowling St, T4992 2212, dungogvc@midac.com.au, open Mon-Fri 0900-1700, Sat/Sun 0900-1500, and Gloucester, Denison St, T6558 1408, gsc@midcoast.com.au, open daily 0930-1630. Look out for the free brochure, *Barrington Tops World Heritage Area*.

Sleeping & eating

The local VICs have full accommodation listings including the numerous quaint B&Bs that surround the park. **LL** *Barrington Guest House*, T4995 3212, wwwbarrington-g-h. com.au, 40 km west of Dungog, near Salisbury. This award-winning guest house is set in a private wildlife refuge. Meals and activities from bush walking to horse riding are included and it is considered the finest luxury option in the region. **LL** *Allyn Riverside Cabins*, T4982 1921, located 3 km from the Park (35 km north of East Gresford). New and self-contained this option is also recommended, offering queen rooms, spa, hand-made furniture and decks overlooking the river. No less popular is **A-B** *Barringtons Country Retreat*, Chichester Dam Rd, 23 km north of Dungog, T4995 9269, www.thebarringtons.com.au A bush resort offering comfortable lodges, an à la carte (BYO) restaurant, pool, spa and organized activities including horse riding. The NPWS can also supply details of the many **campsites** within it. The basic **F** *Gloucester River Camping Area*, Gloucester Tops Rd, T6538 5300, is in a fine riverside spot at the park boundary and comes complete with tame kangaroos but no showers. No bookings required. There are 3 campsites, several viewpoints and picnic areas beyond the Williams River Day Use Area.

Transport

The only way to access the park by public transport is with the *Forster Bus Service* (#308), T6554 6431, which accesses Gloucester, Mon-Fri, from Forster-Tuncurry. If you have your own transport there are various routes. From the south and east, the park and the 2 main fringing communities of Dungog and Gloucester are best reached from Bucketts Way Rd (Highway 2) that heads northwest off the Pacific Highway 33 km north of Newcastle. Alternatively, the northern sector of the park (and Gloucester) can be accessed west off the Pacific Highway at Nabiac, 160 km north of Newcastle. If you have 2WD and are limited for time, the drive up the Gloucester River Valley to Gloucester Tops is recommended. This drive (unsealed) climbs through the varied vegetation types, offers great views down the valley and provides a few good short walks to a waterfall and views at the terminus. Take the Gloucester Tops Rd off Bucketts Way Rd, 10 km south of Gloucester. The climb to the plateau begins at the park boundary and the congenial Gloucester River Camping Area (see above).

The northern sector of the park offers a more extensive 78-km scenic drive (mostly unsealed) from Gloucester to Scone via Scone Road and then Barrington Tops Road, west of Gloucester. This drive provides pleasant diversity from river valleys to the plateau. Sadly, the best views from Carey's Peak and its surrounding campsites can only be reached by 4WD south off Forest Road, just west of the Devils Hole Camping Area. The southern sector of the park is accessed 40 km northwest of Dungog, via Salisbury and the Williams River Valley Rd.

Myall Lakes National Park

*Myall Lakes National Park, or Great Lakes as they are known, combine beautiful coastal scenery with a patchwork of inland **lakes**, **waterways** and **forest** to create one of the best-loved eco-playgrounds in NSW. Only four hours north of Sydney and one hour, twenty minutes from Newcastle, the only drawback is its inevitable popularity in summer holidays and at weekends. However, given the sheer scale of the area, 21,367 ha of park, of which half is water, it seems there is always somewhere to escape the crowds be it camping, walking or perhaps best of all – cruising on its myriad waterways on board a **houseboat**. The main settlements fringing the national park are **Tea Gardens** and **Hawks Nest** that sit on the northwestern shores of **Port Stephens** to the south, **Bulahdelah** on the Pacific Highway to the west and back on the coast, the popular surf spots of **Bluey's Beach** and **Pacific Palms** to the north. If you have at least two days the order of destination and route below, from Tea Gardens in the south to Pacific Palms in north, or vice versa, is recommended.*

Colour map 1,
grid B5
100 km north of
Newcastle, 161 km
south of Port
Macquarie

North Coast NSW

Ins and outs

Myall is best explored by car however *Great Lakes Coaches* (Kings Bros), T49831560, offer regional bus services between Taree and Sydney via Forster-Tuncurry, Bluey's Beach, Hawks Nest and Newcastle.

Getting there

For navigation, whether on foot, by car or paddle Great Lakes District Map ($6) is not only recommended but essential. Copies can be bought in the VIC. *Forster Bus Service*, T6554 6431, offer daily local bus services around the twin towns and south as far as Pacific Palms, Bluey's Beach and Smith Lake (weekdays). Ferry services, T4981 3798, link Tea Gardens (wharf opposite *Tea Gardens Hotel*) with Nelson Bay daily 1000/1200/1430/1630, $17, child $9, return. Boat hire is available in Forster, Tea Gardens and Hawks Nest. Houseboats can be hired from *Myall Lakes Houseboats*, Bulahdelah, T4997 4221, *Luxury Houseboats*, Myall Marina, Bulahdelah, T1800 025 908, www.luxuryhouseboat.com.au, or *Luxury Afloat*, Marine Dr, Tea Gardens, T4997 0307.

Getting around

Great Lakes VIC in Forster serves as the region's principal centre, however there are smaller local VICs in Tea Gardens, Myall St, T4997 0111. Open daily 1000-1600. Bulahdelah, corner of Pacific Highway and Crawford St, T4997 4981. Open daily 0900-1700.

Tourist information

Pacific Palms, Boomerang Dr, Bluey's Beach, T6554 0123. Open daily 1000-1600. All hold NPWS parks and camping information – the nearest NPWS office is in Nelson Bay, T4984 8200. Also visit www.greatlakes.org.au

Tea Gardens and Hawks Nest

Colour map 1, grid B5
Population: 2,200
75 km north of Newcastle,
112 km south of Forster-Tuncurry

The little known but fast developing coastal settlements of Tea Gardens and Hawks Nest, on the northwestern shores of Port Stephens, serve not only as excellent holiday destinations in themselves but as the main southern gateway to the Myall Lakes National Park. Straddling the Myall River and host to beautiful beaches, headlands, coastal wetlands and forest, the twin towns combine to offer a wealth of activities from surfing to koala spotting. But barrel waves and furry ears aside, most come here to escape the crowds and relax, either soaking up the sun on 'The Hawks', quiet swathes of sand, or to quietly rejoice in the areas beautiful aesthetics and congenial, laid-back atmosphere.

Sights The place to be is **Bennetts** (Ocean Beach) at the southwestern end of Hawks Nest. From there you can access the **Yaccaba Walk** (3 km return) that climbs the summit of the Yaccaba Headland affording some memorable views across the mouth of Port Stephens and the numerous offshore islands. To reach Bennetts Beach, cross the bridge from Tea Gardens on Kingfisher Avenue, turn right on Mungo Brush Road, then left to the end of Booner Street. The bridge connecting the two towns is often called 'The Singing Bridge' because of its tendency to 'sing' during a strong southwest wind.

Another excellent but far more demanding walk is the **Mungo Track** that follows the Myall River through coastal forest to the Mungo Brush Campsite (15 km one-way). It starts on the left off Mungo Brush Road, 600 m past the national park boundary. The detailed booklet, *Walkers Guide to The Mungo Track*, breaks the entire walk into sections with additional alternatives and is available from the VIC Tea Gardens, NPWS or Hawks Nest Real Estate on Tuloa Avenue. Look out for koalas along the way, especially late in the day. Dolphin-watching cruises, diving, golf, fishing charters, boat, sea kayak, canoe and surf ski hire are all readily available in the twin towns. The Tea Gardens VIC has full listings.

Sleeping *Hawks Nest Accommodation Centre*, 166 Myall St, T499 0755, and *LJ Hooker*, 203 Myall St, both in Tea Gardens act as holiday accommodation and letting agents. **A** *Tea Gardens Hotel Motel*, on the waterfront corner Maxwell St and Marine Dr, Tea Gardens, T49970203, offers regular value deals especially on doubles with free breakfast. Friendly. **A-E** *Hawks Nest Caravan Park*, Booner St, Hawks Nest, T1800 072 244, www.hawksnestcaravan.com.au, is in a good position next to Bennetts Beach and the town centre. **L-E** *Jimmy's Beach Caravan Park*, Coorilla St, T4997 0466, has a better range of cabins.

Eating Marine Parade in Tea Gardens is the place to sample local fare with the *Oyster Hut*, Marine Pde, T4997 0579, offering fresh, locally harvested oysters and the *Tea Gardens Hotel* and *Waterfront Seafood Restaurant* affordable mains for lunch and dinner. In Hawks Nest, *Beaches Café*, corner of Booner and Tuloa sts, T4997 1022, is both convenient and a local favourite.

Directory Marine Drive in Tea Gardens and Mungo Brush Rd/Booner St in Hawks Nest host the main amenities including **post offices**, **service stations** and **supermarkets**. The post offices act as **bank agents**. Hawks Nest Service Station, Tuloa Avenue, has **bikes** for hire.

Watt?

Despite the original 122,000 candlepower beam of the Sugarloaf Lighthouse forewarning passing ships, there have been 20 shipwrecks around the Seal Rocks area since the light was first installed in 1875. The worst, the Catterthun in 1879, was bound from Sydney to China and accounted for 55 lives. Beyond the increasing and controversial number of refugee ships currently being lost at sea between Indonesia and Australia, this remains one of the worst and most tragic maritime disasters in the nations territorial waters.

From Hawks Nest, Mungo Brush Road heads north, parallel with the Myall River, to meet the southern boundary of the Myall National Park (4.5 km). From there the road remains sealed and cuts through the littoral rainforest and coastal heath for 15 km to the Mungo Brush Campsite beside the Bombah Broadwater, the second largest of the Great Lakes.

Hawks Nest to Bulahdelah

Before reaching Mungo Brush consider stopping and walking the short distance east to the long swathe of deserted beach. There are a number of 4WD tracks, which provide a walkway if you only have 2WD. **Dark Point** is a good option and can be accessed via 4WD track, about 5 km north of the southern boundary at Robinson's Crossing, 4.5 km return. It is an interesting rocky outcrop that is the only significant feature along this 44 km of beach between Hawks Nest and Seal Rocks. It is an interesting spot and the site of a midden (equivalent, yet very different to modern-day refuse tip) used by the Worimi Aboriginal peoples for centuries before they were displaced by invading European cedar cutters. This particular example is thought to be at least 2,000 years old. Lying almost tantalisingly offshore lies **Broughton Island**, accessed by day trip from Nelson Bay.

From Mungo Brush the road skirts the northern shores of Bombah Broadwater, turning inland, past increasingly thick stands of paperbark trees to reach the Bombah Point ferry crossing which runs daily every half an hour from 0800 to 1800 costing $3. **Bombah Point** is dominated by the large, yet unobtrusive, **LL-F** *Myall Shores Eco-tourism Resort*, T4997 4495, resort@myall shores.com.au, which provides a range of accommodation from luxury waterfront villas, en suite cabins and budget bungalows to shady powered and non-powered sites. There is also a small licensed restaurant, a café/bar, fuel, a small store, boat and canoe hire and a bevy of friendly pelicans – not to mention the odd, huge, lumbering goanna (monitor lizard)! Prices rocket at this resort at peak holiday times and at any time in the high season, book ahead. From Bombah Point 16 km of partly sealed roads takes you to the small community of Bulahdelah and the Pacific Highway. Bulahdelah has a helpful VIC and is the main venue for houseboat hire for the region (see above).

Four kilometres north of Bulahdelah, the Lakes Way – the main sealed access road through the Great Lakes region – heads west, eventually skirting Myall Lake, the largest of the lakes. Before reaching the lake, however, you may consider the short diversion 5 km north along Stoney Creek Road. Some 38 km into the southern fringe of the Bulahdelah State Forest, along Wang Wauk Forest Drive, is '**The Grandis**', a towering 76-m flooded gum reputed to be the highest tree in NSW. It's no sequoia but still worth a look.

Bulahdelah, Seal Rocks & Sanbar

Back on The Lakes Way between Myall Lake and Smiths Lake, Seal Rocks Road (unsealed) heads 11 km southwest to reach the coast and the pretty

North Coast NSW

beachside settlement of **Seal Rocks**. The residents of this sublime little piece of wilderness know all to well that it is the jewel in the Myall and do not really want to advertise the fact. There is a superb beach and short rainforest and headland walks – the 2-km stroll to the Sugarloaf Point Lighthouse past the Seal Rocks Blow Hole is well worth it. The views from the lighthouse (no public access to the interior) are excellent and Lighthouse Beach to the south is more than inviting. Seal Rocks lie just offshore and serve as a favourite regional dive site. Home to numerous grey nurse sharks it is clearly not the place to get shipwrecked.

Back on The Lake Way another recommended diversion, 3 km east, ventures to **Sandbar**, 1 km past the turn off to Smiths Lake village. Here you will find some excellent, quiet beaches (500-m walk), good bird watching along the sandbar that holds the lake back from the sea and many lakeside activities based at the delightful caravan park.

Sleeping & eating   **A-E** *Seal Rocks Camping Reserve*, Kinka Rd, T4997 6164, overlooks the main beach and offers a handful of self-contained cabins, powered and non-powered sites. Lakeside **L-E** *Sandbar Caravan Park*, T6554 4095, sandbar@paspaley.com.au, offers self-contained cabins, powered and non-powered sites, BBQ, kiosk, fuel, canoe and bike hire and a 9-hole golf course.

Pacific Palms & Bluey's Beach   Four kilometres north of Smiths Lake is the small community of Pacific Palms fringing the southern shores of Lake Wallis. Two kilometres east are delightful little beachside communities of Bluey's Beach, Boomerang Beach and Elizabeth Beach. While Pacific Palms boasts its lakeside charms and activities, Bluey's and its associates are something of a local surfing Mecca. Bluey's Beach itself is idyllic and further north, beyond Boomerang Point, Boomerang Beach only marginally less attractive. Further north the rather unfortunately named (and not to be verbally confused) Pimply Rock and Charlotte Head give way to Elizabeth Beach, which is an absolute stunner.

Sleeping & eating   **L-B** *Bluey's by the Beach*, 184 Boomerang Dr, Pacific Palms, T6554 0665, blueys@midcoast.com.au, is a good motel option with 9 tidy units an outdoor pool and spa, all within a short stroll from the beach. Campervans are best accommodated at **L-F** *Moby's Beachside Retreat*, Redgum Rd (off Boomerang Dr), T6554 0292, which is the closest to the surf beaches. Campers should look to NPWS Ruins and Green Cathedral campsites, north of Elizabeth Beach off The Lakes Way (see Forster section below). There are a few eateries on Boomerang Drive, Bluey's Beach, including the basic *Pacific Palms Takeaway*, T6554 0452.

Tours & activities   *Sun and Surf*, Boomerang Dr, Pacific Palms, T6554 0929, www.sunandsurf.com.au, offer surfing lessons from $35 (1 hr) and board hire from $30 (half day). *Pacific Palms Windsurfing* (Tiona Park), T6554 0309, offer windsurfing lessons from $40 per hr. *Pacific Palms Kayaking Tours*, T6554 0079, tours@ppkayaktours.com.au, explore the local coast by sea kayak and get to places otherwise inaccessible on half-, full-day or overnight trips from $33. Birders will enjoy the convivial, early morning outings on offer with *Birdwatching Breakfasts*, T6554 0757, from $30, child $15, or the extended half- or full-day rainforest, hinterland and rainy day tours under their *Boomerang Forest Tours* banner, T6554 0757, ppmartin@gl.hardnet.com.au

Directory   Boomerang Drive (Bluey's Beach) offers a wide range of low-key amenities including a **supermarket**, **newsagent**, **service station** and **pharmacy**.

Forster-Tuncurry

The twin coastal towns of Forster-Tuncurry, which straddle **Wallis Lake** and the Cape Hawke Harbour, are a favourite domestic holiday destination forming the northern fringe of the park and providing the northern gateway to the superb **Great Lakes Region**. Although the town itself has some fine beaches and numerous, mainly water-based activities, it is the lakes, beaches and forests of the **Booti Booti** and **Myall Lakes National Parks** to the south that lure visitors time and again. As one of the most appealing coastal regions between Sydney and Byron Bay, a few days here is highly recommended. If you need all the usual amenities then Forster is the place to stay but there are some superb alternatives in the national park and coastal villages to the south (see Myall Lakes National Park, above).

Colour map 1, grid A5
Population: 21,000
140 km north of
Newcastle, 120 km
south of Port
Macquarie

Great Lakes VIC, beside the river on Little St, Forster, T6554 8799, www.greatlakes.org.au, serves Forster-Tuncurry and the Great Lakes (Myall) Region as far south as Tea Gardens and Hawks Nest. Daily 0900-1700. To find your way around the twin towns and region ask for the free Cartoscope Great Lakes Region Map. The Great Lakes District Map ($6) is recommended if you intend to explore the Myall Lakes and National Park fully. The VIC also supplies NPWS camping and national parks information.

Ins & outs
See Transport,
page 178,
for details

Many short-term visitors find ample satisfaction on **Forster Beach**, which sits at the mouth of the Hawke Harbour Inlet, just north of Forster's main drag Head Street, but better beaches await your attention further west. **Pebbly Beach**, which is only a short walk along the coast from Forster Beach (or alternatively accessed by car, just beyond the junction of Head St and MacIntosh St), is a great spot for families and despite the name does possess some sand. At the western end of town, **One Mile Beach** is the towns true favourite offering great views and good surfing at its northern end. It is best accessed via Boundary Street, south off Head Street/Bennetts Head Road, then east down Strand Street. **Bennetts Head**, at the terminus of Bennetts Head Road, also provides good views south along the One Mile Beach, north to Halliday's Point and straight down into almost unbelievably clear waters.

Sights

If you can drag yourself away from the town's main beaches, the **Booti Booti National Park** straddling the The Lakes Way and the distinctly svelte strip of terra firma between Lake Wallis and the ocean, is well worthy of investigation. At the park's northern fringe, head east along Minor Road (just south of Forster, off The Lakes Way) and climb to the top of **Cape Hawke** where there is a superb lookout tower (40 minutes return). **McBride's Beach** sits in almost perfect isolation below and is one of those beaches that instantly has you mesmerised and stripping off uncontrollably at the mere prospect. It is as good as it looks and the ideal place to escape for the day, provided you are up for the 20-minute walk from the parking area just west of the lookout car park. To the south **Seven Mile Beach** stretches to **Booti Hill**, **The Ruins** and **Charlotte Head**. The Ruins has a good NPWS campsite and the southern edge of the park offers some excellent walks, with the 7-km track from The Ruins to Elizabeth Beach being recommended. **Elizabeth Beach** is another regional gem that has the habit of detaining all whom visit – sometimes for days! On the western side of Lakes Way **Wallis Lake** provides saltwater swimming, fishing, boating and numerous picnic sites.

A-C *Great Lakes Motor Inn*, 24 Head St, T6554 6955, is modern, well facilitated and within walking distance of the Forster beaches and town centre. **L** *Tudor House Lodge*,

Sleeping

North Coast NSW

1 West St, T6554 8766. Overlooking Forster Beach itself, this tidy lodge offers standard doubles, ocean-view suites, complimentary breakfast and a good in-house bar/restaurant. **C-E** *Dolphin Lodge YHA*, 43 Head St, T6555 8155, dolphin_lodge@hotmail.com It's quiet, friendly and offers tidy motel-style double/twin/single rooms and dorms, well-equipped kitchen, free use of boogie boards, bike hire and internet. Some 500 m from the beaches, VIC and long-distance bus terminal. **L-E** *Forster Beach Caravan Park*, Reserve Rd, T6554 6269. This centrally placed park is right beside the Harbour Inlet and Forster Beach and is within walking distance of Forster town centre. It has a good range of cabins and BBQs but lacks privacy and has no camp kitchen. **L-F** *Smugglers Cove Holiday Village*, 45 The Lakes Way, T6554 6666. Further south (2 km) is this better facilitated option, but less conveniently located. **NPWS Ruins campsite**, beneath Booti Hill at what is known as the 'Green Cathedral' about 20 km south. This is the best bet if you do not wish to be in town. It is in a great position, beach or lakeside, with good coastal and forest walks. Self-registration, hot showers, but no fires allowed, T6554 0446. Local estate agents can also assist with holiday lettings, including *LJ Hooker*, T6554 6188, www.ljhooker.com.au/forster

Eating   Other than the fish and chip shops, *Lobby's* and *Beach St Seafoods*, you will find more value seafood and pub grub at the popular, *Lakes and Ocean Hotel*, corner of Little and Lake sts, T6555 4117. For fine dining, the intimate *Oyster Rack, Oyster Bar and Restaurant*, in the Pacific Arcade off Memorial Ave, T6557 5577, is a popular choice. *Divino*, T6557 5033, next door, is a congenial and good value Italian. Daily lunch 1100-1500, dinner from 1800. For a great pie and peas and to support the Aussie institution, try *Harry's Café de Wheels*, corner of Beach St and Memorial Dr.

Tours &   *Dolphin Watch Cruises*, Fisherman's Wharf, T6554 7478, are the only local operators per-
activities   mitted to put people in the water (in a boom net) with dolphins, from $38, child $15.
There are plenty of   *Amaroo*, Lakeside, T04 1933 3445 and *Free Spirit*, Tikki Boatshed (opposite the VIC)
water-based activity   T6559 2899, offer general lake cruises and dolphin watching, from $20. There are several
operators in Forster   excellent dive sites in the region including Seal Rocks, *The SS Satara* wreck dive, Bennetts
with most tendering   Head and the Pinnacles which are all well known for their grey nurse sharks. Idol Bay is
for your custom along   also home to Aggro, the inquisitive loggerhead turtle. There are several local dive opera-
Little St and the   tors, including *Underwater Adventures*, Fisherman's Wharf, T6554 7478, which reput-
lakeside   edly have the best boat and offer a good range of packages. *Action Divers*, Shop 4/1-5 Manning St, Tuncurry, T6555 4053, www.actiondivers.com.au, offer value for money, with full gear hire from $38, single dives from $44 and a good trip to Seal Rocks from $95. *Joy C*, Little St, T6554 6321, and *Double-D Deep Sea*, T6554 7189, both offer entertaining half- or full-day fishing trips. *Great Lakes Seaplanes*, T6555 8771, offer scenic floatplane flights, often spotting dolphins and whales, from $40-90. All manner of watercraft, from BBQ boats to canoes, can be hired along the waterfront. *Tikki Boatshed*, 15 Little St, T6554 6321, is one of the major players and are based opposite the VIC.

Transport   **Bus** *Forster Bus Service*, T6554 6431, offer daily local bus services around the twin towns and south as far as Pacific Palms, Bluey's Beach and Smith Lake (weekdays). Long-distance buses stop outside the VIC on Little St. VIC also acts as booking agents. *Greyhound*, T132030, offer services from Sydney or Port Macquarie. *Great Lakes Coaches* (Kings Bros), T4983 1560, also offer services between Taree and Sydney via Tuncurry Forster, Bluey's Beach, Hawks Nest and Newcastle. **Car hire** *Budget*, Traveland Forster Shopping Centre, Breeze Parade, T6555 5700. **Train** The nearest train station is at Taree, *Countrylink* T132232, offer daily services north and south. *Kings Bros* (above) or *Eggins*, Elizabeth St, Taree, T6552 2700, provide links between the station and Forster.

Internet is available at *Leading Edge Computers*, corner Head and Beach sts, T6555 **Directory**
7959 or the YHA.

Forster-Tuncurry to Port Macquarie

Taree, 33 km north of Forster-Tuncurry, is a pleasant riverside town that acts *Distance: 124 km*
as the commercial centre for the picturesque **Manning Valley** and Manning
River District where you can stop in **houseboats** and kick about in dinghies.
They can be hired along Crescent Avene. From Taree, the 160-m sheer-drop,
Ellenbourgh Falls, near the Bulga State Forest, provides good day trip. It is
reached by mainly unsealed roads (46 km) northwest, beyond Wingham.

Back on the coast the **Crowdy Bay National Park** can be accessed
(unsealed) from Moorland off the Pacific Highway, 30 km north of Taree.
There are some good NPWS campsites at **Kylie's Beach**, **Indian Head** and
Diamond Head. Alternatively, a good way to sample the coastal scenery is to
take the short diversion east, to Crowdy Head and Harrington (23 km north of
Taree). Although **Harrington** is pleasant enough, and offers some good fishing
and bird watching around the Harrington Inlet, press on further north to the
tiny fishing village of **Crowdy Head**. Although it provides very little in the way
of amenities, the views from the pocket-sized lighthouse on the headland are
memorable, followed perhaps with a swim or a stroll along the beach at the base
of **Crowdy Bay**.

Back on the Pacific Highway take the road to **Laurieton** from Kew, 51 km
north of Taree. Just before Laurieton itself, take the road to the summit of
North Brother through the **Dooragan National Park**. The views up and
down the coast on a clear day are stunning. Below, Laurieton, and its neighbouring settlements of North Haven and Dunbogan collectively known as
Camden Haven, merge and fringe the **Queens** and **Watson Taylor Lake**
inlets. Boating and fishing are not surprisingly hugely popular with *Camden
Haven River Cruises*, based at the Dunbogan Boat Shed, 46 The Boulevarde,
T6559 6978, providing a range of cruise options. Boats can also be hired from
the *Boat Shed*, T6583 6300. All around the waterways it seems you are never far
from the gaze of friendly pelicans. **Kattang Nature Reserve**, on the headland
beside Dunbogan, offers some good picnic spots and short coastal walks offering more great views. From Laurieton it is another 30 km through the lazy
beachside settlements of **Bonny Hills** and **Lake Cathie** to Port Macquarie.

Port Macquarie

Officially declared as possessing the best year-round climate in Australia, and Colour map 1, grid A5
blessed with a glut of superb **beaches**, *engaging* **historical sights**, **wildlife** *rich* Population: 34,000
suburban nature reserves and a wealth of mainly water-based **activities**, *the for-* 399 km north
mer penal colony of Port Macquarie is rightfully recognized as one of the best holi- of Sydney,
day destinations to be found anywhere in NSW. The strange thing is, for most 589 km south
international visitors, 'found' is not the word, while 'lost' should be. Due perhaps of Brisbane
*to more domestically oriented advertising, or simply the 6 km of road between the
town and the Pacific Highway, it seems the vast majority of international travellers miss Port Macquarie completely as they charge northwards, blinkered with
the hype and prospect of the more high-profile destinations like Byron Bay. However, if you make the effort and the short detour, you will not be disappointed.*

North Coast NSW

Ins and outs

Getting there
See Transport, page 186, for further details
Port Macquarie is 10 km east of the Pacific Highway along the Oxley Highway. The airport is 3 km away. Long-distance buses serve the town and there is a train station 18 km away with connecting buses to the town centre.

Getting around
The town centre is bordered by the Kooloonbung Creek to the west and the Hastings River to the north. To the west the suburbs stretch south off Pacific Drive fringed by the spectacular western beaches. The town centre's main shopping streets are Clarence St which runs parallel with the river and terminating at the Wharf, to the west, and Horton St, which runs north to south off Clarence, to meet Gordon St. Gordon St then connects west with the Oxley Highway.

Tourist information
Port Macquarie VIC is located right in the heart of town on the corner of Clarence and Hay sts, T1300 303155/65818000, www.portmacquarieinfo.com.au Open Mon-Fri 0830-1700, Sat/Sun 0900-1600. NPWS, 152 Horton St, T6586 8300, port@npws.nsw. gov.au Open Mon-Fri 0830-1700.

History

Historically, in European terms, you could argue Port Macquarie to be the most significant town between Sydney and Brisbane. Although first sighted by Captain Cook in 1770 and again in 1802 by Matthew Flinders, the area was first fully investigated at the behest of NSW Governor Lachlan MacQuarie by explorer John Oxley in 1819. MacQuarie's desire was to establish a secondary penal colony to Sydney – one that could handle the most notorious criminals (those that stole the plate as well as the three potatoes) thereby removing such unmentionables from the growing population of free setters further south. Identifying what is now 'The Green', off Clarence Street, as the best site for building 104 souls duly arrived in 1821 (with over half being convicts) and the most northerly European settlement in Australia was born.

After an initial period of relative success and a growing number of free settlers showing an interest in establishing themselves in the area, the penal colony formerly closed in 1840s, with the worst convicts being moved north to Moreton Island, near what would later become Brisbane. Sadly, for Port Macquarie its prefix proved too optimistic and the destructive nature of the river mouth its nemesis. By the late 1880s it could not function as a crucial port and an inevitable decline set in. This decline would last well into the 20th century, until finally, the entrepreneurial representative of a completely new shower of congenial reprobates stood on the green and thought tourism!

Sights

Stewart Street & around
For a full tour of the historic sites pick up the free 'Port Macquarie's Heritage' leaflet from the VIC
Allman Hill on Stewart Street is home to the settlement's first cemetery which was used until 1824. The gravestone will reveal the obvious hardships and life expectancies. The site of the first goal is at **Goal Point Lookout**, just off Stewart Street, that although now offering pleasant views across the harbour and Town Beach once drew crowds to view a far more hideous sight – hangings. If you would to quietly search the heavens the **Observatory** in Rotary Park on William Street has viewing nights. ■ *Wed/Sun in summer from 1930. $2. T6583 1933.* More relaxation can be had on **Town Beach** which fringes Rotary Park and is the most convenient for swimming with good surfing at the northern end. Given the Hastings River's extremely harsh treatment of

North Coast NSW

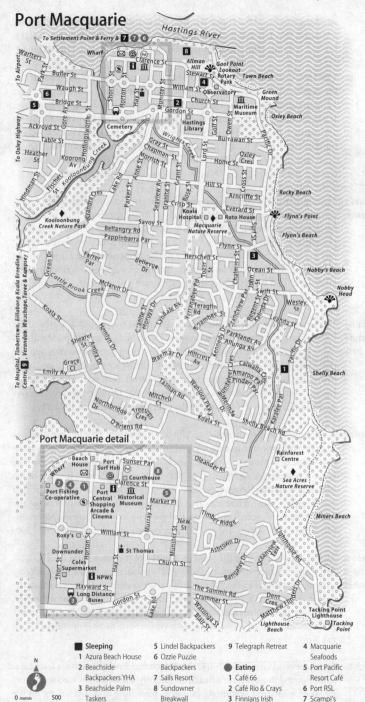

Port Macquarie

Hastings River

To Settlement Point & Ferry &

Wharf

Warlters St

Park St

To Airport

Buller St

Waugh St

Bridge St

Ackroyd St

Table St

Gore St

Horton St

Hollingworth St

Short St

Hay St

Munster St

Cemetery

Allman Hill

Clarence St

Stewart St

William St

Church St

Gordon St

Hastings Library

Gaol Point Lookout

Rotary Park

Observatory

Maritime Museum

Town Beach

Green Mound

Oxley Beach

Wrights Creek

Gray St

Chapman St

Morrish St

Granite St

Anne St

Grant St

Burrawan St

Home St

Oxley Cres

Rose St

Hill St

Arncliffe St

Cross St

Rocky Beach

Koorong Av

Heather St

Hindman St

Fischer St

Kooloonbung Creek

Wanda Cres

Lake Rd

Parker St

Bellangry Rd

Savoy St

Crisp St

Granville Av

Koala Hospital

Roto House

Macquarie Nature Reserve

Flynn St

Flynn's Point

Flynn's Beach

Kooloonbung Creek Nature Park

Ocean Dr

Cattle Brook Creek

Koala St

Farrer Par

Bellevue Dr

Mclaren Dr

Kemyn Dr

Pappinbarra Par

Herschell St

Tozer St

Chalmers St

Ocean St

Nobby's Beach

Nobby Head

To Hospital, Timbertown, Billabong Koala Breeding Centre, Verandah, Wauchope, Taree & Kempsey

Shearer St

Grace Cl

Amita Dr

Grante St

Moruya Dr

Lyndale Av

Teratgin Rd

Thambee St

Swift St

Regent St

Kennedy Dr

Glanview Par

John St

Parklands Av

Altunga Av

Westey St

Leanda St

Kalinda St

Emily Av

Braemar Dr

Hillcrest Av

Wangra Pkwy

Tasman Rd

Mitchell Ct

Calwalla Cres

Amaroo Par

Pindari Par

Blackbutt Rd

Karalee Par

Pacific Dr

Shelly Beach

Northbridge Dr

Treetops Cres

O'Briens Rd

Koala St

Shelly Beach Rd

Oleander Av

Rainforest Centre

Sea Acres Nature Reserve

Miners Beach

Port Macquarie detail

Beach House

Port Surf Hub

Sunset Par

Wharf

Port Fishing Co-operative

Clarence St

Courthouse

Port Central Shopping Arcade & Cinema

Historical Museum

Market Pl

Roxy's

William St

St Thomas

Murray St

New St

Munster St

Downunder

Coles Supermarket

NPWS

Hay St

Short St

Horton St

Church St

Hayward St

Long Distance Buses

Gordon St

Lake Rd

Timber Ridge

Ashtown Dr

Bangalay Dr

The Summit Rd

Crummer St

Dent Cres

Waroma St

Oceanview Terr

Lighthouse Rd

Matthew Flinders Dr

Tacking Point Lighthouse

Lighthouse Beach

Tacking Point

N

0 metres 500
0 yards 500

North Coast NSW

■ Sleeping	5 Lindel Backpackers	9 Telegraph Retreat	4 Macquarie Seafoods
1 Azura Beach House	6 Ozzie Pozzie Backpackers	● Eating	5 Port Pacific Resort Café
2 Beachside Backpackers YHA	7 Sails Resort	1 Café 66	6 Port RSL
3 Beachside Palm Taskers	8 Sundowner Breakwall Tourist Park	2 Café Rio & Crays	7 Scampi's
4 HW Motor Inn		3 Finnians Irish Tavern	8 Toros Mexican

anything that dared float upon it in the 19th century, the **Maritime Museum**, 6 William Street, is worth a look with the emphasis very much on wrecks. It is housed in former pilot station cottages built in 1896. ■ *Mon-Sat 1100-1500. $2.*

Courthouse   The 1869 Courthouse, that dished out the capital punishments, is located at the corner of Clarence and Hay Streets. It served the community for over 117 years and is now refurbished faithfully to the times and open to the public. If you are lucky you may time your visit with a period uniform re-enactment with cannon firing, held on the occasional Saturday at 1130. Ask for up-coming dates from the VIC. ■ *Mon-Sat 1000-1600, $2, child 50c, T6584 1818.*

Across the road is the **Historical Museum**, which is housed in a former convict-built store (1835). It contains 14 rooms of historical artefacts.

St Thomas's   This church, on the corner of Hay and William streets, is the fifth oldest Angli-
Church   can Church still in use in Australia and was not surprisingly built by convict labour through the late 1820s. Its most interesting feature actually lies buried beneath one of the pews, in the form of one Captain Rolland – the Port's former gaol supervisor. He died, believe it or not, from sunstroke. He was buried there, as opposed to outside, through fears that he might be exhumed by convicts, torn limb from limb, and displayed with gay abandon all around the town. ■ *Mon-Fri 0930-1200/1400-1600, donation, T6584 1033.*

Kooloonbung   The Kooloonburg Creek Nature Park sits amidst the western suburbs of the
Creek Nature   town offering a network of walkways and boardwalks through parkland and
Park   mangroves. Several lookout platforms offer some fine bird-watching. The park is well worth a visit in itself, however, the historic cemetery situated at the top of the park, the southern end of Horton Street, is an interesting addition. It took over from the first in Clarence Street and hosts the remains of over 1,500 soldiers, convicts and free settlers buried there between 1824-86.

Koala Hospital   A healthy suburban population clings precariously to the area's nature reserves and parks and numerous roadside signs are testament to this. In town one of the best places to spot wild koala is in Sea Acres Nature Reserve (see below), however, if you have no joy there is alway the Koala Hospital, in the **Macquarie Nature Reserve**, on Lord Street. It almost always is rehabilitating a number of animals for one reason or another and although you cannot see any of the sick animals some permanents and pre-release animals are usually on display. ■ *Daily. Donation. T6584 1522. Feeding takes place daily, 0800 and 1500.*

Western &   The beaches that fringe the western suburbs of the town from the Hastings
northern   River mouth, south to Tacking Point and beyond, are simply superb offering
beaches   some excellent swimming, fishing, surfing, walks and views. Even north of the town the great swathe of **North Beach**, that stretches 15 km to **Point Plomer**, fringed by the diverse coastal habitats of Limeburners Creek Nature Reserve, provides almost total solitude. Access is via the Settlement Point ferry ($2) on the North Shore.

Oxley Beach to   South, beyond Green Mound, **Oxley Beach** and **Rocky Beach** are less acces-
Tacking Point   sible. Beyond those, **Flynn's Beach** and **Nobby's Beach** are two other favour-
Lighthouse   ite spots with good swimming as well as fossicking and snorkelling on the
If feeling energetic   extensive rock platforms. **Flynn's Point** and **Nobby Head** also provide great
stroll down Pacific   views. South of Nobby Head the coastal fringe gives way to **Shelly Beach** and
Drive and catch the   the 72-ha coastal **Sea Acres Nature Reserve**, one of the best places in town to
bus back (#331)

spot wild koala (particularly in the late afternoon). This sublime piece of rainforest is preserved with a 1.3-km boardwalk providing the ideal catalyst for observation of its rich biodiversity. You really feel you are miles from civilization. The boardwalk starts and finishes at the Rainforest Centre which in itself houses an interesting range of displays, a café and shop. Guided tours available. Recommended. ■ *Daily 0900-1630, $10, children under 7 free, family $27. T6582 3355.*

Then on to **Miners Beach** reached by a coastal path from the same car park, which is a favourite spot for naturists. At the terminus of Lighthouse Road is **Tacking Point**, named by Matthew Flinders in 1802, and the pocket-sized **Tacking Point Lighthouse** built in 1879. From there you are afforded great views south, along **Lighthouse Beach** towards Bonny Hills and North Brother Hill.

Taking the road parallel with the nature park out of Port Macquarie you will reach **Timbertown**, in Wauchope, 19 km west. The working 1900s village is a great place for a family outing with its steam train rides, heavy horses and displays of sawing, woodturning, smithing and even a spot of whip cracking. There is a restaurant on site. ■ *Daily 0930-1530. Free (train ride $5, child $3). T6586 1422. Getting there: buses serve Wauchope, see Transport.*

There is also the **Billabong Koala Breeding Centre** which not only provides copious koala patting but also the usual array of hand-out crazed Australian natives including wallabies, wombats and rainbow lorikeets in six acres of landscaped gardens. ■ *Daily 0900-1700. $9.50, child $6. T6585 1060. 61 Billabong Dr, 10 km from the town centre. Café, BBQ and picnic areas.*

Excursions

North Coast NSW

Essentials

There are plenty of accommodation options in and around Port Macquarie from basic NPWS campsites to luxury resorts. *Hills*, 114 William St, are a reputable agent, T6584 1154, www.portmacquarieholidayspecialists.com.au During holiday periods and in the high season you are advised to book ahead.

Sleeping
■ *On map, page 181*
See inside front cover for price categories

Hotels, motels and self-contained apartments LL *Sheraton Port Macquarie (Four Points)*, 2 Hay St, T6589 2888, www.fourpoints.com/portmacquarie New, ideally located in the town centre, overlooking the river, with 126 modern rooms with all the usual facilities and a good restaurant. **LL-L** *Sails Resort*, 20 Park St, T6583 3999, www.sailsresort.com.au, is the town's top resort offering suites and units (some with spa), pool, bar, good restaurant and sports facilities. **L** *Flynn's Beach Village Resort*, 25 Surf St, T6584 2244, flynnsbeach@midcoast.com.au, offers modern, well-appointed, self-contained beach houses and a pool in a great position near the western beaches. For a really chic motel in the ideal position, look no further than **LL-L** *HW Motor Inn*, 1 Stewart St, T6583 1200, www.hwmotorinn.com.au The rooms are well appointed with most offering views across the river mouth and Town Beach. **LL-L** *Country Comfort*, corner of Buller and Hollingworth sts, T6583 2955, sets the usual good standards. **A-B** *Arrowyn Motel*, 170 Gordon St, T6583 1633, is a good cheaper option.

B&Bs In town and handy to the western beaches is the modern **L** *Azura Beach House*, 109 Pacific Dr, T6582 2700, www.azura.com.au, offering en suites, heated pool and spa. **LL** *Telegraph Retreat*, 126 Federation Way (35 km northwest), T6585 0670, www.telegraphretreat.com.au, is a lovely, classy, old-style self-contained country house in a beautiful setting with well-appointed suites, spa, pool and great cuisine. Complimentary pick-ups available.

Hostels **B-E** *Beachside Backpackers YHA*, 40 Church St, T6583 5512. Family run, it is the closest hostel to the beaches, offering dorms, twins and family rooms, spacious facilities, free bikes, body/surf boards (free boogie board lessons), small gym, internet, pick-ups from the bus station. **C-E** *Lindel Backpackers*, 2 Hastings River Dr, T6583 1719, lindel@midcoast.com.au A friendly, family-run historic house with lots of character, dorms, twins and doubles, pool, 24-hr kitchen and TV room, free use of boogie boards, fishing gear, bikes, pool table. Internet and pick-ups. **C-E** *Ozzie Pozzie Backpackers*, 36 Waugh St, T6583 8133, www.nomads world.com More modern, activity oriented back-packers well in tune with travellers needs, good facilities, dorms, doubles/twins, internet, pick-ups, free use of boogie boards, bikes and fishing gear. Shame about the name.

Motor parks There are plenty of motor parks in the area with the vast **L-E** *Sundowner Breakwall Tourist Park*, right beside the river mouth, town centre and Town Beach, 1 Munster St, T6583 2755, www.sundowner.net.au, hard to beat for position. The staff are a bit impersonable but it is well facilitated with a pool and camp kitchen. Another good alternative is **L-E** *Beachside Palms Taskers*, 14 Flynn St, T6583 1520. It is just a short walk to Flynn's Beach and excellent for kids, with the Peppermint Park and Fantasy Glades amusement parks within walking distance. Pool and BBQ, but no camp kitchen. Remote **NPWS camping** is available at Big Hill and Point Plomer in the Limeburners Creek Nature Reserve, T6586 8300.

Eating
● *On map, page 181*
See inside front cover for price categories

Seafood rules in Port Macquarie from the full plate of oysters to humble fish and chips. The main outlets can be found at the Wharf end of Clarence St. The regional vineyards are also worth considering, especially for lunch.

Expensive Both *Cray's*, beside the wharf at 74 Clarence St, T6583 7885, open daily for lunch and dinner, and *Scampi's*, Port Marina, Park St, T6583 7200, open daily from 1800, are the best venues for quality à la carte seafood in congenial surroundings. *Cray's* also serves good steak.

Mid-range *Café 66*, 66 Clarence St, T6583 2484, is recommended for Italian and is open daily for breakfast and lunch and Tue-Sun for dinner. The long-established *Toros Mexican*, 22 Murray St, T6583 4340, is good value and does a wicked fajita, while the lively *Café Rio*, 74 Clarence St, T6583 3933, offers more traditional fare and good coffee. Out of town *Ca Marche*, 764 Fernbank Creek Rd (corner of Pacific Highway), T6582 8320, is a small, award-winning French/Mediterranean restaurant at the Cassegrain Winery with a congenial atmosphere and nice views across the vines. Open for lunch 1030-1600 daily. For Guinness and stew as opposed to chardonnay and salad, try *Finnians Irish Tavern*, 97 Gordon St, T6583 4646, for good pub grub.

Cheap For great fish and chips look no further than *Macquarie Seafoods*, corner of Clarence and Short sts, T6583 8476. Open daily 1100-2100. If you are looking to cook your own, *Port Fishing Co-operative*, beside the wharf, is excellent for buying fresh seafood straight off the boat. *Port RSL*, 1 Bay St, T6580 2300, offers both value for money, outdoor and fine dining (Tue-Sat) as well as a family restaurant and live entertainment. Locals recommend the no-nonsense *Sun Hing BYO Chinese Restaurant*, 112 William St, T6583 5667, for both sit down and takeaway. Open daily for lunch 1130-1430 and for dinner Sun-Tue 1700-2130, 2200 Wed-Sat. *Port Pacific Resort Café*, 14 Clarence St, T6583 8099, offers all-you-can-eat breakfasts for $10.50. *Port Central Shopping Arcade* has a food court.

Entertainment For up-to-date entertainment listings pick up the free, weekly *Hastings Happenings* at the VIC. There are 3 main **nightclubs** in the Port: *Roxy's*, on William St, open Wed-Sat

2000-0400, which attracts a young crowd; the more modern and popular *Beach House*, on the Green, Horton St, T6584 5692, open nightly, free entry until 2300, then $5 (free all night Thu), jazz on Sun afternoons; the small *Downunder Night Club*, next to *Coles*, has karaoke on Wed and attracts a slightly older crowd, open 2000-0300. There is also live entertainment at the very modern *Port RSL*, Settlement City, Bay St, T6580 2300, every Fri/Sat. For a quieter night out try the congenial *Finnians Irish Pub*, 97 Gordon St. They stage live bands at the weekend. The city **cinema** is at corner of Clarence and Horton sts, T6583 8400.

Shopping The main shopping streets are Clarence and Horton sts with the **Port Central Shopping Arcade** at the northern end of the latter. The large, modern **Settlement City Shopping Centre** is near the Marina at the junction of Bay and Park sts. *Camping World*, 133 Horton St, T6583 2390, is the place to buy camping equipment. *Angus and Robertson Bookworld*, Port Central Shopping Centre, Horton St, T6583 4626.

Tours & activities **Aerial** *Alltime Skydive*, T6584 3655, skydive@midcoast.com.au, offer 10,000-ft tandem skydives from $290. *High Adventure Air Park*, Pacific Highway, Johns River, T1800 063 648, www.highadventure.com.au, offer an exciting range of activities including tandem hang gliding (from $195), paragliding (30 mins from $185) and 45-min microlight flights from $130. *Johnston Aviation*, T1800 025 935, *Coastwings*, T6584 1130, and *Wingaway Air*, T65841155, all offer fixed-wing scenic flights from $35. *Seaplane Joy and Charter*, T04 1250 7698, offer float plane trips from $45-275 while for true adrenaline try *Fighter Flight Centre*, T6583 9788, www.fighterflightcentre.com, 35 mins from $450-1,950. *Port Aero Transport and Training*, T6583 4198, also offer scenic flights where you take the controls (be it briefly) on your own, from $55.

Land-based *Camel Safaris*, on Lighthouse Beach, are a local favourite, T6583 7650. Rides are from 20 mins to 1 hr, from $15/28, child $10/18, with breakfast from $33. *Centre of Gravity*, 52 Jindalee Rd, T6581 3899, offer indoor rock climbing, with walls from 5-11 m, bouldering, caves and ladders, from $15 with instruction. Phone for varying seasonal opening hours. Along the same lines and preferably attached to one you can go for a full days abseiling, up to 45 m, with *Edge Experience*, T6585 3531. On 4 wheels you can blat about on an ATV with the all new *ATV Quad Bike Tours*, T6582 3065, on 2, hire a bike and join *Hastings Valley Mountain Bike Riders*, T6583 3633, from $12 (plus hire) or on 4 legs go horse trekking with *Cowarra Forest Trails*, Wauchope, T6585 3531, 1 hr from $30. There are a number of excellent wineries in the region. The VIC can supply details of the North Coast Wine Trail which takes in five of the best. *Macquarie Mountain Tours*, T6582 3065, offer various regional tours including a wine tasting tour on Thu/Sat/Sun afternoons from $29. *Port Explorer*, T6581 2181, offers informative bus tours of the town, from $16, child $15 and as far afield as Bellingen and Dorrigo, from $42, child $36.

Water-based Most of 'The Port's' activities are of course water based with almost everything on offer from sedate river cruises to precarious surf lessons. The Wharf at the western end of Clarence St is a good place to start. There you will find *Port Macquarie River Cruise* (Port Venture), T6583 3058. They carry over 200 passengers onboard the *MV Venture* offering a scenic 2-hr River Cruise, 1000/1400, most days, from $20, child $8; 5-hr BBQ Cruise 1000 Wed, from $37, child $18, and a 4-hr BBQ Cruise, 1000 Mon, from $35, child 415. Also based at the Wharf are *Waterbus Everglades Tours*, T1300 555890, that offer daily river cruises to an oyster farm 1000/1400, from $22, child $9; 5-hr Everglades and Butter Factory Cruise, Tue, 0930, from $50, child $33 and a 4½-hr cruise to Wauchope and Timbertown, Wed 1000, from $38, child $25. *The Pelican* is a historic 30-ft steamboat built in 1949 that offers a very sedate and

North Coast NSW

value range of cruises, from $20, T04 1865 2171. Independent boat and canoe hire is also available at the Wharf, with *Hastings River Boat Hire*, T6583 8811, *Jordan's Boat Hire* in the Caravan Park on Settlement Point Rd (North Shore), T6583 1005, and at Settlement Point itself, T6583 6300. All shapes and sizes of craft are on offer starting at about $20 for 2 hrs. *C-Spray*, northern end of the Wharf, Short St, T6584 1626, also offer jet ski hire from $40 for 15 mins. *Port Water Sports*, T04 1223 4509, offer parasailing, from $55. For offshore fishing charters contact *Odyssey*, T6582 2377, www.odyssey charters.com.au, or *Canopus*, T6585 5474, from $95 half day. *Port Macquarie Estuary Sportsfishing*, T6582 2545, offer full- or half-day estuary fishing from $77 and *Castaway*, T6582 5261, beachfishing trips. Surfing lessons are available with *Dawn Light*, T6584 1477, dawnlight@turboweb.net.au, from $30 per hr. There are a number of dive operators including *Port Diving Academy*, Shop 7 Port Marina, T6584 6062, portdivingacademy@tsn.cc, offering equipment hire, courses and weekend packages with 5 boat dives from $220 and mid-week packages with 8 boat dives for certified divers, from $350. *Rick's Dive School*, T6584 7759, offer courses starting at $220.

Transport Air Port Macquarie Airport is 3 km west of the town centre on Boundary Rd (off Hastings River Dr), T65834382. *QantasLink*, T131313, and Hazelton, T131713, offer daily services to Sydney. **Bike hire** Available from *Graham Seers*, Shop 1, Port Marina, Park St, T6583 2333, from $22 per day. **Bus** Long-distance buses stop at the bus terminal on Hayward St. *Premier Motor Service* have an booking office at the terminal, T6583 1488. Open Mon-Fri 0830-1700, Sat 0830-1200. *McCafferty's*, T131499, and *Greyhound*, T132030, also offer daily state-wide services. *Keans Coaches*, T1800 043 339, run a service from Port Macquarie to Scone (via the Waterfall Way, Dorrigo/Bellingen/Armidale and Tamworth) 3 times a week, Tue/Thu/Sun. *Kings Bros*, 6 Denham St, T6583 3079, www.kingsbrosbus.com.au, offer both local and regional bus services to, Wauchope, Kempsey, with connections to Coffs Harbour and Armidale 3 times a week. To access the eastern beaches jump on the #331. **Taxi** T65810081. **Train** The nearest train station is at Wauchope 19 km west of the city, T132232. The connecting bus to Port Macquarie is included in the fare.

Directory Banks All major branches with ATMs can be found along Clarence and Horton sts. **Car hire** *Budget*, corner of Gordon and Hollingworth sts, T6583 5144; *Hertz*, 102 Gordon St, T6583 6599. **Communications** Internet: *Port Surf Hub Internet Lounge*, 57 Clarence St, T6584 4744. Open daily until late. Or the **Hastings Library**, corner of Grant and Gordon sts, T6581 8755. Open Mon-Fri 0930-1800, Sat 0900-1200. **Post office**: corner of Clarence and Horton sts. Open Mon-Fri 0900-1700. **Medical services** Port Macquarie Base Hospital, Wright Rd, T6581 2000. Police 2 Hay St,T65830199. **Travel agencies** *Port Macquarie Travel Agency*, 110 William St, T6583 1422, porttvl@bigpond.com **Useful numbers** NRMA: Port Central, Horton St, T6584 2050.

Kempsey and Crescent Head

Colour map 1, grid A5/6
Population: 9,000
49 km north of Port Macquarie, 167 km south of Mackay

Kempsey, on the banks of the Mcleay River, is the commercial centre of the Mcleay River Valley. Although a pleasant place with a few notable attractions it serves mainly as a temporary stop before heading further north or east to the coast and the Hat Head National Park. If you are short of time, save your bucket and spade and sunblock for South West Rocks.

Macleay River Museum, next door to the VIC (see page 187), includes a replica of a pioneer settlers cottage. **Wingay Aboriginal Culture Park** offers plenty of cultural insight including traditional bush tucker, boomerang throwing and didgeridoo playing. Entertaining and informative ranges of local tours are also on offer with genuine Aboriginal guides. ■ *Daily. $7. Danger St.*

Although the small village of **Crescent Head**, 20 km northeast of Kempsey, does not have the same aesthetic appeal as South West Rocks and Smoky Cape, 37 km further north, it does offer a quiet escape with some fine beaches with good surfing. To the south of the village, Limeburners Creek Nature Reserve has a number of fine coastal walks featuring historic Aboriginal sites, particularly around Big Hill and Point Plomer.

A-F *Crescent Head Holiday Park*, located on Pacific St, east of the village centre, T6566 0261. Basic but offers a good range of cabins, powered and non-powered sites, BBQ though no camp kitchen. Basic NPWS camping is available at Crescent Head and the Nature Reserve, T6586 8300. **Sleeping & eating**

Bus *Kings Bros*, T6562 4724, run a Kempsey (Belgrave St) to Crescent Head (Country Club) bus service (#345), Mon-Fri at 0835/1230. **Transport**

South West Rocks, Hat Head and Hat Head National Park

South West Rocks is the best-kept secret on the NSW north coast. In comparison to Byron Bay, it has everything except the footprints. Long swathes of golden sand, great fishing and swimming, a cliff-top lighthouse, stunning views and a superb local national park – Hat Head – combine to make South West Rocks the ideal place to get away from the crowds and simply kick back for a few days. Here, you can watch dolphins surfing rather than people. South West Rocks is best reached and explored using your own transport.

Colour map 2, grid C4
Population: 3,500
94 km north of Port
Macquarie, 123 km
south of Coffs
Harbour

South West Rocks Visitors Centre is housed in one of the two historic 'Rocks' Boatman's Cottages on Ocean Drive, next to the caravan park (end of Gregory St), T6566 7099, www.kempsey.midcoast.com.au Daily 1000-1600. Kempsey VIC, South Kempsey Park (off Pacific Highway), Kempsey, T1800 642 480, www.kempsey.midcoast.com.au, is a good source of information. They have NPWS national parks information. Open daily. **Ins & outs**
See Transport, page 188, for details

South West Rocks sits at the southern bank of the Mcleay River mouth and western end of Trail Bay, where the colourful, wave-eroded rocks that earned the village its name form the perfect playground for swimmers and snorkellers. At the eastern end of Trial Bay the charming settlement of **Arakoon** fringes the Arakoon State Recreation Area and Laggers Point which is the site of the pink granite monolith Trial Bay Gaol that was built in 1886 and now houses a small museum that offers some sympathetic insight into the torrid existence of its former inmates. ■ *Daily 0900-1700. $4. T6566 6168.* Trial Bay was named after *The Trial*, a vessel that was stolen by former convicts and was wrecked in the Bay in 1816. Several other vessels with more conventional crew were wrecked in Trial Bay in the 1970s. A few rusting remnants still jut out from their sandy grave. **Sights**

At the terminus of Wilson Street, at the western end of Arakoon, is **Little Bay**, with its sublime beach on which to escape humanity. The car park also provides access to the Graves Monument walking track (2 km return) which provides memorable views back across Trial Bay and the Trail Bay Gaol. Gap Beach, accessed a little further south is another fine spot, especially for the more adventurous surfer. South of Arakoon (3 km) Lighthouse Road provides access to the northern fringe of the Hat Head National Park, Smoky Beach and the Smoky Cape Lighthouse. The 1891 lighthouse is one of the tallest and oldest in NSW and provides stunning views south to Crescent Head and north down to the beckoning solitude of North Smoky Beach.

South of South West Rocks, accessed via Hat Head Village Road and Kinchela, the small village and headland of **Hat Head** sits in the heart of the national park separating the long swathes of Smoky Beach north and Killick Beach to the south. The village has a caravan park, limited amenities and walking access to Hat Hill, Korogoro Point, Connor's Beach and the Hungry Hill Rest Area.

Sleeping

For resort, apartment and holiday house accommodation the best bet is to contact the local real estate agents

Raine and Horne, T6566 6116, randhswr@midcoast.com.au, and *Elders*, T6566 6666, swrps@midcosat.com.au, can assist. The most unusual accommodation in the area has to be the former keepers quarters at **L** *Smoky Cape Lighthouse*, T6566 6301, www.smokycapelighthouse.com.au Totally refurbished in the interior it provides self-contained or B&B options, modern facilities, a '4-poster' and stunning views south across the national park. Book well in advance. Recommended. **L-A** *Rockpool Motel*, 45 McIntyre St, T6566 7755, www.rockpoolmotorinn.com.au, is a modern motel complex 1 km east of the town centre, while the older and cheaper **A-B** *Bay Motel*, Livingstone St, T6566 6909, is right on the main shopping street. The busy and beautifully placed **A-E** *Horseshoe Bay Beach Park*, Livingstone St, T6566 6370, overlooks the river, ocean and the sheltered Horseshoe Bay Beach, within yards of the town centre. It offers cabins, on-site vans and powered sites (some en suite). Hugely popular with locals so book well in advance. **D** *Arakoon State Recreation Area*, T6566 6168, Laggers Point, beside the Trail Bay Gaol. Equally fine aesthetics and more seclusion can be secured here. It's a great spot and the best for camping. There are also good basic NPWS campsites at **F** *Smoky Rest Area*, near the lighthouse (excellent for wildlife) and **F** *Hungry Rest Area*, south of Hat Head village. Pit toilets, no water and fires permitted. Self-registration, fees apply, T6584 2203.

Eating

In Arakoon, overlooking the Trail Bay Goal and beach, *Trial Bay Kiosk*, T6566 7100, provides a superb location, al fresco dining and quality but fairly pricey fare. Good breakfasts and coffee. Open daily for breakfast and lunch 0800-1600 and Thu/Fri/Sat for dinner. Back in South West Rocks *Geppy's*, corner of Livingstone St and Memorial Ave, T6566 6196, is well known for good seafood, Italian and modern Australian cuisine. Live jazz and blues on Wed. Locally recommended *Pizza on the Rocks*, Prince of Wales Ave, T6566 6626, or *Seabreeze Hotel Bistro*, at the top of Livingstone St, T6566 6205.

Tours & activities

The immediate area is well renowned for its excellent dive sites including the 120-m Fish Rock Cave, home to many species including wobbygongs, cod and rays. *South West Rocks Dive Centre*, 5/98 Gregory St, T6566 6474, www.southwestrocksdive.com.au, offer both trips and accommodation. The entrance to the Macleay River also offers some good snorkelling but only at peak tide. *Trail Bay Fishing Charters*, T04 2725 6556, offer fishing and whale/dolphin watching trips and Osprey, T6566 6612, river trips (Boatshed via Gordon Young Dr, 5 km west off Gregory St).

Transport

Bus *Kings Bros*, T65624724, run a Kempsey (Belgrave St) to South West Rocks (Livingstone St) bus #350, Mon-Fri at 0740/1130/1530. *Rocks Travel*, Shop 1/3 Livingstone St, T6566 6770, www.rockstravel.com.au, can assist with onwards travel. **Taxi** T65666677.

Nambucca Heads

Colour map 2, grid C4
Population: 6,000
131 km north of Port Macquarie, 53 km south of Coffs Harbour

Nambucca is a popular domestic holiday destination on the east coast and has been for years. Much quieter than Coffs Harbour but still relatively well facilitated, it provides a good place to escape the crowds and is blessed with some glorious beaches and lookouts. The picturesque Nambucca River also provides some good fishing and boating opportunities.

Nambucca Heads VIC is located on the Pacific Highway at the southern entrance to Nambucca Heads (Riverside Dr), T6568 6954, www.nambuccatourism.com.au Open daily 0900-1700. Town maps are available on request.

Ins & outs
See Transport, page 190, for details

Sights

Nambucca's elevated position gives the town some excellent **views** up and down the coast. The Rotary and Captain Cook lookouts on Parkes Street, east off Bowra and right off Ridge Street, offer fine views south to South West Rocks, across the river mouth and down over Shelly Beach. Further north, at the end of Liston Street, beyond Ridge Street, the Lions Lookout looks north and below to the Main Surfing Beach. No doubt the views will tempt you down to the beaches, which are patrolled in summer and provide some good surfing.

The Nambucca River mouth is fringed by a sea wall – **Vee Wall** – which is good for fishing and dolphin watching. Although the locals snorkel here do not be tempted as the currents are notorious. River boats and canoes can be hired, see Tours and activities for details. Vee Wall shares Port Macquarie's concept of using the rocks as 'postcards' or a 'graffiti forum'. Covered in messages and insights from visitors it makes for some colourful, if repetitive reading. Far more imaginative is the unusual 60m-**mosaic wall** outside the police station in Bowra Street. Created by local artist Guy Crozley; it took two years to complete. See if you can spot the toilet bowl.

Inland from Nambucca the historic villages of **Macksville** and **Bowraville** are worth a look if you have your own transport. Bowraville Folk Museum is considered one of the best folk museums in the state. In **Taylors Arm**, 26 km away, the **Pub With No Beer** is a congenial, historic local made famous by folk singer Slim Dusty. It does in fact sell beer and also a quality lunch.

Sleeping

L *Destiny Motor Inn*, corner of Pacific Highway and Riverside Dr, T6568 8044, is a modern, well-facilitated establishment, right beside the main highway. Closer to the town centre, **A-C** *Max Motel*, 4 Fraser St, T6568 6138, has tidy rooms. Two offer superb views across the river mouth. **A-C** *Bellby's Beach House B&B*, 1 Ocean St, T6568 6466, beilbys@midcoast.com.au Within walking distance of the beach is this friendly and good value B&B. Well-appointed single/double/twin/quad and family rooms with en suites, showers or shared bathrooms, complimentary breakfast, bikes, boogie/surf board, fishing gear hire, internet and a great pool. **C-E** *Nambucca Backpackers Hostel*, 3 Newman St, T6568 6360. The only backpacker in town. Quiet, motel-style with dorms, doubles, twins, singles, and fully self-contained units and can take the odd tent. Good discounts in the low season. Organized trips, free bike, boogie/surf board, snorkel gear hire, internet and pick-ups from the bus stop. **L-F** *White Albatross Holiday Resort*, right next to the Nambucca River mouth and Vee Wall (end of Wellington Dr), T6568 6468. The best motor park in the town, it has just about everything from luxury units with spa, to on-site vans and campsites. Good camp kitchen and excellent bistro/bar.

Eating

Boatshed Seafood Brasserie, 1 Wellington St, overlooking the river, T6568 9292, for seafood and steak. Recommended. Open daily 1200-1430 and 1800. *V Wall Tavern Bistro and Bar*, Wellington St, T6568 6394, is an award winner and popular with the locals. *RSL*, Nelson St, T6568 6288, is a modern option, great value and especially good for budget meals on Thu/Sun, with à la carte Tue-Sat). *Star Fish Café*, 5 Mann St, T6569 4422, good coffee, breakfasts and light lunches, friendly. Open daily 0800-1700. Main supermarkets are off Fraser St, or off Pacific Highway, south of the Riverside Drive junction.

Tours & activities

River boats can be hired from *Nambucca Boatshed*, Wellington Drive, T6568 5550 and *Beachcomber Marine*, Riverside Drive, T6568 6432. Canoes can also be hired for exploring the Warrel Creek, from the *Scotts Head Caravan Park*, 1 Short St, T6569 8122.

North Coast NSW

Transport   **Bus**   The long-distance terminal is located near the VIC and supermarket on the Pacific Highway. *McCafferty's*, T131499, *Greyhound*, T132030, and *Premier*, T133410, all provide drop-offs. *King Bros Buses*, T1300 555 611, run between Nambucca Heads and Bellingen several times daily, Mon-Fri, from $5.40, child $5. *Newmans*, T6568 1296, stop outside the police station on Bowra St and offer daily services to Coffs Harbour. *Keans Coaches*, T1800 043 339, run a service from Scone to Port Macquarie and Coffs Harbour (via the Waterfall Way and Dorrigo/Bellgen) 3 times a week, Mon/Wed/Fri returning Tue/Thu/Sun. **Train**   The station is 3 km north west of the town centre, via Railway Rd (off Bowra). *Countrylink*, T132232, offer state and interstate services. *Nambucca World Travel*, Shop 16, Nambucca Plaza, T6569 4411, acts as the local bus and rail booking agents.

Directory   Internet available at the *Bookshop and Internet Café*, corner Bowra and Ridge St, T6568 5855. Open daily 0900-1700.

Bellingen

Colour map 2, grid C4
Population: 3,000
160 km north of Port Macquarie, 38 km south of Coffs Harbour

Sitting neatly on the banks of the Bellinger River, in the heart of the Bellinger Valley, the distinctly pleasant country village of Bellingen is well renowned for its artistic and alternative community, its markets, music festivals and laid-back, congenial ambience, all of which rightfully lure tired travellers from the hype and heat of the coast. Simple relaxation or country walks are the name of the game in and around Bellingen, before continuing further inland to explore the superb national parks of Dorrigo and New England, or the resumption the relentless journey northwards up the coast. The village has its own nickname used affectionately by the locals – Bello.

Ins & outs
See Transport, page 192, for further details

Getting there   There aren't any long-distance connections to Belligen – you must travel to Nambucca Heads or Uranga and then get a connection. **Getting around** The main areas of interest are within walking distance. **Tourist information** VIC to Bellingen is beside the Pacific Highway, in Uranga, just south of the Bellingen turn-off. Bellingen Visitors Centre, T1800 808 611, www.bellingen.nsw.gov.au/tourism/bellingen.html Mon-Sat 0900-1700, Sun 1000-1400. Ask for a free street map of the town.

Sights   Bellingen's peaceful tree-lined streets are lined with some obvious heritage buildings many of which are protected by the National Trust. The small **Bellingen Museum** in Civic Square, Hyde Street, contains a low-key collection of photos and artefacts that concentrate on the 'cedar-getting' and boat building years of the mid-1800s, as well as detail about the Bellinger Rivers dramatic propensity to flood. ■ *Mon/Wed-Fri 1000-1200, T6655 0289*. **The Old Butter Factory**, Doepel Lane, on the western approach to the village, and the unmistakable **Yellow Shed**, 2 Hyde Street, are the two main arts and crafts outlets in the village selling everything from opals to wind-chimes. The Old Butter Factory also has a café and offers a range of relaxation and healing therapies including iridology, massage and a float tank. Both open daily from 0930 to 1700. The colourful Bellingen craft and produce **market** is considered one of the best in the region and is held in the local park on the third Saturday of the month. The village also hosts a top quality **Jazz Festival** in mid-August, and the equally popular **Global Carnival**, which is an entertaining celebration of world music held in the first week in October.

Nature lovers, or those who need to dispel their irrational fears of bats, should take a look and a big whiff of the large **flying fox (fruit bat) colony** on Bellingen Island, which is now no longer an island beside the river, and within easy walking distance from the centre of the village. The best place to view the colony is from the Bellingen Caravan Park on Dowle Street (cross the Bridge off Hyde, on to Hammond then turn right in to Dowle), while the best time to observe them en masse is around dusk when they depart to find food. But even during the day it is an impressive sight indeed as they hang like a thousand Christmas decorations from almost every tree.

L *Monticello Countryhouse*, 11 Sunset Ridge Drive, (2 km) T6655 1559, www. bellingen.com/monticello and **L** *Bliss Lodge*, 355 Martells Rd (12 km southeast), T6655 9111, www.blissholidays.com.au, are both popular B&Bs, within easy reach of the village. **L-A** *Rivendell Guest House*, situated right in the heart of town on Hyde St (12), T6655 0060. **L** *Fernridge Farm Cottage*, 1673 Waterfall Way (4 km west), T6655 2142, fernridge@bellingen.com.au, provides peaceful, cosy, self-contained accommodation in a 19th-century 'Queenslander' cottage on an 120 ha alpaca farm. **LL** *Kumbaingiri Retreat*, 180 Kalang Rd, T9212 0388, www.kumbaingiriretreat.com.au More contemporary and spacious than *Fernridge*, this is another quality self-contained option.

A-B *Bellinger Valley Motor Inn*, 1381 Waterfall Way, T6655 1599. A good motel option within walking distance of the village centre, with pool, spa and in-house restaurant. **B-F** *Bellingen YHA Backpackers*, 2 Short St, T6655 1116, belloyha@midcoast.com.au, consistently receives rave reviews and deservingly so. Housed in a beautifully maintained 2-storey historic homestead in the heart of the village, with large decks overlooking the river valley, it oozes character and has a great social, laid-back atmosphere. It has a range of dorms, double/twins, family rooms and camping facilities. Internet, musical instruments, hammocks and entertaining trips to Dorrigo National Park are all on offer and donning the hallways are tasteful nude photographs of over 300 guests willing to get genuinely creative and arty. **C-F** *Bellingen Caravan Park*, beside the bat colony on Dowle St, T6655 1338, is basic. On-site vans, powered and non-powered sites but no camp kitchen.

For fine dining *No2 Oak St*, T6655 9000, is recommended. Housed in a 1910 heritage cottage it offers an excellent and innovative menu. Book ahead. Open Tue-Sat, from 1800. There are plenty of excellent cafés in the village with Church St hosting many of them: *Cool Creek Café* has a nice atmosphere, is good value and offers occasional live music. Closed Tue/Wed. Next door, *Good Food Shop* is great for sandwiches, while sweet teeth will chatter with delight in *Swiss Patisserie and Bakery* which offers some irresistible cakes and sweets. Elsewhere, overlooking the river valley, *Lodge 241*, 121 Hyde St, T6655 2470, is a café, gallery combined offering fine local cuisine and good coffee. Open daily 0800-1700. For good-value, wholesome pub grub and live music, try *Diggers Tavern*, 30 Hyde St, T6655 0022. Open Wed-Sat for lunch and Wed-Sun for dinner, and for gourmet pizza, *Café Bare Nature*, 111 Hyde St, T6655 1551. Open Mon-Fri from 1430, Sat/Sun from 1130.

Bellingen offers a fine base from which to explore the numerous excellent rainforest walks of the Dorrigo National Park (see below). The river also offers some exciting opportunities; either by canoe or on a river cruise. *Bellingen Canoe Adventures*, T6655 9955, www.bellingen.com/canoe, offer half-day guided trips from $44, full-day trips from $88, a sunset tour from $66 and independent hire from $11 per/hr, while *Water Rat River Cruises*, based in Uranga, T6655 6439, offer sedate cruises of the lower reaches, from $25. *On the Wallaby*, 18 Hammond St, T6655 4388, offer half- and full-day 4WD eco-tours of the Bellinger Valley and Dorrigo Plateau and also wildlife night spotting from $30. *Gambarri Aboriginal Tours*, T6655 4195, offer local guided tours with lots of cultural insight, activities and entertainment, from $50.

Sleeping
Given the verdant country setting it is not surprising to find plenty of good B&Bs and self-contained cottages in the area

Eating

Tours & activities

North Coast NSW

Transport   **Bus** The long-distance buses do not make the detour to Bellingen, with the nearest stop being either Nambucca Heads or Uranga. *King Bros Buses*, T1300 555 611, run between Nambucca Heads, Uranga, Coffs Harbour and Bellingen several times daily, Mon-Fri, from $5.40, child $5. **Train** The nearest station is in Uranga. *Countrylink*, T132232, offer state and interstate services.

Directory   **Communications** Internet: available free at the *Bellingen Library*, Hyde St, open Tue-Fri 1030-1730 or at the *Bellingen Environment Centre*, 1 Church St Lane (just off Church St) T6655 2599, open Mon-Fri 0900-1715. *Bellingen Travel*, 42 Hyde St, Bellingen, T6655 2055, can also offer some local information and can assist with travel bookings and enquiries.

Dorrigo and Dorrigo National Park

Colour map 2, grid C4
Population: 1,000
188 km north of Port
Macquarie, 66 km
southwest of Coffs
Harbour

From Bellingen the **Waterfall Way** follows the Bellinger River upstream, passing through some beautiful countryside, before making the steep, 1,000-m climb through the lush forested slopes of the **Dorrigo National Park** to emerge at the crest of the **Dorrigo Plateau** and the former timber town of **Dorrigo**. It makes for a strange transition, almost as if you have been raised to some forgotten country in the clouds. It doesn't just rain here – it pours – with 250 mm in 24 hours during a typical subtropical summer downpour, merely raising a single dripping eyebrow. Dorrigo provides the gateway to the World Heritage listed Dorrigo National Park with its excellent views and rainforest walks as well as a scattering of scenic waterfalls. Further west the Waterfall Way resumes its scenic course through gorgeous green rolling hills towards **New England National Park** and Armidale.

Ins & outs   Dorrigo VIC, Hickory St in the centre of Dorrigo, T6657 2202, www.dorrigo.com.au,
See Transport, page
193, for details
offers local accommodation listings. Open daily 1000-1600. Ask for a free street map. NPWS Dorrigo National Park Rainforest Visitors Centre Dome Rd, T6657 2309, supplies national parks, walks and some local information.

Sights   Provided the weather is kind and the clouds do not blind you, you are in for a scenic treat. Even the Dorrigo National Park Rainforest Visitors Centre has an amazing vista. Sitting right at the edge of the escarpment, the view across the forested slopes and across the Bellinger Valley towards the coast, is greatly enhanced with the slightly shaky 100-m **Skywalk** that sits like a jetty out across the rainforest canopy. From its edge, like some eagle in its mountain eyrie, you can survey the glorious scene, listen to the strange and distant calls of illusive rainforest birds. You may also see the odd python curled up in a branch or right next to the handrail. The visitors centre itself has some good interpretative displays and a small café. The main office and shop can provide the necessary detail on the excellent **rainforest walks** (ranging from 400m to 5.4 km) that begin from the centre and descend in to the very different world beneath the forest canopy. ■ *Daily 0900-1700. T6657 2309.*

From the Rainforest Centre it is then a short, scenic 10-km drive along the edge of the escarpment to the **Never Never Picnic Area**, which is not a place of pixies and fairies bearing tasty sandwiches but instead a fine network of rainforest walks, including the 5.5-km Rosewood Creek Track to **Cedar Falls**, the 4.8-km **Casuarina Falls** Track and the 6.4-km Blackbutt (escarpment edge) Track. Before heading into Dorrigo township itself, it is worth taking the short 2-km drive to **Griffith's Lookout** for its memorable views across the Bellinger Valley. The road to the lookout is signposted about 1 km south of

North Coast NSW

Dome Road off the Waterfall Way. Just north of Dorrigo (1.5 km), the **Dangar Falls** may prove a disappointment after long periods of fine weather to many but after rain can become a thunderous torrent of floodwaters.

L *Ridgetop Hideaway*, 193 Old Coast Rd, 5 km northwest, T6657 2243, www.dorrigo. **Sleeping**
com/hideaway, and **A** *Fernbrook Lodge*, 470 Waterfall Way, 6 km west, T6657 2573,
fernbrooklodge@midcoast.com.au, both offer great views and are recommended.
B-C *Historic Dorrigo Hotel*, corner of Hickory and Cudgery sts), T6657 2016, offers traditional pub rooms at affordable prices in the centre. Other comfortable budget (B&B)
accommodation is offered at **A-E** *Gracemere Grange*, 325 Dome Rd, 2 km from the
Rainforest Centre, T6657 2630, helenp@omcs.com.au **C-F** *Dorrigo Mountain Resort*,
on the southern edge of the town on the Waterfall Way, T6657 2564, has standard
self-contained cabins, powered and non-powered sites, BBQs, but no camp kitchen.

For fine dining try *Misty's*, 33 Hickory St, T6657 2855, open Thu-Sun from 1800. For pub **Eating**
grub the hotel is an old classic and for coffee and light snacks the *Art Place Gallery*, 20
Cudgery St, T6657 2622, open daily 1000-1630, or *The Good, the Bad and the Healthy*,
also on Cudgery St, T6657 2304.

Bus *Kings Bros*, T1300555622, offer coach tours to Dorrigo from Coffs Harbour. *Keans* **Transport**
Coaches, T1800 043 339, also run a service from Coffs Harbour (via the Waterfall Way
and Dorrigo/Belligen/Armidale and Tamworth) 3 times a week, Tue/Thu/Sun.

Oxley Rivers National Park

The World Heritage listed Oxley Rivers National Park takes in the dramatic *Colour map 2, grid C3*
gorges and **waterfalls** of the **Macleay River** watershed. The two major attrac- *40 km east and south*
tions are the dramatic 260-m **Wollomombi and Chandler Falls** that plunge *of Armidale*
in to the Wollomombi Gorge, 40 km east of Armidale, and **Dangars Gorge**
(and Falls) to the southeast. The main body of the park however is fairly inaccessible and lies about 50 km southeast of Armidale. The best way to get
around is in your own transport, preferably a 4WD. If you are short for time
the Wollomombi Falls and Gorge are certainly worth a visit with the falls
lookout only 1 km from the main road and a 100-m walk from the car park.
There is also a five-hour strenuous River walk that will deliver you to the base
of the gorge. **Gara Gorge** section of the park, 18 km from Armidale, southeast
on Castledoyle Road, also offers some great **swimming holes**. VIC or NPWS
office in **Armidale** both stock the relevant leaflets and information surrounding
the park, its walks and camping facilities, www.npws.nsw.gov.au

Basic car-based (**F**) camping is available at Wollomombi Gorge, Long Point, Dangars **Sleeping**
Gorge, Budds Mare, Aspley Falls and Tia Falls. *Youdales Hut*, in the southern sector of **& eating**
the park, is another good site for camping. NPWS also have a historic homestead at
East Kunderang that provides comfortable, modern, self-contained accommodation. It
is remote (112 km southeast of Armidale) but accessible by 2WD. For details, T6776 4260.

Waterfall Way Tours, T6772 2018, www.waterfallway.com.au, based in Armidale offer **Tours &**
half-, full- or two-day eco-tours to Oxley Rivers, from $40. **activities**

The Waterfall Way east of Armidale and the Oxley Highway, south (via Walcha) fringe **Transport**
the park and provide the main access points in to the interior. For details contact local
NPWS offices or the website, see above.

North Coast NSW

North Coast NSW

► **Things that go bump in the night...**

Thungutti campsite in New England National Park at night, shrouded in mist and enveloped in bush can be a little scary, but when a Tiger Quoll comes calling its like something out of a Spielberg movie. The Tiger Quoll is the largest surviving marsupial carnivore in NSW and sadly has declined greatly in number since the arrival of Europeans, the subsequent loss of habitat and predation by introduced predators like foxes and, ironically –cats. Although its natural diet is extensive and includes other small mammals, sadly, quolls have taken to the far more accessible handouts (or more often blatant burglary options) on offer in campsites. If you are paid a visit, by all means admire and watch, but by no means feed the little devils. Doing so actually limits the individual's ability to hunt naturally opens it up to human abuse and in essence only promotes their decline.

New England and Cathedral Rocks national parks

Colour map 2, grid C3
85 km east of Armidale, 107 km west from Urunga (Pacific Highway)

The 71, 207 ha **New England National Park** is breathtaking. What makes it so special are not only its sense of wilderness and rich biodiversity, but its stunning vistas, **Point Lookout** being the most popular and accessible, and truly memorable. Do not venture here automatically expecting to see those views however. What adds a very atmospheric and unpredictable edge to this viewpoint is its height, which, at over 1,564 m often results in a shroud of mist or worse still, sheets of rain. It really can be a glorious day in Armidale and along the coast and yet Point Lookout is like Edinburgh Castle in mid winter. Still, if you can afford a couple of days the camping, the views and the varied walks around Point Lookout (2.5 km to full day) are well worthwhile.

Just north of Point Lookout Road, Round Mountain Road (8 km) ventures into the heart of **Cathedral Rock National Park**. The main feature here is the magnificent granite tors – **Cathedral Rocks** – and in spring, vivid displays of wildflowers. The 6-km Cathedral Rock Track from the Barokee Rest Area provides a circuit track with a 200-m diversion to the 'Rocks'.

The VIC in Armidale or NPWS offices in Armidale (see above) or the Dorrigo Rainforest, Centre, T66572309, www.npws.nsw.gov.au, both stock the relevant leaflets and information surrounding the park, its walks, camping and self-contained accommodations.

Sleeping
L *Moffat Falls Cottage*, T6775 9166, Point Lookout Rd, www.moffatfalls.com.au, is comfortable, self-contained with a wood fire and 2 bedrooms. Basic car-based (**F**) camping is available at *Thungutti campsite*, just past the park boundary along Point Lookout Rd (2.5 km from the lookout). Basic facilities, water, a good sheltered BBQ area and firewood. Other accommodation along Point Lookout Rd includes 3 self-contained **NPWS cabins** ($29-51 per person per night, minimum 2 nights stay). Call for details and book well ahead, T6657 2309. There is basic car-based (**F**) camping available at the **Barokee Rest Area** in the Cathedral National Park. Bring supplies for cooking.

Transport
Point lookout Rd is unsealed and accessed (signposted) off the Waterfall Way, 5 km south of the Waterfall Way/Guyra Rd Junction (3 km west of Ebor). It is then 11 km to the park boundary and a further 3 km to Point Lookout. **Bus** *Keans Coaches*, T1800 043 339, from Coffs Harbour (via Waterfall Way and Dorrigo/Belligen/Armidale and Tamworth) 3 times a week, Tue/Thu/Sun.

Coffs Harbour

*Roughly halfway between Sydney and Brisbane and the only spot on the NSW coast where the Great Dividing Range meets the sea, Coffs Harbour is a favourite domestic holiday resort and the main commercial centre for the northern NSW coast. Surrounded by rolling hills draped by lush banana plantations, pretty beaches and hosting a wealth of **activities**, it presents a fine spot to kick back for a couple of days before continuing north to Byron Bay and Queensland, or inland, along the Oxley Highway to Armidale, New England and beyond. The main activities in town are centred around the town's attractive **marina** where regular fishing, whale and dolphin watching cruises are on offer, together with highly popular **diving** and snorkelling trips to the outlying **Solitary Islands**. The island group and surrounding coast is gazetted as a marine park and considered to have one of the most diverse marine bio-diversities in NSW. Other principal attractions include **Muttonbird Island** that guards the entrance to the harbour and offers sanctuary to thousands of burrowing seabirds and, in complete contrast, a huge and far more obvious model banana beside the main highway and the kitschy **Big Banana** complex, on the northern edge of the town.*

Colour map 2, grid C4
Population: 23,000
558 km north of Brisbane, 426 km south of Brisbane

Getting there The airport, 3 km out of town, with services from main cities. Long-distance buses serve the area and there is a train station in the centre of town. **Getting around** Small enough to get around on foot though there are local buses and bike hire. **Tourist information** VIC, corner of Elizabeth and Maclean sts, T6652 1522, www.coffs tourism.com.au Daily 0900-1700. Ask for the free *Coffs Coast Visitors Guide*. NPWS, 32 Marina Dr, T6652 0900, coffs.coast@npws.nsw.gov.au Mon-Fri 0900-1700.

Ins and outs
See Transport, page 200, for further details

Sights

The rather unsightly and uninspiring main drag through Coffs Harbour, Grafton Street, has seen something of an improvement in recently, with the creation of the Palms Centre Arcade, and redevelopment of the Mall and Park Avenue, which combined form the hub of the town centre. From the end of the Mall, High Street heads 3 km west to the coast and the much more pleasant aesthetics and beaches that surround the harbour.

The harbour is hemmed in by the town's three main beaches: **Park Beach**, which straddles Coffs Creek to the north, **Jetty Beach**, beside the harbour and **Boambee Beach** to the south. Park Beach is the most popular generally and is regularly patrolled in summer. Jetty Beach is considered the safest. The view from **Beacon Hill Lookout**, at the end of Camperdown Street, off High Street, offers fine 360-degree vistas across the harbour, the coast, and the green rolling hills of the Great Dividing Range to the west. There are also numerous other, excellent beaches, stretching 20 km north all the way to **Woolgoolga**.

The harbour

Linked to the mainland by the marina's 500-m sea wall is Muttonbird Island Nature Reserve, which offers more than just a pleasant walk, and some memorable views back towards the town. From October to April Muttonbird Island and others in the Solitary Island group are home to thousands of breeding **wedge-tailed shearwaters** (muttonbirds) that nest in a warren of burrows across the entire island. The birds are best viewed just after dusk, when they return in number to feed their mates or chicks hiding deep within the burrows. Although the birds were once easily harvested for food, they are

Muttonbird Island Nature Reserve

now, thankfully, fully protected and for obvious reasons, do not stray from the main pathway. Also keep a lookout for **humpback whales** which are often spotted just offshore from June to September.

Coffs Creek Walk The walk (5.5 km) starts from Coff Street in the centre, fringes both the Botanical Gardens and the creek before terminating at Englands Park. At the beginning of the walk is an opportunity to view a wealth of creative contrast at the **Coffs Harbour Regional Art Gallery**. ■ *Wed-Sat 1000-1600. Free.*

The **Regional Botanical Gardens** are found at the end of Hardacre Street, offering 20-ha of landscaped green sanctity, fringing Coffs Creek and networked with a series of boardwalks. ■ *Daily 0900-1700. Donations.*

At the point where the walk joins the HighStreet is **Cooinda Aboriginal Art Gallery**, The Promenade, 321 High Street, which is worth a look.

Having skirted the creek you reach the family oriented **Pet Porpoise Pool**, with its resident friendly seals, dolphins and penguins, as well as the obligatory kangaroos, emus and cockatoos. There are two shows at 1030 and 1415 where you might be lucky enough to receive a wet, fishy breath, peck-on-the-cheek. ■ *Daily. $17, child $8, family $52, dolphin swimming Sat only $150.*

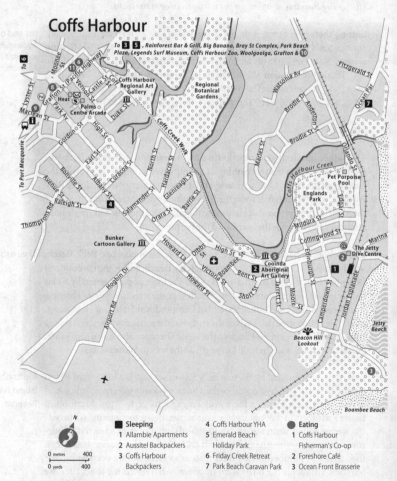

Coffs Harbour

To **3** **5** , Rainforest Bar & Grill, Big Banana, Bray St Complex, Park Beach Plaza, Legends Surf Museum, Coffs Harbour Zoo, Woolgoolga, Grafton & **10**

Sleeping
1 Allambie Apartments
2 Aussitel Backpackers
3 Coffs Harbour Backpackers
4 Coffs Harbour YHA
5 Emerald Beach Holiday Park
6 Friday Creek Retreat
7 Park Beach Caravan Park

Eating
1 Coffs Harbour Fisherman's Co-op
2 Foreshore Café
3 Ocean Front Brasserie

0 metres 400
0 yards 400

Even wider selections of cuddle-crazed natives await your attentions at Coffs Harbour, 12 km north of the town, on the Pacific Highway. For those who have not yet seen a **wild kangaroos** keep your eyes open (especially towards dusk) in the landscaped areas beside the highway and opposite the zoo. ■ *Daily 0830-1700 (1600 in winter). $15, child $12.50. T6656 1330.*

Coffs Harbour Zoo

Also north of the town is this new museum run by enthusiastic and enigmatic Scott Dillon, ex-master of the waves. There are over 120 classic boards on display as well as the odd canoe, photos and other such enlightening memorabilia. ■ *Daily. $5. Tours available. Gauldrons Rd, left off the Pacific Highway.*

Legends Surf Museum

Finally, its incredible that by building an oversize banana next to the main highway, you attract people like bees to honey. Coff's famous icon and monument of marketing genius, the Big Banana, located just north of the town on the Pacific Highway, fronts a banana plantation that hosts a number of activities from a train plantation tour to a lookout, toboggan rides, ice skating and lots of souvenir kitsch. It is however, perhaps entertainment enough, to sit in the café and watch people posing for photos in front of the main attraction. ■ *Daily 0900-1600. Free entry, rides from $5 and tours from $12, child $7.50. T6652 4355, www.bigbanana.com.au*

Big Banana

Essentials

There is a rash of motels and resorts located along the Pacific Highway on the north and south approaches and along the waterfront on Ocean Parade. **LL** *All Seasons Pacific Bay Resort*, T6659 7000, www.pacificbayresort.com.au; **LL-L** *Pelican Beach Centra*, T1800 028 882, www.australishotels.com.au, and **LL-L** *Novotel Opal Cove Resort*, T6651 0510, www.opalcove.com.au, are three of the major all-inclusive resorts located near the northern beaches, just off the Pacific Highway. **L-A** *Country Comfort Motel*, 353 Pacific Highway, T6652 8222, www.countrycomfort.com.au Next to the Big Banana, this modern, convenient and good value motel is a good choice if you are merely passing through. Pool, sauna and spa. **LL-L** *Allambie Apartments*, 22 Camperdown St, T6652 6690, www.stay incoffs.com.au Well positioned close to the beaches, harbour and marina, with superb views, pool and spa. **LL** *Friday Creek Retreat*, 267 Friday Creek Rd, Upper Orara, 17 km west of town, T6653 8221, www.fridaycreek.com.au Sheer luxury, as well as complete peace and quiet in a country setting is offered here. There are 9 superb fully self-contained cottages with

Sleeping
■ *On map, page 196*
See inside cover for price categories

North Coast NSW

Park Beach

South Pacific Ocean

NPWS

Marina Booking Centre

Marina

Muttonbird Island Nature Reserve

4 Rainforest Bar & Grill
5 Shearwater
6 Star Anise
7 Tide & Pilot Brasserie

● **Pubs & bars**
8 Coffs Harbour
9 Fitzroy Hotel
10 Greenhouse Tavern
11 Plantation

spas, open fires, hammocks and great views, free bike hire, complimentary breakfast and dinner by arrangement. Recommended.

The hostels in Coffs Harbour are lively places – very activity and party oriented

C-E *Coffs Harbour YHA*, 110 Albany St, T6652 6462. Friendly, spotless and well managed in a suburban setting half way between the town centre and the beach, offering dorms, doubles, twins and family rooms, pool, internet, cable TV and free bikes, surf/body boards and pick-ups. **C-F** *Aussitel Backpackers*, T6651 1871/1800 330 335. Further towards the beach on High St (312) this a highly social place with emphasis on discounted activities and its own attractive dive packages being a speciality. Dorms, twins and doubles, large kitchen, common area, internet, pool, bikes, surf/body boards, wetsuits etc. **C-E** *Coffs Harbour Backpackers (Barracuda)*, 19 Arthur St, T6651 3514, www.barracudabackpackers.com.au At the northern end of town within a stones throw from the Park Beach Shopping Plaza is the purpose-built, motel-style option offering dorms, doubles/twins (mostly en suite). It's laid-back, social and again very activity oriented with attractive discounts and its own organized outings, pool, spa, internet, free equipment hire and pick-ups. Links with the other hostels for social pub/club outings.

There are plenty of motor parks in the area with the best located north of the town. **A-E** *Emerald Beach Holiday Park*, Fishermans Dr, Emerald Beach, 18 km north of Coffs, has luxury villas, standard cabins, on-site vans, powered and shaded non-powered sites in bush setting with shop, café and pool. The beach is only yards away and is simply superb with headland walks nearby. Recommended. **L-F** *Park Beach Caravan Park*, Ocean Pde, T6651 2465. If you must stay in Coffs itself, this newly renovated option is the best facilitated and beachside.

Eating

● *On map, page 196*
See inside cover for price categories

Foreshore Café, Jetty Strip, 394 High St, T665 23127. Open daily. For a good breakfast, coffee and lunch locals swear by. *Shearwater Restaurant*, overlooking Coffs Creek, 321 High St, T6651 6053. Another relaxed alternative, open daily for breakfast, lunch and dinner (Wed-Sun) from 0800. For fine dining, beyond the classy restaurants in the main resorts, seafood at the Marina complex is recommended. A pre-dinner walk to Muttonbird Island can be followed by quality al fresco dining at the award-winning and congenial *Tide and Pilot Brasserie*, Marina Dr, T6651 6888. Open daily for breakfast, lunch and dinner from 0700. *Fisherman's Co-op*, 69 Marina Dr, T6652 2811, is the place for fish and chips. Open daily until 1800. *Star Ainse*, 93 Grafton St, T6651 1033, is earning a good reputation for its innovative modern Australian cuisine. For cheaper deals around town try the value pub-style food *Rainforest Bar and Grill*, corner of Pacific Highway and Bray St, T6651 5488 (ideal if you are catching a movie across the road afterwards). Open daily for lunch and dinner. *Ocean Front Brasserie*, Coffs Harbour Deep Sea Fishing Club, Jordan Esplanade, T6651 2819, is also good value and offers great views across the harbour. Open daily 1200-1430/1800-2030. **Food courts** and the main **supermarkets** are located in the Park Beach Plaza Pacific Highway, just north of the town centre, or the Palms centre Arcade in the centre of town.

Entertainment

Coffs tries hard to show the backpacker party set a good time with *Plantation*, Coffs Harbour, and *Fitzroy Hotels*, Grafton St, all offering cheap drinks, pool and regular live entertainment. The latter remains open well into the wee hours. The 2 nightclubs in the centre of town (Grafton St) are *Chill*, 76 Grafton St ($5 cover, free for backpackers) and *Heat*, 1st floor, 15 City Centre Mall ($8 cover). *Ex-serviceman's Club*, Grafton St, is also a popular haunt for cheap food and drinks, especially on Fri night, but ID is required for entry. The town's modern **Cinema Complex** is in the Bray St Complex just of the Pacific Highway (corner of Bray St), T6651 5568. *Greenhouse Tavern*, directly opposite, is a more modern pub with live music, a good atmosphere at the weekend.

The VIC has full activity listings and can offer non-biased advice. *Marina Booking Centre* based at the marina also act as booking agents for most regional activities and cruises, T6651 4612. For general activity information visit www.coffscentral.com.au

Coach and 4WD tours There are plenty of local tour operators from private 4WD adventures to coach trips. The well-established *Mountain Trails 4WD Tours*, T6658 3333, offer everything from day-long trips to Bellingen the Dorrigo National Park and a gold mine, from $85, historical and Aboriginal tours, from $55 and also nocturnal wildlife spotting trips. *Blue Tongue*, T6651 8566, offer entertaining town and locality tours from $25, Dorrigo, from $50 and South West Rocks (south) from $60. Recommended.

Cruising and fishing *Spirit of Coffs Harbour Cruises*, Shop 5, Marina, T6650 0155, www.spiritofcoffs.com.au, offer a range of cruise options, from a 3-hr Solitary Island trips/dolphin spotting, departing 0930 Mon/Wed/Fri/Sat/Sun, from $35, child $20: Whale-watching (mid May-mid Nov), from $35 and a 4-hr Luncheon/Waterslide Cruise, departing 0930 Tue/Thu, from $45, child $25. *Pacific Explorer*, T6652 7225, www.pacificexplorer.com.au, offer a sedate half-day island/dolphin and whale watching cruise on board their sailing catamaran with snorkelling and boom netting departing 0900 and 1330, from $49, child $35. *Blue Wing*, T6651 1611, also offer value whale-watching trips in season twice daily at 0830 and 1330, from $44, couple $40 and child $25. *Bluefin II*, T04 2866 8072, *Adriatic III*, T6651 1277, and the classy *Cougar Cat 12*, T6651 6715, all offer entertaining fishing trips from around $70 for a half day and big game fishing, from $140.

Diving *Solitary Islands* offer some fine dive sites with such evocative names as 'Grey Nurse Gutters', 'Manta Arch', and a wealth of marine life, including lots of grey nurse sharks, 90 species of coral, 280 species of fish and the densest colonies of anemones and anemone fish (clown fish) in the world. *Jetty Dive Centre*, 398 High St, T6651 1611, www.jettydive.com.au, offer small group Padi Certification from $185, introductory dives from $137 and snorkelling trips from $50. *Pacific Blue*, 40 Marina Dr, T6652 2033, pacificblue@bigpond.com.au, offer Padi Certification from $175, one-day introductory from $115, half day snorkelling from $55 and certified half day trips from $75 (with gear $105). *ScubaCrew*, T1800 330 335, offer attractive 4-day/4-night packages culminating in four ocean dives, through *Aussitel Backpackers*, from $230.

Coffs Harbour is also one of the cheapest places to get certified on the NSW coast

Horse trekking *Valery Trails*, T6653 4301, is an award winning outfit suited to advanced and beginners, 13 km south of Coffs. They offer 1-/2-hr/breakfast; BBQ, moonlight and camp ride outs from $35. *Busland Trail Rides*, based at Halfway Creek, 50 km north, T6649 4487, bushlandtrails@ ozemail.com.au, offer 2-hr breakfast, family and twilight rides, full day rides upon request. Closer Coffs, *Wyndyarra Estate*, Island Loop Rd, Upper Orara, T66538488, offer similar rides, from $30 with pick-ups.

White-water rafting, sea kayaking and surf rafting *Liquid Assets*, T6658 0850, liquidassets1@yahoo.com.au, offer an exhilarating range of aquatic adventures, including half- or full-day white water rafting, on the Goolang River (grade 3) and the Nymbodia River which is a scenic grade 3-5, from $80. Sea kayaking, half day from $40. Surf rafting, half day from $40 and flat water kayaking in Bongil Bongil National Park, half day from $40. Big Day Out sea kayak, surf rafting and white water rafting combo costs from $135. Recommended. *WoW Rafting*, T66544066, www.wowrafting.com.au, offer a 1-day 9-km trip down the Nymbodia with 25 rapids from $153 and a 2-day trip with 75 rapids with all meals, camping included, from $325. *Whitewater Rafting*, T6653 3500, www.wildwateradventures.com.au, offer similar 1-2 day trips for the same price and extended 4-day and Queensland adventures, from $560.

Other activities *Coffs City Skydivers*, T6651 1167, www.coffsskydivers.com.au, offer tandem skydiving, 10,000 ft, from $275. Surfing lessons are offered with the *East Coast Surf School*, T6651 5515, www.eastcoastsurfschool.com.au, at Diggers Beach (near the Big Banana) 1030-1230, from $35, private lessons, from $50 per hr, group from $45per person and weekend camp/surf from $330.

Transport **Local Bus** *King Bros*, T1300 555 611, are the local suburban bus company with daily, half-hourly services from 0715-1730. To get from Park Ave in the town centre to the jetty, take #365E. *Ryan's Buses*, T6652 3201, offer local services to Woolgoolga and Grafton. **Bike hire** From *Bob Wallis Bicycle Centre*, corner of Collingwood and Orlando sts, T6652 5102, from $20 per 24 hr ($50 deposit). *Coastal Power Bikes* rent out scooter/bike hybrids, free delivery, T6650 9064. **Taxi** T131008.

Long distance Air Coffs Harbour Airport is about 3 km south of the town centre off Hogbin Dr. *Qantaslink*, T131313, and *Hazelton Airways*, T131713, offer regular daily services to Sydney, Brisbane and Newcastle. A taxi into town costs about $7. **Bus** Long-distance buses stop beside the VIC on Elizabeth St. *Greyhound*, T132030, *McCafferty's*, T131499, and *Premier*, T133410, offer daily interstate services. *Keans Coaches*, T1800 043 339, run a service from Coffs Harbour (via the Waterfall Way and Dorrigo/Belligen/Armidale and Tamworth) 3 times a week, Tue/Thu/Sun. **Car hire** *Coffs Harbour Rent-A-Car*, Shell Roadhouse, corner of Pacific Highway and Marcia St, from $44 per-day, T6652 5022, *Thrifty*, T6652 8622, *Hertz*, airport, T66511899. **Train** The station is at the end of Angus McLeod St (right off High St and Camperdown St), near the harbour jetty. *Countrylink*, T132232, offer daily services to Sydney and Brisbane.

Directory **Banks** Major branches with ATMs can be found on the Mall or along Grafton St and Park Ave. **Communications** Internet: *The Internet Room*, Shop 21, Jetty Village Shopping Centre, T6651 9155. Open Mon-Fri 0900-1800, Sat/Sun 1000-1600 or *Jetty Dive Centre*, 398 High St, T66511611. **Post office**: Palms Centre Arcade, Vernon St. Open Mon-Fri 0830-1700, Sat 0830-1200. **Medical services** Hospital: T66567000. **Useful numbers** Police: Moonee St, T66520299. NRMA: 30 Gordon St, T66593401.

Wooli, Minnie Water and Yuragyir National Park (South)

Colour map 2, grid B5
105 km north of Coffs
Harbour, 210 km
south of Byron Bay
For maps, sleeping
and national parks
info visit Grafton VIC,
see next page

Some 70 km north of Coffs Harbour the Wooli Road heads west towards the coast and the two sleepy beachside settlements of **Wooli** and **Minnie Water**. Either provide a relaxing base from which to explore the surrounding, southern section of the **Yuragyir National Park**, renowned for its rich variety of wildlife, secluded beaches and, in the spring, its vivid displays of wild flowers. There are good short walks at the **Illaroo Camping Area**, just north of Minnie Water, or **Wilson's Headland** and **Diggers Camp**, accessed along Diggers Camp Road, just south of the Minnie Water turn off Wooli Road. Four-wheel drive is permitted on the beaches.

Just offshore the **Solitary Islands Marine Park** offers some fine diving and is considered to have one of the most diverse marine bio-diversities in NSW. *Wooli Deepsea Tours* offer dive and snorkelling trips as well as fishing, island sight seeing and whale/dolphin watching.

Sleeping Wooli is the larger of the 2 settlements and hosts a general store (with Eftpos), service
& eating station, newsagents, motel, hotel and two caravan parks. Minnie Water, 15 km north of Wooli, has a store, service station and the modern **C-F** *Minnie Water Caravan Park*, T6649 7693. There is basic **F NPWS camping** at Illaroo and Diggers Camp (see above). If you enjoy seafood try Wooli's famed oysters at the *Wooli Oyster Supply*, T6649 7537.

Grafton

An elegant provincial city on the banks of the Clarence River, Grafton is renowned for its graceful old buildings and tree-lined streets. Despite its aesthetic appeal it is seldom featured in the travellers agenda with the lure of the region's coastal towns and national parks presenting a far more attractive proposition. Grafton was born of the 'red gold'– the cedar cutting industry– in the mid 1800s and is named after the grandfather of Governor Fitzroy.

*Population: 18,500
86 km north of Coffs
Harbour, 162 km
south of Byron Bay*

City maps, accommodation and activity listings can be secured at the Grafton Visitor Centre, just off the Pacific Highway, in South Grafton, T6642 4677, crta@nor.com.au Open daily 0900-1700. For national parks information contact the NPWS office on Level 3, 49 Victoria St, T6641 1500. Open Mon-Fri 0900-1700.

Ins & outs
*See Transport,
page 201, for details*

Grafton Regional Gallery is lauded as one of the best regional galleries in NSW and is housed in one of Grafton's finest historical buildings, **Prentice House** built in 1880. The hallowed walls, in combination with a new annex added in 1999 showcase a dynamic range of permanent and visiting contemporary and traditional exhibitions. The in-house courtyard **café** is a great place for a relaxed lunch. ■ *Tue-Sun, 1000-1600. Donation. T6642 3177. 158 Fitzroy St.*

Sights

Less high-profile, but still worth a visit is the **Shaeffer House Museum** which occupies a historic homestead and displays a wide range of exhibits tracing the history of the city and Clarence River Valley. ■ *Tue-Thu and Sun, 1300-1600, T6642 5212, 192 Fitzroy St.*

For something completely different visit, or keep an eye on, **Susan Island** which sits mid-river in the heart of the city. Part of the island is a nature reserve and home to the largest colony of **flying foxes** (fruit bats) in the southern hemisphere. Dawn and dusk sees most activity when these little 'dogs on a hang gliders' come and go on feeding forays. See below for tours to the island.

A-E *Gateway Village Tourist Park*, 598 Summerland Way (north of the CBD on the Casino Rd), T6642 4225. Modern and best facilitated motor park with deluxe villas, on-site vans, en suite/standard powered and non-powered sites, pool but no camp kitchen. **A-E** *Crown Hotel Motel*, 1 Prince St, T6642 4000, and **D** *Roaches Hotel*, 85 Victoria St, T6642 2866, both offer good budget and standard rooms. There are a dearth of good restaurants in Grafton with the art gallery café (open Mon-Fri 1000-1600), local hotels and motels being the best bet. *Victoria's Restaurant* in the *Clarence Motor Inn*, 51 Fitzroy St, T6643 3444, has a good local reputation. *Great Time Cruises* (see below) offer dinner cruises on Fri/Sat, 1830, from $40.

**Sleeping
& eating**

Grafton is the gateway to some excellent canoeing and rafting opportunities. The VIC has details. *Clarence Islander Rivercat*, 22 Mary St, T6642 5957, can take groups across to Susan Island by private charter. River cruises are offered by *Great Time Cruises*, Prince St Wharf, from $10, T6642 3456. Better still, hire your own houseboat and do some real river cruising, through *Clarence Riverboats*, T6647 6232.

**Tours &
activities**

Bus There is a regular city bus service operating on an hourly circuit, T6642 3111, and the public can also travel on school buses to outlying areas. Long-distance buses stop in South Grafton. *Premier Motor Service*, T133410, offer daily services between Sydney and Brisbane. **Train** The station is on Through St, South Grafton (just of the Pacific Highway). *Countrylink* have an office in the station, T6640 9438/132232. *King Brothers Bus Service*, T6646 2019, provide daily services from Grafton-Yamba-Maclean-Iluka. **Taxi** T6642 4633.

Transport

North Coast NSW

Directory **Communications** Internet is available at *Grafton Health Foods*, 75 Prince St. Open Mon-Fri 0800-1700, Sat 0900-1300.

Mclean

Colour map 2, grid B5   In name alone the small town of Mclean on the banks of the Clarence River gives an inkling of its Scottish roots, if not its relentless desire to keep up the auld traditions. First settled by several shiploads of Scots immigrants fleeing the Highland Clearances in the 1860s, the tartan-clad colony was first called Rocky Mouth, before thankfully assuming the name of its founding father-NSW colony surveyor General Alistair McLean. Now a base for a large fishing fleet and the local sugar industry, as well as tourism, the social highlight of the year are the **Highland Games** held at the end of March featuring the usual burly kilted caber tossers and kilted pipe bands and Scottish Week held every July. At other times the highland links are revealed and celebrated with numerous Gaelic street names, tartan painted power poles, the **Taloumbi Scots Cairn** – a monument in Stamford park made of stones from Scotland and from local Scots families throughout Australia – and the small **Bicentennial Museum** on Wharf Street. ■ *Fri 1000-1600, Wed-Sat 1300-1600. $3.* The **Mclean Lookout** at the end of Wharf Street provides good views across the town and the coast. Heritage and general community Information, as well as all the usual highland gimmick souvenirs can be secured at The Scottish Shop on River Street. Lower Clarence Visitor Centre, Ferry Park, just off the Pacific Highway 5 km south of the Clarence River bridge, T6645 4121, has full accommodation, events and activities listings.

Yamba, Angourie and Yuragyir National Park (North)

Colour map 2, grid B5
Population: 5,000
169 km north of Coffs
Harbour, 132 km
south of Byron Bay

The coastal fishing town of **Yamba**, 13 km west of the Pacific Highway just before the Clarence River bridge, on the southern bank of the Clarence River mouth, is famed for its prawn industry, its enviable climate and its fine surf beaches. Serving mainly as a domestic holiday destination it offers the opportunity to spent two or three days away from the mainstream tourist resorts along the north coast. **Main Beach**, below Flinders Park, is the most popular of Yamba's wealth of golden sands with **Turners Beach** between the main breakwater and lighthouse. **Covent Beach**, between Lovers Point and Main Beach and Pippie Beach, is the most southerly, providing equal, if not better aesthetics. **Clarence River Delta** and **Lake Wooloweyah**, 4 km south, all provide a wealth of boating, fishing and cruising opportunities with the Yamba-Iluka ferry shuttling back and forth daily to **Iluka**, providing access to some sublime beaches, bluffs, a stunning rainforest nature reserve and the wilderness Bundjalung National Park (see below).

Some 5 km south of Yamba is the small, picturesque village of **Angourie**, with its spectacular ocean views and world-class (advanced) surf breaks. The Angourie Lookout provides the perfect spot to watch the 'point-break' surfing and plenty of 'wipe-outs'. **Blue Pool**, reached via a walking track from the car park at the eastern end of The Crescent, is a deep freshwater pool and a favourite spot for swimming and diving (as in the upside down vertical entry variety).

The northern section of the **Yuraygir National Park** encompasses the **Angourie Point headlands**, **Woody Bluff**, **Shelly**, **Plumbago** and **Red Cliff headland**, which are linked by sand dunes and glorious beaches. There are plenty of walking opportunities including Angourie Lookout to Angourie

Point and Back Beach (unofficial naturist beach). A gravel road links the Lakes Boulevarde Road to the Mara Creek car park. From there an excellent and recommended 10-km walking track leads to **Lake Arragan** and **Brooms Head** which takes about three-hours. Walk-in camping is available at Shelly and Lake Arragan.

Maps, accommodation and national parks information can be secured at the Lower Clarence Visitor Centre, Ferry Park, just off the Pacific Highway, 5 km south of the Clarence River bridge, T6645 4121, crta1@nor.com.au

Sleeping & eating

Most of Yamba's amenities can be found along its main drag – Wooli St – or Yamba St (off Wooli St), which terminates at Pippie Beach. **LL-E** *Blue Dolphin Holiday Resort*, Yamba Rd, T6646 2194. An excellent 5-star resort offering luxury/standard self-contained cabins, en suite/standard powered and non-powered sites, café, pool and camp kitchen. **LL-A** *Surf Motel*, 2 Queen St, T6646 1955, is a modern, well-appointed motel option right next to Main Beach. *Restaurant Castalia*, 1/15 Clarence St, T6646 1155, offers good modern Australian fare. Open Wed-Sat for lunch and dinner. *Pacific Hotel*, 18 Pilot St, T6646 2491, overlooking the ocean, also offers budget accommodation and value bistro meals daily. *Beachwood Café/Restaurant*, 16 Clarence St, T6646 9258. Open daily. For breakfast and coffee.

Tours & activities

Action Adventures, Yamba, T04384 61137, are a highly professional outfit offering scenic sea kayaking, half day from $65 and full day from $100. *Yamba Surfing Academy*, T6646 2971, can provide surfing lessons from beginner to advanced. River cruises depart 1100 Wed/Fri/Sun, from $16, chid $8 and there is also an Evening BBQ Cruise on offer at 1645 Wed, from $25, child $12.50 (book ahead), T6646 6423.

Transport

Bus *King Brothers Bus Service*, T6646 2019, provide daily services from Yamba-Maclean-Iluka-Grafton. **Ferry** The Iluka-Yamba ferry departs daily from the River St Wharf at 0930/1100/1515/1645, from $4.

Iluka and Bundjalung National Park

Colour map 2, grid B5
Population: 2,200
156 km north of Coffs Harbour, 119 km south of Byron Bay

North of Chatsworth, on the Pacific Highway, Iluka Rd heads west for 14 km

If you can give yourself at least two to three days to explore the Iluka area, you won't regret it. Other than the superb coastline contained within the southern sector of the Bundjalung National Park and one of the best campsites on the northern NSW coast at Woody Head, the big attraction at the sleepy fishing village of Iluka is the **World Heritage Rainforest Walk** through the **Iluka Nature Reserve**. The 136-ha reserve contains the largest remaining stand of littoral rainforest in NSW – a rich forest habitat unique to the coastal environment that supports a huge number of associated species like the charmingly named lilly pilly tree or noisy pitta bird. The 2.5-km rainforest walk can be tackled either from the north at the Iluka Bluff Car Park (off the main Iluka Road opposite the golf club) or from the caravan park at western edge of the village (Crown Street).

Iluka Beach is another fine quiet spot reached via Beach Road (head west from the end of Iluka Road). Further north, just beyond Iluka Bluff, **Bluff Beach** and **Frazer's Reef** are also popular for swimming and fishing. On the southern bank of the Clarence River mouth, Iluka's twin fishing village of **Yamba** and its equally good, if busier, beaches can be reached by ferry from the end of Charles Street (see Transport below).

Two kilometres north of Iluka and Woody Head, the 18,000 ha wilderness of **Bundjalung National Park** with its 38 km of beaches, littoral rainforest, heath lands, unusual rock formations, lagoons, creeks and swamps is an

North Coast NSW

eco-explorer's paradise. Sadly, access from the south is by 4WD only ($16 permit), or on foot. There is better access from the north along the 21-km unsealed road. Go up to Gap Road, off the Pacific Highway, 5 km south of Woodburn, to the Black Rocks campsite.

Maps, accommodation and park information are available at the Lower Clarence Visitor Centre, Ferry Park, just off the Pacific Highway 5 km south of the Clarence River bridge, T6645 4121, crta1@nor.com.au Daily 0900-1700.

Sleeping & eating Iluka has 3 basic caravan parks. **B** *Iluka Motel*, T6646 6288, Charles St, is in the centre. **F** *Woody Head Campsite*, beside the beach off Iluka Rd, 14 km west of the Pacific Highway and 4 km north of Iluka. T6646 6134. This NPSW campsite is simply superb. It has non-powered sites, toilets, water, hot showers, boat ramp and fires permitted, plus 3 cabins with cooking facilities. The information office and reception is open daily 0900-1000. Book well ahead. *Black Rocks Campsite*, located beside the beach in the heart of the national park, NPSW, it is far more basic and harder to access but an alternative. There is a dearth of eateries. The best bet being the *Golf Club*, Iluka Rd, T6646 5043, open Tue-Sun, or *Sedger's Reef Bistro*, Queens St, T6646 6122, open daily.

Tours & activities River cruises depart Yamba at 1145 Wed/Fri/Sun, from $14, child $7, and there is an evening BBQ Cruise at 1715 Wed, from $25, child $12.50, T6646 6423. Book ahead.

Transport **Bus** *King Brothers Bus Service*, T6646 2019, provide daily services from Yamba-Maclean-Iluka-Grafton. **Ferry** The **Iluka-Yamba** ferry departs daily from the Boatshed and Marina at the end of Charles St, Iluka at 0845/1015/1430 and 1600, from $4.

Directory Most of the main amenities in Iluka are found along the main drag into town or Spenser and Charles sts, where you will find a **service station**, **supermarket** and **ATM**. **Internet** at Lower Clarence Visitor Centre. See above.

Evans Head and Broadwater National Park

Colour map 2, grid B5
Population: 2,600
192 km north of Coffs
Harbour, 62 km south
of Byron Bay

No public transport –
your own vehicle
is essential

From Woodburn the coastal road to Evans Head and back through the Broadwater National Park presents another welcome break from the relentless Pacific Highway. Straddling the mouth of the **Evans River** and separating the two coastal national parks of Bundjalung to the south and Broadwater to the north, Evans Head is a mainly fishing and prawning settlement in an idyllic position, offering a fine spot for a picnic, fishing or a swim. **Main Beach** access is beside the Surf Club at the end of Booyong Street, just off the main drag – Woodburn Street. Also not to be missed is the view looking north from the **Razorback Lookout** which is accessed across the river, then left, at the end of Ocean Drive. Further explorations can be made off Ocean Drive to **Chinaman's Beach** and **Snapper Point**, a favourite spot for serious surfers at the edge of the **Dirrawong Headland Reserve** and the Bundjalung National Park. In the 1870s the population of Evans Head was double that of today when, for a short time, over $200,000 worth of gold was taken through fossicking on the local beaches.

From the northern edge of Evans Head, on Beech Road, you can drive through the heart of **Broadwater National Park** to rejoin the Pacific Highway at Broadwater, 8 km away. Coastal heath and wetland drape a landscape of dunes and swales (gullies) with a wide variety of plants and, in spring, carpets of wild flowers. Salty Lagoon walking track (3 km return) is 2 km north of Evans Head, while 2.5 km south of Broadwater, the **Broadwater Lookout** offers the best views across the park.

B-F *Silver Sands Caravan Park*, near the beach, and *Surf Club*, Park St, T6682 4212, has
self-contained cabins, en suite/standard powered and non-powered sites. *Wood-burn-Evans Head RSL*, beside the river on Woodburn St, T6682 4282, has a bistro
(daily) and an à la carte restaurant (Fri/Sat) offering value meals.

Most of the main amenities in Evans Head are at the end of Woodburn St where you
will find a post office, supermarket and ATM.

Ballina

For most people, in their haste to reach the exalted Byron Bay, their only lasting memory of Ballina is a mammoth roadside crustacean, the mighty 'Big
Prawn' on the town's southern approach. This is a shame since Ballina is a
pleasant enough coastal service centre and domestic holiday town with fine
beaches, scenic headlands and a good range of accommodations worth more
than just a photo of a monstrous google-eyed prawn.

Colour map 2, grid B5
Population: 16,000
210 km north of Coffs
Harbour, 30 km south
of Byron Bay

Ballina's best beaches are found at the eastern end of town across North
Creek and the Richmond River in East Ballina. **Shelly Beach** and **Lighthouse
Beach** both offer good swimming, surfing and can be reached via Compton
Street, just beyond the bridge, off Hill Street. On the way, **Shaws Bay Lagoon**,
next to the river, also provides a pleasant swimming spot. Further north, **Flat
Rock**, between Angels and Sharpes Beach, is good for snorkelling.

The small **Ballina Naval and Maritime Museum**, next to the VIC, displays
some interesting local artefacts and is home to the 1973 Las Balsas Trans
Pacific Expedition Raft (Ballina to South America). ■ *Daily 0900-1600. Entry
by donation. T6681 1002. Regatta Ave.* Still very much afloat is the *MV
Bennelong* which offers an interesting range of scenic and historical cruises on
the Richmond River. See Tours and activities below.

Ballina VIC, at the corner of River Street and Las Balsas Plaza, T6686 3484,
www.tropicalnsw.com.au, opens dalily from 0900-1600/1700.

LL-L *Ballina Manor*, 25 Norton St, T6681 5888, www.ballinamanor.com.au Comfort
with a traditional, historical edge can be secured here with its 4 poster and standard
suites. **L-A** *Ballina Heritage Inn*, 229 River St, T6686 0505. More modern and cheaper,
this motel-style option has singles, doubles and family rooms, with spas and a pool.
YHA Ballina Travellers Lodge, 36 Tamar St, T6686 6737, lenballina@ozemail.com.au
This quiet, motel-style lodge offers backpackers and budget travellers dorm rooms,
doubles/twins with all amenities, close to the town centre. **A-F** *Ballina Lakeside Holiday Park*, Fenwick Dr, East Ballina, T6686 3953. One of the many caravan parks in and
around Ballina, this 4-star option offers the full range of accommodation and facilities.
Close to the eastern beaches and alongside Shaws Bay Lagoon.

Beaches Restaurant, *Ballina Beach Resort*, T6686 8888, is locally recommended for fine
dining with its regional cuisine and al fresco dining. Open daily for breakfast, lunch and
dinner. *Shelly's on the Beach Café*, Shelly's Beach Rd, East Ballina, T6686 9844, offers
value traditional Australian cuisine and great ocean views. Open daily for breakfast and
lunch, from 0730-1500. *Ballina RSL*, at the western end of River St, T6686 2544,
fordown-to-earth value. It offers both à la carte and bistro-style meals and hosts live
bands every Fri and Sat nights, plus Jazz every Sun from 0800. All you can eat breakfasts
also on Sun from 0800. *The Rink's Restaurant*, the Ballina RSL Bowling Club, Canal Rd,
T6686 6888, offers $6 meals Wed/Thu, $10 meals Fri/Sat and $3 mains on Sun. *Paddy
McGinty's Irish Pub*, 56 River St, T6686 2135. For good beer, traditional pub-grub and a
congenial atmosphere.

Tours & activities *MV Bennelong*, T6688 8266, offer cruises including a 3½-hr lunch cruise (1100-1430), from $35, child $17.50 and a day-long cruise, upstream to Lismore (1000-1700), from $70, child $35. *Richmond River Cruises*, T6687 7940, also offer weekly cruises. Much more exhilarating are the fast launch dolphin watching tours offered by *Ballina Ocean Tours*, 24 Smith Dr, T6686 3999, www.ballinaoceantours.ballina.net.au Back on dry land Ballina's waterfront and parks are well renowned for their excellent cycling and rollerblading opportunities. Ask at the VIC for details and a map. *Jack Ransom Cycles*, 16 Cherry St, T6686 3485, rents bikes and *Ballina Indoor Sports and Skate Centre*, Barlows Rd (just past *McDonalds*), T6686 2806, can assist with blades. *Forgotten Country* Eco-Tours, T6687 7845, offer entertaining and informative guided rainforest walks and gold-panning, canoeing, horse riding and white water rafting by arrangement. *Summerland Surf School*, 51 Ocean Dr, Evans Head, T6682 4393, www.surfingaustralia. com.au, can oblige with surfing lessons for both beginners or the advanced.

Transport **Air** Ballina Airport is 3 km to the east of town, off Southern Cross Drive, and served from Sydney daily by *QantasLink*, T131313 and *Hazelton Airways*, T131713. **Bus** *Byron Bay Airbus*, T6681 3355 (from $25 one-way). Long-distance buses stop outside the unmistakable 'Big Prawn' and its dwarfed service centre, 3.5 km south of the town centre. *Greyhound*, T132030, *McCafferty's*, T131499, *Premier Motor Service*, T133410, all offer daily services to Sydney and Brisbane while Lismore based company *Kirklands*, T6622 1499, offer daily services to Lismore, the Gold Coast, Byron Bay and Brisbane. *Blanch's Buses*, T6686 2144, offer local bus services between Byron Bay (Mullumbimby) and Ballina (#640), Lismore (#661/611) and Evans Head (#660). **Car hire** There are several companies based at the airport including *Avis*, T6686 7650, and *Budget*, T6681 4031. **Taxi** *Ballina Taxi Service*, T6686 9999.

Directory Internet is available at the *Ballina Ice Creamery and Internet Café*, 178 River St, T6686 5783. Open Mon-Fri 0930-1800, Fri/Sat 0930-2100.

Lennox Head

Colour map 2, grid B5
Population: 2,400
226 km north of Coffs Harbour, 11 km north of Ballina, 21 km south of Byron Bay

The small, beachside settlement of Lennox Head is world famous for the long **surf breaks** that form with welcome repetition at the terminus of **Seven Mile Beach** and **Lennox Point**. Either with or without a board the village offers a quieter, alternative destination in which to spend a relaxing couple of days, away from the tourist hype of Byron Bay. Just south of the village the namesake heads offer excellent views north to Cape Byron and are considered a prime spot for both hang gliding and dolphin/whale spotting. The Lennox Reef, below the heads, known as 'The Moat', is also good for snorkelling. At the northern end of the village Lake Ainsworth is a fine venue for freshwater swimming, canoeing and windsurfing. Lennox Head Sailing School, beside the lake on Pacific Parade, hires watersports equipment and offers lessons. The lake edge also serves as the venue for the coastal markets that are held on the second and fifth Sundays of the month.

Sleeping
There are a number of low-key resorts and motels in the village ideal for families

L *Headland Beach Resort*, 7 Park Lane, T6618 0000, info@headlandbeachresort.com.au, has modern 1, 2 and 3 bedroom self-contained apartments with a pool, spa and in-house restaurant. Holiday house rentals can be arranged through *Pidcocks*, T6687 7888, www.pidcocks.com.au **C-E** *Lennox Head Beachouse YHA*, 3 Ross St, T6687 7636, backpack@spot.com.au, is a purpose-built hostel with a great laid-back, friendly atmosphere, near the beach and Lake Ainsworth. It offers dorms and small doubles and free use of surf/boogie boards, bikes and fishing gear. Free sailing and windsurfing lessons can also be arranged and there is a natural therapies (massage) clinic on-site and legendary chocolate cake. For campers and campervans the **B-E** *Lake Ainsworth Caravan Park*, Pacific Pde, T6687 7249, is ideally located next to the lake and offers en suite/standard cabins, powered and non-powered sites but no camp kitchen. Activities include windsurfing, sailing and canoeing.

Sullivan's Restaurant, in the *Headland Beach Resort*, is recommended for fine dining. **Eating** Other more affordable options and cafés can be found beachside, at the junction of Pacific Parade and Byron St, including *Ruby's Bar and Restaurant*, 17 Pacific Pde, T6687 5769, which offers both à la carte or casual café dining. Closed Mon.

Bus *Blanch's Buses*, T6686 2144, offer local bus services between Byron Bay and **Transport** Ballina (#640). You can flag them down along Pacific Parade. Long-distance buses stop on Ballina St, including *Premier Motor Service*, T133410.

Byron Bay

Anything goes in Byron Bay. This is a town that would love to have its own passport control to prevent entry to anyone remotely conservative or thinks surfing is something you do in front of a computer. Only three decades ago 'Byron' was little more than a sleepy, attractive coastal enclave. Few strayed off the main highway heading north except a few alternative lifestylers who found it an ideal escape and the land prices wonderfully cheap. But news spread and its popularity exploded. To its infinite appeal, it lacks the glitz of the Gold Coast and the conformity of many other coastal resorts, but there is little doubt it is teetering on that level of popularity and hype that can turn to 'a love it or hate it' experience. No doubt however its ultimate saviour is its beautiful aesthetics and few leave Byron disappointed.

Colour map 2,
grid B5
Population: 6,000
790 km north of
Sydney, 173 km
south of Mackay

Getting there The two nearest airports are Coolangatta (north) and Ballina (south) with good daily services and shuttle buses to town. As you would expect there are plenty of long-distance buses and trains that head in from Sydney, Cairns, Brisbane, etc. Both the train station and bus station are located in the middle of town. **Getting around** You can enjoy all the offerings of Byron Bay on foot, or, to cover more ground, hire a bike. There are local bus services for getting around town and also to local sights such as Ballina and Lennox Head. **Tourist information** Byron Bay VIC, 80 Jonston St, T6680 8558, www.byron-bay.com.au, is open daily 0900- 1700. See also page 214, for travel agents.

Ins & outs
See Transport, page 214, for further details

Beware – Byron Bay attracts thieves

Sights

The main attraction in Byron, beyond its hugely popular social and creative scene, are of course the surrounding beaches and the superb aesthetics of the Cape Byron Headland Reserve. To its eternal credit one thing you will not see in Byron are traffic lights and highrise resorts. For excursions into the hinterland of Byron Bay, including Mount Warning and the arty villages of Nimbin and the like, see page 214.

There are over 37 km of beach around Byron and seven world-class surf **Beaches** beaches stretching from Belongil Beach in the west to Broken Head in the south. As to be expected Byron hosts an extensive array of organized activities to lure you from your beach based somnolence. Surfing is, of course, the most popular pastime. See page 212 for details of activities.

North Coast NSW

Only metres from the town centre **Main Beach** is the main focus of activity, from surfing to the soporifics. It is also patrolled and the safest for families or surfing beginners. West of Main Beach, **Belongil Beach** stretches about 1 km to the mouth of Belongil Creek. About 500 m beyond that (accessed via Bayshore Drive), true to Byron's non-conformist attitudes, there is a designated naturist beach. East of the town centre, Main Beach merges with **Clark's Beach**, which is no less appealing and generally much quieter. Beyond Clark's Beach and the headland called **The Pass**, which is a favourite surf spot, **Watego's** and **Little Watego's Beaches** fringe the northern side of Cape Byron providing more surf breaks and some dramatic coastal scenery with Cape Byron looming above. South of the Cape, **Tallow Beach** stretches about 9 km to **Broken Head**. It is a great spot to escape the crowds but is unpatrolled. Several walks also access other more remote headland beaches within the very pretty **Broken Head Nature Reserve**. In the heart of Byron Bay itself, the small and clearly visible rocky outcrop known as **Julian Rocks** provides a favourite snorkelling and diving spot and is especially noted for its visiting manta rays.

Cape Byron Headland Crowning the Cape Byron Headland is the **Byron Bay Lighthouse** that was built in 1901. It sits only metres away from Australia's easternmost point. Cape Byron was sighted by Captain Cook in May 1770 and was named after the grandfather of the famous 19th-century poet **Lord Byron**. Previous to that is was called 'Walgun' meaning 'shoulder' by the resident **Arakwal Aboriginal People**. As well as the dramatic coastal views east over Byron Bay and south down Tallow Beach to Broken Head, the headland provides some excellent walking opportunities, with the track down from the lighthouse to

Byron Bay

To Julian Rocks

Byron Bay

Main Beach

To Belongil Beach, Pacific Highway, Lismore, Tweed Heads

To Pighouse Flicks & Old Pigpery

To Broken Head & Nature Reserve

Not to scale

■ Sleeping		
1 Amigo's Byron Bay Guesthouse	4 Backpackers Inn	10 Cape Byron Hostel (YHA)
2 Aquarius Backpackers Motel	5 Bamboo Cottage	11 Clark's Beach Caravan Park
	6 Beach	12 First Sun Holiday Park
3 Arts Factory	7 Belongil Beachouse	13 Garden Burees
	8 Byron Bay Bunkhouse	14 Holiday Village Backpackers
	9 Byron Bayside Motel	

Little Watego's Beach being the most popular. **Humpback whales** can often been seen offshore during their annual migrations in mid-winter and early summer, while dolphins and the occasional manta ray can be spotted in the clear waters below the cliffs year round. ■ *Lighthouse open 0800-1930 (1730 in winter). 30 mins walk from the town. Tours 40 mins, daily except Wed and Fri.*

The town has a number of galleries worth seeing including the **Colin Heaney Glass Blowing Studio**, 6 Acacia Street, and the superb works of local photographer John Derrey, at **Byron Images**, on the corner of Lawson and Jonson streets, see www.johnderrey.com.au VIC has full gallery listings, and a tour to meet local artists and see their work and studios is offered by *Studio Arts Tours*, see Tours and activities below. Byron also hosts an arts and crafts **market** on the first Sunday of the month on Butler Street.

Galleries & markets

Essentials

There is certainly plenty of choice in Byron with the emphasis on backpacker hostels and up-market boutique hotels, B&Bs and guest houses. Thankfully, due to building and height restrictions, the multi-storey resort buildings of the Gold Coast and Noosa in Queensland have not yet taken over. While researching options from afar, or on arrival, you are advised to checkout the excellent service and free directories available from *Byron Bay Accommodation* in the VIC.

Sleeping
■ *On map, page 208*
See inside cover for price categories

Pre-booking is advised at all times

North Coast NSW

LL *Beach Hotel*, Bay St, T6685 6402, www.beachhotel.com.au This is the perfect place to be if you like to be in the heart of all the action. It has tidy, spacious rooms and suites (some with spa and ocean views) is only yards from the beach and the bar/restaurant

15 J's Bay Hostel	● **Eating**	6 Expresso Head
16 Julian's Apartments	1 Bay Kebabs	7 Oh Delhi Tandoori
17 Rae's on Watego	2 Beach Café	8 Pass Café
18 Summerhouse	3 Belongil Beach Café	9 Raving Prawn
19 Watego's Watermark	4 Cheeky Monkey's	10 Seven At 13
	5 Dish & Raw Bar	11 Thai Lucy

downstairs is the social hub of the town. **LL** *Garden Burees*, 19 Gordon St, T6685 5390, www.byron-bay.com/gardenburees Near the town centre, this offers something very different with 2-storey, self-contained Bali/Pacific bungalows, beautifully appointed, with spas, in a quiet bush setting. Vegetarian restaurant and massage therapy on site. **LL-A** *Julian's Apartments*, 124 Lighthouse Rd, west of the town centre, near the lighthouse, T66809697. Modern, well-appointed en suites close to the beach. **LL-L** *Nirvana Lodge B&B*, 4 Beach Rd, Broken Head (5 km), T6685 4549, hbrook@bigpond.com.au Luxurious and beautifully appointed, there are spa/en suite and en suite. Out of town, close to Broken Head Beach and Nature Reserve.

LL *Rae's on Watego*, overlooking Watego's Beach, T6685 5366, www.raes.com.au This sits firmly at the top of this price category and is the most luxurious hotel in Byron. It was voted in *Conde Naste Traveller Magazine* (and others) as being in the top 50 worldwide. Although location has a lot to do with that accolade, the place itself is superb and cannot be faulted. It has an in-house restaurant that is also excellent and open to non-guests. **LL** *Summerhouse*, 9 Coopers Shoot Rd, T6685 3090, www.thesummerhouse.com.au The modern aesthetics and views take some beating. It offers 3 luxury suites with spa. **LL** *Watego's Watermark*, 29 Marine Parade, T6685 8999, wategoswatermark@byron-bay.com.au, is in the ideal location only metres from the best surf beach, 5 great 'minimalist' rooms with balcony views and very friendly hosts.

Some excellent, cheaper options, include **A-B** *Amigo's Byron Bay Guesthouse*, corner of Kingsley and Tennyson sts, T6680 8662, with en suite double, double with shared bathroom, bike and body board hire and massage, and **A** *Bamboo Cottage*, 76 Butler St, T6685 5509, bamboocottage@byron-bay.com.au, has a tidy single, twin, double and triple in a quiet garden setting close to all amenities. Of the many motels the 3-star **A** *Byron Bayside Motel*, 14 Middleton St, T6685 6004, bbaymtl@norex.com.au, is well placed in the heart of town, modern, clean and good value.

There are over a dozen very competitive backpackers in town all having to maintain good standards. Mostly the choice comes down to availability – book well ahead. **A-F** *Arts Factory*, Skinners Shoot Rd (via Burns St, off Shirley St), T6685 7709, www.omcs.com.au/artsfactory For the quintessential 'alternative' Byron experience this place takes some beating. It offers a wide range of 'funky' accommodations from the 'Love Shack' and 'Island Retreats', to 'The Gypsy Bus', tepees and campsites. Excellent amenities, pool, sauna, internet, café (plus vegetarian restaurant nearby)', bike hire, tours desk and unusual arts, relaxation or music based activities including didgeridu making, drumming and yoga. The Pighouse cinema is also next door. It may not be everybody's cup of tea, but for an experience it is recommended. **LL-D** *Belongil Beachouse*, Childe St (Kendal St, off Shirley St), T6685 7868, www.belongilbeachouse.com.ault Also east of the town centre and in contrast to the *Arts Factory* this option offers a wide range of modern, well-appointed options from dorms and private double/twins with shared facilities, to luxury motel-style rooms with spas, or two-bedroom self-contained cottages. Quiet setting across the road from the beach. Balinese style café and float/massage therapy centre on site. Internet, bike, body/surf board hire and courtesy bus. Recommended.

A-E *Aquarius Backpackers Motel*, 16 Lawson St, T6685 7663, www.aquarius-backpack.com.au, is a large and lively complex offering dorms, doubles and spa suites (all en suite, with 'proper beds'), pool, good-value licensed café/bistro, internet, free boogie boards, bikes, pool tables and courtesy bus. **A-E** *Cape Byron Hostel* (YHA), T6685 8788, offers modern, clean dorms, double and twins (some en suite/a/c) centred around a large courtyard with pool. Well managed and friendly. Good kitchen facilities, café, free

BBQ nights, large games room, internet and tours desk. Dive shop next door. **A-E** *Holiday Village Backpackers*, 116 Jonson St, south of town centre, T6685 8888. Offers modern dorms, doubles and motel-style apartments (some en suite with TV), large courtyard with pool, spa, well equipped kitchen, all-you-can-eat BBQs, internet, free surf/body boards, scuba lessons, bike hire. If the above are booked up other alternatives include the spotless **C-E** *J's Bay Hostel*, 7 Carlyle St, T6685 8853, jbay@nor.com.au The very laid-back and social **C-E** *Byron Bay Bunkhouse*, 1 Carlyle St, T6685 8311, www.byronbay-bunkhouse.com.au, and the beachside **C-E** *Backpackers Inn*, 29 Shirley St, T668 58231, www.byron-bay.com/backpackersinn

The local council operate 4 local caravan parks that are usually busy and should be booked well in advance. **L-E** *Broken Head Caravan Park*, Beach Rd, Broken Head (8 km), T6685 3245. Further afield and much quieter, the appeal of the park is its friendly atmosphere, beachside position and proximity to the Broken Head Nature Reserve. It has cabins, powered and non-powered sites, small shop, BBQ but no camp kitchen. **L-E** *Clark's Beach Caravan Park*, off Lighthouse Rd, T6685 6496. Further west, with better aesthetics and right beside Clark's Beach, again this place offers self-contained and standard cabins, powered and shady non-powered sites, no camp kitchen just BBQs. **L-E** *First Sun Holiday Park*, Lawson St (200 m east of the Main Beach Car Park), T6685 6544, www.bshp.com.au/first The most convenient to the town centre and Main Beach, it offers a range of self-contained/standard cabins, powered and non-powered sites, camp kitchen.

Although Jonson St and the various arcades host some good restaurants and cafés most folk gravitate towards Bay Lane where you will find plenty of atmosphere.

Eating
● *On map, page 208*
See inside front cover
for price categories

Expensive *Fins*, Beach Hotel, T6685 5029, is a posh, multi-award winning seafood restaurant specializing in really fresh, organic produce. Open daily from 1830, bookings essential. *Dish Restaurant* and *Raw Bar*, corner of Jonson and Marvel sts, T6685 7320, Another award winner, this is a relatively new and very chic place with fine innovative international and Australian cuisine.

Mid-range *Raving Prawn*, Feros Arcade, Jonson St, T6685 6737, this award-winning seafood restaurant is recommended. Open Mon-Sat from 1800, daily in summer. *Asian Oh Deli Tandoori*, 4 Bay Lane (upstairs in the Bay Lane Arcade), T6680 8800, open daily 1200-2200, and *Thai Lucy*, Bay Lane, T6680 8083, open Mon-Sun 1200-1500 and 1730-2200, both offer excellent dishes, good value and lots of atmosphere, but book ahead. *Beach Hotel Bistro*, Bay Lane, never fails to lure in the crowds and wins hands down for atmosphere. Open for lunch and dinner from 1200-2100.

Cheap *Bay Kebabs*, at the bottom of Bay Lane, T6685 5596, offers generous and good value kebabs. Open daily from 1000 until late. *Cheeky Monkey's*, 115 Jonson St, T6685 5886. Backpacker specials (as little as $6) are regularly on offer in order to tempt you to stay late at the bar and nightclub. Open from Mon-Sat, 1900-0300. *Old Piggery*, next door to the cinema, has lots of atmosphere and offers something a little different. Vegetarian. *Arts Factory Backpackers*, 1 Skinners Shoot Rd. Wood-fired pizza restaurant ('noshery'). Open daily from 1800.

Expresso Head, 111 Jonson St, T6680 9783, has good coffee and is popular with the locals. Across the road *Seven At 13*, T6685 7478, in the Woolies Plaza, Jonson St, offers pure, modern organic cuisine in a pleasant al fresco setting. Open daily for breakfast, lunch and dinner. If a beach stroll is in order you will find a refreshing coffee and generous breakfasts at the very congenial *Belongil Beach Café*, just above *Belongil Beach*

Cafés

Café on Childe St, T6685 7144. Open daily 0800-2200. *Beach Café*, Clarks Beach, T6685 7598, is another option in the other direction. *Pass Café*, Off Lighthouse Rd (end of Clark's Beach), T6685 6074, overlooks the ocean and the best surf spots.

Entertainment   The huge bar at *Beach Hotel*, T6685 6402, facing the beach off Bay St, is the place too see and be seen and is popular both day and night, with the lively atmosphere often spilling out on to beer garden. Live bands Thu-Sun. *Cocomangas*, 32 Jonson St, has Retro 80s on Wed and Disco Funk and House on Sat. Open 2100-0300, free entry before 2330. There are 2 other nightclubs in **The Plaza**, off Jonson St, with the rather tired and loud *Carpark Nightclub*, Jonson St, open until 0300, and the far less frantic and congenial *Verve Nightclub*, internet café and bar, tucked in the corner, T6685 6170, www.vervenightclub.com.au The atmospheric and very comfortable *Pighouse Flicks*, Arts Factory, Gordon St (Via Butler), T6685 5828, www.pig-gery.com.au, acts as the local cinema showing both foreign, arts and mainstream films nightly. Meal/movie deals are available in unison with *Old Piggery* vegetarian restaurant next door.

Festivals   The most lauded annual festival in Byron is the popular *Blues and Roots Festival*, held every Easter weekend, www.bluesfest.com.au, which attracts its fair share of international stars, 'wanna-bes' or 'has-beens'!

Shopping   Byron offers a wealth of 'alternative' and arts/crafts oriented shops selling everything from futons to $300 hand-painted toilets seats. For a lasting image of Byron, look no further than John Derrey's photography work at *Byron Images*, corner Lawson and Jonson sts, T6685 8909, www.johnderry.com.au Also don't miss the Asian lanterns and light stars at the end of Bay Lane in the evenings. *Byron Bay Camping and Disposals*, Plaza, Jonson St, T6685 8085, can oblige should you need camping gear and supplies. Self-caterers will find the *Woolworths* supermarket in the Plaza Shopping Centre, Jonson St, while *Supermarket*, 17 Lawson St, is open daily 0700-2100.

Tours & activities   As well as all the activity options that area on offer, Byron Bay also supports a large number of massage, yoga practitioners and health therapists. Look out for the free *Body and Soul* brochure at the VIC for full listings and prices.

Grasshoppers Nimbin Eco-Explorer Tour, run by *Rockhoppers*, Shop1/87 Jonson St, T0500 881 881, is recommended if you want to see some of the hinterland's best sights and to experience Nimbin from the 'right angle', from $35. Recommended. Transport to the Nimbin backpackers is also an additional option. They also offer guided sunrise treks on Tue/Wed/Sun, with breakfast or day treks to the summit of **Mount Warning** from $49. *Jim's Alternative Tours*, T6685 7720, www.byron-bay.com/jimstours, also offers an wide array of entertaining options from simple lighthouse or market trips to dolphin watching and national park eco-tours. Day tour departs Mon-Sat at 0900, from $30. *Rockhoppers* are one of the largest operators, offering an attractive range of single or combination activity packages, from mountain biking to wake boarding.

Arts and crafts   *Studio Arts Tours*, T6680 9797, offers tours to meet local artists and view their work from $30 (2 hrs), $55 (3½ hrs) $98 full day. If you fancy partaking as opposed to merely viewing. **Epicentre Arts Centre**, 1 Border St, T6680 7688, offers art courses from beginner to advanced Tue-Sat.

Diving   Julian Rocks Marine Reserve, 2.5 km from the shore in Byron Bay, is listed in Australia's 'top ten' dive sites, with over 400 species of fish including sharks and manta ray, with turtles and dolphins often joining the party. If you are not a certified diver, a snorkelling trip to the rocks is recommended. *Sundive*, opposite the Court House on Middleton St, T6685 7755, offer courses, trips with gear (from $75) and snorkelling from $45 (0830/1100/1400). *Byron Bay Dive Centre*, 9 Marvel St, T6685 8333, www.byronbaydivecentre.com.au, offer a similar range of trips.

Mountain biking *Rockhoppers*, Shop1/87 Jonson St, T0500 881 881, offers day-long biking adventures on hinterland rainforest trails, taking in the Minyon Falls, from $69-80. *Wanderlust Eco-Adventures*, T6685 7266, also offers biking adventures with more sedate family oriented tours.

Paragliding and hang gliding *Poliglide*, T04 2866 6843, www.poliglide.com.au, offer tandem paragliding from $165 and day-long introductory courses from $220. *Skylimit*, T6684 3711, skylimit@mullum.com.au, and *Flight Zone*, T6685 8768 offer tandem hang gliding and microlight flights and courses, from $70.

Sea kayaking *Dolphin*, T6685 8044, www.dolphinkayaking.com.au, also offer good trips departing at 0900 and 1400 daily from $40. Recommended.

Skydiving *Skydive Cape Byron*, 2/84 Jonson St T6685 5990, www.sky dive-cape-byron.com.au, are a reputable outfit, offering tandems from 8,000 ft (from $229) to 12,000 ft (from $299). *Byron Bay Skydiving Centre*, T1800 800 840, www.skydivebyronbay.com.au, based east of town near Brunswick Heads, is owned by Australian World representative and 'skysurfer' Ray Palmer. He and his colleagues offer a range of professional services including tandems. The views from the jump zone across Byron Bay to the headland and beyond are stunning. Jumps from 8,000 ft ($253) to 10,000 ft ($341).

Surfing and kite boarding With so many superb surf breaks around Byron and subsequently so many local professionals there is no shortage of opportunity to learn – or at least to try to stay upright for more than a nanosecond. Most operators offer a guarantee to get you standing or will refund. *Style Surfing*, T6685 5634, www.byron-bay.com/byronbaystylesurfing, offers a 4-hr beginners package or advanced courses daily at 0900, 1100 and 1300, from $33, or private lessons from $50 per 1½ hrs. *Byron Bay Surf School*, T1800 707 274, www.byronbaysurfschool.com.au, guarantee to get you standing with half-, full-, 3- and 5-day packages, from $45 (3-day $110, 5-day $150, private 2-hr lesson from $85). *'Surf Angels'*, girl's only sessions are also available. *Kool Katz*, T6685 5169, are one of the cheapest in town and also guarantee to get you standing for 4 hrs, from $25 and 3-day from $65. For real enthusiasts or serious learners, *Surfaris*, T1800 634 951, www.surfaris.com.au, offer a week-long Sydney-Byron trip (from $499) or a 4-day/ 3-night Byron-Noosa-Hervey Bay trip, from $365.

Byron Bay Kiteboarding, T1300 888 938, offer half-, 2- or 3-day packages to master the new and increasingly popular art of kite boarding, from $150. No 'keep you standing' guarantees on this one.

These operators offer surf hire with short boards starting at about $5 per hour, $12 for 4 hours and around $20 or 24 hours

Walking Nightcap, Border Ranges and Mount Warning national parks all present some excellent walking opportunities in contrast to the many coastal options. *Byron Bay Walking Tours*, T6687 1112, walknorth@mullum.com.au, offer a range of guided day-trips from the eco-based to historic, taking in both coast and hinterland. Trips range from a basic 8-km day walk along the Evans River, (from $65) and an 11-km trip to see the Minyon Falls, (from $50) to a part guided, part self-guided 20-km walk through the rugged Nightcap National Park, from $70.

Other activities *Byron Boat Charters*, based at The Pass, Brooke Dr, T6685 6858, offer a range of cruise and activity options, including dolphin/whale watching, fishing, snorkelling and general water-based sightseeing, from $35. *Rockhoppers*, T0500 881 881, offer day-long 'triple challenge' waterfall abseiling, rappelling and canyoning adventures in the hinterland rainforest, from $119. For something completely different you might like to try flying trapeze and circus school activities at the *Byron Bay Beach Resort*, Bayshore Dr, T6685 8000, from $25. Safety net included but bring your own fetching pair of tights!

Transport   **Local Bus** *Blanch's Buses*, T6686 2144, offer local services within Byron Bay (#637) and also south to Ballina via Lennox Head (#640) and north to Mullumbimby (#640). **Bike hire** Contact *Byron Bay Bicycles*, 93 Jonson St, T6685 6067, *Byron Bay Bike Hire*, (free delivery), T0500 856 985 or *Rockhoppers*, Shop1/87 Jonson St, T0500 881 881, from $25 per day. **Motorcycle** Hire from *Ride On*, 105 Jonson St, T6685 6304 from $110 per-day. **Taxi** T6685 5008.

Long distance **Air** The closest airports to Byron Bay are Coolangatta to the north (90 km), Gold Coast), see page 226, and Ballina to the south (31 km), see page 206. Both are served by *QantasLink*, T131313. *Airporter Shuttle*, T04 1460 8660 and *Byron Bay International*, T6685 7447, serve Coolangatta from $66 one-way. *Byron Bay Airbus*, T6681 3355, serve Ballina, from $25 one-way. **Bus** The long-distance bus stop is located right in the heart of town on Jonson St. *McCafferty's*, T131499, *Greyhound*, T132030, and *Premier Motor Services*, T133410, offer daily inter-state services north/south. *Kirklands*, T1300 367 077, offer services to Brisbane, Ballina, Lismore and Coolangatta. *Byron Bay Bus and Backpacker Centre*, 84 Jonson St, T6685 5517, act as the local booking agents. **Car** *Byron Car Hire*, T6685 6345, from $40 per day. *Byron Bus*, Transit Centre, T6685 5517. *Byron Odyssey*, T1800 771 244, from $39 per day. Car servicing at *Bayside Mechanical*, 12 Banksia Drive, T6685 8455. **Train** The station is also located in the heart of town, just off Jonson St. *Countrylink*, T132232, offer daily services south to Sydney and beyond and north (with bus link) to *Queensland Rail*, T132232, to Brisbane.

Directory   **Banks** Most major branches with ATMs are represented along Jonson or Lawsons St. Currency exchange is readily available including *Byron Foreign Exchange*, Shop 3/5-7 Byron St, T66857787. Open daily 0900-1800. **Communications** Internet: *Global Gossip*, 84 Jonson St, T6680 9140, open daily 0800-2400, or *Soundwaves*, 58 Jonson St, open daily 0900-2100. **Post office**: 61 Jonston St. Open Mon-Fri 0900-1700. **Medical services** Hospital: Byron Bay Hospital, T6685 6200. **Travel agents** *Backpackers World*, Shop 6 Byron St, T6685 8858. *Backpackers Travel Centre*, Cavanbah Arcade, Jonson St, T6685 7085. *Jetset Travel*, corner of Jonson and Marvel sts, T6685 6554. **Useful numbers** Police: corner of Shirley and Butler sts, T6685 9499.

Byron Lismore Hinterland

*East of Byron Bay and the far north coast of New South Wales, the dramatic peak of **Mount Warning** lures the visitor inland with the desire to climb the summit or explore its associate national parks that all come replete with rugged landscapes of rainforests, waterfalls and rivers. For others, the 'trip' inland is fuelled with the desire to experience that altogether different type of 'high' in a scattering of bohemian, arty villages that are famous for their alternative lifestyle. This very pleasant, scenic area, often called the Northern Rivers, or more aptly perhaps – the **Rainbow Region** – encompasses and stretches from **Murwillumbah** in the* *north to **Kyogle** in the west, Lismore and **Ballina** in the south and Byron Bay on the coast to the east. While Byron serves as the most popular tourist destination, **Lismore** is the largest town and region's commercial capital, with the small villages of **Nimbin** and **Dunoon**, amongst others, providing the alternative edge.*

Geologically the region is dominated by the Mount Warning Shield **volcano** and its vast and associate **Caldera** (crater), which is the largest of its type in the southern hemisphere. The huge volcano, which erupted about 23 million years ago, produced a flat shield-shaped landform with its highest point rising almost twice that of **Mount Warning** (1,157 m), which is all that remains today of the original magma chamber and central vent. If viewed from the air the huge eroded bowl of the Caldera can be seen stretching almost 60 km inland from the coast, with the dramatic peak of Mount Warning in its middle, like an undilated bulls eye. The original lava flows reached as far as Canungra in the north, Kyogle to the west, Lismore and Ballina in the south and almost 100 km out to sea. Today, after millions of years of wind and water erosion, the region is rich in dramatic geological features with Mount Warning having stood the test of time. Around the rim and fringing plateaus lush rainforest covered landscapes have risen form the ashes, while the floor of the Caldera acts as a vast watershed for the **Tweed River** that gives itself up to the ocean at the border of New South Wales and Queensland. There are nine **national parks** in the area including Mount Warning and **Nightcap** that present some of the best scenery and walking opportunities. Then, of course, if it's a 'trip' into orbit you are after it seems that Nimbin is the proverbial launch pad.

Background

Close to Byron Bay is the small historic village of Bangalow, which has a pleasant laid-back atmosphere, a scattering of art galleries, antique and gift shops. It also hosts a good market on the fourth Sunday of each month.

Bangalow

Lismore

The attractive city of Lismore is the capital and commercial centre for the Northern Rivers (Rainbow) Region and far north New South Wales. Straddling the banks of the Richmond River, and hosting the Southern Cross University as well as a wealth of creative talent, Lismore offers a pleasant combination of rural aesthetics and youthful exuberance, far removed from the tourist hype of Byron Bay. It is also a fine base from which to explore the many outlying, alternative lifestyle villages, famous for their weekend markets and some of the states most pristine national parks. The city was first settled by the Europeans in 1850s during the rapacious, ecologically disastrous 'rape' of the regions once-rich stands of cedar trees known collectively as 'The Big Scrub'.

Colour map 2, grid B5
Population: 29,000
47 km west of Byron Bay, 32 km south of Nimbin

Lismore VIC is located at the corner of Ballina and Molesworth sts, just south of the city centre, T6622 0122, www.liscity.nsw.gov.au Open Mon-Fri 0930-1600, Sat/Sun 1000-1500. They can provide city maps and full accommodation and activity listings. The VIC also hosts the small but informative Indoor Rainforest and Heritage Display, $1.

Ins & outs
See Transport, page 216, for details

Lismore Regional Art Museum is one of the oldest in the State and is housed in the 1908 art nouveau Trench Building. It showcases permanent international, Australian and local collections as well as a diverse range of travelling exhibitions. ■ *Tue-Fri 1000-1600, Sat/Sun 1030-1430. Donation. T6622 2209. 131 Molesworth St.*

Sights

A few doors down, **Richmond River Historical Society** is worth a look if only as an attestation of the rise and (literal) fall off the region's cedar-cutting industry. ■ *Mon-Fri 1000-1600, $2, T6621 9993, 165 Molesworth St.* Ironically, one of the last great **cedar** logs sits outside the City Hall (Molesworth Street) and was presented as another proud memorial to local cedar pioneers rather than the wholesale and permanent loss of the trees themselves.

There are several attractive nature reserves in the area many of which contain the last remnants of the 'Big Scrub'– the collective name given to the extensive rainforest that once dominated the region – as well as some interesting wildlife. **Boat Harbour Nature Reserve**, 6 km northeast on the Bangalow Road, is a fine example and also supports a colony of flying foxes (bats), while **Tucki Tucki Nature Reserve**, 15 km south on Wyrallah Road, has the added attraction of a thriving colony of koala. Late afternoon, when they go into their slow-mo-eucalyptus-leaf-feeding-frenzy, is the best time to view them in the wild. But if you are out of luck, you are just about guaranteed a close encounter at the regional **Koala Hospital**, next to the Southern Cross University. ■ *Daily. Donation. T6622 1233. Rifle Range Rd. Booking advised.*

Sleeping **C-E** *Currendina Lodge*, 14 Ewing St, just east of the CBD, T6621 6118, currendi@nor. com.au, serves as the local friendly backpackers, offering tidy dorms, singles, doubles and family rooms with all the standard amenities and courtesy pick-ups. There are 4 caravan parks in and around town with **C-F** *Lismore Palms*, 42-58 Brunswick St (northern, Bangalow Rd approach), T6621 7067, being the best facilitated with cabins, on-site vans, powered and non-powered sites, pool and camp kitchen.

Eating *Café Millennium*, 78 Uralba St, T6622 0925. Open lunch Tue-Fri 1130-1430, dinner Wed-Sat from 1800. If you like Japanese food try this award-winner. BYO. *Hector's Place*, 34 Molesworth St, T6621 6566, is in a fine spot overlooking the river and offering modern Australian, open lunch Tue-Fri 1200-1400, dinner Tue-Sat from 1800. *Mary Gilhooley's*, corner of Keen and Woodlark sts, T6622 2924. Open for lunch and dinner Mon-Sat. For traditional Irish pub grub amidst a congenial friendly atmosphere. Cheaper options include: *Northern Rivers Hotel*, 33 Terania St, T66215797, a traditional venue and *Lismore RSL*, 1 Market St, T6621 2434, a good-value bistro.

Tours & *MV Bennelong* offers an range of scenic and historical cruises on the Richmond and
activities Wilson Rivers with a 3½-hr lunch cruise (1100-1430), from $35, child $17.50 and a day-long cruise, downstream to Ballina (1000-1700), from $70, child $35, T6688 8266.

Transport **Air** Lismore Airport, T6622 2798, is located 2 km southwest of the city centre off the Bruxner Highway and is served from Sydney by *Hazelton Airlines*, T131713, www.hazelton.com.au **Bus** The local and long-distance bus centre is on the corner of Molesworth and Magellan sts, T6621 8620. Open Mon-Fri 0730-1830, Sat 0730-1330, Sun 0730-0830/1600-1700). *Kirklands*, T6622 1499, www.kirklands.com.au, offer regular daily services locally and throughout the region including Byron Bay and Brisbane. *Greyhound Pioneer*, T132030, and *Premier Motor Service*, T9281 2233, offer daily interstate services between Sydney and Brisbane. *Nimbin Byron Shuttle Bus*, T6680 9189, departs Lismore at 1100 and returns at 1500 ($16 return). **Taxi** T131008. **Train** The station is across the river from the bus transit centre on Union St. *Countrylink*, T132232, offer state-wide services including the fast XPT service to Sydney, with regional coach transfers/connections (including the Gold Coast).

Directory **Communications** Internet: Available at *Lismore Internet Services*, 4/172 Molesworth St, T6622 7766. Open Mon-Fri 0900-1700 or **Lismore Regional Library**,

Rainbow region markets

◀

One of the great tourist attractions in the Rainbow Region are its colourful weekend markets that operate in a circuit throughout the region, primarily on Sundays. Byron Bay Market is held in the Butler St Reserve on the first Sunday of the month. Lismore hosts a regional Organic Produce Market at the Lismore Showgrounds every Tuesday between 0700-1000, the less convivial Car Boot

Market at the Shopping Square on the first and third Sunday of the month, and the Lismore Showground Markets every second Sunday. The excellent Channon Craft Market, kicks off in Coronation Park on the second Sunday, while the Aquarius Fair Markets, in Nimbin are on the third and fifth Sunday. Bangalow holds their market in the local show grounds on the fourth Sunday. Worth a visit.

Carrington St, T6621 2464. Open Mon-Wed 0930-1700, Thu/Fri 0930-1930, Sat 0900-1200. Bookings required.

Nimbin

Up until the 1970s, the sleepy dairy village of Nimbin had changed little since its inception by the first European settlers over a century before. Then, in 1973 the Australian Union of Students (AUS) chose the Nimbin Valley as the venue for the 'experimental and alternative' **Aquarius Festival**. The concept was to create 'a total cultural experience, through the lifestyle of participation' for Australian creatives, students and alternative lifestylers. Of course, with many of that generation eager to maintain the ideologies and practices of the 60s, the very concept became like a red rag to the proverbial, 'alternative' bull and when the time arrived it all inevitably went in to orbit. In many ways Nimbin never got over the invasion, the excitement or indeed the hangover and its more enlightened long-term residents have been joined by a veritable army of society's drop-outs, man.

Colour map 2, grid A5 Population: 300 70 km from Byron Bay, 384,000 km from the moon

Nimbin Tourist Connexion, at the northern end of Cullen St acts as the local VIC. It offers bus, train and accommodation bookings, has internet access and village maps, T6689 1764. Open Mon-Fri 1000-1700, Sat 1200-1430, Sun 1000-1700.

Ins & outs
See Transport, page 218, for details

In many ways the colourful main street of Nimbin, **Cullen Street**, is the single collective 'sight' in the village and one that speaks very much for itself. Amidst a rash of laid-back cafés, alternative health and arts and craft shops, is **Nimbin Museum**. Entirely true to the unconventional and the alternative ideology, it goes deliberately beyond any conventional concepts. It is perhaps simply unique in its creative, historical and often humorous interpretations and expressions of the village, its inhabitants and Australia as a whole. A visit is highly recommended. ■ *Daily 0900-1700. $2. T6689 1123. 62 Cullen St.*

Sights

On the other side of Cullen Street, the loudly advertised **Hemp Embassy** is also worth a look but, as you can imagine, has little to do with gardening or fashion wear, free. As well as supporting the multifarious and controversial uses of hemp, the Nimbin Valley is also well known for fruit growing and permaculture. For the visitor the **Djanbung Gardens Permaculture Centre** offers garden tours, herbal crafts, environmental workshops and an organic café. ■ *Daily 1000-1200, Tue-Fri 1000-1500. T6689 1755. 74 Cecil St. Tours Tue/Thu 1030, Sat 1100.*

North Coast NSW

The most obvious volcanic feature around Nimbin are the **Nimbin Rocks**, which are estimated to be over 20 million years old. There is a **lookout** on Lodge Road, 3 km south of the village.

Sleeping Nimbin is a popular haunt for backpackers keen to experience the spirit of Nimbin and you are invited to 'Live the Nimbin Dream' at the unusual, good value and suitably laid-back **C-F** *Rainbow Retreat Backpackers*, 75 Thorburn St, T6689 1262, www.skybusiness.com/rainbowretreat Not surprisingly, it provides a range of highly unconventional accommodation options from Malay-style huts to VW Kombis, dorms and secluded campsites, all set in a quiet 18-acre site near the edge of the village. Both the facilities and atmosphere are excellent with regular musical jam sessions, visiting chefs, $5 meals international, alternative practitioners and performers, not to mention the odd platypus in the creek or harmless python up a tree. Over all, it provides the ideal way to experience the true spirit of Nimbin. *Peterpan* in Byron provide free transport, T1800 252 459. Recommended. **C-F***Nimbin Caravan and Tourist Park*, 29 Sibley St, T6689 1402, has basic, facilities, on-site vans, powered and non-powered sites, within easy walking distance of the village.

Eating Cullen St hosts a number of alternative eateries with *Rainbow Café* being the oldest. **Bush Theatre**, T6685 5074, northern end of Cullen St, is another popular venue, combining a cinema and a café and offering the occasional good value movie/meal deal. Open Fri/Sat 1930, Sun 1830.

Transport If you do not wish to stay in Nimbin and are based in Byron Bay, the best way to see the village and its surrounds is to join one of the various day-tour operators. *Grasshoppers Nimbin Eco-Explorer Tour*, run by *Rockhoppers*, T0500 881 881, (from $35) is recommended. Other operators include *Jim's Alternative Tours*, T6685 7720, and *Mick's Bay and Bush Tours*, T6685 6889. *Nimbin Byron Shuttle Bus*, T6680 9189, operates Mon-Sat, departing from Jonson St Byron Bay at 1000, returning at 1430, from $25 return.

Nightcap National Park and Whian Whian State Forest

Colour map 2, grid A5
50 km northeast
of Lismore, 40 km
west of Byron Bay

The World Heritage 8,145-ha Nightcap National Park is located on the southern rim of the Mount Warning shield volcano caldera and adjacent is the Whian Whian State Forest Park. Combined, the two present a wealth of volcanic features including massifs, pinnacles and cliffs eroded by spectacular waterfalls and draped in lush rainforest. Some unique wildlife also resides in the park including the red-legged pademelon (a kind of wallaby), the Fleay's barred frog and the appealingly named wompoo fruit-dove.

The main physical features of the park are **Mount Nardi** (800 m), which is 12 km east of Nimbin; **Terania Creek** and the **Protestors Falls**, 14 km north of The Channon; and Whian Whian State Forest and 100-m **Minyon Falls**, 23 km southwest of Mullumbimby. The 30-km **Whian Whian Scenic Drive** (unsealed), which can be accessed beyond the Minyon Falls, traverses the forest park and takes visitors through varied rainforest vegetation and scenery including the memorable **Peates Mountain Lookout**. Nightcap National Park also holds the rather dubious but essential accolade of receiving the highest mean rainfall in the State.

Popular long walking tracks include the moderate to hard 7.5-km **Minyon Loop**, which starts from the Minyon Falls Picnic Area that takes in the base of the falls and the escarpment edge, and the moderate to hard 16-km **Historic Nightcap Track** that follows the former pioneer trails that once connected Lismore and Mullumbimby. Other, shorter and easier possibilities are the

North Coast NSW

3-km **Mount Matheson Loop** and 4-km **Pholis Gap** walks, which both start from Mount Nardi and the 1.5-km **Big Scrub Loop** that starts from the Gibbergunyah Range Road in Whian Whian State Forest. It is said to contain some of the best remnant rainforest in the region. **Protestors Falls**, which were named after a successful six-week protest to prevent logging in the late1970s, are reached on a 1.5-km return track from the Terania Creek Picnic Area.

The Mount Nardi section of the park is accessed via Newton Drive, which is off Tuntable Falls Rd west out of Nimbin. The Terania Creek and Protestors Falls are reached via Terania Creek Rd north out of The Channon and the Minyon Falls and Whian Whian State Forest is reached via Dunoon or Goonengerry southwest of Mullumbimby. Camping is available at Rummery Park 2 km north of the Minyon Falls, T6662 4499.

Access & camping
See also Tours, page 213

The little village of Mullumbimby is about as charming as its name suggests and offers a fine stop or diversion on the way to Lismore, Minyon Falls or the Nightcap National Park. There is a scattering of historic buildings along Dalley and Stuart streets that include the 1908 **Cedar House**, that now serves as an antique gallery and the old 1907 **post office** which houses a small museum. **Crystal Castle**, south of Mullumbimby on Monet Drive, has a fine display of natural crystals, gardens and a café. You might also be tempted to checkout your psychedelic colours as seen through the 'aura camera' or try some crystal healing, a tarot card reading or massage. ■ *Daily 1000-1630. Free. T6684 1196, www.crystalcastle.net.au*

Mullumbimby
18 km northwest of Byron Bay

Sleeping F *Maca's Camp Ground*, 12 km west of Mullumbimby, T668 45211. Congenial, basic, set amidst rainforest and a macadamia nut orchard (free nuts to campers!).

Mount Warning National Park

The 1157-m peak of Mount Warning is all that remains of the magma chamber and vent that formed the vast caldera that shaped much of the Northern Rivers region 20 million years ago. Other than its stunning aesthetics and rich flora and fauna, the great lure to Mount Warning is the pilgrimage summit walk to see the first rays of sunlight to touch the Australian mainland. The moderate to hard 4.4-km ascent starts from the Breakfast Creek Picnic Area, 17 km southwest of Murwillumbah at the terminus of Mount Warning Road. To ensure you reach the summit for sunrise you are advised to set off about 2½ hours beforehand. For the less energetic, Lyrebird Track crosses Breakfast Creek before winding 200 m through palm forest to a rainforest platform.

Colour map 2, grid A5 17 km west of Murwillumbah, 80 km north of Lismore

To learn more about the Aboriginal mythology surrounding the mountain and its diverse wildlife, you might like to join either the sunrise or daytime summit walking tours on offer from Byron Bay.

Mount Warning was named from offshore by Captain Cook in 1770 to warn mariners of the dangers of the approaching Barrier Reef. Ironically, he would later run aground of Cape Tribulation in far north Queensland several weeks later.

Access to the park is via Mount Warning Rd, 11 km south of Murwillumbah on the main Kyogle Rd. Camping is available at the privately run **B-E** *Mount Warning Caravan Park* about 3 km up Mount Warning Rd, T6679 5120. It has cabins, on-site vans, powered and non-powered sites and a camp kitchen. Murwillumbah, below, serves as an overnight stop for those undertaking the dawn ascent.

Access & camping
See also Tours, page 213

North Coast NSW

Murwillumbah

Colour map 2, grid A5
Population: 8,000
35 km south of Tweed
Heads, 49 km north of
Byron Bay

The pleasant, sugar cane town of Murwillumbah sits on the banks of the Tweed River, at the eastern edge of the vast Mount Warning shield volcano caldera. It serves as the gateway to the Northern Rivers (or Rainbow) Region with its villages famed for their alternative lifestylers and superb national parks including Mount Warning, Nightcap, Lamington, Springbrook and the Border Ranges. For many the main attraction is the dawn ascent of Mount Warning to see the first rays of sunlight to hit the Australian mainland.

Sights Most people who visit Murwillumbah gather what information they need from the **World Heritage Rainforest Centre** (see below) and then 'head for the hills', however, if you can spare an hour or so the small **Tweed Regional Art Gallery**, on Tumbulgum Road, is worth a look. As well as its permanent collection of Australian and International art, it features some fine works by local artists and also hosts the very lucrative Doug Moran National Portrait Prize. ■ *Wed-Sun 1000-1700, T6670 2790.*

Murwillumbah VIC shares its office with the NPWS and the World Heritage Rainforest Centre, on the corner of Pacific Highway and Alma Street, T6672 1340. Combined they offer insight and information surrounding the region and the parks. Open daily until 1600.

Sleeping **LL** *Crystal Creek Rainforest Retreat*, Brookers Rd, T6679 1591, www.crystalcreekrain
& eating forestretreat.com.au   This award-winning retreat is located on the edge of the Numinbah Nature Reserve, about 23 km west of Murwillumbah, and offers exactly that and much more, with modern aesthetics, 7 well-appointed self-contained bungalows, spa baths, excellent cuisine, local forest walks and even the odd hammock across the creek. Transfers from Murwillumbah by arrangement. Recommended. **C-E** *Mount Warning/Murwillumbah YHA*, 1 Tumbulgum Rd, Murwillumbah (first right across the bridge, 200 m, across the river from the VIC), T6672 3763, mbahyha@norex.com.au Relaxing, friendly and homely place next to the river and overlooking Mount Warning. Dorms and double/twins, free use of canoes and transport to Mount Warning if you stay 2 nights. **B-E** *Mount Warning Caravan Park* (see Mount Warning NP above). *The Imperial Hotel*, on the Main St, offers value pub-style lunches and dinners.

Tours & *RitzRail*, T1300 795 795, www.ritzrail.com.au, offer a range of standard and luxury train
activities trips to Byron Bay and Lismore. *Blue Ribbon Byron Bay Explorer* combines a scenic rail journey and coach tour of Byron (departs Murwillumbah Mon/Tue/Thu, from $90, child $35).

Transport **Bus** Long-distance and local bus company *Kirklands*, T1300 367 077, and interstate *Greyhound*, T132030, stop outside agents *Tweed Valley Travel*, corner of Main and Queen sts, T6672 1031. Northbound buses and trains both stop in Murwillumbah. **Train** The station is opposite the VIC and is served by *Countrylink*, T132232.

Introducing the Gold Coast

From its humble beginnings and the fertile seed of a few
beachside holiday apartments built in the mid-1900s,
the Gold Coast has grown into a mighty forest of apartment
blocks that now stretch up and down the coast like some giant,
manic beaver's house steadfastly holding back the tide.

With almost five million visitors a year the **'Coast With the
Most'** is Australia's most popular domestic holiday destination
and for some inexplicable reason is seen by some native

Gold Coast

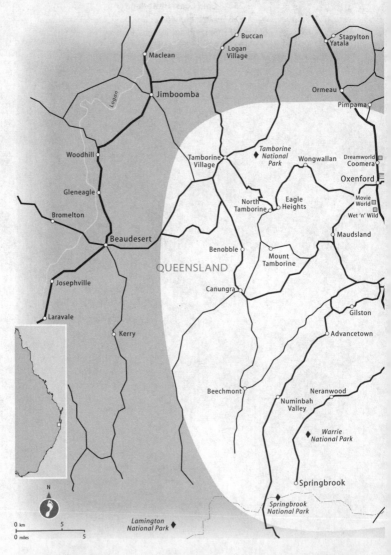

Australians as the perfect piece of real estate. Like any place that is bold and brash, the Gold Coast's reputation precedes it and no doubt those that have never been will already have formed a strong opinion. Sure it's a concrete jungle and a womb of artificiality, but for lovers of the laid-back beach lifestyle, socialites seeking a hectic nightlife, theme park and thrill ride junkies and shopaholics, it can promise more than just a 'surfers paradise'. For those of you just itching to scratch the mighty Gold Coast from your travelling agenda at the mere prospect of such a place – think again. Even for the greatest cynic, the worst (or the best), the Gold Coast can prove utterly infectious and lead to a thoroughly enjoyable experience.

Generally speaking the further north you go the more highrise, high profile and expensive the resorts become, with the truly luxurious real estate havens and holiday resorts like **Sanctuary Cove** located north of Southport. The main focus for tourism is of course **Surfers Paradise**. Festooned with its fair share of the many decked and multi-windowed blocks, all underscored with colourful neon and souvenir shops; it is a fascinating spectacle, especially at night.

Turning your back on the coast, only an hour away, is one of the Gold Coast's greatest assets and the 'Green behind the Gold' in the form of the **Springbrook** and **Lamington national parks**, two of Queensland's best, perfect retreats from the choas.

Gold Coast

Coolangatta and Tweed Heads

Colour map 2, grid A5
Population: 60,000
100 km from Brisbane

What Surfers Paradise is to hype and shopping malls, Coolangatta is to beach aesthetics and surf breaks. Its greatest attractions are undoubtedly its beaches and the mighty surf that breaks upon them. If you are a surfer there will be no mucking about and your intentions will be entirely focused. But if you have never been on a surfboard in your life and your idea of surfing consists of www.com, then this is one of the best places in the world to watch in awe, the true meaning of the word.

Ins & outs
See Transport, page 226, for further details

Getting there The airport servicing the Gold Coast area is 2 km from Coolangatta. Major bus companies have services to the town. **Getting around** Small enough to navigate on foot with local bus services to surrounding sights. **Tourist information** Gold Coast (Coolangatta) VIC, Shop 14B, Coolangatta Pl, corner of Griffith and Warner sts, T55367765, www.goldcoasttourism.com.au/www.tweedcoolvisitorsguide.com.au Mon-Fri 0800-1700, Sat 0800-1600, Sun 0900-1300. Tweed Heads VIC, 41 Wharf St, T55364244, www.tweed-coolangatta.com.au Mon-Fri 0900-1700, Sat 0900-1200. There is a town map in the useful, free brochure *Tweed-Coolangatta Visitors Guide*.

Sights

Coolangatta is fringed with superb beaches that surround the small peninsula known as **Tweed Heads**. The tip of the peninsula was named **Point Danger** by Captain Cook in 1770 and provides a fine starting point from which to survey the scene – be it with a sense of admiration rather than Cook's obvious angst. Below and to the right is **Duranbah Beach** which flanks the sea wall at the mouth of the Tweed River. Like all the beaches around the heads it is popular surf spot and Point Danger provides a good vantage point from which to spectate. You can come here for sunrise and true to the spirit of surfing, already see surfers out riding the waves.

To the left is **Snapper Rocks** which is perhaps the most popular surf break in the southern Gold Coast. This is by far the best place to watch the surfers since you can literally sit on the rocks beside the 'launch zone' only metres away from all the action. The launch zone itself is a place of endless entertainment as surfers of all ages and personalities line up like aircraft taxiing onto the runway. Once out there, often in their dozens, it is a bit like watching an orchestra belting out Beethoven's fifth, in complete harmony and yet, remarkably, without a conductor. Also, the unwritten rules, never mind the skill it must take not to mow each other down and create havoc – for the layman – remains a complete enigma. Just to the west of Snapper Rocks is the pretty little beach called **Rainbow Bay** which is the first of the beaches that combines both good surfing with safe swimming. Continuing west, Rainbow Bay is then separated from **Greenmount Beach** by a small headland that offers fine views from Pat Fagan Park. Greenmount Beach then merges with **Coolangatta Beach**, both of which are idyllic, excellent for swimming and enormously popular with families. At the western end of Coolangatta Beach, **Kirra Point** also provides great views back down Greenmount and Coolangatta beaches and north, beyond North Kirra Beach, to Surfers Paradise.

If you can drag yourself away from the beaches there is yet another fine viewpoint at the **Tom Beatson Outlook** on Mount Toonbarabah. From there, looking north, the twin towns of Coolangatta-Tweed Heads and the Tweed River are laid out before you, while to the west you can see the prominent volcanic peak of Mount Warning. ■ *Getting there: from the centre of Coolangatta and Griffith St, head south down Dixon, then straight ahead up Razorback Rd.*

Gold Coast

Gold Coast gandering

Getting around the Gold Coast is generally very easy, with 24-hour local bus transport and numerous companies offering theme park/airport transfers and car, moped, and bike hire.

Surfside Buslines, T131230, www.gcshuttle.com.au, offer suburban services, theme park and airport transfers ($13) between 0830-2245. For other theme park transfers: Con-x-ions, T55912525, www.con-x-ion.com.au, Active Tours, T55970344, or Coachtrans, T131230.

There are also travel passes available. Surfside Buslines, offer a 3-14 day Freedom Pass, from $40, child $20 includes a return airport transfer and unlimited theme park/local services. A 1-14 day Gold Pass, from $15, child $8, allows unlimited local and theme park transfers, T55745111. Airtrain, T07-3216 3308, www.airtrain.com.au, offer Brisbane City/Airport Transfers with 3-7 day unlimited theme park/local transport from $95.

Beyond the beaches and the views there are two main tourist attractions in the immediate area. **Minjungbal's Aboriginal Historic Site**, on the corner of Kirkwood Road and Duffy Street, offers an insight into the life and times of the local tribe, with various displays including a bora-ring used for initiation ceremonies. ■ *Daily, $6. T55242109.* **Tropical Fruit World**, near Kingscliff, is reputed to house the world's largest selection of tropical fruits. Although that may sound far from ripe, it is actually quite entertaining and educational, and just about guarantees to introduce you to at least one fruit you have never heard of, seen or tasted before. ■ *Daily from 1000-1700. $25, child $15. T66777222, www.tropicalfruitworld.com.au Turn off the Pacific Highway on to Duranbah Rd, 10 mins south of the Gold Coast Airport.*

Sleeping Of the many resorts, **LL-L** *Calypso Plaza*, 87 Griffith St, T55990000, www.mirvac hotels.com.au, and **L** *Bella Mare*, corner of Hill and Boundary sts, T55992755, www.bellamare.com.au, are recommended. There are 2 backpackers in the area. **C-E** *Coolangatta YHA*, 230 Coolangatta Rd, T55367644, is located near the airport and facing the busy Pacific Highway. It offers tidy dorms, doubles/twins, pool, bike and surfboard hire, internet. The emphasis, not surprisingly, is catching the best wave as opposed to the best fish, pool or local tour bus. Having said that *Coachtrans* service direct to the hostel. **B-D** *Sunset Strip Budget Resort*, 199-203 Boundary St, T55995517. Much closer to the beach and the town centre, this is an old spacious hotel with unit style singles, doubles, twins, quads and family rooms with shared bathrooms, excellent kitchen facilities, large pool and within yards of the beach. Basic but spacious, good value. Fully self-contained 1 and 2 bedroomed holiday flats are also available. No internet. Recommended. **A-E** *Kirra Beach Tourist Park*, located on Charlotte St, off Coolangatta Rd, T55817744. Well facilitated offering powered/non-powered sites, cabins, camp kitchen and salt water pool. Another option worth considering is a fully self-contained houseboat with which to cruise the extensive reaches of the Tweed River. *Boyd's Bay House Boats*, T55234795, www.goldcoasthouseboats.com.au, can oblige, from around $745 for the most basic vessel per week in the high season.

Eating For an affordable dinner most are lured by the fine and fishy fare of *The Fisherman's Cove Seafood Taverna*, in the *Calypso Resort*, Griffith St, T55367073. *Raffles Coffee Shop*, 152 Griffith St, T55363888, is good for lunch, coffee and light snacks (try a pancake with real maple syrup). For more healthy snacks and sandwiches *Bayleaf Café*, 1/40 Griffith St, T55365636, is recommended, while for breakfast *Uno Café*, Marine Pde, T55995116, provides the best value and aesthetics.

Gold Coast

Tours & activities For surfing supplies and rentals try *Pipedream*, 24/72 Griffith St, T55991164 and *Zumo*, Shop 233 McLean St, T55368502. For lessons try professionals **Brad Holmes**, T5539 4068, or **Cheyne Horan**, T1800227873. *Gold Coast Surf Schools Australia*, T55200848, can also point you in the right direction. *Tweed River* also offers some good cruising opportunities. Operators include *Perfector*, T55242422, www.catcha crab.com.au, and *Tweed Endeavour*, T55368800, www.goldcoastcruising.com *Blue Juice Diving Centre*, 33 Machinery Dr, T55243683, offer local dive trips, courses and equipment.

Transport **Air** **Gold Coast Airport** is located only 2 km from Coolangatta. **Bus** *Premiere Motor Services*, T133410, *Greyhound*, T55316677, *MacCafferty's*, T55382700, all offer daily inter-State services, while *Coachtrans*, T131230, www.coachtrans.com.au, offer regular shuttles up and down the coast, to Brisbane and to/from the airport. *Kirklands*, T1300367077, www.kirklands.com.au, and *Suncoast Pacific*, T55316000, offer regular services to Byron Bay and the NSW coast. All long-distance buses stop outside the main booking agent, *Golden Gateway Travel*, 29 Bay St, T55361700. *Surfside Buslines*, T131230, www.gcshuttle.com.au, are the main suburban bus company with regular links north to Surfers. **Taxi** For a taxi, T55361144.

Directory **Communications** **Internet**: available at *Coolangatta Internet Café*, beneath *Montezuma's*, corner of Griffith and Warner sts, T55992001, open Mon-Fri 0900-1900, Sat 0900-1800, Sun 1200-1600, or *PB's Internet Café*, Shop 2 Griffith Plaza, Griffith St, T55994536, open Mon-Fri 0830-1900, Sat/Sun 0900-1800.

Currumbin to Surfers Paradise

Currumbin Wildlife Sanctuary is one of the most popular parks in the area. One of the more unique aspects of Currumbin is the small train that takes you into the heart of the park, where you can then investigate the various animal enclosures, that house everything from Tasmanian devils to tree kangaroos. But without doubt the highlight of the day is the infamous rainbow lorikeet feeding. To either partake or spectate at this highly colourful and entertaining, 'avian-human interaction spectacular', is truly memorable and thoroughly recommended. Just before feeding time the air and the trees fill with the radiant hues and excited screeching of the birds, while below the human participants are all given a small bowl of liquid feed. Then, with arms out-stretched, like a hundred desperate and overly expectant Oliver Twists, everyone tries to attract their attention and 'their' particular bird. The great feeding frenzy takes place twice daily at 0800 and again at 1600. Given that 80% of Australia's native wildlife is nocturnal, the 'Wildnight' tour program is also well worth considering. It also includes an Aboriginal dance display. ■ *Daily 0800-1700, $17, child $9.50. T55341266, www.currumbin-sanctuary.org.au Just off the Gold Coast Highway, Currumbin. Dance display Mon/Wed/Sat 1930-2145.*

Burleigh Heads – an ancient volcano – forms one of the few breaks in the seemingly endless swathe of golden sand and offers fine views back towards Surfers, some world-class surf breaks and several good walking tracks through the Burleigh Heads National Park. West of Burleigh Heads, **David Fleay Wildlife Park** is home to all the usual suspects, including koalas, crocodiles, kangaroos, cassowaries and some of the less well known, like bilbies, brolgas and dunnarts. Overall it offers a fine introduction to Australia's veritable treasure chest of native species and is especially well known for it's nocturnal platypus displays, breeding successes and care of sick and injured wildlife. ■ *Daily 0900-1700, $13, child $6.50, T55762411. Signposted 3 km west of Gold Coast Highway on Burleigh Heads Rd.*

Gold Coast

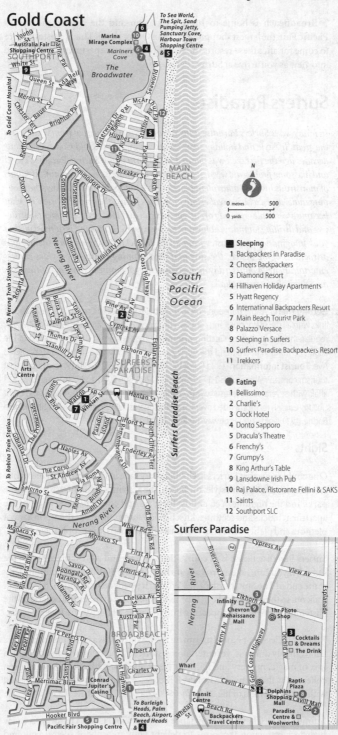

Sleeping
1 Backpackers in Paradise
2 Cheers Backpackers
3 Diamond Resort
4 Hilhaven Holiday Apartments
5 Hyatt Regency
6 International Backpackers Resort
7 Main Beach Tourist Park
8 Palazzo Versace
9 Sleeping in Surfers
10 Surfers Paradise Backpackers Resort
11 Trekkers

Eating
1 Bellissimo
2 Charlie's
3 Clock Hotel
4 Donto Sapporo
5 Dracula's Theatre
6 Frenchy's
7 Grumpy's
8 King Arthur's Table
9 Lansdowne Irish Pub
10 Raj Palace, Ristorante Fellini & SAKS
11 Saints
12 Southport SLC

Surfers Paradise

Gold Coast

Broadbeach is home to **Jupiter's Casino** and the equally monstrous **Pacific Fair** the largest shopping centre in Queensland. This is a taste of more to come for after these resorts the stands of high-rise apartment blocks come into view as you arrive at Surfers Paradise.

Surfers Paradise

Colour map 2, grid A5
Population: 400,000
100 km north of
Byron Bay, 78 km
south of Brisbane

In many ways Surfers Paradise is the raison d'etre and the root from which grew the great 'lifestyle and holiday tree' we now know as the Gold Coast. Over four decades ago the first seed was planted in the form of the Surfers Paradise Hotel *and like some proliferate weed, it gave rise to the endless and all dominant stands of monstrous highrise apartment blocks we see today. In their shadow, the shopping malls and exclusive real estate properties joined the great invasion in what became a veritable grow bag of entrepreneurial and tourist development. Attractive and thrilling for many, abhorrent to some, Surfers has (and is) almost all that your imagination can muster from kitsch to cocktails. Other than the obvious attractions of the* **beach***, the* **surf** *and the* **shopping malls***, it provides endless entertainment 24 hours a day and serves as the gatehouse to more* **activities** *than anywhere else in Australia.*

Ins & outs
See Transport, page 233, for furhter details

Getting there As the transport hub of the whole of the Gold Coast there are transport links with all the major cities and centres. The airport is at Coolangatta, 22 km south, with regular shuttles to Surfers. **Getting around** Surfers is a small place with most of the action centring in and around the Cavill Ave Mall and adjacent nightclub strip, Orchid Ave. **Tourist information** Gold Coast VIC, Cavill Ave Mall, T55384419, www.goldcoast tourism.com.au Mon-Fri 0830-1730, Sat 0900-1700, Sun 0900-1530. An incredibly small affair with several small forests' worth of free 'guides' and maps. The official *Gold Coast Holiday Guide* is recommended over these. The nearest QPWS office is near Tallebudgera Bridge, 1711 Gold Coast Highway, Burleigh Heads, T55353032.

Sights

One could argue that Surfers itself offers very little in the way of notable sights. It is after all, all about lifestyle, the beach, the activities, proximity to the theme parks and the nightlife. Yet, amidst the glass and concrete forest of high-rise apartment blocks and seething, kitsch-filled shopping malls, there is in a way a plethora and plenty to look at. Not least of all perhaps, the people themselves.

Surfers Paradise Beach

Surfers Paradise Beach is of course the big draw and a great place to 'see the sights'. If you can, take a stroll at sunrise along the 500-m sand pumping jetty at the end of The Spit, north of Sea World. It opens at 0600 and for $1 you can walk out to the end and take in the memorable view of the entire beach and the glistening high-rises disappearing into the haze, all the way to Tweed Heads.

Ripley's Believe it or Not Museum

Ripley's Believe it or Not Museum on the Cavill Mall is a collection of displays telling highly dubious, yet entertaining stories of apparent non-fiction, with a mix of magic, mystery and illusion. These any many like them have all been collected by the inimitable Robert L Ripley – a man who was clearly obsessed with the odder facts of life. ■ *Daily 0900-2300. $12, child $8. T55920040.*

Infinity

Infinity, in the Chevron Renaissance Mall, off Gold Coast Highway, is a new high-tech attraction that aims to delight with an array of special light and

Happy New Year(s)

Queensland, Tasmania, Victoria and New South Wales all share the same Eastern Standard Time Zone (EST). However Queensland does not recognize daylight saving between October-March, which means it is 1hr behind NSW during that time. This may cause some inconvenience and confusion for visitors (and presumably residents) in the twin towns of Coolangatta and Tweed Heads, where the State border is not noticeable and largely unmarked. In Coolangatta the official borderline runs down the centre of Dixon St then Boundary St, to Point Danger on the Tweed Heads peninsula. Of course, most of the time everybody, especially the town's residents go about their business oblivious to the fact, adhering either to Queensland time, New South Wales time or indeed, both. But at New Year it is of course another story. In Coolangatta it is possible to officially celebrate New Year on one side of the road, then an hour later do exactly the same on the other.

---

optical affects, from the seemingly bottomless 'Light Canyon' to the rather dubious 'Wobbly'. You will either love it or be deeply disappointed! Good for kids. ■ *1000-2200. From $16.50, child $10. T55382988.*

In the heart of Surfers, on the corner of Cypress Avenue and Gold Coast Highway, there are a number of thrill rides that may appeal or indeed turn your stomach, including the Flycoaster – a sort of huge pendulum swing that promises to exert lots of 'Gs' in appropriate places, a rather tame 46-m bungee and the very popular SlingShot – which promises to send you seemingly into orbit at over 100 kmph. The expressions of the foolhardy at the moment of release are in themselves, well worth seeing. But bring earplugs for the kids; the language is 'choice' to say the least. **Flycoaster & Sling Shot rides**

Gold Coast City Art Gallery, 3 km west of Surfers, offers the opportunity to see if the local lifestyle influences both the colour and content of the collection. The gallery presents a dynamic programme of local contemporary work as well as a more wide-ranging historical collection. International exhibitions are also generated by the gallery itself or displayed with pride as part of national touring schedule. It is also home to one of Australia's longest running art prizes now titled the Conrad Jupiters Art Prize, which has provided an exciting survey of contemporary Australian Art since 1968. The outdoor sculpture walk is also worth looking at though with the 'Surfers' skyline in the background it could hardly be more muted. ■ *Mon-Fri 1000-1700, Sat/Sun 1100-1700. Free. 135 Bundall Rd, T55816567.* **Gold Coast City Art Gallery**

Between Surfers Paradise and The Spit, Main Beach fringes the southern shores of Broadwater Bay and the Nerang River Inlet. Like an assemblage of huge white tepees **Marina Mirage shopping complex** contains some of the best restaurants in the region, most of which offer al fresco dining overlooking **Mariners Cove**, the departure point for most scenic cruises and helicopter scenic flights. Amongst the commercial vessels the sumptuous launches and ocean-going yachts of the wealthy herald the presence of one of the Gold Coast's newest and most luxurious hotels – the very elegant and distinctly 'watery' *Versace*. **Main Beach**

Gold Coast

Essentials

Sleeping
■ *On map, page 227*

Book ahead, especially in peak season

With almost 5 million visitors a year the Gold Coast is well geared up for accommodation of all types to suit all budgets. But even with the 55,000 beds currently available you are advised to book in advance. Prices fluctuate wildly between peak and off peak seasons. Stand-by deals and packages are always on offer so you are advised to shop around and research thoroughly. Resorts and motels naturally predominate with almost 200 high-rises offering very similar self-contained apartments with the obligatory pool fringed with palm trees. Listings and recommendations therefore go well beyond the scope of this guide. The best advice is to decide exactly what you are looking for, and then consult the various accommodation agents for advice, brochures and bookings. Booking at least 7 days in advance will usually work out cheaper. The free *Qantas* and *Sunlover* 'Gold Coast' brochures available from travel agents are also an excellent source of illustrated listings. Accommodation agents include the *Gold Coast Accommodation Service*, Shop 1, 1 Beach Rd, Surfers, T55920067, www.goldcoast accommodationservice.com.au

As you might expect the area is home to copious hotel chains and sumptuous 5-stars

LL *Palazzo Versace*, Sea World Dr, Main Beach, T55098000, www.palazzoversace. com.au, which is simply unbelievable and almost requires a launch to secure a booking. **LL** *Sheraton Mirage Resort*, across the road, T55911488, www.sheratonmirage gc.com.au, which is famous for its incredible landscaped pool and excellent cuisine. Further afield **LL** *Hyatt Regency*, T55301234, www.sanctuarycove.hyatt.com.au, is aesthetically spectacular and dominates the Sanctuary Cove Resort. It is an absolute Mecca for golfers and boaties. **LL** *Marriott*, 158 Ferny Ave, T55929800, reservations@marriott.com.au Back in Surfers and more affordable is this classy option. **L-A** *Diamond Resort*, 19 Orchid Ave, T55701011. Mid-range yet right in the heart of the action, this has no nonsense en suite units, pool and spa. **LL-L** *Hilhaven Holiday Apartments*, 2 Goodwin Terrace, T55351055, www.goldcoastburleightourism.com.au This offers a superb view of the coast, away from the hype of Surfers, at Burleigh Heads.

The choice of backpackers is vast with most very similar and offering gimmick discount deals, party nights activities and pick-ups. **C-E** *Surfers Paradise Backpackers Resort*, 2837 Gold Coast Hwy, T55924677, www.surfersparadisebackpackers.com.au, is a lively, popular purpose-built place on the border of Surfers and Broadbeach. It offers tidy en suite dorms, units (some self-contained with TV) and good facilities, including well-equipped kitchen, bar, free laundry, pool, sauna, gym, volley ball pitch, TV/games room, internet, party and activity tours, pick-ups (as in van) and off street parking. **C-E** *Backpackers in Paradise*, 40 Whelan St, just west of the Transit Centre, T55384344. Again it is lively, colourful, friendly and well facilitated, with dorms and 3 spacious doubles (en suite), café, bar, pool, internet, tours desk and a comfy TV lounge with a huge screen. A few doors away is **L-E** *Sleeping in Surfers*, 26 Whelan St, T55924455, www.sleepinginn.com.au, that offers similar and modern facilities but with a wider choice of room options from dorms and singles to doubles, twins and self-contained units with TV and living room. It can also throw a good party. **B-E** *Cheers Backpackers*, 8 Pine Ave, T55316539. Further north this is the largest in town with a wide selection of rooms, including en suite doubles, pool, spa, a spacious bar and beer garden, free internet and good meal deals. **C-E** *International Backpackers Resort*, 70 Sea World Dr, T55711776, www.britisharms.com.au In Main Beach overlooking the Mirage Marina and Mariners Cove is the YHA affiliated resort. It offers modern facilities, has its own British pub next door and is within yards of the beach. Internet and courtesy bus in to Surfers. **C-E** *Trekkers*, 22 White St, in Southport 2 km north of Surfers, T55915616, www.trekkersbackpackers.com.au, which is without doubt the best backpackers in the region. It is a relatively small traditional suburban Queenslander, offering cosy well

Gold Coast

appointed/facilitated rooms including en suite doubles with TV, nice pool and garden. Great atmosphere, friendly, family run business with the emphasis on looking after each guest rather than the turnover. Recommended.

The Gold Coast City Council operate a number of excellent facilities up and down the coast. Look out for their free *Gold Coast City Council Holiday Parks* brochure or visit www.gctp.com.au In the Surfers area look no further than **A-E** *Main Beach Tourist Park*, Main Beach Parade, T55817722. It offers cabins, en suite/standard powered and non-powered sites, with good facilities and camp kitchens, all nestled quietly amongst the high-rises and across the road from the main beach.

Like the rest of the Gold Coast, Surfers is a sea of every type of international cuisine a stomach can rumble at, from kangaroo steaks to poppadoms and aesthetics that range from the traditional McDonalds to a Victorian-style English. In Surfers, the many, mainly cheap or affordable restaurants, are located along the Cavill Mall, along The Esplanade, Gold Coast Highway or in the new Chevron Renaissance Mall. Elsewhere it is worth looking at the more up-market affairs along Tedder Ave or the Marina Mirage in Main Beach. Further north Sanctuary Cove is a fine spot for a lunch. To the south, Burleigh Heads provides excellent views, while the many surf lifesaving clubs offer great value, views and are undoubtedly in the spirit of the Gold Coast experience.

Eating
● *On map, page 227*

Expensive Many of the major hotels offer excellent fine dining often with an emphasis on seafood. *Sheraton Mirage Resort's*, T55911488, is worth considering for that one-off special, if only to take a pre-dinner peek at the facilities and the amazing swimming pool. Across the road the **Marina Mirage Complex** has some superb al fresco possibilities including *SAKS*, T55912755, *Ristorante Fellini*, T55310300, and *The Raj Palace*, T55311600. Also well worth the trip are *Oskars*, T55763722 (mainly seafood) and Italian restaurant, *Daniele*, T55350822, that sit side-by-side soaking up the memorable coastal views at Burleigh Heads.

Mid-range The various restaurant/cafés in the **Chevron Renaissance Mall**, Gold Coast Highway, all share tempting menus in pleasant Mediterranean-style surroundings. Also in the mall is the *Landsdowne Irish Pub*, T55315599, that offers the traditional wholesome pub food at reasonable prices. At the northern entrance to the Mall, *Clock Hotel*, T55390344, also enjoys a good reputation as a top lunch venue. Tedder Ave in Main Beach is a quieter location with some good al fresco options, including *Saints*, T55284286, that is open daily for breakfast lunch and dinner. Further north around Mariners Cove and the Marina Mirage Complex, you will find *Grumpy's Wharf Restaurant*, T55322900, and *Frenchy's*, T55313030, both of which offer affordable seafood with a casual atmosphere and pleasant views. In Broadbeach, directly opposite Jupiter's Casino, *Bellissimo Italian Restaurant*, T55703388, is earning a fine reputation and has live music Fri/Sat. Nearby, *Donto Sapporo*, 2763 Gold Coast Highway, T55399933, is considered one of the best Japanese restaurants in city.

Cheap There is no end of cheap and cheerful eateries in and around Cavill Ave. The food court in the Dolphins Shopping Mall is a favourite for the seemingly omnipresent all you can eat Asian eateries. *Charlie's Restaurant*, Cavill Ave Mall, T55385285, offers decent meals 24 hours a day and a good breakfast. The many surf lifesaving clubs (SLCs) along the coast, offer great value meals, including the *Southport SLC*, McArthur Pde, Main Beach, T55915083 and the *Palm Beach SLC*, 7th Ave and Jefferson Lane, Palm Beach, T55342180. Self-caterers will find the Woolworths supermarket, Lower Level, Paradise Centre. Coles is located in the Chevron Renaissance Mall.

Gold Coast

For something different consider the dinner cruises on offer from Mariners Cove, T55578800, *Dracula's Theatre Restaurant*, Broadbeach, T55751000, or the Olde English surrounds of the *King Arthur's Table*, Raptis Plaza, Cavill Ave, T55267855.

Bars & clubs
Like activities, the scope for a good night out is endless

If you are staying at any of the hostels you will be well looked after by the staff and will only need to 'follow mi (legless) leader' and 'go with the flow'. The great club crawl has been done a thousand times before and invariably there are fee drinks and the odd free meal thrown in. Sadly, for those not staying at a hostel, the free and readily available 'entertainment' brochures are little more than advertising and business directories and give no indication of which are the best venues, nor what exactly is happening where and when. **Orchid Ave**, off the Cavill Ave Mall, is the main focus for clubbing with most staying open well in to the wee hours. Dress is smart casual, carry ID and be prepared to kiss your money good bye. Entry generally ranges from $5-10, which is manageable, but the drinks and ensuing and almost inevitable cocktails are expensive. *Cocktails and Dreams* and *The Drink*, both on Orchid Ave, have a good reputation but they are two of many. For a more sophisticated night out try *Lansdowne Irish Pub* in the Chevron Renaissance Mall, T55315599. Live music every Fri/Sat.

Entertainment

Casinos Conrad Jupiter's Casino offers 2 floors of gaming tables and pokies, plus one of those strange and illusive 'high-roller' rooms for the filthy rich. Far more accessible and affordable are the numerous bars and restaurants that suit all, 'suits with suits'. Open 24 hrs, T55921133. Off Hooker Blvd, off Gold Coast Highway, Broadbeach.

Cinema and theatre There is a cinema and theatre at the **Arts Centre**, 135 Blundall Rd, T55884000, and other mainstream cinemas in the shopping centres at **Pacific Fair**, Broadbeach, T55722666, **Australia Fair**, Southport, T55312200, and the 14 cinema complex at Harbour Town, corner of Gold Coast Highway and Oxley Dr, north of Southport, T55291734.

Festivals
For a detailed calendar of events visit www.goldcoast tourism.com.au

The Gold Coast hosts a number of exciting annual events most of which involve lots of money, speed under the guise of fireworks and parties, festivals, races and sporting spectaculars. **Jan** kicks off with *Conrad Jupiter's Magic Millions*, a 10-day horse-racing event with (not surprisingly) a very popular fashion event. Ladies fashion then takes a bit of a dive (or a slice perhaps), at the *Australian Ladies Golf Masters*, held in **Feb** at the beautiful Royal Pines course. It attracts some of the world's best (but worst dressed) lady golfers. In **Mar** the beach becomes the main focus with the *Australian Surf Life Saving Championships*, which is perhaps the Gold Coasts most iconic event. It attracts over 7,000 national and international competitors, all trying to out fit, swim, run and row each other, for the lauded Iron Man or Iron Woman trophy. In **Jun** Coolangatta revs it up with the 10-day *Wintersun Festival* that sees Australia's biggest 50s and 60s rock'n'roll event combined with the nation's largest display of hot rods and custom cars. 'Americana' comes to the coast in **Jul** to celebrate the 4th with an *All Star America Football competition*, which gives a few Aussie teams the chance to show them that all the body armour is for 'big Jessies'. Jul also sees the *Gold Coast Marathon* – considered Australia's premiere long-distance running event. In **mid-winter** it's green for go with the ever-popular *Honda Indy 300*, when the streets of Surfers squeal to the sound of racing cars and the evenings to the heady beat of parties, parades and the mardi gras.

Numerous food festivals are also held throughout the year, including the *Gold Coast Food Festival* in **Sep**, the *Broadbeach Festival* in **Oct** and the *Gold Coast Signature Dish Competition* in **Dec**.

Not surprisingly the Gold Coast offers some golden shopping opportunities with 3,500 **Shopping**
shops the region has 12% more retail outlets than the national average, all of which
contribute to over $3 billion of visitor spending per annum. **Paradise Centre** in Cavill
Ave is a focus for mainly tourist based products, with the **Marina Mirage** in Main Beach
and Sanctuary Cove being a little bit more up-market. **Harbour Town Shopping Complex**, corner of Gold Coast Highway and Oxley Dr, north of Southport, is well known for
its bargain shopping and clearance stores, T55291734. The beachfront markets held
every Sun at the eastern end of Cavill Ave are one of many taking place regularly up
and down the coast. The main shopping centres in the region are **Pacific Fair** in Broadbeach (which is the largest in Queensland) and **Australia Fair** in Southport.

Other than the beach, shopping and the theme parks, Surfers presents a mind-bend- **Tours &**
ing array of additional activities, the listings and recommendations of which go way **activities**
beyond the scope of this handbook. In summary, you have the choice of the following
and more: Scenic, harbour, river, canal, island cruises, lunch, dinner and party cruises,
sailing, fishing, whale and dolphin watching; Independent boat hire, gondola rides,
houseboats and speedboats; Surfing and surf schools; Diving, sea kayaking, jet skiing,
water-skiing and paragliding; Skydiving and balloon flights; Scenic flight seeing by
helicopter, float plane or by-plane; Amphibious vehicle trips, 4WD and ATV safaris; Hinterland rainforest, farm and winery tours; Walking and horse trekking; Golf, mini-golf,
tennis and beach volley ball. If anything is to be recommended it is perhaps the pursuit
of sanity and temporary escape in the form of a rainforest tour to the stunning Lamington and Springbrook National Parks, merely an hours drive inland from the chaos. The
resorts on South Stradbroke Island also offer a suitable coastal escape, see Moreton Bay
and Islands, page 259.

Surfing For surf board hire try the *Beach Club House*, 189 Paradise Centre, Cavill Ave,
T552670/7, from $40 per day and for surfing lessons either professionals Brad Holmes,
T55394068 or Cheyne Horan, T1800227873.

Rainforest tours Lamington and Springbrook National Parks: *Bushwacker*
Ecotours, T55257237, www.bushwacker-ecotours.com.au, offer both day walk/
tours and night spotting to Springbrook, from $50. The VIC on Cavill Ave has full listings and the latest prices, though by now you have no doubt already been handed
numerous brochures. For anything water-based, including self-hire, shop around at
the Cruise Terminal, at Mariners Cove (Main Beach) or the wharf at the western end
of Cavill Ave T55383400.

Local Bike hire Available from *Red Rocket Rent-A-Car*, Shop 9, The Mark Orchid **Transport**
Ave, T55389074. **Moped hire** There are a number of central outlets including
Yahoo, 80 Ferny Ave, T55920227, from $25 ($150 deposit), *Rent-A-Jeep*, corner of
Palm and Ferny Ave, T55386900, hire small jeeps from $69 per day.
Taxi *Regent-Gold Coast* T131008.

Long distance Air Gold Coast Airport is located near Coolangatta, 22 km south
of Surfers, T55891100. *Qantas*, T131313, *Virgin Blue*, T136789, *Freedom Air*,
T1800122000 and *Flight West*, T132392, all offer domestic services (and/or international connections). *Gold Coast Tourist Shuttles*, T55745111, and *Surfside Buses*,
T131230, offer local transfers, from $14, child $7. *Con-x-ions*, T55912525,
Coachtrans, T55069777, *Murray's*, T132259, and *Active Tours*, T55970344, all offer
regular shuttles between Brisbane City and/or Airport to the Gold Coast, from about
$50, child $26.

Bus The long-distance bus terminal is located corner Beach Rd and Remembrance Dr. Most of the major coach companies have offices within the complex. Open 0600-2200. *Premier Motor Services*, T133410, *Greyhound*, T55316677, *MacCafferty's*, T55382700, all offer daily inter-State services. *Coachtrans*, T131230, www.coachtrans.com.au, are recommended for Brisbane City/Airport transfers. *Kirklands*, T1300367077, www.kirklands.com.au, and *Suncoast Pacific*, T55316000, offer regular services to Byron Bay and the NSW coast.

Car hire *Avis* T55363511, *Budget* T55365377, *Hertz* T55366133 and *Thrifty* T55366955, all have outlets at the Gold Coast Airport. Numerous companies are located in and around Surfers Paradise, with prices starting from about $30 per day. Petrol 24-hr *Shell* (2824) and *Caltex* (2885), Gold Coast Highway.

Train Both Robina and Nerang train stations, located about 15 km/10 km south-west/west of Surfers are served by *Airtrain*, T131230, from Brisbane (with connections to Brisbane airport), from $50, child $30. *Airtrain Connect*, T55745111 and *Surfside Buslines* (#2/#22) then offer road transport to the coast.

Directory **Banks** All major branches with ATMs and currency exchange are located in and around the Cavill Mall-Gold Coast Highway intersection. *Thomas Cook*, Cavill Ave, T55921166. **Communications** Internet: *1 hour Photo Shop*, 3189 Gold Coast Highway, T55384973. Open daily 0900-2100. *Email Centre*, next door to *Shooters*, Orchid Ave, T55387500. Open daily 0830-2400. **Post office**: Cavill Ave Paradise Mall, T553984144. Open Mon-Fri 0830-1730, Sat 0900-1200. **Medical services** Chemist: *Day and Night*, Piazza On Boulevard (ANA Hotel), 3221 Gold Coast Highway, Surfers, T55922299. Open 0700-2200. **Hospital**: **Gold Coast Hospital**, 108 Nerang St, Southport, T55718211. **Paradise Medical Centre**, Paradise Centre, T55923999 (24-hr). **Travel agencies** *Backpackers Travel Centre*, Transit Centre, 8 Beach Rd, Surfers, T55380444. **Useful numbers** Police: 68 Ferny Ave, Surfers, T55707888. RACQ: T55320311.

Theme parks

The Gold Coast is often labelled as Australia's Theme Park capital, with millions visiting annually to ride the slides, get wet, go wild, meet Batman or pat Tweetie Pie. The stalwarts are **Sea World**, **Dreamworld** and **Movie World**, with other less high-profile parks, like Wet'n'Wild providing 'splashtacular' (or simply 'tackular') back up. Entry for each is expensive from $33-54, but that usually includes all the rides and attractions, which provides a very full day of entertainment. VIC can help you secure the latest discounts (around 12%) and packages on offer, including multi-day trips and transfers. A '3-Park Pass' costs from $141, child $91, which makes no saving on the individual ticket sales but does allow one free return visit.

Sea World For over 30 years Sea World has been successfully developing its sea-based attractions, picking up numerous awards on the way and earning it the reputation as one of the world's best theme parks. Although the main attractions continue to be the incredible dolphin and seal shows, the shark feeding, thrill rides and water-ski stunts, the recent (and controversial) addition of polar bears, Kanook (from Arizona!) and Ping Ping, has breathed new and distinctly cool life into the park. Of course, whether polar bears should continue to be kept in captivity at all these days is now hardly open to debate and true, the main reason for having them there is to draw the crowds, but there is no doubting Sea World's dedication to conservation and the welfare of their fleecy white charges. Polar Bear Shores, which cost a cool $6 million, is certainly one of the Gold Coast's most luxuriant pieces of real estate and the polar bear equivalent of the Gold Coast's 5-star *Versace Hotel*.

Another great and innovative attraction at Sea World is the ability to swim with the dolphins in a new seal/dolphin interactive program, which given their astonishing intelligence and discipline, is highly recommended. There are a range of options, one for kids that involves a shallow water experience with the seals (from $40) and dolphins (from $45) and several for adults – seals from $80 and dolphins from $110. Book well in advance. ■ *Daily 1000-1700. from $54, child $35. T55882205, www.seaworld.com.au Sea World Drive, Main Beach (1 km)*.

Movie World

With the advent of Harry Potter recently adding to the obvious appeal of the older, traditional attractions like Batman Adventure, Looney Tunes, The Police Academy Stunt Show and the breathtaking thrill ride 'Lethal Weapon', Movie World is perhaps the most popular of all the theme parks. Even if you are not spellbound by Harry Potter's world of wizardry, a stroll down the superb recreation of 'Diagon Alley' is truly memorable and as magical as the expressions of joy as thrill seekers hit the water on the Wild Wild West Adventure Ride. Overall, it is a very exciting and stimulating mix of sights, sounds and action that requires at least one full day. There is plenty of opportunity for the kids to meet their old favourites like Daffy Duck, Bugs Bunny and Tweetie and for middle-aged men to secure that much dreamed of peck on the cheek from Marilyn Munroe. ■ *Daily 1000-1730, $54, child $35. T55738485, www.movieworld.com.au   Pacific Highway, Oxenford (21 km)*.

Dream World

The big attraction at Dream World are the adrenaline pumping rides, some of which are reputed to be the fastest and tallest in the world. Paramount amongst them is the new 'Cyclone', which is the biggest high-speed gravity roller coaster in the Southern Hemisphere. And if that does not blow your wig off, then the hair-raising 'Tower of Terror' certainly will. In fact, not only will it send your stomach into orbit it, there is every chance of meeting its contents again on the way back down at a truly memorable 150 kmph. To settle both mind and body there are, thankfully, also plenty of native animals on hand to cuddle and stroke, including koalas and kangaroos. ■ *Daily 1000-1700. $54, child $35. T55881122, www.dreamworld.com.au Parkway Coomera, Pacific Highway (25 km)*.

Wet'n'Wild

The aptly named Wet'n'Wild offers practically every way imaginable to adhere to the laws of gravity and get soaked at the same time. From tubes and slides, to fake waves, it's all there with rides like the 'Mammoth Falls', 'White Water Mountain' and 'Terror Canyon' contrasting with the relaxing surroundings of Calypso Beach. Combined they offer a great water park experience for all ages and an ideal opportunity to escape the Gold Coasts oppressive summer heat. There are plenty of lifeguards on hand to insure children's safety, as well as food outlets and even 'dive-in' film shows. ■ *Daily 1000-1700. $33, child $21. T55732255, www.wetnwild.com.au, Pacific Highway, Oxenford (21 km)*.

Gold Coast

Gold Coast Hinterland

*Less than an hours drive from the Gold Coast are perhaps its greatest theme parks – the great national parks of **Lamington**, **Springbrook** and **Mount Tamborine**. Labelled 'the Green Behind the Gold', individually or combined, they provide their own natural wonder-worlds of pristine subtropical rainforest, waterfalls, walking tracks and stunning views all of which provide a memorable experience in deep contrast to the glitz of that other 'paradise'. The weather here can also be dramatically different with much more rain and the coolest temperatures in the State.*

Ins & outs
See Transport, page 237, for details

The main Gold Coast QPWS office is near the Tallebudgera Bridge, 1711 Gold Coast Highway, Burleigh Heads, T55353032. They stock detailed information surrounding all the national parks throughout the region. Alternatively, a walking track guide with map and details are available from the information offices at Binna Burra, T55333584 and Green Mountains, T55440634. Open Mon, Wed-Fri 0900-1100, 1300-1530. Tue-Fri 1300-1530. For vineyard information visit www.goldcoastwinecountry.com.au

Lamington National Park

Colour map 2, grid A5 60 km southwest of Surfers Paradise, 10 km south of Brisbane

The 20,500-ha Lamington National Park sits on the border of Queensland and New South Wales and comprises densely forested valleys and peaks straddling the McPherson Range and an ancient volcanic area known as the Scenic Rim, about 60 km inland from the Gold Coast. The park is essentially split into two sections: the Binna Burra to the east and the Green Mountains (O'Reilly's) to the west. Combined they offer a wealth of superb natural features and a rich biodiversity that can be experienced on over 100 km of walking tracks. For generations its two most famous guesthouses *O'Reilly's* and *Binna Burra* have introduced many to the complex rainforest environment and its exotic wild residents including the regent bower bird and the continent's greatest avian mimic, the lyrebird.

Green Mountains were first settled in 1911 by the O'Reilly family, who took up a number of small dairy farms before consolidating their assets in 1915 with the establishment of their, now internationally famous, guest house. Other than the sense of escape and the obvious green aesthetics that surround, its most popular draw is the treetop canopy walkway which is an ideal way to see the rainforest habitat. There are also some excellent walking tracks that range from 1 to 20 km offering spectacular views and numerous waterfalls. Guided tours are available, along with a broad range of places to stay.

Binna Burra section of the park is the most accessible from the Gold Coast and like the Green Mountains, also offers a wealth of excellent rainforest walking opportunities and plays host to a historic guesthouse, *Binna Burra Mountain Lodge*. Guided tours are available through the lodge and there is a QPWS information centre and campsite.

Sleeping & eating

LL *Binna Burra Mountain Lodge*, Binna Burra Rd, Beechmont (via Nerang), T55333758/1800074260, www.binnaburralodge.com.au, offers well-appointed en suite cabins with fireplace (some with spa), activities, meals included. **LL-L** *O'Reilly's Rainforest Guesthouse*, Lamington National Park Rd (via Canungra), T55440644, www.oreillys.com.au, offers a range of room options from luxury suites to standard, pool, sauna, spa and restaurant. Package includes meals and some tours. There are **QPWS campsites** at both Binna Burra, T55333584, and Green Mountains (200 m from

O'Reilly's) with water, hot showers and toilets. Fees apply, book ahead through the ranger/information centres at each location.

The most accessible section of Lamington National Park is Binna Burra, 35 km south **Transport** west of Nerang on the Pacific Highway. From Brisbane you can travel south via Nerang or via Mount Tamborine and Canungra. The Green Mountains (O'Reilly's) section is accessed from Canungra. If you do not have your own transport, there are numerous tour operators that provide trips daily to Lamington including *Mountain Trek Adventures*, T0500844100, sherpa@bigvolcano.com.au The VICs have full listings. Alternatively, *O'Reilly's Mountain Coach Company* (Green Mountains section), T55244249, offer transportation to and from the Gold Coast to *O'Reilly's Resort*, daily from $39, child $22 return. *Binna Burra Mountain Lodge* also have their own bus service, (Binna Burra section), T55333758, from both the Gold Coast and Brisbane, from $44, child $22 return.

Springbrook National Park

Springbrook National Park (2,954 ha) is the most accessible to the coast and *Colour map 2, grid A5* sits on the northern rim of what was once a huge volcano centred on Mount *31 km southwest of* Warning. The park is spilt into three sections, **Springbrook Plateau**, **Natural** *Surfers Paradise, 100* **Bridge** and the **Cougals**. Like Lamington, they combine to offer a rich sub-*km south of Brisbane* tropical rainforest habitat of ancient trees and gorges, interspersed by creeks, waterfalls and an extensive system of walking tracks. In addition, the park is well known for its many spectacular views including **Canyon**, **Wunburra**, **Goomoolahara** and the aptly named **Best of All**. Other attractions include the **Natural Arch** (1-km walk) – a cavernous rock archway that spans Cave Creek and the 190-m Purling Brook Falls (4-km walk). Natural Arch also plays host to a colony of glow-worms that, along with the parks many nocturnal animals, are best viewed at night.

For detailed information about the park, including accommodation listings, try to get **Sleeping** hold of the *Springbrook Mountain Handbook* from the Gold Coast VICs, or from the **& eating** Springbrook Mountain Information Centre, Springbrook Mountain Homestead and Observatory, 2319 Springbrook Rd, T55335200, www.maguires.com/spring There is also information available at the historic 1911 schoolhouse, Springbrook Rd. Open daily 0800-1600. **C-E** *Springbrook Mountain Lodge YHA*, 317 Repeater Station Rd, Springbrook (near the Best of All Lookout), T55335366. This small lodge offers a fine retreat and has 1 dorm and 4 double/twins. **LL-L** *Mouses Houses*, 2807 Springbrook Rd, Springbrook, T55335192, www.mouseshouse.com.au Characterful and cosy, recommended. There is a QPWS campsite at Purling Brook Falls.

Springbrook is 29 km south from Mudgeeraba on the Pacific Highway. The Natural **Transport** Bridge section of the park is accessed from the Nerang to Murwillumbah Rd. Several tour operators offer day trips to Springbrook from both Brisbane and the Gold Coast including *Scenic Hinterland Tours*, Tue/Thu/Sun, T55315536, and *Bushwackers Eco-tours* (day and night tours), T55257237.

Mount Tamborine

Mount Tamborine is a name that is used loosely to describe the 17-section *Colour map 2, grid A5* **Tamborine National Park** and the picturesque settlements of **Mount** *47 km west of Surfers* **Tamborine**, **Tamborine Village** and **Eagle Heights**. Combined they offer an *Paradise, 80 km south* attractive escape from the coast with fine coastal views, walking tracks, vine-*of Brisbane* yards, B&Bs, teahouses and arts and craft galleries. One of the most popular

Gold Coast

sections is the **Witches Falls** that was first gazetted as a national park in 1908 making it Queensland's oldest. Other popular spots include Cedar Creek section, with its pleasant 3-km walk to some pretty cascades and waterfalls, or the Joalah section, where if you are lucky, you may see – or more probably hear – one of its best-known residents – the mimicking lyrebird.

The VICs can supply information and accommodation details, while the QPWS at Burleigh Heads (Gold Coast) or the Doughty Park Information Centre, off Main Western Rd, North Tamborine, T55453200, stock walks and national parks information. There are no QPWS campsites.

■ *Getting there: accessed via the Oxenford-Tamborine Rd (Oxenford turn-off) or the Nerang-Tamborine Rd (Nerang Turn-off) both on the Pacific Hwy. No public transport to Mount Tamborine but various tours are available.* O'Reilly's Mountain Coach Company, *T55244249, offer transportation to and from the Gold Coast (via Mount Tamborine) to O'Reilly's Resort in the Lamington National Park.*

Brisbane & around

Introducing Brisbane and around

For a former penal settlement that developed into a fairly anonymous State capital and created the disco sensation *The Bee-Gees*, Brisbane has come an awfully long way! Ever since the city hosted *Expo 88* it seems that both the progressive desire for improvement, as well as the atmosphere of informal pride that proved such a recipe for success, have never left it and, to the contrary, have simply grown from strength to strength.

As Australia's only true tropical city, Brisbane enjoys an almost perfect climate that not only plays a key role in attracting over five million visitors a year but seems to permeate almost every aspect of city life. Wherever you go al fresco restaurants, cafés and outdoor activities dominate, with the most obvious and aesthetically remarkable venue being the **South Bank parklands**. As the site for *Expo 88* they have remained a deserving icon and perhaps the city's greatest tourist draw-card. Complete with numerous cultural attractions and even its own inner city beach, South Bank represents, in many ways, the very essence of modern-day Brisbane. The city's namesake **river** also seems to dominate city life. As it meanders gently through the city's heart it merely echoes the air of casual congeniality that Australia's other state capitals either never had or lost long ago. So welcome to the new Brisbane, the beautiful, tropical river city with its sights set firmly on the future – and one that will certainly 'shake your pants' better than *The Bee-Gees* ever did!

Brisbane also serves as the gateway to the **Moreton Bay Islands**, some of the most beautiful and unspoilt on the Queensland Coast. If time allows try to visit at least one of the island either for a day or for a couple of nights. As the remnants of one vast sand island they offer the perfect precursor and a taste of what awaits on Fraser Island further to the north. With its wilderness areas and shipwrecks Moreton Island is especially alluring and also offers the superb and rare opportunity to physically encounter **wild dolphins**. *Tangalooma Resort*, which is easily accessible by boat from Brisbane, has been introducing people to dolphins (and likewise) most evenings for many years and the experience makes a refreshing change from seeing the regimented captive performers in theme parks and zoos. However, when it does come to captive wildlife Greater Brisbane also hosts a number of excellent wildlife parks and reserves including the world's largest **koala sanctuary** at Lone Pine. Again, easily reached from the city by boat and recommended if you have not yet experienced the almost indescribable feeling of being hugged by a hopelessly cute and vacuous koala like you were some luscious eucalyptus, then this is your chance.

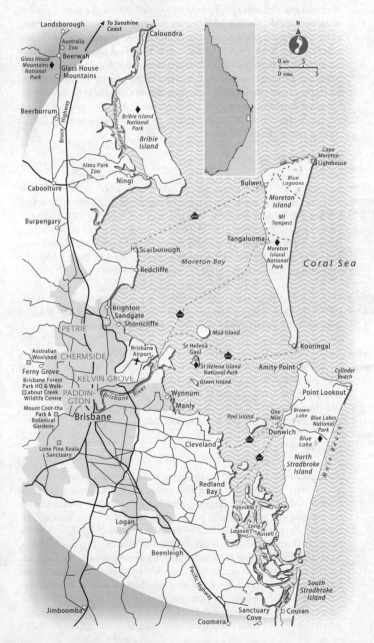

Brisbane

Colour map 3, grid C5
Phone code: 07
Population: 1,300,000
984 km north of
Sydney, 1,710 km
south of Cairns

*For many travellers Brisbane, like the Gold Coast, presents a bit of a dilemma. With the lure of pretty little Noosa and Fraser Island just to the north, let alone the Great Barrier Reef and Far North Queensland, a stop here is usually met with a little trepidation. However, 'Brizzie' is a vibrant tropical city unlike any other in Australia and well worth getting to know. As well as some fascinating, modern attractions like the **South Bank Complex** that over looks the CBD on the banks of the river there are the lesser-known yet wonderfully convivial delights of sub-urbs like **Chinatown**, **Petrie Terrace** and the **West End**. The river is also major attraction in itself, presenting an ideal opportunity for sightseeing and simply get-ting about. Lying on the outskirts of the city a wealth of diverse natural attractions add to the mix with the stunning views from **Mount Coot-tha** to the diverse wild-life of the **Brisbane Forest Park**. Then of course, for sports fanatics, there is always the opportunity to catch a fixture or just pay homage to the famous 'Gabba' cricket and football stadium.*

Ins and outs

Getting there
See Transport, page 256, for further details

Both trains and buses connect the CBD with both airport terminals: *Airtrain*, T131230/32155000, departs from Central (top end of Edward St), Roma (Transit Cen-tre) and Brunswick St (Fortitude Valley) 4 times per hour, from $9, child $4.50. *Coachtrans* (SkyTrans service), T32361000, www.coachtrans.com.au, departs from the Roma St Transit Centre every 30 mins (0500-2100), from $9. Accommodation pick-ups cost about $2 extra. A taxi to the airport will cost about $27. There are frequent long-distance buses and trains to the city from major centres and cities.

Getting around

There is an efficient transport system with the river playing a large part in navigating the city. The main centre is within walking distance. The city tours, see page 255, are a great way to get around and see the sights, especially if short of time.

Tourist information

Queen Street Mall VIC, corner of Albert and Queen sts, T30066290, www.brisbanetourism.com.au, offers free city maps and can assist with accommodation bookings. Open Mon-Thu, 0900-1700, Fri 0900-1900, Sat 0900-1600, Sun 1000-1600. The free *This Week in Brisbane* booklet is also useful. QPWS main office is at 160 Ann St, T32278186. Open Mon-Fri 0830-1700. There is also a VIC behind the lagoon complex, T38672051, www.south-bank.net.au Open Mon-Sat 0900-1800, Fri 0900-2200.

History

Aboriginal tribes frequented the mainland and Moreton Bay islands for over 40,000 years before the first Europeans settled in 1824. Like many east coast frontier settlements, it was first established as a penal colony to keep captive the convicts sent to Australia to pay for their 'evil' crimes. The first explora-tions of the area were made in 1823 by the explorer John Oxley at the behest of the then Governor of New South Wales, the Scot, Sir Thomas Brisbane. Ironically, their first human contact was with a small gang of escaped convicts on Moreton Island who secured some reprieve by showing Oxley a source of freshwater. The first settlement was established on the coast at Redcliffe, but moved shortly afterwards to a better site upriver, now christened 'The Bris-bane', at North Quay. The new and initially notorious penal colony soon grew into an established colony that grew from strength to strength into the 20th century. Shrugging off its backward, non-progressive reputation in recent decades Brisbane has enjoyed phenomenal growth, greatly accelerated with the hosting of internationally important events like the Commonwealth Games in 1982, *Expo 88* and most recently, the 2001 Goodwill Games. Although the source of the name Brisbane is obvious, there are many lesser-known place names that remain from Aboriginal beginnings, including Toowong, Indooroopilly and Mount Coot-tha (meaning 'place of native honey').

Sights

Nestled in the shadows of the glistening modern highrises, there are a number of historical buildings that stand out in stark contrast and grandeur. At the top end of Albert Street, which bisects Queen Street (facing King George Square), is **City Hall**, with its iconic 92-m Italian renaissance clock tower. Built in 1930 it became known as the 'Million Pound Town Hall' due to its huge and controversial construction cost. Ironically, recent renovations to the tower and its senescent lift cost about the same with no questions asked! Once satisfying the irresistible urge to ride the old lift and see the view from to the top, the interior of the building is also worth a muse, housing the **City Art Gallery** and grand ballroom. ■ *Daily 0900-1700. Free. T34038888. Tours by arrangement. Lift Mon-Fri 1000-1500, Sat 1000-1400.*

City Centre
One of the best ways to experience the main historical sights is to join the Brisbane Historical Walking Tour, see page 255

Around the corner on George Street and the riverbank is the grand 19th-century façade of the former Treasury Building. Although still dealing with money matters, it now does so in a far more casual and transitory nature in the form of the city's **Treasury Casino** that echoes to the sound of over 1,100 gaming machines and 100 tables dishing out its disappointment to the ever hopefuls 24 hours a day.

Heading down William Street you reach the **Science centre** housing an entertaining and educational range of interactive exhibits that will keep the little Einsteins or the merely inquisitive amused for hours. ■ *Daily 1000-1700. $8, child $6. T32200166, www.sciencentre.qld.gov.au, 110 George St.*

To the east beside the Botanical Gardens is the 1868 French Renaissance-style **Parliament House** which was commissioned when Queensland was declared a separate colony in 1859. You can watch proceedings when the house is in session. ■ *Mon-Fri 0900-1700. Free. T34067111. Free tours 5 times daily.*

Nearby is the **Old Government House** built in 1862 as the official residence of the state's governers and now housing the HQ of the National Trust. It is also open for public inspection daily. ■ *1000-1630. Free. T32291788.*

Further north, beyond the modern aesthetics and chic restaurants of Waterfront Place, Eagle Street Pier and the Riverside Centre is **Customs House**. Built in 1889, it resembles a miniature version of St Paul's cathedral in London, exuding an elegant Victorian charm. There is also a small art gallery and brasserie. ■ *Tours Mon-Fri by arrangement. Gallery opens 1000-1700 daily. Free. T33658999.*

Directly opposite the Customs House is perhaps the city's most well-known and photographed icon – the **Story Bridge**. It was built between 1935 and 1940 and due to a distinct lack of bedrock has some of the deepest (42 m) foundations of any bridge in the world.

Close to Customs House are Brisbane's two main **cathedrals**, the Gothic-style St John's Cathedral (uncompleted since 1901), 373 Ann Street, and St Stephen's Cathedral (1874), Charlotte Street. Both are open to the public daily and provide a welcome sanctuary from the bustle of the city.

Brisbane

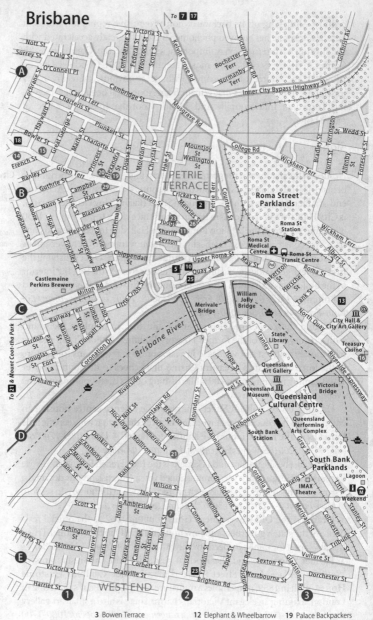

N

0 metres 300
0 yards 300

■ **Sleeping**

1 Astor Motel *B4*
2 Aussie Way *B2*

3 Bowen Terrace
   Backpackers *B6*
4 Breakfast Creek *A6*
5 Brisbane YHA *C2*
6 Caravan Village *A5*
7 Catherine House B&B *A2*
8 Central Brunswick
   Apartment *A5*
9 Chermside Green Motel *A5*
10 City Backpackers *C2*
11 Dress Circle Holiday Village *E4*

12 Elephant & Wheelbarrow
   Backpackers & Pub *A5*
13 Explorers Inn *C3*
14 Globetrekkers *B6*
15 Homestead
   Backpackers *B6*
16 Il Mondo Boutique *C5*
17 Newmarket Gardens
   Caravan Park *A2*
18 Paddington (Waverley)
   B & B *B1*

19 Palace Backpackers
   & Downunder Bar *B4*
20 Powerhouse
   Boutique *B2*
21 Ridge Haven B&B *C1*
22 Royal Albert
   Boutique *C4*
23 Somewhere to
   Stay *E2*
24 Thornbury House *B4*
25 Yellow Submarine *C2*

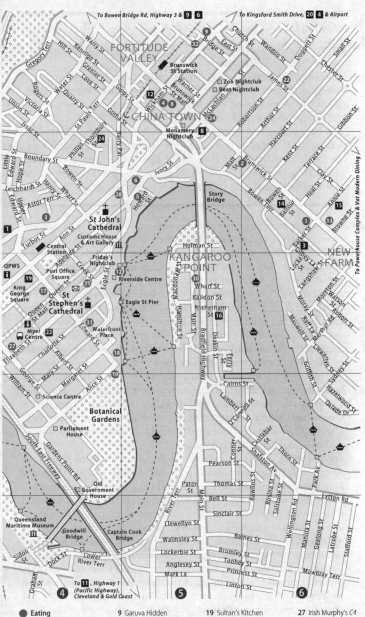

Brisbane & around

● Eating

1 Anise *B6*
2 Arc *B6*
3 Armstrong's *B4*
4 Aya & King of Kings *A5*
5 Circa & Jameson's *B5*
6 E'cco *B5*
7 Expresso Head & Tempo *E2*
8 Fat Boys & Ric's Café Bar *A5*
9 Garuva Hidden Tranquillity *A5*
10 Gianni's & II (2) *C4*
11 Harry's Fine Foods *B2*
12 Il Centro & Pier Nine *C4*
13 Koffie's Expresso Bar *B6*
14 Kookaburra Café *B1*
15 Moorish Dar *B1*
16 Ryan's in the Park *C3*
17 Shingle Inn *C4*
18 Siggi's *C4*
19 Sultan's Kitchen Indian *B1*
20 Tea Shop *B1*
21 Three Monkeys *D2*
22 Vroom Café *A6*

● Pubs & bars

23 Caxton Hotel *B2*
24 Dooley's *A5*
25 Gilhooley's *C4*
26 Hotel LA *B2*
27 Irish Murphy's *C4*
28 Orient Hotel *B4*
29 Paddo Tavern & Fibber McGee's *B1*
30 Story Bridge Hotel *C5*
31 Victory *C4*
32 Wickham Hotel *A5*

▶ **Wishing tree**

In late 2001 the Queensland Art Gallery had the rather novel idea of creating a huge mural called 'The Wish Tree' that was made up of coloured strips of paper on which visitors were asked to write down their greatest wish. It made fascinating reading that in many ways summed up what it is to be human. All our traits were described, both good and bad – humility, courage, sadness, greed, joy, simplicity, shallowness and ignorance, but above all

our unflappable sense of hope! Examples included...

Johnny Depp; gravy on my chips; a sister; a 'Barbie' scooter; to go on a holiday and never come back; a pet penguin; several puppies; a sister; to fly; a good night's sleep, wings; that my dad would come back from overseas; lots of partners; lots of peace; lots of love, and of course, lots of money – and perhaps the best… 'I wish Sophie would think about me for once'.

South Bank Overlooking the all-dominant highrises on the southern bank of the Brisbane River, is the remarkable and superbly aesthetic 17-ha 'oasis in the city' known as South Bank. Built primarily as the showpiece for *Expo 88*, the 1-km stretch of parkland remains as a fascinating and functional recreational space that includes riverside walks, shops, restaurants, open-air markets and – its undoubted highlight – a pristine swimming **lagoon** with its very own beach. To strip off down to your bathers here and join the many Brisbanites under the warming rays of the tropical sun is a truly memorable experience, especially for those from far colder climes. This area is also the venue for the colourful South Bank **markets** held every Friday night, Saturday and Sunday and the **Al Fresco Cinema** in February and March, Wednesday to Saturday.

If you can drag yourself away from the lagoon, the edges of the park also play host to many notable attractions that can provide entertainment for at least half a day. At the northwestern end, straddling Melbourne Street, is the **Queensland Cultural Centre** that encompasses the State Library, Queensland Museum, Queensland Art Gallery and Queensland Performing Arts Complex.

Queensland Art Gallery is considered Brisbane's premiere cultural attraction displaying, in part, an impressive collection of Aboriginal, European, Asian and contemporary Australian art that numbers over 10,000 pieces. Even before exploring the galleries in any detail you are immediately struck but the sheer space and almost minimalist nature of its interior. As the proud repository of the State collection there is a diverse collection of art, from paintings and prints to sculptures and photographs spanning the years since colonial times. Early works include paintings by John Russell and Rupert Bunny, two of the nation's most noted expatriate artists. Added to this are some more familiar internationals names such as Rubens, Degas, Picasso and Van Dyck. Invariably the gallery also hosts major visiting or special exhibitions and also has a reputation of being particularly child friendly. ■ *Daily 1000-1700. Free (except for temporary exhibitions). T38407303, www.qag.qld.gov.au Tours Mon-Fri 1000/1300/1400, Sat 1100/1400/1500, Sun 1100/1300/1500.*

Broadside to the art gallery is the **Queensland Museum**, guarded at the front door by two huge and menacing looking dinosaurs and at the rear by even larger model whales. As these gigantic doorkeepers suggest, the museum is especially noted for its prehistoric and natural history displays – including some monstrous live cockroaches and stick insects. As usual it also hosts the inevitable and absorbing collections of indigenous and early European artefacts. ■ *Daily 0930-1700. Free (except for temporary exhibitions). T38407555, www.Qmuseum.qld.gov.au*

Although not generally considered a tourist attraction the **State Library** offers a wide range of services including free internet (book ahead) and a notable collection of historical treasures in the John Oxley Library. Free guided tours behind the scenes tours to view the most noted historical items. ■ *Mon-Thu 1000-2000 and Fri–Sun 1000-1700. T38407666, www.slq.qld. gov.au Tours Tue at 1015. Riverfront Café on Level 1 overlooks the river and is recommended. Daily from 0900-1700.*

Just on the opposite side of Melbourne Street is the multifarious **Queensland Performing Arts Complex** that houses the Lyric Theatre, Concert Hall, Cremorne Theatre and Optus Playhouse. Combined they offer an exciting and on-going programme of performance events from plays and ballet to modern dance, musicals and opera. See page 254 for details. Further entertainment on a grand scale is also available at the **IMAX Theatre** that provides more two-dimensional entertainment in the form of 45-minute high impact films on its 8-storey screen. See page 254 for details.

At the southeastern end of the South Bank is the **Queensland Maritime Museum** which houses all the usual relics from anchors to lifebuoys. Most of the larger vessels, that include the Second World War warship *The Diamantina* sit forlornly in the adjacent dry dock. ■ *0930-1630, $5.50, child $2.80. T38445361.* The dock and these vessels are best viewed from the new and futuristic **Goodwill Bridge**. This latest addition to the South Bank skyline, built in celebration of the 2001 Goodwill Games, it is entirely in keeping with the parks modern and imaginative aesthetics and offers a convenient route back to the CBD via the Botanical Gardens.

Botanical Gardens & Roma Street Parklands

Another fine retreat from the chaos of the city is the Botanical Gardens. Fringing the river on the southeastern edge of the CBD, they were first established in 1858 as an experimental garden, using convict labour. It has since matured to become a fine showpiece of both native and non-native species. There is a short mangrove boardwalk that takes views across the river and a café. ■ *Tours available Tue-Sun, 1100/1300. T3403888.*

In stark contrast in age and aesthetics is the new Roma Street Parklands at the opposite end of the CBD. Only recently completed and lauded as the world's largest subtropical garden in a city centre, it offers a superb mix of horticultural displays, landscaping, architecture and artworks. Several walks, ranging from half an hour to two hours, encompass numerous interesting features from fossils to bottle trees. Self-guided walking brochures are available from the Activity Centre, next to the Roma Street Rail Station. ■ *Daily dawn to dusk. Free. T30064545, www.romastreetparkland.com.au*

Mount Coot-tha Park & Botanical Gardens

Further afield, but no less spectacular, is Mount Coot-tha Park and Botanical Gardens, west of the city, reached via Milton Road. At the base of the hill are the Botanical Gardens considered Queensland's best, featuring over 20,000 specimens of 5,000 species. To show off this impressive inventory there are 52 ha with numerous features that include a herbarium, tropical dome, bonsai house and water lily ponds. Within the grounds there is also a Planetarium and *Lakeside Restaurant*, open daily 0900-1700. ■ *Daily 0830-1730. Free. T34038888. Tours daily 1100/1300 or pick up a free self-guided leaflet.*

Set high above the gardens is the **Mount Coot-tha Lookout**, which offers superb views across the city and out across Moreton Bay to Moreton, North Stradbroke and Bribie Islands. *The Summit Restaurant* and *Kuta Café* (see page 252) provide an ideal place for lunch, dinner or just a convivial glass of chardonnay, while soaking up both the sun and the city vistas. Backing on to

▶ **Muddy waters**

You will almost immediately notice that the Brisbane River looks distinctly brown in colour. This is not due to pollution, but the lack of bedrock, sediments and the continuous tidal action. Sadly, being so close to the sea it will never be the clear blue that the city authorities would dearly love it to be. The Brisbane has flooded the city on a number of occasions throughout its history, including 1863, 1893 (when both the Victoria and Indooroopilly Bridges were swept away) and 1974 (when 14,000 homes were affected).

the lookout complex is the **Mount Coot-tha Forest Park** which consists of 1500 ha of open eucalyptus forest, networked with walking tracks and containing over 350 weird and wonderful native species from boobooks (owls) to frogmouths (like owls with a mouth the size of a tractor shovel)!

■ *Getting there: by bus take the #471 from Adelaide St (stop #44, opposite City Hall), from $5.20 return, T131230. Alternatively, join the City Sights or City Nights Tours (see page 255).*

Brisbane Forest Park Mount Coot-tha Forest Park is just part of the vast 30,000 ha expanse of the Brisbane Forest Park that backs on to the city, boasting an astonishing range of wildlife and over 30 km of walking tracks. There are also opportunities for horse trekking, mountain biking and bush camping. The park headquarters and information centre is located at The Gap on Nebo Road, west of the city centre. At the same location is the **Walk-about Creek Wildlife Centre**, that features some of the forest wild inhabitants including platypuses and lungfish. ■ *Daily 0900-1630. $3.50, child $2. T33004855.*

Castlemaine Perkins Brewery Back in the city, Castlemaine Perkins Brewery stands out like… well, a brewery, on Milton Road. Established in 1878 and maker of that famous Aussie brand **XXXX**, you can take a tour to see how it is produced and then do some sampling. ■ *T33617597, tour.guides@lion-nathan.com.au Tours last 45 mins, Mon/Tue/Wed 1100/1330/1600 from $8.50. 'BBQ and Beer' Tour Wed 1830, from $18.50.*

Excursions Almost anywhere east of the Great Divide in Queensland, it seems you are never far away from a wildlife sanctuary and the opportunity to see (or cuddle) a koala. Brisbane is no different hosting the **Lone Pine Koala Sanctuary** – the oldest and the largest in the world. Having opened in 1927 and now housing around 130 of the famously adorable, yet utterly pea-brained tree dwellers, it offers a fine introduction, or reminder, of how unique Australia's wildlife really is. Also on display are the equally ubiquitous and marginally more bush-wise wombats, echidnas and kangaroos. ■ *Daily 0800-1700. $15, child $10. T33781366, www.koala.net.au Jesmond Rd, Fig Tree Pocket (southwest via Milton Rd and the western Freeway 5). Getting there: by bus take the #430 from the 'koala platform' in the Myer Centre, Queen St, from $3.40, child $1.70 single. Or Mirimar Boat Cruise departs daily from North Quay at 1000, T32210300, from $25, child $15 (not including admission, returns at 1500).*

Playing second fiddle to Lone Pine is the **Alma Park Zoo** in Dakabin some 30 minutes away. It also features koalas and roos, as well as other non-natives, including deer and water buffalo, all of which would love to make your acquaintance and share your lunch. ■ *0900-1700, $20, child $10, T32046566, www.almaparkzoo.com.au. Getting there: by train on the Caboolture line from*

Brisbane & around

Roma St (daily 0902) where a courtesy bus will pick you up. 30 km north of the city centre off Boundary Road, Bruce Highway.

Australian Woolshed claims to offer a 'a real outback experience without leaving Brisbane' with working dog and sheep shows, whip-cracking, farm-yard animal feeding and milking and yes, more koalas. It is actually quite entertaining and there is an à la carte café or a buffet lunch available where a strange bushman in an Akubra hat swings a 'billy' (that's a sort of tea pot, not a sheep, or a relative) around his person – which apparently improves the taste. ■ *Daily 0730-1600. $15.70, child $10.40. T38721100, www.auswoolshed.com. au Samford Rd, Ferny Hills (north west of the city centre, via Ashgrove).*

Essentials

Brisbane boasts more than 12,000 beds from large 5-star hotels and modern apartment blocks to numerous backpacker and budget options. The only thing lacking are good motor parks within easy reach of the city centre. Although there are plenty of hostels you are still advised to book a budget bed at least 2 days in advance.

Sleeping
■ *On map, page 244*
See insdie front cover
for price categories

Almost all the big hotel chains are represented, but for sheer aesthetics it is hard to beat **LL** *Conrad International Hotel and Casino*, 130 William St, CBD, T33068888, www.hilton.com.au Housed in the former 1890s Treasury Building it offers the full range of luxury rooms, each featuring its own touch of 'heritage' and all the usual amenities including 5 restaurants, numerous bars and of added appeal the Casino downstairs. **LL-A** *IL Mondo Boutique Hotel*, 25 Rotherham St, T33920111, www.ilmondo.com.au Across the river on Kangaroo Point, this modern and chic hotel offers 1-2 bedroom, self-contained apartments, within interesting aesthetics and in relative peace from the city centre. It is also within walking distance of all the action via a typical Brizzie ferry ride from the Holman St Wharf. In-house Mediterranean al-fresco restaurant and a lap pool. **LL** *Powerhouse Boutique Hotel*, corner of Kingsford Smith Dr and Hunt St, T38621800, www.powerhousehotel.com.au Towards the airport and overlooking the river, this is a firm favourite offering great luxury rooms (some with spa), 2 restaurants, gym, sauna and off-street parking. **LL** *Royal Albert Boutique Hotel*, corner of Albert and Elizabeth sts, T32918888, www.atlantisproperties.com.au This hotel offers something a little bit different. Art Deco style with deluxe rooms, suites and self-contained apartments. **LL** *Sheraton*, 249 Turbot St, T38353535, and **LL** *Stamford Plaza*, corner of Edward and Margaret sts, T3211999, are conveniently placed, both within easy walking distance of Queens St. **L-A** *Central Brunswick Apartment Hotel*, 455 Brunswick St, Fortitude Valley, T38521411, www.centralbrunswickhotel.com.au Modern, friendly and ideally placed for the 'Valley' action. **L-B** *Kangaroo Point Holiday Apartments*, 819 Main St, T33916855, www.kangaroopoint.com.au Modern, well appointed and close to the South Bank. **L-A** *Metro Inns*, 239 Wickham St, T38321412, www.metroinns. com.au Sits high on the hill, like a transparent pepper pot, overlooking the CBD and offering tidy standard rooms, each with a balcony and in-house restaurant. **A** *Explorers Inn*, 63 Turbot St, T32113488, www.powerup.com.au/~explorer One of the best value (and certainly the best placed) of the budget hotel options. Friendly, it offers tidy (if small) doubles/twins/family rooms and singles and has a cheap but cheerful restaurant/bar. It is only 500 m from the transit centre and Queens St. Recommended.

Brisbane has a good selection of B&Bs, some of which present an ideal opportunity to experience a traditional 'Queenslander' house. **L-A** *Catherine House*, 151 Kelvin Grove Rd, Kelvin Grove (2 km northwest), T38396988, www.babs.com.au/catherine It is a large Victorian colonial home with 3 beautifully appointed rooms, a self-contained flat, pool and spacious gardens. **L-A** *Paddington (Waverley) B&B*, 5 Latrobe Terrace, Paddington (2 km west), T33698973. A traditional Queenslander with 4 rooms, 2 standard en suites and 2 self-contained suites, right on the main café/restaurant strip. **L-A** *Ridge Haven B&B*, 374 Annerley Rd, Annerley, 4 km south of the city, T33917702, ridge-haven@uq.net.au, is an award-winning Queenslander with 3 very tidy en suites set in a quiet, leafy surroundings. **L** *Thornbury House*, 1 Thornbury St, within walking distance of the CBD, T38325985, www.babs.com.au/qld/thornbury.htm Another traditional Queenslander with 5 recently refurbished rooms, all traditionally furnished with private bathrooms and a self-contained apartment.

There are the usual rash of motels on the main highways north and south into town. **A-B** *Astor Motel*, 193 Wickham Terrace, T38319522. In the CBD, this has tidy modern units and suites close to all amenities. **A-B** *Chermside Green Motel*, 949 Gympie Rd, Chermside, 9 km from the city, T33591041, chermside@futureweb.com.au On the northern approaches, this motel is modern, friendly, with an in-house restaurant and only a short walk from the huge Westfield Shopping Complex.

There are 3 good hostel options on Upper Roma St just 500 m southwest of the transit centre. **B-E** *Brisbane YHA*, 392 Upper Roma St, 500 m southwest of the transit centre, T32361004. It offers plenty of clean, modern dorms, standard/en suite double/twins, good kitchen, restaurant, internet and good activities/information desk, but it lacks the same casual social atmosphere of it's neighbour, *City Backpackers*. **C-E** *City Backpackers*, 380 Upper Roma St, 500 m southwest of the transit centre, T32113221. Deservingly popular and well managed, it offers spotless en suite doubles and dorms, modern kitchen, roof decks, pool, internet and a great bar. It's a very social place that can throw a great party at the weekend and so is ideal if you are travelling alone want company. Also excellent security. **C-E** *Yellow Submarine*, 66 Quay St, T32113424. It's rather tired but characterful multi-level homestead, with dorms and doubles, good kitchen, free BBQs (Sun) and a pool. Friendly, casual, social atmosphere and the staff can also help find work. **C-E** *Palace Backpackers*, corner of Ann and Edward sts, T32112433/1800676340. Right in the heart of the CBD, this large elegant and historic landmark building has been fully revamped offering large dorms, doubles and small singles with all amenities including cable TV, café and the rowdy in-house *Down Under Bar and Grill* that consistently goes off most nights and well into the wee hours. It's well placed but almost too busy and certainly not a place for a shy and quiet bookworm!

There are plenty of choices in and around Fortitude Valley that offer some peace and quiet but are still within walking distance of its popular 24-hr cafés, pubs and nightclubs. **B-F** *Elephant and Wheelbarrow Backpackers*, 230 Wickham St, T32524136. Modern, having recently opened above the popular British-style pub, it has cheap but cheerful dorms, quads/doubles/triples, internet, cable TV, good kitchen and free breakfast. **C-E** *Bowen Terrace Backpackers*, 365 Bowen Terrace, New Farm, T32540458, ceclarke@bigpond.com.au Further south in New Farm, this is quiet and friendly, with a B&B feel, offering good value singles, twins/doubles (some en suite and bath) with TV, fridge, small kitchen and a large relaxing deck. No internet. **C-E** *Globetrekkers*, 35 Balfour St, New Farm, T33581251, globetrekkers.net.au A small, senescent, yet characterful, 2-storey house, it is both cosy and homely, with dorms, doubles (some en suite and one 'four poster'), free internet and off-street parking. Owner, artist, traveller, and all round good guy, Dennis, is usually on hand to offer advice and point you in the right direction. Recommended. **C-E** *Homestead Backpackers*, 57 Annie St, New Farm, T32541609. One of the Valley's liveliest offering tidy 3/4/7 dorms, doubles (some en suite), internet, pool, off-street parking and a whole list of 'freebies' from pick-ups, bike hire, fun-filled day trips to Mount Coot-tha and organized socials with other backpackers.

C-E *Aussie Way*, 34 Cricket St, T33690711. West of the CBD, this hostel is handy to Caxton St nightlife and Paddington. A tidy 1872 colonial house, it offers small but comfortable dorms, singles and doubles, pool, quiet verandahs, free pick-ups and internet. **C-E** *Somewhere to Stay*, corner of Brighton Rd and Franklin St, West End, T38464584, www.somewheretostay.com.au South of the river, this hostel offers exactly that (but needs a good clean) in the form of basic to standard dorms, singles, double/twins with nice views (some with TV and en suite) and lots of youthful energy. Good kitchen, pool, free pick-ups, organized tours, internet.

There are a few motor parks. **L-E** *Caravan Village*, 763 Zillmere Rd (off Gympie Rd), on the northern approach, 12 km from the CBD, T32634040, www.caravanvillage.com.au This is the best bet offering a wide range of options from luxury cabins, en suite/standard powered and non-powered sites, pool, store, internet and an excellent camp kitchen. **B-F** *Newmarket Gardens Caravan Park*, 199 Ashgrove Ave (off Enoggera Rd), T33561458. This is the closest motor park to the city (6 km northwest) and is pretty basic. It has some tidy cabins, powered and non-powered sites in a quiet suburban setting, BBQs but no camp kitchen. Close to main bus route and shops. **L-F** *Dress Circle Holiday Village*, 10 Holmead Rd (Logan Rd exit off SE Fwy), T33416133. South of the city (15 km), this is the best upmarket option in a quiet setting yet close to shops and the main highways. It has luxury apartments, cottages, standard cabins, powered and non-powered sites, pool and a camp kitchen.

They say Brizzie can offer the best of most things and its culinary experiences are no exception. From chic and expensive riverside restaurants and al fresco cafés to historic pubs and paddle steamers, the choice is vast. Outside the city centre and the Riverside (Eagle St) areas the suburbs of Fortitude Valley, New Farm (east), South Bank, the West End (south of the river) and Paddington (west) are well worth looking at. For something uniquely Brisbane try the famed Moreton Bay Bugs (not cause for a rash, but a delicious and very weird looking crab); the stunning view from *The Summit Restaurant* at Mount Coot-tha (see page 252); or a leisurely lunch or dinner cruise on a paddle steamer (see page 256).

Eating
● *On map, page 227*
See inside front cover for price categories

City centre Expensive Some of Brisbane's hotels are well known for their exceptional fine dining including multi award winners, *Siggi's* in the Stamford Plaza, corner of Edward and Margaret sts T32211999; *Ryan's in the Park*, in the *Conrad International*, T33068899 and *Armstrong's, Inchcolm Hotel*, 73 Wickham Terrace, T38324566. Open Breakfast daily, dinner Mon-sat, lunch Mon-Fri. The latter was founded by one of Brisbane's most famous chef Russell Armstrong and is especially well known for its wine list and Asian-style seafood dishes. On Adelaide St, *Jameson's*, (475), T38317633, and *Circa*, (483), T38324722, open lunch Tue-Fri, dinner Mon-Sat, are recommended, with *Jameson's* renowned for its Japanese influences. The Riverside and Eagle St Pier have plenty of fairly upmarket options with great river views including the famous *Pier Nine*, Eagle St Pier, T32292194, with its superb seafood and *Il Centro*, Shop 6, Eagle St Pier, T32216090, which is well renowned for its stunning Sand Crab Lasagne.

Mid-range *Gianni's*, 12 Edward St, T32217655, offers an imaginative Spanish influence and extensive wine cellar. Nearby, *II (Two)* 2 Edward St, T32100600, offers unusual aesthetics as well as excellent meat and seafood dishes. Open dinner Mon-Sat, lunch Mon-Fri.

Cheap For cheaper options in the city centre try the numerous food courts and outlets along the Queen St Mall or one of the city centre pubs (see below).

Fortitude Valley, New Farm and east Mid-range This area offers a truly vast and eclectic range of mainly affordable options from the numerous Asian restaurants that surround Chinatown and the 24-hour café/bars on Brunswick St Mall, to the new and the chic along Brunswick and James sts, in New Farm. Of the numerous Asian choices on Wickham St and the Chinatown Mall, many swear by the large *King of Kings*, (169), T38521122, or for Japanese the *Aya*, (149), T32572399. Another great favourite in the Valley is the recently relocated *Garuva Hidden Tranquillity Restaurant and Bar*, 324 Wickham St, T32160124. It offers imaginative international cuisine with great aesthetics, sitting on comfy floor cushions surrounded by silk screens. In New Farm, *Arc*, 561 Brunswick St, T33583600, is renowned for its modern Australian dishes while *Anise*, 697 Brunswick St, T33581558, is a small and congenial wine bar/restaurant. On the edge of New Farm Park and the river, the *Vat Modern Dining*, in the newly renovated Powerhouse Centre, is also great for a lazy lunch, T33588600. East of Fortitude Valley the *Breakfast Creek Hotel*, 2 Kingsford Smith Dr, T32625988, famous for its ambience and enormous steaks (see pubs below). **Cheap** See cafés below.

South and west Mid-range One of Brisbane's best restaurants is to be found in the West End. The award-winning *E'cco*, 100 Boundary St, T38318344, offers simple yet delicious modern Australian dishes. For something different the *Moorish Dar*, 267 Given Terrace, Paddington, T33690111, offers upmarket, café-style dining with a French/Arabesque influence surrounded by Moorish crafts. Recommended. Also on Given Terrace, *Sultan's Kitchen Indian Restaurant*, (163), T33682194, is a friendly, good value curry house. *The Summit Restaurant*, T33699922, Mount Coot-tha, is another Brisbane classic with its superb views across the city and Moreton Bay (Open daily for lunch/dinner and on Sun for brunch). Next door the *Kuta Café* offers lighter meals. **Cheap** For a really cheap feed well into the wee hours try *Harry's Fine Foods*, corner Petrie Terrace and Caxton St.

Cafés The main focus for Brisbane's al fresco, casual café scene are the Brunswick St Mall in Fortitude Valley, the South Bank parklands, the West End (Boundary St) and Petrie Terrace/Paddington (Caxton and Given Terrace).

Shingle Inn, 254 Edward St, in the city centre, T32219039, is an 'olde-world' teashop with marvellous brews and sweets to die for. *Merlo's*, in the Queensland Art Gallery, is one favourite outlet of this chain which serves great coffee. Nearby, the South Bank parklands also has numerous cafés and outdoor eateries to satisfy the midday munchies or provide that much sought after coffee fix. In Fortitude Valley, the Brunswick St Mall has a rash of good options, many of which are open late or even 24 hrs. *Ric's Café Bar*, T38541772, and *Fat Boys*, T32523789, are 2 favourites. Further south down Brunswick St, *Vroom Café*, corner of James and Dogget sts, Fortitude Valley, T32574455, offers good food and interesting aesthetics, while *Koffie's Expresso Bar* (726), T32541254, is good for value and breakfasts. In Paddington, *Kookaburra Café*, 280 Given Terrace, T33692400, is well known for its excellent pizza, while the *Tea Shop*, 231 Given Terrace, T38766088, serves a hearty, good value breakfast. The West End is a popular café haunt, especially for weekend brunches with *The Three Monkeys*, 28 Mollison St, T38446045, and *Expresso Head* 169 Boundary St, T38448324 and *Tempo*, 181A Boundary St, T38463161, recommended.

Bars Brisbane has a lively and variant pub scene with everything from the historic and traditional Australian to the pseudo Irish and gay friendly.

City Centre For a traditional street corner Australian try *Orient Hotel*, corner of Queen and Ann sts, T38394625, well known for its live music, Thu-Sat, open nightly until 0300.

The Victory, corner of Edward and Charlotte sts, T32210444, is also an old Brisbane favourite with local (free) live bands Thu-Sun and a good beer garden. There are a glut of Irish pubs throughout the city with *PJ O'Briens*, 127 Charlotte St, T32106822, *Gilhooley's*, 283 Elizabeth St, T32218566, and the new and classy *Irish Murphy's*, Treasury Chambers, corner of George and Elizabeth sts, T32214377, all proudly flying the flag in the city centre. Backpackers tend to focus on the *Downunder Bar*, beneath *Palace Backpackers*, 308 Edward St, T30025740, open nightly until 0300.

Fortitude Valley   *Dooley's in the Valley*, 394 Brunswick St, T32524344, is another Irish offering with live music most nights while the new *Elephant and Wheelbarrow*, 230 Wickham St, T32524136, presents some stiff opposition. *The Wickham Hotel*, Wickham St, T38521301, is a well-known gay bar with live music, drag shows and dancing at the weekend.

Petrie Terrace and Paddington   On the corner of Petrie Terrace and Caxton St, *Hotel LA*, T33682560, attracts the loud and pretentious and if you can past the over ambitious 'fashion police' on the door, it will accommodate you well into the wee hours. Further down Caxton St, the huge *Caxton Hotel*, 38, 133695544, is just slightly more casual, with a good restaurant attached. Open daily until 0200-0500. In Paddington *Paddo Tavern*, 186 Given Terrace, T33690044, is another vast offering and a firm suburban favourite, with a fine beer garden and a comedy club. *Fibber McGee's* is an Irish bar/restaurant with entertainment nightly.

Elsewhere   Although a bit of a trek the 111-year-old *Breakfast Creek Hotel*, 2 Kingsford Smith Dr, T32625988, is something of a Brisbane institution. It retains a distinct colonial/Art Deco feel, has a large Spanish beer garden and serves up the best steaks in town. Over in Kangaroo Point, in the shadow of its namesake edifice, is *Storey Bridge Hotel*, 200 Main St, T33912266, www.storeybridgehotel.com.au, a firm favourite at any time, but most famous for hosting the annual *Australia Day 'cockroach races'* and the *Australian Festival of Beers* in Sep.

Clubs
See also the publications listed in Entertainment, below

Brisbane has a happening club scene that echoes the city's reputation for producing some of Australia's best modern musicians. Although it is a far cry from the spectacle of Sydney's diverse and emancipated club scene you can still have a mighty night out and shake your pants to the most modern of vibes. Fortitude Valley, The Riverside Centre (Eagle St, City) and Petrie Terrace are the main club and dance venues. In Fortitude Valley look out for *Zoo*, 711 Ann St, (Wed-Sat until about 0200); *Ric's*, 321 Brunswick St, (Sun-Thu until 0100, Sat/Sun until 0500, free entry); *The Monastery*, 621 Ann St, and *The Beat*, 677 Ann St. At Riverside, *Friday's*, 123 Eagle St, (Sun-Thu until 0300, Fri/Sat until 0500). In the city, backpackers gravitate towards the *Downunder Bar*, under *Palace Backpackers*, 308 Edward St, City, T30025740. Nightly until 0300. In Petrie Terrace and Paddington try *Paddo Tavern* and *The Hotel LA*, see pubs above.

Like most major centres Brisbane has a brash and lively gay scene that mainly centres around the pubs and clubs in 'The Valley' and Spring Hill. In the Valley, *The Wickham Hotel*, Wickham St, T38521301, and *The Beat*, Ann St, T38522661, are especially popular, while in Spring Hill the *Options Nightclub*, *Spring Hill Hotel*, and *Sportsman's Hotel*, Leichardt St, are other favourite haunts.

Entertainment

For up-to-date listings and entertainment news consult the *Courier Mail* on Wed/Sat or the free street press publications, *Rave*, *ShowBriz*, *Time Off* and *Scene*. Street press publications to look out for, for gay and lesbian nights are *Brothersister* or *Queensland Pride*, see also Clubs above.

Brisbane & around

Performing arts Queensland Performing Arts Complex on the South Bank (see Sights above) is the main focus of the city's cultural entertainment. The busy on-going programme includes West End and Broadway musicals, touring productions and Queensland's own ballet, opera, orchestra, theatre and music companies. For programme details check the local press or call *Otix*, T136246, Mon-Sat 0900-2100, www.qtix.com.au/ www.qpac.com.au Brisbane's New Farm Park also hosts the newly restored theatre and performance space, **Powerhouse Complex**, 119 Lamington St, T33588600, while **La Boite Theatre**, 57 Hale St, Petrie Terrace, T33691622, offers mainly Australian themed plays.

Live music From relative obscurity, other than the rather dubious accolade of spawning the disco-era giants, *The Bee-Gees*, Brisbane has now been placed firmly on the international rock music map, with bands such as *Savage Garden, Powder Finger* and *Regurgitator* all being Brisbane bred. As well as its ever changing, yet healthy nightclub scene, Fortitude Valley (alias 'The Valley') is the best place to check out the latest local rock bands, with its many pubs hosting bands from Thu-Sat. Brisbane has a wealth of Irish pubs (see above) with most offering occasional jam sessions and regular live bands at the weekend. *Irish Murphy's* is recommended. *Brisbane Jazz Club*, 1 Annie St, Kangaroo Point, T33912006, has a loyal following with regulars playing on Sat/Sun, from 2030 ($7 cover). Other pubs around Kangaroo Point including *Storey Bridge*, 200 Main St, T33912266, also host jazz sessions mainly on Sun afternoons. *Jazzy Cat*, 56 Mollison St, West End, T38462544, www.jazzycat.com.au, is another good venue.

Casino Brisbane Treasury Casino is housed in the grand, former Treasury Building on North Quay and is open 24 hrs. As well as the usual pokies and gaming tables it has 5 restaurants and 7 bars, T1800 506888. Dress is smart casual and the minimum age is 18.

Cinema IMAX, Queensland Cultural Centre, Melbourne St, has showings 3 times daily, from 1000-2200, $16.20, child $12. T38444222, www.imax.com.au The city centre hosts *Dendy*, 346 George St, T32113244, and 2 *Hoyt's Cinemas*, one at the Myer Centre, 91 Queen St and another at 197 Queen St, T3229554. In Fortitude Valley *Centro*, 39 James St, T38524488, and more alternative *Village Twin*, 701 Brunswick St, T33582021, are other options. As usual Tue night is discount night.

Comedy Several pubs host comedy clubs and evenings, featuring the best of local or visiting talent. They include *Paddo Tavern* (Wed/Thu/Fri/Sat), 186 Given Terrace, Paddington, T33694466 and *The Dockside Comedy Bar* (Thu-Sat) Ferry St, Kangaroo Point, T33911110.

Festivals The year begins with a bang with the New Year celebrations and fireworks display over the river beside the South Bank parklands. This is repeated with even more zeal on **26 January**, *Australia Day*, with other hugely popular and bizarre events (that offer some weight to the more conservative southerner's claim that Queenslanders are as mad as cut snakes) including the annual cockroach races and even a little 'frozen chicken bowling'.

Over **Easter** the *Brisbane to Gladstone Yacht Race*, leaves Shorncliffe, while the *Caxton Seafood and Wine Festival* arrives at the western suburb of Paddington. **May** sees the *Queensland Racing Festival* and **Jun** the annual *Queensland Day* celebrations. Fortitude Valley's Chinatown and Brunswick St becomes the focus for the lively *Valley Festival* in **Jul**, with the *Brisbane International Film Festival* at the end of month. The last week of **Aug** sees the start of the 2-week *River Festival* which celebrates the 'city's lifeblood' with food, fire and festivities, which is echoed in **Sep** with the *National Festival of Beers* (Australia's biggest) held at the *Storey Bridge Hotel*.

A day at the races (Aussie style)

Twenty years ago (or so the story goes) two Brisbanite's were sitting in a bar arguing about whose suburb had the biggest, fasted cockroaches. Unable to reach a settlement, the following day they captured their very best and raced them. And with that the annual 'Cockroach Races' were born (and who said Queenslanders are not as mad as cut snakes!). Now, every Australia Day (26 January), the Storey Bridge Hotel in Kangaroo Point hosts the infamous and truly unique cocky races. Of course the races, along with many other events and live entertainment (much of it involving the removal of blouses), is merely an excuse to get utterly inebriated. Picture the scene for a second… small grandstands surround a central ring, bursting with rowdy punters, many with faces painted in national colours and supporting flags (often as an item – and the only item – of

clothing). The race is called and from deep within the throngs of celebrants the sound of badly played bagpipes herald the arrival of the teams and their roaches. The crowd gives way and the scene is set. On the count of three a plastic container, held in the middle of the ring, is lifted and off the roaches 'zip' in all directions. The crowd goes wild. The squeamish scream as the insects run under bags, shoes and into sandwiches. If the winner is found, or indeed can ever be caught, it is identified and the winning team is announced. Then its drinks all round and more – until we all fall down.

To say it is an experience is an understatement and needless to say, if your visit coincides, it is recommended (but don't plan on doing anything the following day, except that is maybe checking the contents of your shoes). www.storeybridgehotel.com.au

Livid Festival in Oct is Brisbane's biggest live music event with numerous city venues hosting the best of local talent and visiting bands. An up-to-date events listing is available at www.brisbanetourism.com.au

Shopping

Brisbane is without doubt the Queensland Capital for retail therapy with over 1,500 stores and 650 shops in and around Queens St alone. Three department stores, 5 shopping centres and a rash of malls and arcades all combine to provide a vast array of choice from fashion to furnishings, all of which presents a veritable binge for the shopaholic.

The city also hosts a few good markets including the **South Bank markets** on Fri night/Sat/Sun, the **Riverside and Eagle St Pier markets** on Sun and the **'Valley' markets** (Brunswick St) on Sat. For maps and travel books look no further than *World Wide Maps and Guides*, 187 George St, T32214330, www.worldwidemaps.com.au For mainstream bookshops you will find major outlets in around Queens St including *Angus and Robertson Bookworld*, 52 Queens St, T32298899 (also in the Myer Centre, Level A and Post Office Sq) and *The American Book Store*, 173 Elizabeth St, T32294677. For second-hand books try *Bent Books*, 205A Boundary St, West End, T38465004, or *Emma's Bookshop*, across the road at 132 Boundary St, T38444973 (also has internet).

For camping and outdoor equipment *City Camping Disposals*, 157 Elizabeth St, should supply all your needs.

Tours & activities

There are a vast array of tours on offer from the historical to ecological from the culinary to the fearful

City tours Brisbane Transport's CitySights and CityNights Tours are a great way to see the inner city and the views from Mount Coot-tha, with the added bonus of free bus and CityCat travel on the tour day. **CitySights** lasts 1½ hrs, from $20, child $15, T131230. Tours leave every 45 mins from Post Office Square, from 0900-1545. **CityNights** at 1830-2100 Nov-Feb and 1800-2030 March-Oct. Recommended.

Local history expert Brian Ogden leads visitors on a journey into Brisbane's interesting past with 1½- and 2-hr historical walking tours, Sat 0830/1130, Wed 1900, Mon

0930 (2-hr tour including 30 mins guided tour of St John's Cathedral), from $11, T32173673, www.ogdenswalkingtours.com.au

Not for the superstitious is the entertaining **Ghost Tour of Brisbane**, T38446606, www.ghost-tours.com.au, Tue-Thu/Sat 1100-1700, from $25-$61. You can practically eat your way around the city, and sample a Moreton Bay Bug (type of crab) with **Culinary Tour** expert Jan Power, T32683889, or combine fine dining with art gallery tours with **Art Tours**, T38993686, www.artours.coaus.com.au, from $55. Even the shopaholics are well catered for on a **Shopping Tour** with *Brisbane Warehouse Shopping Tours*, T38210438. For bicycle tours contact *Hotel Cycle Tours*, T04 0800 3198, daily 1400/1930, from $30, child $25.

Day tours Numerous bus companies offer a wide range of day tours around the region from the Gold and Sunshine coasts to Fraser Island and the Southern Queensland National Parks including *Coachtrans* (Gold Coast, Sunshine Coast and hinterlands) from $55; T32364165, www.daytours.com.au; *Flight Deck Tours* (City, Moreton Bay and Gold Coast) from $40, T0418735141; *Australia Day Tours* (practically everywhere!) from $60-80, T32364155, www.daytours.com.au, and *Grayline* (the same) from $37, T1300360776. Brochures can be picked up at the various company offices at the Roma St Transit Centre.

Ballooning *Fly Me To The Moon*, T34230400, www.flymetothemoon.com.au, offer flights right over the city with champagne breakfast, Mon-Fri, from $198 (Sat/Sun $218). *Champagne Breakfast Flights*, T33970033, www.possumairtours.com.au, take you out over the city to the Moreton Bay Islands, 0600/0730, from $230. **River cruises** Other than the *CityCats*, that offer casual sightseeing, *Club Crocodile Paddle steamers*, T32211300, www.clubcroc.com.au, have become a familiar sight on the river offering a range of sightseeing/dining options. Lunch 1½ hrs, Mon-Fri 1145, from $36. Dinner 2½ hrs, Mon-Thu 1900, Fri-Sat 1845, Sun 1800, from $52.50. Sunday breakfast with live jazz 0730-1030. *The Island* is Brisbane's biggest party boat, departing from Pier 5, Queens Wharf, North Quay, T32119090. Booking essential. **Rock climing and abseiling** The cliffs on the south side of the river between the maritime Museum and Kangaroo Point offer excellent opportunities for climbing and abseiling. *Worthwild*, T33956450, and *Careflight*, T55980222, offer classes from $70. **Rollerblading** *Blade Sensations* offers guided rollerblade tours including the unusual Full Moon Skate which does not mean you skate in the buff but see the city at night, departs 2000, T38440606. *Skatebiz*, 101 Albert St, T32200157, offers independent hire, from $11 for 2 hr. Group skating Wed 2000, tours Sun from $10. **Skydiving** *Brisbane Skydiving Centre*, T1800061555, www.brisbaneskydive.com.au, offer tandems with Australian team member Brian Scoffell over Brisbane city or Willowbank, from $220 (over the city $290).

Transport
For all public transport enquiries T131230, www.trans info.qld.gov.au

Local Bus Central Queens Street Bus Station is located downstairs in the Myer Centre, Queen St. City *Circle 333* (blue and white) service the city centre circuit, *Citybus* (white and yellow) service the suburbs and *Cityexpress* (blue and yellow stripes) offers half hourly express services within Greater Brisbane area, T131230. Fares work on a 5-zone system from $1.80-3.80/concession, 90c-$1.90. For attractive travel pass deals and saver tickets, see box.

Car Although Brisbane is not as congested as most Australian cities of the same size, the CBD does have a very confusing system of one-way streets and utterly merciless traffic wardens. Given the efficiency of the public transport system you are advised to park the car in a non-metered area and take the bus or ferry into the CBD. Kangaroo Point, just under the Story Bridge on the south bank, is a good spot to park and cross by ferry to the city centre.

Sporting capital

An extraordinary number of Australia's sporting greats hail from Brisbane including recently retired Wallabies (Australia) rugby union team captain John Eales; golfing legend Greg Norman; two-time US Open tennis winner Pat Rafter; former Australian cricket team captain Alan Border; former rugby league legend Wally Lewis; and international swimming champions, Kieran Perkins, Susie O'Neill, Samantha Riley and Hayley Lewis. Sadly, Brisbane could also have had a one-legged boxer champion in 1924, in the form of either C Olsen or E Holmes, but (apparently) both fell down in the fourth round and were unable to stand up, so a draw was declared.

There are also three famous sporting venues in Brisbane: the 'Gabba' in Woollongabba (cricket and Aussie football); the ANZ Stadium in Nathan (home to rugby league's Brisbane Broncos) and Ballymore in Herston (home of rugby union State side, the Queensland Reds). For bookings and tickets contact Ticket master, T32217894 or Ticketek, T131931.

CityCat and ferry Brisbane's famous, sleek blue and white *CityCats* glide up and down the river from Bretts Wharf (Hamilton) in the east, to the University of Queensland (St Lucia) in the west, stopping at selected wharfs on both sides of the river, daily from 0550-2230. The round trip takes about 2 hrs. Fares start at $1.60. A *Day Rover Ticket* costs $8.40, child $4.20. *Ten Trip Saver* and *Off-Peak Saver* tickets also apply in conjunction with city bus services. *City Ferry* operates an inner city and cross river service (every 15-20 mins) at various points along the river. Fares are determined by the number of sectors crossed and start at $1.60. Pick up a copy of the *Brisbane River Experience Guide*, which highlights the main attractions and specialist tours on offer. For general enquiries, T131230.

Cycling Brisbane is very well geared up for cyclists with over 350 km of city cycleways. Most of these have been established around the edge of the CBD along the riverbank, providing an excellent way to take in the sights and to get from A to B. VICs can supply the free and comprehensive *Brisbane Bicycle Maps* booklet. Bike hire is available from *Brisbane Bicycle*, 87 Albert St, T32292433, from $20 per day ($100 deposit for over-night hire); or *Hotel/Valet Cycle Hire*, T0408003198, tours also available.

Taxi *Black and White Cabs*, T131008, or *Yellow Cabs*, T131924.

Train *Citytrain*, T132232, services greater Brisbane with networks to Ipswich (west), Gold Coast and Cleveland (south) and Caboolture and Ferny Grove (north). The main city stations are Central (top end of Edward St), Roma (Transit Centre), South Bank (South Brisbane) and Brunswick St (Fortitude Valley). Fares are based on a zone system and start at $1.65, 'One-Day Unlimited Pass', from $8.60.

Long distance Air Brisbane's international and domestic airports are 16/18 km northeast of the city centre. *Qantas*, T131313, Qantas Office, 247 Adelaide St, T32382953, and *Virgin Blue*, T136789, offer regular daily domestic services to all main centres. *Flight West*, T131300, and *Sunstate* (*Qantas*), offer additional services to Gladstone, Townsville and other outback or coastal destinations.

Bus All interstate and local buses stop at the multi-level Roma St Transit Centre, Roma St, T32363035. Open 0530-2030. Most of the major bus companies have internal offices on Level 3 (Coach Deck) and there are also lockers, internet and a visitors information desk, T32295918. Various food outlets and showers are available on Level 2.

Brisbane & around

Bus and CityCat saver tickets

Brisbane Transport City buses offer an 'Off Peak Saver' ticket with unlimited travel within the city centre, Mon-Fri from 0900-1530 and after 1900, all day Sat/Sun, from $4.60. Additional savings can be made with the 'Day Rover' (from $8.40) and 'Ten Trip Saver' (save 20%), from $13.80,

concession $6.90, which combines travel on CityCat services. City Sights Tours leave every 40min from Post Office Sq, from $20, child $15 (Nights Tour 1830). This then includes unlimited bus and ferry travel for the tour day.

McCafferty's, T131499, www.macaffertys.com.au, *Greyhound*, T132030/T32581670, www.greyhound.com.au, *Premier Motor Services*, T133410, www.premierms.com.au, all offer north/southbound interstate services. *MacCafferty's* services runs as follows: Sydney (3 per day) from $65-235, 15¾ hrs; Cairns (9 per day) from $134-182, 25-30 hrs; Townsville (6-7 per day), from $116-151, 22 hrs; Byron Bay (6 per day) from $25-33, 3 hrs, 10 mins; Gold Coast (6 per day) from $12-16, 1½ hrs; Noosa (*Suncoast Pacific*) daily from $27, 3 hrs.

For a good deal to the **Gold Coast**, catch the *Gold Coast Conrad Jupiter's Casino Bus*, T32224067. Departs Roma St Transit Centre daily 0900, returns 1500, Sat/Sun 1100, returns 1700). For $10 you will be transported to Jupiter's Casino where you will then receive a $5 lunch voucher and $5 gaming voucher. *Coachtrans*, T32361000, offer 4 daily services to the Gold Coast (including the airport) and 'Unlimited Travel Passes' for city sights, airport and Gold Coast. *Crisps Coaches*, T32365266, offer south and west-bound services from Brisbane to **Toowoomba/Moree**, from $29 single and Brisbane to Tenterfield, from $36 single. *Sun Air*, T54782811/1800804340, *Sunshine Coast Sunbus*, T54507888, and *Suncoast Pacific*, T32361901 (latter recommended for Noosa), offer regular daily services to the **Sunshine Coast**. *Brisbane Bus Lines*, T33550034, also service the Sunshine Coast and South Burnett Region.

Car/van hire *Able*, Transit Centre, T131429; *Avis*, 133 Albert St, T32212900; *Budget* 105 Mary St, T32200699; *Britz camper vans*, 647 Kingsford Smith Dr, T36301151; *Maui*, 647 Kingsford Smith Dr, T1300363800.

Train Queensland Rail Travel Centre is located on the Ground Floor, Roma St Transit Centre, T32351331, for general enquiries T132232 (0600-2000). *Citytrain* offer links to the Gold Coast. Northbound services include the *Tilt Train* – the new express service between **Brisbane- Rockhampton** (6½ hrs) and the service recommended for those travelling to Noosa via Nambour or Hervey Bay via Maryborough (free bus connection), departs Sun-Fri 1030 and 1700 (Rockhampton $82/Namour $22/Bundaberg $52 single). *Sunlander* (**Brisbane-Cairns**) departs 0855 Tue/Thu/Sat (Cairns from $201 single). *Spirit of the Tropics* (**Brisbane-Townsville**) departs 1340 Tue/Sat (Townsville from $180 single). *Queenslander* (**Brisbane-Cairns**) is a luxury service departing Sun 0855, from $558.

Directory **Banks** All major bank branches with ATMs are represented in the city centre especially in the Malls Queen, Edward and Eagle Sts. Also *Thomas Cook*, Bowman House, 276 Edward St, T32219422. *American Express*, 131 Elizabeth St, T32292729. **Employment** *Work Travel*, Level 3, Transit Centre, Roma, T32364899. *Centrelink*, T132850. **Communications** Post office: the central Post office is at 261 Queen St (opposite Post Office Sq). Post shops at 44 Roma St, 27 Adelaide St, Wintergarden and Queen St Malls. Open Mon-Fri 0830-1730. Mall post shops open Fri until 1900 and Sat 0900-1600/Sun 1030-1600. Post Restante, Queens St, T34051448. Open Mon-Fri

0900-1700. **Internet**: **International Youth Service Centre**, 2/69 Adelaide St, T32299985, open daily 0800-2400, or the **State Library**, South Bank, T38407666, 30-min free, book a day in advance, open Mon-Thu 1000-2000, Fri-Sun 1000-1700. If you are staying north of the city, *Dymocks* in the Westfield Shopping Centre, Chermside, has free internet with a café purchase. **Medical services** Chemist: *Day and Night*, 245 Albert St, T32218155. **Mater Hospital** (24 hr), Raymond Terrace, Woolloongabba, T38408111. **Roma St Medical Centre**, Transit Centre, T32362988. **Travellers Medical Service**, Level 1, 245 Albert St, T32113611. **Travel agents** *Backpackers Travel Centre*, 138 Albert St, T32212225. *YHA Queensland*, 154 Roma St, T32361680. *Flight Centre*, 170 Adelaide St, T32218900. **Useful numbers** Police: corner of Queen and Albert sts and opposite the Roma St Transit Centre T33646464. Emergency T000. **RACQ**: 261 Queen St, T33612394.

Moreton Bay and Islands

*Almost like an echo of their far more famous and visited relative Fraser Island, the sand islands of Moreton Bay present a superb 'island experience' and opportunity to escape the urbanity and hype of the Gold Coast and Brisbane. Although much smaller than Fraser and hosting marginally less dramatic or variant scenery, the true beauty of the Moreton group lies in the fact that they are so easily accessible and so remarkably unspoilt. Of the 300 odd islands scattered throughout the bay, the two largest and most popular are **Moreton Island** and **North Stradbroke Island**. Moreton, which lies 37 km northeast of the Brisbane River mouth, is almost uninhabited and famous for its **4WD opportunities**, its **shipwrecks** and its pod of friendly **dolphins**. Further south, North Stradbroke (or 'Straddie') is the largest of the islands and a true, yet casual, island resort with three easily accessible **laid-back communities**, world-class **surf beaches** and awesome **coastal scenery**. Also, if you ever thought it possible to stand on a headland and watch breaching whales, dolphins and manta rays gliding past effortlessly beneath the waves, then 'Straddie' will prove that it is.*

Colour map 2/3, grid A5/C5

Brisbane & around

Bayside resorts

Although the islands are deservingly the greatest and obvious lure of Moreton Bay, several of the coastal settlements (essentially suburbs of Brisbane) offer a more relaxed base from which to explore both the islands and the city, as well as presenting some opportunities for sailing, diving and other watersports. North of the Brisbane River mouth you pass through Sandgate and Brighton before reaching Redcliffe. South of the Brisbane River the main coastal settlements are Wynnum, Manly, Cleveland and Redland Bay.

Redcliffe, 36 km northeast of Brisbane, was founded in 1824 and was the first settlement in Queensland, before the small penal colony was moved up the Brisbane River to seed the great capital city we see today. A picturesque peninsula suburb, it boasts a broad range of accommodation, several safe swimming beaches, numerous water sports and activities and also serves as the northerly access point to Moreton Island with '*Combie Trader*', on Mondays, Fridays and Sundays, T32036399.

Redcliffe

Redcliffe VIC is located at Pelican Park, Hornibrook Esplanade, T32843500, www.redcliffe.qld.gov.au Open daily 0900-1600. They stock maps and can assist with general information and accommodation/activity bookings.

Manly Manly is another popular holiday destination and as the host to one of the largest marinas in the Southern Hemisphere, offers some excellent sailing opportunities. *WAGS* (Wednesday Afternoon Gentleman's Sailing) offer free afternoon sailing but book before 1230, T33968666.

Cleveland and **Redland Bay**, to the south of Manly, serve as the main departure points to North Stradbroke Island. See below for details.

The well-organized Wynnum Manly Tourism and VIC is located in the heart of the town at 43A Cambridge Parade, T33483524. Open daily 1000-1500. They stock maps and can assist with general information and accommodation/activity bookings.

Sleeping and eating B-E *Moreton Bay Lodge*, 45 Cambridge Parade, T33963020, offers budget dorms, singles, doubles and family rooms. Good views and a café/wine bar.

Tours *Manly Eco Tours*, T33969400, offer an excellent range of bay cruises, from full day island explorations (from $71, child $35), to Sunday breakfast (from $28) and boom netting parties (from $13.50). **Helena Island** tours also depart from Manly (see below).

Transport For detailed and up-to-date information regarding bus services to Cleveland and Redland Bay (North Stradbroke Island) contact the Roma St Transit Centre, T32363035, or *Citybus*, T131230.

North Stradbroke Island

Colour map 2,
grid A5
Population: 3,000
30 km southeast
of Brisbane;
36 km in length and
11 km at its
widest point

North Stradbroke, or 'Straddie' as it is affectionately known, is the largest, most inhabited and most accessible of the Moreton Bay Islands by ferry. Separated from its southerly neighbour South Stradbroke by a fierce cyclone in 1896, it has become a magical tourist attraction often overlooked due to its proximity to the obvious lures of Brisbane and the Gold Coast. In many ways it is similar to Fraser Island, offering diverse and unspoilt coastal scenery and a rich biodiversity that is so unique to 'sand islands'. A wedge-shaped island, the three pleasant and picturesque villages of Dunwich, Amity Point and Point Lookout offer a broad range of accommodation, play host to some excellent beaches and plenty of water-based activities. Surfing is the obvious speciality.

Ins & outs
See Transport, page
262, for details

Broad based information is available from the VICs in Brisbane, Manly or Cleveland. On the island itself, Stradbroke VIC is located 300 m from the ferry wharf on Junner St, Dunwich, T34099555, www.redland.net.au/redlandstourism Open Mon-Fri 0830-1700, Sat/Sun 1100-1500. They stock island maps and can assist with general information.

Sights **Dunwich**, which was a former penal colony and quarantine station first settled in 1850s provides the main arrival point and is located on the west mid-section of the island. There is a small museum on Welsby Street that explores the island's rich aboriginal and early settler history. Open on Wednesdays and Saturdays. **Amity Point**, first settled in 1825, sits on the northwest corner 17 km from Dunwich, while **Point Lookout**, the main focus for today's tourist accommodation, sights and activities, is 21 km away on the northeast corner. If you only have one or two days on the island the place to be is Point Lookout, with its golden surf beaches and dramatic headland. At the terminus of East Coast Road is the start of the **North Gorge Headlands Walk** (1 km one way). Before you set off take a look at **Frenchman's Bay** below, which gives you a flavour of the dramatic scenery to come. Follow the track, through wind-shorn stands of pandanus palms to **The Gorge**, a narrow cleft in the rock that is pounded endlessly by huge ocean breakers. Further on **Whale Rock** provides an ideal viewpoint from which to spot migrating humpback whales between June and October and all year round manta rays, turtles and dolphins are also a familiar sight.

At the far end of the walk the vast swathe of **Main Beach** comes into view stretching 34 km down the entire length of the island's east coast. It offers some excellent four-wheel driving, fishing, surfing and a few mosquito-infested campsites. **Cylinder Beach**, back along East Coast Road, provides the best recreational spot with great surf breaks and safe swimming. If you do swim always stick to patrolled areas and between the flags.

Other attractions on the island include **Blue Lakes National Park**, which is reached via Trans Island Road, from Dunwich. The lake itself, a 2.5-km walk from the car park, is freshwater and fringed with melalucas and eucalypts, providing the perfect spot for a cool swim. To reach Main Beach from there requires 4WD. **Brown Lake**, which is bigger and only 2 km outside Dunwich is, thanks perhaps to its name alone, is a less popular spot.

There is a broad range of accommodation available on Straddie from apartment-style resorts and self-contained holiday houses to hostels and campsites, with the vast majority being based in Point Lookout. **LL** *Whale Watch Ocean Beach Resort*, 7 Samarinda Dr, T34098555, www.whalewatch resort.com.au, and the slightly cheaper **LL-L** *Islander Holiday Resort*, East Coast Rd, T34098388, (both Point Lookout) are two of the major up-market resorts on the island, both located close to Cylinder Beach and offering the standard self-contained apartments, pool, spa etc. **L-A** *Sunsets at Point*, Lookout, 6 Billa St, T34098829. A B&B in a spacious, modern house with 3 en suites overlooking Home Beach. **A** *Amity Bungalows*, 33 Ballow St, Amity Point, T34097126, www.amitybung alows.com.au, offers 3 well-appointed 1-2 bedroom, self-contained (thatched) bungalows that sleep up to six. **B-F** *Straddbroke Tourist Park*, Dickson Way, T34098127. This is the best-facilitated motor park/campsite. Located in Point Lookout it offers deluxe villas (with spa), en suite/standard cabins, powered and non-powered sites, salt-water pool, BBQ but no camp kitchen. **C-E** *Stradbroke Island Guesthouse* (above and part of the Dive Shop), 1 East Coast Rd, T34098888, www.stradbroke islandscuba.com.au Basic but friendly. Internet and pick-ups from Brisbane. **E** Campsites, Adder Rock and Cylinder Beach in Point Lookout, Amity Point and Dunwich. Camping is also allowed anywhere along the Main Beach foreshore, T34099555.

Sleeping
Pre-booking is recommended in the summer, and on public/school holidays

Straddie Beach Hotel, overlooking Cylinder Beach, T34098188, is a popular spot for value pub meals and has a large outdoor deck space. Open daily for breakfast lunch and dinner from 0730. *The Stonefish Restaurant*, Mintee St, near the headland, T34098549. Open daily from 0800, dinner Wed-Sun. For something a little more intimate. *La Focaccia Italian*, Meegera Pl (off Mooloomba/East Coast Rd), T34098778. Open daily from 0900. For congenial, al fresco dining. *Danny's Chinese*, at the Local Bar, East Coast Rd, T34098519. Recommended by the locals for sheer good value. There are grocery shops at the Centre Point Shopping Centre, Endeavour St and Mintee St. Open 0700-2100.

Eating

Straddie Adventures, T34098414, straddie@ozemail.com.au, offer an exciting range of backpacker based tours and activities, including sand boarding from $28, sea kayaking and snorkelling from $33 and half-, full-day 4WD tours from $50. *Kingfisher Tours*, T34099502, www.straddiekingfishertours.com.au, and *Beach Island Tours* (Tour de Straddie), T34098098, both offer excellent and informative 4WD tours. *Stradbroke Island Tours*, T34098051, specialize in wildlife and eco-based trips, from $30. There are several cruise and fishing charters, including Point Lookout (Mal Starkey), T34098353, from $110 and *Captain Silver*, T34098636 (daily at 1000 from One Mile Jetty, Dunwich).

Tours & activities
VIC has all details of activities and operators

Stradbroke Island Scuba Centre, 1 East Coast Rd, Point Lookout, T34098888, www.stradbrokeislandscuba.com.au, offers daily boat dives at 0900/1130/1330 with manta ray, turtle and dolphin spotting, from $110 (including gear). Snorkelling and dive courses also. *Dive Oceantechniques*, 451 Esplanade, Manly, T33963003, oceantec@stradinet.aunz.com, also offer courses, dives and eco-sightseeing tours, from $45.

Transport

Many mainland car rental companies will not permit their vehicles on the island

Local All major roads on 'Straddie' are sealed and it has its own bus service, *North Stradbroke Bus Services*, T34097151. Buses meet every scheduled ferry arrival or departure and operate between Dunwich, One Mile, Amity and Point Lookout Mon-Fri 0715-1945, Sat/Sun 0715-1830. The return fare from Dunwich to Point Lookout is around $8. For a taxi, T131924/34099800.

The crossing for both services takes about 45 mins

Long distance Cleveland services To reach the Cleveland ferry terminal by car from Brisbane, follow signs from Highway 1 to Old Cleveland Rd, then follow Finucane Rd right through the centre of Cleveland to Toondah Harbour. From the Gold Coast take the Bryants Rd/Cleveland exit, off the Pacific Highway and follow signs to Redland Bay or Cleveland. By train from Brisbane, take *Citytrain* to Cleveland from the Roma St Transit Centre, where a bus (*National Bus*, T32453333) will provide pick-ups to the ferry terminal, T131230. *Stradbroke Ferries*, T32862666, operate both passenger (water taxi) and vehicle services. The water taxi departs every hr Mon-Fri 0600-1915, Sat 0630-1800, Sun 0800-1800, from $12, child $5.50 return. The vehicle ferry also departs every hr, Mon-Fri 0530-1830, Sat 0530-1830, Sun 0530-1930, from $86 return (passenger $10, child $5 return, bikes $4). The crossing for both services takes 30 mins. *North Stradbroke Flyer*, T32861964, also offers a fast passenger service, 9 times daily from 0630-1830, from $12 return. They also offer half-full day tours to the island (from $129, child $85). Their bus 'Bessie' meets the Cleveland train.

Redland Bay services To reach the Redland Bay ferry terminal by car from Brisbane, or the Gold Coast, follow signs from the Pacific Highway to Bryants Rd exit and follow signs to Redland Bay. *Island's Transport*, T38290008, www.islandstransport.com.au, operate both passenger and vehicle services. They depart every 2 hrs, Mon-Fri 0500- 1730 (Fri also 1900), Sat/Sun 0700-1730, from $11, child $5.50 return. The vehicle ferry also departs every hour, Mon-Fri 0530-1830, Sat 0530-1830, Sun 0530-1930, from $82 return.

Directory

Banks The post offices in Dunwich, Amity and Point Lookout all act as Common-wealth Bank agents. Eftpos is available in shops and resorts. There is an ATM at the *Stradbroke Island Beach Hotel*, Point Lookout. **Communications** Internet: *Stradbroke Island Guesthouse*, 1 East Coast Rd, Point Lookout, T34098888. **Post office**: Dunwich, Point Lookout (Megerra Pl). **Useful numbers** Medical: T34099596. Police: T34099059.

Moreton Island

Colour map 3, grid C5
Population: 270
37 km northeast of Brisbane; 38 km in length and almost 20,000 ha

Moreton Island, which lies to the north of the Stradbroke Islands, is often considered the jewel of the Moreton group by virtue of it being uninhabited and its unspoilt beauty. It is another 'sand mass' offering diverse scenery of long, empty beaches, dunes, forest, lagoons and heath lands with abundant wildlife. Other than the sheer aesthetics and solitude, the greatest attractions are its four-wheel drive opportunities, fishing, camping, wreck-snorkelling/diving and above all, for its world famous pod of wild dolphins that put in a nightly appearance at the island's only resort, Tangalooma.

Sights The main attractions and activities on the island accessible without a 4WD are the resort itself, *Tangalooma Wild Dolphin Resort* – which served as a former

◀

Tangalooma dolphins

Tangalooma bottlenose dolphins have had a close almost symbiotic relationship with humans that date back centuries, when Aboriginal fisherman rewarded them for seeking and herding shoals of fish. After the Europeans arrived and a whaling station was established (1952-62), they sensibly kept a low profile, before returning regularly again for free fishy handouts at the new resorts wharf in 1989. From 1992 a research and education programme was established in conjunction with the University of Queensland.

Today that research mainly revolves around nightly feeding during when at least eight to nine dolphins ('Freddy', 'Nari',

'Lefty', 'Tinkerbell' and 'Wedge', to name a few) regularly visit to be fed by visitors under strict supervision. 'Feeding time' is deliberately kept out of daylight hours so as to not interfere with the animal's natural feeding behaviour and also, along with the island destination, prevent the spectacle becoming too commercial. As it stands it has to be one of the best and most accessible wild dolphin encounters in the world and what makes it extra special is the unpredictability and anticipation of their arrival. If you do partake in the experience the actual feeding as opposed to merely watching is recommended (especially for children).

whaling station between 1952-62, the **Tangalooma Desert** – a large sand blow near the resort, the **Blue Lagoons** – a group of 15 deliberately sunken shipwrecks which provide excellent snorkelling, and of course, the immensely popular, nightly **dolphin viewing** and feeding at the resort wharf. If you do have the freedom of the island with a 4WD Cape Moreton at the northeastern tip of the island is worth a visit to see the 1857 lighthouse – the oldest in Queensland. Mount Tempest (285 m) dominates the heart of the island and is reputed to be the highest coastal sand dune in the world (5-km strenuous walk). See Tours.

LL-D *Tangalooma Wild Dolphin Resort*, T1300652250, www.tangalooma.com.au, is a fine resort offering a wide range of beachside accommodations from luxury self-contained apartments and standard rooms/units to new backpacker/budget beds, a restaurant, bistro/bar café, pools and an environmental centre. Recommended. **QPWS campsites** are available at The Wrecks, Ben-Ewa and Comboyuro Point on the west coast and Blue Lagoon and Eagers Creek on the east. The Wrecks campsite is about a 2-km walk from the resort. Each has toilets, and limited supplies of water, cold showers. Fees apply ($3.85 per night), T34082710, moreton_is.qpws@bigpond.com.au
Sleeping & eating

Tangalooma Wild Dolphin Resort offers full/half-day tour options, dolphin feeding/watching and an excellent range of island excursions and activities from sand boarding, snorkelling and diving to scenic helicopter flights. Daily whale-watching cruises are also available Jun-Oct, from $95, child $55. Their website www.tangalooma.com.au, offers all the detail and is a fine introduction to both the resort and the island. *Dolphin Wild*, T54975628, www.dolphinwild.com.au, also offer day cruises to Moreton from Redcliffe, from $129, child $70.
Tours & activities

Local There are no sealed roads on Moreton and access is by 4WD only ($30 fee for 1 month). Vehicular/passenger barge *Combie Trader*, T32036399, www.moreton-island.com.au, offers regular services from Scarborough (Redcliffe) to Bulwer on the islands northwest coast, from around $150 return. *Moreton Venture*, T38951000, www.moretonventure.com.au, runs from Howard Smith Dr, Lytton to Kooringal at the island's southern tip. *Heliquest*, T38802229, www.heliquest.com.au, offer helicopter access. For those without a 4WD vehicle the best way to reach the island is through the *Tangalooma*
Transport

Brisbane & around

Resort, which offers accommodation, day trips, tours and independent transfers, T1300652250, www.tangalooma.com.au Their launch leaves from the terminal on the northern bank of the Brisbane River, at the end of Holt St, and departs Sun-Fri 0930, from $35, child $18 (75 mins). A courtesy coach operates from McCafferty's Bus Bay 26, Level 3, Roma St Transit Centre in Brisbane city centre at 0900.

Other Moreton Bay islands

South Stradbroke Island South Stradbroke Island, which is the most southerly of the Moreton group, sits just to the north of Main Beach on the Gold Coast. Being uninhabited and in such stark contrast to the heady tourist developments on the mainland, it provides an ideal island getaway far from the madding crowd. The island is largely uninhabited apart from two resorts.

Sleeping and eating LL *Couran Cove Resort*, T55979000, www.couran.com.au On the west coast, this luxurious resort provides all that you might expect from a 5-star establishment: a broad range of deluxe accommodations, amenities and island activities and a range of day tours from $55, child $30. **L-A** *South Stradbroke Island Resort*, T55773311, www.southstradbrokeislandresort.com.au, offers more basic facilities, numerous water-based activities and caters for day visitors.

Transport *Couran Cove* launch offers scheduled daily services from their own terminal at the Runaway Bay Marina, 247 Bayview St, Runaway Bay Marina, T55979000. Daily scheduled services to the *South Stradbroke Island Resort* are also available from the Runaway Bay Marina (Gate C), T55773311. Day cruises to the latter are also available from Cavill Ave, Surfers Paradise.

Bribie Island The most northerly of the Moreton group and closest to the mainland, Bribie (14,400 ha) is the only island in the bay that is accessible by car. As such it is fairly well developed with a good infrastructure, amenities and mainly water-based activities. The vast majority of development is located at the southern end of the island while the north is mainly given over to national and conservation parks. These areas are relatively quiet and unspoilt and providing plenty of opportunity to explore the many wildlife-rich areas. The Pummistone Passage, which separates the island from the mainland, is also a fine venue for bird, turtle and dolphin watching.

Sleeping There are 4 designated QPWS campsites, fees apply, T34088451. Bribie Island VIC, Benabrow Ave (on the island), T34089026, can assist with general information, accommodation/activity listings and bookings. Open Mon-Fri 0900-1600, Sat 0900-1500, Sun 0930-1300.

Transport From Brisbane travel north via The Bruce Highway to the Caboolture turn-off, then head 26 km east, via Ningi to the bridge at the southern tip of the island.

St Helena Island
7 km off the mainland

St Helena Island National Park lies near the mouth of the Brisbane River. Often labelled Australia's Alcatraz, it was first utilised as a **penal colony** as early as 1867 and continued to house prisoners until 1932. With many remnants of the former notorious jail remaining, as well as an information centre, displays and artefacts, it offers an interesting insight in to the harsh treatment of the former convicts, many of whom later helped to put Brisbane on the map. Access only by joining guided day cruises or theatrical ghost tours (book) weekend evenings, from Manly, *AB Sea Cruises*, T33963994, www.abseacruises.com.au, from $50.

Sunshine & Fraser coasts

Introducing Sunshine and Fraser coasts

What the Gold Coast is to glitz and theme parks and Far North Queensland to the barrier reef and rainforests, the Sunshine and Fraser coasts are to sand, surf and sunshine. Just an hour north of Brisbane, the spellbinding volcanic peaks known as the **Glass House Mountains** herald your arrival in the aptly named region known as the Sunshine Coast. To the east, on the coastal fringe, is **Maroochy**, with its popular, mainly domestic, holiday resorts of **Maroochydore** and **Mooloolaba**, bathed in over 300 days of sunshine a year. Consistently, these partners in the business of the beach-based lackadaisicals, attract the ever faithful from Brisbane who go there to pitch their beach umbrellas and loose the crowds and hype of the Gold Coast. With the promise of even better things to come, the vast majority of international tourists however, sacrifice a visit to Maroochy and head north, to the much-lauded resort of **Noosa Heads**. Like the 'Belle of the ball', pretty Noosa is without doubt the most popular resort on the coast and one of the most sought after residential postal codes in Australia. With beautiful beaches, namesake national park, numerous activities and a wealth of attractive accommodation to suit all budgets, Noosa rarely disappoints. However, if you can manage to drag yourself away from her heavenly embrace, the hinterland also promises a wealth of refreshing and unusual attractions from dramatic displays of crocodile dentition at the **Australia Zoo** – the home of the infamous 'Crocodile Hunter' – and the waterfalls, dramatic coastal views and cosy B&Bs of the **Blackall Range** to the quality, colourful markets at **Eumundi**. You can even muse with dismay at a plastic pineapple the size of a small house in **Nambour** or bite the head of a freshly made ginger bread man in **Yandina**.

North of Noosa the coastal strip succumbs to the vast expanses of the **Great Sandy Region** – the largest coastal sand mass in the world. With its fascinating expanses of ancient coloured sands, sand blows, freshwater lakes and unusual wildlife to add to its appeal as the perfect place for four wheel driving, and fishing, the mainland (Cooloola) section of the Great Sandy National Park is well worthy of investigation. Yet, it offers only a taste of something even bigger and better, sitting just offshore, to the north. Like a huge trigger cocked off the mainland **Fraser Island** – the largest coastal sand island in the world – is without doubt, the most deservingly popular tourist draw card in Southern Queensland. With its unique and often unexpected range of habitats, natural features and rich biodiversity, all of which can only be fully explored by 4WD, Fraser presents the opportunity for a truly memorable eco-experience and hosts one of the most attractive resorts in Australia – **Kingfisher Bay**. The main gateway and stepping stone to Fraser is the rather unremarkable and transitory resort of **Hervey Bay**, that flies its own touristical banner between the months of July and October, proudly declaring itself as the whale-watching capital of the world.

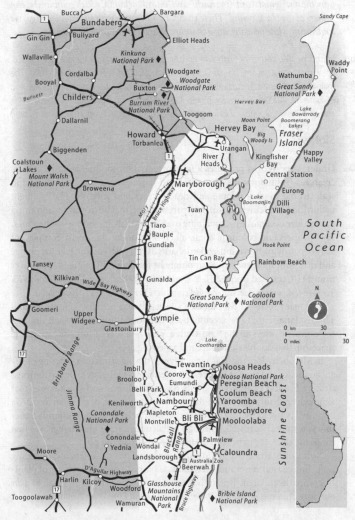

Maroochy

Colour map 3,
grid B5/C5
Population: 112,000
110 km north
of Brisbane

The name Maroochy loosely refers to an area of the Sunshine Coast that encom-passes a string of popular coastal holiday resorts from **Caloundra**, *on the northern fringe of Moreton Bay, to* **Noosa Heads**. *The largest of these is* **Maroochydore**, *the principal business and commercial capital, that sits neatly on the southern shore of the Maroochy River estuary. To the south, Maroochydore practically merges with the neighbouring resorts of* **Alexandra Heads** *and* **Mooloolaba**.

Famous for its long stretches of **pristine beach**, *and of course its climate, the region attracts mainly domestic holiday makers from Brisbane wishing to escape the hype and pretentiousness of the Gold Coast and Noosa. Beyond the beaches and the rivers there is not exactly a wealth of attractions but with some excellent* **surfing**, **fishing** *and a growing number of adrenaline pumping* **activities**, *it may tempt you to stray off the beaten track. The name Maroochydore is thought to have derived from the aboriginal words 'marutchi' and 'murukutchidha' which combined mean 'waters of the black swans'. These graceful birds, along with the equally large, yet contrasting white pelicans, are a common sight on the Maroochy River.*

Ins & outs
See Transport, page 270, for details

Maroochy VIC, corner of Sixth Ave and Aerodrome Rd, Maroochydore, T54791566, www.maroochytourism.com.au Open Mon-Fri 0900-1700, Sat/Sun 0900-1600. The main regional centre. There is also a small booth in Mooloolaba, corner of First Ave and Brisbane Rd, T1800882032, www.mooloolababeach.com.au, open Mon-Sun 0900-1700, and an office in Caloundra, 7 Calondra Rd, T54910202. All can supply free street maps.

Sights

The main tourist attractions, other than the regions surf beaches, centre around the Mooloolaba Harbour and Wharf

Underwater World promises a fine introduction to Queensland's aquatic creatures from stunningly beautiful and harmless sea dragons, otters and seals, to the more fearsome and deadly crocs and jellyfish. The highlight within the complex is an 80-m transparent tunnel that burrows through an 2.5 million litre oceanarium, containing over 20,000 fish, including wobbegongs, rays, gropers and colourful coral, all coming under the steely, complacent stare of patrolling nurse and leopard sharks. If you wish you can take the plunge and dive with these mighty elasmobranchs for about 30 minutes (non-diver from $110, certified from $83). ■ *Daily 0900-1800, from $22, child from $13, T54448488, www.underwaterworld.com.au Parklyn Parade, Mooloolaba.*

The main focus of Mooloolaba's beach based activity, centres around **The Esplanade** that has recently been developed to include such unusual sculptural odysseys as the 'Loo With a View' – a sort of futuristic maritime spaceship that doubles as a toilet and a viewing deck.

In Maroochydore the Maroochy River is the big attraction, offering pleas-ant aesthetics and a range of watersport activities (see below). One of the most striking features of the river are its resident pelicans and black swans that although enchantingly beautiful and refreshingly tame, don't seem to share a brain cell between them! Upstream the **Maroochy Waters Wetlands Sanc-tuary**, features boardwalks through melaleuca swamps and mangroves that fringe the river. It can be reached from Sports Road, Bli Bli.

North of Maroochydore, **Mount Coolum** (208 m) offers a challenging walk, fine coastal views and, incredibly, is home to over 700 species of plants In comparison, Great Britain has only about twice that – in total. ■ *1 hr one-way. Access is off Tanah St, which is off David Low Way, Coolum.*

Sunshine & Fraser coasts

Essentials

Sleeping
See inside cover for price categories

The entire coastal strip is dotted with the obligatory resorts offering comfortable 4-star self-contained apartment blocks with palm-tree fringed pools and spas. Pre-booking is advised during school and public holidays.

Maroochydore Of the many resorts **LL-L** *Argyle on the Park*, 31 Cotton Tree Parade, T54433022, is recommended, offering all the usual comforts in a fine position over looking the river and close to the beach. Most motels are located on the main drags (David Low Ave and Alexandra Parade) north and south of the town. **L-A** *Beach Motor Inn*, 61-65 Sixth Ave, T54437044, has nice units and is metres from the beach. **L-E** *Maroochy Palms Holiday Village*, 319 Bradman Ave, T54438611, www.maroochy palms.com.au Of the many motor parks in the area, this 4-star option is recommended. **C-E** *Cotton Tree Beachouse Backpackers*, Cotton Tree Parade (15), T54431755, www.cottontreebackpackers.com In a fine position overlooking the river, this backpackers is a laid-back, friendly place with a distinctly B&B feel, offering tidy dorms, double/twins, internet and free use of surfboards, kayaks and boogie boards. The Irish/Aussie owners also dish out a mean carrot cake. **C-E** *Maroochydore YHA*, 24 Schirmann St (off Cotton Tree and O'Connor), T54433151. In a more suburban position, this is a quiet, friendly place that looks after its visitors, offering motel-style unit dorms, small double/twins, one family room, large kitchen, pool, internet and free use of surf boards, canoes and fishing gear. Courtesy pick-ups, bike hire and cheap, in-house tours to the Glass House Mountains and beyond. Cheaper alternatives for vans and campers are the beach/riverside **E** *Pincushion*, Cotton Tree Parade, T1800461917, and **E** *Seabreeze*, corner of Melrose Parade and Sixth Ave, T54431167.

Mooloolaba Of the many resort complexes in Mooloolaba: **LL-L** *Agean*, 14 River Esplanade, T54441255, www.ageanmooloolaba.com.au; **LL-L** *Alexandra Beach*, corner of Alexandra Parade and Pacific Terrace, T54750600, www.alexbeach.com.au; **LL** *Nautilus*, 30 River Esplanade, T54443877, www.nautilus-at-mooloolaba.com.au; and **LL** *Zanzibar*, 47 Esplanade, T54445633, www.zanzibarresort.com.au, all offer classy facilities, are close to the beach and all amenities. **L-A** *Aquila Guest House*, 21 Box St (off King), inland near Buderim, T54453681, www.guesthousequeensland.com.au, offers superb aesthetics both inside and out, 4 deluxe en suites, gourmet breakfast and fine views. **L-A** *Mooloolaba Motel*, 46 Brisbane Rd, T54442988. One of the few motels, this modern option is well positioned with spacious 1-2 bedroom units and a pool. **B-E** *Mooloolaba Beach Backpackers*, 75 Brisbane Rd, T54443399. This is the main backpackers in 'Mooloo'. Modern but rather impersonal it offers standard and en suite dorms, standard and en suite doubles with TV and a/c, pool and internet. **E** *Mooloolaba Beach Caravan Park*, Parklyn Parade, T54441201. Powered and non-powered sites close to the beach.

Maroochydore Most of Maroochydore's restaurants and cafés are located between Aerodrome Rd and The Esplanade. *Rusty's Mexican Restaurant*, 68 Sixth Ave, T54431795, is a long-established favourite. Open daily from 1800.

Eating

Mooloolaba The Esplanade and Wharf (Parklyn Parade) are the main restaurant/café spots offering a wide array of options. One of the best is *Mooloolaba Surf Club*, The Esplanade, T54441300, offering good value for money and great views across the beach. Open Mon-Thu 1000-2200, Fri/Sat 1000-2400, Sun 0800-1000. Live entertainment every Thu-Sun in the afternoon. When it comes to fine dining *Harry's Restaurant*, Lindsay Rd, Buderim (8 km west of Mooloolaba), T54456661, is a fine choice, offering fine, modern Australian cuisine in a 120-year-old homestead in a quiet rural setting.

Tours & activities

Sunshine Coast almost rivals that of the Gold Coast for surfing with evocative named breaks such as The White House, The Groyne, Geriatrics Reef, Dead Man's and The Cheese Factory

Abseiling *Adventures Sunshine Coast*, Mooloolaba, T54448824, offer abseiling, rock climbing and rap jumping (and wilderness canoeing), from half-day from $69, full day from $99, 2-day camp from $245. (no experience necessary). **Cruising** From the sedate to the bum-breaking, *Harbour River Canal Cruises*, The Wharf, Mooloolaba, T54447477, offer leisurely trips up the Mooloolaba River 1100/1300/1430, from $13, child $4, while *Ocean Sprinter*, T54446766, offers an exhilarating 50-min blast about the bays in a rigid inflatable, from $50. *Cruise Maroochy Eco Tours*, T54765745, are a good outfit offering a wide range of nature-based cruises, including a nocturnal adventure, from 30 mins to 5½ hrs, from $33, child $21. **Diving** *Scuba World*, next door to Undersea World, Parklyn Parade, Mooloolaba, T54448595, offer shark diving, from $83 and trips to the Gneerings/Murphy Reefs and Mudjimba Island for certified divers only. **Flight seeing** *Suncoast Helicopters*, Caloundra Airport, T54996900, offer a range of scenic flights from the coast to the Glass House Mountains from $85-135. **Jet skiing** The Maroochy River and coast is becoming a top venue for jet ski adventures. *Jet Ski Hire and Tours*, T0412637363, www.jetskihiretours.com.au, offer independent hire from $75 (30 mins), 2½-hr Breakfast Tours, from $150 per ski and Offshore Tours, from $160 per ski. Skis can also be hired independently in Mooloolaba from *Ocean Jet Ski Hire*, Mooloolaba Beach, Parklyn Parade, T0412373356. **Sea kayaking** *The Aussie Sea Kayak Company*, Shop 9, The Wharf, Mooloolaba, T54775335, www.aussieseakayak.com.au, offer everything from sedate 2-hr sunset paddles from $40, to extended trips to Fraser Island and the Whitsundays. **Sky diving** *Sunshine Coast Skydivers*, Caloundra Airport, T0500522533, are a large and reputable operator providing daily 12-15,000 ft Tandems from $260. Excellent backpacker deals. *Skydive Ramblers*, T0407996400, also have a drop zone in Coolum Beach. **Surfing** There are numerous surf shops and hire outlets including *Surf Dog*, 12/110 Sixth Ave, Maroochydore, T54754565; *Bad Company*, Shop 5/6-8 Aerodrome Rd, Maroochydore, T54432457, and *Beach Beat*, 164 Alexandra Parade, Alexandra Head, T54432777. Boards cost from $25-40 per day. **Water-skiing, wake boarding and skurfing** Ski and Skurf Cable Ski Park, 325 David Low Way, Bli Bli (12 km north of Maroochydore), is a purpose-built, lake complex, offering skiing and boarding, from $25 for 2 hrs. Skurfing is essentially kneeling on a body board which, as a beginner, is great.

Transport

Local Bus *Sunshine Coast Sunbus*, T131230, are the local bus company, offering services to the Noosa Heads/Tewantin, (#1), north/southbound throughout the Sunshine Coast (#1), west to Eumundi/Cooroy/Nambour (#2, #1A). The main bus stop in Maroochydore is at the Sunshine Plaza, Horton Parade. **Bike hire** Available from *Skate Biz*, 150 Alexandra Parade, Alexandra Headlands, T54436111, from $22 per day and *Mooloolaba Bike Hire*, 25 First Ave (behind the *Sirocco Resort*), T54775303, from $20 per day. Tandems can be hired from the Maroochy VIC. **Taxi** *Sunshine Coast Taxis*, T131008.

Long distance Air Maroochydore (Sunshine Coast) Airport, www.suncoast-airport.com.au, 6 km north of Maroochydore, is serviced by *Qantas* (*Sunstate*), T131313, several times daily from **Brisbane**. Local northbound bus services stop at the airport and a taxi to Maroochydore will cost about $15. *Henry's*, 12 Noosa Dr, T54740199, www.henrys.com.au, offer express (non-stop) services between Brisbane and Maroochydore Airports and Noosa Heads, 7 times daily, from $27.50. *Sunshine Shuttle*, T0412507937, and *Sun-Air*, T54782811, offer similar services (Brisbane from $33 one-way). **Bus** The long-distance bus terminal is located in the Scotlyn Fair Shopping Centre, First Ave, Maroochydore, T54431011. *McCafferty's*, T131499, *Greyhound*, T132030 and *Suncoast Pacific*, T54431011, offer daily north/southbound services. **Train** The nearest train station is at Nambour, T132232. *Sunbus* offer regular services from there to Maroochy (#2, #1A) and Noosa (#1).

Communications Internet: available at the *Maroochy Internet Café*, Shop 7, King St, T54795061 and *Mooloolaba Internet Café*, Shop 2/22 River Esp, T54775695.   **Directory**

Noosa

*To some the former surfing backwater of Noosa is now little more than an upmarket suburb of Brisbane blighted by a Gold Coast style tourism hype. However, it does have one of the finest **surf beaches** in Queensland, a climate that is 'beautiful one day perfect the next' and is fringed with two magnificent **unspoilt national parks**. In the last three decades, the string of coastal communities known loosely as 'Noosa' have rapidly metamorphosised to become one of the most desirable holiday resorts and residential areas on the entire east coast of Australia. If you can turn a blind eye to the pretentiousness of the place, Noosa it makes it a worthwhile stop on your way north.*

Colour map 3, grid B5
Population: 65,000
145 km north of Brisbane, 187 km south of Hervey Bay

Ins and outs

Noosa's airport is 6 km north of Maroochydore which has regular bus services to the town centre. There are regular long distance buses to major cities and centres and there is also a train station at Cooroy with a bus service to Noosa Heads.

Getting there
See Transport, page 277, for further details

Noosa refers to a string of barely separated settlements that border the Noosa River and fringe the Noosa Heads National Park. From the east along the southern bank of the Noosa River, the mainly residential communities of Tewantin and Noosaville connect with each other and Noosa Heads, at the western fringe of Noosa Heads National Park. To the south of the park Sunshine Beach sits facing the ocean, east of Noosa Junction. With so many vague boundaries to these settlements, finding your way around the area is difficult and made worse by a seemingly endless string of roundabouts and inland waterways. Pick up an area map from the VIC.

Getting around

Noosa VIC is located on Hastings St, Noosa Heads, T54474988, www.noosa.com.au Open daily 0900-1700. The centre has a very helpful 24-hr touch screen display and the free *Noosa Guide* has detailed road and locality maps.

Tourist information

Sights

Noosa Heads forms the main focus for activity, hosting the main surf beach on **Laguna Bay** and the chic tourist shops, accommodation and restaurants along Hastings Street. To the south is **Noosa Junction** with Sunshine Beach Road providing the main commercial shopping area.

To the east of Noosa Heads is the pretty 454-ha **Noosa National Park** that offers sanctuary from all the tourist rumblings and some fine walks. The most popular of these is the 2.7-km **Coastal Track** that starts beside the information office at the end of Park Road, T54473243. The track, which occasionally comes under the bleary-eyed gaze of resident koalas, takes in a number of idyllic bays and headlands, before delivering you at **Alexandria Bay**. From there you can return the way you came, explore the interior of the park, continue south to the very plush northern suburbs of **Sunshine Beach**, or simply spend the day on the beach in relative isolation. Bear in mind that all the beaches that fringe the national park are unpatrolled and swimming is not recommended. The fairly unremarkable **Laguna Lookout**, across Noosa Heads and the river, can be accessed by car from Noosa Drive (Viewland Drive).

The Noosa River runs both west and south from Noosa Heads in a tangled mass of tributaries to join **Lake Weyba** (south) and **Lakes Cooroibah and Cootharaba** (west and north).

Gympie Terrace, in Noosaville, runs along the southern bank of the river and is the focus for most river and lake based activities. To the north of the river is the vast expanse of the **Great Sandy National Park**, in Cooloola, stretches northwards to Rainbow Beach and Fraser Island. As well as a number of interesting natural features, it offers some excellent four-wheel driving, walking, fishing and canoeing opportunities. Access to the park is from beyond Boreen Point, Lake Cootharaba, or Noosa North Shore via the car ferry in Tewantin, and is by 4WD only. See page for 281 further details. Various operators offer tours to the area, see Tours and activities, below.

Eumundi Markets held in the historic village of Eumundi, 23 km west, on Saturday mornings, provides a popular day trip. See page 278 for details.

Essentials

Sleeping
■ *On map, page 272*
See inside cover for price categories

Noosa is very much like a mini Gold Coast without the highrises, yet with the same almost inexhaustible range of 4-star resort complexes, self-contained holiday apartments and backpacker options. Given the sheer number, range and similarity of the resorts the best bet is to pre-book through agents according to your requirements.

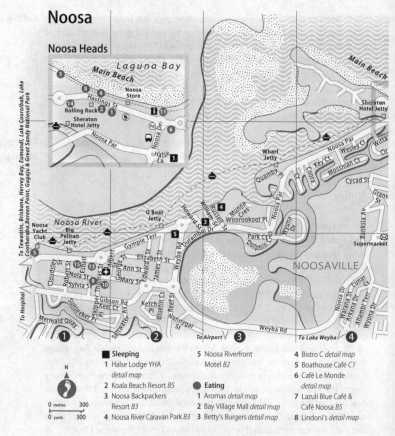

Noosa

Sleeping
1 Halse Lodge YHA *detail map*
2 Koala Beach Resort *B5*
3 Noosa Backpackers Resort *B3*
4 Noosa River Caravan Park *B3*

5 Noosa Riverfront Motel *B2*

Eating
1 Aromas *detail map*
2 Bay Village Mall *detail map*
3 Betty's Burgers *detail map*

4 Bistro C *detail map*
5 Boathouse Café *C1*
6 Café Le Monde *detail map*
7 Lazuli Blue Café & Café Noosa *B5*
8 Lindoni's *detail map*

Sunshine & Fraser coasts

These include **Accommodation Noosa**, T1800072078, www.accomnoosa.com.au; **Noosa Holidays**, T54473811, www.noosare.com.au; **Peter Dowling**, T54473566, www.peterdowlingnoosa.com.au and **Century 21**, T54472919, www.sunzine.net/noosa/century

Noosaville A-C *Noosa Riverfront Motel*, 277 Gympie Terrace, T54497595. Of the various motels in Noosaville, this option offers good value. It's very friendly and close to all amenities. **C-E** *Noosa Backpackers Resort*, 9-13 William St, T55498151, www.noosabackpackers.com.au This is the main backpacker option west of Noosa Heads. It offers tidy 4 bed dorms, en suite doubles, pool, cheap meals, cable TV and internet. **E-F** *Noosa River Caravan Park*, Russell St, T54497050. This is the best motor park/camping option in the area. Hugely popular given its riverside location and views, it offers powered and non-powered sites, modern amenities and BBQ. Book at least 2 days in advance.

Noosa Heads LL *Sheraton Noosa Resort*, Hastings St, T54494888, www.sheraton.com/noosa This is the main high profile hotel complex in Noosa Heads. It offers standard 4-star rooms and suites, pool, spa, gym and a bar/restaurant that front on to Hastings St. **C-E** *Halse Lodge YHA*, Halse Lane, T54473377, wwwhaselodge.com.au At the other end of the scale is this spacious lodge, which is only a short walk from the long-distance bus stop. It is a historic 1880s Queenslander offering a good range of rooms from 6/4 dorms to doubles, twins and triple all with shared bathrooms, bistro/bar, large quiet deck and social areas, good tour and activities desk, surf/body board hire. **C-E** *Koala Beach Resort*, 44 Noosa Dr, just over the hill near Noosa Junction, T54473355, www.koala-backpackers.com Offers fairly tired motel-style en suite dorms and doubles. It does however have its finger on the pulse and is considered the liveliest and most social of the backpackers, with a popular bar/bistro, pool and internet.

Elsewhere D-E *Melaluka/Costa Bella*, Selene St, Sunshine Beach, T54473663/1800 003663, www.melaluka.com.au Offers spotless and spacious apartment-style budget rooms with shared facilities close to the beach. Recommended. **C-F** *Gagaju*, Boreen Point, T54743522, www.travoholic.com/gagaju/ Characterful eco-backpackers-come-bush camp, located between Lakes Cooroibah and Cootharaba, on the Noosa River. Everything is built from recycled timber with dorms, doubles and powered/non-powered, shaded campsites (campfires allowed), full kitchen facilities, TV lounge room and excellent in-house half, 1 and 3-day canoe trips on the river. Pick-ups are offered from Noosa Heads. **L** *Eumarella*

Sunshine & Fraser coasts

Shores, Eumarella Rd, T5449 1254, offers something well removed from the resorts and tourist hype next to Lake Weyba and local horse trekking operation. Fully self-contained colonial and log cabin style cottages sleeping 2-6 in a bush setting overlooking the lake.

Eating
• On map, page 272
There are almost 150 restaurants in the Noosa area with 30 along Hastings St alone. Over the years many top national chefs have set up kitchen in the region, fed by their desire to escape the big cities and the stiff competition. Many foreign chefs have also followed suit adding a distinctly cosmopolitan range of options. Rumour has it that TVs famous 'Naked Chef' Jamie Oliver is looking to establish a casual restaurant in Noosa. But due to the sheer demand for new premises in Noosa, even he was pipped at the post. Other than the expensive offerings on Hastings St in Noosa Heads, the main focus for eateries are along Gympie Terrace and Thomas St in Noosaville. The best budget options are to be found along lower Noosa Dr and Sunshine Beach Rd in Noosa Junction.

Noosa Heads There are plenty of fairly pricey options along Hastings St, offering everything from modern Australian to Italian. *Café Le Monde*, T5449 2366, is one of the most popular socially with its large covered, sidewalk courtyard and live entertainment. It serves generous international and imaginative vegetarian dishes and is also popular for breakfast. Open daily 0630-late. *Lindoni's*, Hastings St, T5447 5111. Of the Italian restaurants in Noosa, *Lindoni's* has the finest reputation, a nice atmosphere and entertaining staff. Open daily 1800-2230. *Bistro C*, T5447 2855, tucked away on the beachfront this classy restaurant offers a good traditional menu and a welcome escape from the main drag overlooking the beach. Open from 0700-2130 daily. *Noosa Heads Surf Lifesaving Club*, 69 Hastings St, T5447 5395, and the Sunshine Beach Surf Club (Spinnakers), corner of Duke St and Belmore Terrace, Sunshine Beach, T5474 5177, both offer value for money and great sea views. **Bay Village Mall** on Hastings St has a food court with several cheap options. *Sierra*, 10 Hastings St, T5447 4800, is a very popular café with rather crammed seating, but a good laid-back atmosphere, good coffee and value breakfasts. *Aromas*, 32 Hastings St, T5474 9788, is spacious and modern also serving excellent coffee and providing a great spot to watch the world go by. Open daily 0700-late. *Betty's Burgers* is an old favourite that is now trading from a caravan beside the beach at the end of Hastings St. The $2 burgers are almost legendary.

Noosaville Gympie Terrace and Thomas St in Noosaville present all sorts of slightly more affordable options including the excellent and healthy *Thai Breakers*, corner of Gympie Terrace and *The Cockleshell*, T5455 5500. Open daily from 0630-1500/ 1700-2130. *The Natural Thai*, Shop 1/10 Thomas St, T5449 0144, is equally good, with excellent service. *Max's Native Sun*, No 1 Islander Resort, Thomas St, T5447 1931, is a small BYO and offers something different in quiet and casual surrounds, with a specialization in duck dishes, from duckling and split pea soup to the generous 'Duck Indulgence'. Open Tue-Sat from 1800. *Magic of India*, T5449 7788, just a few doors down and is reputed to be the best Indian takeaway in Noosa. Open dine-in Tue-Sun from 1730. *Seawater Café*, 197 Gympie Terrace, T5449 7215, offers generous and affordable seafood platters, fish and chips in colourful surroundings. Open daily for breakfast, lunch and dinner. *The Boathouse Café*, 142 Gympie Terrace, T5474 4444, has a loyal following with its casual but stylish Mediterranean dishes. Open Wed-Sat 1000-late, Sun 1000-1900. Live entertainment Sun 1530-1830.

Elsewhere *Jetty Restaurant*, T5485 3167, overlooking Lake Cootharaba at Boreen Point, offers a fine escape from the Noosa hype and is deservingly popular, especially for lunch. It has a mainly traditional menu that changes daily. Nearby *Apollonian Hotel*, Laguna St, Boreen Point, T5485 3100, is also well known for its delicious Sunday spit-roasts. Towards Noosa Junction, on Noosa Dr, *Noosa Reef Hotel*, T5447 4477, offers fine views, value for money and is especially good for families. Nearby, *Lazuli Blue Café*, 9 Sunshine Beach Rd, T54480055, offers all you can eat vegetarian buffets for $8.50, while *Café Noosa*, 1 David Low Way, T54473949, is a popular dine-in/take away pizzeria, offering all the usual toppings from $12.20.

The in-house bar at the *Koala Beach Resort*, 44 Noosa Dr, T54473355, is considered the **Entertainment** liveliest under thirties haunt in town, with *Reef Hotel's Reef Bar*, further up the hill (towards Noosa Heads), taking the overflow after closing at around midnight. On the upper level of the **Bay Village Mall**, on Hastings St, is the fairly unremarkable and pretentious dance and live band venue Rolling Rock. Open 2100-0300 daily, smart/casual, $5 cover. Of the regular pubs the new *Irish Murphy's*, corner of Sunshine Beach Rd and Noosa Dr, T54553344, offers the usual ambience, gimmicks, pub grub and fine, over-priced traditional beers. The main **Noosa Cinema**, is located on Sunshine Beach Rd, Noosaville, T1300366339.

Mary Ryan's Books, Music and Coffee, Bay Village, Hastings St, T54554848, is worth a **Shopping** muse while *Noosaville Disposals*, 249 Gympie Terrace, Noosaville and *Noosa Camping*, Shop 6, 28 Sunshine Beach Rd, Noosa Junction, can supply/hire camping equipment.

There are plenty of mainly water based activities in and around Noosa from surf les- **Tours &** sons to river cruises, as well as the more unusual like multi-day canoe trips and camel **activities** rides. *Noosa 4WD Eco Tours*, T54491400, offer full and half day tours to the Great Sandy National Park (Cooloola) and beyond from $70. *Laguna Bay Tours*, T1800114434, offer a wide range of day tours Mon/Wed/Fri to the Great Sandy National Park (Cooloola), Sunshine Coast Hinterland, including Australia Zoo (from $35), the Blackall Range and the Eumundi Markets (from $10). *Fraser Island Adventure Tours*, T54446957, offer an exciting day trip to Fraser Island, taking in the main sights of the Great Sandy National Park (Cooloola) along the way, from $130, child $90. *Fraser Island Trailblazers Tours*, T1800626673, www.trailblazertours.com.au (*Noosa Backpackers Resort*) offer a good value 3-day Camping Safari, via the Great Sandy National Park (Cooloola section), from $245.

Camel safaris *Camel Safaris*, T54424397, based on Noosa North Shore have a fleet of dromedaries offering safaris of 1- to 2-hr along Forty Mile Beach (Great Sandy National Park/Cooloola) from $42. If you go ask to see 'Rocky' taking a drink? Man what that animal can do with a garden hose!

Cruises and boat hire There are numerous operators that offer sedate cruises up and down the Noosa River from Noosa Heads to Tewantin and beyond. The main ferry terminals are (from west to east): **Harbour Marine Village** (Gympie Terrace, Noosaville), **O Boat Jetty**, **Big Pelican**, **Noosa Yacht Club** and at Noosa Heads – **Sheraton Hotel jetty**. *Noosa Ferry Cruise*, T54780040, run regular services between all these stops, daily, from 0920-1930, from $8.50, child $3.50, family $20 one way. An 'All day pass' costs $12.50. If a spot of Jazz or calypso tickles your fancy then *Noosa Sound Cruises*, T54473466, can oblige, with morning, or sunset cruises from only $20. *Noosa River Cruises*, T54497362, offer a 5-hr trip to Lake Cootharaba daily from $60, while *Cooloola Cruises*, T54499177, offer a similar cruise, with an additional 4WD combo that takes in the main sights of the Great Sandy National Park (Cooloola), from $95, child $62. Recommended. For much faster action try the (small group) *Ecstasea Safaris*, T54472726, half-day from $65, or *Oceanrider*, T1800001386. The latter will hurtle you at over 50 knots (that's 'boatie' speak for 'hold on') around Noosa Heads and up the Noosa River for 75 mins, from $60. At the other extreme you might like to take your sweetheart out for a quiet Gondola Cruise, T0412929369, 1 hr from $90 (including seafood dinner, from $110). Though what happens to the shrimps and chardonnay when the latter two craft pass one another (never mind the gesticulations that result) would surely be worth twice the price! There are numerous boat hire operators along the riverbank (Gympie Terrace) where you can hire U-Drive Boats, BBQ Boats, speed boats, kayaks and jet skis (from $55, for 30 mins).

Diving *Noosa Blue Water Dive*, Boatshed, Gympie Terrace, T54471300, offer 4-day open-water courses form $399 and ½-day charters from $99.

Fishing *MV Trekka*, T54424919, offer ½-, ¾-, full-day deep-sea fishing from $95. *Noosa River Fishing and Crab Tours*, T0407206062, and *Mud Crab Adventures*, T0402834001, offer half day finger nipping adventures, from $70.

Flight-seeing *Noosa and Maroochy Flying Services*, T54500516, www.noosaaviation. com.au, offer a range of scenic flights from coastal trips to Fraser Island and reef safaris, from $45-439. For something different *Dimona Motor Glider Flights* (cross between a light aircraft and a glider), based at the Sunshine Coast Airport, Maroochy, T54780077.

Horse trekking The rather dubiously named *Clip Clop Horse Treks,* Eumarella Rd, Lake Weyba, T54491254, offer a wide range of options from 2-hr treks to 6-day adventures. Full day from $150. *Bush and Beach*, T54471369, based on Noosa North Shore, offers 1- to 2-hr rides suitable for beginners.

Parasailing and kite surfing *Fly High Para flying*, T0500872123, offer short flights from Main Beach, while *Kitesurf*, T54556677, and *Wind 'N' Sea*, T0414727765, will introduce you to the new and exciting experience of kite surfing from $95 for 2 hrs.

Sea kayaking and lake/river canoeing *Elanda Point Canoe Company*, T54853165, www.elanda.com.au, offer a wide range of exciting adventures on the waterways of the Great Sandy National Park (Cooloola), from half-day (from $68), 2-day backpacker special (from $198), to 5-day/4-night (from $880). Independent hire is also available. Recommended. *Noosa Ocean Kayaking Tours*, T0418787577, offer sea kayaking around the Noosa National Park, from $45 (2 hrs) and river trips, from $40 (2 hrs). Independent hire is also available, from $35 per day.

Spas No doubt after a few hours on a camel or a horse your weathered cheeks and other bodily parts would greatly benefit from a spa or a massage. *Newland*, 28 Sunshine Beach Rd, T54748212, the *Noosa Spa* (South Pacific Resort), T54471424 and the 'mobile' *State of Health Company*, T0412181396, can oblige, from $55-70 per hr.

Surfing There are more 'Learn to Surf' operators vying for your custom on Main Beach than there are beach umbrellas. Generally they are all very professional and run by pros and/or experts-or at least those very clever, fit looking folk, who manage to stand up on them. Most claim they will get you doing the same at least for several nanoseconds after a 2-hr session, from about $35. Companies include *Wavesense*, T54749076; *Learn to Surf,* (with world champ Merrick Davies) T0418787577; and for girls only the *Girls Surf School*, T0418787577. *Noosa Longboards*, Shop 4, 64 Hastings St, T54472828, hire long/short surfboards and body boards, from $25/15/10 per hr.

Sky diving *Sunshine Coast Skydivers*, Caloundra Airport, T0500 522533, are a large and reputable operator providing daily 12-15,000-ft tandems from $260. Excellent backpacker deals. *Skydive Ramblers*, T04 07996400, also have a drop zone on Coolum Beach.

Local Bus *Sunshine Coast Sunbus*, T131230, are the local bus company offering services to the Noosa Heads/Tewantin, (#10), north/southbound to the Sunshine Coast (#1), west to Eumundi/Cooroy/Nambour (#12). **Bike hire** Available from *Noosa Bike Tours and Hire*, T54743322, www.noosabikehire.com, delivery and pick-ups and *Mammoth Cycles*, corner of Gympie Terrace and Thomas St, Noosaville, T54743322, both from $20 per day. **Car hire** If you wish to explore the Great Sandy National Park (Cooloola) there are several 4WD hire companies that can oblige including *Henry's*, 12 Noosa Dr, T54740199, www.henrys.com.au; *Thrifty*, Noosa Dr, T136139 and *Coastal 4WD Hire*, T1300726001. *Henry's* also hire 'fun-tops' from $44 per day. The Tewantin car ferries cross the Noosa River (end of Moorindil St) and provide access to the Great Sandy National Park (Cooloola). It operates from Nov-Jan Sun-Thu 0430-2230, Fri/Sat 0430-0030 and Feb-Oct Mon-Thu 0600-2230, Fri 0600-0030, Sat 0500-0030, Sun 0500-2230, from $4. **Taxi** *Sunshine Coast Taxis*, T131008.

Long distance Air The nearest airport is the **Maroochydore (Sunshine Coast) Airport**, www.suncoast-airport.com.au, 6 km north of Maroochydore. *Qantas* (*Sunstate*), T131313, provide daily services from Brisbane. Local northbound bus services stop at the airport and a taxi to Noosa Heads will cost about $55. *Henry's*, 12 Noosa Dr, T54740199, www.henrys.com.au, offer express (non-stop) services between Brisbane Airport/ Maroochydore Airport and Noosa Heads 7 times daily, from $27.50. *Sunshine Shuttle*, T0412507937, offer similar services (Brisbane from $44 one-way). **Bus** The long-distance bus terminal is located on the corner of Noosa Parade and Noosa Dr, Noosa Heads. *McCafferty's*, T131499, *Greyhound*, T132030 and *Suncoast Pacific*, T54431011, offer daily north/southbound services. Services include Rockhampton (2 daily), from $65, 9 hrs; Hervey Bay (5 daily), from $20, 3 hrs; and Brisbane (*Suncoast Pacific or McCaffertys*) daily from $16-27, 3 hrs. *Suncoast Pacific* also offer regular services to Tin Can Bay. *Harvey World Travel*, Shop 2 Lanyana Way, Noosa Heads, T54474077 and *Palm Tree Tours*, Bay Village, Hastings St, T54749166, act as local booking agents. **Train** The nearest train station is at Cooroy, T132232. *Sunbus* offer services from there to Noosa Heads (route #12).

Banks Most major branches/ATMs are on Hastings St, Noosa Heads or Sunshine Beach Rd, Noosa Junction. Currency exchange at *Harvey World Travel*, Shop 2 Lanyana Way, Noosa Heads, T54474077. **Car hire** *Avis*, corner of Hastings St and Noosa Dr, T54474933 (from $43), *Budget*, Bay Village, Hastings St, Noosa Heads, T54474588. **Communications** Internet: *Travel Bugs*, Shop 3/9, Sunshine Beach Rd, Noosa Junction, T54748530 (open daily 0800-2200); *Koala Backpackers*, 44 Noosa Dr, Noosa Junction. **Post office**: 91 Noosa Dr. Open Mon-Fri 0830-1730, Sat 0830-1230 Post Restante, T54473280. **Medical services** *Chemist Night and Day*, Hastings St. Open daily 0900-2100; **Noosa Hospital**, 111 Goodchap St, T54559200; **Noosaville Medical Centre**, corner of Thomas and Mary Sts, T54424922. Open Mon-Thu 0800-2000, Fri-Sun 0800-1800. **Useful numbers** Police: 48 Hastings St, T54745255.

Sunshine Coast Hinterland

With a name like 'Sunshine Coast' it is hardly surprising that the vast majority of travellers take the title literally and head ad nauseam for the beach. But, although the swathes of golden sand will not disappoint, if you allow some time to explore the hinterland you will find a wealth of other attractions and strange enigmas, from colourful markets, quaint villages and giant 'walk-in' fruits, to perhaps the greatest oddity of them all – television's infamous 'Crocodile Hunter'.

Colour map 3, grid B5/C5

Ins & outs

Best visited on a tour from Brisbane or Noosa, see pages 256 and 275, or in your own vehicle

VIC in Noosa, T54474988 and Maroochydore, T54791566, www.maroochytourism.com.au, can provide information on the major attractions, along with accommodation listings and location maps. Montville, T54785544, www.montvillage.com.au, and Maleny, T54999033, information centres offer more localized information. If you are exploring from the south the Caboolture VIC, BP Caboolture North Travel Centre, Bruce Highway, Burpengary, T1800833100, can also be of assistance. Open daily 0830-1700. There is a QPWS office on Sunday Creek Rd, Kenilworth, T54460925.

Sights

Eumundi

The historic 19th-century former timber town of Eumundi, 1 km off the Bruce Highway and 23 km west of Noosa, on Noosa Road, is pretty enough even without its famous markets. But if your timing is right, a visit to this creative extravaganza is well worth it. Every Saturday and, to a lesser extent, Wednesday mornings, the village becomes a bustling conglomerate of over 300 fascinating arts, crafts and produce stalls, that combined offer excellent quality, atmosphere and endlessly colourful aesthetics. It seems everything is on offer from kites and bandanas to neck massages and boomerangs. The markets kick off at about 0700 and start winding up about 1500. The best time to go early is on Saturday early before the day heats up and the tourist buses arrive. It can get busy and a little stressful. A fine place to have breakfast is *Chuckles Café*, on Memorial Drive, across the road from the markets, open from 0600-1700. ■ *Getting there: numerous tours are on offer from Noosa or Brisbane (see below).*

Yandina

In the small town of Yandina, 15 km south of Eumundi, 1 km west off the Bruce Highway, is the **Ginger Factory** which is the largest of its type in the world. Here you can witness the manufacturing process, watch cooking demonstrations, ride the 'Cane Train' and of course, purchase various end products from jam to the obligatory smiley Ginger Bread Men. ■ *Daily 0900-1700. Free. T54467096. 50 Pioneer Rd.*

The historic 1853 *Yandina Station Homestead*, 684 Yandina Creek Road, T54466000, towards the coast via the Yandina-Coolum Road, is one of the best restaurants in the region. Open for lunch on Fridays, Saturdays and Sundays from 1200 and for dinner on Fridays and Saturdays from 1800. Recommended.

Blackall Range Tourist Drive

Blackall Range Tourist Drive that straddles the Blackall Range from Nambour to the Glass House Mountains is highly recommended, offering everything from national parks with waterfalls and short rainforest walks to fine coastal views and cosy B&Bs. From Yandina or the Bruce Highway, head west just north of Nambour on the Nambour-Mapleton Road. **Nambour** itself is a busy agricultural service centre for the sugar cane and pineapple industries.

The latter is celebrated with remarkable over-kill at the rather kitschy **Big Pineapple Complex**, 10 km south and 1 km west of the Bruce Highway. The biggest and unavoidable attraction here, especially for children, is the enigmatic 15-m 'Big Pineapple' that seems, inexplicably, to have the same effect on passers-by as nectar does bees. It is just one of Australia's 33-strong inventory of 'big man-made monoliths' from koalas to bananas. As well as the obligatory photographs, you can loose all your street credibility with a tour the plantation on a miniature train, or worse still spend your money on Percy Pineapple key-rings and fridge magnets. Nearby is the 'Nutmobile' at the Macadamia Nut Factory, but let's not even go there! ■ *Daily 0900-1700. Free. T54421333.*

Back on the Nambour-Mapleton Road you begin the ascent up the Blackall Range to reach the pleasant little town of **Mapleton**. As well as its own great views and attractive B&Bs, Mapleton is the gateway to **Mapleton Falls National Park**. The heady views of the 120-m falls can be accessed 17 km west on Obi Obi Road. Nearby, the 1.3-km Wompoo Circuit walk winds through rainforest and eucalypts providing excellent views of the Obi Obi Valley. Obi Obi was a noted Aboriginal warrior and wompoo refers to a beautiful native pigeon.

From Mapleton the road heads south along the range through the similar aesthetics and amenities of **Flaxton village** and the **Kondalilla National Park**. This 327-ha park is accessed and signposted 1 km south of Flaxton and offers views of the 90-m **Kondalilla Falls**, from the 2.1-km Picnic Creek trail and the 2.7-km Kondalilla Falls circuit, that winds its way down through rainforest to the base of the falls. Neither of the parks offers camping facilities.

First settled by fruit growers in 1887, historic **Montville**, 5 km south of Flaxton, is the main tourist hub along the Blackall Range. Replete with European-style historic buildings, chic cafés, galleries and souvenir shops, selling everything from Scottish shortbread to cuckoo clocks, it provides a pleasant stop for lunch or a stroll. Nearby, **Lake Baroon** also offers a pleasant spot for a picnic. Although undoubtedly very touristy, Montville has not yet been spoilt by all the hype and indeed has seen many visitors so enchanted and so delighted to find such a contrasting and quaint little place away from the coast, that they search out the nearest B&Bs in order to stay longer.

From Montville the road continues south taking in the **Gerrard and Balmoral Lookouts** that offer memorable coastal views from Noosa Heads in the north, to Caloundra and Bribie Island in the south.

Turning inland you then encounter the equally pretty aesthetics of **Maleny** which, like Montville, offers many interesting arts and crafts galleries, good B&Bs and a winery. At the far end of the town turn left down the narrow Maleny-Stanley Road to access Mountain View Road (left). Heading back towards the coast you are then almost immediately offered the first stunning views of the Glass House Mountains to the south from **McCarthy's Lookout**. A few kilometres further on is the 41-ha **Mary Cairncross Scenic Reserve**, the legacy of 19th-century environmentalist Mary Cairncross. If you can manage to drag yourself away from the similar views on offer there, you can also visit the parks environmental centre or take a stroll through the rainforest (1.7 km), T54999907. From the Cairncross Reserve, the road descends the Blackall Range towards **Landsborough**, which is the northern gateway to the spellbinding Glass House Mountains.

Glass House Mountains National Park

The Glass House Mountains provide superb natural aesthetics and are indeed a wonderful sight but they do nothing for safe driving. Somehow, the 13 volcanic peaks that dominate the scene from all directions are utterly absorbing and will, if you are not careful, have you swerving all over the road. Gradual weathering by both wind and water has, over the last 20 million years, created the distinctive mountain peaks named collectively in the passing by Captain Cook in 1770 – who it is believed thought the peaks looked similar to Glass furnaces in his native Yorkshire. The highest peak is **Mount Beerwah** (556 m), while everybody's favourite has to be the distinctly knobbly **Mount Coonowrin** (377 m). Although the best views are actually from Old Gympie Road – which runs north to south, just west of Landsborough, Beerwah and Glass House Mountains Village – there is an official lookout on the southern edge of the park, 3 km west off Old Gympie Road. When it comes to bush walking and summit climbing, **Mount Ngungun** (253 m) is the most accessible (Fullertons Road of Old Gympie or Coonowrin Roads) while **Mount Tibrogargan** (364 m) and Mount Beerwah also offer base viewpoints and two to three rough summit tracks. Sadly, pointy Mount Coonowrin is closed to public access due to the danger of rock falls. There is no camping allowed in the park. Several companies offer walking and climbing adventures (see below).

Australia Zoo Of all Queensland's many wildlife attractions, it is the Australia Zoo that has folks flocking with more enthusiasm than the wildlife does for free handouts within them. The reason for this has resulted from the hype and exposure of the famous (or infamous) Crocodile Hunter (alias Steve Irwin), to whom the zoo is official homebase. Founded by Steve's father, the collection is now – thanks to his son in heir's popularity and antics – developing faster than a crocodile can clamp its jaws around a dead chicken. The zoo houses a wide array of well-maintained displays exhibiting over 550 native and non native species ranging from austere wedge tailed eagles and insomniac wombats to enormous 20-ft pythons and senescent Galapagos tortoises. Of course the biggest attraction of the park are the numerous crocodiles, or more to the incisor point, the crocodile feeding that is enthusiastically demonstrated daily at 1330. Many visitors are unwittingly attracted to the zoo to see Steve himself, in the hope of witnessing first hand, his inimitable (or appalling, depending on your viewpoint) style of feeding the mighty reptiles. However, Steve is rarely there and the job is left to his able staff. Over all, the park is magnificent and the animals are mighty, variant and well looked after. But what most definitely lets the place down is the sheer megalomania so apparent in the shop with its talking 'Steve' and 'Terri' dolls and personal clothing lines that even include a special kids-line after Bindi (their infant daughter). ■ *Daily 0830-1600, $16.50, child $8.50, family $40. T54941134, www.crocodilehunter.com.au Glass House Mountains Rd, Beerwah. Free transportation available from Noosa (Wed/Sat/Sun) and Maroochy, Mooloolaba and Caloundra (daily). Phone for details.*

Essentials

Sleeping There are numerous excellent B&Bs in the region all promising the ultimate country haven or romantic weekend retreat. See the VIC for complete listings. In Mapleton, Flaxton and Montville area are: **LL-L** *Falls B&B and Rainforest Cottages*, 20 Kondalilla Falls Rd, near Flaxton, T54457000, www.thefallscottages.com.au; **LL** *Narrows Escape*, Narrows Rd, Montville, T54785000, www.narrowsescape.com.au and more central and affordable **A** *Montville Mountain Inn*, Main St, Montville, T54429499, www.montville inn.com.au, are all recommended. In and around Maleny the views from **L** *Roseville House*, 226 Maleny-Montville Rd, T54943411, and the 'spa with a view' at the incredible and aptly named **LL** *Eyrie Escape B&B*, 316 Brandenburg Rd, Bald Knob, Mooloolah, T54948242, www.eyrie-escape.com.au, take some beating. There are a small number of motor parks scattered around the area, including **B-E** *Lilyponds Holiday Park*, 26 Warruga St, Mapleton, T54457238, and **C-E** *Glass House Mountains Tourist Park*, Glass House Mountains Rd, Beerburrum, T54960151.

Eating There are many fine restaurants and cafés. *Tree Tops Gallery Restaurant*, Kondalilla Falls Rd, near Flaxton, T1800087330, www.treehouses.com.au, which also has equally excellent cabin-style accommodation. *Poets Café*, 167 Main St, Montville, T54785479, and *King Ludwig's German Restaurant and Bar*, T54999377, overlooking the Glass House Mountains, on Glass House Mountains Rd, are also excellent.

Glass House Mountains Adventure Company, T54749166, offers a day's summit climbing combined with a trip to the Australia Zoo from $100, half-day from $49. *Skydrifter*, Glass House Mountains, T54387003, offers balloon flights over the mountains, from $175-240. *Storeyline Tours*, T54741500, and *Noosa Hinterland Tours*, T54743366, both offer a range of tours to hinterland attractions including the Eumundi Markets (from $12) and the Australia Zoo, from $32. *Tropical Coastal Tours*, T54749200, do the Eumundi market run form Noosa, from $12, child $7 return. *Off Beat Tours*, T54735135, www.offbeattours.com.au, are a reputable outfit offering 4WD eco-tours, from $11.

Rainbow Beach and Great Sandy National Park (Cooloola)

With access limited to 4WD only from Noosa from the south and a 76-km diversion from Gympie on the Bruce Highway from the north, the mainland – Cooloola Coast – section of the Great Sandy National Park and its delightful, neighbouring coastal communities of Rainbow Beach and **Tin Can Bay**, are all too often missed by travellers in their eagerness to reach Hervey Bay and Fraser Island. As well as the numerous and varied attractions and activities on offer within the 56,000-ha park including huge **sand blows**, ancient **coloured sands** and weathered **wrecks**, Tin Can Bay offers an opportunity to feed wild dolphins, and Rainbow Beach an ideal rest stop off the beaten track, as well as southerly access to **Fraser Island**.

Colour map 3, grid B5
Population: 850
144 km north of Noosa, 110 km south of Hervey Bay

See Transport, page 283, for details

Ins & outs

For general information either contact Cooloola VIC, Bruce Highway, Kybong (15 km south of Gympie), T54835554, www.cooloola.org.au, open daily 0900-1700, or an independently run VIC, 8 Rainbow Beach Rd, Rainbow Beach, T54863227, open daily. For more information about Tin Can Bay, T54864855, www.tincanbaytourism.org.au QPWS, Rainbow Beach Rd, T54863160, have detailed information on the Great Sandy National Park (including Fraser Island) and issue camping/RAM Fraser Island permits. Open daily 0700-1600.

Sights

Along with Fraser Island, Great Sandy National Park forms the largest sand mass in the world. For millennia sediments, washed out from the river courses of the New South Wales coast, have been steadily carried north and deposited in vast quantities. Over time the virtual desert has been colonized by vegetation that now forms vast tracks of mangrove and rainforest, which in turn provides a varied habitat for a rich and unique variety of wildlife.

Perhaps the most incredible feature of the park is the magnificent **coloured sands** that extend from Rainbow Beach to Double Island Point. Over 200 m high in places and eroded into ramparts of pillars and groves, the sands colourful palette of over 40 hues, from blood red to brilliant white, glow in the rays of the rising sun. Carbon dating of the sands has placed them well into the realms of the ancients, with some deposits being over 40,000 years old. As such, it is little wonder that they are steeped in Aboriginal legend. According to the Kabi tribe who frequented the area long before the Europeans, the mighty sands were formed and coloured by the Rainbow Spirit who was killed there in his efforts to save a beautiful maiden.

Other features of the park include the **Carlo Sand Blow**, just south of Rainbow Beach, a favourite haunt for hang gliders and the wreck of the cargo ship *Cherry Venture* which ran aground in 1973. The views from the **lighthouse** on Double Island – which is actually a headland, falsely named by Captain Cook in 1770 – will also prove memorable.

All the features of the park can be explored by a network of 4WD and **walking** trails. Other popular activities include horse trekking and fishing. At the

Sunshine & Fraser coasts

southern end of the park (accessed from Noosa), the lakes **Cootharaba** and **Cooroibah** are popular for boating and canoeing.

Located at the northern edge of the park the laid-back, yet fast developing, seaside village of **Rainbow Beach** provides an ideal base from which to explore the park and as a stepping-stone to Fraser Island. **Inskip Point**, 14 km north, serves as the southerly access point to the great island paradise.

Tin Can Bay, located west of Rainbow Beach on the banks of the Tin Can Bay Inlet, is a popular base for fishing and boating but by far its biggest attraction is the visiting pod of **wild dolphins** that almost religiously gather for their free handouts, every morning at 0800 around the Northern Point boat ramp.

Sleeping One of the most unusual and attractive places to stay in the area is on board your own houseboat. This innovative method gives you free access around the Great Sandy Strait and western shores of Fraser Island. *Luxury Afloat Houseboats*, Norman Pt, Tin Can Bay, T54864864, www.luxuryafloat.com.au and *Rainbow Beach Houseboats*, T54863146, www.sunfish.com.au/rbhb/htm, has a range of craft and packages. Alternatively, for yachts, try *Fraser Island Rent-A-Yacht*, Tin Can Bay Marina, T54864814, www.rent-a-yacht.com.au Prices for houseboats range from about 3 nights midweek from $660 to 7 nights from $1,540 (low season) to $825-1,925 (high season).

Back on terra firma in Rainbow Beach is **LL-L** *Rainbow Getaway Apartments*, corner of Rainbow Beach Rd and Double Island Dr, T54863500, a modern complex with 29 self-contained units (some with spa), pool and gym. More secluded is **L** *Rainbow Shores Resort*, Rainbow Shores Dr, T54863999, www.rainbowshores.com.au, a fine eco-resort set in native bush and close to the beach, with fully self-contained villas, bungalows and apartments, a pool and in-house activities. There are 2 backpackers in the village. The newest is the modern, purpose-built **C-E** *Rocks Backpackers Resort*, Spectrum St, T1800 646867/54863711, that offers en suite singles, doubles and dorms, bar/restaurant, pool and internet. **E** *Rainbow Beach Backpackers*, 66 Rainbow Beach Rd, a little further from the centre, T54863288, rainbowbeachback@excite. com.au, which is small but comfortable, dorms, doubles and internet. For a motor park, try 3-star **B-E** *Rainbow Waters Holiday Park*, Carlo Rd, T54863200, set in 23 acres of parkland next to the water, with self-contained cabins, powered and non-powered sites, kiosk but no camp kitchen.

In Tin Can Bay, at the top of the range you will find **L-A** *Dolphin Waters Holiday Apartments*, 40 Esplanade, T54862600, that has 10 modern 1- and 2-bedroom self-contained apartments and a salt water pool. A cheaper option is **C** *Sandcastle Motel*, Tin Can Bay Rd, T54864555. There are 3 motor parks in the area including **D-E** *Golden Trevally Caravan Park*, Trevally St, T54864411, that offers en suite/standard powered and non-powered sites. Great Sandy National Park (Cooloola) hosts 20 varied **QPWS camp-sites**. The main site is the Freshwater camping area, 20 km southeast of Rainbow Beach. It provides water, showers and toilets, but fires are banned. Access is by 4WD only. Booking centre open Mon-Fri 1300-1500, T54497959, otherwise contact the QPWS office in Rainbow Beach.

Tours & activities *Sun Safari Tours*, T54863154, offer day or overnight trips to Fraser Island and the Great Sandy National Park (Cooloola). If you want to go it alone, *Aussie Adventure 4WD*, T54863599, hire 2-9 seat 4WD vehicles. *Fraser Explorer Tours*, T54473845, www.fraser-is.com, a good option if you are visiting Fraser Island from Noosa. Their 2/3-day tour has the added attraction of taking in the sights of the Cooloola section of the Great Sandy National Park on the way, from $170-304. For Fraser Island ferry services, see page 288.

Rainbow Beach is 76 km east of the Bruce Highway at Gympie. Alternative access is by **Transport**
4WD only from Tewantin, 3 km east of Noosaville, Noosa River ferry 0600-2200, from
$4. *Polley's Coaches*, T54822700, offer twice daily (weekday) services from Gympie to
Tin Can Bay and Rainbow Beach.

Fraser Island

Jutting out from the eastern Australian coast is the incredible 162,900-ha land   *Colour map 3,*
mass known as Fraser Island – the biggest sand island in the world. Part of the   *grid A5/6 & B5*
Great Sandy National Park, which extends on to the mainland south of the   *123 km in length*
island, Fraser is now fully protected and was afforded **World Heritage** *listing in*   *and 27 km at its*
1992. It is, without a doubt, a very special place; a dynamic 800,000-year-old   *widest point*
quirk of nature blessed with stunning aesthetics and hosting a rich and unique
biodiversity. For the vast majority of visitors, the island presents a landscape far
from the plays of the imagination. For beyond a few **sand blows***, seemingly end-*
less stretches of **beach** *and, of course, its network of* **4WD tracks** *it is no Sahara*
and certainly no desert. Blanketed in thick and variant **rainforest** *interspersed with*
almost 200 freshwater **lakes** *and numerous small* **streams***, it really does surprise even*
the most knowledgeable of environmentalists or adventure tourists.

As well as its stunning aesthetics, its sheer scale and its rich **wildlife***, Fraser*
presents a great opportunity to try your hand at four-wheel driving and also plays
host to one of the best resorts in the country. And despite the fact the island attracts
over 300,000 visitors annually it is still possible to find a little peace and solitude –
but only just.

Ins and outs

Vehicular access is from Hervey Bay (Urangan) to Moon Point and Kingfisher Bay, River   **Getting there**
Head (20 mins south of Hervey Bay) to Kingfisher Bay and Wanggoolba Creek and from   *See Transport, page*
Rainbow Beach to Hook Point which is the southern most tip of the Island.   *288, for details*

By far the best way to experience Fraser Island is to stay for at least 3 days and to hire   **Getting**
your own 4WD. Other than the sheer freedom it also presents an ideal opportunity to   **around**
get a feel of what an expensive 4WD is all about. Having said that walking is hard to
beat – to experience the sights, sounds and smells that would otherwise be missed.

VICs and QPWS offices on the mainland can provide most of the necessary information   **Tourist**
on the island. On the island itself there are QPWS ranger stations at Eurong, T41279128,   **information**
Open Mon 1000-1600, Tue-Thu 0700-1600, Fri-Sun 1400-1600, Central Station,
T41279191, Dundubara, T41279138 and Waddy Point, T41279190 (all open variable
times). The resorts, especially *Kingfisher Bay Resort*, are also a valuable source of information. A vital piece of kit is the very informative and detailed 1: 130,000 Fraser Island
Tourist Map ($9) supplied by the resorts.

History

Fraser Island has a fascinating human history that may date back as far as
40,000 years. The Butchulla tribe were the first indigenous people to inhabit
the island, which they called K'gari. According to Butchulla legend, Beeral,
the great god who created the land, changed K'gari, his spirit helper, into an
idyllic island with trees, flowers, animals, lakes and people for company. For
thousands of years the Butchulla lived in harmony with their environment,

Fraser Island

Sandy Cape

Sandy Cape Lighthouse

Orchid Beach
QPWS Ranger Station
Waddy Point
Airstrip
Champagne Pools
Middle Head
Indian Head

Wathumba

Hervey Bay

Woralie Rd
Lake Bowarrady
QPWS Ranger Station
Dundubara

Lake Allom
Cathedral Beach **1**

Moon Point
Bullock Rd
Northern Rd

Moon Pt
Boomerang Lakes
Knifeblade Sand Blow
The Pinnacles
Maheno

To Hervey Bay

Happy Valley Rd
Eli Creek

Yidney Scrub

Urangan

Postans Rd
Bogimbah Rd
Fraser Island Retreat **4**
Happy Valley
Sailfish **6**

East Beach

River Heads

Kingfisher Bay **5**

Smith Rd

Mary River Heads

Lake McKenzie
QPWS Ranger Station
Wanggoolba Creek
Lake Wabby

Ungowa

Central Station **1**
Lake Birrabeen
QPWS Ranger Station
Eurong Beach Resort **2**
Fraser Island Beach Houses **3**

Lake Benaroon
Lake Boomanjin

South Pacific Ocean

Dillinghams Rd

Toby's Gap Airstrip
Dilli Village

N

0 km 5
0 miles 5

Hook Point
To Rainbow Beach
Inskip Point

■ Sleeping
1 Cathedral Beach Resort & Camping Park
2 Eurong Beach Resort
3 Fraser Island Beach Houses
4 Fraser Island Retreat
5 Kingfisher Bay Resort
6 Sailfish Apartments

maintaining a sustainable body of natural resources aided by a system of 'totems'. Totems were allocated to each member of the tribe and were usually the rare prey species like parrots or snakes. With every tribe member policing his or her own particular totem, each species was afforded the similar protection that our modern legal system provides today. Tragically, what it took the Aboriginals thousands of years to create; it took the first European settlers decades to dismantle. With their arrival in 1842 and the same wholesale ignorance and arrogance that predominated throughout the whole continent, the indigenous people were gradually pushed out of their lands, or relocated, and the natural resources unsustainably plundered. By 1904 the Butchella lost their ancient foothold on Fraser never to return and within a decade the colonial timber industry was in full swing. For another 70 years the kauri pine, tallowood, blackbutt, hoop pine and later the marine borer resistant satingay, were blundered before timber getting ceased in 1991 and the island was declared a World Heritage area in 1992. Although Fraser is now fully protected and still offers sanctuary to many unique species, its primary usage is recreation and as a playground for tourists. As such, there is an ever-increasing range conflicts of interest that need to be addressed. Perhaps paramount in recent years is the fate of its resident population of dingoes – ironically, the most commonly used mascot of the tourism-marketing gurus. On the covers of numerous glossy leaflets they are depicted as, plump and healthy and even donning boots, an Aussie hat and a camera. Yet in reality the purest race of dingoes on the continent are now utterly confused and starving as a result of scavenging from tourists. And sadly, the age old ethic of Aboriginal sustainability still remains far from the minds of most. The name Fraser derived from one of the island's most famous residents, Eliza Fraser, an 1836 shipwreck survivor.

Sights

The main resorts on the island are at Kingfisher Bay on the west coast and Eurong, Happy Valley and Cathedral Beach on the east. Other small communities on the east coast include Dilli Village to the south and Orchid Beach to the north. The west coast is inundated with small creeks, inaccessible even by 4WD.

East Beach Highway (Eurong to Orchid Beach)

Fringed by pounding surf on one side and bush on the other, barrelling up and down the 92-km natural highway of East Beach is an exhilarating experience in itself. The main access point for those arriving on the west coast is Eurong, where you can fuel up and head north for as far as the eye can see. Of course you will not be alone and at times the beach looks like some weird 4WD version of a 'bikers meet' on their way to a rock'n'roll gig. Although the temptation is to let rip and 'see what this baby can do', it is ill advised since creeks and soft sand have resulted in some nasty accidents. The indecision as to who goes left and who goes right with on-coming traffic can also cause problems, but generally speaking, stick to the usual road rules. There are a number of sights as you head north, the first of which is **Lake Wabby** – 4 km north of Eurong. Reached, by foot – 4 km return on soft sand – Lake Wabby is one island lake that is at war with an encroaching sand blow creating bizarre aesthetics and lots of fun partaking in sand surfing and swimming. For a really stunning elevated view of the 'lake verses blow' you can head inland for 7 km, on Cornwells Road, 2 km north of the beach car park. This in itself will test your 4WD skills. A walking track (5-km return) connects the lookout car park with the lake.

Next stop is **Eli Creek** which offers a cool dip in crystal clear waters. Some 3 km beyond Eli Creek the rusting hulk of the *Maheno* – a trans-Tasman passenger liner that came to grief in 1935 – provides an interesting stop and a welcome landmark along the seemingly endless sandy highway.

A further 2 km sees you at the unusual **Pinnacles** formation, an eroded bank of sand of varying gold and orange hues that look like some bizarre inter-planetary (Star Trek) film set. Somehow you feel it would not be entirely unsurprising to see Captain Kirk and Spock rolling about in a dramatic fist fight.

Just south of the Pinnacles, the 43-km **Northern Road circuit** ventures through ancient rainforest known as Yidney Scrub taking in views of the huge Knifeblade Sand Blow, the pretty, small Lake Allom and Boomerang Lakes, which at 130 m above sea level are the highest dune lakes in the world.

Back on East Beach, the colourful sand banks continue to the *Cathedral Beach Resort* and the *Dundubara campsite* offering the truly fit and adventurous walker an opportunity and access to explore the turtle infested **Lake Bowarrady**, 16 km return. From Dundubara it is another 19 km to **Indian Head**. One of the very few genuine rocks on the island the heads offers a fine vantage point from which to view the odd shark and manta ray in the azure blue waters below (demonstrating why swimming in the sea is ill advised around Fraser). Just beyond Indian Head, at the start of Middle Head, the track turns inland providing access to **Orchid Beach** and **The Champagne Pools**. Named due to their clarity and wave action, they provide a perfect saltwater pool for swimming amongst brightly coloured tropical fish that seem no more shocked at your choice of radiant swimwear as your many fellow bathers.

Beyond the settlement of Orchid Beach and Waddy Point, four-wheel driving becomes more difficult with most hire companies banning further exploration north. But if you have your own vehicle and experience the northern peninsula can offer some welcome solitude and fine fishing spots all the way up to **Sandy Cape**, 31 km away.

The lakes   There are over 40 freshwater lakes on Fraser that form part of a vast and complex natural water storage system, the length and breadth of the island. Surprisingly for a sand island, there is 20 times more water stored naturally here than is held back by the Wivenhoe Dam that supplies the whole of Brisbane. The most popular and aesthetic lakes are scattered around the islands southern interior. By far the most beautiful and frequented is **Lake McKenzie**, which can be accessed north of Central Station or via the Cornwells and Bennet roads from East Beach. With its white silica sands and crystal clear azure blue waters, it is quite simply foolish not to visit just go either early in the day or late, to avoid the throngs of tour buses. Also take sunglasses, sunscreen and insect repellent – there are flies of a size not normally encounted.

Further south, lakes **Birrabeen** and **Benaroon** also offer fine swimming and are quieter than McKenzie but do not share quite the same beauty. Further south still is **Lake Boomanjin** which is the largest 'perched' lake in the world, which does not mean it is full of perch (fish) but that it ranks high on the humus podsol B Horizon with a large pH – very brown in colour, and one of a kind.

Central Station   For those arriving on the west coast, Central Station provides the first glimpse of just how well wooded Fraser Island really is. Shaded by towering bunya pine, satinay and thick with umbrella like palms, this green heart of Fraser beats to the rhythms of a unique and special biodiversity. In the 50-m canopies many of the island's 240 recorded species of birds reside from brightly coloured lorikeets and honeyeaters to tiny fairy wrens. On the ground echidna and dingoes roam and even beneath it there are earthworms as long as your arm! One of the most pleasant features of Central Station are the crystal clear waters and white sandy bed of Wanggoolba Creek which is the main feature on the 450-m boardwalk. Central Station also serves as the departure point for some excellent walking tracks to Lake McKenzie and the Pile Valley where you will find yourself gazing heavenwards wondering if the trees could possibly grow any taller.

Essentials

LL-L *Kingfisher Bay Resort*, on the islands west coast, T1800072555/41255511, www.kingfisherbay.com.au This multi award-winning resort is without doubt one of the best resorts in Australia. In fact more an eco-village than a resort, *Kingfisher Bay* is highly successful in combining unique and harmonious architecture with superb facilities and a wide variety of accommodation options. On offer are a range of modern fully self-contained holiday villas, lodges and luxury hotel rooms, centred around a spacious central lodge with landscaped pools and gardens. Within the main lodge are 2 excellent, if pricey restaurant/bars, with a separate and more affordable bistro/pizzeria and shopping complex nearby. The resort also offers a wide range of activities and tours and hires out its own 4WD vehicles. **A** *Backpacker lodges* with modern facilities, including a lively bar, but can only be accessed on their Wilderness Adventure Tours programme (see below). Recommended.

Sleeping & eating *On map, page 284*

LL-A *Eurong Beach Resort*, on the islands east coast T41279122, www.fraser-is.com.au Older and more traditional, this resort offers a range of tidy self-contained apartments, motel-style units and cabins as well as some aging, budget A-frame houses that can accommodate up to 8. Other budget units are also available. There is a spacious, yet characterless, restaurant/bar, a pool and a range of organized tours and activities. Well-stocked shop, café and fuel on site. Though far less salubrious than *Kingfisher* it is perfectly comfortable and provides easy access to East Beach. **LL-L** *Fraser Island Beach Houses*, T41279207, www.fraserislandbeachhouses.com.au, offer another alternative in Eurong with modern, well-appointed and fully self-contained houses, with pool, spa.

LL-L *Fraser Island Retreat*, Happy Valley, further north (20 km), T41279144, www.fraserislandtours.com.au It consists of 9 fully serviced timber lodges in a quiet bush setting, just off East Beach and near Eli Creek (6 km). Pool, BBQ, Bistro/bar and shop. **LL** *Sailfish Apartments*, Happy Valley, T41279494, www.sailfishonfraser.com.au, offers modern 2-bedroom en suites, with pool and spa. **L-E** *Cathedral Beach Resort and Camping Park*, 13 km further north, T41279177, is the only non-camping permit park on the island. It offers tidy cabins, on-site tents and vans all with fully equipped kitchens and non-powered sites with hot showers and a shop. There are also a number of fine holiday house lets on Fraser that are ideal for groups or families.

QPWS campsites are at Central Station, Lake Boomanjin, Lake McKenzie, Lake Allom, Wathumba, Waddy Point and Dundubara. Facilities include toilets and cold showers. There are coin (50c) operated hot showers at Central Station, Waddy Point and Dundubara. Beach camping is permitted all along the east coast and on a few selected sites on the west coast. A nightly fee of $3.85 ($15.40 per family) applies to all campsites (Dundubara and Waddy Point must be pre-booked, all others cannot be pre-booked). Do not feed the dingoes. QPWS fees do not apply to private resorts or campsites.

Tours & activities

Do not be fooled into thinking you cannot go it alone or need a guide

As you might expect there are more tours on offer to Fraser than you could possibly analyze in great detail from as far away as Brisbane and Noosa. To get the most from the island you really need at least 3 days so a day tour should only be considered if you are hard pressed for time. If you really want to learn about the island you can still do so independently through the excellent guided tours on offer through the resorts, especially *Kingfisher Bay*. Their Wilderness Adventure Tours, of 3 day/2 night (from $270 quad share/ $336 twin) or 2 day/1 night (from $198 quad/ $234 twin) are the most expensive, but for good reason, being very entertaining, professional and with an excellent standard of accommodation, T1800072555, www.kingfisherbay.com.au Other reputable tour companies worth looking in to include: *Fraser Island Company*, Hervey Bay, T41253933, www.fraserislandtours.com.au, offering a good range of 1-3 day safaris, from $82, child $49. *Fraser Venture*, T1800249122, offers day tours (ex Hervey Bay) from $82, child $47 and multi-day packages with accommodation at the *Eurong Beach Resort*. *Fraser Explorer Tours*, T54473845, www.fraser-is.com, are a good option if you are coming Noosa. Their 2/3-day guided adventure tours have the added attraction of arriving on Fraser via Teewah Beach (Great Sandy National Park, Cooloola Section) and Rainbow Beach, from $170-304. *Tasman Venture II*, Hervey Bay, T1800602322/ T41243222, offers something different with a West Coast day tour which explorers the quiet and largely inaccessibly beaches of Fraser's west coast, taking in snorkelling and perhaps a bit of dolphin watching along the way, from $60. *Koala Backpackers*, T1800466444, www.koala-backpackers.com.au, and *Palace Backpackers*, T1800063168, offers specialist multi-day, self-drive, budget packages (camping), from $125.

Transport

There is a spartan taxi service, but due to the terrain and demand it is unreliable to say the least, T41279188. Book well in advance

Local All vehicles on the island require a **RAM 4WD permit** that must be displayed on the windscreen. RAM permits can be obtained prior to arrival for $30 from the mainland **QPWS offices**, Hervey Bay City Council, 77 Tavistock St, T41250222, **Whale Watch Tourist Centre**, Boat Harbour, Urangan, T41289800, or the **River Heads Kiosk-Barge Car Park**, Ariadne St, T41258473. On the island permits cost $40 and can be purchased from the **QPWS Eurong Office**. An information pack containing a detailed colour guide, camping and walking track details is supplied with the permit.

4WD hire One of Fraser Island's greatest assets is that it has virtually no sealed roads and its single lane tracks are all 4WD only. This alone makes it one of the best 4WD venues in Australia (and has protected the island from wholesale development). Although for the layman the tracks take some getting use to and are rough and soft in some places, access around the island is generally good, if slow. On average it takes about 30 mins to travel 10 km on inland roads where a 35 kmph speed limit is in force. East Beach is essentially one very long 90-km sand highway with a speed limit of 80 kmph. Although it is of course great fun and exhilarating to travel at such speeds along a beach, extreme care must be taken at high tide, in soft sand, crossing creeks and negotiating headlands, not to mention of pedestrians, fisherman and local wildlife. Strict guidelines have been put in place for 4WD on the island and these should be adhered to at all times. As you might expect, there are plenty of operators hiring 4WD and plenty of options, but generally hire does not include fuel, ferry, food or accommodation/camping permits, nor does it include the cost of camping gear, which is also an additional extra. Conditions include a minimum age of 21, current drivers license, at least a $500 bond or credit card imprint and a permit (see above). The more professional companies will also give you a thorough briefing and maps. Several of the larger backpackers including *Koala*, T1800466444, www.koala-backpackers.com.au, and *Palace*, T1800063168, offer their own vehicles, guides and package deals, but if you want to get a group together and go independently several Hervey Bay based companies can oblige. *Safari 4WD*, 102 Boat Harbour Rd, T41244244, www.safari4wd hire.com.au, are one of the most professional offering a range of models from $90-130 a day, camping kits from $16 per day and hire/accommodation packages from $573. Other reputable companies offering similar deals include *Fraser Island 4x4*, 10 Fraser St, Torquay, T41256355, Bay 4WD Centre, 54 Boat Harbour Dr, T41282981 and *Aussie Trax*, 56 Boat harbour Dr, T41244433, www.aussietraxfraserisland.com.au *Kingfisher Bay Resort*, TT1800072555/41255511, also provide 4WD hire. *Air Fraser Island* is recommended if you are on your own or are a couple. They will fly you out to Eurong, where you are supplied with a small, economical 4WD (with camping gear if required, fuel not included) from $90 per day. The only drawback is that the vehicles must stay on the island and be dropped of again at Eurong. This option does avoid the expensive vehicular ferry fees and is fine if you want fly back, but it can present problems if you wish to stay at the *Kingfisher Bay Resort* and/or get the ferry back on foot from the island's west coast.

Breakdown If you breakdown there are mechanical workshops at Eurong, T41279173, and Orchid Beach, T41279220. For tow truck, T41279167, and be prepared to wave the contents of your bank account bye bye.

Long distance Air There are 2 small airfields on Fraser (Toby's Gap and Orchid Beach) but most light aircraft land on East Beach at Eurong or Happy Valley. *Air Fraser Island*, T41253600, offer daily services from $50 return. They also offer 'Fly-Drive-Fly' ($110 one-day), 'Fly-Drive-Camp' ($190, 2-days/1 night) packages, scenic flights, from $165. *Noosa and Maroochy Flying Services*, T54500516, www.noosaaviation.com.au, offer shuttle from the Sunshine Coast from $99.

Vehicle barges *Rainbow Venture*, Inskip Point, Rainbow Beach, to Hook Point departs mainland daily from 0700-1630 (15 mins), T54863227 (no bookings required), from $70 return, including driver, passenger-only, from $12. *Fraser Dawn*, Urangan Boat Harbour, Hervey Bay, to Moon Point, departs mainland daily 0830/1530 (1 hr) returning 0930/1630 T4125444 (pre-book), from $82 including driver return, additional passengers $5.50, passenger only $16.50, one-way half price. *Fraser Venture*, Mary River Heads (20 mins south of Hervey Bay), to Wanggoolba Creek, departs mainland Mon-Fri 0900, 1015, 1530, Sat 0700 (30 mins), returning Mon-Fri 0930/1430/1600, Sat 0730, T4125444 (pre book), price as above. *Kingfisher Barge*, Mary River Heads to Kingfisher Bay departs mainland daily 0715/1045/1400, returns 0830/1300/1530, T1800072555 (pre book), price as above. Note the Hook Point and Wanggoolba Creek landings require prior 4WD experience, Moon Point landing is recommended.

Passenger-only ferry *Kingfisher Fast Cat*, Urangan Boat Harbour, Hervey Bay to *Kingfisher Bay Resort*, departs mainland daily 0845/1200/1600, Sun-Thu also 1830, Fri/Sat also 1900/2230, returns daily 0740/1030/1400/1700/2000, Sat/Sun extra at 2330, T41255511 (bookings preferable), from $35, child $17.

Secure parking Buccaneer Dr, Urangan, T4128999, from $5.50 per day.

Food supplies, hardware, fuel, ice and public telephones are available at the *Eurong* **Directory** *Beach Resort*, *Fraser Island Retreat* (Happy Valley), *Kingfisher Bay Resort*, *Cathedral Beach Resort* and Orchid Beach. Additional public telephones are located at Ungowa, Central Station, Dundubara, Waddy Point and Indian Head. There are no banks or ATMs on the island but most major resorts accept EFTPOS. There are no medical facilities, doctors or pharmacies on the island. QPWS ranger stations and major resorts all have basic first aid and can call in an air ambulance in an emergency, T000. Food on the island is expensive so if you are camping, you are advised to take all your own supplies from the mainland.

Hervey Bay

Colour map 3, grid B5
Population: 33,000
290 km north of
Brisbane; 34 km east
of the Bruce Highway
and Maryborough

What it lacks in aesthetics and soul, Hervey Bay more than makes up for in tourist hype, as visitors flood in relentlessly to experience two mighty big attractions. For as Airlie Beach is to 74 Whitsunday Islands, Hervey Bay has become to one made entirely of sand – Fraser Island. Then, between the months of August to October, Hervey Bay itself echoes to the tunes and its waters erupt with the visitations of the great Leviathans. Considered by many to be the whale-watching capital of the world , Hervey Bay tries hard to stand-alone as an attractive coastal resort and congenial retirement destination. Yet sadly, despite the usual low-key attractions, activities and ubiquitous sweep of golden sand, it fails unreservedly. The concerted attempts to keep people on the mainland for anything other than a day or a night seem futile and as a result, it has become one of Queensland's most muddled and soulless tourist transit centres.

Ins & outs
See Transport, page 294, for details

For bias-free information (rare in these parts) visit the accredited Maryborough Fraser Island VIC at the BP South Tourist Complex on the Bruce Highway, before heading for the coast, T41214111, www. frasercoast.org.au Open daily 0900-1700.

Sights

Hervey Bay is essentially a beachfront conglomerate of north facing suburbs, from Point Vernon in the west, through Pialba, Scarness and Torquay to Urangan in the east. Almost all major amenities are to be found along the Esplanade from the junction with Main Street in Pialba to Elizabeth Street, Urangan. The main Fraser Island ferry and whale-watching terminal is just south of Dayman Point in Urangan.

If you have any time to kill between whale watching and getting to Fraser Island, Hervey Bay tries hard to lure you with a few low-key attractions. **Natureworld**, on the corner of Maryborough Road and Fairway Drive, is a

Hervey Bay

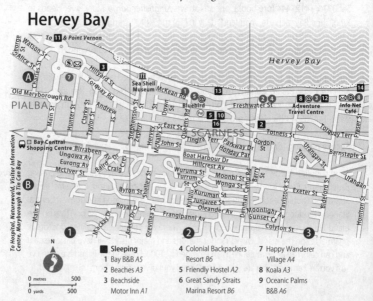

Sleeping
1 Bay B&B *A5*
2 Beaches *A3*
3 Beachside
   Motor Inn *A1*
4 Colonial Backpackers
   Resort *B6*
5 Friendly Hostel *A2*
6 Great Sandy Straits
   Marina Resort *B6*
7 Happy Wanderer
   Village *A4*
8 Koala *A3*
9 Oceanic Palms
   B&B *A6*

small but entertaining animal park, with all the usual natives including wombats, fruit bats, roos and, of course, cuddly koalas. Guided tours kick off at 1130, the koala show at 1200 and you can quake in your boots with snake handling at 1230. Courtesy bus. ■ *Daily 0900-1700. $13.50, child $6.50, family $35.*

Continuing the eco-theme is **Neptune's Reefworld**, on the corner of Pulgul and Kent streets, Urangan, where coral displays provide the aesthetics, turtles and stingrays the interaction and reef sharks the fear factor. ■ *Daily from 0915. From $14, child $8 (shark feed 1400, swim with the sharks from $40, free pick ups). T41289828.*

The 1.5-km long **Urangan Pier** offers a pleasant breezy stroll and good fishing. At the other end of the Esplanade (west) it is worth taking a look at the **Sea Shell Museum** and gift shop, on the corner of Zypher Street and The Esplanade. Even if you do not go into the museum itself and kitsch aside, the range and beauty of the shells in the shop will have you fossicking about until the tide turns.

Essentials

Hervey Bay offers plenty of accommodation options with a very heavy emphasis on backpackers and caravan parks. During the whale watching season and public holidays book well ahead. One option, often overlooked and ideal given the presence of Fraser Island and the Great Sandy Strait, are houseboats. Several companies can oblige, including *Self Sail Holidays*, Great Sandy Straits Marina, Urangan T41253822, www.selfsail.com.au, *Luxury Afloat Houseboats*, Norman Pt, Tin Can Bay, T54864864, www.luxuryafloat.com.au and for yachts, *Fraser island Rent-A-Yacht*, Tin Can Bay Marina, T54864814, www.rent-a-yacht.com.au Prices range from about 3 nights midweek from $660 to 7 nights from $1,540 (low season) to $825/1,925 (high season).

Sleeping
■ *On map, page 290*

LL-L *Great Sandy Straits Marina Resort*, backs on to the boat harbour in Urangan, 141289999, greatsandyresort@bigpond.com.au Set in an ideal position overlooking the bay, it offers fully self-contained units with ocean views, pool, sauna, spa and bike

Sunshine & Fraser coasts

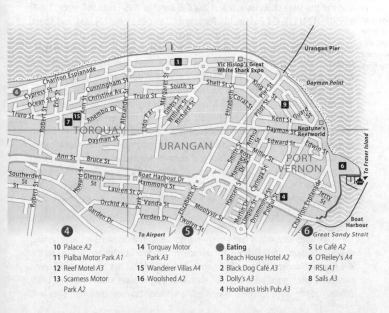

10 Palace *A2*
11 Pialba Motor Park *A1*
12 Reef Motel *A3*
13 Scarness Motor Park *A2*
14 Torquay Motor Park *A3*
15 Wanderer Villas *A4*
16 Woolshed *A2*

● **Eating**
1 Beach House Hotel *A2*
2 Black Dog Café *A3*
3 Dolly's *A3*
4 Hoolihans Irish Pub *A3*
5 Le Café *A2*
6 O'Reiley's *A4*
7 RSL *A1*
8 Sails *A3*

▶ **Up close and personal**

Every year from August to November, while the streets of Hervey Bay are a buzz with the chaotic sounds of humanity, its namesake waters echo to the haunting symphonies of whale song. These whales spend the warmer summer months in Antarctic waters feeding on krill before starting their annual migration north to the central and southern Great Barrier Reef where there calves are born in the warm waters of the Barrier Reef .

Finding temporary heaven in the bay's calm waters, pods of humpback whales stop to socialize and play, often breaching the surface or slapping it with fins and tail, perhaps making the most of the moment, or showing their calves the art of whale fun, before moving on to the far more serious business of returning to their feeding grounds in Antarctica. Through this magnificent annual spectacle they present us – their old time nemesis – the opportunity to show their 'other side' as we muse in awe and admiration. Other marine life including dolphins, turtles and occasionally dugongs, also join the fray and can be seen all year round. See below for tours.

hire. There are many other modern, 4-star, luxury apartment complexes, offering all the comforts of home, including **LL-L** *Alexander Apartments*, 496 Esplanade, T41256555, Alexander@aia.net.au, **LL-L** *Kondari Resort*, 49 Elizabeth St, Urangan, T1800072131, and the very pleasant **LL-L** *Riviera Resort*, 385 Esplanade, T41243344, www.rivieraresort.com.au Slightly different and off the busy Esplanade is **L** *Wanderer Villas*, corner of Ann and Truro sts, T41289048, hwanderer@hervey.com.au, offering peaceful and unusual, well-appointed villas, pool and spa. As you might expect motels flourish in Hervey Bay. They range from the 4-star **L-A** *Beachside Motor Inn*, 298 Esplanade, T41241999, www.beachsidemotorinn.com.au, to the budget **A-B** *Reef Motel*, 410 Esplanade, T41252744. Of the few B&Bs in the city, **A** *Bay B&B*, 180 Cypress St, T41256919, and the more expensive **A** *Oceanic Palms B&B*, 50 King St, T41289562, are popular and handy to the boat harbour.

With over 15 backpackers in the city and more on the way, the choice is huge and competition fierce

Many of the large chain backpackers like **C-E** *Beaches*, 195 Torquay Terrace, T1800 655501/41241322, **C-E** *Palace*, 184 Torquay Rd, T1800063168/41245331, and *Koala*, 408 Esplanade, T41253601, all offer the usual party hype and Fraser Island tour/accommodation package deals. Other alternatives include the excellent **A-E** *Colonial Backpackers Resort YHA*, corner of Pulgul St and Boat Harbour Dr, T41251844, www.coloniallogcabins.com, that offers a fine range of options from luxury villas and 1-2 bedroom cabins, to en suite doubles and dorms, a good bistro/bar, pool, spa, internet, bike hire and tours desk. It is also the closest to the boat harbour. Back in the heart of town and in welcome contrast to the party-hard establishments, is the characterful and friendly **C-E** *Woolshed*, 181 Torquay Rd, T41240677, that has an exquisite range of nicely decorated (and very different) dorms and twin/double cabins and rooms with all the usual facilities and internet. Recommended. Across the road you are certain to get fine traditional Scots hospitality and some peace and quiet at the **C-E** *Friendly Hostel*, 182 Torquay Rd, T41244107, friendlyhostel@hotmail.com It is small and comfortable and more like a B&B, with tidy dorms, doubles/twins with well-equipped kitchen facilities.

There are numerous motor parks to choose from with the decision, as usual, coming down to location and/or facilities. For an excellent range of options and facilities try the **A-E** *Happy Wanderer Village*, 105 Truro St, Torquay, T41251103, hwanderer@hervey. com.au It offers good value fully self-contained duplex villas, studio/standard units, cabins, on-site vans (shared amenities), en suite/standard powered sites and non-powered sites, pool, camp kitchen. Backpacker cabins are also available. Recommended. There are 3 basic, 3-star motor park/campsites (beachside) along the Esplanade, at Pialba, T41281399, Scarness, T41281274, and Torquay, T41251578.

Expensive Many of the up-market resort complexes have restaurants offering fine dining including the popular *Sails Restaurant*, corner of Fraser St and The Esplanade, T41255170, with its wide range of seafood, Asian and traditional Australian dishes. Open lunch Thu/Fri 1200-1430, dinner Mon-Sat 1800-late. Another option to consider (if you are not going on tour to Fraser Island) is the *Dinner Cruise* offered by the excellent *Kingfisher Bay Resort*. Their launch departs the Urangan Boat Harbour Sun-Thu, 1600-2000/1830-2330 (from $39, child $20) for a themed buffet and Fri/Sat, 1600-2200/1900-2330 ($45, child $25) seafood smorgasbord at the resorts *Maheno* and *Seabelle* restaurants. Even without the excellent food the resort itself is well worth the visit.

Mid-range *Beach House Hotel*, 344 Esplanade, Scarness, T41281233, deservingly popular for both lunch and dinner, offers a good range of pub/café style options overlooking the beach. They also have live entertainment and pool tables. Also in Scarness is **Le Café**, 325a Esplanade, T41281793, that offers classy surroundings, value for money and good coffee. Open for breakfast, lunch and dinner, from 0645 Tue-Sun. A few doors down you will find standard hot offerings at the *Tandoori Taj Indian Restaurant*, 355 Esplanade, T41282872. Open lunch Tue-Sun 1200-1500, dinner daily from 1730. Between Scarness and Torquay *The Black Dog Café*, corner of Esplanade and Denman Camp Rd, T41243177, is a modern, classy restaurant with good value Japanese dishes. Open daily for lunch and dinner. *Hoolihans Irish Pub*, 382 Esplanade, T41940099, has a wide range of traditional offerings with an Irish edge. Servings are generous and it's pricey, but then there is always the quality beer! Open 8 days a week from 1100.

Cheap *Dolly's*, 410 Esplanade, T41255633, is a lively backpacker haunt offering regular all you can eat deals, dancing and live music. Further east *O'Reiley's*, 446 Esplanade, T41253100, also offers all you can eat pizza and pancakes on Tue nights and reasonable value at other times. Open daily from 1700 and for value breakfasts Sat/Sun from 0730. At the other end of town *The RSL*, 11 Torquay Rd, Pialba, T41281133, can always be relied on for value for money and sedate entertainment. Open daily. The main supermarkets (*Coles* and *Woolworths*) are in Pialba (open until 2100) and there is a 24-hr convenience store on the Esplanade in Torquay.

Camel safaris *Humpbacks*, T41280055, offer 2-hr jaunts aboard the *Ships of the Desert* from $39. **Diving** Best kept for the Barrier Reef but fanatics or impatient beginners will find value for money with *Divers Mecca*, 403 Esplanade, T41251626. They offer good value certification courses and intro dives from $80/169. **Fishing** *Princess II*, T41240400 and *The Eagle Ray*, T41254957, www.eaglerayfishing.com.au, are the 2 main charters offering local sea, reef and night fishing. *MV Snapper*, T41243788, offers cheap family oriented trips from $33, child $18. **Horse trekking** *Susan River Homestead*, Maryborough-Hervey Bay Rd, T41216846. 2-2½ hrs, 0930/1400, from $50. **Scenic flights** *Air Fraser Island*, T41253600, offer scenic flights from $165 and whale spotting, from $50. **Sea kayaking** *Splash Safaris*, T0500 555580, offer half-, full- and two-day trips exploring secluded beaches on Big Woody and Fraser Islands, from $59/69/165. **Sky diving** *Skydive Hervey Bay*, T41249249, www.skybay.com.au, offer tandems with a beach landing from 10-14,000 ft, from $219. **Watersports** *Fishing World*, 351A Esplanade, T41246375, and *Torquay Beach Hire*, Boat ramp, The Esplanade, Torquay, T41255528, both offer a range of hire equipment from runabouts to jet skis. **Whale-watching** There are now more than 15 whale-watch cruise operators

Eating
● *On map, page 290*

Most of the mainly mid-range options and cheap eateries are to be found along The Esplanade in Torquay, Scarness and Pialba

Tours & activities
For organized tours to Fraser Island, see page 288

based at the Urangan Boat Harbour. There are various options and a variety of boats offering ½, ¾, full and dawn tours, ranging in price from $60-110. The best way to choose is to head for the Whale Watch Tourist Centre at the boat harbour and take a look at the various boats compare the tour details. Open daily 0600-1800. With so many operators, other than cruise time, the differences really come down to minor details like the size of the group. *Tasman Venture II*, T1800620322, *Quick Cat*, T41289611, and *Seaspray*, T1800066404, www.herveybaywhalewatch.com.au, are smaller launches offering two am/pm trips daily from $65, child $40. *Blue Dolphin*, T41203350, offer a 'whales by sail', half-day and sunset cruise option, from $75. *Volante II* is another smaller launch that offers 3/4 day and dawn trips from $70. Then you are moving into large catamaran territory with *Whale Watch Safari* (half-day, from $73), *Whalesong*, T41256222, www.whalesong.com.au, (that also do specialist year-round dolphin cruises), half-day from $70, and *Spirit of Hervey Bay*, T1800642544, www.spiritofherveybay.com.au, which has the added luxury of a smooth glass bottom (half day from $110). Finally you are then getting to the 'floating airport departure lounge with all amenities' department in the form of the *MV Islander* (3/4 day, from $60) and *MV Discovery One*, (day cruise). You can also take to the air, whale spotting with *Air Fraser Island*, T41253600, offer ½-1 hr, from $50pp minimum of 4. Hervey Bay celebrates its visiting Leviathans with an annual *Whale Festival* every Aug.

Transport   **Local Bus** *Bay Bus and Coach*, T41286411, run local hail and ride bus services between Maryborough and Hervey Bay, taking in a circuit of the town through Pialba, along The Esplanade to Urangan and back via Boat Harbour Drive. They operate Mon-Fri every 2 hrs from 0600-1900 and Sat 0720-1800. **Bike hire** Available from *Rayz Pushbikes*, T0417644814, from $12 per day. Free delivery and pick-up. Open daily 0700-1700. **Taxi** T131008.

Long distance   Air Hervey Bay is served by *Qantas* (*Sunstate*), T131313, and *Flight West*, T131300. The airport is located 2 km south of Urangan off Elizabeth St/Booral Rd at the eastern end of the city. Taxis meet all scheduled flights. **Bus** The long-distance bus terminal is located in the Bay Central Shopping Centre, Boat Harbour Rd, Pialba, T41244000. *McCafferty's*, T131499, *Greyhound*, T132030 and *Premier Motor Services*, T133410, offer daily services north/south. Services include Rockhampton (5 daily), from $50-66, 5¾ hrs; Noosa (5 daily), from $20, 3 hrs; and Brisbane (7 daily) from $39, 5½ hrs. *Suncoast Pacific*, T54431011 and *Kirklands*, T1300367077, offer services to Tin Can Bay and *Polley's Coaches*, T54822700, offer onward transfers to Rainbow Beach. **Car** Car hire from *Hervey Bay Economy Car Rentals*, 96 Islander Rd, T41246240, from $44 per day. *Nifty Rent A Car*, 463 Esplanade, T1800627583. 4WD hire (see Fraser Island section). Servicing/repair at *Charlie's*, 92 Boat Harbour Dr, T41241655. **Train** The nearest train station is in Maryborough, Lennox St, T41239264. *Queensland Rail's*, *Spirit of the Tropics*, *Sunlander*, *Capricornian* and fast *Tilt Train* (Brisbane to Rockhampton) offer regular services north and south, T132232. *Trainlink* bus service connects with every *Tilt Train* for transfers to and from Hervey Bay. *Hervey Bay Travel Centre*, 15 Torquay Rd, T41281900/1800 815378, act as booking agents.

Directory   **Banks** *Westpac* and *National* are on the Esplanade Torquay, *Commonwealth* is on Bideford St, Torquay. **Communications** Internet: the cheapest is *Bluebird Internet*, Shop 5/346 Esplanade, Scarness, T41242289. Other alternatives are *The Adventure Travel Centre*, 410 Esplanade, T41289288, and a few doors up *Info Net Café*. All are open daily until late. **Post office**: 428 Esplanade, Torquay. Open Mon-Fri 0830-1700, Sat 0830-1200. **Medical services** Chemist: 418 Esplanade, T41283899. Open 0830-2000. **Hospital**: Nissen St, T41206666. **Useful numbers** Police: 142 Torquay Rd, T41285333 Vehicle Storage Fraser Coast Secure, 629 Esplanade, T41252783.

Capricorn & Central coasts

Introducing the Capricorn and Central coasts

Capricorn Coast begins north of Hervey Bay, where the great sand masses of the Fraser Coast give way to fields of sugar cane and offshore, the start of the Great Barrier Reef. The first of many Queensland towns born of the sugar cane industry, **Bundaberg** – or 'Bundy' as it is known – shares its nickname with the cane's most famous product and subsequent tourist attraction – the Bundaberg Rum distillery. Nearby, on the coast is **Mon Repos**, one of the world's most important and accessible mainland turtle rookeries. Further north, history and beautiful coastline, lure travellers off the highway to investigate the **Town of 1770** – the first place the Europeans (Captain Cook) set foot in Queensland. Touted to become the next booming tourist destination in Southern Queensland, 1770 and **Agnes Water** combine to offer a host of activities centred around two superb coastal national parks – **Eurimbula** and **Deepwater** and also serve as the gateway to the stunning southern reef island of **Lady Musgrave**. Next stop (though rarely for the tourist) is the heavily industrialized coastal port of **Gladstone** which serves as the gateway to arguably the most beautiful and popular Barrier Reef resort islands of them all – **Heron Island**. Straddling the Tropic of Capricorn, north of Gladstone, is Queensland's proud and prosperous 'beef capital' **Rockhampton**, or 'Rocky'. To the east of Rocky the coastal resorts of **Yeppoon** and **Emu Park**, serve as the city's cooling coastal playground, while just offshore **Great Keppel Island** offers many tourists their first taste of Queensland's many beautiful, tropical island resorts.

Central Coast, between Rockhampton and Cairns, is for many the very essence of an Australian beach holiday. **Mackay**, the sugar producing capital of Australia, is used as a base to explore the reef island groups of **Brampton**, **Newry** and **Carlisle**. Just inland the magnificent **Eungella National Park** offers slopes draped in lush rainforest and cloaked in rain-baring clouds that in turn give rise to wonderful waterfalls and unusual wildlife. Back on the coast and beyond the delights of the **Cape Hillsborough National Park**, the rush is on to reach the fast developing, coastal tourist resort of **Airlie Beach** – the gateway to the sublime **Whitsunday Islands**. North of Whitsunday, past the quiet fruit growing, coastal town of **Bowen**, Queensland's 'northern capital', **Townsville**, looms large. Just offshore **Magnetic Island** lives up to its name attacting tourists with its beautiful beaches and infectious laid-back atmosphere. Inland from Townsville, the historic and friendly gold-mining town of **Charters Towers** offers many their first taste of Queensland 'outback'. Between Townsville and Cairns, **Mission Beach** is like a mainland version of Magnetic Island. Offshore, as always, the reef and tropical islands beckon, in this instance in the form of the easily accessible **Dunk Island**.

Capricorn & Central coasts

Capricorn Coast

Bundaberg

Colour map 3, grid A4
Population: 41,000
368 km north of
Brisbane, 321 km
south of
Rockhampton

*The small and congenial city of Bundaberg sits beside the Burnett River amidst a sea of sugar cane. The city relies far more on agriculture than tourism to sustain it and as a result it is either omitted completely from most travel agendas or firmly highlighted as a place to secure agricultural work. Many refer to the city as 'Bundy', however, this affectionate nickname is most often used to describe its famous tipple – rum – that has been faithfully distilled in Bundaberg since 1883. Not surprisingly, therein lies the biggest tourist attraction within the city – the wonderfully sweet smelling **distillery** which offers daily tours. Other attractions nearby are the day cruises to the southern reef islands of **Lady Musgrave and Elliot**. Also not to be missed, and not far away is the fascinating, seasonal action at the incredible **Mon Repos turtle rookery**.*

Ins & outs
*See Transport, page
301, for further details*

Getting there Bundaberg's airport is 3 km from the city centre. All the main bus companies operate services to the city from the north and south. *Tilt train* is the major train service from Brisbane. **Getting around** The city centre nestles on the southern bank of the Burnett River, with its ubiquitous and easily negotiable grid-system of streets. The reef ferries depart from the Bundaberg Port Marina, located on the lower reaches of the Burnett River, about 19 km northeast of the city. The coastal resorts of Bargara, Burnett Heads and the Mon Repos turtle rookery are 15 km due east. Local coach operators run regular services. **Tourist information** There are 2 VICs. The accredited regional centre, 271 Bourbong St, T41522333, www.bdtdb.com.au Open daily 0900-1700. City Council has it's own centre at 186 Bourbong St, T41539289. Open Mon-Fri 0830-1645, Sat/Sun 1000-1300. Little difference between the two.

Sights

**Post office &
Old National
Australia Bank**
*The VIC has a
Heritage Walk leaflet
with over 20 other
fine examples*

Before filling the nostrils with the sweet smell of molasses and titillating the taste buds with the dark spirits at the distillery, it is perhaps worth taking a quick and sober look at one or two of the historical buildings that dominate the city centre. Most prominent is the 30-m clock tower of Post Office building, on the corner of Bourbong and Barolin streets that has been in continuous operation since 1890. A few doors down, west, is the 1891 Old National Australia Bank, with its distinctive colonnades and spacious verandahs embellished with cast iron balustrades.

**Alexandra &
Balwin Swamp
Environmental
Park**

Gracing the bank of the river on Quay Street, west of the road and rail bridges, is Alexandra Park which echoes to the calls of native and exotic birds housed in the small and newly renovated zoo. Entry is free. Slightly further afield, 3 km east, is the Balwin Swamp Environmental Park which is an attractive and peaceful area of natural wetland and open parkland, rich in native birdlife. Boardwalks are provided and entry is also free.

**Botanical
Gardens
Complex**

An equally popular retreat is the city's Botanical Gardens Complex, 1 km north of the city centre. Added to the obvious botanical attractions and landscaped ponds and gardens are the **Fairymead House Sugar Museum**, which documents the history of the region's most important industry, and the

Arson and murder

Sadly, Bundaberg and its neighbouring town of Childers have been subject to storms of controversy in recent years with two terrible tourist related tragedies. The first, an arson attack, on the Childers

Backpackers in June 2000, cost the lives of 15 backpackers. Then, in March 2001, the black clouds extended to Bundaberg, with the assault and murder of a young British backpacker not far from the city centre.

Hinkler House Memorial Museum, which celebrates the courageous life and times of local pioneer aviator Bert Hinkler. Born in Bundaberg in 1892, Hinkler was the first person to fly solo from Australia to England in 1928. Sadly, after going on to break numerous other records, he then died attempting to break the record for the return journey in 1933. There is also a working steam train that clatters round the gardens on Sundays. ■ *Botanical gardens are open daily 0730-1700. Corner of Hinkler Ave and Gin Gin Rd. Both museums are open daily from 1000-1600. $3, child $1.*

Although a relatively small operation, the Bundaberg Distillery, established in 1883, provides a fascinating insight into the distilling process and a delightful bombardment of the senses. The one-hour tour begins with a short video that celebrates the famous Bundy brand before you are taken to view the various aspects of the manufacturing process. First stop is a huge five-million litre well of sweet smelling molasses, that is then gradually drawn through a maze of steel pipes, fermenters, condensers and distillers, before ending up in mighty vats within the maturing warehouses. With one vat alone being worth $5 million (of which $3 million goes to government tax) it is hardly surprising to hear the solid 'click' of lock and key and to be mildly aware of being counted on the way out! Then with a notable increase in walking pace you are taken to an authentic bar to sample the various end products. Generous distillers they are too, allowing four 'shots', which is just enough to keep you below the legal driving limit. With such evocative names as 'Dark and Stormy', 'Dirty Harry' and 'Moonbeam' it is hard to drag yourself away. There is one other thing. Bundy Rum has been described in many ways, all generally good, but most famously with one exception – a short poem, part of which goes… *'Bundaberg rum, over proofed rum, will tan your stomach and grow hair on your bum'*…!
■ *T41508684, www.bundabergrum.aust.com Avenue St (4 km east of the city centre, head for the chimney stack!). Tours run daily on the hour Mon-Fri 1000-1500, Sat/Sun 1000-1400, from $7.70, child $2.20.*

Bundaberg Distillery

Essentials

Beyond the usual rash of motels, Bundaberg has a dearth of accommodation and if you have your own transport you are advised to head for the seaside resort of Bargara (12 km east) where you will find a number of pleasant low-key resorts and beachside motor parks.

Sleeping
■ *On map, page 300*

In Bundaberg itself there are motels located along Bourbong, Takalvan and Quay sts. **L** *Burnett Riverside Motel*, 7 Quay St, T41558777; **L-B** *Villa Mirasol Boutique Motel*, 225 Bourbong St, T41544311; and **L-A** *Reef Getaway*, 11 Takalvan St, T41532255, are all 4-star with the Villa Mirasol being the closest to the city centre. **A-C** *Bargara Gardens Motel*, 13 See St, Bargara, is a good option on the coast with self-contained villas in a quiet tropical garden setting, 3-star. **B** *O'Ryan's B&B*, 25 Water St, T41511865.

Capricorn & Central coasts

The Aussie-Irish style B&B is one of the few in the town and is within walking distance from the city centre. It offers very pleasant, good-value studio en suite, queen and twin with shared bathroom and fine home baking. **E** *Bundaberg Backpackers and Travellers Lodge*, opposite the bus terminal on Targo St, T41522080, is under new management, which should hopefully result in much needed improvements. It is a dorms only hostel, friendly and popular with backpackers seeking work. *Bundaberg Aqua Scuba*, T41535761, located across the road in the bus terminal complex, also offer budget accommodation from $11.

The best motor park in Bundaberg is **B-E** *Cane Village Holiday Park*, Twyford St (2 km south of the city centre, off Takalvan St), T41551022. It has en suite/standard cabins, powered and non-powered sites and a good camp kitchen. **B-E** *Turtle Sands Tourist Park*, Mon Repos Beach, T41592340. This 3-star motor park is a good option if you are visiting the rookery, being within walking distance of the information centre. It has beachside en suite/standard cabins, powered and non-powered sites. **C-F** *Bargara Beach Caravan Park*, The Esplanade, Bargara, T41592228. This spacious option is nearer the amenities in Bargara.

Eating
● *On map, page 300*

Other than the up-market motel restaurants there is not much to choose from. *Numero Uno*, 167A Bourbong St, T41513666, is a licensed Italian restaurant offering value pastas and pizzas. Open Mon-Sat 1130-1400/1700-late, Sun from 1700. *Grand Hotel*, corner of Targo and Bourbong sts, T41512441, has a modern, licensed restaurant offering a traditional pub grub, value breakfasts and good coffee. For a light lunch in quiet surrounds, *Rose Garden Café*, in the Botanical Garden, corner of Gin Gin Rd and Hinkler Ave, T41531477, is recommended. Open daily 1000-1600.

Bundaberg

Sleeping
1 Bargara Beach Caravan Park
2 Bargara Gardens Motel
3 Bundaberg Aqua Scuba
4 Bundaberg Backpackers & Travellers Lodge
5 Burnett Riverside Motel
6 Cane Village Holiday Park
7 O'Ryan's B&B

Capricorn & Central coasts

Transport

Local *Duffy's Coaches*, 28 Barolin St, T41514226, serve the city and the Coral Coast (Rum Distillery/Bargara/Burnett Heads/Bundaberg Port Marina) several times daily. Taxi, T41511612.

Long distance Bundaberg airport is 3 km south of the city centre via the Isis Highway. *Qantas (Sunstate)*, T131313/T41522322, fly daily to Brisbane, Rockhampton, Mackay and Townsville. The long-distance bus terminal is located at 66 Targo St, between Woondooma and Crofton sts. *McCafferty's*, T131499, *Greyhound*, T132030 and *Premier Motor Services*, T133410, offer inter-State services north and south. *The Bundy Express*, T41529700, also runs between Bundaberg and Brisbane Mon/Wed/Fri from $40. The train station is right in the heart of city on the corner Bourbong and McLean sts. *Tilt Train* is the preferred service between Brisbane and Rockhampton but other north/southbound services pass through daily, T132235. *Stewart and Sons Travel*, 66 Targo St, T41529700, act as booking agents for air, bus and train operators.

Directory

Banks All the major branches have ATMs and can be found on Bourbong St. **Car hire** *Thrifty*, T41516222. *Hertz*, on the corner of Takalvan and Twyford sts, T41552403. **Car servicing** *Ampol Canelanders*, corner Barolin and George sts, T41531795. **Communications** Internet: *Cosy Corner*, Barolin St (opposite the post office). Open Mon-Fri 0700-1930, Sat 0700-1700, Sun 1100 1700. **Post office**. corner of Barolin and Bourbong sts, T41532700. Open Mon-Fri 0830-1700, Sat 0830-1200. **Medical services** Chemist: *Bundaberg Day and Night*, 128 Bourbong St, T41515533. Hospitals: Bundaberg Base Hospital, Bourbong St, T41521222. After Hours Medical Clinic, Mater Hospital, 313 Bourbong St, T41539500. Open Mon-Fri 1800-2300, Sat 1200-2300, Sun 0800-2300. **Useful numbers** Police: 254 Bourbong St, T41539111.

Mon Repos Turtle Rookery

8 Reef Getaway
9 Turtle Sands Tourist Park
10 Villa Mirasol Boutique Motel

● **Eating**
1 Grand Hotel
2 Numero Uno
3 Rose Garden Café

12 km east of Bundaberg, near the coastal resort of Bargara

Best viewing times for nesting turtles is subject to night tides between November-February. Turtle hatchlings are best viewed between 1900-2400 from January-March

Capricorn & Central coasts

Supporting the largest concentration of nesting marine turtles on the eastern Australian mainland and one of the largest loggerhead turtle rookeries in the world, the Coral Coast beach known as Mon Repos (pronounced Mon Repo), is a place of near ecological reverence. During the day Mon Repos looks just like any other idyllic Queensland beach and gives absolutely no indication of its conservation value. Yet at night between mid-October and May it takes on a very different aura, and perhaps most incredibly, has done so for millennia. Hauling themselves from the waves, just beyond the tide line, with a determination only nature can display, the often quite elderly females excavate a pit in the sand, then lay over one hundred eggs, before deftly filling it in and disappearing beneath the waves, as if they had never been there at all. To watch this happen, so invasively – apparently there are oblivious – and in the space of about 20 minutes, is a truly memorable experience that ranks as one of the most unique in Australia. And it doesn't end there. Towards the end of the season, from January to March, the tiny hatchlings emerge from the nest and then, almost simultaneously, like tiny clockwork toys wound up to the max, 'run' with unmatched enthusiasm towards the relative safety of the water. Watching this infant spectacle, is both moving and hilarious. Apparently only one in 1,000 of the hatchlings will survive to maturity and ever return to the same beach to breed. Of course like any wildlife watching attraction there are no guarantees that turtles will show up on any given night, so you may need a lot of patience. But, while you wait at the Information Centre to be escorted in groups of about twenty to watch the turtles up close, you can view static displays, or better still, join in the staff's regular and fascinating question and answer sessions, that tell of the turtles remarkable natural history, and sadly, the increasing threats humans are placing upon them.

■ *Open for turtle viewing Oct-May, 1900-0600. Ranger guided tours subject to turtle activity. Information Centre open daily 24 hrs Oct-May and 0600-1800 Jun-Sep). $5, child $2.50. T41591652. Grange Rd (off Bundaberg Port Rd).*

Southern Reef Islands

Lady Musgrave Island Lady Musgrave Island, 83 km northeast of Bundaberg, is part of the Capricornia Cays National Park and the southern-most island of the Bunker Group. With a relatively small 14 ha of coral cay in comparison to a huge 1192-ha surrounding reef, it is generally considered one of the most beautiful and abundant in wildlife, both above and below the water. The cay itself offers safe haven to thousands of breeding seabirds and also serves as an important green turtle rookery between November and March. Then, between August and October, humpback whales are also commonly seen in the vicinity. With such a large expanse of reef, the island offers some excellent snorkelling and diving and being devoid of the usual holiday resort, a very pleasant escape from the mainland.

Sleeping There is a campsite on the island administered by the QPWS, T49716500. No water and fires banned. Bookings essential and need to be arranged well in advance.

Transport *Lady Musgrave Barrier Reef Cruises*, based at the Bundaberg Port Marina, (19 km northeast of Bundaberg), T41594519, www.lmcruises.com.au, offer day trips Mon/Tue/Wed/Thu/Sat (0745-1745), from $130, child $65. Certified diving is available, from $30, introductory dives from $70. Whale watching trips operate between Aug-Oct. Camping transfers are equivalent to 2-day cruise fares. Day cruises are also available from the Town of 1770, see page 305.

Lady Elliot Island Lady Elliot Island sits out on its own, about 20 km south of Lady Musgrave Island and is one of the southernmost coral cays on the Barrier Reef. Although the cay itself is larger in size than Musgrave, the surround reef is smaller, yet both still combine to make it a near equal in aesthetics and wildlife diversity. The island is also a popular diving venue with numerous wrecks lying just offshore (about $30 a dive). The biggest difference between the two is its accommodation and access.

Sleeping and eating LL-L *Lady Elliot Island Reef Resort* is modern and offers affordable suites, units and tent cabins, all the usual facilities and it has it's own airfield.

Transport Day-trips (by air) from Bundaberg cost from $219, child $110. Flight transfers from Bundaberg and Hervey Bay with *Whitaker Air* cost from $168, child $84. T41255344/1800 072200, www.ladyelliot.com.au

Agnes Water and the Town of 1770

*Today both 1770 and Agnes are fast-developing from being fairly inaccessible, sleepy coastal neighbours to potentially becoming the next booming tourist destination on the central, southern Queensland coast. As well as great beaches and its beautiful and varied aesthetics, the area boasts some excellent surfing, boating, fishing, cruising and tour opportunities, centred around the most northerly surf beach in Queensland, two fine national parks, **Eurimbula** and **Deepwater**. and Lady Musgrave Island on the Barrier Reef.*

Colour map 4, grid C5
Population: 300
125 km north of Bundaberg, 120 km south of Gladstone

Despite its increasing popularity the public transport services to Agnes Water and 1770 are generally poor, but now all roads are almost entirely sealed, this situation will no doubt quickly change. There are long distance bus services and a train station at Miriam Vale, 55 km east. Miriam Vale 'Discovery Coast' VIC located on the Bruce Highway in Miriam Vale, T49745428, www.barrierreef.net, open Mon-Fri 0830-1700, Sat/Sun 0900-1700, and the Discovery Centre, Endeavour Plaza, Agnes Water, T49747002, open daily 0900-1700, are the 2 main sources of local information. QPWS have an office on Captain Cook Drive, Town of 1770, T49749350.

Ins & outs
See Transport, page 305, for further details

So why 1770? And who was Agnes? If the intriguing names alone don't persuade you to stray from the Bruce Highway to explore then perhaps their significance in the history books and their sheer aesthetics will! It will be of little surprise that the name 1770 refers to the ubiquitous **Captain Cook**, whom, after landing in Botany Bay (NSW) in April 1770, decided to stretch his legs here, one month later. Finding safe anchorage in the bay off what is now the Town of 1770, Cook and his landing party went ashore to explore in search of fresh water and something refreshingly 'different' for tea. Finding a suitable stream and then blowing the smithereens out of the local birdlife they quickly secured both. Story has it that Cook tucked into a leg of Bustard (a sort of turkey) and so named place –**Bustard Bay**. As for Agnes? Well that remains debatable and is thought to have derived from the name of a local wreck, or more probably, Agnes Clowe, the daughter of the first European settlers.

History

Sights

Agnes Water has a beautiful 5-km beach right on its doorstep, which offers good swimming and excellent surfing. More remote beaches offering more solitude and great walking opportunities can be accessed within the national parks (see below). There is a small **museum** on Springs Road that touches on Aboriginal settlement, Cook's visit and the subsequent visitations by explorers Flinders and King. Other displays document more recent maritime and European settlement history. ■ *Sat/Sun 1000-1200, Wed 1300-1500, $2.*

The Town (village) of **1770**, that nestles on the leeward side of Round Hill Head and along the bank of the Round Hill Inlet, is 6 km north of Agnes and is a popular spot for fishing and boating. It also serves as the main departure point for local national park and reef island tours and cruises. See below.

Deepwater National Park, 8 km south of Agnes, presents a mosaic of coastal vegetation including paperbark, banksias and heath land fringed with dunes and a sweeping beach studded with small rocky headlands. As well as fishing and walking it presents some fine opportunities for bird watching and is often used as a nesting site by green turtles between January and April. There is a QPWS campsite (self-registration) at Wreck Rock, 11 km south of Agnes with toilets, rainwater supply and a cold shower. Fires are banned. As the roads within the park are unsealed and 4WD is recommended. To the northwest of Agnes is **Eurimbula National Park**. Indented by the Round Hill Inlet and Eurimbula Creek it is an area covered in thick mangrove and fresh-water paperbark swamps. As such it less accessible than Deepwater and best explored by boat. Other than the interesting flora and fauna highlights include the panoramic views of the park and coastline from the Ganoonga Noonga Lookout, which can be reached by vehicle 3 km from the park entrance, 10 km west of Agnes Water. Again a 4WD is recommended especially in the wet season. There is a QPWS campsite (self-registration) at Bustard Beach with bore water and toilets. Fires are banned. ■ *For more information on both parks contact the QPWS in Bundaberg, T41311600 or 1770, T49749350.*

Essentials

Sleeping

There is a good range of accommodation but both towns are getting increasingly busy, especially around Christmas and public holidays – book ahead

Agnes Water L *Hoban's Hideaway*, 2510 Round Hill Rd, T49749144, hoban@bigpond.com.au, is an award winning B&B, located just before Agnes, offering 4 spacious en suites in a lovely timber colonial-style homestead amidst a quiet bush setting. **LL-L** *Pacific Crest B&B*, 15 Webster Court, T49021770, www.barrierreef.net/pacificcrest.com.au Closer to town this modern option has 3 suites (one with spa) in a quiet location with good views. **A** *Agnes Palm Beachside Apartments*, Captain Cook Dr, T49747200, offers modern self-contained apartments with in-house restaurant, while the **A-B** *Mango Tree Motel*, 7 Agnes St, T49749132, is slightly cheaper and 150 m from the beach. **C-E** *1770 Backpackers Beachouse*, Captain Cook Drive, T49749849. New and aesthetically unusual, this offers dorms and doubles with modern facilities and is run by a caring manager who has been in the backpacking industry for many years. **B-F** *Agnes Water Caravan Park*, Jeffery Ct, T49749193. A 2 -star option handy to the beach and shops and offering self-contained units, cabins, powered and non-powered sites, but no camp kitchen.

1770 L-A *Beachshacks*, 578 Captain Cook Drive, T49749463, beachshack@1770.net are characterful, spacious and modern fully self-contained bungalows complete with thatched roofs and decks overlooking the beach. **L** *Zamia Lodge*, 3 Zamia Court, T49741101, jeffandpatschmidt@bigpond.com.au A modern 2-storey house with 2 fully self-contained en suites, 1- and 2-bedroom with decks in a quiet location. Good week-end deals. Although there is a basic camping ground with powered and non-powered sites near the beach in 1770, T49749286, **A-F** *Captain Cook Holiday Village*, 300 m further inland on Captain Cook Dr, T49749219, is recommended. Set in the bush it has a good range of options from self-contained en suite cabins to campsites and a good bistro/bar.

Eating

As yet the choice is not exactly vast but things are improving

Agnes Water *Agnes Water Tavern*, 1 Tavern Rd, T49749469, is a popular haunt with locals and offers value counter meals and has a pleasant garden bar. Open daily for lunch and dinner. There is also a bakery (good coffee) and a Chinese restaurant, T49749062. Open Tue-Sun, lunch and dinner. In the Agnes Water's shopping centre next to the post office. **1770** *Deck Restaurant*, Captain Cook Holiday Village (see above). Open Tue-Sat for lunch and dinner. Offers value, local seafood, great views and a nice atmosphere.

1770 Environmental Tours, 1770 Marina, 1770, T49749422, larc@1770.net, offer an exciting and unique eco/history tour/cruise on board an amphibious vehicle, *The LARC*, along the coast north of 1770 to Bustard Head and Pancake Creek. There are 3 tours on offer. *Paradise Tour* (Mon/Wed/Sat/0900-1600) which explores the beaches, Aboriginal middens and the stunning views from the Bustard Head Light Station and neighbouring cemetery, with a spot of sand boarding en route from $88, child $44. The second offering is *Sunset Cruise* (daily, 1630) which is a 1-hr exploration of Round Hill Creek and Eurimbula National Park, from $22, child $11. *Joyride* is the same trip during daylight hours. Book ahead. *Reef Jet*, T49749422, is a new cruise operation (under the same environmental tours banner as the company above) offering exclusive day trips to Fitzroy Reef with snorkelling, sea mammal watching, reef surfing and scuba diving, from $125, child $65. Snorkelling trips to a 20-acre coral reef in Pancake Creek near Bustard Head are also available from $100, child $50. A 2-day Reef and LARC combo costs from $190, child $98. *1770 Great Barrier Reef Cruises*, also based at the Marina, T49749077, spiritof1770@discoverycoast.net~Web, offer day trips and camping transfers to Lady Musgrave Island (51 km east of 1770), from $130, child $65 (plus $4 Reef tax). The cruise, dubbed the 'See More Sea Less' allows a whole 6 hrs on the reef, including a stop on a floating pontoon that acts as an ideal base for snorkelling, diving and coral viewing. Departs 0800 Tue/Thu/Sat/Sun and on demand Mon/Wed/Fri. Lunch included and bookings essential. A shuttle bus is available from Bundaberg. Camping transfers to the island cost $260, child $130. For more information on Lady Musgrave Island see Bundaberg, page 302. *MV James Cook*, T49749422, offer day fishing excursions from $169 per person and *Discovery Coast Detours*, T49747540, offer entertaining 6x4WD day tours to the Discovery Coast Hinterland, Wed, from $75, child $60 and to Deepwater National Park Tue/Thu from $65, child $50. If you want to hire your own 4WD contact 1770 4WD hire, 21 Bicentennial Dr, T49749741. *1770 Adventure Tours*, T49749470, offer half, full-day and overnight canoeing adventures and independent hire.

Tours & activities

The town of 1770 and Agnes Water are best accessed from the Bruce Highway at Miriam Vale (63 km), or from the south via Bundaberg (120 km). All access roads will soon be completely sealed. **Bus** Long-distance bus company *McCafferty's*, T131499, offer part-transfers to Agnes (from the Bruce Highway) stopping at the Fingerboard Junction Service Station (about 30 km south of Agnes and 20 km east of Miriam Vale). The backpackers can pick-up from there. *Barbours Buses*, T49749030, offer twice weekly services from Bundaberg. **Taxi** T49749000. **Train** The nearest station is in Miriam Vale, T132232.

Transport

Banks There is a *Westpac Bank* and ATM facilities in the Agnes Water's Shopping Complex. **Communications** Internet: available at *Daniele's Copy Centre*, Shop 4B Endeavour Plaza, Agnes Water, T49747460. Open Mon-Fri 0900-1700.

Directory

Gladstone

A former penal colony put on the map by unsung naval explorer Matthew Flinders in 1802, Gladstone has grown dramatically in recent years, from being a sleepy coastal town to one of the most industrialized areas in Australia. It now hosts the country's largest aluminium smelter, largest cement operation and Queensland's biggest power station and multi cargo port, all of which combined handle over 50 million tonnes of cargo annually. When the average tourists get the slightest whiff of that dubious accolade, they tend to put the blinkers on and gladly head north. However, though Gladstone is by no means pretty, it is worth joining an 'industry tour' to take a closer look at the processes involved that are, after all, so fundamental to our modern

Colour map 4, grid C5
Population: 26,500
534 km north of Brisbane, 104 km south of Rockhampton

lifestyle. Gladstone is also friendly place with a few worthy and deeply contrasting attractions including one of the best botanical gardens in the state, and lying just beyond the ocean's horizon, one of the most beautiful, picture postcard Reef Islands – Heron Island – for which Gladstone is the main access point. It was named in 1847 after William Gladstone a British statesman who went on to be a British Prime Minister.

Ins & outs
See Transport, page 307, for details

Gladstone VIC is located at the modern Marina Ferry Terminal, Bryan Jordan Dr, T49724000, www.gladstoneregion.org.au Open Mon-Fri 0830-1700, Sat/Sun 0900-1700. Town maps are available. QPWS office is on Floor 3, Centre Point Building, 136 Goondoon St, T49726055. It offers reef island camping permits and information.

Sights
Gladstone lays claim to being the 'Tidiest Town in Queensland'!

By far the best way to see the various industries and industrial complexes in action is to join a one-hour **industry tour** that can be booked through the VIC. Otherwise, if you are pressed for time, a good vantage point (signposted) sits overlooking the **Alumina Plant**, 2 km east of the town centre. The huge complex, which is one of the largest in the world, produces three million tonnes of aluminium oxide a year. Its convoluted mass of rust coloured (bauxite dust) steel certainly looks the part and seems almost alive, making noises like an irate dragon with indigestion. **Auckland Hill**, Flinders Street (just to the northwest of the city centre), also offers expansive views across the busy harbour.

In stark contrast to all the industrial aesthetics is the **Toondoon Botanical Gardens**, Glenlyon Road, on the southern outskirts of town. Considered one of the best in Queensland, the 55-ha site features exclusively native species, a lake replete with turtles and the Mount Biondello bush walk. ■ *Daily (seasonal times) from at least 0900-1700. Free. There is a café on site and guided tours are available weekdays.*

For culture vultures the **Gladstone Regional Art Gallery and Museum** is on the corner of Goondoon and Bramston streets and is worth a muse. Housed in the old 1869 Georgian Town Hall building it features an inspiring collection of Australian art, history and craft. ■ *Mon-Fri 1000-1700, Sat 1000-1600. Free.*

There are (believe it or not) some pretty beaches near Gladstone. **Curtis Island**, which guards the harbour entrance and the neighbouring coastal settlements of **Boyne River** and **Tannum Sands**, 26 km south of Gladstone all have their fair share. **Awoonga Lake** and Dam, detaining the River Boyne, is a popular spot for watersports and walking, while **Mount Larcom** (632 m) to the west of Gladstone (via the Port Curtis Highway and Targinie Road), a five-hour walk, presents more of a challenge. The VIC can provide directions and access details to all of the above.

Other than the excellent industry tours, Gladstone also serves as an excellent and relatively cheap base for **diving**. There are many fine sites around the Capricorn and Bunker groups of reef and coral islands, with Heron Island being considered one of the best dive sites on the reef. See Tours and activities, below.

Sleeping
Goondoon Street is the main drag running northwest to southeast

L *Country Plaza International*, 100 Goondoon St, T49724499, and *Metro Hotel and Suites*, 22-24 Roseberry St, T49724711, www.metroinns.com.au, are the 2 main hotels in the city. Both offer good views and reasonable rates. **L-A** *Auckland Hill B&B*, 15 Yarroon St, T49724907, www.ahbb.com.au, is a conveniently located. 4-star B&B in a restored traditional Queenslander, offering 6 spacious en suites and 1 luxury suite with spa, pool and off-street parking. **A** *Gladstone Reef Motel*, corner of Goondoon and Yarroon sts, T49721000. Of the numerous motels in the city this 3-star option is the

Capricorn & Central coasts

better placed, with a rooftop pool, an à la carte restaurant and good views across the harbour. **C-F** *Gladstone Backpackers*, 12 Rollo St, 750 m southwest of the city centre off Lord St, T49725744, is currently a little tired but very friendly and primed for renovation. It has dorms, singles, doubles, campsites and a good kitchen. Bike hire and pick-ups available. **B-E** *Barney Beach Seabreeze Caravan Park*, Friend St, Barney Bay, 2 km east of the town centre, T49721366. This is the best motor park in town. Enthusiastic staff will escort you to a wide range of en suite/standard cabins, powered and non-powered sites. Good camp kitchen.

Gladstone is renowned for its locally caught seafood and in particular it's Gladstone **Eating** mud crabs and coral trout. Each year in Oct it celebrates this fact with a *Seafood Festival*, but you can have your own quiet celebrations at *Flinders Seafood Restaurant*, Flinders Parade Corner, Oaka Lane, T49728322, open lunch Mon-Fri from 1100, dinner daily from 1730, or *Swaggy's Australian Restaurant*, 56 Goondoon St, T49721653, open lunch Mon-Fri, dinner Mon-Sat. The latter also serves up roo, croc and emu steaks. More affordable meals and $6.50 evening buffet meals are offered at *Yachties* in the Gladstone Yacht Club, 1 Goondoon St, T49722294. Open daily from 1200-1400 and 1800-2030. *Fordy's Seafood*, 18A Tank St, T49721986, is popular for fish and chips. Open Tue-Sun. Other casual dining options with good coffee include *Atrios Café*, Shop 17A Dawson Highway, T49769288. Open daily. *Snoops*, Shop 1/72 Goondoon St, T49722392. Open Mon-Fri 0700-1630.

Backpack and Kayak Outdoor Adventure Store, 1/37 Goondoon St, T49769283, **Tours &** backpackandkayak@bigpond.com.au, offer an exciting range of dive trips, courses and **activities** sea kayaking adventures, from $45 (kayaking) to $450 (certification course). Recommended. Other local dive companies include *Last Wave Dive Centre*, 16 Goondoon St, T49729185 and *Deep Blue Adventures*, (gear hire) T49787069. The VIC has comprehensive listings of local boat and fishing charters. *Sunset Tours*, T49722288, offers a range of day or 2-day (camping). Eco-tours around the region from $90 per day.

The Nightowl convenience store is located next door to *Atrios* and remains open daily **Shopping** until 2400. There are 2 supermarkets in the KinKora Shopping Centre, corner of Dawson Highway and Philip St, T49781045.

Air Gladstone Airport is located in the suburb of Clinton, 7 km south of the city cen- **Transport** tre. *Qantas*, T131313, and *Flight West*, T132392, bookings@flightwest.com.au, offer daily services. **Car hire** *Avis*, T49782633 and *Hertz*, T49784411, are both based at the airport. *Thrifty*, 69 Hanson Rd, T49725999. Car servicing at *Gladstone Service Centre*, 50 Hanson Rd, T49723911. **Bus** *Buslink*, Gladstone Bus and Coach, T49721670, are the local suburban service provider. Gladstone is served by *MacCafferty's*, T131499, and *Greyhound*, T132030. Long-distance buses stop at the 24-hr *Mobil Service Station* on Dawson Rd, just off Glenlyon Rd, T49723888. **Taxi** T49721800/131008. **Train** The station is on Toolooa St, at the end of Tank St (north of the city centre), T49764211. *Queensland Rail* north and southbound services pass through daily. Bookings, T132232, or *Travelworld*, 136 Goondoon St, T49727277, provide a comprehensive booking service for all the above.

Banks Goondoon St. **Communications** Internet: *Arthur's Computer Essentials*, **Directory** 1 Edward St, T49720666. Open Mon-Fri 0830-1800, Sat 0830-1300. **Gladstone Library**, 144 Goondoon St, T49701232. Open Mon/Tue/Wed/Fri 0930-1745, Thu 0930-1945, Sat 0900-1630. **Post office**: corner of Goondoon and Tank sts. Open Mon-Fri 0830-1730. **Medical services** Kent St, T49763200. **Useful numbers** Police: 10 Yarroon St, T49713222.

Coral Sea Islands

Heron Island & the southern coral cays
70 km east of Gladstone

Sitting amongst an extensive complex of reefs is the tiny and idyllic coral cay known as Heron Island. Made entirely of coral – therefore a cay as opposed to a true 'island' – it is world renowned for its wildlife, diving and its upmarket (yet not exclusive) resort. The crystal clear waters, white sands, reef and myriad sea creatures are spectacular and adding to this haven of beauty is a breeding ground of exotic seabirds – like noddy terns and a major green turtle rookery. Humpback whales are also a common sight from June to November. Although much of the focus is on diving, one of the many great attractions of the place is the ability to literally walk from the beach on to the reef. Not surprisingly Heron was declared a national park in 1943 and is not open to day visitors. However, the southern reef does offer some superb cay camping opportunities. The QPWS have bush camps on Masthead, 65 km, and North West Islands, 90 km. Take your own water and gas stove. QPWS office in Gladstone issues permits and can provide the full details. You must book.

Sleeping & eating

LL *P&O Heron Island Resort*, T132469, www.poresorts.com.au Newly refurbished the resort offers all the facilities you might expect for the location from luxury suites to beach houses, swimming pool, an à la carte restaurant, bar, dive shop and a host of other activities. *Harvey World Travel*, 81 Goondoon St, T49723488, or *Travelworld*, 136 Goondoon St, T49727277, can make bookings and often have cheap stand-by rates in the off season.

Transport

Heron is 2 hrs by launch or 30 mins by helicopter. The resort launch leaves daily at 1100 from the Gladstone Marina on Bryan Jordan Dr, Gladstone and costs from $164 return. *Marine Helicopters*, T49781177, www.marineheli.com.au, fly daily from Gladstone Airport from $466 return. Masthead and North West Islands must be reached by private boat charter or helicopter.

Rockhampton

Colour map 4, grid C5
Population: 58,000
630 km north of Brisbane, 348 km south of Mackay; 40 km from the coast

*Straddling both the **Tropic of Capricorn** and picturesque **Fitzroy River**, Rockhampton, or 'Rocky' as it is affectionately known, is the dubbed the '**beef capital'** of Australia. First settled by Scots pioneer Charles Archer in 1855 (yet strangely bestowed the anglicised suffix 'Hampton', meaning 'a place near water'), the city enjoyed a brief gold rush in the late 1850s before the more sustainable plump and horny herbivores finally sealed its destiny. Although most visitors stay only very briefly on their way to sample the coastal delights of Yeppoon and **Great Keppel Island**, 'Rocky' has a truly diverse range of tourist attractions from the historical and cultural to the ecological and even subterranean including the 'must see' **Capricorn Caves** and an elegant city centre that is well worth a muse. Then of course, beyond the sights, are its gastronomical delights in the form of steaks the size of a small continent.*

Ins & outs
See Transport, page 312, for details

Rockhampton VIC, 208 Quay St, T49225339, rdpda@ozemail. com.au, is housed in the grandiose 1902 Customs House overlooking the river. Open Mon-Fri 0830-1630, Sat/Sun 0900-1600. QPWS office is located at the corner of Yeppoon and Norman rds, T49360511. VIC also stocks QPWS information.

Capricorn & Central coasts

Sights

Being a settlement born of considerable mineral and agricultural wealth, there **City Centre** are numerous stately, historical buildings dominating the city centre. These include the 1902 **Customs House** that now houses the VIC, the 1895 **Post Office**, on the corner of East St Mall and Denham Street, the 1890 *Criterion Hotel*, on Quay Street, and the 1887 **Supreme Court**, on East Lane, which has been in continuous use now for over a century. The self-guided walk or drive *Rockhampton Heritage* leaflet available from the VIC lists many others. Train enthusiasts will also find Rockhampton's tram history revealed at the Archer Park Steam **Tram Museum**. ■ *Denison St. Tue-Sun 1000-1600, $5.50, child $2.20. Tram operates Sun 1000-1300.*

The town has a number of art galleries. Paramount amongst them is **Rockhampton Art Gallery** which displays a long-established collection of mainly 1940-70s Australian works and more recent contemporary acquisitions. ■ *Tue-Fri 1000-1600, Sat/Sun 1100-1600, free. 62 Victoria Parade. T49368248.* More contemporary still is the **Attic Gallery** which holds the largest display of handmade crafts and pottery in Central Queensland. ■ *Mon-Fri 0915-1700, Sat 0915-1300. Free. 141 East St.* In contrast, across the river on Musgrave Street, is **Khum Yarn Art Gallery**, (Darumbul Youth Centre) which displays contemporary Aboriginal art. ■ *Mon-Fri 0900-1700.*

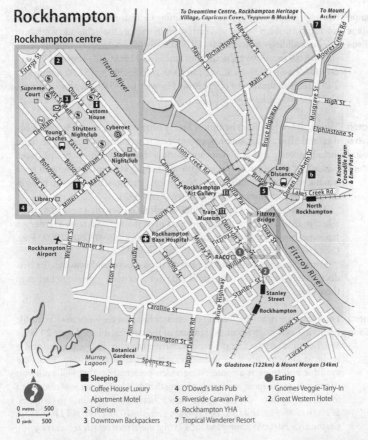

Rockhampton

Rockhampton centre

To Dreamtime Centre, Rockhampton Heritage Village, Capricorn Caves, Yeppoon & Mackay

To Mount Archer

Fitzroy River

Supreme Court

Customs House

Strutters Nightclub

Cybernet

Young's Coaches

Stadium Nightclub

Library

Moores Creek Rd

Haines St

Richardson Rd

Alexandra St

Main St

High St

Bruce Highway

Elphinstone St

To Koorana Crocodile Farm & Emu Park

Lions Creek Rd

Campbell St

Rockhampton Art Gallery

Long Distance

Queen Elizabeth Dr

Bridge St

Lakes Creek Rd

North Rockhampton

Tram Museum

Fitzroy Bridge

Rockhampton Base Hospital

Hunter St

Rockhampton Airport

RACQ

William St

Fitzroy River

Stanley St

Stanley Street

Rockhampton

Caroline St

Botanical Gardens

Murray Lagoon

Pennington St

Spencer St

Upper Dawson Rd

Bruce Highway

Wood St

Lucas St

To Gladstone (122km) & Mount Morgan (34km)

N

0 metres 500
0 yards 500

Capricorn & Central coasts

■ **Sleeping**
1 Coffee House Luxury Apartment Motel
2 Criterion
3 Downtown Backpackers
4 O'Dowd's Irish Pub
5 Riverside Caravan Park
6 Rockhampton YHA
7 Tropical Wanderer Resort

● **Eating**
1 Gnomes Veggie-Tarry-In
2 Great Western Hotel

As well as its numerous historical buildings and in celebration of its status as the beef capital of Australia Rockhampton has ensured that their four-legged friends are duly honoured, with no less than six **bull staTue** in the town. Scattered in parks and on roundabouts several very horny and discreetly endowed characters are in evidence from the 'well done' 'Brahman Bull' to the 'rare' 'Santa Gertrudis'.

Dreamtime Centre Maintaining the Aboriginal theme, though not quite on a par with the award winning Tjapukai Aboriginal Park near Cairns, is the Dreamtime Centre. Set in 30acres of parkland, just off the Bruce Highway, 6 km north of the city centre, the centre and staff offer an entertaining introduction to Aboriginal and Torres Straight heritage using a wide range of displays and hands-on activities. On a guided or self guided tour you can witness some masterful didgeridoo playing, before exploring the various displays outside in the Torres Straight Islander Village, including traditional *gunyahs* (shelters) and the giant Dugong Complex that displays artefacts and building materials. There is also a native plant garden where you can learn about their use as food and medicine. For many the highlight of their visit is the opportunity to throw a boomerang so it actually comes back. It is also interesting to learn about another that is not supposed to. ■ *Mon-Fri 1000-1530. $12, child $5.50. T49361655. Guided tours daily at 1030 and 1300. Dance performances on Mon.*

Rockhampton Heritage Village Also along the Bruce Highway, maintaining the historical theme, is this 'active township museum' where you can faithfully explore the sights and sounds of original buildings, homesteads and businesses of yesteryear. Highlights of the visit are the extensive collections of clocks and beautifully restored vintage cars. ■ *Mon-Fri 0900-1500, Sat/Sun 1000-1600 $5.50, child $1.10, family $11. T49361026. Boundary Rd off the Bruce Highway (north past Yeppoon turnoff). Guided tours available.*

Rockhampton Zoo & Botanical Gardens The small but tidy Rockhampton Zoo is situated between the Botanic Gardens and Murray Lagoon on Spencer Street. There are many natives on hand including koala and tame kangaroos and a charming pair of chimps called Cassie and Ockie (as in Dokie) who will happily demonstrate how to eat a banana with their mouths open. Surprisingly perhaps, there are no bulls in evidence. ■ *Daily from 0800-1700. Free. T49368000.*

Almost next door are the spacious **Botanical Gardens** that were first established in 1869. Amongst its leafy avenues of palms and cycads are a fernery, a Japanese garden and the peaceful garden tearooms. ■ *0600-1800. Free. Guided walks are available Tue/Wed/Thu from 0930, $3.*

Murray Lagoon is also a fine place to stroll around and provides the best duck feeding venue in town – but keep your eyes open – there are turtles in there too.

Koorana Crocodile Farm For a far more dramatic feeding experience head for the Koorana Crocodile Farm on Coowonga Road, 33 km east of the city. Established over 20 years ago, Koorana was the first private croc farm established in Queensland and is home to some mighty large characters with spectacular dentition. Tours are available and there is an interesting video presentation that will avail you of many facts the most memorable being that crocodile dung was once used for contraception, though quite how, thankfully, remains an enigma. ■ *1000-1500. $12, child $6. T49344749. Tours at 1030-1200 and 1300-1430. On the Emu Park/Rockhampton Rd. Getting there: own vehicle is necessary.*

This fascinating limestone cave system, 23 km north of Rockhampton, is well worth a visit. Privately owned and open to the public for over a century, they offer a unique and memorable combination of subterranean sights and sounds and are the home to an array of unusual wildlife. An entertaining guided tour takes you through numerous 'collapsed caverns', beautifully lit caves and narrow tunnels, to eventually reach a natural **amphitheatre** where stunning acoustics are demonstrated with classical music and then, utter silence. The venue is so special it is often used for weddings and Christmas carol concerts. On the way out you can then witness a potentially brilliant and vertical natural light spectacle that captures the full rays of the sun in December and January. The cave system has been home to tens of thousands of bats and the odd harmless python for millennia, and although very few are seen, it adds that essential 'Indiana Jones' edge. The more adventurous can go on an exhilarating two- to four-hour **caving** tour and come face to face with the bats and pythons while squeezing through the infamous 'Fat Man's Misery'. ■ *Daily 0900-1600. Standard tour $13, child $6.50, 3-hr caving with own transport from $45 (1300), with transfers from Rockhampton $55 (not available Tue/Thu). Half-day standard tour with transport daily from $33, full-day standard tour with transfers (Sun/Mon/Wed/Fri) from $64. Accommodation packages also available. T49342883, www.capricorncaves.com.au Olsen's Caves Rd. There is a café and new lodge/campsite within the grounds.*

Capricorn Caves

Mount Morgan, 38 km south of the city, has a steam railway and a small well presented museum celebrating its highly productive gold and copper mining heritage. ■ *Mon-Sat 1000-1300, Sun 1000-1600. $4, child 50c. T49382132.* There is also a bat-infested cave nearby where dinosaur footprints were discovered in 1954. Tours available from the city. **Mount Archer** (604 m), which looms large above 'Rocky's' northeastern suburbs, has a fine summit walk and **lookout**. Access is from the end of Moores Ck Road, north of the Bruce Highway. Vehicular access to the summit is from Frenchville Road (off Norman, which is off Moores Ck Road).

Mount Morgan & Archer

Essentials

There are plenty of quality places in the centre of the city including **L** *Coffee House Luxury Apartment Motel*, corner of Williams and Bolsover sts, T49275722, the_coffee house@bigpond.com.au It is a tidy, modern establishment with well appointed fully self-contained apartments, executive and standard rooms and a fine café on site. Internet. Recommended. **B-D** *O'Dowd's Irish Pub*, 100 William St, T49270344, www.odowds.com.au Clean and good value single, twin, double and family rooms. **C-D** *Criterion Hotel*, Quay St, T49221225. Try this for a traditional, historical edge, overlooking the river, old fashioned and characterful rooms.

Sleeping
■ *On map, page 309*

There are two main backpackers in the city. **C-E** *Downtown Backpackers*, Oxford Hotel, corner of East and Denham sts, T49221837. A clean, no frills place, right in the heart of the city, offering value small dorms, doubles, twins, singles, kitchen and TV room with internet, even a bath! **B-E** *Rockhampton YHA*, located across the river on MacFarlane St, T49275288. Rather plain, it has standard doubles, some with en suite and dorms, a well-equipped kitchen, internet and tours desk. Onward trips to the coast and Great Keppel a speciality.

There are numerous motels and motor parks scattered around the city and along the Bruce Highway. **A-E** *Tropical Wanderer Resort*, 394 Yaamba Rd (Bruce Highway),

Capricorn & Central coasts

T49263822. Urban, 4-star. **B-F** *Capricorn Caves Eco-Lodge and Caravan Park*, Capricorn Caves, 23 km north of the city, T49342883, www.capricorncaves.com.au Handy for visiting the caves. **E** *Riverside Caravan Park*, next to the river just across the Fitzroy Bridge, 2 Reaney St, T49223779. Basic, 3 star. Convenient to the city centre, but only has powered and non-powered sites with limited facilities.

Eating
● *On map, page 309*

Unless you are a vegetarian of almost religious persuasion, then you hardly need a menu in 'Rocky'. Big around here (literally) are the steaks. All the local hotels serve them up on near platters, though the *Criterion*, (*Bush Inn*), Quay St, T49221225 and the *Great* Western, 39 Stanley St, T49221862, are the best bets. Both are open daily from about 1100-late. With all the dribbling carnivores around town it is not entirely surprising to find a fine vegetarian café in the city. *Gnomes Veggie-Tarry-In*, corner of Williams St and Denison Lane (mind the trains!), T49274713, is full of character as well as beaming vegetarians, perfectly content with the extensive blackboard menu. It also has live entertainment. Open Mon-Thu 0930-2200, Fri/Sat 0930-2300. For a good meat eater's breakfast and good coffee, try *Coffee House*, corner of William and Bolsover sts, T49275722. *O'Dowd's Irish Pub* (see above) offers traditional pub grub and live bands at weekends.

Bars & clubs

The aptly named *Strutters Nightclub* is on East St Mall. Wed-Sat from 2000. Sports fans can muse the big screens in the *Stadium Nightclub*, beside *Heritage Hotel* on Quay St.

Tours & activities

Get-About-Tours, T49275977, offer an excellent, value range of full- or half-day and evening tours to numerous locations, including the Capricorn Caves and cattle sale yards, from $30. Accommodation pick-ups. Recommended. *Capricorn Eco-Heritage Tours*, T49361655, offer scheduled tours to the Rockhampton Heritage Village, Dreamtime Centre and Capricorn Caves, from 0900 daily. *Little Bent-Wing Bat Tours*, T49272055, offer trips to see the comings and goings of tens of thousands of cave dwelling bats from Dec-Jan. Call for details. There are several well-renowned farm/station stays in the region, where you can go horse riding, on 4WD adventures and even learn how to milk a cow. They include *Myella Farmstay*, 125 km southwest of the city, T49981290, 2 days-1-night from $143. *Kroombit Station*, T49922186, www.kroombit. com.au, offers a holistic outback nature experience with cattle drives, horse riding and 4WD tours (motor park on site). *Naomi Hills Cattle Station*, 160 km west of the city, T49359121. Mining and aboriginal settlement, backpacker accommodation from $35. Fitzroy River, the largest in Queensland and the second largest in Australia, offers fine fishing with Barramundi, king salmon, grunter and silver dew to name but a few. *Waikari Fishing Charters*, T49288758, offer trips from $66. For a river cruise, *Dowies* Paddleboat, T49391379, plies the river from the Botanical Gardens and Murray Lagoon, 1000 and 1400, from $6, child $4. Lastly you might like to take the bull by the horns, literally, at the *Great Western Hotels* scheduled *Bull Rides*, T49221862, from $5.50.

Transport

Local Bus *Capricorn Sunbus*, T49362133, are the local suburban bus company. *Young's Coaches*, 274 George St, T49223813, offers regular daily services to the train station, Yeppoon (Route 20, from $15, child $7 return), Rosslyn Bay (cruise boats), Emu Park and Mount Morgan (Route 22). The main terminal is on Bolsover St. *Rothery's Coaches*, 13 Power St, T49224320 (bookings T49336744), also offer daily services with accommodation pick-ups to Rosslyn Bay Boat Harbour, from $15.40, child $7.70 return. **Taxi** *Rocky Cabs*, T131008.

Long distance Air Rockhampton Airport is 4 km west of the city centre. *Qantas/Sunstate*, T131313, has regular schedules to main centres north, south and west. A taxi in to town costs about $10. **Bus** Long-distance bus terminal, T49272844, is on the corner of Queen Elizabeth Dr and Bridge St, about 500 m north of the Fitzroy

Bridge. *McCafferty's*, T131499, *Greyhound*, T132030, and *Premier Motor Services*, T133410, offer north/southbound services. **Train** The station is located 1 km south of the city centre at the end of Murray St (off Bruce Highway). *Tilt Train* is the preferred daily service to Brisbane (6½ hrs), from $81. Other slower services north/southbound are the budget *Sunlander* and luxury *Queenslander*. *Spirit of the Outback* heads west to Longreach Wed/Sat. There is a travel centre at the station, T49320234/T132232.

Banks All the main branches with ATMs are centred in and around the Mall on East St.   **Directory**
Commonwealth Bank offer currency exchange services, as do *Travel World*, below the *Leichardt Hotel* on Bolsover St. **Car hire** *Avis*, T49273344, and *Hertz*, T49222500, are based at the Airport, *Red Spot*, 320 Richardson Rd, T49265555, offer some of the best rates in the city. **Communications** Internet: *Cybernet*, 12 William St, T49273633. Open Mon-Fri 0830-1700, or the **Library**, corner of William and Alma sts, T49368265. Open Mon/Tue/Fri 0915-1730, Wed 1300-2000, Thu 0915-2000, Sat 0915-1630. Book in advance. **Post office**: corner of Denham St and The East St Mall. Open Mon-Fri 0830-1730. **Medical services** Chemist: *CQ Pharmacy*, 150 Alma St, T49221621. **Hospital**: Rockhampton Base Hospital, Canning St, T49206211. **Useful numbers Police**: corner of Denham and Bolsover sts, T49321500. **RACQ**: 134 William St (between Kent Lane and Campbell St), T49272255.

Yeppoon and around

Blessed by a cooling breeze and a string of pretty beaches, the small seaside set   *Colour map 4, grid B4*
tlements of **Yeppoon**, **Rosslyn Bay** and **Emu Park**, form the main focus of   *Population: 9,000*
the Capricorn Coast and serve as the region's principal coastal holiday resorts.   *40 km northeast of*
Yeppoon – the largest – offers a wealth of affordable accommodation and safe   *Rockhampton*
swimming, while 7 km south, Rosslyn Bay provides the gateway to **Great Keppel Island**. To the north of Yeppoon, the vast coastal wilderness of the **Byfield National Park** offers sanctuary to a rich variety of water birds and is the venue for some fine 4WD adventures.

Capricorn Coast VIC is beside the Ross Creek Roundabout (Yeppoon Rd), on the approach   **Ins & outs**
to Yeppoon, T49394888, www.capricorncoast.com.au Daily from 0900-1700. VIC and   *See Transport,*
QPWS office in Rockhampton has detailed information on the Byfield National Park   *page 315, for*
and its amenities as well as other sights around the area.   *details*

Although most non-natives only stop briefly on their way to Great Keppel   **Sights**
Island the surrounding coastline also offers plenty to see and do. There are beaches and headlands dotted all along the 16-km stretch of road between Yeppoon and Emu Park. South of Yeppoon the small national parks of **Double Head**, above Rosslyn Harbour, and **Bluff Point** at the southern end of **Kemp Beach** provide short walks and viewpoints across to Great Keppel Island. South of the Bluff, Mulambin Beach stretches south to Pinnacle Point and the entrance to **Causeway Lake**, a popular spot for fishing and boating. From there the road skirts Shoal Bay and **Kinka Beach**, considered by many as the best in the region, before arriving in Emu Park.

West of Yeppoon, just of the main highway, is the distinctly knobbly volcanic peak known as **Mount Jim Crow** (221 m). Who Mr Crow was exactly remains a mystery, but the peak was steeped in Aboriginal legend well before his arrival and can it be surmounted with a bit of scrambling from the old quarry.

To the north of Yeppoon, the seemingly boundless Byfield Coastal Area is one of the largest undeveloped regions on the east coast of Australia and although the vast majority of it is taken up by the inaccessible Shoalwater Bay

Capricorn & Central coasts

Military Training Area, the biologically diverse **Byfield National Park**, on its southern fringe, offers plenty of opportunity for nature based recreation, including camping, walking, boating, fishing, bird watching and 4WD. The heart of the park and its bush campsites are reached via the Byfield Road and Byfield State Forest. To see the park proper and to have any chance of reaching Nine Mile Beach requires a 4WD, which is perhaps what makes the park so special. If such luxuries are beyond your budget then you can still get a feel for the place from the 'wetlands' west, of the *Rydges Capricorn Resort* or the **Sandy Point** Section of the park, to the north. Although the road is unsealed it is easily negotiable by 2WD and offers numerous access points to **Farnborough Beach** where you can have a stretch of pristine sand almost entirely to yourself. *Rydges Capricorn Resort* itself is also well worth a look, see below, and offers numerous activities from bird watching to canoeing.

Sleeping   **LL** *Rydges Capricorn Resort*, Farnborough Rd, T49395111, www.capricornresort.com.au, is a hugely popular resort, set in the perfect beachside spot on the fringe of the Byfield National Park. The focus of its popularity is not surprisingly its superb pool, golf courses and huge range of activities. It offers slightly aging apartments, suites and rooms with all the usual facilities, including 2 restaurants, a bistro and café. Although designed for extended package holidays they often offer very attractive short stay deals, especially on weekdays and in the low season. Bookings essential. In contrast and surpassing even the *Rydges Resort* in near perfect isolation is **L-F** *Ferns Hideaway Resort*, located near Byfield, 50 km north of Yeppoon, T49351235, www.fernshideaway.com.au Set deep in the rainforest and beside a creek the colonial-style resort lodge offers log cabins with open fires and spa, basic budget rooms, campsites and a licensed bar and restaurant.

Yeppoon has numerous mid-range apartment blocks and motels, including the rather unsightly, but affordable and well facilitated, **L-A** *Bayview Tower*, corner of Adelaide and Normanby sts, T49394500. **A** *Tropical Nites Motel*, 34 Anzac Parade, T49391914, centrally located this 3-star motel provides another alternative. **A-B** *Sunlover Lodge*, 3 Camellia St, T49396727, www.sunlover@webcentral.com.au Further afield in Kinka Beach is this excellent lodge that offers a fine range of quiet, modern, fully self-contained cabins and villas, some with spa and all within a short stroll to the beach. **C-E** *Yeppoon Backpackers*, 30 Queen St, T49398080. Although nothing remarkable, this friendly backpackers provides a popular and perfectly comfortable stopover on the way over to Great Keppel Island. It has dorms, doubles, a pool, internet, courtesy bus from Rockhampton and offers range of discounted day tours to Great Keppel and elsewhere.

A-E *Capricorn Palms Holiday Village*, Wildin Way, Mulambin Beach (1 km south of Rosslyn Bay), T49336144. This is the best motor park in the area with everything from deluxe villas to non-powered sites, a good camp kitchen and pool.

Eating   *Rydges Capricorn Resort* is recommended for fine dining, or just breakfast in style(see above). There are 2 in-house restaurants – *The Lagoon* offering contemporary Australian (dinner only) and *The Tsuruya Japanese* (lunch and dinner). *Billabong Café*, T49395111, serves modern Australian and is open for breakfast, lunch and dinner. In Yeppoon there are numerous small affordable eateries along the main drag, James St. Elsewhere, *Keppel Bay Sailing Club*, above the beach on Anzac Parade, T49399500, offers value for money and a great view. Open daily for lunch and dinner. The best fish and chips in the area are to be found at *Causeway Lake Kiosk*, beside the Causeway Bridge (between Rosslyn Bay and Kinka Beach). Open daily until about 2000. *Dreamers Café*, 4 James St, Yeppoon, has good breakfasts, coffee and internet.

Get-About-Tours, T49348555, see Rockhampton page 312, offers 4WD tours to the **Tours &** Byfield Forest from $30. *Central Queensland Camel Treks*, T49395248, offers more **activities** local and sedate camel rides from $10-50, or, alternatively, *Rydges Resort Horse Treks*, Farnborough Rd, take away the hump under the saddle and better accommodate the lump upon it, T49395111. To make all that seem tame, you can also jump out of a plane, tandem, with *Capricorn Coast Skydive*, T49395248.

Bus *Young's Coaches*, 274 George St, T49223813, offers regular daily services to **Transport** Yeppoon (Route 20, from $15, child $7 return), Rosslyn Bay (cruise boats), from $9.45 single and Emu Park. *Rothery's Coaches*, 13 Power St, T49224320 (bookings T49336744) also offers daily services with accommodation pick-ups to Rosslyn Bay Boat Harbour, from $15.40, child $7.70 return. **Taxi** *Capricorn Cabs*, T391999.

Communications Internet: Available at *Dreamers Café*, 4 James St, Yeppoon. **Directory**

Great Keppel Island

Great Keppel Island (1,400 ha) is the largest of 18 islands in the Keppel group, *Colour map 4,* which combined, sit within easy reach of Roslyn Bay. For many, Great Keppel *grid B4/5* provides their first appointment and their first taste of Queensland's profusion of idyllic tropical islands. Although not quite on a par with Magnetic Island, Great Keppel still offers a fine introduction, prescribing a wealth of beautiful sandy beaches, pleasant walks and numerous activities. It is also equally accessible and well facilitated with accommodations to suit all budgets.

There are as many beaches of utter sublimity on Great Keppel as there are **Sights** islands in the entire group. Despite having 17 to choose from, few get beyond the main hub of activity at **Fisherman's Beach** which fronts the main **resorts** and provides ferry access. However, if your bucket and spade, snorkel and flippers are not too cumbersome, then you are far better to be more adventurous and seek out the quieter spots. A 20-minute walk to the south is **Long Beach**, which in turn provides access to **Monkey Beach**, 35 minutes away, across the headland to the west. North of the resort, beyond the spit, is **Putney Beach** which offers pleasant views across to Middle Island. There are numerous **walks** around the island with the most popular being the 45-minute trek to **Mount Wyndam**, the highest point on the island. Longer excursions of around 1½ hours will take you to the realms of solitude and the island's northeast coast beaches, including **Svendsen's**, **Sandhill** and **Wreck Beach**, or further still to the unremarkable light beacon on the island's southeast coast. Walking maps and descriptions are readily available from the ferry companies and resorts.

With so many activities, walks and beaches you will probably have very little time for anything else, but highly recommended are the tame and beautiful **rainbow lorikeets** that frequent the resort's *Keppel Café*. Much to the staff's chagrin, these artful avian dodgers cause absolute chaos with the customers, in their masterful and persistent pursuit of a tasty morsel.

The island is well known for offering a broad range of accommodation from luxury to **Sleeping** budget. Before making a decision on island accommodation budget travellers should **& eating** look into the numerous packages available from each, or from Rockhampton/ Yeppoon backpackers. This will save considerably on independent travelling costs. **LL** *Great! Keppel Island Resort*, T1800 245658/49395044, wwwgkeppel.com.au, is the main resort on the island located at the southern end of Fisherman's Beach. It has all

Capricorn & Central coasts

the usual accommodation options from luxury villas to standard rooms, a restaurant, bar, nightclub, café, pool, spas and over 40 activities. The pricey *Keppel Café*, bar and nightclub are open to non-guests. **L-E** *YHA Great Keppel Island Backpackers Village*, T49275288, yhagreatkeppelisland@bigpond.com.au, is a large complex located at the northern end of Fisherman's Beach. It offers a vast range of options from group cabins sleeping up to 8 to the basic tent village. Part of the complex has just been completely renovated providing modern budget facilities. Bistro, bar and games area. **A-E** *Great Keppel Island Holiday Village* ('Geoff and Dianna's Place'), T49398655, wwwgkiholiday village.com.au, is a laid-back place next door to the YHA complex, offering everything from a fully self-contained house to cabins, doubles/twins, dorms and custom built tents. Fully equipped kitchen, free snorkel gear and organized kayak trips. Other than the resort eateries, there is *Keppel Island Pizza* located on the waterfront. Open daily (except Mon) 1230-1400, 1800-2100. The limited groceries available at the YHA resort are pricey so you are advised to take your own food supplies.

Tours & activities
All the main accommodation establishments offer their own range of activities and tours but day-trippers can access a wealth of water-based activities and equipment from the beach hut directly opposite the ferry drop off. There you can secure anything from parasailing ($60) to snorkel gear ($10) and even a humble beach umbrella for $6. You can also take a camel ride or be suitably embarrassed while being flung about on the bay straddling a large inflatable banana. The island offers some fine snorkelling and diving. *Keppel Reef Scuba Adventures*, have a dive shop just beyond the Spit on Putney Beach, T49395022, www.keppeldive.com.au Qualified dive from $77 including gear, introductory dive from $99, depart 0830 daily. They also offer island and beach drop-offs. *Great Keppel Island Holiday Village*, T49398655, offer excellent sea kayaking trips from $35. See Transport, below, for details of cruises.

Transport
Air Great Keppel has its own airfield with Great Keppel Island Air Service, T49395044, providing transfers from Rockhampton. **Bus** *Young's Coaches*, T49223813, offers regular daily services from Rockhampton to Rosslyn Bay (Route 20), from $9.45 single. *Rothery's Coaches*, T49336744, also offer daily services from Rockhampton (*McCafferty's* bus terminal and YHA) to link with the Keppel Tourist Services departures, from $15.40, child $7.70 return. **Ferry** Both of the major ferry companies are based at Rosslyn Bay Harbour, 7 km south of Yeppoon. *Freedom Fast Cats*, T49336244, www.keppelbaymarina.com.au, are based at the new Keppel Bay Marina. It has a travel centre, shop, café and internet. Yacht charters are also available. The basic return fare to Great Keppel (30 mins) is $30, child $15. Ferries depart daily at 0900,1100 and 1500. *Freedom* (see below) offers a range of cruise packages beyond their basic transfers to Great Keppel. These include a daily *Coral Cruise* in a glass bottom boat with fish feeding, from $49, child $27; an *Adventure Cruise* Tue/Sun with boom netting, beach games, swimming and lunch from $59, child $35 and a daily *Lunch Cruise*, from $59, child $35. Half-day/evening trips that are aimed at backpackers and including transfers to Rockhampton are also on offer weekly, from $40. Book ahead. *Keppel Tourist Services* have a ferry terminal next door to the Keppel Bay Marina, T49336744. They offer a similar range of cruises and provide transfers to Great Keppel at 0730, 0915, 1130, 1530 (and 1800 Fri only), for the same price. Note return times from Great Keppel are around an hour after departure from Rosslyn Bay. **Parking** Secured parking is available 500m from the Rosslyn Bay Harbour, off the main road, T49336670, from $8 per-day.

Other Keppel Islands
While Great Keppel Island is the main focus of activity, some of the other little 'Keppelettes' offer more solitude, good snorkelling and camping opportunities. **Middle Island** that lies just north of Great Keppel is home to an **underwater observatory** that sits above a sunken Taiwanese **wreck** teeming with

monster cod and other bizarre sea creatures. The Rosslyn Bay ferry companies offer cruises daily. There is a QPWS campsite on the island, but you will need to take your own water and a gas stove. Other QPWS campsites are located at Considine Beach, **North Keppel Island**, and **Humpy Island** which is renowned for its good snorkelling. Both sites have seasonal water supplies and toilets. For more details and permits contact the QPWS office in Rockhampton or Yeppoon. All the islands have a complete fire ban. **Pumpkin Island** (6 ha), just to the south of North Keppel, is a privately owned island offering five self-contained cabins sleeping five to six (from $130) and a camping area with fresh water, toilet, shower and BBQ (from $10), T49394413. Other than Middle Island all water transport must be arranged privately through the Keppel Bay Marina, T49336244.

Central Coast

Mackay

Colour map 4, grid A3
Population: 75,000
340 km north of Rockhampton, 732 km from Cairns

Driving towards Mackay at night in early summer is a surreal experience. For miles around the oceans of sugar cane fields are awash with the orange glow of flames that illuminate the heavens. Though the burning of harvested cane fields, in preparation for the next crop, is both a traditional and common practice, for the visitor it can look like the world is on fire. Ever since Scots pioneer John Mackay recognized the regions agricultural potential in 1862 it has grown to become the largest sugar producing area in Australia and now hosts the biggest bulk sugar facilities in the world. Although not particularly tourist oriented, Mackay still provides a welcoming halfway stop between Brisbane and Cairns, and in itself has much to offer. As well as being the gateway to several Barrier Reef and Whitsunday Islands, Mackay is also a fine base from which to explore the superb **Eungella** and **Cape Hillsborough national parks.**

Ins & outs

See Transport, page 319, for details

Mackay VIC is housed in a former sugar mill at 320 Nebo Rd (Bruce Highway), T49522677, www.mackayregion.com.au It offers full bookings services for local and Island accommodation and tours. Open Mon-Fri 0830-1700, Sat/Sun 0900-1600. QPWS office, corner of River and Wood sts, T49447800, offers information and permits for island and national park camping. Open Mon-Fri 0830-1700.

Sights

Although most of the Mackay's attractions are to be found beyond the city limits, the city centre with its tropical palm-lined main street and pleasant river views is worth a muse. The heart of the city boasts some notable historical buildings, including the impressive façades of the **Commonwealth Bank** (1880), 63 Victoria Street, the former **Queensland National Bank** (1922), corner of Victoria and Wood streets, and the old **Customs House** (1902), corner of Sydney and River streets. The VIC stocks a free Heritage Walk leaflet.

Greenmount Historic Homestead, 15 km away near Walkerston, is a beautifully preserved 1912 original built on the land first settled by Captain John Mackay the city's founding father. Gloria Arrow the former owner's maid is still on hand to provide a guided tour and genuine insight. ■ *Mon-Fri 0930-1230, Sun 1000-1500. $6, child $3 (includes tour). T49592250. Signposted from Walkerston (Peak Downs Highway).*

Northern Beaches of Mackay are well known for their tropical aesthetics and fine swimming. They are a great place to recharge the travel batteries. The best spots are at Black's Beach, Dolphin Heads (Eimeo Beach) and Bocasia Beach and are best accessed from Mackay-Bucasia Road of the Bruce Highway.

If you can drag yourself away from the beach, given you have seen and will see so much sugar cane perhaps it would be rude not to visit one of the local sugar mills. **Fairleigh Sugar Mill** in Fairleigh, northwest of Mackay, is open to the public during the crushing season. ■ *Mon-Fri at 1300 Jun-Nov. Access and tour $14, child $7.50, T49574727.* To the southwest **Polstone Sugar Cane Farm** also offer tours. ■ *Mon/Wed/Fri at 1330, Jun-Nov. Masottis Rd, Homebush, T49597298.*

Sleeping
■ *On map, page 318*

LL *Ocean International Hotel*, 1 Bridge Rd, T49572044, is considered the best hotel in town, due as much to its beachside position as its level of hospitality. It offers luxury rooms with spa bath, standard rooms, a restaurant, bar, pool, sauna, and so on. **L** *Whitsunday Waters Resort*, Beach Rd, Dolphin Heads, about 12 km north of the city centre, T49549666, www.whitsundaywaters.com.au On the beach, just about as classy as the former but a little less pricey. A good option.

A *White Lace* (73-75), T49514466, **A-B** *Rose Motel* (164) and, opposite the bus terminal in Peel St, **B** *Paradise Lodge*, T49513644, are reasonable motels on Nebo Rd (Bruce Highway). **B-E** *Larrikin Lodge YHA*, 32 Peel St (200m south of the bus terminal), T49513728, larrikin@mackay.net.au The mainstay of the backpacker offering standard dorms, doubles and one family room with all the usual facilities in a traditional 'Queenslander'. Internet and entertaining in-house tours to Eungella National Park (*Jungle Johno's*).

There are several good motor parks within the city limits. **B-F** *Bucasia Beachfront Caravan Park*, 2 Esplanade, Bucasia Beach, T49546375. To the north (10 km) is this 3-star option offering self-contained villas, cabins, powered and non-powered sites and memorable views across to the Whitsunday Islands. **B-E** *Beach Tourist Park*, 8 Petrie St, Illawong Beach, T49574021. In the south, 4 km to the city centre, this 4-star motor park offers villas, cabins, powered and non-powered sites, a good camp kitchen and internet. It is beachside but don't expect to go swimming at low tide or you'll have a 3-km walk to reach the water!

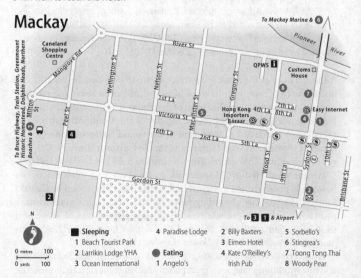

Mackay

■ **Sleeping**	4 Paradise Lodge	2 Billy Baxters	5 Sorbello's
1 Beach Tourist Park		3 Eimeo Hotel	6 Stingrea's
2 Larrikin Lodge YHA	● **Eating**	4 Kate O'Reilley's	7 Toong Tong Thai
3 Ocean International	1 Angelo's	Irish Pub	8 Woody Pear

0 metres 100
0 yards 100

Sorbello's, 166B Victoria St, T49578300, and *Angelo's*, 29 Sydney St, T49535111, fight it out as to who is the best Italian restaurant, with just about a fair match. Open lunch/dinner daily from 1130. Nearby, the *Woody Pear*, 7 Wood St, T49574942, tries to keep the peace with a nice interior and congenial ambience. Its varied international fare is also popular with the locals. Open Tue-Fri 1200-1400, Tue-Sat 1800-late. *Toong Tong Thai*, 10 Sydney St, T49578051, is said to offer both quality and value while *Kate O'Reilley's Irish Pub*, 38 Sydney St, T49533522, the best for pub grub. *Billy Baxters*, corner of Sydney and Gordon sts, T49440173. Go for good coffee and breakfast. Open daily from 0700-late. *Eimeo Hotel*, Mango Ave, Dolphin Heads, 12 km away, T49546106, offers cheap counter meals with spectacular views over Eimeo Beach and the Whitsunday Islands. Open daily 1200-2000. Recommended. *Stingrea's*, Mulherin Dr, beside the new Mackay Marina development north of the city centre, offers casual alfresco dining from 0700 daily, T49555600.

Jungle Johno Tours, T49513728, is a popular outfit, offering entertaining eco-tours and camping trips to Eungella National Park and the Finch Hatton Gorge. Platypus spotting is a speciality, from $75. *Mackay Reeforest Tours*, T49531000, offers a wider range of day tours to Hillsborough and Eungella National Parks and the Moranbah open cast coal mine, from $85, child $53, family $255. The waters of Mackay offer some fine diving including such evocatively named sights as the 'Catacombs' and 'Credlin'. *Pro Dive Mackay*, T49511150, www.prodivemackay.com.au, offers 2-dive trips for certified from $149. Open water courses from $195 and 3-day/3-night trips from $355 or 5-day courses from $499 (Discount 2 dive/2 night package from $209). *Mackay Adventure Divers*, 153 Victoria St, T49531431 also offers courses, reef and wreck dives. *Reef Flight Seaplanes*, T49530220, offers a wide range of reef adventure flights and trips including the popular Bushy Reef lagoon trip with stopover and snorkelling from $194. *Osprey Air*, T49533261, whitsundayheli@bigpond.com, also offers helicopter flights over Mackay and the reef. *Mackay Parachute Centre*, 9 Elamang St, T49576439, straps you to a qualified parachuter and jump from a plane at 10,000ft. Prices on application.

Victoria St **markets** are held every Sun from 0900-1230 and are noted for their local arts and crafts. Alternatively you can shop til you drop at the new **Caneland Shopping Centre**, corner of Victoria and Mangrove rds, T49513311.

Local Bus *Mackay Transit*, Casey Ave, T49573330, www.mackaytransit.com.au, is the local hail 'n' ride suburban bus service offering services to the Northern Beaches (Mon-Fri, route 7) and Mirani (Pioneer Valley) on Thu only. A Day Rover ticket costs $5.60, child $3.40. **Taxi** *Mackay Taxis* (24 hrs), T131008

Long distance Air Mackay Airport, T49570255, is 2 km south of the city centre, along Sydney St and is served by *Qantas*, T131313 (4 flights daily to Brisbane). *Whitsunday Island Air Taxis*, T49469933, www.heliaust.com.au, offer shuttle services to Proserpine and Hamilton Island from $120 one-way. Taxis meet all flights and cost about $9 in to town. **Bus** Served by *McCafferty's*, T131499, and *Greyhound*, T132030, which stop at the terminal on Milton St (between Victoria and Gordon St), T49513088. **Car** Car hire from *Avis*, Mackay Airport, T136333, *Network Rentals*, 196 Victoria St, T49531022, *AAA Rentals*, 6 Endeavour St, T49575606. Car servicing at *Automotive Repair and Towing Service*, 35 Evans Ave, North Mackay, T49573555. **Train** The station is 5 km southwest of the city centre on Connor's Rd (between Archibald St and Boundary Rd of the Bruce Highway). *Queensland Rail*, T132332. Again taxis meet most trains and will cost about $10 in to the city centre. Regular buses to city centre from Nebo Rd (Bruce Highway).

Eating
● *On map, page 318*

Tours & activities

Shopping

Transport

Capricorn & Central coasts

Directory **Banks** *Commonwealth* (currency exchange), *Westpac*, *National* and *ANZ* branches are centred around the intersection of Victoria and Sydney sts. **Communications** Internet: *Hong Kong Importers Bazaar*, 128 Victoria St, T49533188. Open Mon-Fri 0845-1715, Sat/Sun 0900-1400, or *Easy Internet*, 22 Sydney St, T49533331. Open Mon-Fri 0830-1730, Sat 0800-1300. **Post office**: corner of Sydney and Gordon sts. Open Mon-Fri 0800-1700. **Medical services** Chemist: *Night and Day*, Sydney St (next door to the post office). Open daily 0800-2100. **Hospital**: *Mackay Base Hospital*, Bridge Rd, T49686000. **Useful numbers** Police: Sydney St, T49683444.

Around Mackay

Brampton & Carlisle islands
The islands of Brampton (464 ha) and Carlisle (518 ha) are part of the Cumberland Islands National Park that lie 32 km northeast of Mackay. Both are practically joined by a sandbank that can be walked at low tide and have a rich variety of island habitats, rising to a height of 389 m on Carlisle's Skiddaw Peak and 219 m on Brampton's namesake peak. The waters surrounding both islands are part of the Mackay/Capricorn Section of the Great Barrier Reef Marine Park, offering some excellent dive sites. There are 11 km of walking track on Brampton that give access to Brampton Peak as well as several secluded bays and coastal habitats. In contrast walking on Carlisle Island is rough with no well-formed paths. Instead you are better to explore the beaches or take to the water with a snorkel and mask, especially in the channel between the two islands. Day trips aren't available and the minimum stay is one night.

Sleeping and eating **LL-L** *Brampton Resort*, T1800737678, www.brampton.com.au A family-oriented resort, no camping allowed. **QPWS campsite**, on Carlisle Island. Basic. All supplies must be imported. There is a seasonal water tank but a back-up supply should be taken anyway. Basic bush campsites are also available on Goldsmith, Scawfell, Cockermouth, Keswick and St Bee's Islands. Permits apply to all sites.

Transport Local companies also offer flights to and from **Hamilton Island** (see page 331) and a daily service to and from **Mackay**. A launch service for resort guests is available from Thu-Mon, at 1130 from Mackay Marina, T49514499. Campers can take the scheduled launch (from $50 return) and walk to the QPWS campsite or, alternatively arrange to be ferried directly to the island through the resort. *Qantas*, T131313, offer daily flights to Brampton from major Australian capital cities. For more information contact the QPWS office in Mackay.

Newry Islands
The Newry group consist of six national park islands, 50 km northeast of Mackay. Like the Cumberlands, they are hilly, diverse in coastal habitat types and rich in wildlife, including sea eagles, ospreys, echidna and bandicoots. Green sea turtles also nest between November and January on the largest of the group – **Rabbit island**. There are 2-km of walking track on Newry Island that lead through rainforest and open forest to elevated viewpoints. Again the waters that surround the islands are part of the Great Barrier Reef Marine Park.

Sleeping and eating Newry Island plays host to a small, low-key **resort** with basic cabin-style accommodation, T49590214. **QPWS campsite** with toilets and a seasonal water tank on Rabbit Island and a hut (maximum of 10 at any one time) on Outer Newry Island.

Transport *Seaforth Fishing Tours*, Seaforth (23 km north of Mackay), T49590318, offer transfers for campers.

The Leap

◀

Just north of Mackay the small community and mountain peak known as The Leap has long been immortalised in Queensland folklore. According to local legend, in 1867, an Aboriginal woman leapt to her death while being chased by racist white policeman. Surprisingly she made the leap clinging tightly to her baby, which miraculously survived the ordeal and continued to live in the district until her own death in 1928. A statue of her mother can be seen outside the Leap Hotel.

Although positively petite compared to most of Queensland's other mainland national parks, Hillsborough is no less impressive, boasting some superb coastal habitats, views and beaches. It is also particularly lauded for its tame, beach loving wildlife, that includes grey kangaroos, the aptly named pretty-faced wallabies and the distinctly more ugly faced scrub turkeys. There are four diverse walking tracks ranging from 1.2 km to 2.6 km in length, including the 1.2-km Juipera Plant Trail, which highlights the food plants once utilised by the Juipera Aboriginal people.

Cape Hillsborough National Park

Sleeping and eating B-F *Cape Hillsborough Nature Resort*, Casuarina Bay T49590262, www.capehillsbor oughresort.com.au, has beachfront cabins, motel units or powered and non-powered sites. There is a small store and restaurant on site. **QPWS campground** is available at Smalley's Beach at the western end of the park, T49590410. Small with limited fresh water.

Eungella National Park and Pioneer Valley

The 80-km inland excursion from Mackay via the Pioneer Valley to Eungella, pronounced 'young-galah', offers an excellent diversion from the coast and access to what the aboriginal people once called 'the land of the clouds'. And whether shrouded in mist or gently baking under the midday sun, Eungella and its exquisite national park possess a magic as special as the wildlife that lives there and the aboriginals that once did.

Colour map 5, grid C2/3

Immediately west of Mackay, the Mackay-Eungella Road branches of the Peak Downs Highway and follows the southern bank of the Pioneer River to the small settlement of **Marian**. Born of the vast sea of sugar cane that surrounds it little Marian plays host to the largest mill in the district that rumbles and groans to life during the crushing season from June to November. In **Mirani**, 10 km further west of Marian, you can find out why the two were so called, and if they were indeed sisters, at the small **museum** on Victoria Street. ■ *Mon-Fri 1000-1400, Sun 1000-1500.*

Sights

Just beyond Mirani is the **Illawong Fauna Sanctuary**. Although a fairly low-key affair it is well worth a stop exhibiting all the unusual suspects from 'Princess Dribbles' the koala to 'Vincent Van Gough' the half-eared, hairy-nosed wombat! Included is a walk through enclosure full of plump and leggy emus, wallabies and roos, that will either sit in the shade and gaze at you in utter contempt, or, expertly investigate the interior of your pockets or bags for the feed pellets. The sanctuary also has accommodation, a café and its own tour company, *Gem Tours*. ■ *Daily 0900-1730. $11, child $5.50. T49591777.*

A further 29 km past Mirani, beyond the small hamlet of Gargett and 1 km east of Finch Hatton Township, is the turn-off to the **Finch Hatton George** section of the Eungella National Park. In the dry season the 10-km road is

Capricorn & Central coasts

suitable for 2WD, but in the wet when several creek crossings are subject to flooding and the final 6-km gravel road often requires 4WD. At the gorge there is a private bush camp (see below), picnic site and access to the memorable **Wheel of Fire Falls**, 5-km return, and **Araluen Falls** walks, 3-km return.

Back on the main highway, the road then seems to head towards the hills with almost worrisome terminability before ascending suddenly and dramatically, 800 m up to the small and pretty township of **Eungella**. At the crest of the hill, and past a few holes in the roadside barriers to boot, is the historic **Eungella Chalet**, with its spacious lawns, swimming pool and views to blow your wig off. As well as being an ideal spot for lunch, it is also the perfect venue for hang-gliders, whom launch themselves with intrepid glee into the valley below.

From the chalet the road veers 6 km south, following the crest of the hill, before arriving at **Broken River**. Here you will find a picnic area, QPWS campsite and the associate Eungella National Park Ranger Station which opens daily 0800-0900/1130-1230/1530-1630, T49584552, who can give you all the necessary detail on the numerous and excellent short walks in the vicinity. There is also a **platypus** viewing platform nearby but bear in mind they are seen at just about the same time as the average cock crows. The park is also home to a host of other unique species including the Eungella honeyeater, the brown thornbill and the infinitely wonderful Eungella gastric brooding frog. The latter, as its vaguely eyebrow rising name suggests, has the unenviable habit of incubating its eggs in the stomach before spitting the young out of its mouth.

Sleeping & eating

Finch Hatton Gorge C-F *Platypus Bush Camp*, Finch Hatton Gorge Rd, T49583204, www.bushcamp.net.au Offers a superb and authentic bush camping experience. Created and maintained by a friendly and laid-back bushman called 'Wazza', it features a characterful assemblage of basic open-air huts and campsites, set amongst the bush and beside the river. The huts range from single, through doubles to the notably more distant 'Honeymoon Hut', with its 'no need to move in the morning platypus spotting'. Other camp features include an open-air communal kitchen a sauna (all constructed from local cedar wood) and a fine swimming hole. Campfires are also authorised. Recommended (especially in the rain!).

Eungella A-D *Historic Eungella Chalet*, T49584509. As well as the magnificent views, it has a wide range of options from self-contained cabins with open fires to motel rooms and backpacker (weekday only) beds, an à la carte restaurant, public bar and swimming pool. **B-F** *Eungella Holiday Park*, North St (take the first right beyond the chalet), T49584590, www.eungella-holidaypark.com.au Has a self-contained cabin, powered and non-powered sites. Internet. *Hideaway Café*, just beyond the chalet, T49584533, is well worth a stop. Here the delightful Suzanna has single handedly created her own little piece of paradise, with spacious gardens, home-made pottery and a unique wishing well. Take a tour of the imaginative and truly international menu while supping a coffee and soaking up the views across the valley. Open daily 0800-1700.

Broken River L-B *Broken River Mountain Retreat*, T49584528, www.brokenrivermr. com.au, has a range of studio, 1- and 2-bedroom self-contained cabins, restaurant (open to the public) and an exciting range of in-house activities from night spotting to canoeing. There is also a delightfully tame 'out-house' pet kangaroo. **QPWS campsite**, across the river, has toilets, drinking water, showers and gas BBQs. Permits available at the Ranger Station, T49584552. There is a small food kiosk attached to the Ranger Station.

Transport

There is no public transport to Eungella, though it is possible to make arrangements with local tour operators, particularly *Jungle Johno Tours*, T49513728, see page 319.

Airlie Beach

*From a sleepy coastal settlement, Airlie Beach and is neighbouring communities of **Cannonvale** and **Shute Harbour** (known collectively as Whitsunday) have developed into the principal gateway to the **Whitsunday Islands**. With over 74 islands, many home to idyllic resorts plus a glut of beaches like Whitehaven (often hailed as among the worlds best), it is comes as no surprise that little Airlie has seen more dollars spent in the name of tourism in recent years than almost anywhere else in the State. With all the offerings of the Whitsunday Islands most people simply use Airlie as an overnight stop but amidst all the hype, 'Airlie' itself can be a great place to party and meet people, or just relax and watch the touristical world go by.*

Colour map 5, grid B3
Population: 3,000
160 km north of Mackay, 308 km south of Townsville

Getting there The nearest airports are at Proserpine and Hamilton Island. Long-distance bus services run from Cairns and Sydney, stopping at all major centres and cities on the way. Both north and south services run 3 times weekly. The train station is at Proserpine. **Getting around** The main centre is small and can easily be explored on foot. Bikes are readily available for hire to explore the outlying resorts. See page 326 for tours to the Whitsunday Islands. **Tourist information** Whitsunday VIC, Bruce Highway, Proserpine, T49453711, www.whitsundayinformation. com.au, is the main accredited VIC for the region. QPWS office, corner of Mandalay St, is very helpful and can supply the latest island camping information and issue the necessary permits, T49467022. Open Mon-Fri 0900-1700, Sat 0900-1300.

Ins & outs
See Transport, page 328, for further details

Sights

Right in the heart of town, and the focus for many, is the new and glorious lagoon development. In the absence of a proper beach and the insidious threat of marine stingers (October to May) it has to be said that the local authorities have created a fine substitute.

Lagoon

On Waterston Road, off Shute Harbour Road, and accessed through the huge gaping jaws of a model shark, is this museum. It is a somewhat egocentric display of Hislop's personal vendetta against the mighty Great White – driven most definitely by the 'fear factor'. Although presenting a highly biased standpoint against these ancient and complex creatures and very pro the 'killing machine' image, Hislop does present some intriguing and debateable arguments as to why sharks attack both humans and whales, and what should be done about it! There is a wealth of information and statistics on display, as well as the obligatory pictures of bitten limbs, torsos and half eaten surfboards. The highlight is supposed to be a real shark deep frozen for your viewing pleasure, however it is clearly well past its use-by date and looks more like Jabba the Hut. ■ *Daily 0900-1800. $16.*

Vic Hislop Great White Shark Expo

From one enormous and alarming set of gnashers to another, one can have a more varied, if no less scary wildlife experience at this wildlife park in Cannonvale, a fairly non-descript settlement just north of Airlie Beach. Here you can acquaint yourself with wide array of nasty natives from the ubiquitous crocodile or taipan to the more folk-friendly, and eminently more cuddly, koala or roo. The park is home to Rob – 'the barefoot bushman' – who, thankfully, is not nearly as excruciating as the 'poke it, jump on it and annoy the crap out of it' Crocodile Hunter, Steve Irwin. ■ *Daily 0900-1630. $20, child $10.*

Barefoot Bushman's Wildlife Park

Capricorn & Central coasts

Snake show 1100, croc-feeding 1200/1400. T49461480, 7 km west of Airlie on Shute Harbour Rd.

Conway National Park To spot your own wildlife or simply use your limbs, as opposed to seeing how easily they might be removed, you can always take a quiet and congenial walk in a section of the Conway National Park between Airlie and Shute Harbour. There is a self-guided 6.5-km circuit walk through mangrove forest on the way to a lookout on the slopes of Mount Rooper.

Essentials

Sleeping
■ *On map, page 324*

Despite having numerous smart resorts, apartments and a backpackers aplenty, Airlie can hardly keep pace with its own popularity – you are still advised to book ahead. Many backpackers offer accommodation and activity combo deals, often booked from afar, however though these can be attractive in price, they can severely limit your choice.

LL *Coral Sea Resort*, overlooking the Abel Point Marina, 25 Oceanview Dr, T49466458, www.coralsearesort.com.au Airlie's most exclusive, high profile resort satisfying all the expectations, from oceanview suites to a fine pool and à la carte restaurant. **LL-A** *Airlie Beach Hotel*, corner of the Esplanade and Coconut Grove, T49641999, www.airliebeachhotel.com.au Having undergone renovation, this offers standard motel units and new, well-appointed hotel rooms in the heart of the town. Good in-house bar/bistro (*Capers*). There are plenty of plush apartment complexes, including the new **LL-L** *Martinique Resort*, 18 Golden Orchid Dr, T49480401, www.martiniquewhitsunday.com.au, that has fully self-contained, 1-3 bedroom

Airlie Beach

Sleeping ■
1 Airlie Beach
2 Airlie Waterfront B&B
3 Backpackers by the Bay
4 Beaches
5 Club 13
6 Club Habitat
7 Coral Sea Resort
8 Flame Tree Tourist Village
9 Island Getaway Caravan Resort
10 Koala Backpackers
11 Magnums Backpackers
12 Martinique Resort
13 ReefO's
14 Whitsunday Wanderers Resort

Eating ●
1 Boltz Café & Bar
2 Burgers in Paradise
3 Chatz Bar & Brasserie
4 Courtyard
5 KC's Bar & Grill
6 Paddy Shenanigans & Tricks Nightclub
7 Sidewalk Café

N
0 metres 100
0 yards 100

Capricon & Central coasts

apartments with fine views and a 'wet edge' pool and spa. One of the better value, well positioned and spacious resorts in the town is **L** *Whitsunday Wanderers Resort*, Shute Harbour Rd, T49466446, which is attached to the (chain) **C-F** *Koala Backpackers*, T49466001, www.koala-backpackers.com.au Together they offer the full range of accommodation from a/c suites with spa to campsites with several pools and a host of activity bookings. In the heart of town **A** *Airlie Waterfront B&B*, corner of Broadwater and Mazlin sts, T49467631, www.airliewaterfrontbnb.com.au, is one of the best B&Bs in the region and certainly the best located for all amenities.

There is no paucity of backpackers in Airlie all of which can broadly placed in to one of three categories – good value, party places and the more relaxed and peaceful. **C-F** *ReefO's*, 147 Shute Harbour Rd, T49466137, www.reeforesort.com.au For sheer value for money the spacious and tidy *ReefO's* cannot be beaten. Dorm beds go for as little as $8, with breakfast. En suite cabins with a/c and TV for under $50. There is a bar/restaurant and small communal kitchen on site, as well as an excellent (and honest) tour/activities desk. Its only drawback is the walk into town but regular shuttles are available. **C-E** *Club Habitat*, 394 Shute Harbour Rd, T49466312. YHA members will get the usual discounts at this friendly and motel-style option.

All the major party oriented backpackers are located right in the heart of the town and in many ways are the heart of the town. At the end of the day (or night) they are all pretty similar and certainly fiercely competitive, always trying to outdo each other on the small details. But in essence almost all have the full range of dorms, singles and doubles, boast lively bars, nightclubs, a pool, good-value eateries and internet. They can also advise on the best activities and trips but note that advice will almost certainly be biased. **C-E** *Beaches*, 362 Shute Harbour Rd, T1800 636630/49466244, **C-F** *Koala*, Shute Harbour Rd, T1800 354535/49466001, and **C-E** *Magnums Backpackers*, 366 Shute Harbour Rd, T1800 624634/49466266, are the main players.

C-E *Bush Village Backpackers Resort*, 2 St Martins Rd, Cannonvale, T1800809256. For a little bit more peace and quiet this is an excellent option. It is friendly with tidy and spacious, a/c self-catering cabins, en suite doubles, dorms, pool and a regular shuttle in to town. **C-E** *Club 13*, 13 Begley St, T49467376, www.whitsundaybackpackers.com.au Another quiet option, in an elevated position in the heart of Airlie. Spacious with good a/c doubles, a pool and a fine, free cooked breakfast (YHA discount). **C-E** *Backpackers by the Bay*, 12 Hermitage Dr, T49467267, bythebay@whitsunday.net.au At the eastern end of town, this is well facilitated with dorms and doubles and glorious bay views.

There are plenty of motor parks in and around town. **B-F** *Island Getaway Caravan Resort*, a short walk east of the town centre (corner of Shute Harbour and Jubilee Pocket rds), T49466228. 4 star, this is a popular option, offering units, cabins, camp-o-tels and powered and non-powered sites. Good camp kitchen and very tame possums. **B-F** *Flame Tree Tourist Village*, Shute Harbour Road (near the airfield), T49469388. Further east, this is low-key in a quiet bush setting, with a characterful camp kitchen and within easy reach of the ferry terminal. Both Koala and Magnums Backpackers in Airlie also have powered sites.

There are over 30 **QPWS campsites** throughout the Whitsunday Island group and beyond. QPWS office on Shute Harbour Rd, T49467022, can provide up-to-date information, advice and issue permits. Note to obtain a permit you must have proof of return transportation. *Island Camping Connections*, T49465255, offers independent transportation by water taxis and hire out camping gear. The Shute Harbour scheduled ferry services stop on most major island resorts.

Eating

● On map, page 324

Expensive *Courtyard Restaurant*, 301 Shute Harbour Rd, T49465700. This award winner is recommended for fine dining. Open for dinner daily (except Mon). **Mid-range to cheap** Both *Magnums* and *Beaches Backpackers* (see above) have popular bar/bistros offering a wide variety of good-value dishes (including the obligatory 'roo burgers') and have a lively atmosphere. Both are open for both lunch and dinner. *Irish Pub Paddy Shenanigans*, 352 Shute Harbour Rd, T49465055, also offers value bar meals and is a fine place to remain for a night out. *KC's Bar and Grill*, 382 Shute Harbour Rd, T49466320, is popular for seafood and meat dishes and has live entertainment daily from 2200. *Boltz Café and Bar*, 7 Beach Plaza, The Esplanade, T49467755, offers a varied Mediterranean lunch and dinner menu in modern surroundings and is also open for breakfast. Open daily 0700-late. *Chatz Bar and Brasserie*, at the eastern end of Shute Harbour Rd, T49467223, also offers value lunches and dinner and is open daily until 0200. **Cheap** *Burgers in Paradise*, 269 Shute Harbour Rd, can ease the post-party munchies and is open 24 hr. *Sidewalk Café*, on The Esplanade, for good coffee and breakfast. Open daily from 0730. Self-caterers will find the *5-Star Supermarket*, right in the centre of town, on Shute Harbour Road. Open daily until 2100.

Bars & clubs

The street side bars at *Magnums* and *Beaches Backpackers* are both popular and the best place to meet others for the almost obligatory wild night out. At *Magnums* you don't have to stumble too far to 'shake your pants' in its own nightclub *M@ss*, that rips it up well into the wee hours (sometimes quite literally, with wet tee-shirt competitions and foam parties). Neighbours *Tricks Nightclub* and *Paddy Shenanigan's* (see above) can also go in to orbit, almost simultaneously, well beyond midnight.

Tours & activities

With numerous dive shops, umpteen cruise operators, over 74 islands and almost as many vessels, the choice of waterbased activities and trips is mind bending (see box, page 327). The two big day trip attractions are Whitehaven Beach and *Fantaseas* floating 'Reefworld' pontoon. Whitehaven Beach on Whitsunday Island is world famous for its glorious white sands and crystal clear waters, while Reefworld offers the chance to dive, snorkel or view the reef from a semi-submersible or underwater observatory. However that both these popular options are also the most commercial and most crowded. The main ferry companies also offer island transfers and island 'day-tripper' specials. See Whitsunday Islands section, page 332.

Cruising (Fast catamaran) The major players are *Whitsunday All Over*, 398 Shute Harbour Rd, T49466900 www.whitsundayallover.com.au, and *Fantasea* (Blue Ferries) Cruises, Shop 10, Whitsunday Village, T49482300, info@fantasea.com.au Both have offices at the Shute Harbour Ferry Terminal. Other operators include *Reefjet* (see Diving below) and *Whitehaven Express*, T49466922, www.whitehavenxpress.com.au All offer a wide array of day cruises to the islands or the outer reef, or indeed, both. A day cruise will cost anywhere between $60-150.

Remember that the outer reef offers the clearest water and most varied fish species

Diving There are numerous options with all local dive shops and most of the larger cruise companies offering day or multi-day trips and courses. Shop around, confirm exactly where you are going and how long will actually be spent on the reef. Also consider whether you wish to be with a small or large group and what kind of vessel you would like to be on. Bear in mind that generally the faster the vessel the more time you will have on the reef. *Reef Dive*, Shute Harbour Rd, T49466508, www.reefdive.com.au, offer 3-day/3-night packages and certification from $325 *Kelly Dive and Sail*, 1 The Esplanade, T49464368, www.kellydive. com.au, offer 3-day/3-night trip, en suite cabin, with 10 dives from $490. *Oceania Dive*, 257 Shute Harbour Rd, T49466032, www.oceaniadive.com.au, offer 5-day open water course from $535 and 10 dive certified diver trip from $500). *Pro Dive*, 344 Shute Harbour Rd, T49481888,

Choose a cruise

Airlie Beach is attractive enough, but in many ways it can seem characterless and to an extent, almost 'parasitic' – a glorified 'tourist transit centre', where hundreds of operators vie for your tourist dollar, with the promise that 'their island resort' or 'their sailing trip' is the 'one and only'. Our advice in choosing a cruise is not to walk with blank expressions and carrying your bulging wallets!

First decide as an independent, or as a group what exactly you would like to do- whether it be diving, snorkelling, cruising, sailing, island hopping, camping or combinations thereof. Then ask yourself what kind of vessel you would like to go on – is it a fast catamaran, a sail catamaran, a modern racing yacht, a square-rigger, a rigid inflatable or a pink dinghy? Then ask yourself how long you want to be out there – a day or several days? Is a 3-day/3-night package actually three whole days or in real terms much less? If the trip is several days – what is the on board accommodation like? Do you have an en suite to yourself or are you on deck with someone who snores like a bull warthog? Then ask yourself where exactly you would like to go – to the outer reef, the islands or all over the place? Then there is the minor detail – will you be with a small group or large group? What kind of food is offered? And so on.

Then, armed with these preferences, go shopping. Of course ultimately everything comes down to your budget or the money you are willing to spend. But clued up accordingly you are far less likely to be coerced with sales speak and by being assertive, far more likely to find exactly what you are after.

For those who are short of cash – there is the economical and independent option of island camping. QPWS have numerous campsites on the islands that can be reached by scheduled ferries or by group charter boats for under $100. Do it this way, under the stars and in near solitude and you will really find out what the Whitsundays have to offer! Island Camping Connections, *T49464255,* offer water taxis and hire out camping gear.

www.prodivewhitsundays.com.au, offer a 5-day Open Water Course from $499. *Reefjet*, Shop 2, Abel Point Marina, T49481838, www.reefjet.com.au, offer an excellent day cruise to the Bait Reef (outer reef) and Whitehaven Beach with dive and snorkelling options from $110 (snorkel only). *Tallarook*, Shop 1 Beach Plaza, T49464777, also offer packages but also hire dive equipment for independent divers, snorkelling gear from $4 daily and stinger suits from $6 daily.

Fishing *MV Jillian*, T49480999, offer entertaining half/full-day trips from the Abel Point Marina at 0830, from $99 (full day). The *MV Moruya* ,T49467127, is another popular option, from $97, child $48.

Flight seeing Most of the region's flight seeing operators are based at the airfield between Airlie and Shute Harbour where there is also a good café. *HeliReef Whitsunday*, T49468249, www.heliaust.com.au, offers a range of flight seeing options by helicopter and are also often in evidence on the waterfront in Airlie offering short scenic flights around the bay, 10 mins from $65, 40 mins Whitehaven Beach flight with 1-hr stopover from $239. *Air Whitsunday*, T49469111, www.airwhitsunday.com.au, and *Coral Air*, T49469130, greatbarrierreef@bigpond.com, both have a fleet of seaplanes and offer both tours and island transfers, 3 hrs from $190. *Island Air Taxis*, T49469933, www.heliaust.com.au, offers fixed-wing scenic flights of 30 mins – 5 hrs from $79.

Horse trekking *Morrison's Trail Rides*, T49465299, are based in the Conway Ranges and offer bush trekking to Cedar Creek Falls, from $66 (includes transport).

National parks *Fawlty's 4WD Tropical Tours*, T49480999, offer entertaining and value day tours to the rainforests of the Conway National Park and Cedar Creek Falls, from $42, child $25.

Ocean rafting *Ocean Rafting*, T49466848, www.oceanrafting.com.au, offer a 7-hr fast cruise around the islands and Whitehaven Beach on board their rigid inflatable. Includes snorkelling, guided rainforest and aboriginal cave walk from $70, child $42, family $203.

Quad biking *Whitsunday Quad Bike Bush Adventures*, T49481008, www.bush adventures.com.au, are a new operation offering not only a lot of fun but great views, wildlife and history. From $110.

Sailing Again the choices are mind-boggling. A whole host of vessels from small dinghies to world-class racing yachts are available to take you at a more leisurely pace to your island and/or reef. Day, night or multi-day adventures are available. To provide a comprehensive list or make accurate recommendations is beyond the scope of this guide. The simple advice is to shop around (see box, page 327). A day cruise will cost about $70 while a 3-day/2-night trip around $250.

Transport **Local Bus** *Whitsunday Transit*, T49461800, offers regular daily bus services from **Proserpine** to Shute Harbour (through Airlie). Services between **Cannonvale** and Shute Harbour operate daily between 0600-1845, from $4.50 one way, with further services between Airlie Cove and Adventure Whitsunday from 1900-2230. A day pass costs $8. **Cycle** Can be hired from some backpackers and *Water's Edge Luxury Apartments*, 4 Golden Orchid Dr, T49482655, full-day $20. Mokes and scooters can be hired from *Whitsunday Moke and Scooter Hire*, 1 Laurence Cl, Cannonvale, T49480700. **Taxi** *Whitsunday Taxis*, T131008.

For island ferry connections see Whitsunday Islands section below

Long-distance Air The nearest airports are in Proserpine, 36 km west, and Hamilton Island, Whitsunday Islands. Both are served by *Qantas*, T131313, and *Flight West* (from Brisbane daily), T1300 130092. *Island Air Taxis*, T49469933, provide local island transfers. Again, Whitsunday Transit buses meet all incoming flights in Proserpine.

Bus Long-distance buses stop in the car park beside the lagoon right in the heart of town or next to the Sailing Club in the Recreation reserve to the east. Either way most accommodation is within walking distance or you will be met by private shuttle. *McCafferty's*, T131499, and *Greyhound*, T132030, offer regular daily services. *Aussie Magic Bus*, T1800449444, offers northbound services to Cairns (via Townsville and Mission Beach) on Sat/Mon/Thu and southbound services to Sydney (via all major coastal centres) on Mon/Wed/Sat.

Train The nearest station is in Proserpine, 36 km west of Airlie, which receives 8 trains weekly. For bookings *Queensland Rail*, T132232. The station is served by *Whitsunday Transit*, T49461800, that link Proserpine with Airlie Beach and Shute Harbour and meets all arrivals, from $6.50.

Directory **Banks** Almost all branches (with ATMs) are represented on Shute Harbour Rd in Airlie (*Commonwealth*/*National*) and Cannonvale (*Westpac*/*National*/*ANZ*). Currency exchange at *Travelex* by the post office. **Communications** Internet: access is everywhere including *Beaches Backpackers* (open until late) and *Destination Whitsundays*, upstairs, corner of Shute harbour Rd and The Esplanade, T1800644563. Open daily 0800-2200. **Post office**: Whitehaven Village, Shute Harbour Rd (near *McDonald's*).

Open Mon-Fri 0900-1700, Sat 0900-1100. Post Restante, T49466515. **Medical services** Hospital: **Whitsunday Medical Centre**, 400 Shute Harbour Rd, T49466275 (24 hrs). **Whitsunday Doctors Service**, Shute Harbour Rd, T49466241. Chemist: *Night and Day*, Shute Harbour Rd, Airlie. **Travel centres** *Backpackers Travel Centre*, 257 Shute Harbour Rd, T49465844, or *Destination Whitsundays*, upstairs at the corner of Shute harbour rd and The Esplanade, T1800 644563. Open daily 0800-2200. **Useful numbers** Police: 8 Altmann Ave, Cannonvale, T49466445.

Whitsunday Islands

*With over 74 islands blessed with all the sun-soaked sublimity that the imagination can muster, the Whitsundays are not only the largest offshore island chain on the east coast of Australia but the biggest tourist draw between Brisbane and Cairns. It is hardly surprising. Many of the islands are home to idyllic resorts from the almost unimaginable luxuries of **Hayman** to the much hyped **Hamilton** or quieter, more affordable **South Molle**, plus a plethora of pristine beaches like **Whitehaven** on Whitsunday Island – often hailed as among the worlds best. Here, for once, the term paradise is not an exaggeration. Captain Cook bestowed the name Whitsunday upon the islands when he sailed past on Whit Sunday (seventh Sunday after Easter), 1770.*

Colour map 5, grid B3

Whitsunday VIC, Bruce Highway, Proserpine, T49453711, www.whitsundayinformation.com.au, is the main accredited VIC for the islands. QPWS office is very helpful and is located south of Airlie Beach on the corner of Mandalay St T49467022. Open Mon-Fri 0900-1700, Sat 0900-1300. They can supply the latest information regards island camping and issue the necessary permits, from $3.50 per night.

Ins & outs
See Transport, page 332, for details

Inner Islands

South Molle (405 ha) is one of three little 'Mollies' (South, Mid and North) that sit about 8 km from Shute Harbour. Being in such close proximity to the mainland, and therefore relatively cheap to reach, South Molle is deservingly popular with day-trippers. With its varied habitats and hilly topography, the island offers some excellent walking and sublime views. The best of these is undoubtedly the 6-km Spion Kop walk that climbs through forest and over open grassland to some superb viewpoints across to the outer islands. The resort on the island is both pleasant and casual, offering all the usual mod cons to in-house guests and allowing day-trippers access to the pool, bar/bistro and some activities. It is also noted for its evening entertainment.

South Molle Island

Sleeping and eating LL *South Molle Island Resort*, T49469433, www.southmolle island.com.au There are 2 **QPWS campsites** on South Molle at Sandy Bay and Paddle Bay with toilets but no water supply. There are 2 other sites on small offshore islands and at Cockatoo Beach on North Molle but if the resort cannot offer you a lift in one of its vessels, independent access must be arranged. Cockatoo Beach site has seasonal water supplies.

Aptly named Long Island is the closest island to the mainland running parallel with the uninhabited coastal fringes of the Conway National Park. A national park in its own right, much of its 2,000 acres of dense rainforest is inaccessible, save a loose network of tracks that connect a number of pretty beaches near the major resorts at the northern end.

Long Island

Sleeping and eating There are 3 established resorts on the island and 1 **QPWS** campsite. **LL** *Club Crocodile Resort*, T49469400, www.clubcroc.com.au Offering its guests the perfect arrival point in Happy Bay, both atmosphere and amenities are casual but stylish and ideal for the courting couple. **LL-L** *Palm Beach Hideaway*, T49469233. Less than 1 km south this more eco-friendly option is peaceful, beachside, en suite units and cabins, surrounded by the all the usual amenities. **LL** *Whitsunday Wilderness Lodge*, T49469777, www.southlongisland.com.au In almost perfect isolation on the island's western side, this is an architects dream realized. It strives very successfully to create a relaxing eco-friendly retreat with a focus on the place rather than the amenities. Although expensive and deliberately basic in design, clients very rarely leave disappointed. The accommodation is comfortable but basic: en suite beachfront units. The hosts are very professional and friendly and there is a moody, yet enchanting pet kangaroo. The lodge has its own yacht which is part of an optional, and comprehensive, daily activities schedule. Recommended. *QPWS campsite* is situated on the western side of the island at Sandy Bay. It is a fine, secluded spot backed by rainforest, through which there is a track allowing you to explore and reach viewpoints overlooking the other islands. There are toilets but no water supply.

Daydream Island One of the smallest of the Whitsunday Islands and blessed with a name almost as nauseating as the staffs corporate shirts are colourful, Daydream is one of the closest and most accessible islands to the mainland, just 5 km away. As such its congenial, if compact, surrounds and newly renovated resort have become a popular holiday venue. On offer for guests are a host of activities including sail boarding, jet-skiing, parasailing, reef fishing, diving, snorkelling, tennis and even croquet. But don't expect a plethora of walking tracks, except of the very short variety to the bar. Walking on little Daydream is like circling a small buffet table trying to decide what to choose. It is best just to sit back by the pool; shade your eyes from the staff's shirts and, well… daydream.

Sleeping **LL** *Novotel Daydream*, T49488488, www.daydream.net.au Another resort courtesy of the French chain which has now opened its facilities to day-trippers. Packages must be booked through *FantaSea Cruises* who operate the ferry over to Daydream. Contact *FantaSea*, T07 49465111.

Outer Islands

Whitsunday Island At over 100-sq-km Whitsunday Island is the biggest in the group, boasting perhaps their biggest attraction – the 6-km white silica sands of **Whitehaven Beach**. Repeatedly, aerial views of this magnificent beach and the adjoining **Hill Inlet** turn up in the pages of glossy magazines and on postcards as the epitome of the word 'tropical'. Though best seen from the air the beach is easily accessed by numerous day trips and island cruises, which in many ways is its downfall. Thankfully uninhabited and without a resort Whitsunday's only available accommodation comes in the form of eight QPWS campsites that are scattered around its numerous bays and inlets.

Sleeping Of the 8 QPWS campsites the most popular is Whitehaven Beach, southern end, that can accommodate up to 60 and has toilets, but no water supply. The only campsites with water are Sawmill Beach and Dugong Beach, both of which fringe Cid Bay on the island's western side. They are connected by a 1-km walking track.

Set right in the heart of the Whitsundays, Hamilton Island in many ways nearly breaks it. With its small yet all dominating group of eye-sore tower blocks – that one is amazed were ever allowed to get beyond the mezzanine – it is seen by many as the proverbial fly in the otherwise pure and tropical ointment. But despite its enemies Hamilton, like its tower blocks, is bold and belligerent and for many outsiders it offers an ideal holiday resort with all a body could ask for.

Hamilton Island

Whitsunday Islands

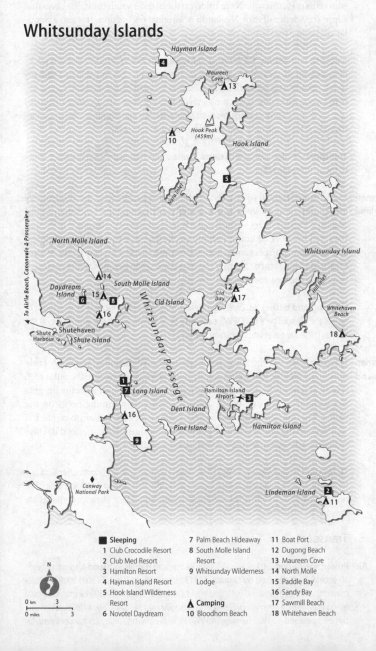

Capricorn & Central coasts

■ Sleeping

1 Club Crocodile Resort
2 Club Med Resort
3 Hamilton Resort
4 Hayman Island Resort
5 Hook Island Wilderness Resort
6 Novotel Daydream
7 Palm Beach Hideaway
8 South Molle Island Resort
9 Whitsunday Wilderness Lodge

▲ Camping

10 Bloodhorn Beach
11 Boat Port
12 Dugong Beach
13 Maureen Cove
14 North Molle
15 Paddle Bay
16 Sandy Bay
17 Sawmill Beach
18 Whitehaven Beach

Sleeping and eating LL *Hamilton Resort*, T0283538468, www.hamiltonisland.com.au Though day-trippers are welcome, there are no campsites on Hamilton Island.

Hook Island Hook is the second largest island in the group and the loftiest, with **Hook Peak** (459m) being the highest point of all the islands. Like all the others it is densely forested and inundated with picturesque bays and inlets. The most northerly of these, like **Maureen Cove**, has fringing reef that offers excellent snorkelling. Picturesque **Nara Inlet**, on the island's south coast, has caves that support evidence of early Ngalandji Aboriginal occupation. It is also a popular anchorage for visiting yachties.

Sleeping and eating L-E *Hook Island Wilderness Resort*, T1800 248824, www.oz horizons.com.au, located towards the southeastern end of the island, is a low-key resort, popular with budget travellers. It offers en suite cabins, standard cabins and dorms along with numerous activities, an underwater observatory, café/bar, pool and spa. There are 5 **QPWS campsites** with Maureen Cove and Bloodhorn Beach (Stone-haven Bay) being the most popular. None have a water supply.

Transport Transfers are with *Seatrek Cruises*, which depart 0830 daily from Shute Harbour, from $36 return.

Lindeman Island Lindeman Island, 20 sq km, is one of the most southerly of the Whitsunday group and the most visited of a cluster that make up the Lindeman Island National Park. It offers all the usual natural features of picturesque inlets and bays and has over 20 km of walking tracks that take you through rainforest and grassland to spectacular views from the island's highest peak, **Mount Oldfield** (7 km return, 212 m). The island has seven beaches, with Gap Beach providing the best snorkelling.

Sleeping and eating LL *Club Med Resort*, T079469333, is located at the northern end of the island. There is a **QPWS campsite** at Boat Port, which is the only one on the island. There are toilets but no water supply.

Hayman Island Hayman Island is the most northerly of the Whitsunday Island. A fairly mountainous little jewel, clad mainly in eucalyptus and close to the outer reef, it is most famous for its world-class resort, which amongst its many delights has without doubt one of the most magnificent swimming pools on the planet. The domain of the wealthy and costing over $300 million to create, it is well beyond the budget of most people, but for those that can afford it, Hayman offers the epitome of a tropical island paradise.

LL *Hayman Island Resort*, T49401234, www.hayman.com.au (worth checking out for the photos), has all you might expect for tariffs that start at $560 a double. The resort's own luxury launch *The Sun Eagle* departs from Shute Harbour or guests are flown in by seaplane.

Transport

Air **Proserpine Airport**, 36 km west of Airlie Beach, and **Hamilton Island Airport**, provide air access. Both serviced by *Qantas*, T131313, and *Flight West*, T1300130092. Lindeman is the only other island with an airfield. *Island Air Taxis*, T49469933, provides local island transfers by fixed wing, *HeliReef Whitsunday*, T49468249, www.heliaust.com.au, by helicopter and *Air Whitsunday*, T49469111, www.airwhitsunday.com.au, or *Coral Air*,

T49469130, greatbarrierreef@bigpond.com, by seaplane. The fare (fixed-wing) to Hamilton costs about $60 one-way. All local fixed-wing, helicopter and seaplane companies also offer scenic flights.

Whitsunday Transit, T49461800, offers regular daily bus services from Proserpine to Shute Harbour (through Airlie Beach). Taxi, T131008. Available at Whitsunday Airport, T0419790995, and the Shell Station near the Shute Harbour ferry terminal, T49469666, from $11 per day. There are 2 car parks at the terminal. The lower car park is paid parking and expensive. The upper car park (accessed just beyond the petrol station) is free. **Road**

Shute Harbour, east of Airlie Beach, is the main departure point for ferry services to the Whitsunday islands. *Blue Ferries* (*Fantasea*), T49465111, www.fantasea.com.au, offer daily scheduled services to Hamilton (6 per day, from $42 return), South Molle /Daydream (6 per day, from $22 return) and Long Island (Club Croc), 3 per day, from $25 return. Their main office is located at the ferry terminal, with an additional office located at Shop 10, Whitsunday Village, Shute Harbour Rd, Airlie Beach, T49482300. Ferry schedules are available in all VICs and travel/tour agent offices. *Whitsunday All Over*, T1300366494, www.whitsundayallover.com.au, is also based at the ferry terminal and offers regular services to Daydream, South Molle, Long, Lindeman, and Hamilton Island. They meet every *Qantas/Flight West* arrival and departure from Hamilton Island airport (book ahead). Transfer rates are priced per sector and start from $15.50. Both companies offer a range of 'Day-tripper' and adventure cruises from $40. *Whitehaven Express*, T49466922, www.whitehavenexpress.com.au, offers a daily trip to Whitehaven Beach (includes snorkelling) from Abel Point Marina (Cannonvale) from $80, child $40, family $230. *Mantaray*, T49464579, www.mantaraycharters.com.au, offers a similar day trip taking in Whitehaven Beach and snorkelling the reef at Mantaray Bay. *Island Camping Connections*, T49465255, are based at the ferry terminal and offers island transfers for campers by water taxi. Book ahead. **Sea**

Bowen

Back on the mainland, Bowen, a lazy atypical Queensland coastal town, is the next stop. Named after the first Governor of Queensland, it is often dubbed the 'Climate Capital of Australia' and enjoys an average of around eight hours of sunshine a day. Having such a warm climate it is also known as the 'Salad Bowl of the North' and amongst other fruits and vegetables, the surrounding soils produce over 80,000 tonnes of tomatoes annually, as well as enough mangoes to feed several small armies. Other than a suntan, there is not a great deal on offer for the time-pressed tourist in Bowen. Most visitors that stay any length of time are cash strapped backpackers for horticultural work, however, other travellers find its atmosphere and its beaches the ideal getaway from the more hyped resorts along the coast.

Colour map 5, grid B2
Population: 9,000
200 km south of Townsville, 188 km north of Mackay

The best beach is arguably the sublime cradle of **Horseshoe Bay** but others, namely Grays Bay, Murray Bay, Rose Bay and King's Beach, are all quite magnificent. Queen's Beach immediately to the north of the town is the most heavily utilised, yet is the least attractive. Murray's Bay is the most remote. They are all quite easy to reach and lie to the north and east of the very orderly town centre. One fine way to get your bearings on arrival is to drive to the top of **Flagstaff Hill**, which offers fine views of the coast and back across the town. Drive into the centre of town then from the waterfront head east on to Peter Wyche Road.

Bowen is also well known for its **murals** that adorn numerous walls in the centre of the town and depict various historical scenes.

Sleeping & eating

F *Barnacles Backpackers*, 16 Gordon St, T47864400, **F** *Bowen Backpackers*, corner of Herbert and Dalrymple sts, T47863433, and the best-placed **F** *Trinity's At The Beach*, 93 Horseshoe Bay Rd, T47864199, all offer basic budget accommodation and can help find work. **A-F** *Horseshoe Bay Resort*, Horseshoe Bay, T47862564, is the best placed motor park in the area and offers a wide range of good-value accommodation from beach units and caravans to powered and unpowered sites. *Horseshoe Bay Café*, T47863280 is nearby offering breakfast, lunch and dinner. Out of town **L-E** *Bogie River Bush Lodge*, T47853407, www.bogiebushhouse.com.au, offers the ideal country get-away with luxury or budget accommodation in a quiet setting, friendly hosts and a wide range of activities. Book ahead.

Transport

Bus Long-distance buses including *McCafferty's*, T131499 and *Greyhound*, T132030, stop on William St near the VIC. **Train** The station is located south of the town centre on Bootooloo Rd. *Bowen Travel*, 40 Williams St, T47862835, are booking agents for both bus and rail.

Ayr, Home Hill and Bowling Green Bay National Park

Colour map 5, grid A1
Population: 9,000
175 km north of Proserpine, 90 km south of Townsville

The small sugar cane town of Ayr and Home Hill, located on the banks of the Burdekin River, offer two main attractions. Connecting the two settlements is the 1,097-m **Burdekin River Road and Rail Bridge**, also known as the 'Silver Link', which for many years was the longest in Australia. Located on the corner of McKenzie and Wilmington streets (turn left at the police station) is the **Ayr Nature Display** with its vivid collection of over 60,000 (dead) Australian butterflies. It is a remarkable sight but one cannot help feeling a sense of dismay and that such displays perhaps miss the point. ■ *Mon-Fri 0800-1700, Sat/Sun 0800-1200. $2.50, child $1. T47832189.*

Alva Beach, on the fringe of the largely inaccessible and fragmented **Bowling Green Bay National Park** (Cape Bowling Green and Mount Elliot), 18 km north of Ayr, offers a great spot for a swim or a picnic. There are walking tracks and the only QPWS campsite in the park, at **Alligator Creek**, 25 km south of Townsville.

Townsville

Colour map 6, grid B6
Population: 130,000
1,370 km from Brisbane, 386 km from Mackay, 345 km Cairns

*Considered the capital of Queensland's north coast and the second largest city in the state, Townsville, until recently, shunned the way of its northerly neighbour, Cairns, and turned its back on tourism. Recently, however, after seeing the success of Cairns, Townsville has made an effort to attract visitors and those efforts are clearly working. Beyond the city centre, with its drab mall and eminently bizarre 'sugar dispenser' tower block, the **waterfront** has been transformed into one of the most attractive in Australia. And what it may still lack in aesthetics, it more than makes up for with its tropical climate, friendliness and increasing touristical opportunity. With a wealth of activities now on offer, local sights and the nearby sublime **Magnetic Island**, Townsville is certainly becoming a fine tourist base, worthy of investigation.*

Ins & outs
See Transport, page 339, for details

The principal VIC is several kilometres south of the town, on the Bruce Highway, T47783555. Open daily 0900-1700. If you miss that, the information booth in the Flinders Mall, T47213660, can also be of assistance. Mon-Fri 0900-1700, Sat/Sun 0900-1300. Alternatively see www.townsvilleonline.com.au QPWS information can be secured within the Reef HQ Complex, see below.

Head-eating potato cod

Other than several notable reef sites, the big diving attraction in these parts is the wreck of the SS Yongala, a passenger ship that sank with all 121 crew – and a racehorse called Moonshine – during a cyclone in 1911. Located about 17 km off Cape Bowling Green, Yongala is often touted as one of Australia's best dives, offering diverse habitats and a huge range of species, including enormous manta rays, colourful coral gardens and even the odd human bone. Since the wreck sits at a depth 29 m and is subject to strong

currents the dive presents a challenge and requires an above average level of competency. Also, in recent times some of its fishy residents are posing a threat and have become too accustomed to visits of the human kind – as one unfortunate diver experienced in 2001 when one of the huge and supposedly friendly potato cod decided to try and swallow his head. Luckily it didn't taste too good and was quickly rejected and whether malicious, a simple mistake or 'jolly japes' remains open to debate.

Sights

Although due for a multi-million dollar refurbishment, and therefore, as yet, not on a par with Sydney Aquarium's remarkable Reef Exhibit, the long-established Reef HQ still provides an excellent land-based introduction to the reef and its aquatic who's who. Centrepiece within the facility is a huge 750,000-litre 'Predator Exhibit' that comes with genuine wave action, a part replica of the famous (local) *Yongala* wreck and a myriad of colourful corals, fish and, of course, the obligatory sharks. Shark feeding takes place on most days at 1500, but what is equally if not more interesting is the 'Danger Trail', which is guided presentation, daily at 1300. This talk is a truly 'underwear wetting' introduction to some of the most deadly and dangerous creatures on the reef. The most nasty of the lot are on show from the infamous box jellyfish, to the harmless yet potentially lethal cone shell – yes, even the shells round here can kill you! However, the star of the show, and indeed the entire region, has to be the stonefish. This is without doubt, the ugliest fish on the planet. Within the same complex is the enormous **Imax Dome Theatre** which is 'an overwhelming experience of sound and screen'– all 18-m of it! See page 339. ■ *Daily 0900-1700, $16, child $7, family $38, T47500800, www.reefHQ.org.au Flinders St East.*

Reef HQ

Next door to Reef HQ, the newly renovated Museum of Queensland provides an impressive insight into the regions maritime history, with the story of **HMS Pandora**, the British 17th century tall ship that is closely linked with that of the betterknown *HMS Bounty* (Mutiny on the Bounty). It was the *Pandora* that was dispatched by the British Admiralty in 1790 to bring the Bounty mutineers to justice, but her own voyage to the South Pacific proved no less notorious. Having captured 14 of the mutineers on the island of Tahiti and then going in search of those that remained on the *Bounty*, the *Pandora* ran aground on the Barrier Reef, with the loss of 31 crew. The wreck was rediscovered near Cape York in 1977 resulting in a frenzy of archaeological interest and the many exhibits and artefacts on show in the museum today. The collection and the presentation of the *Pandora* story is an impressive and imaginative mix of old and new, with the stunning scale replica section of the ship itself providing a memorable centrepiece. Other, no less impressive and imaginative, displays explore and promote the Queensland environment and people.

Museum of Queensland

Capricorn & Central coasts

As ever, there is also an interactive science centre to keep the less young and the less nautically inclined suitably engaged. The café is also notable due to its views across the river. ■ *Daily 0900-1700. $9, child $5, family $24. T47260606, www.mtq.qld.gov.au Flinders St East.*

If you are really (really) nutty about shipwrecks and need further exposure, then the **Maritime Museum of Townsville** will oblige, with its low-key exhibits of more local wrecks, including the most famous, the *SS Yongala*. ■ *Mon-Fri 1000-1600, Sat/Sun 1200-1600, $5, family $4, T47215251, 42-68 Palmer St, South Townsville.*

The Strand   Fringing the shoreline east of the city centre is The Strand, which along with the Museum of Queensland, is the new 'showpiece' of the city and part of its recent multi-million pound facelift. Said by some to be the most attractive public waterfront development in Australia, it provides both locals and visitors an ideal spot to soak up the rays, take a stroll or break a leg on rollerblades. It is also designed to serve as protection against cyclones, but you won't find any signs advertising the fact. One of the most attractive features of the Strand are the 50-year old **Bunyan Fig Trees** that look like columns of melted wax. At its westerly terminus – Kissing Point – there is a man-made **Rock Pool**, which provides safe swimming, year round, and complete protection from the infamous 'marine stingers'. Sunset and nighttime will doubtless reveal why it is called Kissing Point. There is also a

Townsville

■ Sleeping		● Eating		7 Quarterdeck Bar &
1 Aquarius	7 Rowes Bay Caravan Park	1 Covers		Bistro
2 Civic Guest House	8 Southbank Village Backpackers	2 Gauguin & Bar		8 Taj Mahal & Thai International
3 Coral Lodge	9 Walkabout Palms Caravan Park	3 Heritage Café & Bar		9 Tim's Surf & Turf
4 Globetrotters		4 La Bamba Café		
5 Jupiter's Townsville & Casino	10 Yongala Lodge	5 La Cucina		● Pubs & bars
6 Rocks Guesthouse		6 Molly Malone's		10 Seaview Hotel

N

0 metres 200
0 yards 200

popular fish and chip shop and seafood restaurant next to the pool, but unless you want an enforced hunger strike, while you wait in line, it is best avoided. For rollerblades hire, see page 339.

Housed in a former bank, built in 1885, is the Perc Tucker Gallery on Flinders Mall which houses an extensive collection of national and regional art. ■ *Mon/Tue/Wed/Thu 1000-1700, Sat/Sun 1000-1400. Free. T47279011. Corner of Denham St.*

Perc Tucker Gallery

As well as the enigmatic 'sugar shaker' building, Townsville's skyline is dominated by Castle Hill, which is said to glow orange in the rays of the rising sun. But if you cannot drag yourself out of bed to find if that is indeed true, then you can always make the climb to the summit by car or on foot and take in the memorable day or nightime views. Access by car is at the end of Burk Street, off Warburton Street. The aptly named 'Goat Track' to the summit is off Stanton Street, at the end Gregory Street, also off Warburton.

Castle Hill

For a more leisurely stroll with nature head to one or all of Townsville's 'trilogy' of Botanical Gardens: the shady **Palmetum** off University Road, Douglas; **Anderson Park** off Gulliver Street in Mundingburra; and **Queens Gardens** off Burke Street in North Ward. **Town Common Conservation Park**, at the end Cape Pallerenda Road, west of the Strand, is another fine walking spot and a mecca for local birdwatchers. Pick up a leaflet from the QPWS in Reef HQ, T47741382.

Botanical Gardens

Billabong Wildlife Sanctuary, 17 km south of the city, next to the Bruce Highway, is undoubtedly one of the best in Queensland. Fringing an authentic billabong (lake) replete with sandwich-crazed ducks, it houses an extensive collection of natives, from the extraordinary and leggy cassowary, to the adorable and somnolent wombat. There are many tame and oblivious roos and emus lazing on paths around the park and as with all other parks, the more dangerous individuals are keenly highlighted, including the ubiquitous crocodile and a host of poisonous and all embracing snakes. Various shows and talks throughout the day give you an opportunity to learn about the animals and if you wish, to handle the more docile serpents and baby crocs. Don't miss the wild and wonderfully smelly fruit bat colony next to the lake. ■ *Daily 0800-1700, $20, child $10, family $48, T47788344, www.billabongsanctuary. com.au Airport transfers, T4775554, offer twice daily shuttles to Billabong from $32, child $16 return (0915-1330).*

Billabong Wildlife Sanctuary

Essentials

LL *Holiday Inn*, Flinders Mall, T47722477, www.holiday-inn.com.au If you have ever had the slightest inclination to stay in a hotel that looks remarkably like a giant sugar dispenser, then this is your chance. It certainly lacks external aesthetics, but it is centrally located, offering all the usual comforts, good weekend rates and has some of the best views in town. **LL** *Jupiter's Townsville Hotel and Casino*, off Sir Leslie Theiss Dr, T47222333. The most upmarket hotel in the city, which sits in isolation overlooking the new marina and Magnetic Island.

Sleeping
■ *On map, page 336*

There are plenty of modern motels on The Strand overlooking the ocean, including **L** *Aquarius*, 75 The Strand, T47724255, www.aquarius-townsville.com.au Again it is something of an eyesore from the outside but is good value and offers great views across to Magnetic Island. **A** *Yongala Lodge*, off the Strand on Fryer St, T47722477, info@historicyongala.com.au Named after the famous local shipwreck it offers a range of basic motel units from single to 2-bedroom, has a pleasant Greek/international restaurant and is a stone's throw from the waterfront.

There are very few B&Bs and guesthouses in the city, however both **L** *Rocks Guesthouse*, 20 Cleveland Terrace, T47715700, www.therocksguesthouse.com, **A** *Coral Lodge*, 82 Hale St, T47715512, urwelcome@ultra.net.au, are reputable and good value for money.

There are plenty of backpacker beds in town, though most struggle to keep their guests any longer than 1 night in their desire to get to the much more attractive surroundings of Magnetic Island. **C-E** *Globetrotters*, 45 Palmer St, T47713242. One of the closest to the transit centre. Small and popular. **C-E** *Civic Guest House*, 262 Walker St, T47715381, www.backpackersinn.com.au A little less convenient, but the pick of the bunch has to be this tidy option. It has a wide range of rooms (some with TV and a/c), good general facilities and regular and interesting in-house trips. **D-E** *Southbank Village Backpackers*, McIlwarth St, T47715849. Just around the corner from *Globetrotters* and equally convenient and somewhat improved since refurbishment.

B-E *Rowes Bay Caravan Park*, west of The Strand on Heatley's Parade, T47713576. Close to town, this 3-star park has villas, cabins, powered and un-powered sites and is close to the beach however it is in severe need of a camp kitchen. **B-E** *Walkabout Palms Caravan Park*, 6 University Rd, Wulguru, T47782480. This 4-star park is well facilitated and connected to the 24-hr petrol station. Although not central to the city it is in a good position for the transitory visitor right on the main north/south highway.

Eating
• *On map, page 336*

• On map, page 336

Expensive   There are reputable, upmarket restaurants in most of the major hotels and motels, including *Flutes* (*Reef International*, 63 The Strand, T47211777), *Aqua* (*Jupiter's Hotel*, Sir Leslie Theiss Drive, T47831283) and the *Zoui Alto* (top floor of the *Aquarius* – superb views). The best bet for fine dining and dining in general, is along Flinders St East, Palmer St and along the waterfront. On Flinders St East is the award-winning, 2-storey *Covers Restaurant*, 209 Flinders St, T47214630, offering an eclectic range of International and Australian dishes from quail to roast roo. On a recent visit *Covers* was the choice of the less than charismatic Prime Minister 'Johnny' Howard. The restaurant is upstairs with an attractive balcony, while at the street level there is a café and wine bar. Open lunch Mon-Fri, brunch Sat and Sun, dinner Mon-Sat.

Mid-range   Flinders St East offers a wide range of international, affordable options, including the popular Indian *Taj Mahal*, (2/235), T47723422, and just above it, *Thai International*, T47716242. Open daily 0530-late. A few doors down the Italian *La Cucina*, (215), T47211500, is also good value. Open daily 1800-late. For pub grub try the tidy surroundings, menu and congenial atmosphere of *Molly Malone's Irish Pub*, corner of Wickham and Flinders St East, T47713428. Otherwise, meat lovers will love the generous steaks at *Tim's Surf and Turf*, overlooking the river on Ogden St (behind Flinders Mall), T47214861. Towards the water and overlooking the marina (off Sir Leslie Theiss Dr), is *Quarterdeck Bar and Bistro*, T47222261. It offers good-value seafood dishes in a nice setting, with live jazz on Sun from 1600-2000. Further along The Strand is *Gauguin Restaurant and Bar*, Gregory St Headland, T47245488, another fine venue for seafood and in the perfect spot overlooking the ocean. It's open daily for lunch and dinner.

Cheap *Heritage Café and Bar*, 137 Flinders St East, T47714355, has a nice atmosphere and variant, good-value blackboard, while the colourful *La Bamba Café*, 3 Palmer St, T47716322, does cheap breakfasts and good coffee. For self-caterers the *Woolworths* supermarket is conveniently located on Sturt St, behind the Flinders St Mall. Open weekdays till 2100.

The Bank, 169 Flinders St, T47716148, open Wed-Sat till 0500. Across the road the rather unfortunately named *Mad Cow*, T47715727, is a little less formal and also remains open well into the wee hours. *Molly Malone's*, corner of Wickham and Flinders St East, has a happy hour daily from 1700-1800 and provides the usual live 'diddly-dee' or local rock bands at the weekend. During the tropical afternoons and balmy evenings the *Garden Bar* at the *Seaview Hotel* along the Strand, corner of Gregory St, is also popular. Otherwise you might like to try your luck at *Jupiter's Townsville Hotel and Casino*, Sir Leslie Theiss Dr, T47222333. Open Sun-Thu 1000-0200, Fri/Sat 1000-0400.

Bars & clubs
Flinders St East is the place to head for a steamy tropical night out

Townsville Entertainment and Convention Centre, Entertainment Dr, T47714222, www.tecc.net.au, Is the main entertainment venue in the city. Also home to the fiercesome Townsville Crocodiles NBL team. **IMAX**, Reef HQ, T47211481, have shows, usually with lots of noise and action, every hour from 1000 1600. $12. Opening hours are reduced from Oct-May. See also *Jupiter's Townsville Hotel and Casino*, above.

Entertainment

Diving There are several companies located in Townsville or on Magnetic Island (which is often the preferred location) that offer a wide variety of trips for certified divers wishing to experience the *Yongala*, see box, page 335. Basic and advanced training that can culminate with the 'ultimate wreck dive' is also available. *Diving Dreams*, 252 Walker St, T47212500, www.divingdreams.com.au, offers reputable 2-5 day trips from $350. Others include *Pro-Dive*, T47211760, www.prodive-townsville.com.au, who offers a 5-day advance course which includes 2 dives on the *Yongala* from $515 and *Adrenaline Dive*, 121 Flinders St, T47240600, www.adrenalindive.com.au, who offers 2 dives on the wreck from $179 as well as other day trips to the reef from $130. **Fishing** Townsville is well known as a premiere venue for sea and big game fishing. Local charters include *Gladiator*, T04 12073606, that offer trips around Magnetic island from $67, child $34 and family $182, the 42-ft *Fringe Benefits*, T47715579, that offer day, half-day, overnight or extended trips with all mod cons, aboard the 75-ft luxury yacht, Pacific Coast, T04 28778458. **Horse trekking** *Woodstock Trail Rides*, based along Flinders Highway, T47788888, www.woodstocktrailrides.com.au, offers authentic rides on a working cattle station, half-day $40, full-day $90 and overnight camp $120 (includes transfers). **Rollerblading** Rollerblades can be hired from *Street Dreams*, 30 Palmer St, T47716477, from $6 per hr. **Skydiving** *Coral Sea Skydivers*, 14 Plume St, South Townsville, T47724889, www.coralseaskydivers.com.au, offers daily tandem dives on to the Strand Beach from between 8-12,000 ft, from $240. **White water rafting** *Raging Thunder*, T40307990, www.ragingthunder.com.au, provides pick-ups for a range of rafting trips and packages on the Tully River, from $155.

Tours & activities
See page 344 for Magnetic Island diving operator listings

Local Bus *Townsville's Sunbus*, T47258482, www.sunbus.com.au, offers regular daily suburban services. There is a main town centre bus terminal with posted information in the heart of the main Flinders St Mall. Fares are from $2.50, Day Pass from $10. Townsville Taxi T131008 (24 hr). **Cycles** Can be hired from *Townsville Car Rentals*, 12 Palmer St, South Townsville, T47721093, from $10 a day.

Transport

Long distance Air Townsville is serviced from all major cities by *Qantas*, T131313, and *Virgin Blue*, T136789. *Flight West*, T47253855, www.flightwest.com.au, offers

Capricorn & Central coasts

regular onward services throughout Queensland. *Macair*, T40359722, www.macair. com.au, services several locations including Cairns, Cooktown and Dunk Island. The airport, T47273211, is located about 5 km west of the city in the suburb of Garbutt. *Airport Transfers and Tours*, T47755544, offers regular services into town, from single/return, $7/11. **Bus** Townsville is serviced by *Premier Motor Services*, T133410, *McCafferty's*, T131499, and *Greyhound*, T132030. Westbound destinations include Charters Towers and Mount Isa. Transit centre is located at the corner of Palmer and Plume sts, T47725100. Open daily 0430-2000. **Car** Hire from *Hertz*, T47755950, *Delta*, T131390, and *Thrifty*, T47254600, have outlets at the airport. *Townsville Car Rentals* have an outlet at 12 Palmer St, South Townsville, T47721093. **Train** The railway station is located on Blackwood St, just south of the Flinders Mall, next to the river. It has a travel centre, T47728358 (bookings T132232), www.traveltrain.qr.com.au *The Sunlander* operates 3 weekly services between Brisbane and Cairns (northbound Tue/Thu/Sat, southbound Mon/Thu/Sat); *The Spirit of the Tropics* operates a twice-weekly service from Brisbane to Townsville (northbound Tue/Sat, southbound Wed/Sun) and *The Inlander* operates twice-weekly services from Townsville to Mount Isa (westbound Sun/Wed, eastbound Mon/Fri). Contact the travel centre for confirmations, latest fares and departure times.

Directory **Banks** Most bank branches (all with ATMs) are represented in and around the Flinders Mall. Currency exchange at *Wespac Bank*, 337 Flinders Mall. **Communications Internet**: *Internet Den* (opposite the VIC), 265 Flinders Mall, T47214500. Open 0800-2400; *Ripples Café* in Great Barrier Reef Wonderland, Flinders St; *Infinet*, Castletown Shopping World, Woolcock St, Kings Rd (3 km southeast of the town centre), T47727666. Open Mon-Fri 0900-1800, Thu 0900-2100, Sat 0900-1600. **Post office**: Sturt St. Open Mon-Fri 0830-1730, Sat 0900-1230. Post Restante. Open Mon-Fri 0830-1630. **Medical services** Townsville Hospital, 100 Agnes Smith Dr, T47819211. **Useful numbers** Police: corner of Sturt and Stanley sts, T47607777. RACQ: 202 Ross River Dr, T47255677.

Magnetic Island

Colour map 6,
grid B6
Population: 2,250

*Magnetic Island is Townsville's biggest tourist attraction and the most easily accessible 'tropical island escape' on the reef. Lying only 8 km offshore and baking in over 320 days of sunshine a year, 'Maggie' has always been a popular holiday spot, but adding to its charm is the discrete permanent population that negates the resort feel of most of the other reef islands. As such, the island is considered by many in the region as the most desirable suburb in Townsville. Blessed with a fine range of amenities in a fairly compact area – in the eastern and north eastern fringes of the island itself – the most striking feature is that surrounding both the resort and the beaches is a much larger area of wild and fairly inaccessible terrain giving an over all impression of wilderness and escape. With over half the island given over to **national park**, encompassing over 40 km of **walking tracks**, 20 picture-postcard **bays** and **beaches**, as well as a wealth of **activities** and some great budget accommodation, not to mention a resident population of **koala**, Magnetic Island is well named. The island was named by Cook. Apparently, while passing the island in 1770, his compass had a small fit, hence the 'Magnetic'.*

Ins & outs
See Transport, page
344, for further details

Getting there There are regular ferry services from Townsville to the two arrival points, Picnic Bay and Geoffrey Bay. **Getting around** The best way to explore the island is to hire a 4WD or moke, throw your snorkel and walking boots in the back and just 'croooozz'! The 4 main villages, spread along its eastern coastline, are served by public transport. Tours are also available. **Tourist information** VIC is located a short walk from the ferry at the Island Travel Centre, T47785155, www.townsvilleonline.com.au They offer transportation, accommodation and activities bookings. Daily 0800-1630.

Sights

With over 20 beaches to choose from there are plenty of places to set up camp and just relax. Although there is excellent swimming and some good snorkelling spots – most notably the left hand side of **Arthur Bay** – care must be taken during the stinger season from October to May, when you are advised to swim only in the netted areas at Picnic Bay and Horseshoe Bay. The most popular beaches are **Rocky Bay**, between Picnic Bay and Nelly Bay, and **Alma Bay**, just north of Arcadia, though the most remote, secluded and perhaps most beautiful are **Arthur Bay**, **Florence Bay**, **Radical Bay** and **Balding Bay** at the northeast corner of the island. All four are accessed down the unsealed Radical Bay Track, 8 km north of Picnic Bay, but note all the vehicle hire companies place restrictions on unsealed roads, so you may have to walk. Beyond these bays is **Horseshoe Bay** the biggest on the island, and a popular spot for swimming and watersports.

There are many excellent **walking tracks** on the island with the two most notable being the Horseshoe Bay to Arthur Bay track (3 km, two hours one-way) and in the same vicinity, the Forts Walk (2 km, 1½ hours return). The Horseshoe Bay to Arthur Bay track can be tackled in either direction and takes in all the secluded bays and some low lying bush. Many allow themselves extended stops at one of the beaches since it can be very difficult to drag yourself away. The Forts Walk starts at the Radical Bay turn-off and follows the ridge past some old gun emplacements to the old observation tower lookout. This track is also one of the best places to observe **koalas**. Late afternoon (when they are awake and feeding) is the best time to see them. Another short walk to **Hawking's Point** lookout above Picnic Bay is also worthwhile. It starts at the end of Picnic Street (600 m, 30 minutes). To visit the more remote areas on the south and west coast

Magnetic Island

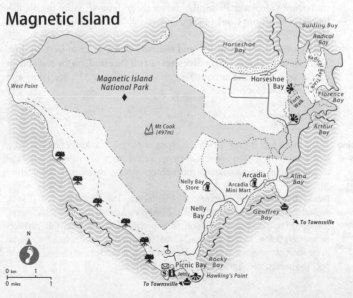

▶ ## Marine stingers

Although the Queensland Tourism Board are reluctant to advertise the fact, 2001-02 saw the worst year on record for fatalities from the seasonal 'marine stingers'. Sadly, two tourists died from the horrific (but secondary) symptoms that resulted from the stings of these notorious jellyfish.

The most well-known and prevalent species is the rather banal looking **Box Jellyfish** – a sort of floating custard pie with highly poisonous tentacles, which trail several metres behind it. Other lesser known and poisonous species include the **Irukandji** – a particularly insidious character, about the size (remarkably) of your thumb nail and another very aptly named the Snotty! All stingers pose a significant threat during the period in their life cycle (October and May) when they are in the open sea. Of course, like almost all the well known nasties, marine stingers are not out to get you. What is unfortunate is the collective absence of both your senses and theirs and the regretful fact that you simply don't belong in the ocean.

If a Box Jellyfish stings you, your blood pressure triples, CPR is administered and an ambulance is duly called to the scene. Although there is an antivenin widely available at hospitals for the Box Jellyfish, an antivenin for the less lethal Irukandji has yet to be developed. However, rest assured that even without antivenin, provided you are quickly and liberally soaked in vinegar, are young and fit, and reach a hospital as soon as possible, you will have every chance of surviving the ordeal. But if ever there was a case of prevention being better than cure this is it, and provided the following sensible precautions are taken your chances of injury fall well below that of simply crossing a road:

1 Do not swim in the sea (outside the 'stinger nets' provided at most major beaches) during the 'stinger season' (October to May).

2 Do not swim alone during the stinger season.

3 Be aware of the effectiveness of vinegar for immediate treatment and call the emergency services as soon as possible.

4 Seek local knowledge as to the best locations to swim.

---

requires your own 4WD, a boat or a very long trek. The unsealed track west, starts from Yule Street, Picnic Bay, beside the golf course. Sadly, the island's highest peak **Mount Cook** (497 m) is inaccessible to anything other than the local wildlife.

Magnetic Island is a superb and relatively cheap venue to learn to dive. There are also some excellent **dive sites** just off the island, on the reef and, of course, over the world famous *Yongala* wreck, see page 335. See Tours and activities below, for details.

Essentials

Sleeping
■ *On map, page 341*

As the main arrival point Picnic Bay offers most amenities bar accommodation which is evenly spread mostly down the east coast

As you might expect there is plenty of choice on Maggie from luxury poolside apartments to your very own hammock – most are virtually self-contained. For budget accommodation, and during school and public holidays, you are advised to book ahead.

Picnic Bay A *Dunoon Beachfront Apartments*, The Esplanade, T47785161, www.dunoon.com.au, has good-value 1/2-bedroom, fully self-contained apartments, surrounded by gardens with pool and spa, especially good for families. **C-E** *Travellers* Backpackers Resort, 1 The Esplanade, T47785166, www.travellers-on-magnetic.com.au In the heart of the village, it offers en suite a/c rooms and dorms, all centred around a pool and beer garden. Internet and close to all amenities.

Nelly Bay LL-L *Magnetic International Resort*, Mandalay Ave, T47785200, www.magnetichotel.com.au This upmarket 4-star resort offers luxury rooms, suites and family suites, licensed restaurant and pool, all set in its own 10-acre gardens. **L-C** *Magnetic Island Tropical Resort*, Yates St, T47785955. An excellent choice has en suite chalet-style cabins with restaurant/bar, pool and spa, amidst a bush setting. **B-E** *Coconuts Backpackers*, 1 Nelly Bay Rd, T1800 065696, www.bakpakgroup.com.au South of Nelly Bay on beach, this backpackers is regaining popularity after renovations. It has an interesting range of accommodation options from dorms and 'camp-o-tels' to ocean-view doubles. Camping. In house dive courses. Beach party every month.

Arcadia A *Beaches B&B*, 39 Marine Parade, T47785303, is a small and pleasant beachside cottage in a quiet location, ideal for couples. **A** *Magnetic North Holiday Apartments*, 2 Endeavour Rd, T47785647. Peaceful, 2-star, offering standard, tidy, self-contained apartments close to Alma Bay. **B-C** *Marshall's B&B*, 3-5 Endeavour Rd, T47785112, www.moonshine.com.au This eco-friendly option next door to *Magnetic North Apartments*, offers basic, but good value singles and doubles in a traditional Queenslander house and is surrounded by spacious gardens with the odd congenial wallaby to share lunch with. Fans and free night stand-by special (ie buy 2, get 3) from Oct-Jun. **B-F** *Arcadia Hotel Resort* ('Arkies'), 7 Marine Parade, T47785177. A busy, sprawling place with 30 a/c motel style units (including dorms) close to all local amenities. Pool, spa, restaurant/bar and bistro. Internet.

Horseshoe Bay LL *Shaw's Apartments*, 7 Pacific Dr, T47581900, www.shawsonthe shore.com.au Although the decor may not be to everyone's taste this new fully self-contained 2-3 bedroom, luxury apartment block, has all the mod cons. Right above the main grocery shop and facing the beach. Minimum 2-nights. Good for families. **A-E** *Maggie's Beach House*, 1 Pacific Dr, T47785144. A modern purpose built facility next to the beach and although the most remote and expensive of the backpackers is, deservingly, the most popular. It offers a wide range of rooms from ensuites to dorms, has a pool, bar and internet café. Free, direct transfers by boat from Townsville adds to its appeal. **C-F** *Geoff's Place*, 40 Horseshoe Bay Rd, T1800 285577, www.geoffsplace.com.au It is an YHA affiliate, set in spacious grounds, offering everything from basic air-con chalets to camp and powered sites. Regular, mass lorikeet feeding. Lively place with popular late night bar and bistro, pool, spa and internet but a little further away from the beach.

The restaurants and cafés on Maggie tend to be very casual affairs and close early. Most of the major resorts and backpackers have cafés, bistros, or à la carte restaurants all open to the public.

Eating
● *On map,
page 341*

Picnic Bay In the Mall, *Gossip Café*, T47581119, has an extensive blackboard menu and does good breakfasts and coffee. Nearby, is *MI Chinese Restaurant*, T47785706. Open daily from 1100.

Nelly Bay *Mexican Munchies*, Warboys St, T47785658, offering vegetarian dishes. Open daily (except Wed) from 1800. Next to the supermarket is *Pizza Tonite*, T47581400, which offers sit down, takeaway or deliveries (closed Mon).

Arcadia *Bannister's Seafood Restaurant*, 22 McCabe Cr, T47785700, claims to offer the best fish and chips on the island. Open daily until 2000.

Horseshoe Bay *Cotters*, on the waterfront, T47785786, is another place offering fine seafood and overlooks the beach. Self-caterers will find grocery stores in all the main centres, that open daily until about 1900.

Bars & clubs The major backpackers provide most of the island's entertainment and open late bars. *Picnic Bay Hotel* (Thu) and backpackers (*Arkie's*/Fri, *Geoff's*/Mon) are the places to go for full on pool competitions. There are also live bands most nights at *Arkie's Resort*, Arcadia.

Tours & activities *Magnetic Island Bus Service*, T47785130, offers 3-hr guided tours from Picnic Bay at 0900 and 1300 from $30, child $15, family $75. *Tropicana Tours*, 2/26 Picnic St, T47581800, www.tropicanatours.com.au, offers an excellent and highly entertaining 8-hr '7 Days in 1' adventure around the island, from $125. Recommended. But book ahead. *Pleasure Divers*, 10 Marine Parade Arcadia, T47785788, www.pleasuredivers@ austarnet.com.au, offers 3 or 4-day PADI Open Water Courses from $179, a 2-day Advanced Open Water Course (for the *Yongala*) from $279. Accommodation packages are also available. *Magnetic Island Dive Centre*, Shop 7/4 Picnic Bay Mall, T47581399, www.mag.is.dive@austarnet.com.au, offers similar deals. *Bluey's Ranch*, 38 Gifford St, Horseshoe Bay, T47785109, offer horse treks from 1 hrs to half-day, from $30. If you must create havoc *Adrenalin Jet Ski Tours*, T47785533, offers a guided 85-km half-day circumnavigation of the island, from $115. Jet skis can also be hired independently from Horseshoe Bay, from $38 for 15 mins, T47581100. *Magnetic Island Sea Kayaks*, T47785424, offers half-day sea kayaking adventures from $45 (includes beach breakfast). *Watersports*, T47581336, www.jazza.com.au, based at Horseshoe Bay, offers a range of activities from parasailing (from $60) to water skiing (from $25). Closed Tue. *Jazza's Sailing Tours*, 90 Horseshoe Bay Rd, T47785530, offers a good value, 6-hr cruise aboard the 12-m *Jazza* from $75, child $50 (includes lunch). *Magnetic Palm Islands Rent-A-Yacht*, T47785644, www.miray.com.au, for hire of 32-ft and 43-ft yachts from $660 for 3 days/2 nights. *Ocean Runner*, T47785774, is a new outfit offering a range of enjoyable cruises around the island, including a sunset cruise from $90. Magnetic Island has a small 9-hole golf course in Picnic Bay, visitors welcome, $11, T47785188.

Transport

The island speed limit is 60 kmph and this should be adhered to at all times

Local Bus *Magnetic Island Bus Service*, T47785130, runs up and down the east coast, between Picnic Bay to Horseshoe Bay every hour or so from 0620-2350. Tickets are sold on the bus from $2. One-day ($11) and two-day ($13) unlimited passes are generally the preferred option. They also offer 3-hr guided tours from Picnic Bay at 0900 and 1300 from $30, child $15, family $75. **Moke and 4WD** One of the highlights of 'Maggie' is exploring the island by mini-moke or small toy-like 4WDs. *Tropical Topless Car Rentals*, Picnic St, Picnic Bay, has a fleet of colourful (and indeed topless) 4WD that are comfortable, good value and economical, from $60 per day, flat rate, unlimited kilometres. Credit card deposit. Book at the *Photo Shop* at the end of the jetty. Recommended. Alternatively, *Moke Magnetic*, 4 The Esplanade, T47785377, hires mokes and vehicles seating up to 8 from $47 per day. Note however that there is a 44c per/ km charge (including petrol) on top of that. Deposit $100. *MI Wheels*, 13 Pacific Dr, Horseshoe Bay, T47785491, hire mokes on a sliding scale rate from $42 per day, with 33c per/ km (excludes petrol). Scooters and trail motorbikes can be hired from *Road Runner Scooter Hire*, Shop 3, Picnic Bay Mall, T47785222, from $28 per day. Bikes can be hired from some hostels and from *Magnetic Island Photos*, Picnic Bay Mall, and T47785411. Petrol from *Petrol Arcadia Mini Mart*, 5 Bright Ave, T47785387, daily 0800-1900, and *Nelly Bay Store*, 36 Madalay Ave. **Taxi** T131008.

Long distance **Ferry** Passenger ferries arrive at the wharf off the settlement at Picnic Bay and vehicular ferry and other passenger services arrive at the passenger and car ferry terminal at Geoffrey Bay next to Arcadia. *Sunferries Magnetic Island*, T47713855, www.sunferries@ultra.net.au, offers regular daily sailings from both the **Flinders St Ferry Terminal** and **Bayswater Terminal** to Picnic Bay from 0550-1855 and from $16, child $8, family $33 return. *Magnetic Island Car and Passenger Ferries*, based on Ross St, Townsville South, T47725422, www.riversidemarine.com.au, offers regular sailings to Geoffrey Bay (Arcadia) Mon-Fri 0600-1720, Sat 0745-1540, Sun 0745-1720, from $115 (vehicle with up to 6 passengers), $16, child $7 (passenger only), both return.

Banks The post office, Picnic Bay, acts as Commonwealth Bank agents. There are
ATMs at *Picnic Bay Hotel*, *Arkie's Resort* and *Horseshoe Bay Store*. *EFTPOS* is widely available throughout the island. **Communications** Post office: Picnic Bay Mall. Open
Mon-Fri 0830-1700, Sat 0900-1100. **Internet**: VIC (Island Travel Centre), Picnic Bay,
offers free internet with bookings. *Cybercafé*, Courtyard Mall. Open daily 0900-1700. In
Picnic Bay, most backpackers including *Arkie's*, 7 Marine Parade, T47785176. Open daily
0900-2100 and *Maggie's Beach Café*, Horseshoe Bay (Open from 0900-2100). **Medical
services** Medical Medical Centre, Sooning St, Nelly Bay, T47785107. **Chemist**: *Magnetic Island Pharmacy*, Shopping Centre, Sooning St, Nelly Bay, T47785375. Open
Mon-Fri 0900-1730, Sat 0900-1300. **Useful numbers** Police: T47785270.

*(margin: **Directory**)*

The Flinders Highway

*The Flinders Highway – sometimes referred to as the Overlander's Highway –
from Townsville to Mount Isa and beyond provides the most direct route from the
Queensland coast to the Northern Territory. It is an interesting option and has
the added attraction of **Ravenswood** and **Charters Towers**, two historic settlements that can be easily visited on a day trip from Townsville. If you are short for
time they can both provide an authentic **outback experience** and certainly possess
enough allure to encourage you to venture further west, well beyond the horizon.*

(margin: Colour map 6, grid C4-6 889 km from Townsville to Mount Isa)

Ravenswood

A former gold-mining town, there is little left of what once was a thriving, cosmopolitan community. What does remain offers an interesting, if bleak, reminder of more prosperous times. Gold was discovered here quite by chance in 1868 and by 1869 it was in full production, two years ahead of its big brother to be – Charters Towers. The stark outback horizon affords little except overgrown slag heaps dotted with old machinery and crooked old chimneys, that once heralded mines with such evocative names as the 'General Grant', 'The Deep', 'Eureka' and 'The Sunset'. The latter alone produced over 6.6 tonnes of gold. Of the 48 hotels and pubs that once dominated the town – and doubtless life in general – only two still remain, *Imperial Hotel* and the *Railway Hotel*. As if stuck in a time warp, they have changed little and still offer accommodation, meals, and a welcome 'coldie' away from the blazing sun. The former 1837 **Courthouse** has been fully restored and now houses a local museum. ■ *Daily (except Tue) 1000-1500, $2*. Ravenswood Post Office, Macrossan Street, is a good source of information, as well as supplies and fuel. Look out for the pet magpie that sits like a miniature vulture watching visitors and Ravenswood's nemesis – 'Father Time' – go by.

One of the areas most unique natural landscape features is the **White Blow** – a large quartz outcrop located 2 km east via Deighton Street. It is gazetted a national park so nothing must be taken, including any glistening gold bits.

(margin: Colour map 6, grid C6 Population: 100 122 km southwest of Townsville, 84 km southeast of Charters Towers, 34 km off the Flinders Highway)

Some 80 km south of Ravenswood is the Burdekin Falls Dam, which holds back an area of water larger than Sydney Harbour. It can provide an impressive sight during floods, floods the scale of which can scarcely be imagined when you look at the flood marker on the west side of the bridge across the Burdekin River, back on the Flinders Highway.

*(margin: **Burdekin Falls Dam**)*

(vertical margin text: Capricorn & Central coasts)

Charters Towers

Colour map 6, grid C5
Population: 27,000
132 km west
Townsville, 770 km
east of Mount Isa

When a young aboriginal boy discovered gold in the hills of the newly christened Burdekin River Valley in 1871, there is little doubt he would not have been able to anticipate the consequences of his find – that almost overnight, it led to the creation of Queensland's second largest city, a place once called 'The World', a little piece of 'the planet' that soon after buzzed with the rapacious activity of over 30,000 hopeful souls, and resounded to the constant thud of almost 30 crushing batteries. In its heyday Charters Towers (which was named after mining warden WESM Charters and the hills that surround it) produced over six million ounces ($25 million) of the precious metal. Although it is now better known for its beef production than its mineral resources, it remains proud of its golden heritage and is a fascinating example of a quintessential outback town. You may also sense a once familiar twinkle in the local eye, since the old 'world' is once again successfully extracting the most famous metal therein.

Ins & outs

See Transport, page 348, for further details

Getting there Bus and train services stop here on the way to, and returning from, Mount Isa. **Getting around** The town can be navigated on foot. A guided tour is the best way to experience the town. **Tourist information** VIC is housed in the former band hall building between the former Stock Exchange and City Hall, 74 Mosman St, T4752 0314, www.charterstowers.qld.gov.au Open daily 0900-1700.

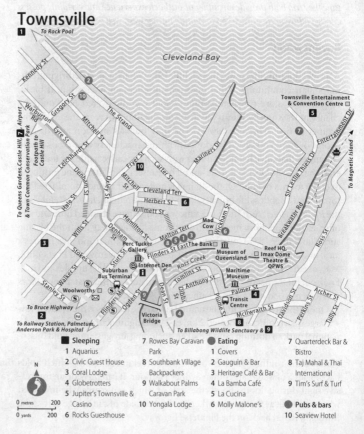

Townsville

Sleeping
1 Aquarius
2 Civic Guest House
3 Coral Lodge
4 Globetrotters
5 Jupiter's Townsville & Casino
6 Rocks Guesthouse
7 Rowes Bay Caravan Park
8 Southbank Village Backpackers
9 Walkabout Palms Caravan Park
10 Yongala Lodge

Eating
1 Covers
2 Gauguin & Bar
3 Heritage Café & Bar
4 La Bamba Café
5 La Cucina
6 Molly Malone's
7 Quarterdeck Bar & Bistro
8 Taj Mahal & Thai International
9 Tim's Surf & Turf

Pubs & bars
10 Seaview Hotel

0 metres 200
0 yards 200

Charters Towers is rightfully proud of its gold-mining heritage and with the help of the National Trust has made some sterling efforts in the restoration and conservation of its heritage buildings and mining relics. In the centre of the city, on Mosman Street, is the former 1888 **Stock Exchange Building**. Built originally as a shopping arcade it was converted into a stock exchange in 1890 and then, after the decline of mining activities, fell into disrepair. In 1970 it was restored back to its original purpose and now hosts a number of small businesses, a gallery, café and an assay room filled with mining memorabilia, including a fascinating working model of a stamping battery. ■ *Mon-Fri 0830-1300/1400-1630, Sat/Sun 0900-1500. $2.20, $1.*

Next door is the aesthetically magnificent, former 1892 **Australian Bank of Commerce** building. For many years after its original purpose it served as a private residence before being purchased by the local council in 1992 and restored and cleverly incorporated into the $8 million **World Theatre** Complex. Even without a performance it is well worth a look inside. ■ *Mon-Fri 1000-1330, Sat 1000-1200. Tours daily, from $6.60, child $4.40, T4787 4337.*

Zara Clark Museum houses an array of historical artefacts and collections donated by local residents. ■ *Daily 1000-1500. $5, child $2.20.* **Miners Cottage**, at 26 Deane Street, is an 1890 original that now houses antiques, arts and crafts and jewellery. ■ *Wed-Fri 1000-1630. Free, gold panning $5.50, child $3.30.* Other heritage buildings and points of interest in the city include the 1892 **Post Office** and 1910 **Police Station** on Gill Street, 1882 **Pfieffer House** on Paul Street and the interior of the 1886 **Civic Club** on Ryan Street, which was once the haunt of 'the world's male elite'. Nearby, don't miss the **Relic Shop** on Ryan Street, which although hardly historical is now a very quirky second-hand mart – or the overflowing nest of a hopeless kleptomaniac?

On the outskirts of the city, east via Gill Street and Millchester Road, are the remains of the **Venus Battery Mill**. This is perhaps the best of all the former mining relics because it remains almost untouched in its gradual decay. As you wander around its eight huge stampers and former cyanide ponds it certainly stirs the imagination back to the days when it was in full production. Days indeed when the mere sound of it must have carried for miles in to the outback. ■ *Daily 0900-1500. Fairly half-hearted guided tours are available at 1000 and 1400. $5, child $2.* Just south of the city on the Flinders Highway there are two modern day features worth seeing. **Dalrymple Sale Yards** which is regularly in action with countless head of beef cattle and surrounding it, the regular sight of the monstrous **road trains** – a true indication that you are now in outback country. Nearby, **Towers Hill** provides excellent views across the city and beyond, especially at sunrise or sunset. It is also home to numerous rock wallabies. Access is south end of Mosman Street, off Black Jack Road. The gates close after sunset.

Sights
Given the depth of its history, as well as its sheer friendliness, by far the best way to experience the town is to join a guided tour

Sleeping
■ *On map, page 346*

In its heyday there used to be almost 100 hotels in Charters Towers, but now although traditional hotel beds are still offered most visitors stick to the motels, guest houses or caravan parks. **A-B** *Heritage Lodge Motel*, 79-97 Flinders Highway, T4787 4088, www.heritagelodge.com.au, is the most upmarket place in town offering modern self-contained units in a park setting. **A** *Cattleman's Rest Motel*, corner of Bridge and Plant sts, T47873555, comes recommended by transitory 'truckies' and business people, and as such, is a good place to get away from tourist hype. Some units have baths and there is a good in-house restaurant. **A-D** *York St B&B*, 58 York St, T4787 1028, yorkstreetbb@httech.com.au, is an old, spacious Queenslander with welcoming hosts, offering doubles, singles and backpacker units and a pool. Recommended. **C-F** *Mexican Tourist Park*, corner of Church and Tower sts, T4787 1161, is the closest motor park

Capricorn & Central coasts

to town and offers self-contained, a/c cabins, standard a/c cabins, powered and non-powered sites.

Charters Towers is the stepping-stone to 2 popular outback stations that offer comfortable accommodation mixed with the quintessential outback experience. Charters Towers VIC has full details. Book ahead. Recommended. **A-D** *Bluff Downs*, T4770 4080, Bluff_Downs@hotmail.com, is a historic 40,000 ha working cattle station, set around the spectacular deep water lagoons of the Basalt River, 80 km north of the city. It offers a range of activities from mustering to fossil hunting and accommodation ranging from a/c backpackers quarters to homestead rooms and a self-contained cottage. **A-E** *Plain Creek Station*, located to the south, half way between Charters Towers and Clermont (5 kms off the Great Inland Way), T4983 5228, plaincrk@cqhinet.net.au and **L-A** *Redlands Station Country Guesthouse*, 50 km west off the Flinders Highway, T478 76617, offer similar outback experiences and farmstays.

Eating
• *On map, page 346*

Lawson's Bar and Restaurant, World Theatre Complex, T4787 4333. Open lunch Wed-Sun 1130-1430, dinner Wed-Sun from 1800. Recommended along with the value *Gold City Chinese*, 118 Gill St, T4787 2414. Open daily (except Mon) from 1130. **Stock Exchange Café**, 76 Mosman St, T4787 7954. Open Mon-Thu 0830-1700, Fri/Sat 0830-2100, Sun 0830-1600. For a coffee and light snacks in historical surroundings.

Festivals

Charters Towers hosts 2 notable annual events, *Charters Towers Country Music Festival*, every May Day weekend, T4787 4500, where you can go line-dancing Matilda and the *Outback Ashes Cricket Carnival*, every Australia Day Weekend, when more than 100 teams bat it out for glory.

Tours

Long-term local Geoff Philips provides an excellent insight into Charters Towers old and new through *Gold City Bush Safari Tours*, T4787 2118, from $16. Recommended. Multi-day trips and adventures in remote outback areas are also a speciality. The currently active Mount Leyshon Mine south of the city also offer guided tours every week morning. Book through the VIC.

Transport

Bus The city is served by *McCafferty's*, T131499, and *Greyhound*, T132030, daily on the Townsville/Mount Isa run. From Townsville it takes 1 hr, 40 mins and costs from $26. **Train** *The Inlander* operates twice weekly services from Townsville to Mount Isa (westbound Sun/Wed, eastbound Mon/Fri). It takes 3 hrs and costs from $23. The station is on the corner of Gill St and Enterprise Rd, T132232, www.traveltrain.qr.com.au *Traveland*, 13 Gill St, T4787 2622, acts as bus and rail booking agents.

Directory

Banks Most branches have ATMs and are housed in heritage buildings on Mosman or Gill sts. **Communications** Internet: VIC, or the painfully slow *Charters Towers Computers*, 59 Gill St. Open Mon-Fri 0900-1700. **Post office**: Gill St, T47871047. Open Mon-Fri 0900-1700. **Medical services** Hospital: 145 Gill St, T47871099. **Useful numbers** Police: 49 Gill St, T47871333. **RACQ**: Gold City Wreckers, 21 Dundee Lane, T47872000.

Townsville to Mission Beach

*North of Townsville, from just beyond Ingham, the scenery changes quite dramatically with the magnificent vista of **Hinchinbrook Island** heralding a distinctly greener and more mountainous landscape. To go beyond this point is to perhaps satisfy the imagination of what the words 'tropical' and 'wet season' actually mean. From April to October (winter) it hardly rains at all but during 'the wet'*

(November to March) the skies can be as angry looking as any on earth and inflict an aquatic onslaught on the green and pleasant land that turns roads into rivers. As well as the dramatic scenery and allure of Hinchinbrook Island the coastal stretch between Townsville and Mission Beach offers a number of worthy attractions.

Paluma National Park

Paluma National Park straddles the summit and escarpments of the Paluma Range and supports one of the most southerly tracts of tropical rainforest, affording it World Heritage status. It is host to the Mount Spec/Crystal Creek and Jourama Falls. **Mount Spec/Crystal Creek Section** is accessed via the small township of Paluma, 20 km off the highway. There is a picnic site and some pleasant walking tracks near McClelland's Lookout. Well facilitated camping, suitable for campervans, is available at Big Crystal Creek, 6 km west of Mutarnee, at the foot of the range (advance bookings, deposit and key collection required, T47773112).

Colour map 6, grid B5 65 km north of Townsville

Jourama Falls Section is accessed 24 km south of Ingham and 6 km off the Bruce Highway. The falls that feature a series of pink-coloured granite cascades along Waterview Creek are reached with a short walk and there are two lookouts. Camping facilities are available (self-registration).

Ingham

Born of the sugar cane industry, Ingham is home to both the oldest and the largest sugar mills in the country. Like many sugar towns in the far north it has an erstwhile Italian connection and still celebrates the fact with the Australian-Italian Festival each May. Although a pleasant place in itself it is most often used as a base for exploring the Lumholtz National Park and 305-m Wallaman Falls – the highest in Australia – or as the southern gateway to Hinchinbrook National Park via Lucinda, 25 km east. There are guided tours of the Victoria Sugar Mill, Forrest Beach Road, available during the crushing season, July to November. There is also the world's largest sugar loading jetty at Lucinda, 5.6-km long.

Colour map 6, grid B5 109 km Townsville

Hinchinbrook VIC, 21 Lannercost Street, T47765211, www.acecomp.com.au/hinchinbrook, is open daily but closes for the afternoon at 1400 at the weekend. It can assist with accommodation and local attractions, while the QPWS office, 49 Cassidy Street, T47761700, can provide detailed national parks information.

Lumholtz National Park

The biggest attraction of the Lumholtz National Park – named after nineteenth-century Danish naturalist Karl Lumholtz – are the **Wallaman Falls**, which are the tallest, but not necessarily the most spectacular falls in Australia. From a height of over 300 m, **Stony Creek** – a tributary of the Herbert River – flings its contents over the edge of water resistant rock known as ignimbrite in to the cavernous gorge below. The falls are naturally best viewed in the wet season, from November to March, when the regions 2-m annual rainfall provides ample ammunition. The falls can be accessed by 2WD but conditions in the wet can be treacherous and you are advised to check with the QPWS before departing. From Ingham travel 8 km west to Trebonne then turn left, then right over Stone River, then left again. After a steep climb the road terminates at the QPWS campsite (self registration and gas BBQs). Just before the

Colour map 6, grid B5

campsite there is a 2-km track to the right that takes you to the falls lookout. From here it is another 2 km by foot on a steep track to the base of the falls.

Cardwell

Colour map 6, grid B5
109 km Townsville

From Ingham the Bruce Highway crosses the Herbert River and climbs to reach the breathtaking lookout across to Hinchinbrook Island. Its mountainous outline and velveteen green cloak of rainforest seems almost connected to the mainland by the huge expanses of impenetrable mangrove swamps and islands to the fore. The beachside town of Cardwell, a further 40 km north, is, to many long-term residents chagrin, is fast developing into a tourist resort and provides a welcome stop on the route north as well as a base from which to explore Hinchinbrook Island National Park, or to sample its fishing, cruising, flight seeing or wildlife watching activities.

The obvious wildlife star and mascot in these parts is the very rotund and congenial looking sea cow – or dugong – which clings precariously to existence in local waters and is without doubt one of nature's most unusual sea creatures.

The lengthy main drag of Cardwell, Victoria Street, hosts most amenities and accommodations as well as the QPWS Rainforest and Reef Centre, at no 142, half way through the town by the jetty, T40668601, hinchin brook.camp @env.qld.gov.au it opens daily 0830-1630 and provides local tourist information, details of seasonal eco-cruises operations and issues permits for Hinchinbrook Island National Park.

Sleeping & eating
Although fast developing there are as yet limited accommodation options in Cardwell

A-E *Kookaburra Holiday Park and Hinchinbrook Hostel*, 175 Victoria St (north of the jetty), T40668648, www.hinchinbrookholiday.com.au YHA affiliated, this has everything from self-catering villas to campsites as well as dorms, doubles and twins in the well-facilitated hostel section. Pool, tours and activities bookings, internet and free bike hire for guests. *Port Hinchinbrook Motel* is a modern option located at the southern end of town in the new marina complex. For eating *Muddies Café and Bar*, 221 Victoria St, T40668907, can offer wholesome mains with a seafood edge as well as takeaways and sandwiches. It also shows free movies for patrons every second Thu night. Open daily from 1100 till late. Happy hour daily from 1600-1800.

Tours & activities

Eco-Cruises, Fishing and Tours Hinchinbrook Island Ferries, T40668270, www.hinchin brookferries.com.au, are the main operator in Cardwell and offer day cruises from $85, child $42. Fri/Sun/Wed Nov-Jun (no sailings in Jan/Feb). *Hinchinbrook Explorer Fishing and Eco-Tours*, T40689716, offer full day national park or estuary fishing trips from $120 and eco-cruises from $66. For Hinchinbrook Island transportation and tours see below. *Cardwell Air Charters*, T40668468, www.oz-e.com.au/cardair, offer a wide range of scenic flights over Hinchinbrook Island (40 mins, $80), the Reef (1 hr, $120) and 'outback' to the Undara Lava Tubes (half-day $255). They also offer a trip to see where the much-hyped TV series 'Survivor II' was filmed over the rugged Herbert River Gorge (45 mins, $95). Children half price. The more adventurous can reach the location and 280-m Blencoe Falls by road (2WD in winter only, 81 km). Details from the VIC.

Transport

Interstate buses stop outside the *Seaview café* on Victoria St south of the jetty.

Hinchinbrook Island National Park

From the moment you first see it, Hinchinbrook Island casts its irresistable spell. Even from afar, the green rugged peaks possess a dramatic air of wilderness. At almost 40,000 ha, Hinchinbrook is the largest island national park in the world and, having changed little since white settlement in Australia, remains one of the most unspoilt. Crowned by the 1142 m peak of **Mount Bowen**, it is a wonder world of sheer cliffs, forested slopes and pristine beaches inhabited with some of Queensland's most weird, wonderful and dangerous wildlife. But, true to its appearance and stature and unlike many of its island family along the Queensland coast, Hinchinbrook presents more of a challenge than a relaxing excursion, with few designated access points and limited walking opportunities. Most who choose to visit the island do so for a day, but you can stay longer at one of two designated campsites, or in the lap of luxury at its one and only (expensive) resort. *Hinchinbrook Resort* is an oasis of sublimity, located at the remote Cape Richards and is the only habitation on the island. But for true explorers there is only one mission – the famed **Thorsborne Trail**. This 32-km, minimum four-day/three-night bushwalk, also known as the East Coast Trail, is lauded as one of best in the country and takes in a wide range of habitats along the east coast from Ramsay Bay in the north east, to George Point in the south. Given its obvious popularity, only 40 intrepid souls are allowed on the track at any one time and you must book sometimes up to a year in advance. The best time to attempt the hike is from April to September, which avoids the very wet and the very dry, but again, true to form, the topography of Hinchinbrook can create inclement weather at any time. The track is not graded and in some areas is rough and hard to traverse and since flamethrowers are sadly barred, insect repellent is an absolute must. QPWS provide detailed information on the track and issue the relevant camping permits, see page 350. Their excellent broadsheet *Thorsborne Trail* is a fine start and will soon have you applying the dubbin to your walking boots.

LL *Hinchinbrook Island Resort*, T40668270, www.hinchinbrookresort.com.au, offers an excellent, if not expensive sanctuary, with eco-friendly aesthetics and all mod cons. Do not expect a party atmosphere or a place over run with activities. This is a resort proudly in tune with the wilderness and environment that surrounds it and a congenial establishment at which to indulge, relax and pamper yourself. There are **camping facilities** (with toilets and gas fireplaces) at Scraggy Point (The Haven) on the Islands north west coast and Maucushla Bay, near the resort. Basic bush camping sites have been established along the Thorsborne Trail with Zoe Bay offering toilets and water. Open fires are not allowed and you will require a gas stove and water containers. Camping permits for all sites must be obtained from the QPWS Rainforest and Reef Centre, see page 350, for contact details. **Sleeping & eating**

Hinchinbrook Island Ferries, T40668270, www.hinchinbrookferries.com.au, based in Cardwell provides the northerly access to the island (including the resort) while *Hinchinbrook Wilderness Safaris* (Bill Pearce) T47778307, provides southerly access from Lucinda east of Ingham. Both also offer a range of day tours and cruises. Most people doing the Thorsborne Trail attempt it from north to south using the former company for the northerly drop-off (from $60) and the latter for southerly pick up (from $45). Note sailings vary according to season. There are no sailings in Jan/Feb. **Transport**

Mission Beach

Taking its name from a former Aboriginal Mission established in the early 1900s, Mission Beach is a loose term given to an idyllic 14-km stretch of the Queensland coast from Bingil Bay to the north to the mouth of the Hull River to the south. The area is not only noted as the principal and rapidly developing tourist attraction between Townsville and Cairns, but for the importance of

Colour map 6, grid A5
Population: 1,000
137 km from Cairns,
250 km from
Townsville

Capricorn & Central coasts

its **rainforest** biodiversity, being home to many unique plants and animals. These include the almost umbrella like Licuala Palm and a distinctly rare and leggy bird called the **cassowary**. Between Mission Beach and the superb off-shore resort of **Dunk Island**, see page 355, there is plenty to see and do here, but it is as much a place to relax from the rigours of the road, as it is to explore its many natural delights.

Ins & outs
See Transport, page 354, for further details

Mission Beach VIC is at the end of the El-Arish-Mission Beach Rd, on Porter Promanade and the northern end of Mission Beach, T40687099, www.mymissionbeach.com Daily 0900-1700. It is a powerhouse of information fuelled with the management and volunteers' great enthusiasm for the region. The area is hard to navigate, so be sure to secure the free *Street and Business Directory*.

Sights
The two main centres of activity are Mission Beach village (just south of the VIC) and Wongaling Beach

Wet Tropics Environmental Centre offers a fine introduction to the rainforest ecology and habitats of the region and if you plan on doing any rainforest walks, this is the place to get directions and avail yourself of all the detail. The centre also acts as a nursery for rainforest plants, collected, by all accounts, with unenvying enthusiasm from cassowary droppings! Also of note are the records kept of the great bird's all too regular disagreements with local automobiles – sadly an argument that, despite their size, they always seem to loose. ■ *Daily 1000-1700. Next door to the VIC*. Before leaving this area, take a look at the large tree just to the south of the VIC and Environmental Centre. It is home to a large colony of **metallic starlings** and in spring becomes a hive of activity when the birds return to their own extensive and exclusive piece of real estate, in the form of countless, beautifully woven nests.

The main tracts of accessible rainforest are to be found in the **Tam O'Shanter State Forest** that dominates the region and contains one of the largest tracts of coastal lowland rainforest in northern Queensland. There are a number of excellent walks on offer. The best and the most moderate of these is the **Licuala Walk**. Accessed and signposted of the Tully-Mission Beach Road. It is a 1.2-km, 45-minute, stroll under the canopy of the rare and beautiful Licuala Palms. On a hot day the torn lily pad-like leaves offer a cool and quiet sanctuary. There is also a special 350-m section designed for kids, where they can 'follow the cassowary footprints' to find a surprise at the end of the walk. If you are fit for a longer walk the 7-km, two-hour, **Licuala-Lacey Creek Track** also starts at the car park. As the name suggests this track, that cuts through the heart of the Tam O'Shanter Forest, links Licuala with **Lacey Creek** where there is another short rainforest walk (1.1-km, 45-minute), accessed and signposted off the El-Arish – Mission Beach Road. Just north of Mission Beach and Clump Point is the 4-km, two-hour **Bicton Hill Track**. It is a stiff, yet pleasant climb to the summit but you are rewarded with a rather disappointing view of the coast and Dunk Island. Yet another option is the historic, 8-km, four-hour return **Kennedy Track**, named after local explorer Edmund Kennedy, that heads from South Mission Beach to the mouth of the Hull River. However, if you are a courting couple you may get no further than the beachside palms of **Lovers Beach**.

Of course other than the rainforest and **Dunk Island**, the big attraction in these parts are the **beaches**. There are over 65 to choose from, but in essence it is one 14-km long stretch of sublimity, backed by archetypal coconut palms. Of course while soporific sunbathing in their shadows might be heavenly enough, you may also be tempted into the water to swim and to snorkel. But if your visit is between October to May, to avoid 'stingers', play it safe and stick within the netted areas off Mission and South Mission beaches.

◀

Big bird

Mission Beach is only a short drive from the main highway and you will doubtless be anxious to reach it. But bare in mind the local residents are rightfully proud and protective of their diminishing isolation and their cassowaries (large flightless bird). So please adhere to the omnipresent road *signs requesting you be vigilant and slow down for the 'Big Bird'. Road kills are a principal killer of this rare and bizarre avian and if you were to hit one it is, apparently, not so much like hitting a rabbit as an enormous, 50 kg black wig with a bad attitude.*

Although there are a scattering of resorts in the area, the many excellent and **Sleeping** characterful B&Bs and self-contained accommodation are recommended. Of the resorts the beachside **L** *Castaways on the Beach*, corner of Pacific Parade and Seaview St, Mission Beach, T40687444, www.castaways.com.au, is well placed while the centrally located, backpacker friendly **L-E** *Mission Beach Resort*, Wongaling Beach, T40688288 and the luxury **LL** *Horizon*, Explorer Dr, South Mission Beach, T40688154, www.thehorizon.com.au, provide two other options.

For a spot of colour and striking architecture try the one-off **LL** *Perrier Walk Guesthouse*, Perrier Walk, Mission Beach, T40687141, www.perrierwalk.nq.nu It offers a choice of 3 superbly appointed en suites in a quiet garden setting with a pool and an outdoor shower, and is only a short stroll from the beach. **L** *Licuala Lodge*, 11 Mission Circle, Mission Beach, T40688194, www.licualalodge.com.au, is an award-winning, pole house B&B with doubles, singles, and a memorable 'jungle pool' and spa. Slightly cheaper but no less enjoyable is **B** *Honeyeater Home stay*, 53 Reid Rd, Wongaling Beach, T40688741, www.uniquevillas.com.au/honeat, which offers a friendly welcome and separate accommodation in a spacious en suite. It also has a pool, guest library and offers bike hire. For an interesting eco-retreat, wildlife enthusiasts should look no further than the value **C** *Sanctuary Retreat*, Holt Rd, Bingil Bay, T40886064, www.sanctuaryatmission.com, which offers secluded, minimalist forest huts in a setting designed to actively nurture and attract the local wildlife rather than scare it away. Restaurant, Internet and pick-ups. **A** *Sejala*, 1 Pacific St, Mission Beach, T40687241, www.sejala.com.au For a self-contained option, try the colourful comforts and boutique beach huts of *Seyala*.

Backpackers options from north to south include **C-D** *Treehouse*, Bingil Bay Rd, Bingil Bay, T40687137, missionbeach@yha.qld.org It is a pole house with doubles, twins and dorms a pool and all the usual amenities. Its only drawback is its distance from the beach but shuttle buses regularly ply the route. Also in Bingil Bay is the **C-E** *Bingil Bay Backpackers*, Cutten St, Bingil Bay, T40687208, www.nomadsworld.com.au, that offers a/c motel style units in an elevated position with good views a pool and lively bar/bistro. Further south in Wongaling Beach is the **C-E** *Mission Beach Backpackers Lodge*, 28 Wongaling Beach Rd, T40688317, www.missionbeachbackpacker.com Although aesthetically nothing special, it is a popular place with a social atmosphere, offering 10/8 and 4 share dorms and separate doubles with fans or a/c, a well-equipped kitchen. It is also close to the happening bar in the Mission Beach Resort and the main shopping complex. Closer to the beach is the well established and popular **C-E** *Scotty's Beachouse Hostel*, 167 Reid Rd, T40688676, scottys@znet.net.au, which offers a range of unit style dorms and doubles surrounding a fine pool. It has a very relaxed atmosphere, a restaurant and reputedly the best bar in town.

There are several motor parks in the area with the very tidy and beachside **L-F** *Beachcomber Caravan Village*, Kennedy Esplanade, Mission Beach South, T40688129 being recommended.

Eating   Most of the eateries in the area are concentrated in and around the Village Green Shopping Complex, Porter Promenade, Mission Beach. For fine dining with an international menu try the award winning *Blarney's By The Beach*, 10 Wongaling Beach Rd, Wongaling Beach, T40688472. Open Tue-Sat for dinner and Sun for lunch. Recommended. In the far south on the shores of Lugger Bay *Ulysses* at the *Horizon Resort*, *Explorer Drive* is also a good restaurant and has a seafood buffet on Fridays. For value *Scotty's Beachhouse Bar and Grill*, 167 Reid Rd (off Cassowary Drive) Wongaling, has a lively atmosphere and offers budget bistro meals. *Port O Call Café*, Shop 6, The Hub, Porter Promenade, T40687390, run by the Odd couple is open daily from 0800 and offers the best coffee and value breakfasts in town. There are supermarkets in the Village Green, Mission Beach and at the Wongaling Beach Shopping Complex. Open daily 0800-1900.

Tours & activities   **Diving** *Mission Beach Dive Charters*, Shop 8a, The Reef Centre, Mission Beach, T40687277, offers wreck dives to the *Lady Bowen* and general reef exploratory dives and all-day cruises from $136 (cruises only Mon/Tue/Thu/Fri/Sat from $96) as well as diver certification from $325. *Quickcat Dive*, T40688432, www.quickcatdive.com, offers similar trips. **Fishing** *Bounty Hunter*, T40886007, offers day-long sea-fishing trips from $150. In contrast *FNQ Fishing Adventures* head up the tidal river systems to catch crabbies and barramundi (amongst other things), promising a bit of crocodile spotting along the way. Half-day from $70, full-day $125. **Horse trekking** *Bush 'n' Beach*, T40687893, offers 1½-hr rides along the beach from $50. **Sea kayaking** *Coral Sea Kayaking*, T40689154, www.coralseakayaking.com, and *Sunbird Adventures*, T40688229, offers full-day voyages to Dunk Island with plenty of time to explore from $84 (half-day coastal exploration $49). **Skydiving** *Skydive Mission Beach*, based next to the *Castaways Resort* on Pacific Parade, T40521822, www.jumpthebeach.com, offers tandem jumps on to Mission Beach or Dunk Island, 8000ft from $248, 14,000 from $363. **White water rafting** *RnR Rafting*, T40517777, www.rnrrafting.com.au, and *Raging Thunder*, T40307990, www.ragingthunder.com.au, provides pick-ups for a wide range of rafting trips and packages on the Tully or North Johnstone rivers, from $135. **Wildlife night spotting** *Sunbird Adventures*, T40688229, offers a fascinating night walk in the Lacey's Creek Rainforest from 1900-2130 from $25. Recommended.

Transport   **Local Bus** *Mission Beach Bus and Coach*, T40687400, operates daily servicing Bingil Bay to South Mission Beach single fare $1.50 day ticket $10, child $5. **Taxi** For a taxi call T131008 (24 hrs). **Long distance Bus** *Greyhound*, *McCaffertys*, *Premier Motor Services* and *Coral Coaches* offers regular daily services from north and south stopping outside the post office on Porter Promenade in Mission Beach. *Island Resort Travel*, Homestead Centre, Mission Beach, T40687187, acts as the local ticketing agents. *Mission Beach Connections*, T40592709, also offer daily shuttles from Cairns at 0730 and 1400, from $31 single (backpacker special $22) and Tully from $9. **Car** Car servicing and breakdowns from *Mission Beach Discount Tyres*, Stephen St (off Cassowary Drive), T40687013.

For Dunk Island cruises and water taxis, see below

Directory   **Banks** The post office, Porter Promenade acts as the Commonwealth Bank Agent. ATMs are available in the *Mission Beach Supermarket* and at the *Mission Beach Resort*. **Communications** Internet: *Cybernet*, Campbell St, Mission Beach. Daily 0900-1800. *Zola's*, across the road in the Village Green, Mission Beach, and *Mission Beach*

Information Station (tour and accommodation bookings), shop 4, Mission Beach Resort Shops, Wongaling Beach. **Medical services** Medical Centre, Cassowary Dr, T40688174. **Useful numbers** Police: corner of Cassowary Dr and Web Rd, T40688422.

Dunk Island

Once far more aptly named 'Coonanglebah' by the Aboriginals meaning 'The Island of Peace and Plenty', it was renamed Dunk by Captain James Cook in 1770 after Lord Dunk, First Lord of the Admiralty. But whatever its official label this 730-ha national and marine park, lying less than 5 km off Mission Beach, certainly offers plenty and is one of the most beautiful island parks and resorts north of the Whitsundays. But what is perhaps most attractive for the visitor is the fact that it is so easily accessible and actively encourages day visitors. Oh and just wait till you see the swimming pool!

Colour map 6, grid A5

Whether staying at the resort or as day visitors the vast majority of people come to Dunk to relax – big style. But if you can drag yourself away from the beautiful stretch of palm-fringed beach either side of the wharf in **Brammo Bay**, you can explore the island and its rich wildlife or sample some of the many activities on offer.

Sights

The island has 13 km of walking tracks and the reception in the main resort building can offer free maps and information. There are plenty of options, from the short 15-minute stroll to see **Banfield's Grave** (see box) at the eastern end of the resort complex, to a complete **Island Circuit** (9.2 km, three hours) which takes in the remote **Bruce Arthur's Artists Colony/Gallery**. ■ *$4, Mon-Thu 1000-1300.* The energetic may also like to attempt the stiff climb (5.6 km, three hours return) to the summit of **Mount Kootaloo** (271 m) that looms large above the resort and is the island's highest peak.

The resort itself offers an attractive day visitors' package that includes lunch and access to the bar, some sports facilities and the very attractive **Butterfly Pool** from $28, child $17, tickets available at *Watersports*, see below for details.

Finally, if you really want to go off the scale on the 'relaxometer' book a session at the heavenly **Spa of Peace and Plenty** where you can choose from a wide-range of alluring treatments, with such evocative names as the 'Floral Rain' or 'Taste of Tahiti'. Book at *Watersports*.

LL *Dunk Island Resort*, Brammo Bay, T40688199, www.poresorts.com.au This 4-star resort offers a delightful range of units and suites, excellent amenities and a wealth of activities and sports on offer. Book well ahead and from Sydney office, T1800737678. Children welcome. For the budget traveler **QPWS camping ground** which is discreetly located next to the resort. Permits can be purchased from *Watersports* on the island. BBQs and showers.

Sleeping

The resort has 2 licensed restaurants, *EJ's on the Deck* (lunch) and *Beachcomber Restaurant*, which offers breakfast and table d'hote dinner. BBQs are also available next to the pool. *BB's On The Beach* is a relaxed and rather expensive affair that is open to the public and located next to the wharf. Open 1100-1700.

Eating

Watersports, located next to the wharf, offers independent day visitors a host of equipment and water-based activities from a mask and snorkel hire ($15 a day) to windsurfing ($20 per hr), water skiing (lesson $25, 15 mins) and even parasailing (from $55). Snorkeling on the island is poor compared to the reef.

Tours & activities

Capricorn & Central coasts

▶ **A place to die for**

Dunk Island's most famous resident was English author and beachcomber Edmund. J Banfield 1952-23. In 1897, Banfield, having been diagnosed with a terminal illness, arrived on the island to live out his final weeks in peace and solitude. He died 26 years later and is buried on the island! His grave is well worth a visit. 'onfessions of a Beachcomber' which was published in 1908 has become (not surprisingly) a celebrated text for escapists, romantics and no doubt, doctors.

Transport   **Air**   Dunk has its own airport and regular flights are available from major Australian cities with *Qantas Link*, from Cairns 4 times daily with *Macair*, T131528, www.macair.com.au **Ferry** *Dunk Island Ferry and Cruises* (*MV Kavanagh*), T40687211, departs Clump Point, twice daily at 0845 and 1030, from $22, child $13 return. They also offer cruise options with diving, snorkeling and boom netting. *Dunk Island Express*, T40688310, departs from the beach opposite their office on Banfield Parade, Wongaling Beach, daily at 0930, 1100, 1230, 1430, 1630, from $22, child $13 return ($26 if overnight). *Dunk Island Ferry and Cruises* and *Dunk Island Express* offer local courtesy pick-ups. **Launch and water taxi** *Quickcat*, T40687289, departs Clump Point daily at 0730, from $29, child $14.50 return. As well as Dunk Island *Quickcat* also visit the outer reef and Beaver Cay which is a beautiful spot offering much better snorkeling than Dunk Island, from $140. *Quickcat* offers coach pick-ups from Cairns. In general prices vary and are fiercely competitive, so shop around.

Cairns to Cape York

Introducing Cairns to Cape York

Without doubt, Far North Queensland offers more to see and do than any other region in Australia, and although the 'Far' and the 'North' may be felt in both distance and climate, the effort will not only guarantee a memorable experience, but almost certainly a return visit.

The bustling tourist-driven city of **Cairns** acts as the gateway to two of the richest most aesthetically stunning biodiversities on earth: the **Great Barrier Reef** and **Wet Tropics Rainforest**. Practically, nowhere else on earth do two such incredible natural wonderlands and World Heritage listed eco- systems literally meet, nor offer the tourist such a wealth of activities or ease of access. From world-class **diving** to wilderness **outback tours** the choice of activities seems almost endless.

North of Cairns, is the smaller yet equally sophisticated resort of **Port Douglas**, then on to the small village of **Daintree** and coastal strip of **Cape Tribulation**. Few venture north beyond CapeTribulation to the proud and historic settlement of **Cooktown**, let alone **Cape York**, but for those adventurous souls that try, they will experience the very best that **4WD** has to offer, and be exposed to some of Australia's true wilderness. West of Cairns the lush, green plateau known as the **Atherton Tablelands** serves as the regions 'other garden' and not only supports a remarkable range of agricultural practices, but equally memorable vistas, unusual wildlife and perhaps most refreshing of all, a cool retreat from the coast. Beyond the Tablelands (since in Australia it seems there is always a 'beyond') the dusty brown horizons of the **Gulf Savannah**, again, beckon the true adventurer.

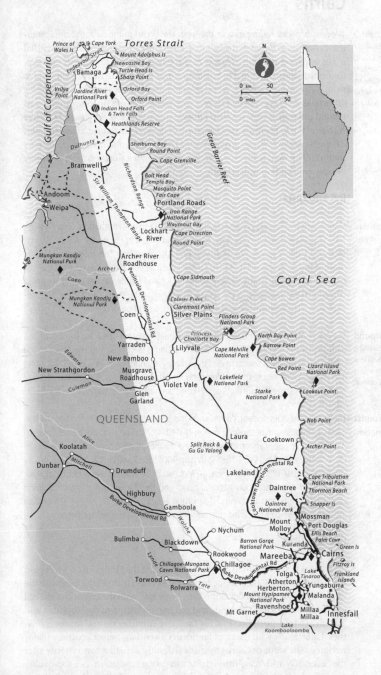

Cairns

Colour map 7, grid C3
Phone code: 07
Population: 130,000
349 km from
Townsville; 1,084 km
from Rockhampton;
1,733 km Brisbane;
2,684 km from Sydney

Wedged between rolling hills to the west, the ocean to the east and thick mangroves swamps to the north and south, Cairns is like a blossoming tourist tree that is fast outgrowing its pot. Thanks to the **Great Barrier Reef** *on its doorstep, Cairns was always destined to become a world-class tourist destination. And so today, after Sydney, it is the second most important city in Australia. But the big attractions don't begin or end there. Cairns is blessed with two other world-class natural assets: its warm* **tropical climate** *and its ancient rainforest,* **Daintree National Park**. *There are very few places in the world so unique, where two such environmentally rich and diverse World Heritage listed national parks literally connect. Or, indeed, where the visitor is offered such ease of access or opportunity to experience and enjoy them both.*

Ins and outs

Getting there
See Transport, page 374, for further details

Many hotels and hostels provide shuttle services to and from the airport. *Coral Coaches*, T40317577, offer regular services to and from the city, from $8. *Airport Shuttle*, T40995950, offers services to and from Port Douglas, Cape Tribulation and Mission Beach. A taxi costs about $15, T131008. The interstate coach terminal south of the city, beside Trinity Wharf. Cairns Railway Station is located beside Cairns Central Shopping Complex, to the southwest of the centre. As a major centre there are coach and rail services from all major towns nearby and from Brisbane and beyond.

Getting around
Maps are available from Absells Map Shop, Andrew Jecks Arcade off Lake Street

The centre of Cairns is compact and easily negotiable on foot. The attractive waterfront with its many hostels, hotels and restaurants fringes the ocean and Trinity Bay to the northeast. At the city's southern end the Trinity Pier complex gives way to Trinity Inlet and Trinity Wharf, where the reef ferry and interstate coach terminals are based. Local bus operators serve the outskirts of the city. Bike hire is readily available.

Tourist information

The number of independent 'commission based' information centres and operators in Cairns is famously out of control. For non-biased information and advice on accommodation and especially activities, look no further than Tourism Tropical North Queensland accredited VIC, 5 The Esplanade, T40513588, F40510127, www.tnq.org.au Open daily 0830-1730. QPWS office, 10 McLeod St, T40466600, www.env.qld.gov.au, has detailed information on national parks and the Barrier Reef Islands, including camping permits and bookings. Open Mon-Fri 0830-1630. Other useful websites include www.welcometocairns.com.au and www.greatbarrierreef.aus.net.au

Background

Cairns was first established as a tiny port serving the Hodgkinson River gold fields during the 1870s. Despite fierce competition from Port Douglas to the north, it was Cairns that developed at a faster rate, with the creation of the rail link to the Atherton Tablelands and the ports subsequent development and growth as a transportation link for the more enduring tin and timber industries. Later, along with much of far north Queensland, sugar became a major resource. The seeds of Cairns touristical destiny were first sown shortly after the Second World War, through its increasing reputation as a top quality venue for big game fishing, however this was dramatically and rapidly taken over with the invention of the aqualung and the inevitable explosion of interest in the Great Barrier Reef. When Cairns airport 'went international' in

1984, further tourist development was inevitable. With the turn of the new millennium there is much concern levelled towards this almost manic development. Many long-term residents feel that the congenial town of old has already been ruined and that it will become the Gold Coast of the north. Scientists also fear for the sustainability of the Great Barrier Reef and the effects of both tourism and increased infrastructure. So, now with the floods of rain in wet season followed by floods of tourists in the dry, perhaps the only hope is that tourism and conservation can develop in harmony and to mutual benefit.

The Aboriginal name for the area was 'Gimuy'. Captain Cook who visited the region in 1770 on Trinity Sunday named Trinity Bay and the city itself is named after William Wellington Cairns the third Governor of Queensland.

Sights

The majority of tourist activities in Cairns are of course centred over, on or indeed under the waters of the Great Barrier Reef. The choice is simply vast, from the most popular activities of diving and snorkelling, to cruising, sailing, kayaking and flight seeing. On land the choices are no less exciting with everything from bungee jumping to ballooning. See page 369 for details. The city itself, however, does offer a number of colourful attractions.

Undersea World Located in the far corner of the plush Pier Shopping Complex is Undersea World, which offers a 'shallow' introduction to the living reef and its inhabitants. There are over 140 species on show, including seahorses, giant wrasse, stingrays, corals and of course, the ubiquitous sharks. Divers hand feed the fish daily at 1000, 1200, 1300 and 1500 and if you have an interest in prosthetics, you can even swim, with 'Linda' the leopard shark and her friends from 1530. $85. ■ *Daily 0800-2200. $12.50, children $7. T40411777. Pier Point Rd.*

Cairns Regional Gallery Less scary but no less colourful is the Cairns Regional Gallery housed in the former 1936 Public Curators Offices. Since 1995 the gallery has been an excellent showcase for mainly local and regional art as well as national visiting and loan exhibitions. ■ *Mon-Fri 1000-1800, Sat/Sun 1300-1800. $4, child $2. T40316865. Corner of Abbott and Shields sts.*

St Monica's Cathedral For even more colour head to St Monica's Cathedral to see the unique stained glass windows known as the 'Creation Design'. The huge and spectacularly colourful display is said to 'combine faith, science and art into one undivided expression of the mystery, the wonder and the beauty of Creation'. What is particularly appealing of course is the inclusion of the reef. Where else in the world would you find stained glass windows depicting tropical fish? ■ *Daily. Donation. Leaflets are on hand to guide you through the design. 183 Abbott St.*

Flecker Botanical Gardens These gardens on the northwestern fringe of the city offers a small but interesting collection of tropical favourites including such evocatively named blooms as Sexy Pink and Stairway to Heaven! The gardens are set amongst fresh and saltwater habitats and intersected with boardwalks and tracks. ■ *Daily 0930-1630. T40443398. Collins Ave, Edge Hill. Informative guided walks are offered at 1300 Mon-Fri. Café and shop on site.*

Cairns to Cape York

Cairns

To 14

James St
Little St
McKenzie St
Cairns St
Law St
Thomas St
Sheridan St
Digger St
Lake St
Esplanade
Charles St
Gelling St
Charles St
Beryl St
Grove St
Trinity Bay
Draper St
Cairns Base Hospital
Dunn St
McLeod St
Captain Cook Highway
Gatton St
Gatton St
Gatton St
Kerwin St
Abbott St
Parramatta St
Martyn St
Grafton St
Upward St
Mary St
Nellie St
Water St
St Monica's Cathedral
Minnie St
Maranoa St
Maranoa St
Florence St
To 8 & Mission Beach
Cairns to Cape York
Mulgrave Rd
Prewitt St
Water St
Aplin St
Johno's Blues Bar
The Chapel
Cairns
Warrego St
Cinema
Library
Esplanade
Grimshaw St
Cairns Central Shopping Complex
Terminus St
Club Five Nine
Scott St
Abbott St
Shields St
Transit Centre
Cairns Regional Gallery
Lumley St
Bunda St
McLeod St
QPWS
Pierpoint Rd
Spence St
Fogarty Park Rd
Sheridan St
Grafton St
Marlin Bay
Hartley St
Dutton St
Casino
Hartley St E
Draper St
Interstate Terminal
Wharf St
Trinity Wharf

```
0 metres        200
0 yards         200
```

Harbour

Pier
Market-   Undersea
place   World

Marlin
Marina

Trinity Inlet

⑤

To Port Douglas, Green Island, Fitzroy Island & Frankland Islands

Cairns to Cape York

A track located next to the gardens, near MacDonnell Street, takes you to the Mount Whitfield Environmental Park with its 7-km of walking tracks through unspoilt rainforest to take in impressive city and ocean views. Alternatively, you might like to combine your walk with a look at the Tanks Art Centre which is a trio of former diesel storage tanks located on the edge of the park now used as a dynamic exhibition and performance space for the local arts community. ■ *Daily 1100-1600. Free. A market day is held on the last Sun of every month from Jun-Nov 0900-1300. 46 Collins Ave.*

Mount Whitfield Environmental Park

Also in Edge Hill is this visitors centre, which offers a broad introduction and history of this vital and almost iconic aspect of outback life. ■ *Mon-Sat 0900-1630, $5, child $2.50, T40535687, 1 Junction St.*

Royal Flying Doctor Service Visitors Centre

Excursions

The award winning Skyrail Rainforest Cableway is highly recommended in both fine or wet weather and is perhaps best combined with a day tour package to Kuranda via the Kuranda Scenic Railway (see below).

Skyrail Rainforest cableway

The once highly controversial Skyrail Gondola project was completed in 1995 and at 7.5 km is the longest cable-gondola ride in the world. It gives visitors the unique opportunity to glide in serenity just metres above the pristine rainforest canopy and through the heart of the World Heritage listed Barron Gorge National Park. From the outset the mere prospect of such an intrusion in to the ancient forest, and the perceived clash of commercial tourism verses conservation, caused international uproar. Conservationists and botanists the world over were immediately up in arms and high profile local demonstrations took place. But for once, all the fears and protestations proved groundless and now

Skyrail provides an highly impressive project that effectively encompasses both environmental sensitivity and education, with a generous dash of fun mixed in.

The journey encompasses two stops, one to take in the views and guided rainforest boardwalk from **Red Peak Station** (545 m) and another at **Barron Falls Station** where you can muse at the entertaining Rainforest Interpretive Centre, before strolling down to the lookouts across the Barron River Gorge and Barron Falls. The interpretative centre offers a range of displays that encompass some clever computer software depicting the sights and sounds of the forest both day and night, while the short walkway to the falls lookout passes some rather unremarkable remains of the 1930s Barron Falls hydro-electric scheme construction camp. One word of warning here – prepare to be disappointed. Ignore the postcards or promotional images you see of thunderous, 'Niagara-like' falls. True, they can sometimes look like that, but only ever after persistent heavy rain and/or during the wet season. Sadly for much of the year – from April to December – the falls are little more than melodic trickle. From the Barron Falls Station you then cross high above the Barron River before reaching civilization again at the pretty Kuranda Terminal. When you are crossing the rainforest you may be lucky enough to see the huge and unmistakable, azure blue Ulysses butterfly, which has become a fitting mascot of the North Queensland rainforest.

■ *Daily 0800-1700. $30 one-way, child $15, return $45, child $22.50. Price includes Cairns transfers, T40381888, www.skyrail.com.au Skyrail can be combined with a return trip via the Kuranda Scenic Railway for around $59, child $30. Skyrail Caravonica Terminal is located 15 mins north of Cairns on the Captain Cook Highway. Skyrail tickets can be bought on the web, travel agents, tour desks, hotels, motels, caravan parks and at the VIC.*

Kuranda Scenic Railway

Kuranda Scenic Railway wriggles its way down the Barron Gorge to Cairns and provides an ideal way to reach the pretty village of Kuranda. To add to the aesthetics you are transported in a historic loco and stop at various viewpoints, which provides some respite from the rambling commentary. ■ *Departs Kuranda 1400, 1530 Sun-Fri, 1530 Sat. $30 single, child $15. T40313636. For Cairns departures see Transport, page 374.*

Tjapukai

Pronounced 'Jaboguy' this award winning, multi-million dollar Aboriginal Cultural Park is lauded as one of the most professional and diverse of its type in Australia and is the culmination of many years of quality performance by the local Tjapukai tribe. The 11-ha site, located next to the Skyrail terminal, in Smithfield offers an entertaining and educational insight in to Aboriginal mythology, customs and history, and in particular, that of the Tjapukai. The complex is split in to various dynamic theatres that explore dance, language, story telling and history and there is also a mock up camp where you can learn about traditional tools, food and hunting techniques. For many, the highlight is the opportunity to learn how to throw a boomerang or to play a didgeridoo properly without asphyxiating. To make the most of the experience give yourself at least half a day. Recommended. ■ *Daily 0900-1700, $27, child $13.50, T40429999, www.tjapukai.com.au There's a quality restaurant and shop on site.*

Northern Beaches

North of the airport the thick mangrove swamps give way to the more alluring northern beaches and the expensive oceanside resorts of **Trinity Beach** and **Palm Cove**. Both offer the fine and natural sandy beaches that the waterfront in Cairns lacks and so make an attractive base to stay outside the city, or a fine venue in which to swing a golf club or to catch some rays. The VIC in Cairns has detailed accommodation listings. Other than Trinity Beach and Palm Cove the most northerly of the beaches, **Ellis Beach** is recommended. If you are looking for a nice spot to have lunch look no further than the new marina at Yorkey's Knob, Buckley Street.

The northern beaches also boast the city's local captive wildlife offering. The Wild World Tropical Zoo at Clifton Beach houses all the usual suspects, like crocodiles, snakes, wombats and koala, as well as a range of species unique to tropical North Queensland. Various shows are on offer throughout the day with everybody's favourite- the 'Cuddle a Koala Photo Session'- taking place daily at 1100 and 1430. The Night Zoo kicks off at 1900 every Monday to Thursday and Saturday and combines a sing along around a campfire with an introduction to other less vocal, bright-eyed creatures of the night. Includes BBQ and refreshments. Bookings essential. ■ *Daily 0830-1700. $22, child $11. T40553669, www.wildworld-aus.com.au Captain Cook Highway.*

Wild World Tropical & Night Zoo

Essentials

Like everything else touristy in Cairns, there is plenty of choice and something to suit all budgets. Almost all the major hotels and countless backpackers are located in the heart of the city, especially along The Esplanade, while most motels are located on the main highways in and out of town. If you are willing to splash out, want access to a proper beach, and wish to escape the heady buzz in the city, ask at the VIC about the numerous apartment and resort options at Palm Beach and other northern beach resorts (about 20 mins north of the city). Prices fluctuate according to season, with some going through the roof at peak times (May-Sep). Prices are often reduced and special deals are offered through 'the Wet' (Jan-Mar). Despite the wealth of accommodations pre-booking is still advised. *Cairns and TNQ Accommodation Centre*, 36 Alpin St, T40514066, Free call T1800807730, www.accomcentre.com.au, can also be of assistance.

Sleeping
■ *On map, page 362*
See inside cover for price categories

Almost all are multi-storey and located overlooking the ocean on The Esplanade or its neighbouring streets. **LL** *Cairns International*, 17 Abbott St, T40311300, F40311801, www.cairnsinternational.com.au It is the largest 5-star hotel in the region, located right in the heart of town. Elegant colonial style architecture and the full range of luxury rooms and facilities. Fine award winning restaurant and café and bar staff masters in making cocktails with such alluring names as 'swirling passion'. **LL** *Hotel Sofitel*, 35 Wharf St, T40308888. Another top range option but markets itself as a boutique hotel and is a lot smaller than the *International* or *Radisson*. As well as the added bonus (for some) of housing the casino it also has a very aesthetic restaurant with tiered seating and a great rooftop pool and spa. **LL-L** *Holiday Inn*, corner of Esplanade and Florence Sts, T40506070, F40313770, www.holiday-inn.com.au Most notable for its huge rainforest atrium but elsewhere in the quality of both its rooms and facilities it won't disappoint. It is a little further from all the action but still within a short stroll from the town centre and cruise departure points. **LL** *Radisson Plaza*, The Pier, T40311411, F40313226, www.radissoncairns.com.au Spacious rooms with great views and giant bathtubs with separate showers. Excellent pool and restaurant overlooking the marina. Another attraction is the varied shopping and aquarium at the Pier Marketplace complex immediately under the hotel. **L** *Country Comfort Outrigger*, corner of Abbott and Florence Sts, T40516188, F40311806, reservations@touraust.com.au, or the **L-A** *All Seasons Esplanade*, corner of Esplanade and Alpin sts, T40512311, F40311294, www.allseasons.com.au

There are endless options, with the vast majority offering the standard clean, spacious rooms and usual facilities, including the almost obligatory tropical flower paintings and palm-tree fringed swimming pools. Most of the motels are located on the main drags in and out of town (Sheridan St). Some, that are particularly appealing both in quality and/or price, include **L** *Regency Palms*, 219-225 McLeod St, T40314445, F40315415, www.regencypalms.com.au, **A** *Coral Cay Villa*, 267 Lake St, T40465100, F40312703, www.coralcay.com.au, and the **L** *Cairns Queenslander*, corner of Digger and Charles Sts, T40510122, F40311867, www.cairnsqueenslander.com.au Of the many cheaper options, try the 'colourful' **A-B** *Cairns Rainbow Inn*, 179 Sheridan St, T40511022, or the historic and well placed **A** *Hides*, corner of Lake and Shields sts, T40511266.

LL *Trinity On the Esplanade*, 21 Vasey Esplanade, T40576850, F40578099, www.trinity esplanade.com.au This beautiful and beachside B&B comes with four poster bed and pool. Highly recommended. **A** *Fig Tree Lodge*, 253 Sheridan St, T40410000, F4041-0001, www.figtreelodge.com.au Although more like a motel than a lodge, this offers fine facilities and a warm Irish welcome and a good congenial bar attached. **A** *Cairns B&B*, 48 Russell St, Edge Hill, T40324121, F40536557, www.cairnsbnb.com.au (5 km from city centre). A traditional modern option where locals Bernie and Norah promise to impart lots of local knowledge.

There is plenty of choice of backpackers with over 30 establishments almost all of which are within easy reach of the city centre. Most people gravitate towards The Esplanade where a string of places sit almost side by side, but you are advised to look in to other options beyond that. Another small cluster of quieter hostels lies just west of the Cairns Central Shopping Plaza and railway station. All offer the usual facilities and range of dorms, twins/doubles (occasionally singles) and will tender for your custom with attractive tour or longer stay discounts, gimmicky giveaways or simply a good sense of humour. Always look for rooms with a/c or at the very least a powerful fan and windows that open and check for approved fire safety regulations. Internet is readily available.

On The Esplanade are **C-E** *Carravella Hostels-Carravella 77*, (77), T40512159, and *Carravella*, (149), T40315680, www.caravella.com.au, both modern, well facilitated with good a/c doubles and free meals. Recommended. **C-E** *Bel-Air*, (155-157), T40314790, offers singles and girls dorm, spa, and characterful **B-E** *Florianna*, 183, T40517886, flori@cairnsinfo.com.au, which are both worth looking at. **B-E** *Bellview*, (85-87) , T40314377. Basic with single rooms, motel style doubles, good for families.

In the city centre is **C-D** *Global Palace*, corner of Lake and Shields sts, T40317921, www.globalpalace.com.au, which is more like a modern boutique motel than a traditional backpackers. It has great facilities including a rooftop pool and large deck from which to watch the world go by. The only criticism is that most of the a/c rooms do not have windows and may feel a bit claustrophobic. Otherwise it gets a big thumbs-up.

West of the centre there are a crop of good hostels, all very similar, with a more cosy, quiet atmosphere. **C-E** *Travellers Oasis*, 8 Scott St, T40521377, www.travoasis.com.au, is a large place that still maintains a nice quiet atmosphere, offering a good range of air con rooms including value singles ($30) and pool. **C-E** *Dreamtime Travellers Rest*, 4 Terminus St, T40316753, www.dreamtimetravel.com.au, is homely and friendly with a great atmosphere, well equipped facilities and a great pool and spa, as well as proper beds, not bunks. Ask about their sister hostel in Yungaburra and the Tablelands tour package. Nearby, the well-managed **C-E** *Ryan's Rest*, 18 Terminus St, T40514734 shares a similar quiet and homely feel. **C-E** *Geckos*, 187 Bunda St, T40311344, www.geckobackpackers.com.au, is new on the block. It's a rambling and spacious

Queenslander with good facilities, caring staff and 2 great dogs Digger and Ruby! Rooms have fans not a/c but they are well ventilated. Good for doubles. Free meals at *The Woolshed*. The better of the two YHAs in the city is the **C-D** *McLeod St YHA*, 20-24 McLeod St, T40510772, www.yha.com.au, where the facilities are fine, but it's a bit characterless. Good tours office.

North of the centre is the popular **C-D** *Cairns Beach House*, 239 Sheridan St, T40414116, www.cairnsbeachhouse.com.au It has all the usual knobs and knockers and is especially noted for its pool, beer/bistro garden and party atmosphere. A little further out is the new and excellent **B-E** *Bohemia Resort*, 231 McLeod St, T40417290, www.bohemiaresort.com.au It is more like a tidy modern motel with great doubles and a pool and other facilities to match. Recommended. Regular shuttles in to town. **B-E** *Inn The Tropics*, 141 Sheridan St, T40311088, www.cairns.net.au/~innthetropics A quality options with single rooms, good motel style doubles. Also suited for families.

If you are looking for a caravan park, **C-E** *Cairns City Caravan Park*, corner of James and Little sts, T40511467, for sheer convenience this basic option is within walking distance of the town centre. **L-F** *Cairns Coconut Caravan Resort*, on the Bruce Highway (about 6 km south, corner of Anderson Rd), T40546644, www.coconut.com.au Sheer class and with all mod cons this is one of the best in the country.

In tune with just about everything else in Cairns there is plenty of choice. Many of the mid-range eateries best suited for day or early evening dining are located on The Esplanade. Don't forget the options on offer in the major hotels and in the Pier Complex. Generally speaking seafood or traditional or specialist Australian fare is recommended. Ever eaten a 'bug' without being in a moving car with your mouth open? If not, now is your chance – look for them in seafood restaurants.

Eating
● *On map, page 362*
See inside cover for price catgegories

Expensive The luxury hotels come complete with plush restaurants and the options are many. Two of the best are *Breeze's* in the *Hilton*, Wharf St, T40526786 and *Siroccos* in the *Radisson*, The Pier T40311411. Dinner Tue-Sat 1800-2300. Also at the Pier is *Pesci's*, which overlooks the Marina, T40411133. It is a great spot to dine on the traditional and quality Aussie fare with a seafood edge. Elsewhere, *Red Ochre Grill*, 43 Shields St, T40510100, is an award winning Australian restaurant, offering the best of Australian 'game' fare including kangaroo, crocodile and local seafood favourites Open daily for lunch and dinner. For a bit of a novelty you might like to try the $70 Dinner Cruise on offer with *Ocean Spirit* a large modern catamaran based at the Marlin Marina, 33 Lake St, T40312920, www.oceanspirit.com.au, 2½ hrs, departs 0700 Wed/Fri/Sat.

Mid-range *Dundee's*, 29 Spence St, T40510399, is a well-established favourite, that offers good value Australian cuisine in a relaxed atmosphere. Meat lovers will love the buffalo, roo, croc and barramundi combos-which thankfully comes in bits as opposed to the whole. The seafood platters are also excellent. *Barnacle Bills*, 65 The Esplanade, T40512241, is another well-established seafood favourite. For Italian *Verdi's*, corner of Shields and Sheridan sts, T40521010, open Mon-Fri 1200-2300, Sat/Sun 1100 and *La Fettucina*, 43 Shields St, T40315959, are both recommended. *Yanni's Taverna*, corner of Alpin and Grafton sts, T40411500, is a good Greek place offering attractive discounts between 1800 and 1900. When it comes to Asian fare *Yamagen Japanese*, corner of Grafton and Spence Sts, T40521009, is recommended. For good Indian fare try the *Tandoori Oven*, 62B Shields St, T40310043, while the award winning *Café China*, is considered the best of the Chinese restaurants, corner of Spence and Grafton sts, T40412828. Open daily from 1030.

Cairns to Cape York

Cheap *Woolshed*, *Sports Bar* and *PJ O'Briens* (see Bars and clubs, below) all offer cheap backpacker meals and are open daily from about 1000. For value pub grub in a quieter Irish atmosphere try **Willie McBride's** in the *Fig Tree Lodge*, corner of Sheridan and Thomas sts, T40410000. Open daily from 1800.

Seriously cheap *Gypsy Dee's Café*, 41A Shields St, T40515530, is a lively wee place that offers value Aussie/traditional meals but is best known for its large vegetarian selections. *International Food court*, The Esplanade and *Meeting Place*, round the corner in Alpin St, has a number of cheap outlets if you are looking for the old dine and dash option.

Cafés   *Perrota's*, corner of Abbott and Shield sts, next to the Art Gallery, T40315899, is a fine place to watch the world go by for breakfast, lunch or dinner. Good coffee. Open from 0730. *Coffee Club*, The Esplanade, T40410522, is also a popular spot and they can serve up a good breakfast for about $10. *Tiny's Juice Bar*, 45 Grafton St, T40314331, is a popular venue for the health conscious, with light snacks and a fine range of cool and colourful juices to cure all ills. Open daily 0730-1700.

Bars & clubs   With so many backpackers descending on the city the nightlife is very much geared to the get dressed up (or down), get drunk and fall over mentality. Finding somewhere to have a few good beers and a good conversation can be more difficult. With the party set in mind Cairns now offers a great value **Ultimate Party** on Sat for $45. The 'party' sometimes of up to 200 rapacious souls tours 5 local pubs with free transport, free entry tickets, a free meal and a free drink in each pub. Sadly, free hangover cures and condoms have still to be included! Tickets are freely available or T40410332. If the party is heavily booked there is a re-run on Wed. While wondering around the city you will inevitably be approached by destitute and persuasive backpackers touting the various nightspots and businesses with free drink vouchers. *Barfly*, www.barfly.com.au, is the local entertainment rag.

Bars There are a good range of pubs in the town from the traditional Aussie street corner hotels to sports bars and, of course, some pseudo Irish offerings. The best of the Irish pubs is the popular *PJ O'Brien's*, Shields St, T40315333. Open daily 1000-0300. It offers live music most nights and is not too shabby in the food department either! Along the same lines is *Frog and Firkin*, corner of Spence and Lake sts, T40315305. It's nicely laid back, offers live music, a bistro and has a good balcony overlooking the main street. For something a little classier try the cool (as in temperature) atmosphere of the *Courthouse Bar and Bistro*, in the former courthouse on Abbott St, T40314166. It is great during the heat of the day or for a little more decorum and offers live Jazz on Sunday nights and al fresco dining, T40314166. Open daily until late. For a traditional Aussie pub experience try *Pier Tavern*, Pierpoint Rd, T40314677.

Clubs There are almost a dozen on 'the circuit' with the following currently enjoying the best reputation. Topping the list is *Woolshed*, 24 Shields St, T40316304. It is very much backpacker oriented, offering very cheap drinks and it generally goes off well into the wee hours. *The Sports Bar*, 33 Spence St, T40412533. Also lures in the younger crowds with cheap drink and has live bands from Thu-Sat. *The Chapel*, 91 The Esplanade, T40414222, might offer tourist sanctuary and meals that include bread and wine during the day, but at night turns more in towards the confessional over cocktails and shooters. Open until 0200. *Johno's Blues Bar*, corner of Abbott and Alpin sts, T40518770, is a bit seedy but is a well-known live music venue. Entry is free before 2100 and on Sun there is the opportunity to show off your talents (or not) at the *Talent Quest* or on Mon the chance to win the best didgeridoo player competition worth a

Diving dilemmas

◀

There are a mind boggling number of reef and reef island sailing and cruise trips based in Cairns, with all sorts of craft, from skiffs to deluxe catamarans. Most give you the opportunity to dive, even for the first time, with a minimum of training, or at the very least to don mask, snorkel and goggles and enter the incredible world beneath the waves. The most popular day trips are to Green or Fitzroy Islands and to the 'outer reef'. These are listed and described in the Northern Reef Islands section, page 375. The 'outer islands' and 'outer reef' offer the best water clarity and the larger fish species and even if you are attempting your first dive, you are advised to choose an operator that goes there. But that does not mean that the 'inner islands' and 'inner reef' like Green or Fitzroy Islands are any less fascinating, or indeed that the waters that surround them are at all lacking in life. Generally speaking, for relaxation, soporific sunbathing, water activities and the odd bit of snorkelling, visit the busier inner islands, but for the best hardcore diving and snorkelling head for the outer reef.

cool $100. One of the newest clubs in the city is *Club Five Nine*, corner of Shields St and The Esplanade, which is earning a fine reputation for modern music. The well established *Tropos*, corner of Lake and Spence St, T40312530, offers regular theme nights, while the *Playpen*, Lake St, T40518211, has 3 separate bars offering various levels of mayhem and a huge dance floor. *Club Trix*, 53 Spence St, T40518223, is essentially a gay bar, but it welcomes both straight and gay and has sexy vibes and highly entertaining drag shows.

Cinema and casino *5 Cinema* is located at 108 Grafton St, T40511222. Cairn's fairly unremarkable *Reef Casino* is located at the bottom of the Esplanade and behind the Wharf. Open all hours.

Shopping Cairns offers some excellent shopping. The 2 main centres are **Cairns Central Shopping Arcade**, McLeod St, T1800646010, and **Pier Marketplace** beneath the *Radisson Plaza Hotel*, The Pier, T40517244. Open daily 0900-2100. There you can buy everything from opals to art works. Don't miss *Reef Gallery* and *Ric Steininger Photo Gallery*, www.steininger.com.au **Cairns Night Markets**, 54-60 Abbott St, T40517666, offer over 100 stalls selling a rather predictable array of arts, crafts, clothing, food and souvenirs. Open daily 1630-2300. More entertaining is *Rusty's Bazaar*, an eclectic conglomerate of colourful consumables located between Grafton and Sheridan sts. Open Fri evening and Sat/Sun morning. For classy colourful panoramic photographs don't miss *Peter Lik's Wilderness Gallery*, 4 Shields St, T40318177, www.peterlik.com.au For Australiana and traditional attire including iconic 'Akubra' hats try *Cairns Hatters*, 4-8, Orchid Plaza, Abbott St, T40316392. For books *Angus and Robertson*, Shop 141, Cairns Central Shopping Arcade, T40410591. Camping equipment can be found in several outlets on Shields and Grafton sts, including *Adventure Equipment*, 133 Grafton, T40312669. For second-hand camping equipment head for *City Palace Disposals*, corner of Shields and Sheridan sts.

Tours & activities There are a vast range of activities and over 600 tours on offer in the region, so shop around, take your time in choosing and avoid the human sharks. Do remember that we are guests in the underwater garden and with too much disturbance, without wanting to be dramatic, it will cease to be.

With literally hundreds of operators in the city vying (sometimes quite aggressively) for your tourist dollar, you are advised to seek unbiased information at the official and

Cairns to Cape York

accredited VIC. Then armed with some outline shop around, before choosing a specific activity, trip, or tour (or combination thereof) to suit your desires, your courage and the wallet. Many of the larger cruise and activity operators offer combination deals, which offer attractive savings. Adrenaline junkies should ask about the **Awesome Foursome** deals which can combine such adventures as an island visit, a rafting trip, a bungee jump and a skydive for around $400 (saving about $40), T40513588.

If you know very little about the reef and its myriad of fascinating and colourful inhabitants, and especially if you are going snorkelling or are a first-time reef diver, you would greatly benefit from an appointment with *Reef Teach*, Spence St, T40317794, www.reefteach.com.au Hosted by the rather over-animated Irish marine biologist and diver Paddy Cowell and his equally gesticulatory staff, it offers an entertaining 2-hr lecture on the basics of the reef's natural history, conservation and fish/coral identification. Show starts 1815, Mon-Sat, $13. Recommended.

Companies that are based in Port Douglas north of Cairns also offer transfers from the city

Cruises There are many other companies that offer half, full or multi-day cruise options that concentrate on sailing, diving or just plain relaxing, and again with various islands stops and other water based activities. Competition is fierce so you are advised to visit the accredited VIC to look at what is on offer before deciding on what best suits your taste and your budget. In general, for a basic inner reef island trip without extras, expect to pay anywhere between $36-55. For an Outer Reef Cruise with snorkelling, anything from $70-150. For an Outer Reef Cruise with introductory Dive from $120-200 and for a luxury 3-day cruise with accommodation, meals and all activities included about $1000. It all boils down to the type of vessel, its facilities, numbers, optional extras and the actual time allowed on the reef.

Reef Island Cruises Great Adventures, T40449944 www.great adventures.com.au, and *Big-Cat Green Island*, T40510444 and *Reef Magic*, T40311588, www.reefmagiccruises.com.au, are the main cruise operators in Cairns and are based at Trinity Wharf. They offer a range of tour options to Green Island, and beyond that, include certified dives, introductory dives, snorkelling, sightseeing and other water based activities. *Great Adventures* in Cairns and *Quicksilver*, T40872100, www.quicksilver-cruises.com.au, based in Port Douglas both have huge floating pontoons moored on the outer reef where you can dive, snorkel, view the reef from a glass-bottom boat or simply sunbathe or watch the world and the fish go by. Although this offers a fine introduction to the reef, don't expect to find any solace. *Compass*, T40500666, www.reeftrip.com.au, offer an attractive alternative with a good value trip on board a modern vessel to Michaelmas and Hastings Reef (both on the outer reef). Also offered are free snorkelling, boom netting and optional dive extras, from $60.

Generally speaking the smaller sailing companies offer the most attractive rates and perhaps more peace and quiet, but lack the speed, convenience and razzmatazz of the fast, modern catamarans. *Falla*, T40313488, www.fallacruises.com.au, is a charming, former Pearl Lugger that allows 4-hr on Upolo Reef 30 km from Cairns, with free snorkelling. Departs 0830, returns 1730, $60, child $35 (introductory dive only $50). *Passions of Paradise*, T40500676, www.passionsofparadise.com.au, is a larger, modern catamaran that also goes to Upolo Cay and Paradise Reef. From $70 (introductory dive $55). Departs daily 0800, returns 1800. *Ecstasea*, T40413055, www.reef-sea-charters.com.au, is a modern 60-ft luxury yacht that once again goes to Upolo Cay with free snorkelling, from $89 (Introductory dive $55). An even more luxurious trip to Michaelmas Cay on the outer reef is offered on the beautiful, all mod cons *Ocean Spirit*, T40312920, www.oceanspirit.com.au, though you will pay the extra at $150, (introductory dive $85).

Diving Cairns is an internationally renowned base for diving and so there are hundreds of dive shops, operators and schools. Cairns of course is an ideal place to learn but certainly not the cheapest (from $300, basic no accommodation to $500 on board all inclusive). However, given all the training required, amazingly perhaps, for as little as $50 on top of a the price of a day cruise you can experience an introductory dive that will blow you out of the water. The big question of course – is it safe? Providing you are fit and healthy, choose a reputable company, with qualified instructors and do exactly what they say, generally it is. Once you have considered your preferences, shop around. As already mentioned the best diving is to be had on the outer reef where the water is generally clearer and the fish species bigger. The following are just a sample of the main operators in Cairns, but there are many more on offer and prices vary. Almost all offer competitive rates and options for certified divers and snorkellers.

Refer also to Northern Reef Islands, page 375

ProDive, corner of Abbott and Shields sts, T40315255, www.prodive-cairns.com.au, offer a range of trips including a 3-day/2-night certification with 11 dives from $510, 1-day Introductory dive from $145. *Cairns Dive Centre*, 121 Abbott St, T40517531, www.cairnsdive.com.au, offer certification from $297 and introductory dives from $120 *Reef Encounter*, 100 Abbott St, T40500688, www.reeftrip.com.au, offer 3-day/2-night certification, from $320. *Down Under Dive*, 287 Draper St, T40528300, www.downunderdive.com.au, offer 3-day/2-night certification from $400. Other reputable companies include *Tusa Dive*, corner of Shields St and The Esplanade, T40311248, www.tusadive.com.au; *Taka Dive*, 131 Lake St, T40518722; *Deep Sea Divers Den*, 319 Draper St, T40312223; *Mike Ball Dive Expeditions*, 28 Spence St, T40315484, www.takadive.com.au; *Ocean Spirit*, 33 Lake St, T40312920, www.oceanspirit.com.au; *Aquarius III*, T40516449, www.aquarius3.com.au; *Adventure Company*, 1st floor, 13 Shields St, T40514777, www.adventures.com.au, offer longer trips from 6-day/5-night from $1000.

Fishing Cairns has been a world-class big game fishing venue for many years and as a result there are many excellent charters with experienced guides to take you on what can be a superb experience in awesome surroundings. Black Marlin are the biggest species, capable of reaching weights of over 1,000 pounds, which we can safely say would be a bit like landing an irate sumo wrestler. Another commonly caught species is the Wahoo. One of the best charter companies is *Cairns Reef Charter Services*, T40314742, www.ausfish.com/crcs They have a fleet of ocean going vessels and also offer an exciting range of inland trips to catch the famed barramundi. Two other reputable local companies are *Cairns Travel and Sports fishing*, T40316016, and *VIP*, T40314355, both offer a wide range of fishing trips targeting both salt and freshwater. Prices start at about $75 for a half-day and $200 a day per person for big game fishing.

For many years until his death the actor Lee Marvin came to Cairns annually to fish for Marlin. He loved the place so much that half his ashes were cast on the reef

Rafting Cairns is the base for some excellent rafting with a wide range of adrenaline pumping trips down the Barron, North Johnstone and Tully Rivers. The minimum age for rafting is usually 13 years. *Raging Thunder*, T40307990, www.ragingthunder.com.au, offer half, full, and multi-day trips, as well as heli-trips and many other activity combos. Half-day Barron River from $83, full-day Tully River, $145, 2-day Tully River $350. *R'n'R*, Abbott St, T40517777, are a similar outfit offering full-day trips down the Tully for $141, half-day on the Barron for $81. *Foaming Fury*, 19-21 Barry St, T40313460, tackle the Barron, half-day $77 and also offer a full-day 2-man 'sports rafting' experience on the Russell River, from $118. *Extreme Green*, Level 11, 15 Lake St, T0409273009, offer a half-day trip down the Barron for $70.

River and sea kayaking *Raging Thunder*, T40307990, www.ragingthunder.com.au, offer river kayaking on the Tully from $128, full-day sea kayaking around Fitzroy island

Cairns to Cape York

from $110, overnight from $135 and an extended 3-day/2-night adventure. *The Adventure Company*, 1st Floor, 13 Shields St, T40514777, www.adventures.com.au, offer a good 3-day/2-night trip crossing King Reef and out to the North Barnard Islands from $535.

Other watersports and activities For a good value attempt at water-skiing or wakeboarding try *Skii-Mee Tours*, a small and friendly family owned operation based in Brinsmead, T40313381, www.skiimee.com.au Scheduled day tour and instruction on Tue/Thu and half/full day tours on other days by appointment, full day from $145. Parasailing is available with *Watersports Adventures*, T40317888 (10min) from $72. Predictably perhaps Cairns has jet boat trips, T40575884, from $70.

Bungee jumping Not to miss out on the massive tourism development in Cairns, Kiwi bungee jumping guru AJ Hackett has created an attractive jump complex in Smithfield 15 mins north of Cairns. It offers a 50-m jump and also the popular jungle swing, a sort of half free-fall/half swing that makes what you did when you were a toddler in the park seem awfully tame. Bungee $109, Swing $79, T40577188, www.ajhackett.com.au Open daily 0930-1730. McGregor Rd, Smithfield. Pick-ups.

Golf The Cairns region has many a good golf course with *Paradise Palms Course*, Clifton Beach, T40591166, being on of Australia's best. The clubhouse alone is worth a look. For a practice hit before your round head for the very plush golf range, 10 mins north of the city, on the Captain Cook Highway, T40550655.

Horse trekking *Blazing Saddles*, T40590955, www.blazingsaddles.com.au, run a half-day trek suitable for beginners, from $85, child $65. They also offer entertaining and delightfully muddy half-day ATV safaris from $110. *Springmount Station Stables,* T40934493, offer a more conventional approach with half to full day, farm stays and camp-outs, from $88, 2-day $242.

Scenic flights Fixed wing flights over the reef and surrounding islands are offered by *Reefwatch Air Tours*, T40359808, www.reefwatch.com.au, and *Daintree Air Services*, T40349300, www.daintreeair.com.au, 30 mins, from $135. *Aquaflight*, T40314307, www.aquaflight.com.au, operate a fleet of seaplanes which have the added attraction of island and reef cay landings, from $179. Recommended. Several companies offer helicopter flights, half-day trips and safaris, including *Cairns Heli Scenic*, T40315999, www.cairns-heliscenic.com.au, 15 mins from $140 and *Kestrel Aviation*, T40352206, www.kestrelaviation.com.au, 10 mins from $89. For a sedate balloon ride *Champagne Balloon Flights*, T40581688, www.champagneballoons.com.au, 30 mins from $135 with a glass of bubbly. *Raging Thunder*, T40307911, www.ragingthunder.com.au and *Hot Air*, T1800800829, offer similar trips from $130. For another silent near flight experience you might also like to try the *Flying Leap*, T40362127, www.flyingleap.com.au – a sort of hang-glider attached to a 300-m wire, 60 m above ground. Two flights, with pick-ups, from $50.

Most of these companies also offer combination packages with other major activities or attractions

Skydiving *Paul's Parachuting*, McLeod St, T1800225572, www.paulsparachuting.com.au, offer tandems from up to 14,000 ft, training and scenic flights from $228 (8,000 ft). Their combination skydive and certified dive package is good value at $320. *Skydive Cairns*, T40521822, offer a similar jumps.

Sightseeing *Cairns Discovery Tours*, T40535259, offer a half-day tour of city sights including the Botanical Gardens, Flying Doctor Service Visitors Centre and Northern Beaches, from $50, child $26. *Terri-Too* and *Calm Water Cruises*, T40314007, offer a cruise exploring the harbour and mangrove, $33 and another tour option in combination with a visit to a Crocodile Farm from $49, children half fare.

Daintree and Cape Tribulation One-day, 4WD tours to Daintree and Cape Tribulation generally leave Cairns at about 0700 and return about 1800 and cost in the region of $115-125. *Billy Tea Bush Safaris*, T40320055, www.billytea.com.au, have friendly entertaining guides, day tour from $125, child $85. *Tropical Horizons*, T40552630, www.tropicalhorizonstours.com.au, and *Suncoast Safaris*, T40552999, www.suncoast-safaris.com.au, both offer very comfortable, quality, small group tours, from $119, child $73. *Trek North*, T40514328, www.treknorth.com.au, take small groups to Daintree and Mossman Gorge and includes a cruise on the Daintree River. Good value, from $99, child $60. *Foaming Fury*, T40313460, www.foamingfury.com.au, and *Jungle Tours*, T40325600, www.jungletours.com.au, are mainly backpacker oriented and offer value day-trips from $89 and overnight trips from $100, staying at the Capes various backpacker establishments.

Cooktown Most of the tours on offer combine both the inland and coast roads to Cooktown. *Wilderness Challenge*, T40556504, www.wilderness-challenge.com.au, offer all-inclusive 1-day (fly/drive, via Daintree Coast), from $265, a 2-day from$330 and 3-day from $732. *Queensland Adventure Safaris*, T40412418, www.qastours. com.au, offer a 2-day 4WD trip offering a range of accommodation from $195-310 as well as a fly/drive from$250. *APT*, T40419419, www.aptours.com.au, and *Tropic Wings*, 278 Hartley St, T40353555, www.tropicwings.com.au, are 2 companies offering 'Cooktown-in-a-Day' from $124, child $62.

Kuranda *Tropic Wings*, 278 Hartley St, T40353555, www.tropicwings.com.au, offer an excellent tour to Kuranda that combines the Kuranda Scenic Railway and Skyline Gondola with the addition of many exciting diversions and activities, from $149, child $75. Recommended.

Atherton Tablelands *On The Wallaby Tablelands Tours*, T40500650, are recommended offering entertaining guided tours of the Tablelands sights with excellent wildlife canoeing trips as a further option, from $60. Their 2-day/1-night accommodation/activity package based at their hostel in Yungaburra is good value and recommended. *Northern Experience Eco Tours*, T40414633, are another good company that also offer a wildlife edge to their day tour, from $99, child $71. *Jungle Tours*, T40325600, also offer a good waterfalls day trip from $79.

Specialist wildlife Given the habitat and abundance of wildlife almost all tours have a heavy emphasis on the environment and wildlife, but for specialist wildlife trips in the region try *Wait-a-while Rainforest Tours*, T40987500, www.waitawhile.com.au, or *Wildscapes Safaris*, T40576272, www.wildscapes-safaris.com.au *On the Wallaby Backpackers*, in Yungaburra, T40500650, www.dreamtimetravel.com.au, offer an exciting range of tours to the Atherton Tablelands and day/night wildlife canoeing trips on Lake Tinaroo, from $70. *Wooroonooran Rainforest Safaris*, T40310800, www.wooroonooran-safaris.com.au, also offer sightseeing and trekking trips with a wildlife bent in the beautiful Wooroonooran National Park south of Cairns. For an interesting insight in to geology consider the *Undara Experience*, T40971411, www.undara.com.au In conjunction with *Savannah Guides* they offer day trips and excellent multi-day package deals by coach, self-drive or rail to view the 190,000 year old volcanic Undara Lava Tubes with additional activities and accommodation in their unique railway carriages or swag-tent village. Day-trip from $119, 2-day, from $393 and 3-day rail, from $624. Recommended.

Transport **Local Bus** The main suburban bus operator is *Sunbus Marlin Coast*, T40577411, www.sunbus.com.au, offering regular services north, as far as Palm Cove and south as far as Gordonvale, from $1. Day/week passes available. The bus transit centre is on Lake St (City Place) where schedules are posted. **Cycle** Hire is readily available in Cairns, with many of the car hire companies and hostels offering rentals from $12 a day. Companies include *MiniCar Rentals*, 47 Shield St, T40513030 or *Bandicoot*, 59 Sheridan St, T40510155. **Taxi** *Black and White*, T131008, T40488333 (24-hr).

Long distance Air Cairns International Airport is located 6 km north of the city centre, on the Captain Cook Highway, T40523888, www.cairnsport.com.au International, domestic and state air carriers are all represented, including *Qantas*, T131313, *Air New Zealand*, T132476, *Cathay Pacific*, T131747, *Malaysia Airlines*, T132627, *Virgin Blue*, T136789, *Air Niugini* (Papua New Guinea), T1300361380, *Qantas* (Sunstate), T40860457, and *Flight West*, T132392. Other local charter flight companies also provide inter-island services throughout the Great Barrier Reef and to the Whitsunday Islands.

Bus The interstate coach terminal is at Trinity Wharf, Wharf St. Open daily 0600-0100. *McCafferty's*, T131499, www.mccaffertys.com.au, and *Greyhound*, T132030, have offices within the terminal and operate regular daily services south to **Brisbane** and beyond (including onward connections to **Darwin** from Townsville). *Premier Motor Service*, T133410, www.premierms.com.au, also operate daily services to **Brisbane** and beyond. Cairns to Brisbane takes about 28 hrs, $134-182 one-way. *Coral Coaches*, T40317577, www.coralcoaches.com.au, run regular local services to the **Airport**, **Port** Douglas, **Mossman**, **Daintree** and **Cape Tribulation** and long-distance services to **Cooktown** (Wed/Fri/Sun) and **Karumba/Mount Isa** (Mon/Wed/Thu). *Whitecar Coaches*, T40519533, www.whitecarcoaches.com.au, service the Atherton Tablelands daily.

The wet road conditions around Cairns and far north Queensland can be, in a word, aquatic. For up-to-date conditions and flood warnings, T131111

Car Car rental at the airport and Abbott and Lake sts in the city have most outlets. *Avis*, 135 Lake St, T40515911. *Budget*, airport, T40359500 and 153 Lake St, City, T40519222. *All One Rentals*, 72 Abbott St, T40311788. *National*, 143 Abbott St, T40514600. *Delta*, 403 Sheridan St, T40322000. *MiniCar Rentals*, 150 Sheridan St, T40516818. *4WD Hire*, T1300726001. For a standard car and 7-day hire expect to pay from $33 a day. Some of the larger companies like *Avis* also offer 4WD hire from around $146 per day. For campervan rentals and purchase (second-hand), *Travellers Auto Barn*, 123-125 Bunda St, T40413722, www.travellers-autobarn.com.au Offer guaranteed buy-backs in Sydney. *Britz*, 411 Sheridan St, T40322611, www.britz.com.auIn Car servicing at *Mac Peak Automotive*, Lot 2, Mac Peak Cr, Smithfield, T40577100.

Ferry *Quicksilver* run a daily ferry, *Wave Piercer*, service to Port Douglas from Marlin Marina, Cairns, $23 one-way, T40872100.

Train The station is located next to Cairns Central Shopping Complex, Bunda St. Travel centre is open Mon-Fri 0900-1700, Sat 0900-1200, T40369249/ T1800620324. For other long-distance enquiries, T132232, 24 hr, www.traveltrain.qr.com.au There are 4 coastal train services to/from Brisbane and beyond, ranging in standards of luxury and price. *The Sunlander* (departs 0835, Mon/Thu/Sat, from $162, child $82), *The Queenslander* (departs 0835, Tue, First Class from $558, child $335), *Tilt Train* departs Mon, Wed and Fri, taking 25 hrs, from $280 one-way) and *Great South Pacific Express*, costing a staggering $2,830. There is one 'Outback' service, *The Savannahlander*, from Cairns to Forsayth (from $95), with connecting coach services to Chillagoe, Croydon and Normanton, (from $138). A local scenic service also operates to Kuranda, from $30, child $15 ($48/26 return). Ask about the various holiday and 'Discover Passes', for price reductions and packages.

Airline offices *Qantas*, corner of Lake and Shields sts, T40504000. **Banks** All the **Directory** major bank branches are represented in the city centre especially at the intersection of Shields and Abbott sts. For currency exchange *Travelex* have offices at the airport and in the city at 13 Shields St, T40414286 and 12 Spence St, T40417696.*Thomas Cook*, 69 Abbott St, T40316860/50, Lake St, T40516255/ 59, The Esplanade, T40411000. *American express*, Shop 29 Orchid Plaza, Abbott St, T40518811. Some hostels offer commission free exchange. **Communications** Internet: Omnipresent, including *Global Gossip*, 125 Abbott St, T40316411; *Backpackers World*, 12 Shields St, T40410999 and *Travellers Contact Point*, 1st floor, 13 Shields St, T40414677. *Internet Outpost*, Shields St, is recommended. All are open until at least 2200. **Post office**: 13 Grafton St, T40314382. Open Mon-Fri 0830-1700. Post restante facility. There is a smaller post shop office in the Orchid Shopping Plaza (2nd floor), Abbott St. Open as above and on Sat 0900-1500. **Library** Cairns City Public Library, 151 Abbott St, T40443720. Free internet. **Medical services** Chemist: *After Hours*, 29B Shields St, T40512466. Open 0800-2100. **Hospitals**: Cairns Base Hospital, Esplanade (north), T40506333. **Cairns City 24-hr Medical centre**, corner of Florence and Grafton sts, T40521119. **Useful numbers** Police: Emergency T000, 5 Sheridan St, T40307000. RACQ: *Coral Motors*, 138 McLeod St, I40516543. Breakdown T131111.

Northern Great Barrier Reef Islands

Cairns is the principal access point to some of the best islands of the northern Great Barrier Reef, famed for their desert island aesthetics, abundant sea creatures, corals and clear waters. If **diving** is not your thing, then you must at the very least take a **day-cruise** to one of the islands and for a few hours sample the good life and supposing you do nothing else – go **snorkelling**. If you seek solace there are also a number of islands that can be visited independently and where camping is permitted, but all transportation must be arranged independently. Bookings and permits are essential. For information contact the QPWS Office in Cairns.

Colour map 7, grid C3 'Northern' is a loose description of southern sectors of the reef that stretches 2,000 km from Cape York to the Tropic of Capricorn (Rockhampton)

Once you arrive in Cairns it won't take long before you see postcards of Green **Green Island** Island – a small outcrop of lush vegetation, fringed with white sand and surrounded by a huge tapestry of azure blue and green reefs. These images look like something that has perhaps, until now, existed only in your imagination.

Green Island is a text book 'coral cay' formed by dead coral and will – its human activities and development aside – fulfil most of those fantasies as to what a tropical island is all about. Being a mere 45 minutes (27 km) away by boat, part of the inner reef, it is the closest island to Cairns and at 15 ha, is one of the smallest islands on the reef. It is home to an exclusive resort but, in essence, is designed more for the day tripper in mind, with concrete pathways leading to food outlets, bars, dive and souvenir shops, a pool and of course – some well trodden beaches. The wealth of facilities may suit some people, or for others, be the only thing to disappoint. But despite it's small size you can still grab a snorkel and mask and find a quiet spot on the bleached white sand and from there enter that infinitely more beautiful and quiet world, beneath the waves. The best place to snorkel is around the pier itself, where the fish love to congregate around the pylons. If you do go snorkelling there and see what appears to be a large shark – it's a shark ray or 'bucket mouth', a charming and congenial bottom feeder that is totally harmless. Another fine set of teeth can be seen at the **Marineland Melanesia**, in the heart of the island, with its small collection of aquariums and marine artefacts all presided over by 'Cassius' a very old and rotund crocodile with plenty of attitude. ■ *Daily 0900-1600. $8. T40514032.*

Cairns to Cape York

If you are physically unable to go diving or snorkelling, you can still experience the vast array of colourful fish and corals from a **glass-bottom boat** or a small **underwater observatory** ($5) both located by the pier. Although nothing remarkable in itself it is interesting to note that this was reputedly the first underwater observatory in the world.

The island was named not as you might think due to its appearance but after Charles Green who was the chief observer and astronomer on board Captain Cooks ship, *Endeavour*.

Sleeping and eating LL *Green Island Resort*, T40313300, F40521511, www.green islandresort.com.au Exclusive and the only accommodation on offer. Rooms and facilities are all mod cons and prices include many of the islands activities.

Tours and activities There are a number of tour options that give you the opportunity to combine, diving and/or snorkelling to the outer islands with a few hours exploring Green Island. Alternatively you may just want to pay the ferry fare and use the islands facilities, go snorkelling, or laze on the beach. You can also walk right round the islands' 1.5-km circumference in 20 mins. Snorkel, mask and fins can be hired from the *Dive Shop* ($12). They also offer introductory dives to non-guests (30 mins) from around $55 and full 3-4-day certification from $320. Pool access costs $5 for those with children or an inability to stray to far from the well-stocked bar. There are two main tour operators to Green Island: *Great Adventures*, The Wharf, Cairns, T40449944, www.greatadventures.com.au, offer basic transfers from $46, child $23 and a wide range of tour options with activity inclusions and optional extras, from half day $54, child $27/ full day $92, child $46. Additionally there is a Green Island and Outer Reef (pontoon) tour from $160, child $80. Added extras include snorkel tour from $15, intro dive from $94 and 3-4 day certification from $320. *Big Cat Green Island Reef Cruises*, The Pier Market Place, T40510444, www.bigcat-cruises.com.au, also offer half and full-day cruises with optional extras from, $52, child $29.

Transport All ferries leave from Trinity Wharf, Cairns with transfers from Port Douglas.

Fitzroy Island Fitzroy Island, part of the inner reef just 6 km off the mainland and 25 km south of Cairns, is, unlike Green Island, a large 339-ha continental island, formed of rock not coral and more mountainous, yet still surrounded by coral reef. It therefore offers more of an escape with pleasant walking tracks through dense eucalyptus and tropical rainforests, rich in wildlife. One of the most popular walks is a circuit to the islands highest point 269 m, with its memorable views and 1970 lighthouse (4-km round trip). A scattering of quiet beaches provide good snorkelling and diving. The best beach on the island is **Nudey Beach** which is not, as the name suggests, a base for soporific naturists. It can be reached in about 20 minutes from the island's resort. Fitzroy was used by the Gunghandji Aboriginal people as a fishing base for thousands of years and in the 1800s by itinerants harvesting 'beche de mer' sea cucumber. It is named after the Duke of Grafton who was the British Prime Minister when the 'Endeavour' left England.

Sleeping and eating A-D *Fitzroy Island Resort*, T40521335, www.fitzroyisland resort.com.au, offers accommodation to suit all budgets from camping to hostel-style bunkhouses to beach cabins. **F Camping** requires a permit from the QPWS in Cairns. Check to see if the campsite is open before departure. Bookings essential. There is a kiosk on the island that offers cheap fairly unremarkable fare, while slightly pricier quality meals can be secured at the resorts *Rainforest Restaurant* (bar attached).

Tours and activities A dive shop at the *Fitzroy Island Resort* offers introductory dive trips, for a great value $65, 3-day certification from $325 and snorkel hire from $12. Other watersports are also available from multi-day kayaking trips from $274 and day-long fishing trips from $150. These activities come as part of the resort accommodation packages, but are also offered to independent visitors. *Raging Thunder*, T40307990, www.ragingthunder.com.au, offer good value day, overnight and multi-day sea kayaking trips to Fitzroy the mainland.

Transport *Fitzroy Island Ferries*, T40307911, depart Cairns at 0830, 1030 and 1600, from $36, child$18. *Sunlover Cruises*, T40311055, and *Great Adventures*, T40449944, also service Fitzroy daily, from $80.

A further 20 km south of Fitzroy Island are the Frankland Group, a small cluster of continental islands of which 77 ha are national park. Once again they are covered in rainforest and fringed with white sand beaches and coral reef. The islands offer a wonderfully quiet retreat in comparison to the larger, busier islands. There are QPWS camping areas on **Russell** and **High Islands**. Permits and bookings through the QPWS in Cairns. Access is by charter boat or with *Frankland Islands Cruise and Dive*, T40316300, www.franklandislands. com.au They offer camp transfers from $146 and day tours to Normanby Island from $140, which ends with a pleasant cruise up the Mulgrave River. Also on offer is certified/introductory diving from $60 and a range of combo multi sight/tour package deals. The ferry departs daily from Cairns at 0800. **Frankland Islands**

Lizard Island hosts Australia's most northerly reef island resort, one of the best and inevitably perhaps one of the most exclusive. The island itself lies 270 km north of Cairns, 27 km off Cooktown and is almost 1,000 ha, with the vast majority of that being national park. All the delights of the other popular islands are on offer without the welcome absence of over commercialism and the hoards of tourists. There are over 24 tranquil beaches, backed by lush forests, mangroves and bush, all abounding in wildlife, while just offshore, immaculate, clear water reefs offer superb diving and snorkelling. The famous **Cod Hole** is lauded as one of the best dive sites on the reef and the island is also a popular base for big game fishermen in search of the illusive Black Marlin. **Lizard Island**

A delightful walking track leads to **Cook's Look**, which at 359 m is the highest point on the island and the place where Captain Cook stood in 1770 trying to find passage through the reef and back out to the ocean. The island was named by Joseph Banks, ship's naturalist, who, as Cook struggled to achieve his goal, obviously had far more success searching for lizards.

Sleeping and eating **LL** *Lizard Island Resort*, T1800737678, www.poresorts.com, is pretty spectacular and offers lodges and chalets with all mod cons, fine resort facilities and a 5-star restaurant. The resort offers an exciting range of guest complimentary activities from windsurfing to guided nature walks. **Camping** is available on the island, but facilities are basic and you must of course get there. Permits and bookings essential. Contact the QPWS in Cairns.

Transport Various regional air operators and vessel charter companies service Lizard Islands but prices and times vary. VIC in Cooktown is the best place to enquire for the most up-to-date options. *Daintree Air Services*, T40349300, www.daintreeair.com.au, offer a day-trip package from $390, from Cairns. *Skytrans Airlines*, T40695446, www.skytrans. com.au, also offer air charters from Cairns or Cooktown.

Cairns to Cape York

Atherton Tablelands

Colour map 6/7, grid A4/5, C2/3

The Atherton Tablelands – sometimes referred to as the Tropical Tablelands – extends inland roughly in a semi-circle from the Cairns coast, to the small mining settlements of Mount Molloy in the north and Chillagoe in the west, to Mount Garnet in the south. In total it is an area almost the size of Tasmania – which in Queensland terms could be roughly translated as 'Cairns backyard'. The regions capital is the rather unremarkable town of Atherton, while the far more characterful and closer townships of Yungaburra, Mareeba and Kuranda successfully satisfy the tourist and day-tripper's inquisition.

In the imagination, while the words 'Australia' and 'tablelands' may conjure up a dry and dusty landscape of rocky outcrops, parched eucalyptus, and bounding kangaroos, when it comes to the heart of the Atherton, you are in for a big surprise. At an average height of over 800 m and subsequently the wettest region in Queensland, the Atherton Tablelands are in fact most extraordinary. Here, you will find a countryside with lush fields and plump cattle, tropical forests busting with birdsong huge brimming lakes and melodic, or at times, thunderous waterfalls. And believe it or not, here, there are kangaroos that actually live in trees. Inevitably of course the further west you go the drier it gets until, at the edge of the Great Divide Range, the vast and traditional 'outback' takes over.

Background

The Atherton Tablelands were once the domain of the rapacious gold miner and are christened after John Atherton, who in 1877 first linked the tin mines of Herberton, to the then sleepy coastal port of Cairns. Today however, although some nominal mining activity remains, it is agriculture and horticulture that dominates. The list of produce is indeed impressive and includes such tropical delights as coffee and tea.

Given its inherent beauty the Tablelands, and especially the small and pretty settlements like Yungaburra, are the favourite retreats of Queensland's coastal dwellers, and tourists whom welcome the peace and quiet, the greenery and perhaps above all, the cooler temperatures. Believe it or not, during winter in the Tablelands it is quite normal and necessary to cosy up near the fire, or even to put a coat on.

Ins & outs

See Transport in each town section for further details

Getting there There are many day and multi-day tours to the Atherton Tablelands mainly from Cairns and if you are short for time this is the best way to see the region. Time constraints aside the region is best toured using your own transport. There are four access roads inland from the coast. From the south the Tablelands can be reached via the Palmerston Highway (just north of Innisfail) through the scenic tropical rainforests of Wooroonooran National Park and Millaa Millaa. From Cairns you can either access the region, south, via Gordonvale and the steeply climbing Gillies Highway, or north via Smithfield, the Kuranda Range Rd and Kuranda. From Port Douglas the region is best reached via the Rex Range Rd and Kennedy Highway via Mareeba. Bare in mind it is an ascent of around 700 m, which is fine by car but a monstrous effort if you are on a bicycle. *Whitecar Coaches*, Trinity Wharf Terminal, Cairns T40519533 www.whitecar coaches.com.au, provide daily services to Atherton, Yungaburra, Mareeba and Kuranda. For transport to The Tablelands via Kuranda and the Kuranda Scenic Railway or Skyrail Gondola, see page 363. **Tourist information** You are advised to research the region from the VIC in Cairns. Tropical Tableland Promotion Bureau, 42 Mabel St, Atherton, T40917444, F40917144, www.athertontable land.com.au, is the principal accredited regional VIC. For national parks information contact the QPWS office in Cairns.

Kuranda

The small, arty settlement of Kuranda has, thanks to proximity to Cairns, its scenic railway and its markets, become the principal tourist attraction – though not necessarily the jewel – of the Atherton Tablelands. Every day the streets flood with visitors who are then wooed to part with their tourist dollars. There is no doubting the veneer of its appeal, its rustic charm or its stunning location. There is plenty to see and do and a place could hardly be accessed by more spectacular methods but it has become a victim of its own popularity. Kuranda was

Colour map 7, grid C3
Population: 750
27 km from Cairns

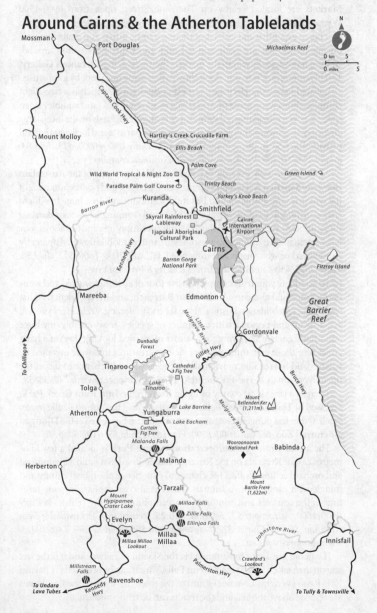

Around Cairns & the Atherton Tablelands

N

Mossman

Port Douglas

Michaelmas Reef

0 km   5

0 miles   5

Captain Cook Hwy

Mount Molloy

Hartley's Creek Crocodile Farm

Ellis Beach

Palm Cove

Wild World Tropical & Night Zoo

Green Island

Paradise Palm Golf Course

Trinity Beach

Barron River

Kuranda

Yorkey's Knob Beach

Smithfield

Skyrail Rainforest Cableway

Cairns International Airport

Ijapukai Aboriginal Cultural Park

Kennedy Hwy

Cairns

Barron Gorge National Park

Fitzroy Island

Mareeba

Edmonton

Great Barrier Reef

To Chillagoe

Little Mulgrove River

Gillies Hwy

Gordonvale

Dunballa Forest

Tinaroo

Cathedral Fig Tree

Bruce Hwy

Tolga

Lake Tinaroo

Mount Bellenden Ker (1,211m)

Mulgrove River

Atherton

Yungaburra

Lake Barrine

Lake Eacham

Curtain Fig Tree

Malanda Falls

Wooroonooran National Park

Babinda

Herberton

Malanda

Tarzali

Mount Bartle Frere (1,622m)

Mount Hypipamee Crater Lake

Millaa Falls

Zillie Falls

Evelyn

Ellinjaa Falls

Johnstone River

Millaa Millaa

Millaa Millaa Lookout

Crawford's Lookout

Innisfail

Millstream Falls

Palmerston Hwy

To Undara Lava Tubes

Ravenshoe

Kennedy Hwy

To Tully & Townsville

Cairns to Cape York

first put on the map in 1891 with the completion of the railway, providing a vital link between the Hodgkinson Gold Fields and the coast.

Ins & outs
See Transport, page 381, for details

Kuranda VIC is located in Centenary Park, Therwine St, T40939311, F40937593, www.kuranda.org.au Daily 1000-1600. It has maps and a comprehensive list of accommodation, tours and activities.

Sights

The main attraction in Kuranda are its permanent markets. **Heritage Markets** are just off Veivers Drive and open daily from 0830-1500, while the **Original Markets** are located nearby on Therwine Street, open from 0900-1500 Wednesday to Sunday. The emphasis here is of course on souvenirs, with much of it being expensive and tacky, but there are some artists and craftsmen producing pieces that are both unusual and good quality, so shop around. Although not actually part of the markets themselves, the **Terranova Gallery**, 15 Therwine Street, is worth a look showcasing some fine work by local artists.

Located below the Heritage Markets is **Birdworld**, which is a free-flight complex showcasing some of Australia's most colourful (and audible) avian species. Given its endangered status there is much emphasis on the local, large and leggy Cassowary, though it is the numerous parrots and lorikeets that will provide the best in photo opportunities. ■ *Daily 0900-1600, $11,child $4, family $28. T/F40939188, www.birdworldkuranda.com.au*

Almost impossibly even more colour is added by virtue of the **Australian Butterfly Sanctuary**. It is reputedly the world's largest and houses hundreds of the countries most brilliant and beautiful 'Lepidoptera'. In a huge free-flight enclosure hundreds of species like the huge and stunning Ulysses, or dazzling Birdwing join in graceful aerial choreography or simply fuss and flirt above your head – perhaps in the hope you are some gargantuan mobile flower. Apparently a bright red or white hat is recommended. ■ *Daily 1000-1600. $12, child $6. T40937575, www.australianbutterflies.com.au 8 Veivers Drive.*

To complete your truly comprehensive tour of all things winged and wonderful you could also consider a visit to **Batreach**, and independent wild bat rescue and rehabilitation hospital at the far end of Barang Street. Here you will get close up and personal with a number of species, most notably, the huge and utterly enchanting flying fox – a sort of startled looking dog on a hang glider. For those who think they are vicious creatures that were invented by witches and horror film moviemakers, this is your big chance to dispel the unequivocal myth. ■ *Tue-Fri/Sun 1030-1430. Donations expected. T40938858.*

There is a large local colony of flying foxes in the **Jum Rum Creek Park**, accessed of Thongon Street. Follow the noise – and the unmistakable musty smell. Other less pungent creatures of the night can be viewed at the **Djungan Nocturnal Zoo**. ■ *Daily 1000-1500. From $11, child $5. 8 Coondoo St.*

The award-winning **Rainforestation Nature Park** is located a few kilometres east of Kuranda on the Kuranda Range Road. Set amidst a rainforest and orchard setting it offers the chance to experience aboriginal culture and mingle with captive native animals. There is also an exhilarating one-hour tour of the complex and rainforest in an amphibious army vehicle. ■ *Daily 0900-1600. Attractions $32.50, child $16.25. Return transfers available from Kuranda, $6, and Cairns, $22. Day tours from $55, child $27.50. T40939033, www.rainforest.com.au*

If you did not arrive in Kuranda via the Skyrail or railway and it is the wet season then take a look at the **Barron Falls**, which can be accessed via Barron Falls Road (Wrights Lookout) south of the town. In 'the wet' the flood gates are opened above the falls and the results can be truly spectacular.

Although Kuranda attracts the tourist hoards like bees to honey, once the last train puffs out the station and peace returns, it can be a wonderful place to stay away from the usual coastal haunts. But don't expect a wealth of options. **L-A** *Cedar Park Rainforest Retreat*, Cedar Park Rd, T40937022, www.cedarparkresort 18 km away this 4-star retreat offers studio type apartments in a pleasant bush setting home to 2,500 year old Acacia Cedars. **L** *Kuranda B&B*, 28 Black Mountain Rd, T40937151, F40938012, kurandabed@tpgi.com.au Also some distance away (25 mins) but no less attractive with 4WD tours available. For something completely different try the quirky **A** *Tentative Nests*, 26 Barron Falls Rd, T40939555, tentnest@internetnorth.com.au It is a charming, colourful and eco friendly retreat where guests stay in self-contained nests' on platforms in the forests. Breakfast included, good value and not just financially. Recommended. **A-D** *Kuranda Rainforest Park*, Kuranda Heights Rd, T40937316, F40937316, www.kurandatouristpark.com.au 3-star, it has cottages, cabins, powered and non powered sites. Facilities include kitchen and pool. **C-D** *Kuranda Backpackers Hostel*, 6 Arara St, T40937355, www.kurandabackpackershostel.com.au Near the railway station, newly renovated this is a fine retreat with dorms, doubles and singles and good facilities. Pool, bike rental and pick-ups from Cairns.

Sleeping
See inside front cover for price categories

For something more luxurious you have to look further afield than the town

Rainforest View Restaurant, 28 Coondoo St, T40939939, offers a wide range of fare and rainforest views funnily enough but it does get packed with tour groups. *Wangal Café*, 40 Coondoo St, T40939339, for something different and a cut of croc or roo. *Monkeys Restaurant*, 1 Therwine St, T40937451, is a more traditional and cosy option. *Frogs*, T40937405, in the heart of Coondoo St, open daily 0900-1600, is the most popular café with the locals. *Oomph Restaurant*, 14 Thongon St, is a recent addition and is certainly the most friendly, T40939144. Good coffee. Open 0830-until too tired.

Eating
Kuranda is awash with affordable cafés and eateries so you will not be short of choice

Kuranda Rainforest Eco-Tours, based on the riverside of the rail bridge, offer 45-min river cruises every hour from 1030-1430 from $12, child $6, family $30, T40937476. Canoe hire is also available, T0408980016. See also Transport, below.

Tours & activities

Most visitors to Kuranda make the village part of a day-tour package from Cairns, with the highlight actually accessing it via the Barron Gorge and the Skyline Gondola, the Scenic Railway or both. Prices and schedules for the *Skyrail*, T40381555 and *Scenic Railway*, T40313636, are also listed in the Cairns section, page 363. *Coral Coaches*, T40317577, www.coralcoaches.com.au, and *Whitecar Coaches*, Trinity Wharf Terminal, T40519533, www.whitecarcoaches.com.au, fight it out to service Kuranda at the most competitive price, sometimes for as little as a $1. *Whitecar Coaches* is a smaller, more personable company and therefore are recommended.

Transport
There are numerous operators many of which are listed in the Cairns section, page 369

Communications Internet: available at *Kuranda Arts Co-op*, Red House, Coondoo St (next to the Ark), T40939026. Open daily 1000-1600.

Directory

Mareeba

Mareeba was one of the first towns in The Tablelands and was founded by John Atherton in 1880. It was originally used as little more than a stopping point for gold miners coming and going from the coast, until 1928 when the first **tobacco** plantation was established. Today the rather drab agricultural service town continues to thrive mainly on the infamous weed and more recently that other great addiction – coffee, but it does spring to life every July when it hosts the region's largest **rodeo**. For a coffee plantation tour, Arabicas Coffee Plantation at 136 Mason Street, T1800355526, www.arabicas.com.au Available from Monday to Friday for $5. Bookings essential.

Colour map 7, grid C3
Population: 7,000
64 km from Cairns

There are two natural attractions around Mareeba worth looking at: **Granite Gorge**, with its inviting swimming holes, is 12 km west of the town – on private land with a small fee for entry – and **Mareeba Wetlands**, a 5,000-acre reserve located 7 km north of Mareeba, then west on Pickford Road from Biboohra, which boasts an impressive list of species, including brolga, sea eagle, frilled lizard and the superbly named bumpy rocket frog. Recommended. ■ *Daily 0830-1600 and guided tours are available, T40932304, www.mareebawetlands.com.au*

Mareeba Heritage Museum and **Tourist Information Centre** is located in Centenary Park, 345 Byrnes Street, www.mareebaheritagecentre.com.au They can assist with local accommodation bookings.

Chillagoe

Colour map 7, grid C2
Population: 500
205 km from Cairns

Chillagoe is somewhat out of character with the rest of the Atherton Tablelands. Given its isolation, yet proximity and access from Cairns, the former mining settlement of Chillagoe presents and ideal opportunity to experience the 'outback' proper, without having to embark on long and often difficult journeys from the coast by 4WD.

Chillagoe is a fascinating little place that combines **mining history** with natural **limestone caves** and **Aboriginal rock paintings**, not to mention some rather eccentric inhabitants. Chillagoe was formerly a cattle station before the discovery of gold in the late 1880s dramatically transformed both the settlement and the landscape. The establishment of rail link in 1900 and a smelter a year after that, gave rise to a resident population of over 1,000 miners. For the next 40 years the area produced almost 10 tonnes of gold and 185 tonnes of silver, as well many more tonnes of copper and lead. Now of course, the boom days are long gone and the population has declined dramatically, yet beyond the hearts of its older residents, it retains a hint of its former importance, in the many wind blown, and sun baked mining relics that remain.

Chillagoe Heritage Museum on Hill Street and the **Queensland Parks and Wildlife Service** office, corner Cathedral and Queen streets, are the best sources of local information. The former offers the best introduction to the settlements mining history and minimal present day operations and they can provide directions to the most obvious mining relics. ■ *Daily 0830-1700. T40947163.* Foremost are the old **smelters** that are located beyond Queen Street, north across Chillagoe Creek, past the lime works. Information is provided at various points for self-tours. QPWS offer 1½-hour guided tours of the limestone caves at 0900 and 1500 from $6. There are more caves and old copper mines about 10 km west of the town at Mungana which is also the location of the Aboriginal **rock paintings**. While in Chillagoe try to visit Tom Prior, the BP Fuel Agent, Aerodrome Street. Old Tom has an interesting collection of old cars, each with a very intriguing story attached, but it is the man himself that is truly entertaining?

Sleeping & eating   A *Chillagoe Cabins*, 22 Queens St, T40947206, chillcab@fastinternet.net.au, offer the best self-contained options. **C-D** *Chillagoe Caves Lodge*, 7 King St, T40947106, is the best budget option, also offering powered and non-powered sites and a restaurant. There are 2 hotel/pubs: *Post Office Hotel*, 37 Queen St, T40947119 and *Chillagoe Hotel*, Tower St, T40947168.

Transport   During the dry season it is negotiable by conventional vehicles and can also be reached by train from Cairns and via Almaden, T132232.

Lake Tinaroo and Danbulla Forest

Barron River Tinaroo Dam was completed in 1958 creating a vast series of flooded valleys that now make up Lake Tinaroo and provide the region with essential irrigation. The lake itself has an astonishing 200 km of shoreline and is a popular spot for watersports, especially fishing for the mammoth barramundi. Some say the lake contains the biggest 'barra' in Australia. The Danbulla Forest that fringes its northern bank, hosts an excellent 28-km unsealed scenic road that winds its way from the dam slipway, from Tolga, to Boar Pocket Road, northeast of Yungaburra.

Colour map 7, grid C3
15 km east of Yungaburra and 61 km southwest of Cairns

Other than the various campsites, viewpoints and short walks on offer, other highlights include **Lake Euramoo**, a picturesque 'double explosion' crater lake, **Mobo Creek Crater**, something of a geological odyssey, and the not to be missed **Cathedral Fig**. Signposted and reached by a five-minute walk this superb example of the strangler fig species is indeed a sight to behold, looking not so much like a cathedral, but like some huge altar stand from which a 1,000 giant candles have slowly melted. The tree – though it is hard to see it as such – is 500-years-old, over 50 m tall and 40 m around the base and is especially worth visiting at dawn, when its many avian inhabitants are full of chatter. Several types of nocturnal possum also inhabit the tree and are best seen with a torch after dark.

From the Cathedral Fig you emerge from the forest on to Boar Pocket Road. The short diversion to the **Haynes Lookout**, left on Boar Pocket Road, heading from the forest towards Gillies Highway, is worthy of investigation. The track itself passes through some beautiful woodland before emerging at the edge of the mountain and the memorable views across the Mulgrave River valley and Bellenden Ker Range. When the winds are right the site is often used by hanggliders. Check out the message written on the launch pad.

For more information on the Danbulla Forest, scenic drive and self-registration campsites ($2) contact the Department of Natural Resources (QPWS), 83 Main Street, Atherton, T40911844 or their Tinaroo Office, T40958459. The area is best explored in your own vehicle or a regional tour.

Sleeping & eating

L *Tinaroo Waters*, 61 Bluewater Dr, T40958425, F40958025, www.tinaroowaters.com.au, is a spacious homestay set lakeside that also offers guided fishing trips. **C-D** *Tinaroo Holiday Park*, Tinaroo Falls Dam, T40958232, offers cabins, units powered and non-powered sites. Basic. 3-star. There is a licensed restaurant nearby, T40958242.

Atherton

Atherton is a major service centre for the Tablelands and was first settled by European and Chinese cedar-cutters in the 1880s. Today its primary industry is dairying and the production of maize, potatoes, nuts and avocados. There is not a great deal to lure the visitor here, except perhaps the unusual **Crystal Caves**, an impressive display of natural crystals and fossils collected over the last 40 years by mineralogist Rene Boissevain. A 45-minute tour of the artificial cave like grotto reveals some spectacular examples including the giant Amethyst geode. ■ *Mon-Fri 0830-1700, Sat 0830-1600, Sun 1000-1600. $11, child $9. T40912365, www.crystalcaves.com.au Shop on site.*

Colour map 7, grid C3
Population: 5,700
94 km from Cairns

The Atherton to Herberton **Historic Steam Railway**, at Platypus Park, is good value with an old loco making the 44-km trip on Wednesdays to Sundays at 1030, returning 1500. It costs from $25. For a little insight into the towns Chinese influence take a look at the **Chinese Temple** next to the **Old**

Post Office Gallery on Herberton Road. The view from **Haloran Hill Lookout**, immediately behind the town is also worth the climb.

Tropical Tableland Promotion Bureau's is located at 42 Mabel Street, Atherton, T40917444, F40917144, www.athertontableland.com.au They can assist with local accommodation and activity bookings.

Sleeping & eating

A *Atherton Blue Gum B&B*, 36 Twelfth Ave, T40915149, www.bnbng.com.au/bluegum, offer, 4WD tours of the area and transfers from Cairns. Non-guests $75 per couple, tours from $180. **C-D** *Mountain View Van Park*, 152 Robert St, Highway One, T/F40914144. 3-star, this option has tidy units, powered and non-powered sites in a nice setting. When it comes to eating options are limited, however given the Chinese influence in the town it is perhaps rude not to try one of the Chinese restaurants: *Atherton*, 18 Main St, T40912585, or *Pagoda*, Maunds Rd, T40914555.

Yungaburra

Colour map 7, grid C3
Population: 1,000
81 km from Cairns

While Kuranda may be the most visited and high profile town in the Atherton Tablelands, sleepy little Yungaburra is without doubt the jewel. Formerly called Allumba it has changed little for over a century and offers a wonderful combination of history and alternative lifestyle and a cool and tranquil retreat from the coast. Added to its impressive gathering of listed **historical buildings** it has a good places to stay, eat and shop and is surrounded by some of the best scenery in the Tablelands. **Lakes Tinaroo**, see page 383, **Barrine** and **Eacham**, see below, are all within a short drive of the village and are a focal point for a number of walks, scenic drives and water-based activities. Yungaburra is also one of the best and most accessible venues in country in which to see that almost surreal quirk of nature, the duck billed **platypus**.

Ins & outs
See Transport, page 386, for details

There is currently no official visitor information centre in the village, however the locals are always glad to help. There is also a useful website, www.yungaburra.com.au Local QWPS office is located at Lake Eacham, T40953786 providing information about campsites and all things environmental.

Sights

Most of the listed historical buildings are constructed from local wood and were built between 1910 and 1920. Two of the finest examples are **St Mark's** and **St Patrick's churches**, on Eacham Road both of which were erected in 1913. Other fine examples are evident on Cedar Street, next to the *Lake Eacham Hotel*. Look out for the Yungaburra Heritage Village leaflet, available from the VICs in Cairns and Atherton, or from most local businesses.

Just a few minutes southwest of the village on Curtain Fig Tree Road is, no surprises here, the **Curtain Fig Tree**, another impressive and ancient example of the strangler species. It is quite different in shape than its close neighbour, the Cathedral Fig in the Dunbulla Forest, see page 383. Again this specimen looks more like the steps of a huge candle factory after a fire than any living thing and it is this perhaps this particular 800-year old tree that is the 'root' of Yungaburra's name, which is Aboriginal for 'fig tree'.

Peterson Creek, that slides gently past the village, is home to several pairs of platypus. The best place to view them is from the bottom and north of Penda Street, at the end of Cedar Street, and the best time is around dawn or sometimes at dusk. Sit quietly beside the river and look for any activity in the grass that fringes the river or on its surface. They are generally well submerged but once spotted are fairly obvious. Provided you are quiet they will generally go about their business, since their eyesight is fairly poor.

A few kilometres east of the village are two volcanic lakes, **Lake Barrine** and **Lake Eacham**. Lake Barrine is the largest and has been a tourist attraction for over 80 years. It's fringed with rainforest and circumvented by a 6-km walking track. Two lofty and ancient kauri pines that are amongst Australia's largest species are located at the start of the track. The long-established *Lake Barrine Rainforest Cruise and Tea House* is nestled on the northern shore and offers 40-minute trips on the lake. ■ *Tours 1015, 1130, 1330 and 1530. $8.50, child $5.50. T40953847. Just off the Gillies Highway.* Just south of Lake Barrine and accessed off the Gillies Highway, or from the Malanda Road, is Lake Eacham. Once again it is surrounded by rainforest and a 3.5-km-walking track and is a favourite spot for a picnic and a cool dip. The most southerly fingers of Lake Tinaroo can also be accessed northeast of the village via Barrine Road.

Sleeping

On Gillies Highway right in the heart of the village you will find a trio of excellent options owned by proud and friendly locals. **LL** *Allumbah Pocket Cottages*, 24-26 Gillies Highway T40953023, F40953300, www.allumbahpocketcottages.com.au, are a cluster of new, spacious and well-appointed, 1-bedroom and fully self-contained cottages complete with spa. The friendly and welcoming owners also offer two other exceptional 2-bedroom cottages, 7/9 Pine St, ideal for the romantic couple. **LL-L** *Eden* House Garden Cottages, 20 Gillies Highway, T40953355, F40953377, www.edenhouse. com.au, is an excellent historic option, offering either deluxe spa cottages or standard cottages which are equally spacious, classy in a quiet garden setting. Fine restaurant and bar on site. **A** *Curtain Fig Motel*, 16 Gillies Highway, T40953168, F40952099, www.curtainfig.com.au Good value spacious self-contained units and one large fully self-contained apartment. A little way out is **LL** *Crater Lakes Rainforest Cottages*, Lot 1, Eacham Close (off Lakes Drive), T40952322, www.craterlakes.com.au In the wooded surrounds of Lake Eacham you will find this luxurious and cosy option.

Back in Yungaburra **C-E** *On the Wallaby Backpackers*, 34 Eacham St, T40500650, www.dreamtimetravel.com.au It is an excellent little backpackers offering dorms, doubles and camping for $10 (pair $15). The decor is all wood and stone giving it a cosy ski-lodge feel, very different from the bustling modern places in Cairns. Plenty of activities are on offer including an exciting range of wildlife and day/night canoeing tours on Lake Tinaroo from $25. Mountain bikes for hire. Pick-ups from Cairns daily. The best budget option. **C-E** *Peeramon Hotel*, located south of Yungaburra on the Gillies Highway, Malanda Rd, T40965873. Historic and congenial, they have perfectly comfortable if basic doubles and singles plus units out the back for only $15 a night. **C-E** *Lake Eacham Caravan Park*, Lakes Drive, 1 km south of Lake Eacham, T40953730. The nearest motor park to Yungaburra. Basic but good value, it has cabins, powered and non-powered sites.

Eating

Eden Garden Cottage Restaurant, 20 Gillies Highway, T40953377. This colonial-style restaurant is the best place in town. Here you can tuck in to such local delights as blue gum steak in a rustic interior or pleasant garden surroundings. *Nick's Swiss-Italian Restaurant*, also on Gillies Highway, T40953330, www.nicksrestaurant.com.au, is another more stylized alternative with live music at the weekends. Open daily (except Wed) for lunch and dinner 1100-2300. For a cheap steak the size of a small continent head for the *Peeramon Hotel* (see Sleeping). *Flynn's Internet Café*, beside the food market on Eacham Rd, T40952235. Good coffee and a value breakfast. Open 0700-1700.

Shopping

Yungaburra markets held on the fourth Sat of the month have a good reputation for homemade arts, crafts, home-grown produce and the odd farm animal. Open 0700-1200. There are a number of quality arts and crafts outlets on Eacham Rd and Gillies Highway including the *Gem Gallery*, 44 Eacham Rd, T40953455.

Cairns to Cape York

Tours & activities Other than the Lake Barrine cruises and walks surrounding both Lake Barrine and Lake Eacham there are also a number of wildlife and canoeing tours on offer. For a spot of night possum spotting contact *Wait-a-while Rainforest Tours*, T40987500, www.wait awhile.com.au, and for excellent backpacker oriented wildlife and day/night canoeing trips contact *On the Wallaby Backpackers* (see Sleeping below). *Wildscapes Safaris*, T40576272, www.wildscapes-safaris.com.au, also offer wildlife tours and specialize in platypus spotting.

Transport The most spectacular way to reach Yungaburra is via the Gillies Highway and Mulgrave River valley just south of Cairns. From the valley floor the road climbs almost 800 m up to the top of the Gilles Range. *Whitecar Coaches*, Trinity Wharf Terminal, T40519533, www.whitecarcoaches.com.au, run daily services to Yungaburra from $26.

Directory **Communcations** Internet: *Flynn's Internet Café*, 17 Eacham Rd, T40952235.

Malanda and Millaa Millaa

Colour map 6, grid A5
18 km south of
Yungaburra

The small village of **Malanda** heralds the start of the famous Tablelands water-falls region. Malanda has its own set of falls but they are actually amongst the least impressive in the group and the village is more famous for milk than water. Dairying in Malanda has always been its raison d'etre. The first herds of cattle were brought by foot from the north of NSW – a journey that took a gruelling 16 months. Today, there are over 190 farmers in the region producing enough milk to fill glasses and breakfast bowls as far away as Alice Springs. The main attraction in Malanda other than a cool dip in the **swimming hole** below the falls is the neighbouring **Malanda Environmental Centre** which has some interesting displays on the geology, climate and natural history of the Tablelands.

A further 24 km south of Malanda is the sleepy agricultural service town of **Millaa Millaa**, which like Malanda has its own waterfalls and is surrounded by fields awash with herds of black and white Friesian cattle. The Millaa Millaa Falls are the first of a trio – the others being the **Zillie Falls** and **Ellinjaa Falls** – which can be explored on a 16-km circuit accessed (and signposted) just east of the town on the Palmerston Highway. The Palmerston Highway, which is a very pleasant drive in itself, then links with the Bruce Highway just north of Innisfail. There are a few lesser-known waterfalls on the way and **Crawford's lookout**, on the left, with its dramatic view through the forest to the North Johnstone River – a favourite spot for rafting.

Sleeping & eating
Your choice of restaurants are confined to a couple of fairly unremarkable options on Main St

Between Malanda and Millaa Millaa (2.5 km on Hogan Road east of Tarzali) are the delightful **LL** *Fur 'n' Feathers Rainforest Tree Houses*, T40965364, rainforest@north. net.au They are a trio of charming fully self-contained pole houses set in the bush offering real peace and quiet and all mod cons including a spa. Perfect for couples. There is also a separate fully self-contained, semi-detached cottage. In Millaa Millaa itself is the cheap and cheery **B** *Millaa Millaa Hotel*, Main St, T40972212, that has basic motel-style units. Home-cooked dinner and light breakfast included. **C-E** *Falls Holiday Park*, Malanda Rd, T40972290. 2 star, basic cabins, powered and non-powered sites and a café.

Mount Hypipamee National Park

Colour map 6, grid A5
24 km south of
Atherton

Mount Hypipamee National Park is a small pocket of dense rainforest with a volcanic **crater lake**, waterfalls and some very special wildlife. During the day the dense forest is a buzz with many exotic avians, like the tame Lewin's honey-eaters, but it is at night that it really comes alive. Armed with a torch and a little

A road with a view

Millaa Millaa Lookout, just to the west of Millaa Millaa on the recently upgraded East Evelyn Road, is said to offer the best view in North Queensland. On a clear day it is indeed memorable encompassing a vast 180-degree vista from the Tablelands to the coast, interrupted only by the Bellenden Ker Range and the two highest peaks in Queensland Mount Bartle Frere (1,622 m) and Mount Bellenden Ker (1,591 m). At a height of 850 m the viewpoint itself offers the best insight as to why the Tablelands are so lush and cool in comparison to the coast.

patience (preferably after midnight) you can see several of the 13 species of **possum** that inhabit the forest, including the coppery brush tail, the green ringtail, and the squirrel glider who leaps and flies from branch to branch. If you are really lucky you may also encounter the parks most famous resident the **Lumholtz's tree kangaroo**, one of only two species of kangaroo that live in trees.

The 95,000-year-old Crater Lake that is in fact a long water-filled volcanic pipe blasted through the granite is a short 10-minute walk from the car park. With its unimaginable depths, algae covered surface and eerie echoes it is quite unnerving spectacle, and seems almost like some horrific natural dungeon. The park has picnic facilities but no camping.

Herberton

Like so many other settlements in the region Herberton owes its existence to mining with the discovery of tin in 1880. For a few decades Herberton was the largest community in the Tablelands with a population of over 8,000, before the resource inevitably was exhausted and the towns of Atherton, Malanda, Mareeba and Millaa Millaa succeeded on the back of agriculture and timber. Although the main street itself could hardly be more timeless or Australian, the town boasts an interesting **Historical Village and Museum**, Broadway Street, from $10. It has over 20 listed buildings, including a single composite of the original 17 pubs. Although not often touted as its main tourist attraction it is perhaps the copious purple flowering **jacaranda trees**, that flower during September and October, that prove to be Herberton's major draw card. The Atherton to Herberton **Historic Steam Railway** provides an attractive alternative to arriving by road, with return trips from Atherton on lovingly restored loco on Wednesdays to Sundays, at 1030 returning at 1500, from $25. It allows about an hour in the village.

Colour map 6, grid A4
Population: 1,500
122 km from Cairns

Ravenshoe and beyond

At over 900 m Ravenshoe is the highest settlement in Queenstown. Although once a bustling and at times controversial timber town, it is now a fairly sleepy little place used as a base to explore the surrounding waterfalls and rainforest. **Millstream Falls**, 5 km west of Ravenshoe on the Kennedy Highway (on the right), are the widest in Australia, while further west the steamy **Innot Hot Springs** offer ideal therapy for the weary driver. *Railco* operate a lovingly restored 1920's steam loco called the **Millstream Express** from Grigg Street, Ravenshoe, north to Tumoulin 7 km away, at weekends from April to January. Although not meant as a tourist attraction, the recently developed **wind farm** close to town on Windy Hill, of all places, is proving popular. VIC has details of accommodation, Moore Street, T40977700, toptown@ledanet.com.au

Colour map 6, grid A4
Population: 850
147 km from Cairns

From Ravenshoe the Kennedy Highway leaves the Atherton Tablelands behind and turns its attentions west in to classic outback country and the endless horizons of the **Gulf Savannah**.

Undara Lava Tubes on the edge of the **Undara Volcanic National Park**, 150 km south of Ravenshoe, are an amazing 190,000-year-old volcanic feature that is well worth the journey. There are regular guided tours available, also available from Cairns, as well as a licensed restaurant, pool and five standards of accommodation (A-E) from charming train carriages to a swag tent village and powered sites, www.undara.com.au

Cairns to Port Douglas

The 70-km drive from Cairns to Port Douglas provides spectacular ocean views beyond a string of Northern Beach resorts the largest and most popular of which is **Palm Cove** offering something that Cairns does not in the form of a pretty beach and safe swimming. Just beyond Buchan Point is **Ellis Beach** a popular spot for swimming and camping.

Hartley's Creek Crocodile Farm, 40 km north of Cairns, is one of the best wildlife attractions in the region. Long-term resident and near octogenarian croc 'Charlie', was, until his death in September 2000, the star exhibit. Despite the loss, there are still plenty of heavyweights of equally rebellious attitude that are fed daily at 1100 and 1500. This spectacle, involving half a chicken and an awful lot of teeth, provides a very fine example of why you should always follow government advice to never dangle your legs or arms over the sides of boats! There are of course plenty of other animals on show. At the entrance to the farm is the rather monstrous plastic model of 7.9-m saltwater croc, which we are reminded pales into insignificance in comparison to one that was shot by local croc hunter Mrs Palowski in Kurumba in 1957. ■ *Daily 0830-1700. $18, child $9. T40553576, www.hartleyscreek.com.au*

Just north of Hartley's Creek is the **Rex Lookout** from where you can get your first glimpse of Port Douglas and the forested peaks of the Daintree National Park and Cape Tribulation in the distance. If the winds are right you may also encounter hanggliders launching themselves off the cliff.

Sleeping
& eating

LL *Thala Beach Lodge*, T40985700, F40985837, www.thalabeach.com.au A very popular, award-winning establishment, that enjoys its very own peninsula and beach just south of port Douglas. 85 bungalows are scattered around the impressive main lodge in a quiet bush setting. It is very popular with couples and honeymooners, so therefore not ideal if you are single or love lost. Perhaps the only criticism is the restaurant that is a tad too expensive for what is offered. **L-F** *Ellis Beach Oceanfront Bungalows and Caravan Park*, 30 km north of Cairns, T40553538. A fine range of options from fully self-contained bungalows and cabins, to units, powered and non-powered sites, all close to the beach. There are cooking facilities and a restaurant nearby.

Port Douglas

Colour map 7, grid C3
Population: 3,600
61 km from Cairns,
1,794 km from
Brisbane

Almost since their inception the coastal ports of Cairns and Port Douglas have slugged it out as to who is the most important. Although Cairns has gone on to become a world famous heavyweight, Port Douglas, lesser known and lighter weight with a village feel, has put up a good fight given it's equal proximity to the **Barrier Reef***, its own swathe of* **golden sand***, and being just a stones throw from the wonderful Mossman Gorge, Daintree and Cape Tribulation just around the* *corner. Port Douglas is a classier option than its rival, however it has lost much of its youthful charm with the building of massive developments and multi-million dollar resorts. With its boutiques, fine restaurants and upmarket accommodation, isn't particularly a place for the budget conscious.*

Getting there Port Douglas is easily accessed from Cairns with regular airport shuttle buses from Cairns International Airport and frequent bus services from the city itself. There are also regular connections with Mosman, Daintree, Cape Tribulation and Cooktown. **Getting around** The main amenities are on and around Macrossan St. To visit areas further afield bike hire is a good option. **Tourist information** Port Douglas Tourist Information Centre, 23 Macrossan St, T40995599, F40995070, is an independent and can therefore, sometimes, be biased. Open daily 0800-1800. Port Douglas and Daintree Tourism official website is www.pddt.com.au The nearest QPWS office is in Mossman, 1 Front St, T40982188.

Ins & outs
See Transport, page 394, for further details

History

Surprisingly perhaps, Port Douglas was at one time the largest port in far North Queensland and in direct competition with Cairns, equally if not more important. This was thanks to one Christie Palmerston, whom in 1877, cut a vital link through the rainforests to the newly discovered Hodgkinson River gold fields on the northern fringe of the Atherton Tablelands. Almost before the last tree was felled, hoards of itinerant hopefuls descended on the new port and within a single decade the population reached over 8,000 souls – over twice that of today. But history also tells us that the new settlement was a very disorganised and transitory place, with little in the way of civil authority. Nowhere, was this more evident than in the inability to settle on a name. For many years it enjoyed a level of anonymity through various names including Island Point, Terrigal, Port Owen and Salisbury, before a posse of government officials arrived to christen it Port Douglas in honour of John Douglas, the then Governor of Queensland.

Sights

Like Cairns, Port Douglas places great emphasis on reef and rainforest tours with only a few attractions in the town itself pulling in the crowds. See page 392 for details of the activities available in the area.

Rainforest Habitat, located at the southern entrance to the town, is well worth a visit, offering a fine introduction to the regions rich biodiversity and natural habitats. There are over 180 species housed in three main habitat enclosures – 'wetlands', 'rainforest' and 'grassland' with many of the tenants being tame and easily approachable. As usual the true stars are the crocs, the koalas and the very leggy and endangered cassowaries. 'Breakfast with the Birds' presents a unique way to start the day. ■ *Daily 0800-1730. $20, child $10. Breakfast with the Birds is available 0800-1100. $34, child $17. T40993235, www.rainforest habitat.com.au Getting there: 6 km from the town centre at the junction of Captain Cook Highway and Port Douglas Rd – self drive or as part of a regional tour.*

Rainforest Habitat

Given Cairns man-made excuse for a real beach, Port Douglas is rather proud of its Four Mile Beach, which is both scenic and inviting to cosmopolitan crowds of topless backpackers and the more conservative resort clients. Many water-based activities are on offer for those not satisfied with merely

Four Mile Beach

Cairns to Cape York

Port Douglas

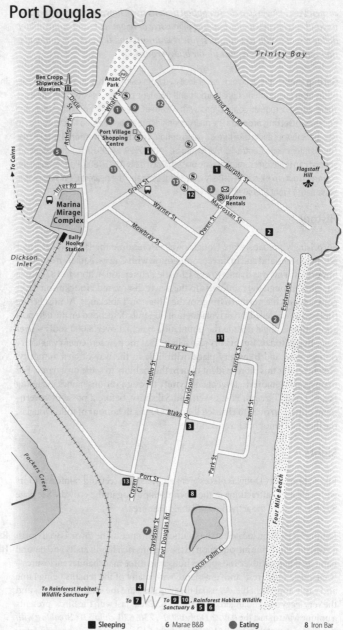

Trinity Bay

Ben Cropp Shipwreck Museum

Anzac Park

Wharf St

Dixie St

Ashford Av

To Cairns

Antet Rd

Marina Mirage Complex

Bally Hooley Station

Dickson Inlet

Port Village Shopping Centre

Island Point Rd

Murphy St

Flagstaff Hill

Uptown Rentals

Grant St

Warner St

Owen St

Macrossan St

Mowbray St

Esplanade

Beryl St

Mudlo St

Davidson St

Garrick St

Sand St

Blake St

Park St

Port St

Craven Cl

Packers Creek

Four Mile Beach

Port St

Davidson St

Port Douglas Rd

Cocos Palm Cl

To Rainforest Habitat Wildlife Sanctuary

To 7   To 9 10, Rainforest Habitat Wildlife Sanctuary & 5 6

N

| 0 metres | 200 |
| 0 yards | 200 |

■ Sleeping
1 Boathouse
2 Coconut Grove Motel
3 Coral Apartments
4 Dougie's Nomads Backpackers
5 Glengarry Caravan Park

6 Marae B&B
7 Port Douglas
8 Port Sea
9 Radisson Treetops Resort
10 Sheraton Mirage
11 Tropic Breeze
12 Villa San Michele
13 YHA Port 'O' Call

● Eating
1 1878 Court House Hotel
2 Beaches Café
3 Café Macrossan
4 Catalina
5 Combined Club
6 EJ's Takeaway
7 Going Bananas

8 Iron Bar
9 Java Blue
10 Mangiare
11 Mocas Pies
12 Nautilus
13 Portofinos

sunbathing or swimming. A net is placed just offshore to ward off box jellyfish and other stingers (October to May) and lifeguards are usually in attendance (always swim between the flags). Before picking your spot on the sand you might like to enjoy the picture postcard view of the beach from Flagstaff Hill, turn right at the bottom of Mossman Street, then follow Wharf Street on to Island point Road.

Back down off Wharf Street on the Anzac Park Pier is the **Ben Cropp Shipwreck Museum**, which displays an interesting collection of material about local shipwrecks. ■ *Daily 0900-1700, $5.50.* Anzac park also hosts the weekly **market** held every Sunday. It is a colourful affair that offers everything from sarongs to freshly squeezed orange juice. More expensive permanent boutiques are housed in the delightfully cool **Marina Mirage Complex**, Wharf Street. For further informtion see www.marinamiragepd.com.au

Anzac Park Pier

Essentials

As you might expect there is plenty of choice in Port Douglas with the emphasis placed heavily on a mind-boggling choice of very samey 4-star resorts and apartments. Thankfully however, budget travellers are also well catered for with a scattering of good backpackers, cheap motels and motor parks. Rates are naturally competitive and more expensive in the high season but at any time you are advised to shop around for special rates, especially in the 'wet' (Dec-Mar).

Sleeping
■ *On map, page 390*
See inside front cover
for price categories

LL *Sheraton Mirage*, that takes up a large portion of the eastern side of the peninsula, T40995888, F40994424, www.sheraton.com.au/mirageportdouglas This is the jewel in the crown of resorts and the one that started it all in the mid 1980. Sumptuous, it offers just about all a body could want, all within yards of Four Mile Beach, including top-class restaurants, a golf course and a pool that just has to be seen to be believed. At the top end of this range. Davidson St is lined with other slightly cheaper options including **LL** *Radisson Treetops Resort*, T40304333/F40304323, www.radisson.com/ treetopsau, and the very congenial **LL** *Port Sea*, 76 Davidson St, T40872000, F40872001, www.theportsea.com.au In the centre of the village there are a number of well appointed, self-contained, boutique apartment blocks with **LL** *Boathouse*, 41-43 Murphy St, T40998800, F40998855, www.boathouse.com.au, and the **LL** *Villa San Michele*, 39-41 Macrossan St, T40994088, F40994975, www.villasanmichele. com.au, both recommended. For a cheaper fully self-contained apartment option try the excellent **L** *Coral Apartments*, corner of Blake and Davidson sts, T40996166, F40996177, wwwportdouglascoralapartments.com.au The place is great value, has a nice quiet atmosphere, attractive pool and very friendly, helpful hosts. **L** *Marae B&B*, Lot 1, Ponzo Rd, Shannonvale, T40984900, F40984099, www.internetnorth.com.au/ marae This B&B provides an ideal sanctuary, yet is still within reach of Port Douglas. A beautiful place offering 3 very comfortable en suite rooms, 2 king and 1 double.

A *Port Douglas Motel*, 9 Davidson St, T40995248. 3 star, well-positioned. **A-B** *Coconut Grove Motel*, 58 Macrossan St, T40985124. 2 star. There are 2 good backpackers in the town, almost within a stone's throw of one another, just off Davidson St. **A-E** *YHA Port 'O' Call*, Port St, T40995422, F40995495, www.portcall.com.au, has excellent motel style doubles, budget dorms and a fine restaurant/bar, internet. **C-F** *Dougie's Nomads Backpackers*, 111 Davidson St, T40996200, www.dougies.com.au, has a/c doubles/twins, dorms and van/camp sites, bar, bike hire, internet. Both hostels provide free pick-ups from Cairns. Other than *Dougie's* there are several choices for powered/non-powered sites and motor parks. **B-F** *Glengarry Caravan Park*, Mowbray

Cairns to Cape York

River Rd, just short of Port Douglas, off the captain Cook Highway, T40985922, Glen-garry@internetnorth.com.au It has fully self-contained en suite cabins, pow-ered/non-powered sites, with a good camp kitchen and a pool. **C-E** *Tropic Breeze Van Village*, 24 Davidson St, closer to the centre of town, and only a short stroll from Four Mile Beach, T40995299. 3 star, it offers cabins, powered/non-powered sites and a camp kitchen.

Eating

● On map, page 390
See inside front cover
for price categories

Plenty of options,
mostly centred along
Macrossan Street

Expensive *Nautilus Restaurant*, 17 Murphy St, T40995330. Touted as providing a unique outdoor tropical, culinary experience and the choice of Bill Clinton during his recent stay. Here you can dine on exquisite dishes with an emphasis on local seafood, under the stars and a canopy of palms. For wildlife of a different nature why not con-sider dinner at the **Rainforest Habitat Wildlife Sanctuary**, T40993235. They offer an entertaining 'Habitat after Dark' dining experience under the gaze of creatures of the night, from $39,child $19.50. Bookings essential.

Mid-range *Going Bananas*, 87 Davidson St, T40995400. Aptly named this more laid back and infamous option is the highly entertaining The owner is a true eccentric and it will almost certainly prove to be a memorable experience. Open daily from 1800. Other more centrally located options worth considering are *Portofinos*, 31 Macrossan St, T40995458 (daily from 1800), with its traditional dishes of seafood and excellent cur-ries; *Mangiare*, 18 Macrossan St, T40994054, an Italian with a good reputation, and the long-established *Catalina*, 22 Wharf St, T40995287, Tue-Sun from 1800, that offers a varied and imaginative menu.

Cheap *The Combined Club*, Wharf St, T40995553, down on the wharf is unbeatable for the waterfront view and for value . *Port' O Call*, at the *YHA*, is also excellent value and has a nice laid-back atmosphere. *Court House Hotel*, corner of Macrossan and Wharf sts, T40995181, for pub food, popular. *Iron Bar*, 5 Macrossan St, T40994776, is well known for its imaginatively named and generous Australian dishes. *Beaches Café*, on The Esplanade, over looking Four Mile Beach, T40994998 (daily from 0700). For a value breakfast and lots of tropical atmosphere. *Java Blue*, Shop 3, 2 Macrossan St, T04995814, and *Café Macrossan*, 42 Macrossan St, T40994372, currently have the edge for good coffee.

Seriously cheap *EJ's Takeaway*, next to the VIC on Macrossan St, for no nonsense, post pub munchies. And what ever you do don't leave Port Douglas without trying the famous and delicious *Mocas Pies*, Warner St (behind *Coles Supermarket*).

Bars & clubs Although rumour has it that major renovations are afoot, as it stands, *1878 Court House Hotel*, corner of Macrossan and Wharf sts, T40995181, www.courthousehotel. com.au, is a fine place to enjoy a cool 'stubbie' (beer) or lunch/diner in the beer garden, listening to the dulcet tones of local musoes singin' the blues (Mon evenings). Wed-Sun sees the more traditional contemporary bands (with an Aussie slant). Open daily 1000-2400. Almost next-door is the highly characterful and aptly named *Iron Bar*, 5 Macrossan St, 40994776. On top of its regular live musical offerings it demonstrates the rather dubious art of Cane Toad Racing, Tue/Thu at 2100 $3 (daily 1000-0200). There are 2 restaurant/clubs in **Mirage Marina Complex** that will keep you 'boppin' well in to the wee hours – *The Vue* (*Maximus Café*), T40995323, open until 0200, and *Nicky G's Sports Saloon*, which closes at 0500.

Tours & activities **Diving and snorkelling** All the major reef operators are based at the Marina Mirage Wharf, Wharf St. Almost all of the Cairns based companies listed in the Cairns section, page 369, also provide transfers from Port Douglas. The vast majority combine cruising with snorkelling and/or diving with others being dive specialists. The main operator in Port Douglas is the long established and highly professional **Quicksilver**, T40872100, www.quicksilver-cruises.com.au, that shuttle tourists out to their own pontoon on the edge of Agincourt Reef, where you can spend the day diving, snorkelling or sunbathing. The basic day-cruise with a buffet lunch costs $161, child $83. Introductory dives from $113, certified dives from $71, scenic flights from $98. Departs 1000 daily. *Quicksilver* also operate a luxury sailing catamaran, the *Wavedancer* to the Low Isles on the inner reef where independent (or guided) snorkelling and guided beach walks are available. Day package from $110, child $57.50, lunch included (transfer only $65, child $35). Departs 1000 daily. Other options on board slightly smaller vessels include: *Aristocat*, T40994727, www.aristocat.com.au, from $129, child $89, intro dive from $175, certified from $169, 2 1-day cruises with 4 dives from $339; *Calypso*, T40993377, www.calypsocharters.com.au, from $125, child $90, introductory dive, from $175, certified from $165, departs 0845, returns 1645. Another option are the more personable cruises on board smaller vessels including *Wavelength* (30 passengers max, launch), from $130, child $90, departs 0830, returns 1630, T40995031, www.wavelength-reef. com.au; *Sailaway* (27 passengers maximum, sail catamaran), 4 hr to Low Isles, (equipped for boom-netting) from $99, child $59, T40995599, www.reefandrainforest. com.au; *Personal Touch* (16 passengers maximum, launch), snorkel and dive specialists (including night dives), from $125, child $85, T40994158, www.divingport douglas.com; *Animal Farm* (12 passengers maximum ocean racing yacht), half-day $60, child $42, full-day $115, child $84, T40996277, www.pdsail.com.au; *Haba Dive*, Bally Hooley Train Station, Marina Mirage, T40995254, www.habadive.com.au, enjoy a good reputation in the region. Intro dive from $190, certified from $170 and snorkelling from $130.

Fishing   There are a posse of charter boats available to take you fishing for a range of exotics including coral trout and red emperors, including the daringly named *Hooker Too*, T40995136, *MV Norseman*, T40995031 and compact *Dragon Lady*, T0418298412. A full day will cost around $130. To hire your own pontoon boat or dinghy contact *Port Douglas Boat Hire*, T40996277, or *Out 'n' About*, T40985204, from $20 per hr.

Horse trekking   *Wonga Beach Equestrian Centre*, T40987583, offer entertaining rides along Wonga Beach (20 km north), including Port Douglas transfers from $75, 3 hr. For inland adventures including the early pioneer 'Bump Track', contact *Mowbray Valley Trail Rides*, T40993268, half-day from $88, child $77, full day from $125, child $110. Suitable for beginners.

Para sailing and jet ski   *Extra Action Water Sports*, based on the first jetty north of the Marina Mirage Complex, T40993175, offer 'fast' 6-hr trips to the Low Isles and the wonderfully quiet Snapper Island from $130, parasailing from $70, and jet bike hire from $70 (30 mins). Combination packages are also available. For a similar range and a spot of 'bumpa tubing' contact *Get High Parafly*, Mirage Marina, from $30, T40996366.

Wildlife   Port Douglas based companies include *BTS Tours*, 49 Macrossan St, T40995665, www.btstours.com.au, that offer full day trips to Kuranda (from $90), Daintree/Cape Tribulation (from $122) and 2-day 4WD Cooktown trips from $210. *Reef and Rainforest Connections*, 8/40 Macrossan St, T40995599, www.reefandrainforest. com.au, offer a wider range of trips at a similar price. *Daintree Adventures*, T40982808, offer a range of 'wildlife attraction' packages from $35. For a personalised, authentic and informative look at the Mossman Gorge through aboriginal eyes, contact Hazel, *Native Guide Safari Tours*, T40982206, www.nativeguidesafaritours.com.au, full-day from $120, child $80 ($130 includes ferry transfer from Cairns).

Almost all the tour companies mentioned in the Cairns section offer pick-ups in Port Douglas

Transport

During the wet season (November- March) road conditions can be treacherous. For up-to-date conditions and flood warnings, T40516711

Air Port Douglas is accessed from **Cairns International Airport**. Airport Shuttle, T40995950, offers services at least every hour daily from 0630-1630, $22, child $11. **Bus** *Coral Coaches*, Port Douglas Local Shuttle, T40995351, www.coralcoaches. com.au, run regular local bus services to the **Cairns City**, **Cairns Airport**, **Mossman**, **Daintree** and **Cape Tribulation** and also long-distance services to **Cooktown** (Wed/Fri/Sun). *Express Chauffeured Coaches*, 5 Opal St, also offer transits to/from **Cairns**, T40985473. The main bus stops are on Grant St and at the Marina Mirage (Wharf) Complex. **Car** Hire from *Port Douglas Car Rental*, 2/79 Davidson St, T40994988, from $64 per day, 4WD from $99. *Crocodile Car Rentals*, 2/50 Macrossan St, T40995555. *Holiday Car Hire*, 54 Macrossan St, have 4WDs from $72 per day and mokes from $50. Car servicing and breakdown from *Mossman Towing*, 23 Mill St, Mossman, T40982848. **Cycle** Hire from *Port Douglas Bike Hire*, 40 Macrossan St, T40995799. Half-day from $10, full-day from $14, week from $59. *Bike 'n' Hike* (specialist mountain bikes), T40994000. Full-day from $16.50. **Ferry** *Quicksilver* run a daily ferry ('Wave Pierce') service from Marina Mirage, Wharf St, Port Douglas to Marlin Marina, **Cairns**, $23 one-way, T40872100. **Train** The quaint *Bally Hooley Train* runs regularly from the Mirage Marina Complex to Rainforest Habitat Wildlife Sanctuary, from $4 return. **Taxi** *Port Douglas Taxis*, 45 Warner St, T40995345, (24 hr).

Directory

Banks Macrossan St or in the Port Village Centre. **Communications** Internet: *Uptown Rentals*, Macrossan St, T40995568. Open daily 0900-2200. *Cyberworld Internet Café*, 38 Macrossan St, T40995661. **Post office**: 5 Owen St,T40995210. Open Mon-Fri 0900-1700, Sat 0900-1200. **Medical services** Chemist: *Macrossan St Pharmacy*, 13/14 Port Village Centre, T40995223. **Medical centres**: Port Village Medical Centre, Shop 17, Port Village Shopping Centre, Macrossan St, T40995043, 24 hrs. Open Mon-Fri 0800-1800, Sat/Sun 0900-1200. **Hospital**: Mossman, T40982444. **Useful numbers** Police: Wharf St, T40995220. RACQ: T131111.

Mossman

Colour map 7, grid C3
Population: 1770
21 km from Port Douglas, 75 km from Cairns

Built on the back of the sugar cane industry in 1880s Mossman sits on the banks of the Mossman River and has one of the world's most exotic tropical gardens on its back door in the form of the **Daintree Wilderness National Park**. Although the 80 year old, fern covered, **Tall Raintrees** that form a cosy canopy on its northern fringe are a sight in themselves it is the **Mossman Gorge**, located 5 km west of the town that is its greatest attraction. Here, the Mossman River falls towards the town fringed with rainforest and networked with a series of short walks. Many combine a walk with another big attraction – the cool swimming holes. Although the walks are excellent, if you are fit and careful, try following the river upstream for about 2 km. This will give you an ideal opportunity to see perhaps the forest and the region's most famous mascot – the huge Ulysses blue butterfly. They regularly flit and fuss up and down the river's corridor in search of food plants and, of course, each other. For Daintree National Park and local walks information contact the QPWS office in Cairns, T40466600.

Sleeping & eating

LL *Silky Oaks Lodge*, located just north of the town, T40981666, F40981983, www.poresorts.com.au The most up-market accommodation in the immediate. It offers 60 excellent freestanding en suite chalets doubles (some with spa) and a fine restaurant. Complimentary activities and pick-ups are also available. **A-E** *Red Backs Resort*, 17 Oasis Dr, a short stroll from Wonga Beach north of the town, T40987871, F40987520, www.redbacks.com.au, This little-known, excellent budget resort has modern, spotless and great value suites, en suite doubles and dorms rooms, with excellent facilities. Pool, café, internet. Tour bookings and pick-ups are available. There is no campsite at Mossman Gorge. *O'Malley's Irish Pub and Hotel*, 2 Front St, Mossman, T40981410, is something of a local institution, serving good value pub meals.

Just short of the gorge car park is the base of ***Kuku-Yalanji Dreamtime Tours*** that offer excellent Aboriginal cultural awareness walks that will enlighten you on the use of certain plants for medicinal purposes. Walks depart at 1000/1200/1400, 2 hrs, from $16.50, child $8.25. There is also a shop, gallery open daily 0900-1600. Pick-ups from Port Douglas 0930, from $40.70, includes walk and refreshments, T40982595, www.internetnorth.com.au/yalanji

Tours & activities

Coral Coaches, 37 Front St, T40995351, offer regular services to Cairns and Port Douglas. The tour companies in Mossman, like most others, include the Mossman Gorge on most of their northbound tours.

Transport

Daintree

The tiny, former timber town of Daintree sits at the end of the Mossman- Daintree Road, sandwiched between the western and eastern blocks of the **Daintree National Park**. The village exudes a quaint and original charm, quite unlike the touristical metropolis to the south. At the edge of the village lies its biggest local attraction – the croc infested meanderings of the **Daintree River**.

Colour map 7, grid C3
Population: 100
111 km north of Cairns

Centred around Stewart Street – and an enormous model barramundi fish – is a general store, Bushman's Lodge, a small timber museum, a couple of restaurants, a school and a caravan park. All combine to make a brief visit, until embarking on a leisurely cruise on the river in search of 'Salties' – the gargantuan **crocodiles** that make it their camouflage and their home. There are now nearly ten cruise options/operators available, all of which ply the river from Daintree village to the coast, several times a day. You can either pick up the cruise near the village itself or at various points south to the Daintree/Cape Tribulation ferry crossing, but most people arrive on pre-organized tours. For independent choice and bookings call in at the General Store.

There are two sources of information in Daintree, both independent and both on Stewart Street: Daintree Tourist Information Centre, T40986120, www.daintreevillage.asn.au and the older General Store Information Office, T40986146, www.daintreestore.com.au Both open daily.

LL *Daintree Eco Lodge and Spa*, 20 Daintree Rd (3 km south of the village), T40986100, F40986200, www.daintree-ecolodge.com.au It enjoys a good reputation and has 15 luxury, serviced villas set in the rainforest, a specialist spa and a top class restaurant. There are a few good B&Bs in and around the village. **A** *Red Mill House*, T/F40986233, redmill@internetnorth.com.au Right in the heart this very pleasant and friendly option offers various well-appointed rooms, some with shared facilities and some with en suites (separate from the main house). Overall the place has a wonderfully peaceful atmosphere with lovely gardens and plenty of wildlife that you can watch from the deck. Good value. **A** *Kenadon Homstead Cabins*, Dagmar St, T/F40986142, kenadon@internetnorth.com.au, has neat, double and single self-contained cabins. Breakfast included. **L** *River Home Cottages*, Upper Daintree Rd, 5 km the west of the village, T40986225, www.riverhomecottages.com.au There are 3 good fully self-contained cottages on a working farm in very quiet surroundings, spa. **D-F** *Daintree Riverview Caravan Park*, 2 Stewart St, T40986119, is aging a little but has on-site vans, powered and non-powered sites right in the heart of the village.

Sleeping

Cairns to Cape York

Eating   *Baaru Restaurant*, *Eco Lodge Resort*, T40986100. The priciest in town offering good contemporary Australian cuisine. *Big Barramundi BBQ Garden*, 12 Stewart St, T40986186, is more affordable and convenient situated in the centre of town and offers fine barramundi dishes . *Jacana's Restaurant*, across the road, T40986146, also offers good barramundi dishes and serves fine bottomless cups of local Daintree tea. *Daintree Tea House*, near Barrats Creek Bridge, Daintree Rd, T40986161, long-established and so something of a local institution. *Daintree Coffee Shop*, Stewart St, next door to the booking and information offices in the village. Good coffee.

Tours &   The largest and longest serving operator is *Daintree Connection*, T40986120, offer-
activities   ing 2 cruises. The most popular is their 1½-hr River Cruise that departs from the vil-
Pick-ups and day   lage on the hour from 1030-1600, from $20, child $7. The second is a 2½-hr Estuary
tours from Cairns or   Cruise that explores the lower reaches and the mouth of the river. It departs from the
Port Douglas are   ferry crossing at 1330 daily, from $28,child $13. *Daintree Wildlife Safari*, based at the
available   General Store, 1 Stewart St, T40986125, dwsafari@internetnorth. com.au, offer 1½-hr
Croc Spot cruises on the hour from 0930-1530, from $20, child $7 and 1-hr cruises on
the hour from 1000-1600, from $17, child $6. Cruise and walk options, 0800-1000 or
1600-1800, cost from $30, child $20. *Daintree Rainforest River Trains*, T40907676,
dntrain@oze mail.com.au, operate a sort of multiple carriage affair from the ferry
crossing on a 2-hr cruise at 1030 and 1330, from $28, child $14. Smaller operators
include *Daintree Lady*, T40986138, www.daintreerivercruises.com.au, which is a
modern 2-storied vessel offering more elevated views. It departs from Daintree Village, 7 times a day on either a 1-hr or 1½-hr tour, from $16.50 ($22), child $7 ($10).
Lunch cruises are also available daily at 1245, from $32. *Chris Dahlberg's River Tours*,
T40987997, chris@internetnorth.com.au, offer an excellent dawn cruise (departs
0600 Nov-Mar and 0630 Apr-Oct), with an emphasis on bird spotting, from $35. Rec-
ommended. *Nice 'n' Easy Cruises*, T40987456, also offer 1½-hr cruises from $22, or a
Sunset Dinner Cruise with BBQ barramundi from $60. *Daintree River Fishing and
Photography Tours*, T40907776, based in Mossman, offer half or full day/night
tours/cruises (including crocodile night spotting) from $65, coastal fishing from
$120. Daintree born and bred **Jamie Beitzel**, T40907638, offers fishing and sightsee-
ing trips, from 4 to 8 hrs, from $65 ($120).

Transport   *Coral Coaches*, 37 Front St, Mossman, T40995351, offer regular bus services to **Cairns**
and **Port Douglas**. Like most other tour companies *Coral Coaches* include Daintree and
its various river cruise options on most of their north bound tours. Note road conditions
around Daintree can be treacherous in the wet season (Dec-Mar). For road information, T40516711.

Cape Tribulation

Colour map 7, grid C3   *Although Cape Tribulation is the name attributed to a small settlement and
Population: 600*   *headland that forms the main tourist focus of the region, the term itself is loosely
140 km from Cairns*   *used to describe a 40-km stretch of coastline within* **Daintree National Park** *and
the start of the* **Bloomfield Track** *to Cooktown. Captain Cook bestowed the label
'Tribulation' upon the region, just before his ship Endeavour ran aground
off-shore in 1770, when, in his own words "all our troubles began".*

*In many ways Cooks misfortune, the name and others like it – Mount Sorrow,
Mount Misery and Darkie's Downfall – are indeed fitting for a place of such wild
and, at times, inhospitable beauty. A place that is still remote and unconquered,
where we can only celebrate and muse with awe at the meeting of dense primeval
rainforest and the Great Barrier Reef. Rainforest so rich in flora and fauna that*

new species are still being discovered today and collectively, a biological 'spring' so rich, that it is now known to have created the watershed of much of Australia's modern day biodiversity. So whether it is the spectacle of nature's palette, or chance encounters with resident wildlife, or merely perhaps, the near constant, uneasy feeling that if you stray too far off the road you would never be seen again, the inherent atmosphere of this place will, in no uncertain terms, remind you that you are indeed, just a tiny mark on the surface of nature's bigger picture.

Detailed information can be obtained from the VICs in Port Douglas or Cairns. Local information is available from Daintree Rainforest Environment Centre or Bat House (see below). For walks information contact the QPWS office in Cairns, T40466600. Australian Rainforest Foundation website, www.wettropics.com.au, is also useful.

Ins & outs
See Transport, page 400, for details

Cape Tribulation

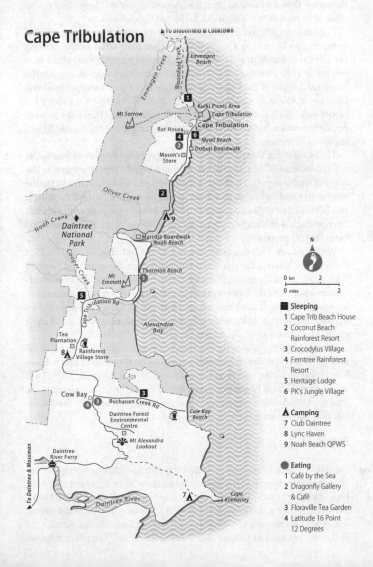

▲ To Bloomfield & Cooktown

Emmagen Creek
Bloomfield Track
Emmagen Beach

Mt Sorrow ▲

1 Kulki Picnic Area
Cape Tribulation
Cape Tribulation

Bat House
4
2
6 Myall Beach
Dubuji Boardwalk
Mason's Store

Oliver Creek
2
▲ 9

Noah Creek
Daintree National Park
Cooper Creek
Marrdja Boardwalk
Noah Beach

Thornton Beach
Mt Emmett ▲
1

5
Cape Tribulation Rd

Alexandra Bay

Tea Plantation
Rainforest Village Store
8 ▲

Cow Bay
3
4 3 Buchanan Creek Rd
Daintree Forest Environmental Centre
Cow Bay Beach
Mt Alexandra Lookout

Daintree River Ferry
▲

To Daintree & Mossman

Daintree River

7 ▲
Cape Kimberley

N
0 km 2
0 miles 2

■ Sleeping
1 Cape Trib Beach House
2 Coconut Beach Rainforest Resort
3 Crocodylus Village
4 Ferntree Rainforest Resort
5 Heritage Lodge
6 PK's Jungle Village

▲ Camping
7 Club Daintree
8 Lync Haven
9 Noah Beach QPWS

● Eating
1 Café by the Sea
2 Dragonfly Gallery & Café
3 Floraville Tea Garden
4 Latitude 16 Point 12 Degrees

Cairns to Cape York

Sights

Five kilometres beyond the ferry crossing, the Cape Tribulation Road climbs steadily over the densely forested Waluwurriga Range to reach the **Mount Alexandra Lookout**, that offers the first glimpse of the coast and the Daintree River mouth. Turning back inland and 2 km past the lookout, is the turn-off (east) to the **Daintree Forest Environmental Centre**, that features excellent displays on the local flora and fauna, with the added attraction of a 400-m boardwalk where guided walks are available and a 25-m tower set amidst the forest offers a bird's-eye view of the forest canopy. There is also a very congenial café on site from which to sit back and let the forest wildlife pervade the senses. ■ *Daily 0830-1700, $15, child $7.50.*

Back on Cape Tribulation Road and just beyond the centre, is the small settlement of **Cow Bay** with its attractive, namesake bay and beach that can be reached by road 6km to the east on Buchanan Creek Road.

Continuing north you are then given another interesting reminder of being in the tropics by passing a well-manicured **tea plantation** before crossing Cooper Creek and hitting the coast below Mount Emmett. Oliver Creek then sees the first of a duo of excellent boardwalks, which provides insight into the botanical delights of the forest and mangrove swamps. **Marrdja** boardwalk takes about 45 minutes and is well worth a look. From here it is about 9 km before you reach the settlement of Cape Tribulation. Here, the second, equally interesting boardwalk **Dubuji** features a 1.2-km walk, once again taking about 45 minutes.

The headland at Cape Tribulation is also well worthy of investigation, as are its two beautiful beaches – **Emmagen** and **Myall** – that sit either side like two golden bookends. The Kulki picnic area and lookout is located at the southern end of Emmagen Beach and is signposted just beyond the village. Just beyond that the Kulki turn-off, 150 m, heralds the start of the **Mount Sorrow** track, a challenging 3.5-km ascent rewarded with spectacular views from the 650-m summit.

While in Cape Tribulation be sure to visit the **Bat House**, opposite *PK's Backpackers*. There, although you won't encounter the saviour of Gotham City, you will find the saviours of the local bat population, in the form of volunteers whom tend the needs of injured, orphaned and, very aptly named 'flying foxes'. To watch these enchanting creatures suckling on a pipette goes beyond cute. A range of interesting wildlife displays are also to hand. ■ *Daily except Mon, from 1030-1530. $2 donation at least. T40980063.*

Beyond Cape Tribulation the road gradually degenerates to form the notorious, controversial blot on the landscape known as **Bloomfield Track**. From here you are entering real 'Tiger Country' and 4WD is essential. A 2WD will only get you as far as **Emmagen Creek** that offers a limited incursion into the fringes of the dense rainforest and some good swimming holes, thankfully, too clear and too shallow for local crocodiles.

Essentials

Sleeping　There are a wide range of choices in and around The Cape, with most prices, not surprisingly perhaps being elevated well beyond the norm. At the upper end there is the **L-LL** *Heritage Lodge*, Turpentine Rd (near Coopers Creek), T40989138, www.home.aone.net.au/heritagelodge, offering, spacious, tidy en suite cabins, a pool and an à la carte restaurant on site. Further up towards Cape Tribulation itself, is the classy, yet expensive **LL** *Coconut Beach Rainforest Resort*, Cape Tribulation Rd,

T40980033, www.coconutbeach.com.au It offers an attractive range of en suite villas and units in a quiet bush setting with a pool. The impressive *Long House* – a huge A-frame log cabin – is located next to the beach and boasts a reputable à la carte restaurant and a pool. Just to the south of Cape Tribulation is **LL-D** *Ferntree Rainforest Resort*, Camelot Close, T40980000, www.ferntreeresort.com.au, a large 3-star complex, with fine facilities and, for a resort, a pleasantly quiet and intimate feel. The wide range of rooms, villas and suites are well appointed, the restaurant and bar is a fine place to relax and the pool is truly memorable. Occasional good deals on offer and budget accommodation with full access to facilities from $33.

There are 3 main backpackers in the region, all different. In the south, near Cow Bay Village (along Buchanan Creek Rd and the beach), is the YHA affiliated **B-E** *Crocodylus Village*, T40989166, www.crocodylus@austarnet.com.au By far the most ecologically 'in tune', it is essentially a glorified bush camp, with an interesting array of huts (some en suite) centred around a large communal area and a landscaped pool. You get the feel not a tree has been uprooted and its only drawback perhaps is the 3 km distance from the beach. Regular shuttle buses are however offered, as are regular daily Cairns and Port Douglas transfers, tours and activities. In Cape Tribulation itself: **B-D** *PK's Jungle Village*, Cape Tribulation Rd, T40980040, www.pksjunglevillage.com.au, is a well-established, mainstream hostel, popular with the social and party set. It offers all the usual including a lively bar, restaurant, pool and a host of activities. **L-D** *Cape Trib Beach House*, Cape Tribulation Rd, T40980030, www.capetribbeach.com.au At the top end of Cape Tribulation just before the tyres fall off a 2WD is this new and very congenial option. It offers a range of modern cabins (some en suite) from dorm to 'beachside'. The most attractive aspects are the bush setting, its quiet atmosphere, the communal bar and bistro (with internet) allocated right next to the beach. A wide range of activities and tours are also available. The only drawback is the inability to park your vehicle near the cabins. This is definitely the best budget option for couples.

Camping and powered sites are available at **A-F** *Club Daintree*, T40907500, off Cape Tribulation Rd on Cape Kimberly, which may be too far south for most. Alternatively, **A-F** *Lync Haven*, T40989155, www.lynchaven.com.au, is located about 4 km north of Cow Bay Village. It is very eco-friendly and also has a reputable restaurant. *PK's Jungle Village* (see above) is the only option in Cape Tribulation. The **QPWS campsite** at Noah Beach, 8 km south of Cape Tribulation, is basic. It is closed during the wet season.

Eating Almost all the resorts and backpackers listed above have their own restaurants or bistros, most of which are open for breakfast lunch and dinner. The most upmarket and aesthetically impressive is the à la carte restaurant in *Long House*, *Coconut Beach Resort* (see above, bookings essential). Alternatively you can also enjoy a more intimate al fresco dining experience at *Ferntree Resort* (see above). For cheaper options, you can certainly leave your best Hawaiian shirt and fetching accessory necktie in your room for all of the backpackers. There are also basic, but perfectly acceptable, offerings at **Daintree Forest Environmental Centre** (see above), *Floraville Tea Garden*, Cape Tribulation Rd, T40989100, *Latitude 16 Point 12 Degrees*, T40989133, Bailey's Creek Rd, both in Cow Bay or the *Café by the Sea*, T40989118, 4 km south of Noah Creek on Thornton Beach. *Drangonfly Gallery and Café*, T40980121, across the road from *Ferntree Resort*, in Cape Tribulation, offers tasty lunches and diners with the added attraction of local artworks and an internet loft.

Tours & activities
For more adventurous day-trips consult the VICs in Cairns or Port Douglas

It is overloaded with a plethora of mainly Cairns and Port Douglas based tour operators. For their daily tour options see pages 369 and 392. Some do not operate in the wet season (Dec-Mar) when access can be severely affected. There are many environmental based activities on offer in the region, including crocodile spotting (from $17); sea kayaking (from $34); horse riding (from $55) and even candlelit dinners deep in the rainforest (from $90). Most activities are best arranged through any of the main backpackers including *Beach House* (see above) outlining all that is currently available. The guided rainforest walks with ***Jungle Adventures*** T40980090, or ***Mason's Tours***, T40980070, www.masonstours.com.au, are recommended. Their night walk spotting the doe-eyed possums is a well worth while (from $28). A 4WD day trip exploring the Bloomfield Track with Mason's Tours costs from $115.

Transport
Self-drive is recommended but all roads in the area can be treacherous in the wet season (December-March). For road information, T40516711

Bus *Coral Coaches*, 37 Front St, Mossman, T40995351, offer daily scheduled services and tour packages from Cairns and Port Douglas, from $32, one-way (Cairns), tours from $52. *Freedom Bus Company* also offer limited transfers from Port Douglas, T055504044. **Car** *Daintree River Ferry*, 15 km southeast of Daintree village, runs daily from 0600-2400, pedestrian $2 return, vehicle $16 return. Beyond Cape Tribulation (36 km), the road degenerates into the strictly 4WD Bloomfield Track that winds its precarious 120 km way to Cooktown. Fuel is available 4 km east of Cow Bay village and 6 km north at the *Rainforest Village Store*. In the event of breakdown contact the RACQ (Cow Bay), T40982848.

Cooktown

Colour map 7, grid C3
Population: 1,500
334 km from Cairns

Like its big cousins Cairns and Port Douglas, the town has grown in stature as an attractive lifestyle proposition and a popular tourist destination. With more 4WD vehicles than your average shopping mall car park in the USA, one gets the impression the locals are as hardy as they are friendly and proud. There is plenty to see and do in and around Cooktown, with the James Cook Museum the undeniable highlight.

Ins & outs
See Transport, page 403, for details

Cooktown Tourism, T40696100, and the Cooktown Travel Centre T40695446, cooktowntravel@bigpond.com, looks after local visitor information services and can provide town maps. Both are located in the heart of the town on Charlotte St.

History

No prizes for guessing who put this place on the map. After coming to grief on the Barrier Reef just off Cape Tribulation on his 1770 voyage of discovery, Captain Cook grounded his ship *The Endeavour* near what is now the Endeavour River – the banks of which would later form Cooktown. For almost two months he tried to make good his misfortune and in so doing he and his crew essentially created the first 'white' settlement in Australia – something the modern day town, with no less than six monuments dedicated to the man, is clearly proud to boast. Once Cook resumed his voyage the site lay dormant until the rapacious gold rush of the Palmer River basin in the 1870s. In a matter of months the cosmopolitan population grew to a staggering thirty odd thousand with probably as many rum glasses and over sixty hotels. As fate decrees the boom naturally did not last. Another blow to the town was two devastating cyclones (the worst in 1907).

Sights

A good place to start your own discoveries of Cooktown is from the **Grassy Hill Lighthouse**, which is reached after a short climb at the end of Hope Street, north of the town centre. Here you can take in the views of the coast and town from the same spot Captain Cook reputedly worked out his safe

Cooktown Olympics

They say that Queenslanders are as 'mad as cut snakes', or as one former Australian Prime Minister put it... 'Queensland, it's not a State – it's a condition'! Whether you find this to be true will depend on your viewpoint and your experiences. However, one true story does demonstrate not so much a tendency towards mild insanity, as devilish individualism, admirable initiative and considerable character. In 2000 during the lead up to the Sydney Olympic Games, SOCOG (Sydney Organising Committee for the Olympic Games) left Far North Queensland and the proud outpost community of Cooktown off the route of the much hyped national Torch Relay Run. This was of course met with much derision and outrage. But instead of lobbying the 'southern powers that be' the good and imaginative people of Cooktown decided instead to organize their own torch relay and without delay created NOCOG (The Not the Organising Committee for the Olympic Games). In due course a substitute torch was made and the race duly ran from the tip of Cape York to Cooktown. But the high jinx didn't end there. NOCOG also decided to organize their own Olympic Games – The Relaxation Games, which in true Queensland style and character included events like 'Armchair Sleeping' and 'Watching the Grass Grow'. Both the Torch Relay Run and the games were such a success that it attracted international media attention promoting Australia and Queensland in way only SOCOG, New South Wales and the Australian Capital Territory could dream of! What is even better is that no public funds were spent whatsoever and it was all done for charity, raising over $40,000 for the Flying Doctors Service. At the highly colourful closing ceremony even the torch was auctioned for $2,500 to a group of fishermen from Sydney, who promised to return it for permanent display in Cooktown after carrying it with pride, most probably all the way to the steps of SOCOG. So are Queenslanders as 'mad as cut snakes'? Most certainly not.

passage back through the reef to the open sea. The old corrugated iron light-house that dominates the hill was built in England and shipped to Cooktown in 1885. For decades it served local and international shipping before being automated in 1927 and becoming obsolete in the 1980s.

From Hope Street it is then a short walk south to the **James Cook Museum**. Housed in a former convent built in 1889, just one of many historical build-ings in the town, the museum is touted as one of the most significant in Aus-tralia. Of course the main reason for this is the towns association with Cook, admirably displayed with striking exhibits in the Endeavour Gallery that include the HMS *Endeavours* anchor and one of her cannons, supplemented with references to Cooks journals and oral tales from the local aboriginals. But the museum is not dedicated solely to Cook, also housing many more inter-esting displays covering the towns' colourful and cosmopolitan history. The significance and influence of the Palmer River gold rush and the Chinese community, and in more recent times, the devastating cyclones that the town has endured are all well worth a muse. ■ *Daily Apr-Jan 0930-1600 (reduced hours Feb-Mar phone first), $5.50, child $2. T40695386. Corner of Furneaux and Helen St.*

The **waterfront** – Webber Esplanade – also hosts a number of interesting historical sites and plenty of reminders. The site of Cooks landing at what is now Bicentennial Park is marked with a small cairn and commemorative bronze statue of the man himself. Nearby is a cannon cast in Scotland in 1803 that was brought to the town in from Brisbane in the 1880s. It's arrival, along with three cannon balls, two rifles and one officer was – supposedly – to ward

Cairns to Cape York

off the perceived threat of Russian **invasion**. As you stand beside it, one can only admire their confidence (if not their naivety) and despair at the contrast of what a threat or act of invasion in the world a century later now entails in the scale of military response and technology.

Other sites of historical interest include the **Cooktown Cemetery**, which is at the southern edge of town along Endeavour Valley Road. There you will notice the huge contrast in nationalities and as ever the young age at which many former pioneers died. Although a **Chinese** shrine is now a dominant feature in the cemetery, the absence of marked graves of both Chinese and the local Aboriginals is a sad indication of their perceived social standing in the community at the time.

If ecological insight is more appealing than the historic, call in at **Nature's Powerhouse** in the **Botanical Gardens** that house an excellent display about the regions reptiles and an art gallery. The core of the reptilian collection was the bequest of local Charlie Tanner who dedicated his life and no doubt a few scars to recording the various snakes, crocodiles and their associates through-out the region. ■ *Daily. $2. T40696004. Walker St (East of the town centre).*

Sleeping   **L-A** *Sovereign Resort Hotel*, corner of Charlotte and Green sts, T40695400, sovereign_resort@cooktown.tnq.com.au This 4-star colonial-style hotel is the most upmarket place in town offering modern 2 bedroom apartments, deluxe and standard units. It also has a reputable à la carte restaurant and a fine pool. **L-A** *Milkwood Lodge Rainforest Cabins*, Annan Rd, at the southern edge of town, T40695007, www.milkwood-lodge.com, offers 6 excellent, luxury self-contained cabins in an elevated position with fine views. One of the best motel options in the heart of town is the value **A** *River of Gold Motel*, corner of Hope and Walker sts, T40695222, while **C-E** *Pam's Place*, corner of Charlotte and Boundary sts, T40695166, pamplace@tpg. com.au, is the principal backpackers in town. It offers dorms, singles and doubles and has all the usual facilities including a pool, tour desk and bike hire. There is a scattering of 3-star motor parks around town with **A-E** *Tropical Breeze*, corner of Charlotte St and McIvor Rd, T40695417, being recommended and well placed. Further afield **B-E** *Peninsula Caravan Park*, Howard St, T40695107, offers on-site vans, powered and un-powered sites in a quiet bush setting next to the Mount Sorrow National Park.

Eating   *Sovereign Resort* is perhaps your best bet for fine dining along with *Segrens Inn*, Charlotte St, T40695357, both of which specialize in local seafood and Australian fare. The usual standard, value bistro meals can be found at the local *Cooktown Bowls Club*, Charlotte St, T40696137, and pub fare at the locally popular *Top Pub* (*Cooktown Hotel*), corner of Charlotte and Walker sts, T40695308. *Cooks Landing Kiosk*, T40695101, on the Webber Esplanade. Congenial, waterfront, for good coffee and breakfast.

Festivals   If you are in Cooktown in **mid Jun** (Queens Birthday weekend) your visit may coincide with the colourful Cooktown *Discovery Festival*, when Cooks landing is commemorated with a re-enactment and a host of other events and celebrations.

Tours & activities   As well as the obvious historical attraction Cooktown offers a number of activities from self-guided local walks and historic town tours to reef fishing, cruising and snorkelling. If you can afford it, a trip to Lizard Island by sea or air is recommended. The information centres have details and can arrange bookings. *Cooktown Cruises*, T40695712, offer a sedate 2-hr historical and Eco-cruise on the Endeavour River from $25, child $12. Many tour operators in Cairns and Port Douglas offer day or multi-day trips to Cooktown some combining road travel with a scenic return flight (see Cairns, page 369 and Port Douglas, page 392).

Air *Skytrans Airlines*, T40695446, www.skytrans.com.au, are one of a number of companies offering regular transfers to **Cairns** from $82 one-way (with 3-day advance pur-
chase). **Bus** *Coral Coaches*, T40982600, ply the inland route from Cairns to Cooktown
on Wed, Fri and Sun taking 5½ hrs and the coastal route Tue, Sat (all year) and Thu
(Jun-Oct), taking 8 hrs, from $115, child $57.50 round trip. **Car** Car hire and 4WD hire
from *Cooktown Car Hire*, 1 Charlotte St, T40695694. **Taxi** T40695387.

Bank *Wespac*, Charlotte St, T40695477. **Communications** Internet: *Computer*
Stuff, Charlotte St, T40696010. **Post office**: Charlotte St. **Medical services** Hospital:
Hope St, T40695433. **Useful numbers** Police: 170 Charlotte St, T40695320. RACQ:
Cape York Tyres, corner of Charlotte and Furneaux sts, T40695274.

Cape York

Beyond Cooktown the great wilderness of Cape York beckons like some for- *Colour map 7*
bidding mountain – mysterious, challenging and dangerous. There are essentially two ways to reach the most northerly tip of Australia. The first and by far
the most sensible for those inexperienced with 4WD, is to join a professional
4WD tour operator, while the second is, of course, to go independently with
an experienced group. Whichever way you go, then one thing is guaranteed –
a true Aussie wilderness adventure and memories of remote landscapes,
lagoons, deserted coastline and perhaps the odd croc sighting that combined
will last a lifetime.

Whether you go as a group or independently, the trip is not for the faint hearted and **Ins & outs**
requires detailed planning, a reliable vehicle, proper equipment and a dogged sense of
adventure. It is almost 1,000-km of unsealed road taking 10-14 days return. It must be
made in the dry season from Apr-Oct, when the numerous riverbed crossings are
negotiable. For those that do go it alone, it most certainly requires research and information well beyond the scope of this handbook. VIC in Cairns can supply up to date
information about the Cape and can also provide a few pointers long before departure.

The first significant settlement along the Peninsula Developmental Road is **Sights**
Laura where you will find basic hotel and caravan park accommodation, fuel
and a café. Laura provides the base for the investigation of the beautifully preserved **Split Rock** Aboriginal rock paintings located 13 km to the south.
Tours are available with the Ang-gnarra Aboriginal Corporation, T4060
3200. An undoubted highlight of the Cape York is the **Lakefield National
Park**. Queensland's second largest, it offers a remote wonderland of diverse
landscapes from grass savannah to quiet billabongs and a very impressive
range of avian residents. Another highlight of the park is the **Old Laura
Homestead** built in the 1880s during the Palmer River Gold rush. Access to
the park is north of Laura and the **Musgrave Roadhouse**. For park information contact the local ranger, T4060 3271. See Sleeping below.

Beyond Musgrave, the tiny settlement of **Coen** provides the next base for
accommodation and supplies and 65 km beyond that is the **Archer River**
where you will find a roadhouse with a café and campsite. The fairly unremarkable mining town of **Weipa** on the shores of the Gulf of Carpentaria then
marks the end of the Peninsula Developmental Road. But those heading for
the tip leave the Peninsula Developmental Road well to the east and continue
north on the most challenging section of the journey to reach (eventually) the
most northerly settlement in Queensland – **Bamaga** and **Jardine National
Park**, its most northerly park before popping the cork overlooking

Endeavour Strait and **Thursday Island**. Before heading north to Bamaga it is well worth taking the diversion east to the remote and beautiful **Iron Range National Park**, but like the journey north 2WD is not an option.

There are several good books about Cape York including the excellent *Cape York – An Adventurers Guide* by Ron and Viv Moon, Kakirra Guides that are almost invaluable. Hema Regional Map of North Queensland is a good general map.

Sleeping & eating

LL *Lotus Bird Lodge*, between Musgrave and the western fringes of the park, T4095 0773, www.cairns.aust.com/lotusbird, offers fine, modern lodge-style accommodation with pool, restaurant, bar and organized national park tours. Beyond Cooktown there is obviously a dearth of amenities and when it comes to accommodation there is little choice beyond basic roadhouses, hotel pubs and basic campsites. QPWS in Cairns can supply detailed national parks and camping information.

Tours & activities

Cairns based tour operators offering reputable trips to the Cape include *Oz Tour Safaris*, T40559535, info@oztours.com.au, 7-day tour from $1495 (twin share). *Billy Tea Bush Safaris*, T0740320077, www.billytea.com.au, also offer attractive options. Another fascinating alternative are the air tours and mail run available with *Cape York Air*, T40359399, www.capeyorkair.com.au, from $297-471.

Background

History

"Australian history is almost always picturesque; indeed, it is also so curious and strange, that it is itself the chiefest novelty the country has to offer and so it pushes the other novelties into second and third place. It does not read like history, but like the most beautiful lies; and all of a fresh new sort, no mouldy old stale ones. It is full of surprises and adventures, the incongruities, and contradictions, and incredibility; but they are all true, they all happened."

Mark Twain, *More Tramps Abroad*, London, 1897.

The arrival of man

From their evolution in Africa, *Homo erectus*, and then *Homo sapiens*, walked into Asia but their expansion from these strongholds to the 'new worlds' was barred by either water or ice for hundreds of thousands of years. Although parts of New Guinea and northwest Australia are tantalizingly close to the islands of Southeast Asia, even during the severest of ice ages there have always been deep channels between them. It has never been possible to walk from Asia to Meganesia. This was one of the most profound clues to continental drifting ignored by most geologists of the early 20th century. Alfred Russell Wallace, Darwin's co-formulator of the theory of natural selection, noticed in the 1860s that these channels marked an invisible line, a threshold that heralded an incredible and inexplicable shift in types of terrestrial animal life from one landmass to the other. It is known today as *Wallace's Line*.

There are three relatively new concepts that have changed the traditional picture of Aboriginal history. Firstly, the idea that Aboriginal people arrived by boat and secondly, when this happened. There are no dates, not even any folk memories of the first coming of humanity to Meganesia (in geological terms the islands of Tasmania, Australia, the Torres Strait, and New Guinea), this is because the time of first migration has been pushed back by slowly accumulating evidence to over 45,000 and possibly as much as 60,000 years ago. Thirdly anthropologists are now certain that Australian Aboriginals and the original New Guineans are one and the same people, separated by just a few thousand years of cultural divergence, and New Guineans were amongst the earliest and most intensive farmers on the planet.

Anthropologists have identified a general 'great leap forward' in human culture, a time when our ancestors first refined their previously clumsy stone tools, clearly invented boats, experimented with art and perhaps agriculture, and probably first became superstitious and intellectually curious. There is no geographic site as yet identified with these first cultural stirrings, but some scholars have been struck by the coincidence that these beginnings seem to coincide with humanity's first escape from its long enclosure on the Africa-Asia landmass. Tim Flannery, the Director of the South Australian Museum, has suggested that the peoples of Southeast Asia that first began their island-hopping progress toward Meganesia were perhaps the principal pioneers of the great leap. As they finally crossed Wallace's Line they encountered totally new environments and fauna for the first time in human history, and swiftly developed new technologies and social structures to exploit and interpret them to the full. Once developed, the benefits of these new cultural advances would have caused the ideas to spread rapidly, both onward with their authors and back to the Asian peoples and beyond to Europe, Africa and eventually the Americas.

Whether or not this is the case, there is little doubt that the peoples who finally crossed from Asia to Meganesia around 55,000 years ago carried with them one of the most, if not the most, technologically advanced cultures of the time. It seems likely that they already had a grasp of the potential of agriculture, as some of those that settled in the northern highlands – later to become isolated as island New Guinea – had developed intensive farming systems by as much as 10,000 years ago. Population expansion amongst the early settlers in the new fertile New Guinean lands would have been exponential, and it cannot have been long before groups were heading south in search of new land.

The early Aborigines carried with them a notable firepower. Stone, bone and wooden weapons were honed to perfection during the many generations of island-hopping from Asia. These hunter-gatherers had encountered, for the first time in human history, lands where they were the undisputed top predator. One of their new weapons would have been psychological, a new feeling of unbridled power, a sense of their own dominance. The Australian animals they met would have been woefully ill-prepared for such an encounter.

The few mammalian predators could not hope to compete with such a powerful new force, either in direct confrontation or for prey as the human population increased. As for the giant reptiles, the awesome *Megalania* and the giant snake *Wonambi* (6 m long with a head the size of a serving tray) were ambush predators, strictly territorial. They would have been a serious hazard to the lone hunter, but in the face of collective competition were as doomed as their mammalian counterparts. The only large Australian predator to survive to the present day is the feared 'saltie' ,the saltwater crocodile, probably protected by its primarily aquatic habitat.

As for the herbivores, the now vanished giants of the vast Australian plains, there can surely be little doubt that the coming of humanity was the decisive factor in the extinction of so many. On virtually every island and landmass outside of Africa Asia a wave of faunal extinctions has followed hard on the heels of human occupation. Ecologists in both America and Australia have argued for a climate-driven cause, linking the disappearances with some phase of the last ice age, but in both cases the bulk of the fauna had previously survived dozens of ice ages and inter-glacial periods. Climate change may have weakened some species, even driven them to relatively small strongholds, but the evidence is almost overwhelming that humans, either directly or indirectly, delivered the final *coup de grace*.

An ecological crisis?

Evidence is also mounting that the coming of humanity had an extraordinarily profound effect on Australian flora. First indirectly and then, in the face of calamity, purposefully. Core samples from around Australia, but particularly in the east, seem to indicate that the now dominant **eucalyptus** were surprisingly rare prior to around 60,000 years ago. These cores also sometimes show high concentrations of carbon – ash – at the point at which the gums began their ascendancy. Could this be another climate-driven coincidence? Again, some researchers think not.

A powerful, and frightening scenario may well have followed the local demise of the large herbivores. Without munching herbivores the forest undergrowth and plains brush would have proliferated; in wet times an impenetrable green morass, in the dry a huge store of kindling. Forest fires are natural, lightening-ignited phenomena on every continent, and especially common in hot and dry Australia. Massive build-ups of combustible fuel would have resulted in equally massive, and quite catastrophic, fires raging through the forest and bush, deadly to the native flora and fauna and humans alike.

In the face of this crisis the early peoples of Australia would have realized that they had to artificially keep the bush low. They would have been forced to fight fire with fire, continuously lighting small-scale blazes to prevent large-scale conflagrations. Whatever the cause, the adoption of fire for more than just cooking and heating was to have many and widespread consequences.

Most important for the first Australians was the realization that fire could have multiple uses. Not only did it prevent life-threatening bushfires, but they could be used for offence or defence against antagonistic neighbours, or to signal to distant groups or family members. They could also be used to drive and herd game to favoured trapping areas, and burn-offs encouraged new grass growth of the succulent shoots favoured by many of the Aboriginals' prey. It would also not have been lost on them how much more easily they could navigate, travel and hunt across burnt-off land.

A more-or-less constant regime of small-scale bushfires had other less useful consequences. Crucially for the future development of Australian flora, it naturally favoured fire-resistant and fire-promoting species. Foremost amongst these are the eucalyptus, the ubiquitous gum trees that once were minor players in the ecology of the continent, but are now almost all-pervading. Dry and wet rainforests have been driven back to relatively tiny refuges around Australia's eastern periphery, while the great gum woodlands have marched on triumphant.

The catch-22 of the Aboriginal's fire regime locked Australia into another ecological cul-de-sac. The total number of animals a landmass can support, its *faunal biomass*, depends on a number of factors. Two of these Australia already had a paucity of – water and nutrients. The fire regime would have accelerated erosion, further depleting soil nutrient levels, and would also have significantly lowered the amount of water and nutrients locked up within the plants themselves. Most obviously of all, the potential number of animals is crucially constrained by the sheer biomass of plant material available as foodstuff. With much of this being continually burned off, the amount of prey available to both humans and their competitors would have had a much-reduced upper limit.

Partnership with the land

The early pioneers into each part of the continent would have had a relatively easy time of it, but once the honeymoon was over the challenges that faced the first Australians were immense. The extinction of the large herbivores and the bushfire crisis were huge blows to an already very specialized, and hence vulnerable, ecology. Without human intervention, massive bushfires could have decreased the viability of many other animal species. As it was, the introduction of the fire regime seems to have stabilized the situation and prevented further degradation of the environment. It was a fix, but a fix that stood the test of time.

As well as coping with a damaged environment and a much reduced quantity of game, most Aboriginal peoples faced challenges never previously faced by humanity. Paramount among these was the scarcity and unpredictably of water supply, and the consequent boom-and-bust fluctuations of many of the species of animals hunted for food. Paradoxically this actually seems to have resulted in a better standard of diet than that experienced by many peoples in more stable environments.

There are two chief reasons for this. The relative scarcity of food resulted in the early Australians becoming experts in everything that could possibly have nutritional value, from roots to roos, and moths to mussels. In most parts of the continent people could draw on their knowledge of a variety of in-season fruits and animals, more than sufficient to sustain them. In the process they also discovered an extensive natural medicine chest that helped keep them healthy.

This pegging of population and resultant 'abundance' of food is perhaps one of the reasons why farming was rarely employed by Aboriginal peoples. ENSO also makes farming extremely difficult, with attempts at planting crops frequently foiled by drought conditions, but one of the key factors that mitigated against Aboriginal agriculture was the lack of suitable species. It is now becoming accepted that under the experimental conditions of our early ancestors only a handful of plants and animals would have had exactly the right characteristics for domestication. In Australia all the large herbivores that may have been suitable quickly disappeared and to this day only one indigenous crop has been cultivated to any extent – the macadamia nut. The unrelated factors of no domesticated animals and continental isolation would later combine to make the Aboriginals tragically susceptible to European diseases.

As is now widely appreciated, it is agriculture that has provided human cultures with the excess labour required to build the urban trappings of civilization. Leading a hunter-gatherer lifestyle with little incentive or opportunity for farming, the Australian peoples rarely created permanent settlements. Over much of the continent not even clothes, let alone buildings were required for warmth. Buildings were also unnecessary for either safety, keeping animals, or the storage of foodstuffs. Only in the colder south were some of these trappings adopted. Here some groups built stone huts, sewed together blankets and clothes from animal skins and embarked on intensive aquaculture, building sophisticated canals and traps to catch fish and eels.

With strong parallels with the peoples in North America, the Aboriginal cultures came to place a great value on their relationship with the land. Disturbances to their environment, or deviation from the fire regime (sometimes called 'fire-stick farming'), were recognized as threats to survival, and this relationship came to be regarded as a sacred custodianship. Nomadic peoples rarely develop the concept of land ownership in the western sense, but the first Australians maintained strict territories, each carefully tended and managed by its resident people. Embarking on a journey through another group's land involved careful negotiation.

In environments as difficult as most that Australia has to offer, isolation can be lethal. Inter-tribal contact was maintained through constant trading, mostly for ochre or precious materials. These were mined in a large number of sites across Australia. There were also great regional meetings, social corroborees that usually coincided with an abundant, seasonal food source such as the bogong moths in the Victorian Alps. Over tens of thousands of years this helped maintain a remarkable consistency of culture across such a vast area.

Given such a prodigious tenure it is hardly surprising that a folk memory of the original coming to America of the ancestors' of the Aboriginal people has been lost. Aboriginal history is passed from generation to generation in the form of oral stories, part of the all-pervasive culture of 'dreaming' that also encompasses law, religion, customs and knowledge. These creation myths talk of a period when powerful ancestors, both human and animal, strode the land, creating natural features, plants, animals and peoples alike. Parts of the dreaming were also immortalized, and illustrated to younger generations through songs and dances, rock art and carvings. It is probable that Australia now has the oldest such art on the planet.

Aboriginal culture is the longest uninterrupted culture the modern world has witnessed. Over tens of thousands of years the first peoples of Australia developed unique strategies to ensure their survival in the face of some of the world's most difficult environments. They built a rich cultural heritage, a phenomenal knowledge of their land and its natural resources, prodigious internal trade routes, a carefully managed environment, and a stable population, which was in harmony with that environment rather than in conflict with it.

The most significant event in Australia of the last 50 millennia was almost certainly the ending of the ice age about 9,000 years ago. Rising sea levels severed both New Guinea and Tasmania from the mainland, leaving the latter island with a population of about 5,000 people. Anthropologists now believe such a small population left the Tasmanian people vulnerable to disease, disaster and the subsequent loss of valuable cultural knowledge, contributing to the islanders' distinctive differences from mainland Aboriginal culture. At the time of first European contact with the Tasmanians they had no bone implements, no stone tools, boomerangs, spear throwers or dingos, and no clothing. Surprisingly, in such a coastal environment, they did not eat fish and indeed reacted with horror when offered some by early European explorers. They also lacked the ability to make fire. A firestick was always kept burning and carried from place to place. If this should be extinguished a group would have to seek out another tribe possessing a firestick who were obligated to give fire, even to a traditional enemy. It is thought that Tasmanian Aboriginals may have lost knowledge when skilled individuals died unexpectedly. Ancient middens (campsites or refuse dumps) reveal that fish were eaten and bone tools such as needles used until about 3,500 years ago, indicating that later people lost the ability to sew warm skin cloaks similar to those worn in southern Australia.

Old and new worlds collide

Elsewhere around the world, other peoples were finally wrestling for mastery of their own environments. Conditions for agriculture were perfect in the 'fertile crescent', and its development enabled large-scale urban cultures for the first time. Like shock-waves, the ideas and technologies that these peoples developed spread from their Middle-eastern epicentre to Europe and many parts of Asia. These in turn fuelled population explosions that then allowed for even greater technological and agricultural advances. Fierce competition between rival empires resulted, a process that shunted populations around the vast landmass. For a variety of reasons much of the pressure was exerted on the peoples of Europe, and those in the far west were the most squeezed of all, with nowhere to go but the sea. By 1400 AD they had developed impressive maritime and military technologies. They also began to experience a growing need for raw materials and extra living space, nurtured a great thirst for personal and national wealth, and, incidentally but critically, had inherited one of the most crusading religions the world has ever seen.

It is little known that the Europeans weren't the first foreign visitors after Australia. Macassans from the Indonesian island of Sulawesi were visiting the northern coasts by around 1500, possibly for centuries earlier. Later, following economic and political destabilization caused by the coming of the Portuguese, the Macassans became the first outsiders to regularly visit Australia, their primary purpose to harvest 'trepang', the sea slug. They also traded with the local Aborigines, and this regular contact with foreigners helped the local indigenous peoples of the north to cope far better with European culture, aggression and diseases when they finally began to arrive in earnest in the 1860s.

Some would argue that the first significant date in the European exploration of Australia is 1493. In that year, in one of the most breathtaking carve-ups in history, Pope Alexander VI apportioned the right of exploration of everything west of a certain meridian to the Spanish, and everything in the opposite direction to the Portuguese. The fact that the world is a sphere seems to have been overlooked and the newly encountered 'spice islands' of the Far East were soon the subject of a squabble. It now seems possible that the Portuguese knew a little more about the landmass south of New Guinea than they were letting on.

Whatever the case, by the end of the 16th century the published information on the much conjectured upon *Terra Australis* (southern land) was negligible, consisting of just a few charts that clearly relied more on guesswork than actual knowledge, and a small passage written in 1598 by one Cornelius Wytfliet that begins *"The Australis Terra is the most southern of lands, and is separated from New Guinea by a narrow strait."* In a nearly aborted voyage of discovery in 1606 the Spaniard Luis de Torres negotiated his way through this strait, and is the first European we know by name to have glimpsed the Australian mainland, even though he mistook it for a group of islands. That the certain knowledge of Torres Strait remained, for whatever reason, unavailable to the other sea-faring nations for over 150 years, had a profound effect on how the exploration of Australian shores proceeded.

This is to jump the gun, however, for we need to look at the first really important date of 1584. In that year the overbearing king of Spain, Phillip II, decided to punish the Dutch for their religious heresies by barring their ships to Lisbon, a port that had latterly come under his control. Hitherto the Dutch had done a roaring trade as the hauliers of Europe, picking up the goods the Portuguese brought back from the Far East and transporting them all over the western seaboard. Phillip, having failed to subjugate them with the sword, was now trying to cut their economic base from under them. The Dutch were nothing if not wilful, however, and instead they set about fetching the goods from the Far East themselves. In 1597 the first fleet returned in triumph and in 1611 Hendrik Brouwer discovered that sailing due east from the Cape of Good Hope for 3,000 miles, and then turning north, cut about two months off the Holland-Java journey time. Five years later Dirk Hartog overshot the mark and found his namesake island off Shark Bay. A visible landmark really opened the route up, and soon the Dutch were establishing a fair picture of the west coast of what came to be called New Holland, wrecking many of their ships on it in the process.

In 1642, a generation after Torres found his strait, Dutchman Abel Tasman, failed to find it. As a result of his failure, however, he retraced his steps, properly charted the northwest coast of New Holland, headed south and found Tasmania (he called it Van Diemen's Land after his Governor-General), then west to 'discover' New Zealand. With equal enthusiasm, but less success, an English buccaneer, William Dampier, convinced the English government to fit him out a ship for exploration in 1699. Had he followed his original plan and travelled via Cape Horn rather than Good Hope, he could easily have been the one to sail into Botany Bay, but he took the traditional route, also failed to find the strait and instead sailed the now well-worn western trail.

There things stood for 70 years until Captain James Cook was sent by the English government to observe a transit of Venus in Tahiti. By now the English were very much caught up in the spirit of European exploration and he was instructed, while in the area, to check out New Zealand and, if possible, chart the hitherto unexplored east coast of New Holland. In all this he was completely successful, spending six months charting New Zealand and then sailing west as planned. This east coast was sufficiently far from the western coast that it was entirely possible the two were actually unconnected, and he named the 'new territory' New South Wales. He must have seen the Australian environment at its best and gave glowing descriptions of it in his reports to his government. His positive, though fateful and misinformed opinions, were summarized in *The Voyages of Captain Cook*:

> "*The industry of man has had nothing to do with any part of it, and yet we find all such things as nature hath bestowed upon it in a flourishing state. In this extensive country it can never be doubted but what most sorts of grain, fruit, roots, etc., of every kind, would flourish were they brought hither, planted and cultivated by the hands of industry; and here is provender for more cattle, at all seasons of the year, than can ever be brought into the country.*"

Two of the most different cultures imaginable of their day were now on an inevitable collision course.

The process of colonization

No sooner had the British Empire nonchalantly claimed a large new territory than it was ignominiously turfed out of an old one. In 1782 the American colonies successfully gained independence, thus creating all sorts of problems for the British government, not least of which was what to do with tens of thousands of convicts, who continued to be sentenced to 'transportation'. The other colonies swiftly declined to accept them, and the practice of dropping them off in West Africa was abandoned on the grounds that this simply meant a nastier death for the transportees than they could have otherwise enjoyed at the end of a noose back home.

Sir Joseph Banks, Cook's botanist on the *Endeavour*, had suggested New South Wales as early as 1779, but it wasn't until 1786 that Prime Minister William Pitt agreed to the suggestion, then formally put forward by Lord Sydney, the minister responsible for felons. The following year Arthur Phillip's 'first fleet' set out, less a grand colonial voyage than a handy solution to a pressing problem.

Botany Bay was not to Phillip's liking so he explored the harbour just to the north, Port Jackson, that had been noted, but not entered, by Cook. A quick scout round revealed that this was just the spot and Sydney Cove was duly named as the site for the new penal colony. On the 26 January 1788 the British flag was unfurled and a toast was raised to the King's health. Governor Phillip must have been a very strong-willed and fair man to have seen the colony through its first five years as well as he did. Livestock and cereals fared worse than expected and rationing was necessary for over two years, until another settlement (Parramatta) set amidst more fertile soils was established a few miles inland. Almost from the start convicts were motivated by grants of land in exchange for good conduct and the local Aborigines were by and large not treated too badly, though how they really viewed this usurpation of their land can only be guessed at. They did not know that this trickle of white men was the prelude to a flood. Had they had the slightest inkling it is likely that resistance would have been fierce, but instead a straightforward curiosity and casual acceptance of gifts seem to have been the most common response in the first few years.

The rag-tag make-up of the early 'settlers' – the soldiers and thieves, forgers and murderers, Irish rebels and English farmers – made for an eclectic mix. Most, as the eloquent pickpocket Barrington reminds us, were unwilling pioneers:

> *"True patriots we, for, be it understood,*
> *We left our country for our country's good.*
> *No private views disgraced our generous zeal,*
> *What urged our travels was our country's weal."*

But unwilling or not, there were soon fortunes to be made. When Phillip had to resign through ill-health the government of the colony temporarily passed into the hands of the military commanders sent to guard the convicts. The military (the 'rum corps') saw this as an opportunity to really open up various trades, particularly in land, sheep and alcohol, and line their pockets in the process. Emancipated convicts with an eye for the main chance also took every advantage that came their way. For nearly 15 years Phillip's civic successors tried to bring the soldiers to heel, a period that had its dramatic conclusion with the virtual mutiny of the new economic masters, and the arrest and expulsion of Governor Bligh in 1806.

In 1810 it took the Scotsman, Governor Lachlan Macquarie, over a decade to instill some order to the chaos with the establishment of a proper infrastructure, the construction of some of Sydney's oldest and finest buildings (using convict labour) and in essence the creation of some domestic pride and international respect for the new colony.

There were two things that further spurred both the expansion of the New South Wales colony beyond that of a simple penal settlement and the establishment of other Australian colonies. The most immediate was an expanding population of convicts, free-settlers and their offspring, all of whom required land for grazing, cultivation and speculation. The other was the possibility that the French, once more the arch enemy, would muscle in on 'British' turf. At some point the apparent potential of this vast new land sank into the minds of colonial secretaries and New South Wales governors alike. It was quickly conceived that the French should have none of this scarcely explored territory and that the British Empire should have all of it. Exploration, both publicly and privately sponsored, was encouraged.

The Blue Mountains proved an amazing obstacle, the crossing of them only accomplished after 20 years of repeated effort. Explorers elsewhere progressed more swiftly. The most important maritime explorer of his time was Matthew Flinders who arrived at Port Jackson in 1795 as a midshipman. It was Flinders, and his associate George Bass, who first demonstrated that Van Diemen's Land was separate from New South Wales, Flinders who first charted the unknown southern coasts and circumnavigated the whole continent in 1801-03, proving it at last to be one vast island. It was also Matthew Flinders who suggested the name 'Australia' for this new continent, a name that quickly caught on in preference to New Holland and became more or less official in 1817. Flinders did his work in the nick of time, for the French were indeed very interested in this new land and their explorers Nicholas Baudin and Louis de Freycinet also made many key discoveries.

The interior of Australia proved far more arduous, and was almost solely undertaken by the British or under British auspices with substantial help from indigenous recruits. There were high hopes of vast swathes of rich land in the interior, even of a substantial inland sea. The cracking of the Blue Mountains opened the way to the Bathurst Plains and beyond. By 1830 explorers such as John Oxley, Hume and Hovell, and Charles Sturt had helped give white Australians a mental picture of much of the southern and eastern parts of the continent.

Territorial conquest

For the first 40 years only a trickle of free-settlers had journeyed out with the convicts, despite the lure of free passage, but from 1830 numbers steadily increased. New South Wales slowly came to be seen as a land of opportunity and by the mid-1830s the inbound ships carried more free-settlers than convicts. Many of the new settlers had a better knowledge of agricultural and trade development than the soldiers and convicts, and better links with Britain.

Hard on the heels of the explorers were the new pastoralists, ambitious men who claimed vast areas of land on which they might prosper, largely by might rather than right. These 'squatters', given to scorn the laws and edicts of distant authorities, were a severe bane to more fair-minded colonial governments, a boon to less scrupulous ones. Farmers had quickly discovered that cattle and vegetables fared a lot more poorly than was expected in the new lands, but the more experimental soon imported strains of grain and sheep that might be better suited to the relatively arid climate. Even then the poor soil meant huge acreages were required to raise profitable quantities of wool and wheat.

Wool soon became the single most important industry in the colonies. With a large and expanding British market, hungry for every bale, the Australian sheep population simply exploded during the 1830s. Millions of them teemed over the countryside, tended by thousands of mostly convict shepherds. The effect of the wool industry was huge: fortunes for hundreds of men; the main catalyst for the Murray steamboats and later the railways; it helped lay the foundation stones of new, non-penal towns; it caused the felling and waste of mile upon mile of forest and scrub; and finally it hugely aggravated conflict with the Aboriginals. Land won for the sheep was land lost to the indigenous peoples and it is estimated that an area the size of Ireland was invaded by the pastoralists every year during the 1830s.

It took decades for Europeans to even begin to understand the Aboriginals' complex relationship with their land. It is ill understood even today. Most people simply didn't care and some, particularly the poor or emancipated, were happy that there were people on a rung lower than theirs. It was assumed that as the Aboriginals did not farm they had no concept or right of ownership, that since they were nomadic they could simply move out of the way, and that as their technology was inferior so was their culture and indeed so were they as people. From the very beginning there were settlers who considered them sub-human, and right up to the 1960s many Aboriginals believed themselves regarded as 'fauna'.

Today it is vigorously debated how much the early authorities were guided by the policy of *terra nullius*, the idea that Australia was an empty land, free for the taking. *Terra nullius* was a legal fiction based on the premise that land ownership was only proved by land cultivation. The colonial authorities did not think for a second that Australia was empty but rather that Aboriginal people had no legal claim upon it. At the time it seems likely that whatever angst was occurring in the minds of liberal societies and authorities in England or urban Australia, the reality on the crucial frontier was promoted by the pioneering settler, over which the authorities had little control. For many that reality was one of conflict. *Terra nullius* was immaterial, there was a future to secure and it was 'either us or them'.

Disease did a lot of the damage, with thousands of Aboriginals undoubtedly dying of smallpox and flu, syphilis and typhoid. The Europeans' long association with domestic animals had fermented a rich brew of transmissible infectious diseases against which, like the native Americans before them, the native Australians had little defence. Sometimes, however, there were survivors, some of whom could not be persuaded to join a Christian mission, work as a farm hand or join the native police. Then some of the of the most intense confrontations took place. A minority of Aboriginals fought back, spearing settlers and attempting to drive them back from whence they had come. The response, both official and not, was often savage. There are known instances of whole groups being rounded up and shot wholesale as retribution for something as trivial as the death of a bullock. On the other hand some groups simply tried to maintain their existence, living off the land as their ancestors had done. Here less brutal tactics were sometimes employed by the Europeans, such as the poisoning of their waterholes.

By 1850 it was all over bar the shouting. Aboriginal peoples reached some of their lowest populations ever, driven almost entirely from Tasmania and Victoria and with hugely reduced numbers in New South Wales and South Australia. Aboriginal people in the northern regions simply had to wait longer for dispossession. By the 1870s and 1880s many had suffered a similar fate to the southerners, although they survived in greater numbers with a more intact culture. When a little later Charles Darwin's theories gained widespread notice (reinforced after his visited the new colony in 1836 during his circumnavigation of the world in HMS Beagle), it was widely expected that these peoples would become extinct. Their perceived inferiority surely meant they could not survive in the face of a more 'advanced' people. It was simply a case of the 'survival of the fittest'.

Land of golden opportunity

Where the indigenous peoples had lost, the invaders had gained. The wool and grain industries were booming, coal and copper were being profitably mined, and there were many towns adopting the trappings of a civilized life. Even the convicts had for the most part outlived their usefulness and there were repeated calls for the end of transportation.

The middle of the 18th century was a landmark moment in Australian history. Wool was the bedrock of the economy of the colonies, and would remain so for another 125 years, but it was the discovery of gold that caught the world's attention. Gold was actually discovered in the Australian colonies, mostly by shepherds and station-hands, at least as early as 1842, but during the 1840s neither the governments nor squatters welcomed the social upheaval that a gold rush would bring and the knowledge of gold-bearing land was vigorously suppressed.

The Californian rushes of 1849 were the eventual trigger for the Australian finds. Some returning diggers may not have come back to the colonies with riches, but they certainly came with knowledge. Even while in the USA, many Australian diggers were casting their minds back to the foothills and geology of the Great Dividing Range, wondering at their similarity to the terrain in California. A good find meant more than a supplement to a poor income – a man could make a fortune overnight. With such prospectors abroad, public awareness of Australian gold was inevitable.

Gold was first publicly found in New South Wales in 1851 and soon after in Victoria. The discoveries created a worldwide sensation with hundreds taking passage to the colonies within days of the arrival of the news. In theory any gold found was crown property, but as with the squatters, the colonial governments knew they had a flood on their hands that could only be regulated, not stopped. In a surprisingly egalitarian move both colonial governments instituted rules that opened up the new goldfields to all comers. Any gold-seeker had to buy a licence for the privilege of searching, and could select a plot of a small given size. After the easy stuff had mostly gone the system proved unworkable and heavy-handed regulation provoked a mini-revolution, but at first it had given everyone the 'fair go' that Australia has become famous for.

By 1860 the transportation of convicts to the eastern colonies had finally ceased. Nearly 160,000 had made the enforced trip over the previous 60-odd years, with few returning to their homelands. The accusation is often jokingly levelled at Australians that they're all descended from thieves. In fact the number of gold-seeking immigrants between 1850 and 1860 dwarfed the number of earlier convicts. It may have been founded on a penal colony but Australia is no felon nation, it's a nation of entrepreneurs.

The next 30 years were ones of considerable consolidation in the Australian colonies. Wool had set the ball rolling, and would keep it rolling for decades, but gold was the catalyst that really sped the pace of progress. Mining corporations and agriculturalists eagerly took to the new technology of steam, fuelling Australia's own industrial revolution, and irrigation was equally enthusiastically introduced. Railways were built and telegraph lines constructed in the face of incredible physical difficulties. The urbanization of the country continued apace with huge city populations living off the vast but poorly populated agricultural regions.

Technological progress was matched by important social advances, in many cases pioneering the way for the rest of the world. Colonial governments almost competed to bring in new democratic legislation and extend free education. In 1861 about one in four European immigrants were illiterate, a figure reduced to one in forty by 1891. The unions forced a shorter working day, then a shorter working week, opening up Saturday afternoons for sport and leisure. The outdoor climate, large accessible spaces, and huge urban populations contrived to ensure that sport itself became almost a religion, and those competing successfully at international level were the new gods. By 1900 Australians were avid followers of home-grown boxers, skullers, jockeys, cricketers, athletes and footballers. Crowds at some football and cricket matches could be measured in the tens of thousands, dwarfing those in other countries. With the rise in sport came a rise in gambling, a habit Australia has never lost.

At the same time artists of the talented Heidelberg school were finally seeing the landscape in an Australian light, and interpreting it realistically for the for first time to the fascination of the largely urban population. They also led the way to a growing appreciation of indigenous flora and fauna. Bushwalking societies formed and there were moves to form reserves around outstandingly beautiful natural landmarks. These forerunners of the national parks began to be declared in the 1870s and 1880s.

Background

Societies very much at odds with the natural environment were also formed. A nostalgia for 'home' led groups of misguided amateur naturalists to import countless species of plants and animals in the hope that the alien landscape of Australia could be transformed into one huge English garden. Other animals were brought over as pets or for stock, and these too often escaped into the wild. Foxes were introduced, for example, so that people could participate in an authentic hunt. Today dozens of these species have gone feral, each one disturbing the native ecology to a greater or lesser degree.

That much of this progress was at the expense of the traumatized indigenous peoples and the environment they had so carefully managed went largely unnoticed and unremarked. The surviving Aboriginal population watched from the fringes, driven either to the very margins of society or out into the near-deserts of the Outback. Their cultures were almost fatally fractured and reservoirs of knowledge were disappearing fast. They were rarely actively hunted down any more, though cold-blooded massacres did occur until at least 1928, but a decline in aggression did not mean an increase in acceptance. That they would themselves soon disappear entirely still seemed entirely likely to the white population, so there was little need to include them in the future of the colonies.

The lustre wanes

In the 1890s falling global prices for the principal Australian exports coincided with the topping out of a spiralling frenzy of stock and land speculation. The combination of a drop in income with huge borrowings, loss of British investment with over-valued stock, led to an economic crash of unprecedented proportions in 1893. Soaring the highest, Victoria had the furthest to fall and Melbourne faced a crisis that saw people literally starving to death.

Just two years later a sapping drought gripped the country, decimating grain harvests and halving the sheep population by 1903. Australia has for much of its recent history been one of the world's most important grain exporters. In 1902 the usual flow was reversed with wheat being imported for the first time since the height of the gold rushes.

Its an ill-wind that blows nobody any good, however, and the crisis of the 1890s was the period when Western Australia finally became a colony of note. In 1885 Perth could have barely mustered 5,000 souls where Melbourne had over 400,000. Its initial low population meant that the effects of the drought, less significant than in the east anyway, were a relatively minor problem. A stricken and restless population in the east also provided a pool of labour and talent should the western colony become more attractive.

Federation and nationhood

Up to about 1890 the six Australasian colonies and New Zealand had jealously guarded their independence from each other. Proud of their differences, they each operated their own institutions, governments, services and military forces, united only solidly by currency, the environment and a shared heritage.

Their military forces were scant, however, and the colonies still relied heavily on the navy of the British Empire for defence. During the late 1800s other nations such as France, Germany, Japan and Russia were becoming powerful, challenging the Empire for hegemony over maritime and continental trade routes. In Australia there were very real fears that some of these powers might have designs on Australian territory, and in the late 1880s Britain pointed out that the colonies' military forces were hugely inadequate and would be far more effective if united under as single command structure.

In 1889 the prime minister of New South Wales made a bold step. He suggested that the proposed federation of armed forces be given far greater scope, that it should be widened to a political federation of the colonies. Two years later he had helped bring together a convention of delegates from most of them, including New Zealand, to draw up a draft constitution.

There things stood until the economic downturn of 1893 when Victoria in particular revived the idea, noting that an open internal market might help revive her fortunes. In that year John Quick devised a three-step strategy for federation. A poll in each state would elect delegates to another convention; this convention would then draw up a full constitution; the people of each colony would then vote on whether they would want to be included in the new Commonwealth of Australia.

The delegates first met in 1897. There were none from Queensland, which stayed ambivalent to the end, and also none from New Zealand. An economic recovery across the Tasman Sea had resulted in the view that joining with the Australian colonies was unnecessary, and they opted for political independence. In the referendums of 1898-1900 the southern states were the most enthusiastic. New South Wales was less so, but endorsed federation when promised the capital territory. Queensland's 'yes' vote was by a whisker, just 4,000 people deciding the outcome. Had it not been for the recent influx of goldminers from the eastern states to Western Australia, to a man keen on the idea, that colony might also have remained aloof.

The Commonwealth officially came into existence on 1 January 1901. Until Canberra was decided upon and built, Melbourne was the first federal capital, remaining so until 1927. The flag adopted was a well-received combination of the British Union Jack and the constellation of the Southern Cross.

Federation effectively ushered in nationhood, colonies became states, and now the relationship with the 'mother country' became more complex. On the one hand ties had never been stronger. Many who held high office in 1914 were British born, Britain was still Australia's biggest market for most of its exports, and British rather than Australian history was still considered more important in schools. On the other hand a British visitor to the new nation had to be careful not to offend local sensibilities. He or she would perhaps be called a 'pommy' (suspected to be a cockney derivative of 'immigrant' from 'pomegranate') instead of the warmer 'new chum' that had been in vogue since the gold rushes of the 1850s.

They would also have noticed signs encouraging people to 'buy Australian' and shun imported goods from the Empire and elsewhere, which was a sign of Australia's growing self-sufficiency and a renewal of confidence lost in the 1890s.

Federation also ushered in a raft of legislation that smoothed out policy across the nation. Paramount among this was the law that gave women the vote in 1902. Another piece of legislation result in the formal introduction of a 'White Australia' policy which, although in line with many nations of the day, seems shocking now and also jars given that the island continent was so manifestly 'Non-White Australia' just 115 years before. Immigration restarted in earnest in the mid-1900s, an integral part of the process being a dictation test in the European language of the immigration official's choice! In the northern regions of Australia, where the colonial frontier was still advancing, Aboriginal people were increasingly devastated by violence, disease, starvation and exploitation. Shortly before the federation the colonial governments had finally begun to worry that they were witnessing the destruction of Aboriginal people and introduced a raft of legislation to 'protect' them by confining them to certain areas away from Europeans. The Queensland Aborigines Act of 1897 meant that Aboriginal people could be forced to move to a reserve, were denied alcohol and the vote, and were paid for work under conditions and wages stipulated by the act. The State Protector was to be the legal guardian for all Aboriginal people under 21. Later amendments included the prohibition of sexual relations between Aborigines and Europeans and the need to seek permission for a mixed race marriage. This act was largely mirrored by the Aborigines Acts of WA (1905), NT (1911) and SA (1911). In NSW and Victoria, governments followed different policies, trying to get Aboriginal people off reserves, and the Tasmanian government refused to accept that it had any Aboriginal people.

Old wars, new purpose

When initiatives for peace in Europe failed after the Balkan crisis of 1914, and Britain swiftly came to the aid of its southern neighbours, Australia also quickly threw its hat in the ring with that of the Empire.

The Australian Imperial Force (AIF) were all either regular army or volunteers, but had still mustered 300,000 by the end of the First World War. They figured in many theatres of the war, the most celebrated of which has come to be known as Gallipoli. On 25 April 1915 the Anzacs (Australia and New Zealand Army Corps) constituted a large part of a force sent to win control of the banks of the Dardanelles, the narrow channel that connects the Aegean and Marmara seas. The expedition's success would open the allies supply line through the Mediterranean to the Black Sea and so to Russia.

Unfortunately the operation was compromised before it even started, with a squadron of ships trying to force the passage without silencing the Turkish guns on either flank. Pre-warned of a landing force, the Turks were well dug in and prepared. In addition the ground was hellishly difficult to attack and the Turks were tenacious and brave. The landing force did manage to create a number of toe-holds, however, and hung on to these for eight months, all the time trying not to forget the original objective.

Though forced to retreat, the chief legacy of the campaign was profound for the Australian psyche. The Anzacs were seen to display a degree of bravery, mateship and humour not expected in such an untried force. In a seminal moment for the nation its unbloodied and untested soldiers had faced the fire for the first time and had not been found wanting. It is sometimes thought that these expressions of national character were forged on the beaches of Gallipoli, but it is truer to say that it was during the campaign that foreign journalists first saw and publicised these traits that had been slowly maturing for decades. Unseen by the rest of the world, and even by many urban Australians, Australian toughness, independence and co-operation had been won on the pastoral and mining frontiers decades before.

Of the 300,000 who went to war over 50,000 were killed, a greater number than was lost by America. Many of these were the bravest, most resourceful, most inspiring men of their time. Their loss was profoundly felt, eliciting a huge outpouring of national pride and grief, given substance by literally thousands of memorials erected all over the country.

In the aftermath of victory, and the knowledge that they had played a substantial part, Australians' pride in themselves and their country increased, and they began to believe they possessed a prodigious future. EJ Brady summarized this optimism in a huge tome, *Australia Unlimited*. Most influential politicians and commentators loudly voiced their uninformed opinions that Australia was a land of virtually unlimited resources, that could sustain a population of 100 million, perhaps half a billion. A subtext was that these people should be European, preferably British, to keep out the Asian hordes. One unusual realist, Professor Griffith Taylor, sounded several notes of caution and made the remarkably astute prediction that the population would be less than 20 million by 2000. Derided and scorned, he left for America in 1928.

By the late 1920s Melbourne and Sydney could both boast over a million residents and over half a million cars travelled Australia's roads. In 1927 Canberra's Parliament House was opened to much fanfare but few spectators. One who was a poignant and tragic witness for his people was an Aboriginal street entertainer called Marvellous. After the ceremony he walked the 10 km back to Queanbeyan and bedded down, blanketless, on a dirt pathway. The night was freezing and in the morning he was found frozen to death.

Depression and consolidation

The early 1930s saw the worldwide Great Depression. This was exacerbated in Australia by large outstanding loans from Britain which the government simply stopped trying to repay. The unemployed (nearly 30% of the workforce by 1932) generally received enough food to avoid starvation, but little else. In the resulting political melee Joseph Lyons became prime minister and held the position until 1939. His right-wing United Australia Party was fiercely anti-communist, a stance that helped blind it to the ambitions of Japan and the European fascist states for a decade.

There were two events in 1932 that each added another ingredient to the mix of moods in the country. The completion of the Sydney Harbour Bridge was greeted with immense pride. This was tangible evidence of the nation's unbroken spirit and continued optimism. The other, oddly, was the visit of the English cricket team for what came to be called the 'bodyline' series. In the face of terrific talent in the Australian batting line-up, including a young Donald Bradman, the English bowlers were coached to aim for the body rather than the stumps. Relations with the 'mother country' soured considerably and the sporting wound has still not entirely healed.

The 1930s were marked by increased misery for many Aboriginal people. Influenced by popular notions of eugenics and racial purity in Europe, state governments thought that 'full bloods' would eventually die out and 'half castes' could be bred out. It was thought that if a woman of both Aboriginal and European descent took a European partner, and her children did the same, then the 'Aboriginal blood' would eventually become so diluted as to be invisible. It was also thought that if children of mixed descent with fairly pale skin could be taken from their Aboriginal mothers at an early age and raised within the white community it would give the child every material advantage and help 'half-castes' be absorbed into the community. As a result, in the Aboriginal Acts of NT (1933, 1936) WA (1936) QLD (1939) and SA (1939) provisions relating to permission to marry and sexual relations between Aboriginal people and Europeans were strengthened. The states' powers of guardianship were increasingly used to remove children of mixed descent from their mothers and rear them in missions, orphanages or foster homes. In 1937 a conference of the state government Protectors decided that, *"the destiny of the natives of aboriginal origin, but not of the full blood, lies in their ultimate absorption by the people of the Commonwealth, and it therefore recommends that all efforts be directed to that end."* However anthropologists working with Aboriginal people in the 1930s began to educate the rest of society about their culture, and various humanitarian groups and Aboriginal protest groups also began to agitate for a change in attitudes.

When war again broke out in 1939 the country was pitifully ill-prepared, probably less so than in 1914, but once again backed Britain to the hilt, sending troops to Europe. For the first 18 months the war seemed distant to those in Australia, with life going on as it did in the First World War. If anything, conditions for the average family improved as unemployment fell. The Japanese attack on Pearl Harbour shattered any illusion that Southeast Asia might go untouched, with waves of the Emperor's forces sweeping out across the region in an unremitting campaign of expansion. Britain, over-extended after a year of orchestrating the battle against Hitler virtually alone, was almost powerless to try to stop them. Singapore was captured and with it tens of thousands of allied troops. For the first time in 50 years invasion seemed possible.

For Australians 1942 was the most important year of the war in many ways. Japanese bombers and warships shelled Darwin, Sydney and Newcastle, but in truth it was their swan-song. In that year too, Australian troops finally halted the enemy advance on the Kokoda Trail, preventing what could have been a fatal occupation of Port Moresby in New Guinea, and the US fleet seriously bloodied the Japanese nose at the Battle of the Coral Sea. Just as courageous as Gallipoli, Kokoda also has the virtue of being a victorious campaign and by rights it should be as widely remembered as its First World War counterpart. Australians witnessed other tangible effects of war. Rationing was introduced and there were floods of fascinating newcomers in the guise of American troops, prisoners of war and European refugees.

Australia had a population of around seven million in 1939. A little under one million of these enlisted or were conscripted, of which under 40,000 were killed. It is estimated that about 500 Aborigines enlisted in the First World War and over 2,000 in the Second World War. More in the north, plus many Torres Strait Islanders, rendered valuable assistance in the defence of the country. At the close of both wars their reward was scant. Some returned only to find their ancestral lands closed to them. White Australia may have discovered a fierce wartime gusto towards its overseas enemies, but the conflicts also helped cement a deep mistrust and fear of all non-Europeans.

'White Australia'

Prime Minister Ben Chifley's Australia of the late 1940s was a careful nation. Beaten by the bomb, it was felt that Japan still had considerable potential for aggression and Australia played a leading role in garrisoning the defeated country and prosecuting its war leaders. There was a deep feeling that peace could not last. Russia and China were deemed the major new threats and it was universally felt that a large population would be the best disincentive to invasion, and defence against any such attempt.

The old 'White Australia' policy was energized once more. Chifley's chief minister for immigration, Arthur Calwell, instigated and pursued the most vigorous population programme Australia has ever seen, stating that the nation must "populate or perish". It was originally thought that the Brits, still seen as the best 'stock', could make up 90% of the numbers but this proved over-ambitious – they eventually made up around a quarter of the immigrants of the period, and some of those were unwittingly expatriated orphans. Calwell had to relax his criteria and was soon fishing in the vast refugee camp that central and southern Europe had become. However the net would be thrown no wider: those of African or Asian origin were definitely not welcome.

In continental Europe Calwell found a more enthusiastic audience, keen to escape the ravages of the war. Soon tens of thousands of Poles and Greeks, Jews and Germans, Italians and Yugoslavs were pouring into the country. All of them had to work for the government for a minimum of two years, many at large schemes such as the Snowy Mountains Hydroelectric Scheme to generate power and irrigate the inland plains. Some had to wait years before being able to properly apply their skills. Historian Phillip Knightley tells the story of one immigrant with medical experience being given the job of an ambulance driver. On witnessing a tracheotomy he suddenly cautioned the doctor "No. No. Not there. Cut here!" The doctor scornfully responded that he was following the manual of a respected international expert. "Yes," replied the driver, "but there've been developments since I wrote that."

Non-British immigrants also had to put up with a fair amount of social antagonism. 'Refos' (refugees), 'DPs' (displaced persons) and 'dagos' were taunts frequently slung at the newcomers. With sometimes only a scant grasp of English, people from the same country frequently banded together, forming distinct enclaves and giving some suburbs, particularly in Sydney and Melbourne, a decidedly international flavour. The few non-European immigrants and descendants of the earlier Chinese gold miners fared much worse, suffering at times outright racial vilification. The non-British were, however, to form the foundation of a vibrant and successful urban multi-cultural society.

In 1949 the giant of 20th-century Australian politics, Robert Menzies, strode back into the limelight, leading his new Liberal party to election victory. A staunch monarchist, he welcomed Queen Elizabeth II to Australia in 1954, the first reigning monarch to make the trip. Under Menzies the immigration policies continued apace, and between 1945 and 1973 about three and a half million people came to live in Australia. With dramatic developments in technology the 1950s saw a renewed thrust in mineral prospecting and mining. In the following decades new discoveries were repeatedly made, with a long list of metals being added to Australia's already rich list, metals such as aluminium, nickel, manganese, uranium and bauxite. Oil and black coal were also discovered in great quantities.

The post-war period, greeted initially with trepidation, had proved a boom time and the good times were neatly encapsulated by Melbourne hosting the Olympics in 1956. Television had been quickly put in place to promote the games and soon people all over the world had the opportunity of seeing, in their own homes, moving pictures of the 'land down under'.

Culture clash

There was a flip-side to all this post-war optimism, however, itself a product of the war. The Nazis had been vanquished and the Japanese firmly re-confined to their island home, but communism now stood even larger on the world stage. Although the Japanese had failed to establish a modern Asian Empire, the 'western' world became convinced that either China or the Soviets might succeed, and many Australians believed that their homeland would be firmly in the sights of any nation with such ambitions.

This fear of communism had two profound effects, which between them later engendered a counter consequence of equal, if not greater, importance. Anti-communist hysteria goes a long way to explaining the firm grip that conservative governments were to have on Australian politics for a quarter of a century, with Labor Party members and supporters frequently suspected of being communist sympathizers and even spies. In 1950 Robert Menzies held a national referendum on whether the Communist Party should be banned outright and its members jailed. To the nation's credit the result was a comfortable 'no'. The other major effect of the national mood was an enthusiastic willingness to back up any Asian military efforts against the 'red tide' with practical support. The same year as the referendum saw Australian troops join those from the USA and their other allies in fighting the 'commies' in Korea. A little later, in the year of the Melbourne Olympics, the Soviet Union invaded Hungary and anti-communist fears in Australia were bolstered further by a stream of frightened refugees.

The conservative cauldron simmered on through the height of the Cold War in the late 1950s and early 1960s, thus ensuring that Australia, unlike Britain, was ready to send troops in support of another Asian crusade, this time in Vietnam. The Australian commitment was never huge in military terms, committing some 8,000 people, but Prime Minister Harold Holt's famous statement, "all the way with LBJ", neatly illustrates the depth of conservative political support. It was also an indication that Australia was shifting from British influence to follow an American lead. Although only a few troops made the journey, some of them were conscripts. This sat uneasily with much of the general public, and when conscripts started getting killed some of that public started getting visibly angry.

The nation became embroiled, for the first time in decades, in serious discussions about the direction and fitness of the government and its policies. Demonstrations against the war were organized and some marches became violent. Governments frequently clamped down hard, prompting further discussion and protests on the subject of civil liberties. Some people demonstrated simply to express their view that they had a right to demonstrate. A heady brew of general anti-establishment feeling began to ferment, particularly amongst the youth of the day, inspired by their cousins in Europe and the USA who were discovering a new independence from their 'elders and betters'.

Aboriginal people were also part of the protest movement and increasingly demanded change. In the early 1960s new legislation appeared in all states that largely removed the paternalistic and restrictive laws relating to Aboriginal people. The federal government enfranchised Aborigines of the Northern Territory (the only region under their control) and the rest of the states followed the federal lead. Previously citizenship had only been available to those who applied for it and was subject to certain conditions; in Western Australia that meant not keeping company with any Aboriginal people except the applicant's immediate family for two years before applying and after being granted citizenship. In 1967 a total of 89% of Australians voted in a referendum to allow the federal government to legislate for Aboriginal people. The ad-hoc and self-interested approach of the states was over.

The granting of rights such as equal wages had to be fought for in some cases, even when the legislation existed, and this could be the catalyst for further activism. When the Gurindji people failed to obtain equal wages from the powerful Lord Vestey of Wave Hill Station in the Northern Territory they walked off the land, led by stockman Vincent Lingiari, and decided to make a land rights claim for some of Vestey-owned land. As one of his people later said; *"We were treated just like dogs. We were lucky to get paid the fifty quid a month we were due, and we lived in tin humpies you had to crawl in and out on your knees. There was no running water. The food was bad – just flour, tea, sugar and bits of beef like the head or feet of a bullock. The Vesteys were hard men. They didn't care about blackfellas."* Just 10 years earlier Lingiari and his Gurindji people would probably have been ignominiously, forcefully and quietly evicted, but this was 1966 and sections of society were prepared to listen and help. The ruling conservative Liberal-Country Party rejected the Aboriginals' claim, wary of their own land-owning voters and perhaps of the effects a positive outcome might have on future mineral exploitation. The political wind was, however, changing. The Australian people had soon had enough of the conservatives and were ready for a new broom. In 1972 they finally elected the Labor Party back into power, and with it the charismatic and energetic Gough Whitlam.

Modern Australia

There is much discussion as to when Australia really became a nation. Looking back Federation seems a likely candidate, but at the time it probably meant little to most people, and certainly nothing to its indigenous people. The return of the Anzacs from the First World War is also considered a seminal moment: they went out as boys from New South Wales, Western Australia and the other states, but came back as Australians. There was still a profound sense of kinship with Britain, however, and many people, though born in Australia, would call themselves British and held a British passport. Another war brought with it the shocking realization that good ol' Britannia could no longer defend Australian shores, and another emotional tie was severed when Britain first lobbied to join the European Union in 1962. By then Australia knew it had to stand alone both economically and politically but, Tarzan-like, it had leaped from the British vine only to grasp desperately at the American one.

In many ways the brief tenure of Gough Whitlam as Prime Minister was the coming of age for Australia. He came to power unencumbered by decades of the politics of fear, and with a zeal to be his own man and make Australia her own nation. Within days the troops were recalled from Vietnam and conscription ended, women were legally granted an equal wage structure, 'White Australia' formally abandoned, and a Ministry of Aboriginal Affairs created. Whitlam's stated policy was "to restore to the Aboriginal people of Australia their lost power of self-determination in economic, social and political affairs". Whitlam spurned the prime ministerial Bentley, ended the old imperial honours system and dumped 'God Save the Queen' as the National Anthem. He was a political dynamo, and exacted an unprecedented work-rate from his colleagues. His policies were not everyone's cup of tea, but no one could argue that his every effort was not aimed at the betterment of Australia and Australians. In 1975 the Gurindji people were given 2,000 sq km from the Vestey leases and Whitlam flew to Wave Hill to personally hand over the deeds, symbolically pouring a handful of sand into the palm of Vincent Lingiari as he did so. Even Whitlam's sacking a few months later, a controversial affair involving the Governor-General, and consequently the British Crown, had the effect of galvanizing public opinion on the subject of republicanism. Whitlam had also permanently altered the mood of the nation, and of Australian politics.

The late 1970s and 1980s continued to be a time of rapid and shifting changes. The fledgling Green movement had failed to stop the damming of Lake Pedder in Tasmania in 1972, but did stop the similar Franklin River scheme a decade later. Sydney's first Gay and Lesbian march in 1978 was met with derision, vilification and police violence – its annual successor, the Mardi Gras, is now the biggest event of its kind in the world and Sydney's wildest party, enjoyed by gays and straights alike. Following the demise of 'White Australia', the country again opened its doors to Asian migrants, and to thousands of Vietnamese 'boat people'. Once again, the new peoples and cultures hugely enriched urban society. In 1988 the country celebrated the Bicentennial – 200 years of white settlement. Aboriginal people found little to celebrate and used the event to draw political attention to Aboriginal issues such as the high rate of Aboriginal deaths in custody, the subject of a Royal Commission enquiry throughout that year, and the question of a treaty between indigenous and non-indigenous Australians.

The 1990s was a tumultuous decade for issues involving Aboriginal people. In 1992 the High Court made what was probably the most important decision of the century in the Mabo land rights case. The court ruled that native title (or prior indigenous ownership of land) was not extinguished by the Crown's claim of possession in the Murray Islands of Torres Strait. In other words the legal fiction of *terra nullias* was overturned after 222 years, and the decision was later enshrined in the Native Title Act (1993). This was a major victory for Aboriginal people although landowners had to be able to prove a continuous relationship to the land and claims could only be made on Crown land. A land fund was suggested to buy land for the majority of Aboriginal people who were unable to claim land under the Act. Despite the limited nature of native title conservatives were horrified and lobbied hard against it.

In 1996 there was further uproar from conservatives and pastoralists when the High Court ruled in the Wik case that pastoral leases and native title could co-exist. However, as there are many different types of leaseholds, the court stated that every case would have to be decided on its own merits. This meant there was no certainty for those holding pastoral leases, covering 40% of Australia and at that time making up two-thirds of all land claims. Those bitterly opposed to land rights wanted the government to legislate to extinguish native title over pastoral leases. The Howard government responded with a 10 Point Plan to amend the Native Title Act that favoured pastoral interests and limited the powers of native titleholders. Neither group was happy with the plan (it wasn't extreme enough for pastoralists) and the Australian Law Reform Commission and Labor politicians called it racially discriminatory. The Native Title Amendment Bill was passed in 1998 with the help of an independent senator.

Amid the turmoil over land rights in 1997, the Human Rights and Equal Opportunity Commission produced the report of their National Inquiry into the Separation of Aboriginal and Torres Strait Islander Children from their Families. This report, titled *Bringing Them Home*, estimated that between one in ten and one in three indigenous children were removed between 1910 and 1970. Its recommendations were compensation, counselling and an official apology. The Howard government described the report as flawed and refused to apologize or pay compensation but later announced a package to pay for counselling, family support and cultural programmes. The children who were the subject of this report are now known as the 'stolen generation'.

As Australia moved toward a new century, two campaigns aimed at moving the country in a new direction built a considerable head of steam – that for a republic and another for reconciliation. One sought to sunder further the ties with Britain, the other to build better ties between white and black Australians. Reconciliation was seen as important for the future health of the nation, a gesture that would heal the divisions between black and white and allow Australians to move into the future together. The Council for Aboriginal Reconciliation worked on a Declaration of Reconciliation that was presented to the government in 2000. In the same year there were large reconciliation marches all over the country by sections of the community who wanted to say 'sorry' for past injustices, despite the government's refusal to do so. The issue of the republic was to be decided by a 1999 national referendum. The question asked, however, was controversially worded in a way that prevented many republicans assenting to it, and the result was 'no', despite polls showing a majority in favour of a republic.

A new century

The Olympics were held in Sydney in 2000, and must be ranked as one of the greatest games ever. The Aboriginal athlete Kathy Freeman won gold in the women's 400 m track sprint, sending the nation into a frenzy of joy. Following the reconciliation movement the victory seemed, to many, serendipitous. However, the huge optimism created by the successful staging of the Olympics seemed to fizzle out with the failure of the republic and the failure to achieve any meaningful reconciliation between indigenous and non-indigenous Australians. Aboriginal people are still coming to terms with the effects of dispossession and the government policies that have affected their lives from 1788 until the present day. By almost every measure of social welfare they are less well off than non-indigenous Australians, for example the life expectancy of an indigenous person is 20 years less than other Australians, and rectifying this inequality is the great challenge of the future for all Australians.

With the turn of the century there is an increasing recurrence and concern throughout Australia and especially in NSW and the East Coast of an age-old natural phenomenon – drought and bush fires. In 1994, 1996, 1997 and most recently in 2001 and 2002, fires ravaged the surrounding national parks and the fringes of Sydney, destroying numerous properties, taking several lives and dulling Sydney's vivid colours with a cloak of grey, acrid smoke. The fires are also not just confined to NSW. In 2002, again, exacerbated by severe drought conditions, both Victoria and Western Australia suffered their most widespread and protracted fires for years. Whether these fires were started by lightening, human accident or malice, they provide a powerful reminder of modern man's disastrous impact on the Australian environment in modern times and his fragile place within it.

In November 2001 the Liberal-National coalition government under John Howard was returned to power despite the unpopularity of the Goods and Services Tax introduced in 2000. The campaign was run amid the uncertainty caused by the terrorist attacks of September 11 and issues of border protection highlighted by the government's handling of the *Tampa* crisis. The *Tampa's* Norwegian captain had rescued boat people claiming to be refugees from Afghanistan but the government refused to allow the 'illegal immigrants' to land on the mainland. Since the election, border protection and the detention of asylum seekers have become even hotter issues. Asylum seekers who are refused residency may appeal the decision but while awaiting appeal they (and their children) are held in remote detention centres for as long as three years. The UN High Council for Refugees has criticized government policy on asylum seekers and detention centres, as have prominent Australians such as former conservative prime minister, Malcolm Fraser, but the government stands by its policies. This issue has affected Australia's international standing and still polarises Australian society today.

Throughout 2002 Australian political affairs were dominated by the international threat of terrorism rather than local issues. In October 2002 terrorism hit very close to home and Australia suffered its own 9/11, when two nightclubs were bombed in Bali, killing around 200 people, almost half of which were Australian. Although the bombers were reputedly trying to target Americans, Bali has for many years been the traditional haunt of Australians, especially youngsters. Regardless of target and nationality, the country and the world was outraged.

With the ousting of the Taliban in Afghanistan by a coalition of US lead forces and the hunt for Bin Laden unsuccessful, America under the Bush administration turned its fevered attentions to Saddam Hussein, Iraq and his reputed weapons of mass destruction. Frustrated by the lack of any evidence of such weapons being unearthed by a new round of UN weapons inspections and after unsuccessfully securing an international mandate and a revised Security Council resolution for the use of force, Bush and his hawks took the highly contentious decision on a pre-emptive invasion of Iraq with a 'coalition of the willing'. Only two Prime Ministers agreed to support the US logistically in the war, Great Britain's Tony Blair and John Howard. For both Blair and Howard that decision was made despite majority public opposition domestically and throughout the world. Undoubtedly once the dust settles such extrovert support for the US will bring considerable economic gains to both Australia and Great Britain. However, quite how it affects the country politically, socially and as a target for terrorism, both at home and abroad, remains the paramount issue for most ordinary Australians.

Politics

Although Australians are not typically political animals, Australian politics are hard to ignore. This is partly because of the sheer volume of government the country bears, partly because of the colourful characters and events Australian politics seems to throw up, and partly because everyone, by law, has to vote.

Australia's head of the state is the reigning monarch of England, a throwback to when the monarch was the head of the British Empire, which the Australian colonies were very much part of. The Queen's representative in Australia, now usually Australian born, is the Governor-General, appointed by the Australian prime minister. The role is largely ceremonial, though in theory invested with considerable powers.

In practical terms the business of governing the whole country is undertaken by the Federal ('Commonwealth') Parliament based in Canberra. Its 'lower' House of Representatives is constituted by members directly elected from electorates with approximately equally sized populations. The electorates range in size from a small city suburb to that of Kalgoorlie which encompasses most of WA and is, in fact, the largest constituency anywhere in the world. The 'upper' house, the Senate, is elected by a form of proportional representation that guarantees each state 12 members, and each territory two. The lower house formulates government policy and the upper house either vetoes or passes it. Both houses are voted for every three years.

There are two major parties which sit either side of the political fence. The Australian Labor Party (ALP) and the Liberal Party are the two chief protagonists, the ALP being the rough equivalent of the British Labour Party or American Democrats, the Liberals the equivalent of the Conservatives or Republicans. Over the last 70 years the ALP have generally polled slightly higher than the Liberals, but have usually been kept out of office by the latter's alliance with the smaller Country and National parties. The leader of the majority in the lower house forms the country's government and is its Prime Minister. In 2001 John Howard's Liberal/National coalition won their third consecutive election and are currently in office. The upper house is even more finely balanced, and here the voting system allows the smaller significant parties, the Democrats and the Greens to win more seats and so to effectively hold the balance of power.

Most of the nation's tax dollar ends up in the Commonwealth coffers. About a third of the Federal budget goes in benefit payments, about a fifth on the machinery of government and state institutions, and about a quarter is distributed as payments to individual states. A constant source of grievance between Federal and state governments is the relative proportion of each state's Federal income compared to the amount of tax its residents have paid, with bitter (and not untruthful) claims that some states subsidize the others.

In a second tier of government most states also have their own upper and lower houses, and also Governors. These too are elected on a three-year cycle, and much the same political parties vie for election. All state governments are currently ALP.

Culture

Aboriginal art and culture

From the beginning Aborigine is a Latin word meaning 'from the beginning'; the Romans used it to describe the first inhabitants of Latium and it can be used to apply to any people living in a country from its earliest period. It may seem strange that the first Australians are known by a generic name but its meaning is certainly appropriate for Australian Aboriginal people. Although anthropologists believe that Aboriginal people arrived in Australia 50,000-60,000 years ago from Southeast Asia, Aboriginal people believe that they have always been here, that they were created here by their spirit ancestors. Before Europeans arrived in Australia, Aboriginal people had no collective sense of identity. Their identity was tied to their own part of the country and to their extended family groups. Hence no name existed to describe all of the inhabitants of Australia, in the same way that until relatively recently the inhabitants of Europe would have had no conception of being 'European'.

A continent of many nations When the First Fleet arrived with its cargo of convicts in 1788 there were between 300,000 and 750,000 Aboriginal people living in Australia, who belonged to about 500 tribes or groups. It is difficult to make generalizations about Aboriginal people because each group had its own territory, its own language or dialect and its own culture. There were broad cultural similarities between these groups just as different nationalities in Europe had more in common with each other than they had with Chinese or African people for example. Naturally, neighbouring groups were more similar to each other; perhaps speaking dialects of the same language and sharing some 'Dreamtime' myths linked to territory borders such as rivers and mountains. However, if a man from Cape York had found himself transported to the Western Desert he would have been unable to communicate with the desert people. He would have found them eating unfamiliar food and using different methods to obtain it. Their art would have been incomprehensible to him and their ceremony meaningless. If he had been able to speak their language he would have found that they had a different explanation of how they came into existence and his own creation ancestors would have been unknown to them. Each group was almost like a small state or nation.

Dreaming Every traveller in Australia will encounter the concept of the 'Dreaming' or the 'Dreamtime'. These words attempt to explain a complex concept that lies at the heart of

Aboriginal culture and should not be understood in the English context of something that is not real. Most Aboriginal groups believe that in the beginning the world was featureless. Ancestral beings emerged from the earth and as they moved about the landscape they shaped it. Some of them created humans by giving birth to them or moulding them from incomplete life forms. Ancestral beings were sometimes human in form but also often animals, rocks, trees or stars, and could transform from one shape to another. Nor were they limited by their form; kangaroos could talk, fish could swim out of water. Wherever these beings went, whatever they did left its mark on the landscape. A mountain could be the fallen body of an ancestor speared to death, a waterhole may be the place a spirit emerged from the earth, a rock bar may show where an ancestor crossed a river, yellow ochre may be the fat of an ancestral kangaroo. In this way the entire continent is mapped with tracks of the ancestor beings.

Although the time of creation and shaping of the landscape is associated with the temporal notion of 'beginning', it is important to understand that Dreaming is not part of the past. It lies within the present and will determine the future. The ancestral beings have a permanent presence in spiritual or physical form. Ancestor snakes and serpents still live in the waterholes that they created; this is why visitors are sometimes asked not to swim in certain pools, so that these ancestors will not be disturbed. This is also why mining or development can cause great distress to Aboriginal people if the area targeted is the home of an ancestral being. The ancestors are also still involved in creation. Sexual intercourse is seen as being part of conception but new life can only be created if a conception spirit enters a woman's body. The place where this happens, near a waterhole, spring or sacred site, will determine the child's identification with a particular totem or ancestor. In this way Aboriginal people are directly connected to their ancestral world.

Aboriginal people belonged to a territory because they were descended from the ancestors who formed and shaped that territory. The ancestral beings were sources of life and powerful performers of great deeds but were also capable of being capricious, amoral and dangerous. Yet in their actions they laid down the rules for life. They created ceremony, song and designs to commemorate their deeds or journeys, established marriage and kinship rules and explained how to look after the land. In the simple forms related to outsiders, Dreaming stories often sound like moral fables. Knowledge of the land's creation stories was passed on from generation to generation, increasing in complexity or sacredness as an individual aged. With knowledge came the responsibility to look after sacred creation or resting places. Ceremonies were conducted to ensure the continuation of life forces and fertility. Aboriginal people had no idea of owning the land in the sense that it was a possession that could be traded or given away, but saw themselves as custodians of land in which humans, animals and spirits were inseparable – in fact, one and the same. Consequently Aboriginal people of one group had no interest in possessing the land of another group. Strange country was meaningless to them. To leave your country was to leave your world.

The bonds of kin

In their daily life Aboriginal people usually hunted, gathered and socialized within a small band, perhaps 50 people belonging to one or two families. These bands or clans only came together to form the whole group of several hundred people for ceremonial reasons and at places or times when food was plentiful. Group behaviour and social relations were governed by an intricate kinship system, and guided by the superior knowledge and experience of the elders. This is one of the reasons that the word 'tribe' is not used to describe groups of Aboriginal people, as a tribe by definition is led by a chief and Aboriginal society did not operate in this way. The rules of kinship are far too complicated to explain here, and also vary in different regions, but in essence the kinship system linked the whole group as family. You would call your birth mother 'mother' but you would also call your mother's sisters 'mother' and they would take on the obligations of that role. The same applied for sisters, fathers, uncles and so on. There were specific codes of behaviour for each kin relationship so you would know the appropriate way to behave towards each member of your group. For example, in many Aboriginal societies mothers-in-law and sons-in-law were not allowed to communicate with each other. A neat solution to an age-old problem in human relations!

Kinship also determined whom an individual could marry. In one type of kinship system each person in a group belongs to one of several sections or moieties. The moiety category is inherited from the father and so contains all of an individual's patrilineal relations. That individual can only marry someone from another moiety. Kinship links also exist between people of the same totem or ancestor. People born from the goanna ancestor would be related to all other 'goannas'. Each kinship relationship carried specific responsibilities and rights such as initiating a 'son' or giving food to a 'sister', creating a strong collective society where everyone is tied to each other. By this method food and possessions are distributed equally and because of these kinship obligations it is almost impossible for an individual to accumulate material wealth. This major difference between Aboriginal culture and the dominant ethic in Australian society of Western materialism still creates problems for those trying to live in both worlds. For example a young Aboriginal footballer will often move from his close-knit rural community to Melbourne to play in the AFL, and find it very difficult to balance the material demands of his family against the demands of his team who teach him to pursue personal wealth and glory.

Environment The laws of the Dreaming provided a broad framework for spiritual and material life, but of course Aboriginal culture was not static. Although their society valued continuity above change, parts of their culture were the result of adapting to their environment. Aboriginal people have lived in Australia for so long that they have seen major environmental changes such as climate change, dramatic changes in sea level caused by the last ice age and even volcanic eruptions in southern Australia. The picture that many people have in their minds of an Australian Aboriginal is of a desert-dwelling nomad with few possessions and only a roof of stars over his head at night. Of course some people lived like this but others sewed warm skin cloaks, built bark or stone huts and lived in the same place for several seasons. The ways in which Aboriginal people differed from each other very much depended on the environment that they lived in. The wetlands of Arnhem Land were particularly rich in food resources throughout the year and were thought to have supported a large and fairly settled population. The Warlpiri people of central Australia had to range far and wide to find their food and move on quickly so as not to over-exploit the resources of a single area. Naturally, tools were developed to match the territory; boomerangs were not known to people who lived in areas of dense woodland, nor elaborate fish traps known to inland people. Conversely, Aboriginal people also changed their environment with methods such as 'fire-stick farming' (see page 409).

Hunting & gathering Aboriginal people were generally semi-nomadic rather than true nomads but they did not wander about aimlessly. They moved purposefully to specific places within their territory to find food that they knew to be ripening or abundant at certain times of the year. Their long tenure and stable society meant that they knew the qualities of every plant, the behaviour of every animal and the nature of every season intimately. Men hunted large game such as kangaroos with their toolkit of spears, clubs or boomerangs, and women gathered fruit, vegetables, seeds, honey, shellfish and small game such as lizards using their own kit of bags, bowls and digging sticks. Each gender had its own responsibilities and knowledge, including the ceremonies to ensure continuing fertility by commemorating the Dreaming. The need to 'look after country' in this way also determined their movements. Although men were generally more powerful than women, having more authority over family members and ritual, women had their own power base because of their knowledge and the reliability of the food they provided. Although hunting and gathering was labour intensive, anthropologists estimate that Aboriginal people only had to spend three to five hours a day working for food, leaving plenty of time for social life and ceremony.

Ceremony and art were at the very heart of life for these were the ways in which Aboriginal people maintained their connection with the ancestors. During ceremonies the actions and movements of the ancestors would be recalled in songs and dances that the ancestors themselves had performed and handed down to each clan or group. Not only did the ancestral beings leave a physical record of their travels in the form of the landscape but also in paintings, sacred objects and sculptures that might be shown or used as part of a ceremony. Ceremonies maintained the power and life force of the ancestors thus replenishing the natural environment. Some ceremonies, such as those performed at initiation, brought the individual closer to his or her ancestors. Ceremonies performed at death made sure that a person's spirit would re-join the spiritual world. Some were public ceremonies or art forms, others were secret and restricted to those who were responsible for looking after a certain piece of country and the ancestors and stories associated with it.

Ceremony & art

When a person painted and decorated his or her body, they did so with designs and ornaments that the ancestral beings had created. The individual was almost transformed into the ancestor, thus bringing these beings to life in the present, in the same way that carvings and paintings of spirit beings such as the Rainbow Serpent can do. Art was also a product of the kinship system as one of its obligations was the giving and receiving of goods. The value of the gift was not important in fulfilling this obligation, only the act of giving. As a result Aboriginal people were continually engaged in making material objects such as body ornaments, baskets, tools and weapons, all of which can be considered secular forms of art or craft. Of course these items also needed to be made again as they wore out. One of the features of Aboriginal art was its ephemeral nature; it existed to perform a function rather than be hoarded or kept as a perfect example of the form. Elaborate body paintings that took hours to complete could be smudged by sweat in minutes. They were also sometimes deliberately wiped off to hide or lessen the power of the ancestral image. The same applied to bark paintings which would be discarded or destroyed. Ground sculptures were often temporary, made in sand, or left to decay like the carved and painted pukunami burial poles of the Tiwi people. The most permanent forms were rock engravings and paintings but even these were eroded or painted over in time. Some Aboriginal art was like a blackboard, used to teach and then wiped clean.

Function of art

The most immediately obvious feature of Aboriginal art is its symbolic nature. Geometric designs such as circles, lines, dots, squares or abstract designs are used in all art forms and often combine to form what seems to be little more than an attractive pattern. Even when figures are used they are also symbolic representations: an emu may be prey or an ancestral being. The symbols do not have a fixed meaning; a circle may represent a waterhole, a camping place or an event. In Aboriginal art symbols are put together to form a map of the landscape. This is not a literal map where the 'key' relates to the topography of a piece of countryside, but rather a mythological map. Features of the landscape are depicted but only in their relation to the creation myth that is the subject of the painting. A wavy line terminating in a circle might represent the journey of the Rainbow Serpent to a waterhole. That landscape may also contain a hill behind the waterhole but if it is not relevant to the serpent's journey it will not be represented, although it may feature in other paintings related to different ancestral beings. Unlike a

A symbolic landscape

conventional map, scale is not consistent. The size of a feature is more likely to reflect its importance rather than its actual size or there may be several scales within a painting. Nor is orientation fixed.

Artistic licence As art was a means of expressing identity it follows that only those who belonged to an area of landscape and its Dreaming stories could paint those stories. No one else would know them. An artist must have the right to paint the image he has in mind and these rights are carefully guarded. This idea is refined further within the clan or group. A father and son of the same clan may know the same story but the father will be able to paint more powerful ancestral beings with more knowledge and detail, because it can take a lifetime to learn all of the knowledge connected to an ancestral being. Rights to paintings can also be established through kinship links, living in an area or taking part in ceremony. To many people Aboriginal art is recognized by its style – dots, X-ray or cross hatching – but what is painted is just as important as how it is painted. Aboriginal people working in traditional forms simply do not paint landscapes, figures or people that they are not spiritually connected to. The idea of painting a landscape simply because it is pretty is utterly foreign to Aboriginal art. Even an artist like Albert Namatjira who painted European landscape watercolours in the 1940s never painted anything but his own Arrernte land in central Australia, although he travelled widely outside it.

Interpretation How does the viewer understand the meaning of a work of Aboriginal art? Because of the use of symbols and the fact that Dreaming stories are only known to the ancestral descendants, only the painter, and perhaps his close relatives will be able to fully understand the meaning of a painting. In some areas the whole group may be able to interpret the painting. When you look at Aboriginal art in a gallery it will be labelled with the name of the artist, and often his clan or group name, dates and location but the meaning of the painting is not usually revealed. As knowledge of the creation myths illustrated relates to ownership it is not appropriate for the artists to pass on important cultural knowledge to strangers, although sometimes a very simple or limited explanation will be given to buyers. Some artists do interpret their paintings in more detail to anthropologists, land rights lawyers or art experts in order to educate non-indigenous people about Aboriginal culture. Looking at examples of Aboriginal art alongside an interpretation is the best way to comprehend the many layers of meaning possible. These can be found in art books such as the excellent *Aboriginal Art* by **Howard Morphy** (Phaidon, 1998).

Culture in the 21st century After the British arrived in Australia, many Aboriginal people died from unfamiliar diseases. Those who did not were often moved off their land to missions or reserves, or killed while resisting the strangers attempting to farm or live on their land. The British acted as they did for a variety of reasons; sometimes for their own material gain, sometimes just following orders and sometimes from the genuine desire to help or protect Aboriginal people. Unfortunately the British had no understanding of Aboriginal culture and did not comprehend that separating Aboriginal people from their land was about the most destructive action possible. In unfamiliar country there was no land to look after, no reason to perform ceremony, hand down knowledge or maintain kinship ties. In missions and reserves people had to live with groups who were perhaps recent enemies, who spoke another language, who did not share their religious beliefs. In the missions they were often forbidden to speak their own language and to practice any aspects of ceremonial life that had survived the sundering from their source. It says much for the strength of Aboriginal culture that many aspects of it still exist. Since the paternalism of the Australian government was abandoned in the 1970s and a policy of self-determination implemented, many Aboriginal people from northern and central

Australia have moved from government reserves back to their land to live in small remote communities. The production of art for sale in these communities helps them achieve financial independence and also revives their cultural life as the art is used to instruct young people in their Dreaming. Art has always been an integral part of the life of Aboriginal people and all over Australia people continue to express their Aboriginality in a variety of art forms. Aboriginal culture survives but continues to change and adapt as it has for countless thousands of years.

Rock art

Rock paintings and rock engravings found all over the country constitute Australia's most ancient and enduring art form. It is possible that rock engravings were being made 40,000 or even 60,000 years ago. Common forms are circles, lines, and animal tracks or animal figures. Many are so ancient that Aboriginal people of the area cannot explain their meaning. Rock painting can also be dated back to many thousands of years ago and was practised until the last few decades. The finest and most extensive rock-painting galleries are found in the great rocky escarpment and range country of the north. The paintings of the Arnhem Land escarpment reflect environmental changes that enable them to be dated to about 15,000 years ago. The Pre-Estuarine period dates from the last ice age until a rise in sea levels between 700 and 900 years ago and demonstrates drier conditions with paintings of kangaroos and boomerangs. Paintings of the Estuarine period, when the plains were inundated, include marine and estuarine species such as barramundi and crocodiles. Paintings made after 1788 are referred to as belonging to the Contact period and these include images of ships and guns.

Painting styles have also changed over the millennia and these help to date paintings too because paintings are generally layered on top of each other. The earliest art forms are stencils, where a mouthful of ochre is spat over the hand, foot or tool to leave a reverse print on the wall. Figures in red ochre (or blood) are also some of the oldest works as red ochre lasts longer than any other colour, seeping into the rock to bond with it permanently. Some of the most intriguing figures are the red ochre Bradshaws in the Kimberley and Mimi spirits in Arnhem Land who wear elaborate ceremonial dress such as tassels and head-dresses and carry feather fans. These are known as dynamic figures for their graceful sense of movement and are thought to be 6,000-10,000 years old. Perhaps most spectacular are the finely drawn and colourful X-ray figures of the last 3,000 years, where the internal structure of a figure, such as vertebrae or stomach, is represented. Gallery walls covered in barramundi, turtles, kangaroo and other food sources are thought to be a kind of hunting magic – to ensure a successful hunt. Sorcery paintings of inverted figures are commonly found in the superb galleries around Laura-Cooktown in Cape York. One of the responsibilities of the custodians of a rock-art site would be to retouch the painting to keep its power bright and strong.

Bark paintings

Although bark paintings are now identified with Arnhem Land and nearby islands, the only places in which this art form survives, bark was used as a painting surface in other parts of Australia. It is not known how long people had been producing bark paintings but it is thought that sheets may have been used in ceremony and hut walls used as a teaching tool, perhaps to instruct initiates in private. The bark comes from the stringybark tree and is stripped off in the wet season when most malleable, then scraped and uncurled by heating it over a fire. The 'canvas' is then painted upon with ochres using brushes made of bark or hair, and a fine stick. Arnhem Land barks usually depict their landscape and its creation myths in a more figurative form than art from central Australia, but still remain inherently symbolic. Paintings also differ in that they are less map-like, tending to represent the events of one place rather than the whole journey. Every clan owns a design representing the creation myth of their ancestors and these are often as abstract as an elongated diamond or a line of diamonds broken by an oval. A geometric pattern may also signify many things. The same pattern could represent a flowing river or smoke from a bushfire depending on the context in which it is used. In this way the bark paintings of Arnhem Land contain incredible depth of meaning, comprehensible only to those who know the landscape and story represented.

Dot paintings   These are the most widely recognized of Aboriginal art forms, highly sought after by international collectors, but also one of the newest forms. Dot paintings are made in the western and central desert regions and relate to an older form used by desert people. In the desert there are few rock surfaces and no trees suitable for stripping off large pieces of bark so the desert people used the ground to commemorate the travels and actions of their ancestral beings. Drawings, or perhaps more correctly sculptures, were created by placing crushed plant matter and feather down on a hard-packed surface. The material would be coloured with ochre or blood. Common designs were spirals or circles and lines. These works were always ceremonial and created by old and knowledgeable men. In the 1970s many desert people were living at Papunya, a community northwest of Alice Springs. An art teacher, Geoff Bardon, encouraged local men to paint a mural on the school wall. A Honey Ant Dreaming painting was created, leading to great interest and enthusiasm from men in the community. They began painting their stories on boards, using ochres or poster paints, in the symbolic manner of ground sculptures and ceremonial body painting. Over the next few decades these paintings, increasingly on canvas using acrylic paints, were offered for sale and became incredibly successful, both in Australia and outside it. There is great diversity of colour and style in contemporary desert paintings but the qualities of symbolism and ownership discussed earlier also apply. They are popularly known as dot paintings because the background is completely filled in by areas of dots. These can represent many elements of a landscape; for example clouds, areas of vegetation, the underground chambers of a honey ants nest, or all three at once. In galleries look out for the incomparable work of **Clifford Possum Tjapaltjarri** and **Kathleen Petyarre**.

Baskets & string work   Aboriginal people all over Australia produced string and fibre from the plants in their region to make functional and ceremonial objects. These have only recently been considered works of art as non-indigenous fibre and textile work has gained in status and as the importance of these objects is increasingly understood. Fibre work is a woman's art, although men sometimes made strong ropes for fishing. Palm leaves, reeds, vines, bark, and hair were all used to make string and fibre which was then made into a variety of baskets and bags. These were primarily used to carry food collected during a day's foraging but also held personal possessions. In the tropical north the common pandanus palm is used to make strong baskets or mats woven with dried strands of palm and a bone needle. Fine narrow bags of twined pandanus are called *dilly bags*, and in Arnhem Land play an important part in ceremony and are often depicted on rock art being worn by ancestral beings. String is spun from bark or palm leaves and knotted into bags or fishing nets in Cape York, Arnhem Land and nearby islands. String was also used to made body ornaments such as belts and fringes, armbands and necklaces. Baskets and bags are still made by the women of Northern Australia and today's techniques show how new technology is adapted to continue traditional ways. Before the British arrived Aboriginal people had no steel or clay containers and therefore were not able to boil water. Fibre work was coloured by rubbing ochre into the fibre when making it or by painting the finished object with ochre. Now the fibre is dyed in boiling water but the dyes are still made by the weavers from natural sources, such as roots and grasses, with great skill and subtlety.

Works of wood   Weapons and utensils made of wood were often carved with designs that symbolized an ancestor, thus identifying the land of the owner. The beauty of these carvings carries them beyond the purely functional, as does their origin in the Dreaming. Carvings of ancestral figures were also made to be used in ceremonies such as funeral rites. The Tiwi people of Bathurst and Melville islands make wooden *pukunami* poles that are placed at the gravesite, carved and painted with symbols relevant to the deceased person. The Yolgnu of Eastern Arnhem Land placed the bones of the deceased in hollow logs, usually painted with clan designs and sometimes carved at one end, and these log coffins would stand upright in the bush. There is a moving display of 200 log coffins in the National Gallery in Canberra, created as a memorial to the Aboriginal dead in the bicentennial year. Groups in NSW carved geometric designs into living trees to mark ceremonial grounds or burial sites.

In many communities weapons are no longer made because Aboriginal people now hunt with guns. Shields and clubs are not needed, but nothing has replaced the spear, and people still make clapping sticks or carrying dishes. As well as making the pukunami poles, the Tiwi carve wonderful wooden sculptures of totemic animals and ancestral beings for sale, as do people along the coast and islands of Arnhem Land. People in central Australia also make wooden animal carvings and these are often decorated with pokerwork, a burn from a hot wire. The didgeridoo is still made and used in ceremony in Arnhem Land, where it is called the *yidaki*. The didgeridoo is made from a tree trunk that has been hollowed out by termites so each one is unique and the bumps and knots inside influence the sound it makes.

Although it has its foundation in an ancient culture, contemporary art is also shaped by the present and is produced by Aboriginal people who live in the urban societies of the south and east, as well as in the north and central areas. These people may have lost their land, language, religion and families but they still have an Aboriginal identity. The people sometimes called urban Aboriginal artists may have trained in art school and their art possesses the 'Western' quality of reflecting the experience of the individual. They are united in their experience of surviving dispossession, by their personal history and experience of being Aboriginal in a dominant non-indigenous society. Some of the common themes in their work are events of the colonial past, such as massacres, or contemporary issues that affect Aboriginal people such as the fight for land rights or the disproportionately high number of Aboriginal prisoners. Some urban artists have tried to reconnect with their past or, like the late **Lin Onus**, establish links with artists working in more traditional forms and to incorporate clan designs or symbolic elements into their work. To see powerful contemporary Aboriginal art look for the work of **Robert Campbell Jnr**, **Sally Morgan**, Lin Onus, **Gordon Bennett**, **Trevor Nikolls**, **Fiona Foley** and **Donna Leslie**.

Contemporary Aboriginal art

Other Australian art

Australia was colonized during the century of Romanticism in Western Europe when interest in the natural world was at its height. Much of the earliest colonial art came from scientific expeditions and their specimen drawings. Most of these early images look slightly odd, as if even the best draughtsman found himself unable to capture the impossibly strange forms of unique Australian species such as the kangaroo. Indeed art from the whole of the first colonial century portrays Australia in a soft northern hemisphere light and in the rich colours of European landscapes. In these finely detailed landscapes the countryside was presented as romantically gothic or neatly tamed, even bucolic with the addition of cattle or a farmer at work, as seen in the work of **John Glover**, **Louis Buvelot** and **Eugene von Guérard**. In some there would also be quaint representations of a bark hut or black figure belonging to the peaceful 'children of nature'. Given the violence of what was happening to Aboriginal people at the time and the British impression that the new colony was a nasty, brutish place full of convicts, these paintings can be seen as an attempt to portray Australia as peaceful, beautiful and civilized. Things began to change in the 1880s and 1890s, by which time a majority of colonists had been born in Australia.

The Heidelberg School & Australian Impressionism

Increasing pride in being Australian and the influence of European Impressionism inspired Australian artists to really look at their environment and cast away conventional techniques, prompting a dramatic change in how the country was portrayed. Truth in light, colour and tone was pursued by artists such as **Arthur Streeton**, **Charles Conder**, **Tom Roberts** and **Frederick McCubbin**, who began painting *en plein air*. In their paintings bright light illuminates the country's real colours; the gold of dried grass, the smoky green of eucalypts and the deep blue of the Australian sky. These artists were known as the Heidelberg School because they painted many of their bush scenes around Heidelberg and Box Hill, just outside Melbourne. Some of Australia's most iconic and popular images were painted at this time. *Down on his luck* (1889) by Frederick McCubbin is a classic image of a bushman and his swag, staring into his campfire among gum trees. In Tom Roberts' *A break away!* (1891) a heroic lone horsemen tries to control the rush of sheep to a waterhole in drought-stricken country. The same painter's *Shearing the Rams* (1888-90) again celebrates the noble masculinity of the bush with a shearing-shed scene portraying the industry and camaraderie of the pastoral life. These paintings all represent a golden age that belie the end of the boom times in Victoria, where the economy crashed in the early 1890s, and the reality that most Australians were urban workers rather than bushmen.

Modernism & the Angry Penguins

After Federation in 1901 Australian landscapes became increasingly pretty and idyllic, typified by the languorous beauties enjoying the outdoors in the work of **E Phillips Fox** or **Rupert Bunny**. However, the trauma of the Great War had a cataclysmic effect on the art world and Australian artists once more followed the lead of Britain and Europe in embracing Modernism. **Margaret Preston** was influenced by the modernist focus on 'primitive' art to incorporate elements from Aboriginal art into her works, *Aboriginal flowers* (1928) and *Aboriginal Landscape* (1941). **Grace Cossington Smith** looked to Van Gogh for works such as *The Lacquer Room* (1936). **Hans Heysen** worked in the tradition of Streeton and McCubbin, glorifying the South Australian landscape with images of mighty old gum trees and the ancient folds of the Flinders Ranges, but other painters of the 1940s and 1950s were looking at the landscape differently. The Outback is presented as a harsh and desolate place in the work of **Russell Drysdale** and **Sidney Nolan**. During the 1940s Nolan produced a famous series of paintings on bushranger Ned Kelly in a whimsical, naïve style in which he expressed a desire to paint the "stories which take place within the landscape" – an interesting link to Aboriginal art. Nolan belonged to a group of artists called the 'Angry Penguins', along with **Albert Tucker**, **Joy Hester** and **Arthur Boyd**. These artists worked under the patronage of John and Sunday Reed at Heide outside Melbourne, the same area that had inspired the Heidelberg School. Tucker painted the evil that the Second World War had brought to society in paintings like *The Victory Girls* (1943). Boyd worked on moral themes set among light-sodden landscapes. Other artists were portraying the alienation of urban lives, in paintings like **John Brack's** *Collins Street 5 p.m.* (1955).

Contemporary art

During the 1960s and 1970s Australian artists were influenced by the abstract movement. Artists such as **John Olsen** and **Fred Williams** still produced landscapes but in an intensely personal, emotional and unstructured way. **Brett Whiteley** painted sensuous, colour-drenched Sydney landscapes and disturbing works such as the *Christie Series* (1964) in a surreal or distorted manner reminiscent of Salvador Dali or Francis Bacon. Painting became a less dominant form in this period and the following decades with many artists working in sculpture, installations, video and photography. The 1980s and 1990s were also marked by an intense interest in Aboriginal art, leading to its inclusion within the mainstream venues and discourse of contemporary Australian art.

Literature

Australia has a rich literary culture and an admirable body of national literature. Until recently this reflected only the European experience of the country, but increasingly includes Aboriginal voices and those of migrants. Awareness and exploration of the Asia-Pacific cultures of the region is also a new theme. It is not surprising that the main concern for Europeans has been the alien nature of the country they had so recently arrived in – to examine how it was different from their own country and to find both meaning and their own place within it. As in so many cultural fields it has taken a long time for an Australian identity to develop and in literature it has been primarily within the last 50 years. As questions of national identity are resolved Australian writers move towards regional and local identity. One of the features of contemporary Australian literature is the strong sense of place it conveys. The writers and poets discussed below are significant figures of Australian literature who have built up a substantial collection of work but of course there are many more fine writers. See also page .

A B 'Banjo' Paterson & Henry Lawson Paterson and Lawson were both journalists of the 1890s and have done more to define the character of the Australian bushman than any other writers. Both were nationalists, although there were important differences in their work. Paterson wrote the country's most famous bush ballads such as *Waltzing Matilda*, *Clancy of the Overflow* and *The Man from Snowy River*. The latter still outsells all other volumes of Australian poetry. Paterson's was a romantic vision; brave and cheerful men on noble horses working companionably across Australia's vast land or standing firm against figures of authority. Lawson criticized Paterson in the literary journal, *The Bulletin*, for his idealism, saying "the real native outback bushman is narrow minded, densely ignorant, invulnerably thick-headed", and that heat, flies, drought and despair were missing from Paterson's poetry. Lawson was a part of the republican movement of the late 1880s and a prolific writer of poetry and prose based on the people of the bush. His well-crafted short stories present the bush in the clear light of realism and their qualities of understated style, journalistic detail, sympathy for broken characters and ironic humour mean that Lawson's stories are considered among the finest in Australian literature. His best stories are found in the collections *Joe Wilson and His Mates* and *While the Billy Boils*.

Patrick White Patrick White detested what he saw as the emptiness and materialism at the heart of Australian life yet it inspired his visionary literature with its characters searching for meaning. He wanted to convey transcendence above human realities, a mystery and poetry that could make an ordinary life bearable. His major novels are *The Tree of Man*, *Voss*, *Riders in the Chariot*, *The Solid Mandala*, *The Vivisector*, *Eye of the Storm* and *Fringe of Leaves*. Never very popular in Australia because of his critical eye and 'difficult' metaphysical style, White won the Nobel Prize for Literature in 1973 for *The Tree of Man* and began to receive more attention at home. His original vision, the dynamism and poetic language of his work are some of the elements that make him a giant of Australian literature.

Thomas Keneally An energetic and prolific writer with a great store of curiosity, Keneally has ranged all over the world in subject matter yet at the core of his fiction is the individual trying to act with integrity in extreme situations. One of his most important 'Australian' novels is *The Chant of Jimmy Blacksmith*, a fictional representation of the late 19th century figure, part-Aboriginal Jimmy Governor, who married a white girl and was goaded into murder. Other subjects include Armistice negotiations (*Gossip from the Forest*), Yugoslav partisans in the Second World War (*Season in Purgatory*) and the American Civil War (*Confederates*) but Keneally's best-known novel is *Schindler's Ark*. He won the *Booker Prize* for this novel, although some complained that the book was hardly fictional, and it was made into the highly successful Spielberg film, *Schindler's List*. Keneally manages to capture historical moments vividly and is that rare kind of writer who is popular yet serious.

Les Murray   Contemporary poet Les Murray can be linked back to the 1890s poets Paterson and Lawson in his central theme of the bush as the source of Australian identity. Respect for pioneers, the laconic and egalitarian bush character, the shaping influence of the land and dislike for the urban life all run through his work. The city verses country theme is informed by Murray's own experience of moving between the two; he grew up on a farming property in NSW, leaving it for university and work, but later managing to buy back part of the family farm in the Bunyah district. The larger-than-life poet is often called the 'Bard of Bunyah'. Murray writes in an accessible and popular style, but is a contemplative and religious thinker of great originality. Murray's reverence for land has led to an interest in Aboriginal culture, expressed in *The Bulahdelah-Taree Holiday Song Cycle*, a series of poems echoing the style and rhythm of an Arnhem Land song cycle. Other major works include the collections *The People's Otherworld* and *Translations from the Natural World*.

Peter Carey   Carey grew up in Victoria, lived for a while in Sydney, but now lives in New York. Being an expatriate writer has only focused his view of Australia, a fairly dark vision that wonders what can grow out of dispossession, violence and a penal colony. Carey is a dazzling writer; each novel is entirely different in genesis, period and character. His earlier novels had magic-realist elements, such as *Bliss* in which advertising man Harry Joy is re-born several times into new realities. Other qualities include surrealism, comedy, the macabre, and a concern for truth and lies. Carey won the Booker Prize in 1988 for *Oscar and Lucinda*, a Victorian novel with echoes of George Eliot and Edmund Gosse, set in 19th-century NSW and centering on the love between two unconventional gamblers. *True History of the Kelly Gang* won Carey the Booker Prize again in 2001 for a feat of language and imagination that is simply breathtaking. Carey puts flesh on the bones of history by getting inside the mind of bushranger Ned Kelly. His other novels are *Illywhacker*, *The Tax Inspector*, *The Unusual Life of Tristan Smith*, and *Jack Maggs*.

David Malouf   An elegant and lyrical writer, Malouf is preoccupied by the question of Australian identity. He believes writers need to create mythologies that are the means of a spiritual link between landscape and lives. Places need to be mapped by imagination to acquire meaning or belonging. His own themes are often played out against the background of his own childhood in Brisbane, a richly imagined slow and lush city of the past. In his novels characters are forced by circumstance to find a new way of seeing. *The Great World* follows the lives of Vic and Digger through Second World War prisoner of war camps to examine layers of history and identity. *An Imaginary Life* deals with the Roman poet Ovid in exile from Rome and his relationship with a wolfchild, a poetic novel that explores Australian issues of exile, place and belonging. These themes are continued in *Remembering Babylon*, set in the 1840s when a white boy who has lived with Aborigines for 16 years encounters the first settlers to reach northern Queensland. Malouf also writes poetry and short stories; forms that suit his economic yet powerfully descriptive language.

Kate Grenville   Grenville's novels are sharply observed, funny and sometimes gothic explorations of what makes people tick and how they create their own destiny. This writer sees

Australian history as a rich source of material; full of stories still to be told, landscape to be described and ways of being 'Australian' to explore. For *Lilian's Story* Grenville was inspired by Sydney eccentric Bea Miles to write the story of an uninhibited woman who makes her own myth at a time when women are supposed to be passive. *Dark Places* is about Lilian's monstrous father and how he distorts truth and reality to justify his actions. *Joan Makes History* re-writes Australian history in the image of women. Joan imagines she is present at all the big moments of Australia's past. *The Idea of Perfection* is about two middle-aged and unattractive people drawn together because they value history and its imperfections. It won the Orange Prize for Fiction in 2001.

Music

Australian popular music has been heavily influenced by the British and American music scenes but has also produced exciting home-grown sounds that are distinctively Australian. The industry suffered from the 'cultural cringe' for some time – the idea that anything Australian is only any good if Britain and America think so. In the last three decades, however, Australians have embraced their own music and there have been many bands that are extremely successful in Australia but unknown outside the country. Australian musicians are limited by their tiny market – if they want to make serious money they must pursue success overseas.

Australian music first came to the notice of the rest of the world in the 1970s, when glam rock outfits **Sherbert** and the **Skyhooks** toured America. **Little River Band** did well in the US with their catchy commercial pop while punk outfit **The Saints** were simultaneously making it big in the UK. However the real success story of the decade was **AC/DC**, one of the greatest heavy-rock bands in the world. Their album *Highway to Hell* was a huge success in 1979 though they lost their lead singer Bon Scott in 1980 to a tragic rock-star death.

The 1980s was the decade of the hardworking pub rock band, the sexy funk rock of **INXS**, the stirring political anthems of **Midnight Oil**, and the working-class onslaught of **Cold Chisel**. Of these bands INXS had the most success overseas while Midnight Oil and Cold Chisel were huge at home, singing about Australian places, issues and experiences. **Men at Work** had a hit with the quirky *Down Under* and **Crowded House**, led by the master singer-songwriter and New Zealander **Neil Finn**, seduced the world with tracks like *Don't Dream It's Over*. Singer-songwriters **Richard Clapton** and **Paul Kelly** also came to prominence at this time and both continue to influence the music scene. Paul Kelly's album *Gossip* is a classic – full of finely observed stories about life in Sydney and Melbourne.

Record companies became less willing to take a chance on unproven Australian bands in the 1990s and the decade was marked by developments on the local scene. Strangely, there was a rash of success for ex-soap stars **Kylie Minogue** and **Natalie Imbruglia**, but more so in the UK than at home. Kylie even got serious when she teamed up with ex-**Birthday Party** frontman, **Nick Cave** on a track for his typically downbeat *Murder Ballads* album. Cave's dark, philosophical stylings have always gone down better in the UK and Europe than down under. **The Whitlams**, meanwhile, appealed to sophisticated punters with witty and melodic funk. At the noisier end of the spectrum **Regurgitator** appeared with an influential and original sound; **Spiderbait**, **Powderfinger** and **Savage Garden** also all made it big. The band that really caught the public imagination though was **Silverchair**, a trio of schoolboys who won a competition to record their grunge classic *Tomorrow*. Aboriginal musicians also had commercial success; look out for bands **Yothu Yindi**, **Saltwater** and **Coloured Stone**, and the soulful ballads of **Archie Roach** or energetic pop of Torres Strait Islander **Christine Anu**.

Popular music

Background

In the first few years of this decade Kylie Minogue just got bigger, Savage Garden split up but singer Darren Hayes started up a solo career. **Superjesus**, **Bodyjar**, **Even**, and **Killing Heidi** are all doing well locally.

Classical & country
About three million Australians a year attend classical concerts and the country has a strong classical music culture, with a dedicated national classical radio station and symphony orchestras in every state. Contemporary classical is also healthy, as demonstrated by composers such as **Peter Sculthorpe** and **Liza Lim**. Conductor **Simone Young** is considered one of the most talented conductors of her generation and was the first woman to conduct at the Vienna State Opera and the Paris Opera Bastille. She is now conducting at *Opera Australia*. Opera singer **Dame Joan Sutherland** is one of the world's best sopranos.

Country music is very popular in Australia, although highly derivative. **Slim Dusty** has represented Australian country music since 1945 and is still going strong. Younger performers include **James Blundell**, **Lee Kernaghan**, **Gina Jeffreys** and **Troy Cassar-Daley**.

Cinema

First steps
Although Australia produced the world's first feature film in 1906, *The Story of the Kelly Gang*, its budding film industry was soon overwhelmed by a flood of British and American films. It wasn't until the 1970s, when Australia was exploring its cultural identity, that the industry revived. Government funding commonly paid for as much as half of the production costs of a film and Australian themes were encouraged. During this period some classics were made, such as *Picnic at Hanging Rock*, directed by **Peter Weir**. This is a story of a schoolgirls' picnic that goes horribly wrong when some of the girls disappear into the haunting and mysterious landscape, one of many Australian films to suggest that perhaps the Outback has the spiritual power that Aboriginal people believe it does. Weir went on to become a very successful Hollywood director (*Witness*, *Dead Poets Society*, *Truman Show*). *My Brilliant Career* was the beginning of brilliant careers for director **Gillian Armstrong** and actor **Judy Davis**. Davis played an independent young woman of the late-19th-century who wanted to escape from the farm and live an intellectual life. The decade was also marked by 'ocker' films made for the home audience portraying the crass, uncouth and exaggerated Australian, like *The Adventures of Barry McKenzie*.

Glamour & heroes
Things changed in the 1980s when the government brought in tax incentives to encourage private investment in the film industry. Direct government funding dropped away to low levels. Naturally under these conditions the emphasis switched to profit rather than artistic merit and many big-budget commercial films were made such as *Crocodile Dundee*. In 1981 Peter Weir's *Gallipoli* was a much-loved film about the sacrifices and stupidity of events at Gallipoli, starring a young **Mel Gibson**. In a completely different role Gibson also starred in another successful film that year, *Mad Max II*, shot around Broken Hill in Outback NSW. Australian high-country life was romanticised in *The Man from Snowy River*, featuring a lot of handsome, rugged horsemen and spectacular scenery. In 1987 the thriller *Dead Calm* brought **Nicole Kidman** much attention and *Evil Angels* did the same for Uluru in a film about Lindy Chamberlain who claimed that a dingo took her baby from the campsite at the base of the rock in 1980. Even Meryl Streep, however, failed to master an Australian accent to play Chamberlain. Despite these big flashy films, Australian filmmakers also managed some interesting smaller-scale films looking at relationships, such as *Monkey Grip*, *High Tide*, *My First Wife*, and the extraordinary *Sweetie* in 1989. The first feature film directed by New Zealand born **Jane Campion**, it focuses on the sisters Sweetie and Kay

in their dysfunctional suburban family life. Sweetie is perhaps the first of the freaks and misfits that would feature in films of the nineties.

The industry changed again in the 1990s when the generous tax concessions of the 1980s were retracted and the country suffered through economic depression in the early years of the decade. Australian filmmakers had to look overseas for finance and increasingly encourage American producers to use Australian facilities and locations. The new *Fox Studios* in Sydney attracted *The Matrix*, *Star Wars Episode II* and *Mission Impossible II*. The joint finance and production arrangements made it difficult to define an 'Australian' film. Cross-fertilisation of talent and general optimism in the industry led Australian filmmakers to produce some bold and risk-taking films in the nineties. Issues of identity and gender came to the fore in films that weren't afraid to celebrate the daggy, the misfits or oddballs like *Strictly Ballroom*, *The Adventures of Priscilla, Queen of the Desert*, and *Muriel's Wedding*. In less subtle films, like *The Castle* or *Holy Smoke*, Australians were portrayed as well-meaning but hopelessly naïve fools and bumpkins. Other films pursued more serious issues but got less attention outside the country, like *Romper Stomper*, a harrowing look at a gang of racist skinheads in Melbourne starring **Russell Crowe**, or *Dead Heart*, a confronting look at the clash of cultures in central Australia starring the ubiquitous **Bryan Brown.**

Despite the successes and attention of the 1990s, the Australian film industry still struggles against the behemoth of Hollywood. International financing is still a feature of the industry and it is difficult for distinctively Australian films to get made as they are still perceived as not very marketable outside the country. There is no shortage of superb talent but many of the best Australian actors and directors need work overseas to get the most opportunities. Indeed at present Australian actors are better known than Australian films; Nicole Kidman, Cate Blanchett, Russell Crowe (who was actually born in New Zealand and raised in Australia), Guy Pearce, Toni Collette, Geoffrey Rush, Judy Davis, Hugh Jackman and more are all in huge demand in Britain and America. The most recent standout film was *Moulin Rouge*, made by visionary director **Baz Luhrmann** and starring Nicole Kidman and Ewan McGregor. This love story set in the Paris of Toulouse-Lautrec is a riot of colour and music. Luhrmann has single-handedly reinvented the musical film in *Strictly Ballroom*, *Romeo and Juliet* and *Moulin Rouge*. Other films worth looking out for are *Lantana*, an immensely sophisticated tangle of love and betrayal, and *Rabbit Proof Fence*, a film bringing alive the trauma of the 'stolen generation' in recreating the true stories of three Aboriginal girls escaping from their mission and walking thousand of miles to find their mother. *Yolngu Boy* is an interesting look at contemporary Aboriginal society, following three teenage boys in Arnhem Land as they try to exchange petrol sniffing for something better. In 2003 *Matrix Reloaded*, once again filmed in Sydney, was released.

Language

When Europeans arrived in Australia there were about 250 Aboriginal languages and many more dialects. Many of these were as different from each other as English and Bengali. Most Aboriginal people spoke three or four languages; those of neighbouring groups, kin or birthplace. Because Aboriginal languages were oral they were easily lost. About 100 languages have disappeared since 1788, another 100 are used only by old people and will die out within 10-20 years. Only about 20 languages are commonly spoken today. Many Aboriginal people still speak several languages, of which English may be their second or third language. Aboriginal English is widely spoken; this is a form of English with the structure of Aboriginal languages or English words that do not correspond to the English meaning.

English is the official language of Australia, and it has developed a rich vocabulary all its own in its two centuries of linguistic experimentation. American visitors will find a lot of unfamiliar British terms and slang words also in use. Unfortunately many colourful Australian phrases are gradually disappearing under the dominant influence of American television and film.

Religion

Despite the almost total domination of religions imported since the arrival of the Europeans in modern Australia it is important to remember that for over 98% of Australia's human history – that's at least 40,000 years out of the last 200 – the aboriginal peoples of Australia developed and practiced their own highly effective form of religion, based not on Gods in the human form, but on spirit beings inextricably linked with the natural world. In the 1996 census 70% of Australians (just over 12.5 million) were Christians and an increasing 16% agnostic, or having no religion. Around 10% were unknown and 'other religions' including Islam made up the remaining 4%.

Land and environment

The shaping of the continent

There are bits of Australia that are staggeringly old. Some rocks found in the southwest date back over four billion years, a time when the world was still in its geological nappies. In fact most of that corner of the continent is made up of something called the Yilgarn Block, a vast chunk of bedrock over two billion years old, and much of the Pilbara is half as old again. The coastal areas are a little younger, and a couple of the deserts, including the great limestone Nullarbor, are composed of more recent sedimentary rocks, but most of the continent is at least a billion years old. There have been periods of excitement, such as the central faulting which created the MacDonnell Ranges, but on the whole the landscape of the west is truly ancient. It is estimated that the Finke River has more or less run its present course for a 100 million years, and a resurrected dinosaur taken back to Uluru might be curious about the visitor centre, but would be completely at home with the rock.

This ancient provenance goes a long way to explaining why Australia, compared with all the other continents, is so flat. Hundreds of millions of years of weathering have steadily taken their toll, relentlessly grinding down mountain ranges and flattening out the plains. This isn't the whole story, however. Around 250 million years ago geological activity of the faulting and folding variety pretty much ceased everywhere, except on the very periphery, as the continent began to stir. It was then part of the super-continent Gondwana, a huge landmass that broke up to become South America, Antarctica, Africa, India, and the Middle East, as well as the Australasian islands. The 'dividing' ranges that are now such a dominant feature of Australia's east coast were formed when New Zealand made its break for independence about 90 million years ago. This pulling and pushing helped create great vertical movement as well as

Size matters

Australia's land mass in comparison to Western Europe

horizontal. Several eastern and southern parts of the continent sank, creating huge depressions that were periodically deluged. The biggest of these depressions is the Great Artesian Basin, an area the size of South Australia centered on the junction of that state with New South Wales and Queensland. During the periods that these depressions were under water huge sheets of sediment were laid down, the other major cause of much of Australia's bewildering flatness.

If we take a broader view, however, we can see that Australia is involved in some pretty spectacular, and ongoing, mountain-building. Island Australia is actually just the biggest part of a greater continent. In geological terms the islands of Tasmania, Australia, the Torres Strait, and New Guinea are one continuous mass, a super-island sometimes called Meganesia. The slightly lower areas of this landmass are usually sunk beneath sea-level, splitting the continent up as we see it today, but for ecological and human history it is important to note that this has not been the normal state of affairs for the last couple of million years. The current, slightly submerged state dates back only a few thousand years to the end of the last ice age.

Meganesia has some terrific mountains, including the central ranges of New Guinea that reach over 5,000 m and carry some of the world's last 'tropical' glaciers. The whole landmass has been heading north ever since breaking with Antarctica, and is still doing so, speeding along at about seven centimetres a year. It is now crashing into the crustal plates of south Asia and the western Pacific. New Guinea has been colourfully, and accurately, described as Australia's bow wave, absorbing the immense contact forces and building its highlands in the process.

Even along the Great Dividing Range of the East Coast there is evidence of more tumultuous times that are at odds with the rest of the continent. The vast, bush-clad crater that now surrounds Mount Warning on the border of NSW and Queensland is a fine example. This distinct mountain is essentially the eroded plug of what was a sizeable volcano that erupted around 23 million years ago. The more recently formed Undara Lava Tubes near Mount Surprise in northern Queensland are an even more striking example and without doubt, one of the most unusual geological features in Australia (besides that great big orange rock in its middle, of course).

The landscape

Although much of the Australian landscape seems utterly vast and timeless; unaffected by the progress of humanity, it is the east coast that is perhaps the most distinct exception. Walking amidst the high-rise forests of Sydney, Brisbane and the Gold Coast, it is hard to imagine you are in fact roaming one of the least populated and flattest countries on earth. Much of the continent is dry, red and flat to an almost mind-boggling degree. The east coast, with its almost constant string of headlands and beaches and varied topographies of the Great Dividing Range that feature up and down its entire length, always seems to offer a sense of scale, space and a varied horizon. The cooler climate and rainfall is of course what sustains all life here and this has resulted in the wildly disproportional levels of human development and population along all the coastal fringes of the continent, especially in the south and the east. But as well as the basic essentials for life, it seems we humans (well the modern versions anyway) can subconsciously find some strange 'positional security' in our surroundings here – the understated notion that if you got lost you would be fine, you would survive. Head west across the Great Dividing Range and in to the outback where horizons become featureless and skies oceanic, and a strange sense of angst begins to suffuse the soul. The eyes begin to search the horizon for something – anything – and we become like the proverbial fish out of water! This may be one of the less obvious reasons the east coast is so popular as a tourist destination or as the base for the more adventurous.

Background

What is far more obvious, and instantly appealing, is without doubt the sheer range of natural habitats and associated rich and varied biodiversity of Australia's East Coast. Host to almost every conceivable kind of landscape from bush to billabong it is here that you will find the greatest concentration of national parks in the country as well as the most intense agriculture and the highest mountains. Furthermore, in tropical north Queensland, the neighbouring World Heritage Parks – Daintree and Great Barrier Reef – are the fragile homes to one of the richest biodiversities on Earth.

Combined these are predominantly the Australia the casual visitor sees – the vibrant colours and vivid shapes, fabulous forests and sublime shores. But spare a thought for the other Australia, the land and ecology under attack from repeated human onslaughts. Huge areas of native vegetation have been cleared for agriculture, and to a small extent urbanization. There are country-sized blocks of land in Western Australia, South Australia, Victoria and New South Wales where practically nothing grows but wheat. Some soil has been improved by fertilizers, but much has been degraded. In some places the removal of trees has led to a rising of the water table, and in turn the salination of the soil, a dreadful affliction that renders the land fit for nothing but the most specialized of plants. Where the land was cleared for grazing sometimes a few trees were left but the effects of hoofed animals have been nearly as damaging, causing erosion in some areas on an unprecedented scale. Where native vegetation has been left untouched or has recovered it can now suffer dramatically from a *reduction* of human interference, that of fire management. Fuel loads build to such an extent that dramatic bushfires flare up every decade or so, many in national parks close to city suburbs. The 'Black Christmas' of 2001 was simply the latest in a succession of such fires that have seen hectares of bush turn to ash and homes turn to cinders.

Flora and fauna

The isolation, age and position of Australia have had a tremendous impact on the flora and fauna that has evolved. Until Australia started heading north 40 million years ago, much of it lay within the Antarctic Circle and had done so for hundreds of millions of years before that. The Antarctic was not glaciated at this warmer time, but was still very cold with average temperatures of no more than 10°C, and a long dark polar winter. Thus, although animals and plants could in theory migrate from South America to Australia and vice-versa until about 70 million years ago, any such migration would have been extremely slow compared to movements on other landmasses. So, for many types of plants and animals, the effective isolation has been far longer than is immediately apparent.

There have been three particularly decisive factors in the subsequent history of life on the landmass. The first is the relative degradation and leaching of the soils compared with all the other continents. Nutrient rich soils are formed through three primary agents: mountain-building, volcanic activity and glaciation. Western Australia particularly has seen very little of these for hundreds of millions of years. At the same time the constant weathering and extraction of nutrients by plants and animals has steadily leached nutrients from the soils. In short, there is little goodness to go around.

The second major effect on the evolution of Australian life is the long-term climatic stability of the continent. The world has gradually cooled over the last 40 million years. On most continents this has resulted in successive waves of appropriately evolved creatures and plants. Australia, however, has been drifting north towards the equator, more-or-less counterbalancing the cooling. The paucity of nutrients encourages intense specialization, for example some plants settle for more saline soils, others for sandier soils. The long-term climate stability has allowed evolution to experiment to an astounding degree, creating thousands of different species.

The third major factor is the type of climate the continent experiences. First and foremost it is dry. Even with the monsoonal rains of the far north this is still the world's driest landmass after Antarctica, and has been for millions of years. During the recent ice ages it became dryer still, most of the interior becoming one vast dune-covered desert. To make matters worse the short-term climate dances only weakly to a seasonal tune, and is crucially affected by one of the world's most powerful weather phenomena, ENSO (El Niño Southern Oscillation). This delivers rain and drought to the continent in unpredictable cycles of two to eight years, though the effects are weaker in the west than the east.

Both plants and animals have had to develop unique strategies to cope with this combination of low nutrient levels and sparse, unpredictable rainfall. Palaeontologists have found evidence for both placental and marsupial mammals on the early island continent, and indeed a few placental rats and mice have survived down to the present day, but it is tempting to suspect that Australia's unique harsh conditions actually favoured the marsupial way of life. Kangaroos and wallabies have a fascinating approach to procreation. As soon as she has given birth, a mother will conceive but the embryo is not necessarily immediately developed. If drought conditions are in play it will be held in a sort of suspended animation until rains come, and only then will it be born and make its way to the pouch.

When it comes to vertebrate creatures, Australian conditions seem to have favoured reptiles rather than mammals. This is hardly surprising as reptiles live on around 20% of the food required by mammals of a similar size, and can go without food and water for considerable periods when they have to.

Mammalian carnivores have long found the conditions difficult with prey species following boom-and-bust population cycles, but some evolved, mostly from vegetarian ancestors. Most impressive was the 'marsupial lion', *Thylacoleo*, while one of the most extraordinary in terms of evolutionary convergence was the *Thylacine*, commonly known as the Tasmanian Tiger, which survived on that island until at least the 1930s. However, these would probably have fled at the sight of the average human tourist, and certainly at the approach of the real top dog in the Australian hierarchy. That was *Megalania prisca*, an awesome relative of the Komodo dragon that could reach 7 m in length and a tonne in weight. It was probably an ambush predator like its cousin, capable of taking practically anything it wanted.

Wildlife

Wildlife is inevitably very much a part of the Australian holiday experience. It seems icons like the koala and kangaroo are just as ingrained in our psyche as the famous Opera House or Uluru (Ayers Rock). Then of course, there are the utterly bizarre species like the platypus and the echidna – a half duck, half mole and an industrial-sized hedgehog, both of which lay eggs. So unbelievable they are that when the first dead platypus specimen was sent to the Natural History Museum in Great Britain in 1798, the spectacle resulted in gales of laughter and cries of 'Okay, who was the seamstress'?

There is no doubt that Australia's rich bio-diversity is among the most remarkable and specialist on the planet. Despite the wholesale, destructive affects that humans have had on the Australian ecosystem for 40,000 years and in particular, in the last 200 years since the arrival of the Europeans, much of that unique ecology, with all its incredibility remains.

The list of species reads like a who's who of the marvellous, bizarre and highly unlikely. There are over 750 bird species alone. Deadly creatures do inhabit Australia. However, provided you have just a modicum of common sense you are about as likely to be bitten by a snake, eaten by a shark, or stung by a jellyfish as choking on your minted lamb on the plane in transit to Australia. Sharks for example, especially the great whites or pointers, occasionally attack but the odd individuals that do are just as maladjusted and as common as your average human serial killer and generally only mistake humans for seals. The reality is they find us very unpalatable. Then, when it comes to snake bite fatalities there is this one little statistic worth your contemplation: In Australia there are between one and three deaths a year, compared to a staggering 30,000 in India.

Dingoes are also infamous, especially after that well documented and particularly nasty 'Ayers Rock baby incident', when a dingo reputedly carried off a couple's new-born. The case went to trail, since foul play on the parent's part was suspected, but they were acquitted and it seems the jury is still out. Recently there have been a number of well documented attacks by dingoes on Frazer Island off Queensland, but they are due to the fact that visitors feed them scraps to such an extent they loose their natural hunting abilities, starve and through desperation attack. Despite the almost unbear-able temptation, do not feed any wild animals, since this merely makes them more dependent on humans and indirectly places them under greater threat.

The following is a very brief description of the species you are most likely to encoun-ter on your travels, with a few interesting facts and statistics added, but it is in no way comprehensive. To describe the majority is well beyond the scope of this handbook and even a scant description of that other incredible world, beneath the waves, or indeed, all things botanical, must sadly be left to your own investigation. Those realms, after all, are another story.

Marsupials   The words 'pouch', 'Joey' and 'Skippy' spring to mind? Marsupials (derived from the Latin word *marsupium*, meaning 'pouch') can be described as mammals that have substituted the uterus for the teat. Their reproductive system is complex, the females have not one, but three vaginas and there is a short gestation and a long lactation. It is a specialist system, almost opportunistic, that is developed to meet harsh environ-mental demands. At any one time when it comes to kangaroos (as the saying goes), 'there is a bun in the oven, one in the pouch and one young at foot'.

Kangaroos and wallabies   The most famous of the marsupials are of course the kangaroos and wallabies. There are over 50 species of kangaroos, wallabies and tree kangaroos in Australia. The most well known and commonly seen are the eastern grey, western grey and the red. The eastern grey can be seen almost anywhere in NSW, Queensland and Victoria, especially along the coast (they are also the only kan-garoo species present in Tasmania). The red kangaroo, which is the largest, is the one most synonymous with the outback and giving you a good punch on the nose. The tree kangaroos live deep in the bush and are notoriously shy and are therefore very seldom seen. Your encounters with these, the most famous of Australian creatures, will be frequent and highly entertaining, especially with the greys in the wildlife parks and a national park campsites around the coast. In wildlife parks they are notoriously tame and obsessed with the contents of your pockets, while in the national parks you can sit and have breakfast with them nibbling the grass nearby. It is so-oo Australian and worth several films through the camera. Sadly in the outback your encounters with kangaroos will most likely be of the dead variety. There are literally thousands of road kills each year involving kangaroos, since they are very inept at avoiding moving vehicles. When traveling in the outback you should avoid dawn and dusk and about an hour either side, since this is the worst time for accidents.

Koala   Equally famous is the koala. One word of advice – never call a koala a koala **bear** in Australia. It is a bit like calling an American a 'yank' or a Scot a 'jock'. Koalas are not bears, never have been, never will be, and are about as closely related as Pope John Paul is to Ozzie Osborne.

Koalas are not only adorable and eminently cuddly but also incredibly well adapted to the Australian environment. How an animal can evolve to eat one of the most toxic of leaves – eucalyptus – and survive quite happily, is remarkable to say the least. There is a catch however. They may be cute but they have a brain about the size of a walnut, which should come as no surprise considering their diet resulting in slow movements and a need to sleep the vast majority of the time. Coping well in captivity, koalas are easily encountered in the many wildlife parks throughout the country. And there is no doubt what so ever that being hugged by a koala is the most seminal Australian experience. Bare in mind though the wild variety is a very different animal that would take to a camera or open arms like a bull to a red rag. Not only does the courting male have a call that would make the Hounds of the Baskervilles run with his tails between his legs, if captured for research purposes, they will, with their sharp tree trunk grappling claws, make a fair attempt at ripping your arms to shreds. Sadly, koalas are on the decline in most regions of Australia and over 80% of their natural habitat has been destroyed since white settlement began.

Tasmanian devil   The belligerent Tasmanian devil may look like a terrier with a penchant for postmen, but are in fact much misjudicated. Although once found all over Australia, they are now, thanks to competition from the introduced dingo, confined to the state of Tasmania. They are the largest meat-eating marsupial and are only really aggressive when it comes to food. It is the horrendous noise they make when protecting it that earned them the name 'Devil'.

Tiger quoll   Another meat-eating marsupial, the tiger quoll is about the size of a cat with a brownish coat dotted with attractive white spots. If you are very lucky, they may be encountered in the wild.

Wombat   Everybody loves a wombat and even the name delights the imagination. Also marsupials, there are three species: the common, northern and southern hairy-nosed wombats. They are infinitely adorable creatures that like their counterparts the koala, are very well adapted to the Australian environment and their specialist vegetarian diet. They are, in essence, somnolent, beaver-like lawn mowers, that can (and do) go where they want, when they want and generally with great success. Like sheep they are also consummate grass-eaters and as a result have the largest colon in relation to size of any mammal. Like the koala, they also sleep much of the time and are essentially nocturnal. Campsites are the best place to see them where burrows and small piles of dung will provide testimony to their presence. Sadly, like kangaroos and koalas, they are far more commonly seen as road kills.

Possums   Another very familiar family of marsupials, there are numerous species with the most commonly encountered being the equally doe-eyed brushtail possum and the smaller ring-tailed possum. Both are common in urban areas and regularly show up after dusk in campsites. Ironically the brushtail possum is protected in Australia, but after being introduced for the fur trade in New Zealand in the 19th century have reached plague proportions there with an estimated 70 million causing havoc to native species. Another magnificent little possum that may be seen is the squirrel sized feather tailed glider, which as the name suggests can glide from tree to tree. All the possum species are nocturnal hence the huge eyes. The best way to see them is by joining a night spotting tour, especially in Queensland, where in only a few acres of bush there may be as many as 18 different species.

Other marsupials   These include the delightful quokka (like a miniature wallaby), bandicoots (21 species most of which are like an attractive rat with a nose like Barry

Manilow), the numbat (endangered) and the bilby (with ears bigger than 'Yoda' from Star Wars). Remarkably, although maybe not for Australia, there is also a marsupial **mole** that lives in the desert.

Monotremes There are only three living species of monotremes in the world: the duck-billed platypus and the short-beaked echidna, both of which are endemic to Australia, and the long-beaked echidna that is found only on the islands of New Guinea. They are unique in many ways, with the word *monotreme* meaning 'one hole' giving an obvious clue (and we are not talking mouth). But suffice to say, the most remarkable feature is that they are mammals that lay eggs. They have also been around for over 100 million years.

The **platypus**, the enigma, the pariah, the very essence of natural stupefication and absurdity. A creature that is the living epitome that nature is, and always will be, the greatest architect, and one that when first introduced to natural science, grabbed the scientist by his inferior privates, swung him around the room and said indirectly, 'now take that'. The duck-billed platypus is only found in rivers and freshwater lakes in eastern Australia. They live in burrows, are excellent swimmers and can stay submerged for up to ten minutes. The duck-like bill is not hard like the beak of a bird, but soft and covered in sensitive nerve endings that help to locate food. The males have sharp spurs on both hind leg ankles that can deliver venom strong enough to cause excruciating pain in humans and even kill a dog. They also have a penis divided into two with foliate papilla – or petals. Platypuses are best seen just before dawn.

As if the order monotremes were not weird enough, the two families within it look completely different. Although the **echidna** is in no way related to the hedgehog, it looks decidedly like one, crossed perhaps with Concorde. You will almost certainly encounter the echidna all over Australia, even in urban areas, where they belligerently go about their business and are a delight to watch. If approached they adopt the same defence tactics as hedgehogs by curling up, erecting their spines and growling. They are immensely powerful creatures not dissimilar to small spiny tanks. They are mainly nocturnal and hunt for insects by emanating electrical signals from the long snout, before catching them with a long sticky tongue.

Eutherians Although you may be an avid *Star Trek* fan and think you know your Klingons from your Vulcans, you may still not be aware that you yourself are not only a Homo sapien, but also a Eutherian – a placental mammal.

Perhaps the most well-known placental mammal in Australia (after Kylie Minogue) is the **dingo**. Although not strictly endemic to Australia, having being introduced, most probably, by Aboriginals over 3-4,000 years ago and derived from an Asian wild dog, they are now seen to be as Australian as *Fosters*. Found everywhere on the continent, but absent in Tasmania, they are highly adaptable, opportunist carnivores, which makes them very unpopular with farmers. Two interesting features of the species are that they do not, like other dogs, hunt or live in packs and cannot bark. The best place to see dingoes is on Frazer Island, off Queensland, where sadly they have come into conflict with humans due to scavenging.

The mighty **fruit bat** is another placental mammal and a remarkable creature you will almost certainly see (or smell) on your travels. Indeed, you can even see them flying around at dusk on the fringes of Sydney's CBD (especially the Botanical Gardens) giving it a wonderful 'Gotham City' feel. With a wingspan of about one metre, they are pretty hard to miss! If you are fearful of bats or have been misled into thinking that they are dirty, blood sucking creatures, Australia, and the fruit bat, will certainly dispel the myth. Observed at close quarters they look like small, cute, hang-gliding foxes (hence the name), hanging upside down in large numbers from tree branches like decorations on a Christmas tree. Contrary to popular belief they are fastidiously clean and feed purely on fruit, flowers and flower products. There are 85 other species of bat in Australia.

With one of the most impressive bird lists in the world, Australia is a bird watchers' paradise and even if you are indifferent, you cannot fail to be impressed by their diversity, their colour and their calls. All across the vast continent you have species like the rainbow lorikeet, as colourful as any artists palette; the lyrebird that can mimic almost any sound and even penguins that need no ice. Let's face it, where else on earth can you see a large white cockatoo perched on the garden fence and not feel obliged to call the RSPCA or the Humane Society thinking it is an escapee?

As a result of everything from children's books to folk songs, perhaps the most famous of Australian birds is the **Kookaburra**. Both cheeky and enchanting, they look like huge kingfishers and are indeed related. Other than their prevalence, their fearlessness and their extrovert behaviour, it is their laughing call that will remain forever in your psyche. At dawn when a family group really gets going, it can sound so much fun that you almost feel inclined to rise immediately and join in. Also, in the wild, when they catch live prey, they automatically take it to the nearest branch and beat the poor thing to death.

Next up is the equally melodic Australian **magpie**. Looking like some smart waiter or wedding groom in their black and white attire they are another common sight, but again it is their fluid carol-like call that remains truly memorable. In the breeding season they are also known to attack people that have the misfortune to stray in to their territory by swooping with angst ridden determination at your head. Just how many bad hair days the dear magpie has caused one can only imagine.

About the same size as the magpie is the **tawny frogmouth** that frankly looks like a cross between an owl and a frog, with cryptic camouflaged plumage, fiery orange eyes and a mouth the size of the Channel Tunnel. Due to its nocturnal lifestyle it is hard to observe in the wild and is best seen in zoos and wildlife parks.

From the cryptic to the colourful, Australia is famous for its **psittacines** – the parrot family, including parakeets, lorikeets, cockatiels, rosellas and budgerigars. There can perhaps be no better demonstration that these species should not be confined to cages, like goldfish are to bowls, than the vast outback of Australia – their true and natural domain. Out there, against oceanic skies, vast flocks roam in search of food – the **cockatoos** like ghosts against thunderclouds, the **budgerigars** like a shimmer of green and yellow in a heat haze and the **crimson rosella** like a firework in the forests. In urban areas the **rainbow lorikeet** that looks like some award-winning invention by some manic professor of colour, is a common sight (and sound), while in rural areas and forests the graceful red, white and yellow tailed **black cockatoos** are also a pleasure to behold. Others include the pink **galah**, the breathtaking **king parrot** and the evocatively named **gang-gang**.

Almost as colourful and yet remarkably obsessed by the phenomenon themselves are the bowerbirds. There are several species in Australia with the most notable being the beautiful, but endangered, **regent bowerbird** with its startling gold and black plumage, and the **satin bowerbird**. Remarkably, the latter builds a nest on the ground with an avenue of twigs decorated with objects, especially blue objects, to attract the female. A nest near an urban area can look like the ultimate in the lost and found, with anything from blue clothes pegs and sweetie wrappers to toy soldiers and flowers. Another member of the bowerbird family is the **catbird**, which once heard, proves to be very aptly named. Surpassing even the bower bird and its kleptomaniac's stash of blue, are the metallic, iridescent hues of the tiny **fairy wrens** that when first seen simply take your breath away and a bird that could hardly be more aptly named.

In the bush one of the commonest of birds is the **brush-turkey**, about the size of a chicken, with a bare head and powerful legs and feet. They are usually completely indifferent to your presence as they rake about for food amongst the leaf litter. They also use leaf litter to build a large mound in which to lay their eggs. Another well-known bird of the bush is the **lyrebird** of which there are two species in Australia.

Birds

Unremarkable in appearance (rather like a bantam) though truly remarkable in their behaviour, they are expert mimics often fooling other birds into thinking there are others present protecting territory. Their name derives from the shape of their tail (males only) which when spread out looks like the ancient Greek musical instrument, the lyre.

A far larger, rarer bird of the tropical rainforest is the **cassowary**, a large flightless relative of the emu with a mantle of black hair-like plumage, colourful wattles and a strange blunt horn on its head. It is a highly specialist feeder of forest fruits and seeds. Tragically, road kills are common. Their last remaining stronghold in Australia is in far north Queensland, especially around Mission Beach, where they are keenly protected. They are well worth seeing but your best chance of doing so remains in wildlife sanctuaries and zoos.

Almost as large, yet flighted, and more often seen around lakes and wetlands, are the **brolga** and the black-necked stork, or **jaribu**. The brolga is a distinctly leggy, grey character with a dewlap (flap of skin under the chin) and a lovely splash of red confined to its head. The brolga is equally leggy but has a lovely iridescent purple-green neck set off with a daffodil yellow eye and a very impressive rapier-like beak.

Equally impressive in the beak department – in fact, perhaps possessing the most remarkable of all – is the **pelican**, that large, doleful, webby white character so synonymous with a day at the beach. They are simply wonderful to watch, behaving as if they would love you forever for a mere fish scrap. As well as hanging around wharfs and boat ramps for free handouts they are also regularly seen sleeping on the top of lampposts, seemingly oblivious to the chaotic urbanity beneath.

Lakes and harbours are also the favourite haunt of the **black swan**, the faunal emblem of Western Australia. The Australian black swan is the only uniform black swan in the world with the other seven species being predominantly white. One interesting feature of swans is that they actually have more vertebrae in their neck than the lofty giraffe. While giraffes use that anatomy to reach leaves high up in the trees, swans use it to reach deep in to the water to sift the bottom, or to reach weed. Almost a match when it comes to wingspan is the white-breasted **sea eagle**, which is a glorious sight almost anywhere along the coast, or around inland lakes and waterways. Like any eagle they are consummate predators and in this case are highly adept at catching fish with their incredibly powerful talons.

Like some interminably cute, chubby little pigeon in a wetsuit, the **fairy penguin** is found all along the southern coastline of Australia and without an iceberg in sight. Their scientific name '*Eudyptula*' is Greek for 'good little diver' and they are the smallest penguins in the world. The largest colony is on Philip Island near Melbourne where over 20,000 are known to breed in a vast warren of burrows.

The **emu**, with its long powerful legs, are prevalent yet quite shy, usually running off like a group of hairy basketball players on a first-time shoplifting spree. Were they human you can only imagine the huge **wedge-tailed eagle** (or 'wedgie'), that other giant of the outback, smug and smirking, knowing for them, there is absolutely no need to flee from anyone, or anything. Wedgies are most commonly sighted feeding on road kills, especially kangaroos, which is an ironic twist of our impact on nature, the outback and the Australian environment.

Reptiles, amphibians & insects   The range of reptile, amphibian and insect species is, not surprisingly, as diverse as any other in Australia and perhaps the group of animals most feared by visitors. Many myths and misconceptions exist but it is true to say that within this group there are some creatures that could bring down a horse, eat it and spit out the empty skin!

First up is the largest and a living dinosaur: the **crocodile**. There are two species in Australia, the saltwater crocodile (or 'saltie' as they are known) found throughout the Indo-Australian region, and the smaller freshwater crocodile, which is endemic. It is only the saltwater crocodile that is partial to meat and could not care less whether there is a fishing rod or a Rolex watch attached. The largest was measured at a fearsome 10 m and the largest human 'feeding frenzy' occurred when one thousand Japanese soldiers vanished in a swamp between Burma and Romree Island to escape the British during the Second World War. By morning only 20 were left! Greatly hyped by films and television since the creation of Tarzan, there is no doubt the mighty 'saltie', is, along with the great white shark, the most feared creature on earth and perhaps deservingly so. Maybe it is their size generally, or their admirable dentition, but either way, there is no doubt they demand our respect. Although you will undoubtedly encounter crocodiles in zoos, wildlife parks and crocodile farms throughout the Australia, you may also be lucky to spot one in the wild in the northern regions. However be aware that there is no doubt as to whom is more successful when it comes to hide and seek. In Queensland warning signs next to rivers and estuaries are a common sight, extolling various recommendations for your due safety, including… 'If out in a boat, DO NOT dangle arms or legs in the water'.

Moving on from the thoroughly dangerous and XXL department, to the relatively harmless and medium range – the enchanting **goanna**, or monitor. A common sight, especially in campsites, where their belligerence is legendary. There are actually many species of goanna in Australia. They can reach up to 2 m in length, are carnivores and if threatened, run towards anything upright to escape. Of course, this is usually a tree, but not always, so be warned!

There are many other species of lizard that you may encounter on your travels. In urban areas these include the **bearded dragon** (also called the water dragon) and the **blue-tongued lizard** (six species), both about 50 cm in length. It is not unusual to be out jogging in Sydney for example and have to side step one of these. They are also commonly kept as pets. Two of the most well known lizards in the outback are the **frilled lizard** and the **thorny devil**. As the name suggests the frilled lizard has a flap of skin around the neck that can be extended like some marvelous colourful orange umbrella, while the wonderfully named thorny devil is indeed a little devil that looks like a mobile cactus. From outback to 'out-house'. **Geckos** are a common sights, especially in the tropics, when you will notice these tiny flesh-coloureds lizard plastered to the roof or busy catching insects. There are many species in Australia. They manage to cling to smooth surfaces using an incredible adaptation, in the form of tiny hairs on their feet called *setae*. On a single toe there can be over one million.

There are many species of frogs and toads in Australia including the commonly seen **green tree frog**. They are a beautiful lime-green colour and support a facial expression of one who has eaten so much they are unable to move, yet are thoroughly proud of the fact. If you find one do not handle them since the grease on our hands can damage their sensitive skin. Another character worth mentioning is the **banjo frog**. If you are ever in the bush and are convinced you can hear someone plucking the strings of a banjo, it is probably a banjo frog singing to its mate.

Insects are well beyond the scope of this handbook, but there are two, that once encountered, will almost certainly reside in your memory forever. The first is the **huntsman spider**, a very common species seen almost anywhere in Australia, especially indoors. Although not the largest spider on the continent, they can grow to a size that would comfortably cover the palm of your hand. Blessed with the propensity to shock, they are an impressive sight, do bite, but only when provoked and are not venomous. Of the huge variety of glorious butterflies and moths in Australia perhaps the most beautiful is the **Ulysses blue**, found in the tropics, especially in far north Queensland. They are huge, incredibly graceful in flight and are quite simply like some precious gem glowing in the rainforest. Once seen, never forgotten.

Background

Marine mammals & turtles Although whaling was once practiced in Australia with the early white settlers playing a considerable role in the slaughter of several whale species to the very point of extinction, it is now thankfully whale watching that is big business. Hervey Bay in Queensland is one of the most remarkable and touts itself as the whale watching capital of the world.

Along both the eastern and western seaboards of Australia, **humpback whales** are commonly sighted on passage between the tropics and Antarctica between the months of July and October. Occasionally they are even seen wallowing in Sydney Harbour or breaching in the waters off the famous Bondi Beach. The **southern right whale** is another species regularly seen in Australian waters, likewise the **orca**, or killer whale. Several species of dolphin are present including the **bottlenose dolphin**, which are a common sight off almost any beach surfing the waves with as much skill and delight as any human on a surfboard. There are also a few places in Australia where you can not only see wild dolphins, but also encounter them personally, including the **Tangalooma Dolphin Resort** on Moreton Island, near Brisbane.

Another less well-known sea mammal clinging precariously to a few locales around the coast is the **dugong** or sea cow. Cardwell and the waters surrounding Hinchinbrook Island, in Queensland, remains one of the best places to see them. Australia is also a very important breeding ground for **turtles**. The **Mon Repos** turtle rookery, near Bundaberg, Queensland, is one of the largest and most important loggerhead turtle rookeries in the world. A visit during the nesting season from October to May, when the females haul themselves up at night to lay their eggs, or the hatchlings emerge to make a mad dash for the waves, is a truly unforgettable experience.

The future In Australia, when it comes to wildlife and the environment, it is far from a case of 'no worries'. It seems that wherever man has gone throughout his own evolution he has done so with all the grace, due care and respect of your average bull elephant in a china shop, and sadly, Australia is no different. The introduction of a whole host of non-native animals has had the greatest and most negative impact on the Australian environment since its very inception and separation from Gondwanaland some 80 million years ago.

Species that are currently causing havoc and have done so for some time include the **rabbit**, the **fox**, the **cat** and most recently, the **cane toad**. The greatest fear is that Australia is a very fragile environment hosting many specialist species extremely antipathetic to unnatural imbalances or disturbance. Many extinct species are testament to that including the most recent and one of the most tragic, the **Thylacine**, or Tasmanian tiger lost to the world forever in the 1940s. Others currently teetering precariously on the brink, include the northern hairy-nosed wombat, the smoky mouse, the dibbler, several bandicoot species, the night parrot and the eastern bristlebird. There are many others.

There is no doubt that sterling conservation efforts are being made to halt the destruction and that eco-tourism plays an important role in conservation generally. However, since conservation is a drain on money and not a money maker, it inevitably suffers and it does not auger well. Nowhere is this becoming more apparent than the **Great Barrier Reef**, which some scientists fear is already doomed to destruction. It is poignant perhaps that the reef is the single largest living entity on earth and has been for millions of years. Yet still, we have the ignorance and the power to destroy it. When in Australia tread carefully.

Books

Diamond, Jared, *Guns, Germs and Steel*. A fascinating explanation of why it is that the **History** British invaded Eastern Australia in 1788, rather than the other way round.
Flannery, Tim (edited by), *The Birth of Sydney*. An amazing insight into the minds of the early European pioneers is given in the eyewitness accounts.
Hughes, Robert, *Fatal Shore*. Probably the most read Australian history book, it concentrates on the detailed story of the convicts and the penal colonies.
Macintyre, Stuart, *A Concise History of Australia*. For general history.

Books detailing the impact of the British invasion on the indigenous peoples include **Richard Broome**'s *Aboriginal Australians*, a good general history of what has happened to Aboriginal people since 1788 and how they have responded to their situation, while the very fine work of **Henry Reynolds** utilises a lot of compelling primary sources. Look out for his *The Other Side of the Frontier* or *An Indelible Stain*. The Aboriginal voice itself is starting to be heard in books such as *Contested Ground*, edited by **Ann McGrath**. Australia would be a very different country today were it not for the gold discoveries that fuelled the growth of Sydney and the other major cities. *Robyn Annear*'s lively **Nothing but Gold** details life on the goldfields.

Berndt, Ronald and Catherine, *The World of the First Australians*. The classic work on **Culture** Aboriginal culture.
Flood, Josephine, *Riches of Ancient Australia*. A superb look at archaeological and art sites by region. Also, *Archaeology of the Dreamtime*, an account of how people first came to Australia and how they lived. Her, *Rock Art of the Dreamtime*, for those interested in rock art.
Knightley, Phillip, *Australia: A Biography of a Nation*. Short but snappy, this is in essence, a modern history book but it also goes a long way to getting inside the minds of today's Australians.
McCulloch, Alan and Susan, *The Encyclopedia of Australian Art*. The major reference book at a hefty 800 pages.
Morphy, Howard, *Aboriginal Art*. An excellent overview of its subject.
Sayers, Andrew, *Australian Art*. A new history of all Australian art forms from 1788 to the present.
Penguin, *Good Australian Wine Guide*. This annual guide may be useful for those intending to drink a lot of Australian wine.

Bryson, Bill, *Down Under by American*. This is probably the best-selling account of a **Travelogues** journey around Australia, and certainly one of the funniest. His account of Sydney and **& memoirs** a trip to the Barrier Reef areincluded.
Cockington, James, *Secret Sydney*. A fine Sydney-based work that focuses on walks within the city featuring particular quirks and oddities.
Connolly, Billy, *World Tour of Australia*. The Scot comes good again with this very funny account of Australia, with a chapter on Sydney.
Jacobson, Howard, *In the Land of Oz*. This Englishman's account was written in the 1980s but it is an amusing, perceptive and thoughtful account, and still pertinent.
James, Clive, *Unreliable Memoirs*. One of Australia's best-loved celebrities, novelists and broadcasters offers an entertaining insight into his Sydney childhood.
Park, Ruth, *Sydney*. An updated version of the famous novelist's 1960s city guide.
Phelan, Nancy, *Setting Out on the Voyage*. A combination of two books relating the adventures of the author from her idyllic Sydney harbourside home to wartime Britain.

Background

Eastern Australia in fiction

See also Australian writers and poets on page 435

One of the best ways of getting a flavour of Australian history and culture is to dive into a great novel.

Alderson, Maggie, *Pants on Fire*. For something contemporary, try this entertaining, modern, 'Bridget Jones's Diary' style 'chick' novel, following the life and loves of magazine editor Georgina Abbott set in Sydney.

Astley Thea, *The Multiple Effects of Rainshadow*. Explores frontier violence.

Bail, Murray, *Eucalyptus*. A gum tree fable.

Carey, Peter, *Oscar and Lucinda Bliss* and *Thirty Days in Sydney*. Past and present New South Wales comes alive in this Booker Prize novelist's two works.

Malouf, David, *12 Edmonstone St* and *Harland's Half Acre*. His novels and stories allow you to soak up the steamy lushness of Queensland.

Park, Ruth, *Harp in the South*. For a slice of incestuous inner-city life in Sydney, this work provides a classic fictional tale of one family's struggle against inner city poverty set in the 1940s.

Ecology, the outdoors & wildlife

Flannery, Tim, *Future Eaters*. A fantastic ecological history of the continent, focusing on its fauna, flora and people, and how they have shaped, and been shaped by the environment. Essential reading.

Low, Tim, *Feral Future*. An interesting and alarming study of the current biological invasion of Australia.

Menkhorst, Peter, et al, *Field Guide to Mammals of Australia*. Another fine field guide. For fine wildlife and landscape photographer look for the names of Ken Duncan, Peter Lik and David Doubilet (Great Barrier Reef).

Simpson, Ken, *Birds of Australia*. A good generalist wildlife book, new and comprehensive that is on a par with the tried and trusted *Slater Field Guide – Australian Birds* by Peter Slater et al (now out of print but worth searching for).

Thomas, Tyrone T. This indefatigable hiker has penned the best series of walking guides.

Zborowski, Paul, *Australia's most dangerous spiders, snakes and marine creatures: Identification and First Aid*. Those who are a little nervous of getting close to Australia's wildlife may be soothed (or terrified) by this useful field guide.

Footnotes

Index

Shorts

Map index

Map symbols

Administration
- ⟲⟳ State border
- ○ City/Town

Roads and travel
- ═══ Freeway
- ─── Main highway
- ── Sealed road
- - - - Unsealed roads of variable quality
- ······ Footpath
- ━■ Railway with station

Water features
- ≈ River
- ⬭ Lake
- ▦ Beach, dry river bed
- ≋ Ocean
- ⦚ Waterfall
- ~∿~ Reef
- ⛴ Ferry

Cities and towns
- ▫ Sight
- ■ Sleeping
- ① Eating
- ▭ Building
- ═══ Main through route
- ═══ Main street
- ─── Minor street
- Σ Ϲ Tunnel
- ▦▦▦ Pedestrianized street

One way street and symbols
- → One way street
- ⋈ Bridge
- ▨ Park, garden, stadium
- ✈ Airport
- ⑤ Bank
- ⛟ Bus station
- ⊕ Hospital
- ⊞ Market
- 🏛 Museum
- ⊚ Police
- ⊠ Post office
- ⊡ Tourist office
- ♦♦ Cathedral, church
- ⓒ Petrol
- ⓐ Internet
- ⚳ Golf
- Ⓟ Parking
- Ⓐ Detail map
- ◁Ⓐ Related map

Topographical features
- ⬭ Contours (approx), rock outcrop
- ⋔ Mountain
- ⊥⊥⊥ Escarpment
- ⟨⟨⟨ Gorge

Other symbols
- ⁂ Archaeological site
- ♦ National park/wildlife reserve
- ✻ Viewing point
- ▲ Campsite

Credits

Footprint credits

Text editor: Stephanie Lambe
Map editor: Sarah Sorensen

Publishers: James Dawson and
Patrick Dawson
Editorial director: Rachel Fielding
Editorial: Alan Murphy, Sophie Blacksell,
Sarah Thorowgood, Claire Boobbyer,
Felicity Laughton, Caroline Lascom,
Davina Rungasamy, Laura Dixon
Production: Jo Morgan, Mark Thomas
Cartography: Claire Benison, Kevin
Feeney, Robert Lunn
Design: Mytton Williams
Marketing and publicity:
Rosemary Dawson, La-Ree Miners
Advertising: Debbie Wylde,
Lorraine Horler
Finance and administration:
Sharon Hughes, Elizabeth Taylor,
Leona Bailey

Photography credits

Front cover: Imagebank
(Coogee Beach, Sydney)
Back cover: Darroch Donald
(Blue Mountains)
Inside colour section: Alamy,
Darroch Donald, Impact Photo Library,
Art Directors and TRIP, Travel Ink

Print

Manufactured in Italy by LegoPrint
Pulp from sustainable forests

Footprint feedback

We try as hard as we can to make each
Footprint guide as up to date as possible
but, of course, things always change. If you
want to let us know about your experiences
– good, bad or ugly – then don't delay, go
to www.footprintbooks.com and send in
your comments.

Publishing information

Footprint East Coast Australia
1st edition
© Footprint Handbooks Ltd
August 2003

ISBN 1 903471 73 7
CIP DATA: A catalogue record for this
book is available from the British Library

® Footprint Handbooks and the Footprint
mark are a registered trademark of
Footprint Handbooks Ltd

Published by Footprint

6 Riverside Court
Lower Bristol Road
Bath BA2 3DZ, UK
T +44 (0)1225 469141
F +44 (0)1225 469461
discover@footprintbooks.com
www.footprintbooks.com

Distributed in the USA by

Publishers Group West

Neither the black and white nor coloured
maps are intended to have any political
significance.

Every effort has been made to ensure that
the facts in this guide book are accurate.
However, travellers should still obtain
advice from consulates, airlines etc about
travel and visa requirements before
travelling. The authors and publishers
cannot accept responsibility for
any loss, injury or inconvenience
however caused.

Acknowledgements

Darroch Donald would like to thank all the staff and representatives of the many regional visitor information centres and regional tourism offices who provided invaluable advice and assistance, in particular Far North Queensland Media Representative Dion Eades and Alison Crump of Townsville Enterprise Ltd.

Also a huge thanks to Sally Van Natta and Tony and Brigitte in Santa Barbara, California, for their invaluable help, valued friendship and for providing sanctuary from the rigours of the road.

Also thanks to all the team at Footprint and Alan Murphy and Rachel Fielding in particular for their much appreciated patience, support and hard work.

Finally a special thanks, as ever, to my mother Grace for her steadfast encouragement and support, my brother Ghill for assisting with frequent cashflow problems and for the many 'tonic' email attachments and my partner Rebecca, whom knows that although she is unable to join me on the road is always with me in my thoughts and in my heart.

Complete title listing

Footprint publishes travel guides to over 150 destinations worldwide. Each guide is packed with practical, concise and colourful information for everybody from first-time travellers to travel aficionados. The list is growing fast and current titles are noted below.

Available from all good bookshops and online

www.footprintbooks.com

(P) denotes pocket guide

Latin America & Caribbean
Argentina
Barbados (P)
Bolivia
Brazil
Caribbean Islands
Central America & Mexico
Chile
Colombia
Costa Rica
Cuba
Cusco & the Inca Trail
Dominican Republic
Ecuador & Galápagos
Guatemala
Havana (P)
Mexico
Nicaragua
Peru
Rio de Janeiro
South American Handbook
Venezuela

North America
Western Canada
Vancouver (P)
New York (P)

Africa
Cape Town (P)
East Africa
Libya
Marrakech & the High Atlas
Marrakech (P)
Morocco
Namibia
South Africa
Tunisia
Uganda

Middle East
Egypt
Israel
Jordan
Syria & Lebanon

Australasia
Australia
East Coast Australia
New Zealand
Sydney (P)
West Coast Australia

Asia
Bali
Bangkok & the Beaches
Cambodia
Goa
India
Indian Himalaya
Indonesia
Hong Kong (P)
Laos
Malaysia
Myanmar (Burma)
Nepal
Pakistan
Rajasthan & Gujarat
Singapore
South India
Sri Lanka
Sumatra
Thailand
Tibet
Vietnam

Europe
Andalucía
Athens (P)
Barcelona
Barcelona (P)
Berlin (P)
Bilbao (P)

Bologna (P)
Britain
Copenhagen (P)
Croatia
Dublin
Dublin (P)
Edinburgh
Edinburgh (P)
England
Glasgow
Glasgow (P)
Ireland
Lisbon (P)
London
London (P)
Lyon (P)
Madrid (P)
Marseille (P)
Naples (P)
Northern Spain
Paris (P)
Reykjavík (P)
Seville (P)
Scotland
Scotland Highlands & Islands
South Italy
Spain
Tallinn (P)
Turin (P)
Turkey
Valencia (P)
Verona (P)

Also available
Traveller's Handbook (WEXAS)
Traveller's Healthbook (WEXAS)
Traveller's Internet Guide (WEXAS)

Check out...

WWW...

100 travel guides, 100s of destinations,
5 continents and 1 Footprint...
www.footprintbooks.com

For a different view of Europe, take a Footprint

"**Superstylish travel guides – perfect for short break addicts.**"
Harvey Nichols magazine

Discover so much more...
Listings driven, forward looking and up to date. Focuses on what's
going on right now. Contemporary, stylish, and innovative
approach, providing quality travel information.

CityRail's Sydney Suburban Network

North

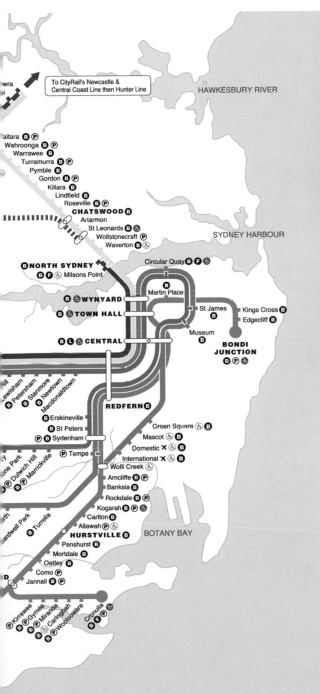

Sydney Suburban Lines

Eastern Suburbs & Illawarra Line
(Waterfall / Cronulla - Bondi Junction)

Bankstown Line
(Liverpool / Lidcombe - City via Bankstown)

Inner West Line
(Liverpool / Bankstown - City via Regents Park)

Cumberland Line
(Campbelltown - Blacktown)

Airport & East Hills Line
(Macarthur - City via Airport / Sydenham)

South Line
(Macarthur - City via Granville)

North Shore Line
(Berowra - Parramatta via Central)

Western Line
(Emu Plains / Richmond - North Sydney)

Carlingford Line
(Carlingford - Clyde)

Northern Line
(Berowra - North Sydney via Strathfield)

To CityRail's Newcastle &
Central Coast Line then Hunter Line

HAWKESBURY RIVER

SYDNEY HARBOUR

Waitara **B** **P**
Wahroonga **B** **P**
Warrawee **B**
Turramurra **B** **P**
Pymble **B**
Gordon **B** **P**
Killara **B**
Lindfield **B**
Roseville **B** **P**
CHATSWOOD **B**
Artarmon
St Leonards **B** ⬤
Wollstonecraft **P**
Waverton **B** ⬤

B **NORTH SYDNEY**
B **F** ⬤ Milsons Point

B ⬤ **WYNYARD**
B ⬤ **TOWN HALL**
B ⬤ **CENTRAL**

Circular Quay **B** **F** ⬤
Martin Place
St James
Museum
Kings Cross **B**
Edgecliff **B**

BONDI JUNCTION
B **P** ⬤

Lewisham
Petersham
Stanmore
Newtown
Macdonaldtown
Erskineville **B**
St Peters **B**
Sydenham **P** **B**
Tempe **P**

REDFERN **B**

Green Square ⬤ **B**
Mascot ⬤ **B**
Domestic ✈ ⬤ **B**
International ✈ ⬤ **B**
Wolli Creek ⬤
Arncliffe **B** **P**
Banksia **B**
Rockdale **B** **P**
Kogarah **B** **P** ⬤
Carlton **B**
Allawah **P** ⬤
HURSTVILLE **B**
Penshurst **B**
Mortdale **B**
Oatley **B**
Como **P**
Jannali **B** **P**

Dulwich Hill
Marrickville
Turrella

BOTANY BAY

Kirrawee **P**
Gymea **B** **P**
Miranda **B** **P**
Caringbah **B** ⬤
Woolooware **B**
Cronulla **B** **P** ⬤

CityRail
© Copyright CityRail
January 2003

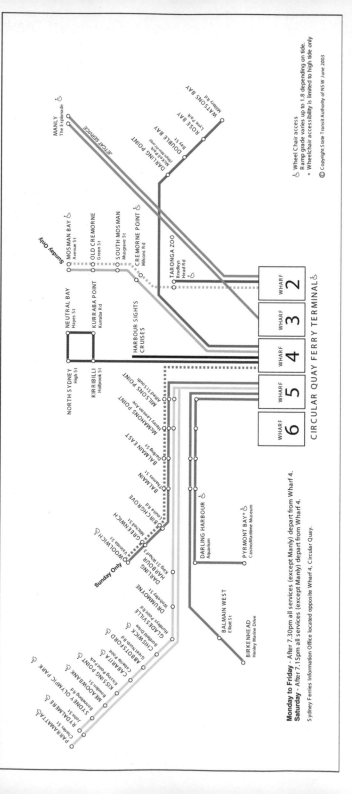

Sydney Ferries
getting there is half the fun

Network Map

Monday to Friday - After 7.30pm all services (except Manly) depart from Wharf 4.
Saturday - After 7.15pm all services (except Manly) depart from Wharf 4.

Sydney Ferries Information Office located opposite Wharf 4, Circular Quay.

Wheel Chair access
Ramp grade varies up to 1.8 depending on tide.
* Wheelchair accessibility is limited to high tide only

© Copyright State Transit Authority of NSW June 2003

CIRCULAR QUAY FERRY TERMINAL

WHARF 2
WHARF 3
WHARF 4
WHARF 5
WHARF 6

MANLY
The Esplanade

JETCAT SERVICE

DARLING POINT
McKell Park
(steps access)

DOUBLE BAY
Bay St

ROSE BAY
Lyne Park

WATSONS BAY
Military Rd

MOSMAN BAY
Avenue St

OLD CREMORNE
Green St

SOUTH MOSMAN
Musgrave St

CREMORNE POINT
Milsons Rd

TARONGA ZOO
Bradleys
Head Rd

NEUTRAL BAY
Hayes St

KURRABA POINT
Kurraba Rd

HARBOUR SIGHTS
CRUISES

Sunday Only

NORTH SYDNEY
High St

KIRRIBILLI
Holbrook St

MILSONS POINT
Alfred St South

MCMAHONS POINT
Henry Lawson Ave

BALMAIN EAST
Darling St

BALMAIN
Thames St

BIRCHGROVE
Louisa Rd

GREENWICH
Mitchell St

WOOLWICH*
Valentia St

DARLING
HARBOUR
King St

Sunday Only

DRUMMOYNE
Wolseley St

GLADESVILLE
Punt Rd

CHISWICK
Great North Rd

ABBOTSFORD
Blackwall Point Rd

CABARITA
Cabarita Point

KISSING POINT
Kissing Point Pk

MEADOWBANK
Bowden St

SYDNEY OLYMPIC PARK
Hennningsbroog Rd

RYDALMERE
John St

PARRAMATTA
Charles St

DARLING HARBOUR
Aquarium

PYRMONT BAY*
Casino/Maritime Museum

BALMAIN WEST
Elliott St

BIRKENHEAD
Henley Marine Drive

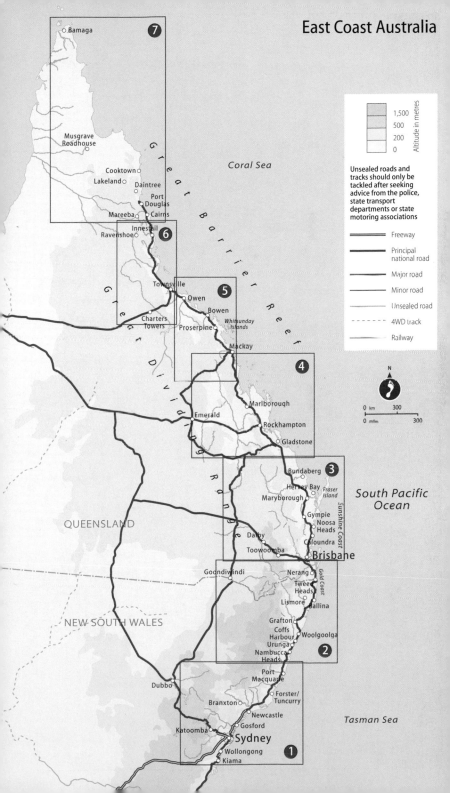

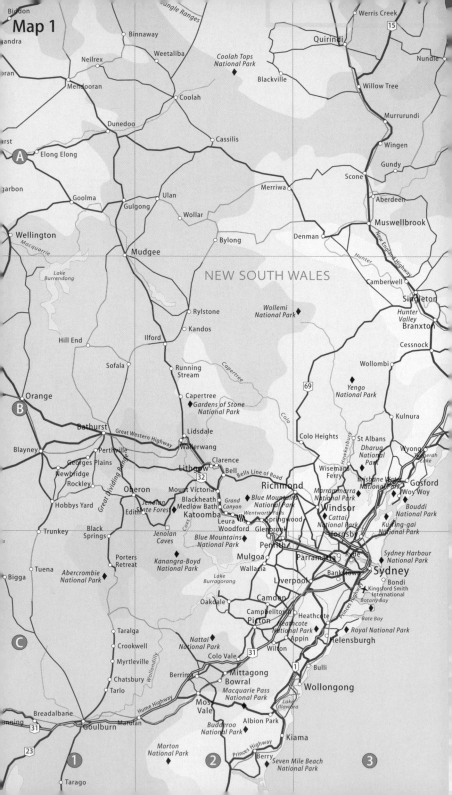

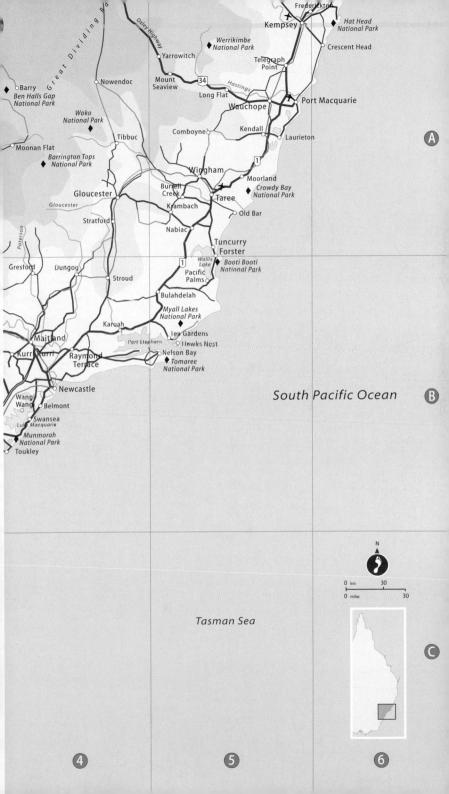

Map 2

34

Gore Highway

85

Millmerran

Map 1

Pittsworth

Greenmount

Ellangowan

Clifton

Leyburn

Allora

Karara

Gore

Lake Leslie

Warwick

Toobeah

Goora

Inglewood

Lake Coolmunda

A

Macintyre

Goondiwindi **42** Yelarbon

Boggabilla

Dumaresq

Limevale

Stanthorpe

39

Yetman

North Star

Texas

Bruxner Highway

Lake Glenlyon

Pike Creek

Wallangarra

Girraween National Park

Bald Rock National Park

shley

Bonshaw

Tenterfield

Coolatai

Kwiambar National Park

Ashford

Kings Plains National Park

Emmaville

New England Highway

Bolivia

e

Pallamallawa

Bukkulla

Deepwater

Gravesend

Warialda

Delungra

Wellingrove

Dundee

Gibralter Range National Park

B

a

Bingara

Inverell **38** Matheson

Glen Innes

Tingha

Glencoe

Newton Boyd

NEW SOUTH WALES

Cobbadah

Bundarra

Guyra

Guy Fawkes River National Park

Barraba

Aberfoyle

oggabri

Cathedral Rocks National Park

Ebor

37

Manilla

Armidale

Wollomombi

C

Uralla

New England National Park

Gunnedah

New England Highway

Nymboida National Park

Wondai

Bendemeer

15

Curlewis

34

Kootingal

Walcha Road

Bellbrook

Tamworth

Nemingha

Walcha

Breeza

Warral

Dungowan

Oxley Rivers National Park

Werris Creek

Map 3

Oxley Highway

Werrikimbe National Park

15

Quirindi

1 **2** **3**

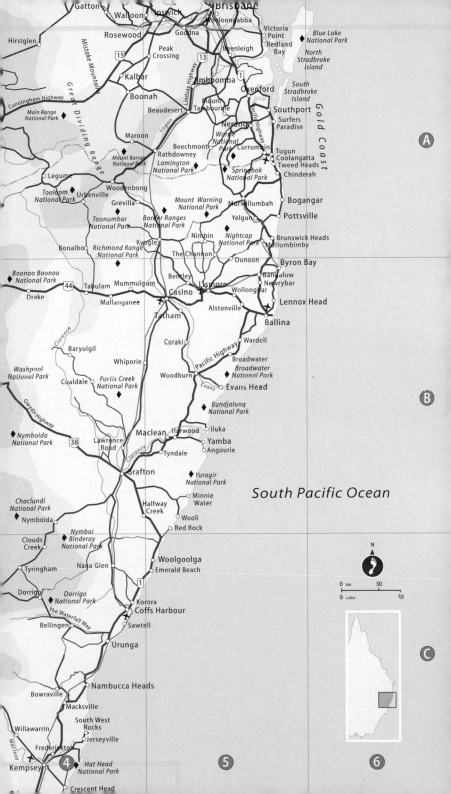

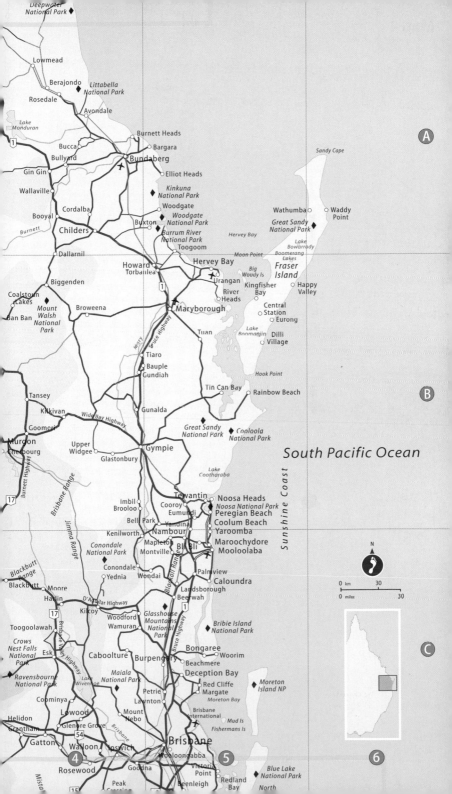

Deepwater National Park

Lowmead

Berajondo
Littabella National Park

Rosedale
Avondale

Lake Monduran

Bucca
Bullyard
Burnett Heads
Bargara

A

Sandy Cape

Gin Gin
Bundaberg
Elliot Heads

Wallaville

Booyal
Cordalba
Kinkuna National Park
Woodgate
Woodgate National Park
Wathumba
Waddy Point

Childers
Buxton
Great Sandy National Park

Burnett

Dallarnil
Burrum River National Park
Toogoom
Hervey Bay
Moon Point
Lake Bowarrady
Boomerang Lakes

Howard
Torbanlea
Hervey Bay

Coalstown Lakes
Biggenden
Broweena
Mount Walsh National Park
Urangan
River Heads
Kingfisher Bay
Fraser Island
Happy Valley

Ban Ban
Maryborough
Big Woody Is

Central Station
Eurong

Tuan
Lake Boomanjin
Dilli Village

Tiaro
Bauple
Gundiah
Hook Point

Tansey
Kilkivan
Tin Can Bay
Rainbow Beach

B

Goomeri
Wide Bay Highway
Gunalda

Murgon
Cherbourg
Upper Widgee
Great Sandy National Park
Cooloola National Park

South Pacific Ocean

Glastonbury
Gympie
Lake Cootharaba

Brisbane Range

Imbil
Brooloo
Tewantin
Noosa Heads
Noosa National Park
Peregian Beach

Cooroy
Eumundi
Coolum Beach

Jimna Range

Burnett Highway

Bell Park
Yandina
Yaroomba
Sunshine Coast

Kenilworth
Nambour
Maroochydore

Conondale National Park
Mapleton
Bli Bli
Mooloolaba

Montville

Blackbutt Range
Conondale
Yednia
Wondai
Palmview
Caloundra

Blackbutt
Moore
Landsborough
Beerwah

Harlin
D'Aguilar Highway
Kilcoy
Glasshouse Mountains National Park

C

Toogoolawah
Woodford
Wamuran
Bribie Island National Park

Crows Nest National Park
Esk
Caboolture
Burpengary
Bongaree
Woorim
Beachmere

Ravensbourne National Park
Maiala National Park
Lake Wivenhoe
Deception Bay

Coominya
Petrie
Lawnton
Red Cliffe
Margate
Moreton Island NP

Helidon
Lowood
Mount Nebo
Moreton Bay

Grantham
Glenore Grove
Brisbane International
Mud Is
Fishermans Is

Gatton
Walloon
Ipswich
Brisbane

4
Rosewood
Mooloongabba

5

Goodna
Victoria Point
Blue Lake National Park

6

Peak Crossing
Beenleigh
Redland Bay
North

N

0 km 30
0 miles 30

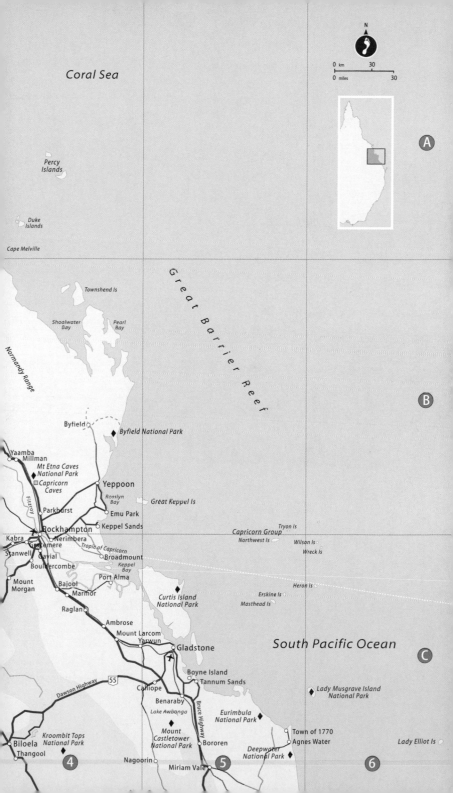

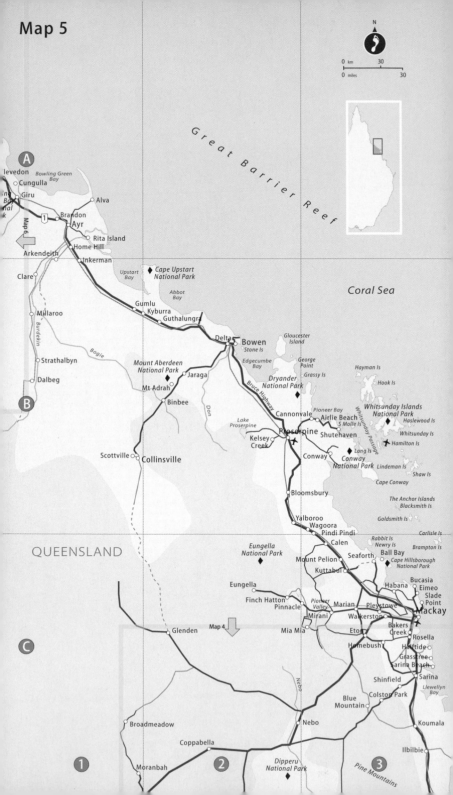

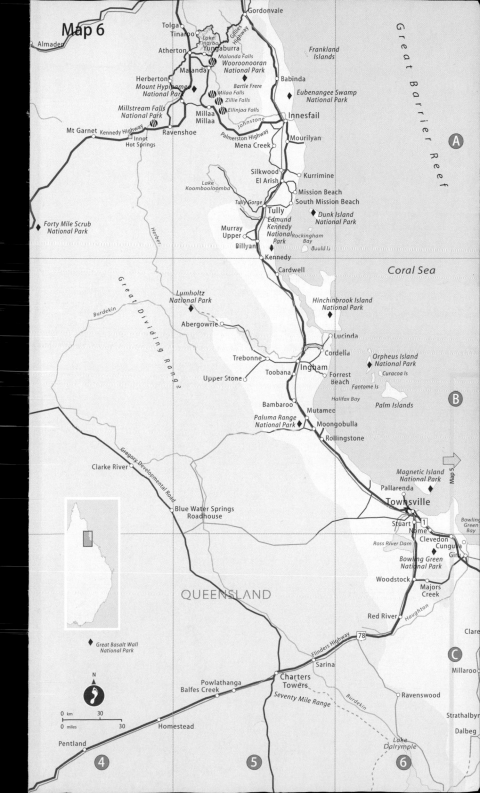